The Writer's Handbook

The Writer's Handbook

EDITOR
Barry Turner

First published 1987 by
THE MACMILLAN PRESS LTD
London and Basingstoke

This edition published 1989

Associated companies in Auckland, Delhi, Dublin, Gabarone, Hamburg, Harare, Hong Kong, Johannesburg, Kuala Lumpur, Lagos, Manzini, Melbourne, Mexico City, Nairobi, New York, Singapore, Tokyo

British Library Cataloguing in Publication data is available for this book from the British Library.

ISBN 0-333-51236-7

Typeset by Media Conversion Ltd, Ruislip
Printed by Richard Clay Ltd, Suffolk

Contents

Introduction

If the size of our postbag is anything to go by, *The Writer's Handbook*, now into its third edition, is beginning to make an impact. The editor may not reply to letters quite as promptly as correspondents might wish but this does not imply a lack of appreciation – simply a shortage of time. To all readers who have contributed advice, ideas and information goes a heartfelt vote of thanks. They are in large measure responsible for the expanded coverage of this latest edition.

This year the brunt of the research has been borne by Michèle Roche who combines a rare talent for tapping information that other reference books cannot reach, with a sharp eye for essential detail. Jill Fenner organised the mailing of questionnaires, a task which gets bigger by the year, and Thea Bennett led the way on compiling new material, notably the section on picture libraries.

As ever, Josephine Pullein-Thompson of PEN, Mark le Fanu of **The Society of Authors**, and Walter Jeffrey of the **Writers' Guild** have responded quickly and generously to requests for help and advice. If there is one thing I have learned from three years association with *The Writer's Handbook*, it is the huge debt of gratitude all writers owe to their professional associations.

Among those who have contributed articles, special thanks must go to Peter Finch, John Spiers, A.P. Kernon and Brian Shuel.

The Editor alone bares his breast to any assaults for negligence or inaccuracy.

Publishing in Turmoil

The Saga Continues

Why do they do it? At a time when booksellers are complaining of too many volumes chasing too few customers, the big publishers are spending vast sums to expand their empires.

Early in the year we saw the once proud William Collins fall to Rupert Murdoch's News International; in June Century Hutchinson was absorbed into Random House, the New York based publisher who, two years ago, acquired Chatto, Bodley Head and Cape; a month later, Chambers was sold to Groupe de la Cité, recent purchasers of Grisewood and Dempsey, and Gollancz is open to offers, (by the time this article appears it almost certainly will have been sold for £7 million plus).

The word is, they haven't finished yet. The giants – Bertelsmann (Doubleday and Bantam), Paramount (Simon and Schuster, Prentice Hall), News Corporation (Harper and Row, Collins), Random House (Random Century, Hutchinson, Cape), Pearson (Penguin, Longman, Viking), International Thomson (Routledge, Methuen), Reed International (Octopus), Maxwell Communications (Macmillan America), Groupe de la Cité (Grisewood and Dempsey, Chambers) and Hachette (Grolier) – are still not satisfied. It is a fair bet that it won't be long before another batch of independent publishers fall victim to the predators.

But the question is still unanswered, why?

Those who remain loyal to traditional publishing – a close, even easy relationship between editor and author, a faith in the literary novel as the highest form of communication and a reluctance to talk about money – predictably assume that the new boys are besotted by Mammon.

The latest buying spree is described by Nicholas Berry, Chairman of Harraps as a 'dance of megalomaniacs to the music of the stock market'. Tom Rosenthal, joint chairman of André Deutsch concurs: 'Book publishing has become a macho business. When people pay absurdly inflated prices for publishers all they are saying is my chequebook is bigger than yours.'

A variation on that theme is provided by Christopher Sinclair-Stevenson, late Managing Director of Hamish Hamilton and a self confessed hater of corporate life. 'If they (the conglomerates) were being truthful they are buying to stop another great corporation from doing the same. Bigness is protection.'

But listen to Anthony Cheetham, founder of Century Hutchinson for a few years the flagship of prosperous middle range companies, and now chairman and chief executive of the mighty Random Century. 'Trade Publishing is an unprofitable activity, a general publisher needs to run alongside a niche or specialist publisher and in conjunction with a paperback operation in order to thrive.' In this context, unprofitable does not increasingly imply a loss, just a very low return. According to Cheetham, general publishing makes 5 per cent in a good year, a case of surviving on the margin. But there is a 15 per cent return in mass market paperbacks and a good 20 per cent in specialist publishing. Add them all together and you have an enterprise to impress the bank manager.

From the author's point of view there are benefits in belonging to a conglomerate. Publishers who operate worldwide can exploit new markets while achieving huge economies of scale; and not just for blockbuster romances and thrillers. Imagine the sales figures for a standard college text which is simultaneously available to every university campus. Then there are the rewards from publishers' overlaps into other media sectors – film, television, newspapers and magazines, supplementing the already large advances that saleable books can attract. It is a revealing fact of life that authors who kick up a fuss when their favourite publisher is taken over, usually go along with the change of ownership, once they find out what is in it for them.

Where does this leave the writers who are not big money makers – first novelists, poets, short story writers, literary critics? For them the small to medium sized company is a natural first stop. But aware of their own best interest they may well decide to stay once they are established in the market place. As summarised by Christopher Sinclair-Stevenson, the second rank of publishers have much to commend them.

'Independence of mind and taste could be assets. Availability on the telephone, the absence of interminable meetings designed to emphasise the corporate reality, the involvement of the author in matters like design, production and marketing – all these quaint, old fashioned ideas may actually bring benefits.'

It has been argued that all this can be provided within the framework of a conglomerate; that an independent can thrive by being part of a list subtlely distinct from big brother. Max Reinhardt did it by leaving Random House and moving with his illustrious author Graham Greene to Reinhardt Books, a change made possible by a distribution deal with Penguin. This means say Reinhardt that, 'we can offer authors both the highly individual treatment of a small house and the distribution clout of a major player.' Maybe. But Graham Greene on the list does constitute a special case.

More a sign of the times, is the decision by Anthony Cheetham, on taking over as Chief Executive of Random Century to close Bodley Head as a separate entity, presumably because it was not living up to its profit targets. Something similar has happened at Penguin with the execution order on Hamish Hamilton and Michael Joseph, companies which having lost their Managing Directors, Christopher Sinclair-Stevenson and Alan Brooke, will now fall directly under the command of Penguin executives.

The problems of staying small within a conglomerate are confirmed by Conrad Goulden who left the managing directorship of Arrow to set up a joint-venture project with Century Hutchinson. His idea was to supply titles to existing Century Hutchinson imprints while offering close attention 'from contract to cover' to the needs of authors. But then came the merger with Random House. Conrad Goulden called it a day. 'Such a venture', he concedes, 'does not live with corporate life... it would be inconsistent for me to stay'.

The good news is that there are independents who survive and prosper. Publishers of indisputed excellence – André Deutsch, Bloomsbury, Fourth Estate, Souvenir Press – the list could stretch to at least a dozen, have found a secure niche in the market. This is not to say they are inviolate, simply that if they are to be dislodged, it will be more by choice than by compulsion. And there will always be others ready to take their place.

An Optimist's Guide to Publishing

John Spiers

It is easy to be a writer: a 3B pencil will equip you. Some 43,000 new titles come out every year – nearly double the number published in the UK in 1960 – and the published titles are only a fraction of what is actually written. What are *you* writing? And for whom? I'm sure, of course, that you are all good writers, and many are already published. So perhaps you will share my interest in the psychology of those – unlike you – who write books that don't come out; those people who insist on spending their lives' energies uncritically producing – with no notion of a market or audience, or costs. For there are an immense number of manuscripts that trudge round publishers in hope and despair; in and out of Jiffy bags; journeying nowhere. Even now someone is hard at work on *The Annotated Diary of Great Aunt Gwen, Chairman of Bognor Regis Thespian Guild, 1919-1948* ('she was such a character'), and *From Therm to Full Term: My 50 Years with Thames Gas* ('people are always saying I should publish it').

But however vast the number of duds, it cannot deter publishers from the excitement of the chase, nor authors from their typewriters. And there can be some wonderful surprises.

I have in mind the idiosyncratic J.L. Carr, whose *A Month in the Country* is one of the two great books I have published. It was runner-up to the Booker Prize; it won the Guardian Fiction Prize, and then it was filmed. Yet it came to me entirely out of the blue – the result of a chance letter – a reward for fifteen years of looking for a potential classic.

Better known is the story of the dry, old salt with a stutter, in the traditional dirty mac, who had never written anything but an Anglo-Saxon Grammar. One day he slipped into Allen & Unwin with something written to read to his grandchildren, obscurely and cryptically entitled *The Hobbit*.

And what about the civil servant who carried a 400-page parable about rabbits all over London until publisher number 47, a specialist in Africana, who knew nothing of fiction, lost his senses and published it – *Watership Down*, of course.

The key point here is that no one could have predicted these very unlikely successes. They were out of the ordinary because the publishable novel found among the touring Jiffy bags is a very rare gem indeed. The unsolicited and publishable non-fiction title is even rarer. Very few non-fiction titles are completed without a publisher's commitment beforehand; moreover the shaping hand of the publisher is very often evident from the start.

Authors seem very complicated people. And publishers do try to understand the mind of the writer. We often wonder why do people write anyway? Why are *you* doing it? To feed yourself? To feed us? To feed posterity? Is your objective to be an individualist? To be knighted? To be a professor? To get even with your mother? Is it a voyage of self-discovery or have you a grudge against society? Do you want to propound a theory and promote a revolution? Are you with Voltaire: 'To hold a pen is to be at war'? Or with Sterne: 'Writing is a different name for conversation.' And is your writing *writing* or just typing?

Goethe said writing was busy idleness. Albee said it was an act of optimism. Tom

Clancy, whose comment on writing has an attractive levity, says: 'Writing is so much damned fun. I play God. I feel like a kid at Christmas. I make people do what I want, and I change things as I go along.' Most writers take their writing and themselves very seriously. And most people who write *do* want to get published. So how is it done?

Amongst their complex mental equipment, authors have two stereotypes of publishers and power, and of the choices between them. First, the local publisher – out of London – small, nice, relatively powerless. Second, the big London houses: Bertelsmann, News International, Newhouse, Pearson, International Thomson, Maxwell, Reed, Gulf and Western – powerful, but brutes.

Local versus London

Is it better to be published by a local publisher, who will be kind to you, and understands you as a person? Or by the London mafia, who will launch your book with such force as to leave you cowering in the corner?

The trouble with these stereotypes is that they are a fantasy. Local, smaller houses and the big London ones have more in common than you would expect. In a hi-tech interconnected world, geographical location is virtually irrelevant except in the case of certain highly perishable popular books, which, if unsuccessful, have a shelf-life of somewhere between fresh fish and yoghurt. Your friendly local house in Sussex is not necessarily small, powerless and inadequate. The dispersal from London due to technology, lower rents and the availability of skills, does not mean that local equals parochial. But it will usually mean specialist. In publishing, 'local' is a word unburdened of most of its meaning, except for co-operatives and small presses.

For the record, most provincial houses have:

- Specialist knowledge and specialist lists, which is not the same as being narrow, or having small sales.
- A network of agencies overseas – often shared with the 'big boys'.
- A network of UK reps.
- A modern computerised warehouse and delivery system.
- Effective and cost-controlled production.
- Relevant marketing strengths – especially in international markets.
- Adequate sources of funds.
- Competent, experienced, knowledgeable management.
- A list of satisfied authors who tell me the above.

In the big houses, if you are at the very top of the list, you will be fussed over rotten. Your book will have cost everyone a great deal of money. And you may have to fight your way out of Langan's Brasserie to get to your word processor. If you're at the bottom of the list, you'll end up in the queue at the Big Whopper Burger and eat the plastic plate too. *Your* book will not have cost everyone a lot of money. You are an overhead absorber.

Consider the worst

These past five years you've hardly left your study. The struggle is over. Now you must sell your manuscript. Fame beckons. Reviews. Signing sessions. A prize. A big cheque ...?

You approach the big house of your choice. The red-letter day is in March 1989. Your letter and manuscript are acknowledged by a Mr Panzer in early May. In July you are advised that it has gone to a reader for appraisal. Then silence. You imagine a traditional process of literary appraisal – the equivalent of William Plomer studying it in a deck chair at a Charleston weekend. After seven months you wonder if it could happen a little more quickly. You ask for Mr Panzer. Problem! Mr Panzer does not have a desk or an office, but a 'work station'. He doesn't actually go there often. He is either 'in a meeting', 'just slipped out', or 'out to lunch'. You leave your name, which you have to spell four times, and no one calls back.

Another call finally produces a letter, saying they are checking to see if your manuscript has ever been received. Accidentally attached to the letter is an internal note: 'Jill – Help! Never heard of this bloke! God knows where this is. It's not logged in the manuscript book. Have we had it? If so, any idea where we sent it? Looks more like a Picture Puffin project to me.' This worries you a lot. You recall the quote that a manuscript is something submitted in haste but returned at leisure. You contact **The Society of Authors** who advise a more threatening tone. Ten weeks later ... a new letter, a brief reader's report, and an offer to publish on rather modest terms. With it, a covering, *xeroxed* letter, saying unfortunately the delay was all due to difficulties with your initial editorial contact who was made redundant due to the takeover. *What* takeover?

It is now early January 1990. You don't want to start again elsewhere so you sign the contract, with its option on your next two books. You revise a little and in September you deliver the manuscript in nice neat Croxley Bond boxes (three copies). A new shock. The person you now regard as your editor doesn't write back. Instead, a new bright-spark editorial assistant fresh down from Oxford, writes to say how she looks forward to *learning* about publishing while working on your exciting book. She has so much admired your previous work on Colette. Working with you on your new book 'Jane Austen and Female Motives' is going to be such fun ...

This puzzles you. This is your first book. You are a military historian. (You have never heard of Jane Austen!) Next, you receive a welcoming letter from the Head of something called the Pan-European Division, a Mr Authorcruncher, and a 10-page sales questionnaire which terrifies you. You discover that the big firm you signed up with is now part of the Pan-European Division of an even bigger conglomerate, Megathing Films and Book. The old name is just visible in the list of firms at the top of the paper – in the typesize usually reserved for lists of mourners in *The Times*. All the original directors have vanished. Nearly two years have gone by. You retain only a little innocence, optimism and hope. You await your book, which is being printed in Hong Kong. Copies are delayed, alas, as Megathing titles are gang-printed, and until 100 separate titles are ready, shipping would not be cost-effective. You do, however, receive the new Megathing catalogue. Are you in it?

On page 104, you find your book. What happened to the expensive photographs of paintings of Napoleon's marshalls that you sent in for the cover? The dust jacket, which you are not asked to approve, is abstract in design and looks like two dolphins making love in a washing-up bowl. In the UK, the book has its original, sober title: *Napoleon's Battles*. For the US, it has been retitled as *Mistresses, Medals and Military Power as Erotic Drive: Lessons from History*.

Unfortunately, the anniversary of Waterloo goes by once again before publication. You then receive a bill for author's corrections and Index which 'please settle promptly within 14 days to avoid unpleasantness'. This bill exceeds the advance by £200. And you still owe £350 in permissions fees.

Welcome to publication ... But your book is treated like a State secret. The title does not appear in the literary columns of the national press. The bookshops don't seem to have heard of it. Another year passes and a computerised royalty statement arrives, two yards long, with 35 lines of print. It's as easy to understand as an astrological forecast in a

Tibetan dialect. There is *no* cheque in the post. Next, big piles of your book appear in the remainder shops. Your friends, who really did want to buy it at £15.95, can now do so at 99p. Goodbye book. Goodbye fame. Hello experience! Like signing up with Customs and Excise, the Inland Revenue, the VAT man and Gatwick Baggage Handlers simultaneously.

Getting It Right

Is publishing like Roulette? Totally arbitrary? Or like chess – a game with no definite answers, just different ways of playing? In fact, there are good things to be said for the big boys. Remember, I was looking at the worst that can happen. But the smaller houses are not without their faults either. I do argue, though, that in order to survive, a small publisher must:

- care about his authors.
- have high intellectual, commercial and production standards.
- try to be the best in his field.
- know how to select, produce, price and sell a book.

Here are some signposts for first-time writers. Do you know who publishes what? And for which market? Look at the books. Look at reviews. Look at catalogues. Try to meet an editor or a publisher, and take advice. Study form. Who does what well? Publishers know what *they* can sell, and want more of the same. They will give you honest advice, if an idea is not for them. They are not predatory or aggressive. Horses for courses. I am a Defence Publisher. Don't send me *How to Teach Your Cockatoo to Dance* or a *Photographic Guide to Feminist Wrestling.*

Publishers want talent. They take it seriously. The editor is the key link. He is the hunter, commissioning regularly. He keeps in touch with the market in which his firm operates. He looks for ideas that can be turned into writing; or writing that can be turned into saleable books. The editor needs you, and you need the editor who will pick you, sell you, nurture your work, and try to make sure that the myriad things required are done in the right way at the right time so that your book comes out right – looking good, reviewing good and selling good.

When you meet an editor, listen as well as talk. Let the editor encourage you to write the book you meant to write but didn't; or the book the market needs you to write and should. *The Comma in Jane Austen, A Psychological Study.* No! *The Life of Jane Austen*; 'ah, that's better!'

For the beginner there is much to be said for mixing with others. Literary societies have a lot to offer; so, too, do the national organisations like **The Society of Authors**, **The Writers' Guild** and **PEN**. Then there are the writers' journals. A new one on the market which looks promising is *Flairnews*, a bi-monthly 'by writers, for writers' (see **Magazines** section).

Approaches to publishers. The old advice was: 'First write your book. That's the easy part done. Now find a publisher.' Perhaps so. But, more usefully, first don't write your book. It is then easier to find the right publisher, who will help you and himself more effectively. Start with a proposal and a c.v., neither to be more than a page long. Imagine you are writing advertising copy. Get across the message in the shortest, simplest way; make an impact.

Other advice in brief:

- Once you have a publisher, try to stay put. Loyalty pays. All books under one imprint from an author sell more.

- Trust your publisher and his judgement. Sometimes he is right; sometimes often enough to stay in business. He is doing one of the most difficult jobs – combining creative and business talent.
- Don't ring up and say you were 'just passing' and would it be helpful if you dropped in. It won't. Your publisher is busy and has to spread his day among all his writers and all his business work.
- Do send return postage with an unsolicited manuscript. Do not send an envelope just big enough to accommodate your manuscript if returned. It's too tempting!
- Don't write self-consciously for posterity. Write for now. Posterity is what you write for after being turned down by ten publishers.

Somehow, in all this, retain your individuality. Richard Ingrams tells us that John Stewart Collis, author of *The Worm Forgives the Plough*, one of the finest pieces of work in the language, demonstrated this essential. The first volume was turned down by 12 publishers and even Jonathan Cape, which did accept it, demanded revisions. Collis was proud of the tactics with which he fended off this criticism. After an interval, he returned the manuscript pretty well unaltered. But he thanked Cape for the substantial amendments they had suggested and Cape replied that they were 'delighted with the improvements'. Volume One came out in 1946; the second volume in 1947; and they were republished together in 1970. It is now an accepted classic.

Finally, here are the words for a poster to be put up on the wall just above your typewriter:

> It is said that literary success of any enduring kind is made by refusing to do what publishers want, by refusing to write what the public wants, by refusing to accept any popular standard, by refusing to write anything to order. Dickens ignored this precept.
>
> It is also said that the rarest thing in literature and the *only* success is when the author disappears and his work remains. Dickens took no notice.

It is at all events necessary to eat. We, like you, get hungry. It is surely no bad thing to be a literary giant; preferably in one's own lifetime; and in ours, please. Remember, we often pay the bills.

John Spiers is Chairman of John Spiers Publishing Ltd.

The Bottom Line

Signing the Contract

The efforts of **The Society of Authors** and **The Writers' Guild** to introduce some sort of order into the complex and often chaotic world of publishers' contracts have met with a predictable counterblast from Kingsley Amis. The champion of freedom condemns the Minimum Terms Agreement (now signed by seven publishers) as a benefit to those in work at the expense of those who are not. If the MTA were to be made universal, he argues, at least 'one highly reputable firm well known for scooping up writers who have failed to achieve publication elsewhere and getting them into print on terms below the minimum set by the MTA ... would go out of business, and a number of writers would be prevented from reaching the public'.

I wonder. Another possibility is that the firm in question might be compelled to raise its efficiency to a level at which it could afford to pay its authors a decent return on their labours.

That there is room for improvement, Amis is the first to admit. Switching from *The Spectator* to *Telegraph Magazine*, we find that his faith in the free market is less than absolute.

He feels about publishers, he tells us, 'the way troops used to feel about generals, that anybody who could merely hold his own in another line of business could rise to the top of this one in five minutes. I have been lucky enough to make a decent living out of authorship for 25 years, but if publishers in the mass have handled my finances with the same competence as my jackets, blurbs, printing, proof-correcting, catalogue entries, publicity and other more visible matters, I sometimes feel I could have done better out of market gardening.'

With such stringent views on the competence of his trade, Kingsley Amis must count it as at least a possibility that the ease with which publishers can foist unfair contracts on their authors encourages them to be lackadaisical in other departments. In any event, it can surely be no coincidence that the companies adopting the MTA (**BBC Books, Bloomsbury, Century Hutchinson, Faber & Faber, Headline, Hodder & Stoughton**) are among the most favourably rated by *The Writer's Handbook* correspondents.

Even if other companies are slow to follow their example, the MTA serves as a standard against which a publisher's offer can be judged. When it comes to signing on the bottom line, you may feel you have had to give way on a few points, but if the general principles of the MTA are followed the chances of securing a reasonable deal are much enhanced.

Probably the most important break from tradition contained in the MTA is the clause allowing for the length of licence granted by the author to the publisher to be negotiable. The custom is for the licence to run for the duration of copyright (i.e. the author's lifetime plus 50 years). Originally the writers' unions pressed for a maximum of 20 years but have since compromised on a review procedure which permits the contract to be revised every 10 years. This gives the author the opportunity to claim, for example, improved royalties if the book has been a success.

Other basic principles covered by the MTA include:

- *Reversion of Rights* As well as the author being able to recover rights after a book goes out-of-print (which is defined in more detail than in most contracts), the author may also terminate the contract if sales fall below certain figures. This gives the author the opportunity to leave a publisher if he feels that the book is not being properly marketed or that the publishers are simply clinging on to rights unnecessarily.
- *Accounting* The publishers will pay over to the author income from sub-licences straight away, once the advance has been earned.
- *Indexing* The cost of indexing, if not done by the author, is shared equally with the publishers.
- *Free Copies* The author will receive twelve free copies of a hardback and twenty free copies of a paperback.
- *Print-run* The author will be informed of the size of print-runs.

Author Involvement

The MTA confirms the extent to which authors should be involved in the publication of their books. For example:

- There will be full discussion prior to signing the contract of illustrations, quotations, etc., the costs thereof, and the party responsible for paying them. Normally, the publishers will pay some or all of the costs involved.
- There will be full consultation on all the illustrations, the jacket, blurb and publication date.
- The author will be invited to make suggestions for publicity and will be shown the proposed distribution list for review copies.
- The author will be fully consulted before any major sub-licences are granted by the publishers (e.g. paperback, American, film, television and merchandising deals).

Royalties

On the touchy question of royalties:

- The basic hardback scale is 10% to 2500 copies, $12\frac{1}{2}$% on the next 2500 copies and 15% thereafter – on the published price (home sales) or the publisher's receipts (exports). On certain small reprints the royalty may revert to 10%.
- On home (mass-market) paperback sales the minimum royalty is $7\frac{1}{2}$% of the published price, rising to 10% after 50,000 copies. On exports the minimum royalty is 6% of the published price. If paperback rights are sub-licensed, the author receives at least 60% of the income, rising to 70% at a point to be agreed.
- The author receives 85% of the income from the sale of American rights and 80% from translations.
- The author receives 90% from first serial rights, TV and radio dramatisations, film and dramatic rights, etc. Other percentages to the author include: anthology and quotation rights, 60%; TV and radio readings, 75%; merchandising, 80%.

Bear in mind however, that the royalty percentages do not necessarily apply to all books. For example, heavily illustrated book's are excluded and there are certain exceptional circumstances in which publishers may pay lower royalties (e.g. long works of fiction published in short print-runs for libraries).

As a spot check on the acceptability of a contract confirm four essential points before adding your signature:

First, there should be a firm and unconditional commitment to publish the book within a specified time, say twelve months from delivery of the typescript or, if the typescript is already with the publisher, from signature of the agreement. It is also as well for the approximate published price to be specified.

The obligation to publish should not be subject to approval or acceptance of the manuscript. Otherwise what looks like a firm contract may be little more than an unenforceable declaration of intent to publish. It is equally important to watch that the words 'approval' or 'acceptance' do not appear in the clause relating to the advance payment. For example, if the advance, or part of it, is payable 'on delivery and approval' of the script, this might qualify the publishers' obligation to publish the work.

This point about the publishers' commitment to publishing a book is of vital importance, particularly since publishers' editors change jobs with increasing frequency. An author who has started a book with enthusiastic support from his editor may, when he delivers it, find he is in the hands of someone with quite different tastes and ideas. The publishers should satisfy themselves at the outset that the author is capable of writing the required book – if necessary by seeing and approving a full synopsis and sample chapter. Provided the book, when delivered, follows the length and outline agreed, the publishers should be under a contractual obligation to publish it (subject possibly to being entitled to ask the author to make reasonable and specified changes to the typescript before publication).

However, even when the contract contains a firm undertaking to publish, the publishers cannot be compelled to publish the book. But should they fail, the author is legally entitled to compensation for breach of contract.

Secondly, there should be a proper termination clause. This should operate when the publishers fail to fulfil or comply with any of the provisions of the contract or, if, after all editions of the work are out-of-print or off the market, the publishers have not within six months of a written request issued a new edition or impression of at least 1500 copies.

When, in any of these circumstances, rights revert to the author, this should be done without prejudice to any claims you may have for monies due. Occasionally termination clauses state that if the publishers fail to reprint a new edition after due notice from the author, the agreement shall terminate provided the author refunds any unearned balance of the advance and buys back blocks, stereo-plates, etc., at a proportion of their original cost. You should insist on the deletion of such a proviso.

Thirdly, there should not be an option clause that imposes unreasonable restrictions on future work. The best advice is to strike out the option clause but if this proves impossible, an option should be limited to one book on terms to be mutually agreed (not 'on the same terms'). The publishers should be required to make a decision within, say, six weeks of delivery of the complete work in the case of fiction, or of submission of a synopsis and specimen chapter in the case of non-fiction. (An option clause which provides for publication 'on the same terms', or which states that the author shall grant 'the same rights and territories' as in the original agreement, can be most disadvantageous to the author and should certainly be altered or deleted.)

It is as well to specify the type of work covered by the option, for example, your next work of fiction, non-fiction or children's books, since you may want to publish different types of book with different publishers. Another wise precaution is to exclude works you may be invited to write for a series published by another firm. Very occasionally, in the case of a new author, the publishers may try to obtain a two-book option. If you accede, it is important to provide that, if the publishers reject the first option book, they should automatically lose their option on the second.

Every Little Helps

The Latest Returns From PLR

Last year Public Lending Right paid out £3,107,000 to 16,034 authors or 1.45p per loan as against 1.12p in 1988. Just 67 writers collected the maximum payment of £6000 (Catherine Cookson, Dick Francis, Jeffrey Archer, Jack Higgins and Barbara Taylor Bradford among them), while another 3000 received between £100 and £499. By far the biggest group, close on 9000, had cheques under £99. A sorry band of 2823 registered authors got nothing at all.

So much for the statistics. So much, too, for hoping that PLR might help towards paying the mortgage. (I am assuming that Catherine Cookson, Dick Francis et al don't have mortgages to worry about).

In fact, for the full-time author on a middle income, which is low income by most standards, there is little overall to cheer about. It is not just that PLR looks set to continue at its current modest level (the last increase, in 1988, barely made up for the loss by inflation since the scheme was introduced a decade ago) but there is evidence to suggest that book borrowing is on the decline. A recent Mori poll for *The Sunday Times* reported fewer people visiting their public libraries (62% in 1988 compared to 64% in 1987).

Book buying is also dropping off – those in the Mori poll admitting to not having bought any books at all in the previous year going up from 37% to 40% in 1988. And this at a time when more books are being published than ever before. Under the old system of computation, which took in late returns, the total number of books launched on to the market in 1988 rose to 62,023, close on twice as many as twenty years ago.

Ironically, the only consolation for the hard pressed author is the steep increase in book prices which has not so much depressed sales as increased the amount earned by royalties.

Since no one is predicting a dramatic change in current trends, it is small wonder that individual authors are looking at ways of increasing their share of the existing cake.

With PLR, the bone of contention is the sampling procedure which seems to underscore some writers. It is based on all loans from a selection of public libraries (about 1% of the national total). These figures are then multiplied in proportion to total library lending to produce, for each book, an estimate of its annual total loans throughout the country. Libraries in the sample change every two to four years. This can lead to some puzzling results. Writing in *The Weekend Guardian*, David Holbrook cited his own experience:

> 'A novel which had over the previous five years been issued from 2,265 times to 3,734 times, suddenly slumped to 95 issues. I was pleased, of course, that a new novel, *Nothing Larger Than Life*, went out 4,727 times (earning me the magnificent sum of £68.54). But there seems to be no explanation of why another novel, *Flesh Wounds*, should be issued only 1,103 times this year instead of 3,828 in 1982–3 or 1,512 last year.'

More curiosities are thrown up by the sampling of Holbrook's critical works:

> 'My *Gustav Mahler And The Courage To Be*, usually borrowed between 1,200 and 1,400 times in previous years scores a duck this year, and my study of Sylvia Plath, issued in previous years from 1,300 to 2,400 times, slumps to 502.'

The latest report from John Sumsion, the PLR Registrar, admits that 'the sampling error estimated from actual PLR loans reported was found (after research at Reading University) to be considerably greater than was estimated in 1981'. To improve matters, the statistical sample is to be enlarged from twenty to thirty libraries, with more small and medium-sized service points observed. Whether this is enough to satisfy David Holbrook remains to be seen, though the promise to include a mobile Welsh library may do wonders for his critical study of Dylan Thomas.

Registering for PLR

To qualify for PLR an author must be resident in the United Kingdom or West Germany (the latter as part of a reciprocal deal). For a book to be eligible it must be printed, bound and put on sale. It must not be mistaken for a newspaper or periodical, have more than three writers or illustrators named on the title page or be a musical score. Crown copyright is excluded, also books where authorship is attributed to a company or association. But – and this is where mistakes often occur – the author does *not* have to own copyright to be eligible for PLR. Anyone who has disclaimed copyright as part of a flat fee commission, for instance, will still have a claim if his name is on the title page.

Under PLR, the sole writer of a book may not be its sole author. Others named on the title page, such as illustrators, translators, compilers, editors and revisers, may have a claim to authorship. Where there are joint authors, two writers say, or a writer and illustrator, they can strike their own bargain on how their entitlement is to be split. But translators may apply, without reference to other authors, for a 30% fixed share (to be divided equally between joint translators). Similarly, an editor or compiler may register a 20% share provided he has written 10% of the book or at least 10 pages of text. Joint editors or compilers must divide the 20% share equally.

Authors and books can be registered for PLR only when application is made during the author's lifetime. However, once an author is registered, the PLR on his books continues for 50 years after his death. If he wishes, he can assign PLR to other people and bequeath it by will.

If a co-author is dead or untraceable, the remaining co-author can still register for a share of PLR so long as he provides supporting evidence as to why he alone is making application. The PLR office keeps a file of missing authors (mostly illustrators) and help is available from publishers, the writers' organisations and the Association of Illustrators, 1 Colville Place, London W1P 1HN.

Apart from widening the sample of loans, the latest changes in the calculation of PLR include the registration of books published up to ten years after the author's death and a share of monies to translators whose names appear on the verso of title pages. Moreover, in future, the minimum payment will be £1 per author rather than £1 per book. It's enough to make you want to book first class to the Caribbean.

PLR application forms and details can be obtained from:

The Registrar, PLR Office, Bayheath House, Prince Regent Street, Stockton-on-Tees, Cleveland TS18 1DF. Tel 0642 604699.

UK Publishers

AA Publishing

The Automobile Association, Fanum House, Basingstoke, Hants RG21 2EA
☎ 0256 492929
Telex 858538 AABAS G Fax 0256 493389

Managing Director *J. V. Howard*
Approx Annual Turnover £10 million

Publishes maps, atlases and guidebooks, motoring and leisure. About 100 titles in 1988.

Editorial Director *Michael Buttler* Unsolicited mss not welcome.

AB Academic Publishers

PO Box 42, Bicester, Oxon OX6 7NW
☎ 0869 241825

Managing Director *E. Adam*

Mainly a publisher of journals; only a few books. *Publishes* learned journals and books in the fields of agriculture, economics and related subject areas, education, forestry, material science and metallurgy, mathematics, medicine, nutrition. New journals coming out regularly. 1988 releases included the *International Journal of Catering and Health* (hygiene and nutrition in food service), and *Bioacoustics* an international journal of animal sound and its recording (in association with the British Library National Sound Archive). New journals scheduled for 1989 include *The International Review of Victimology.* Unsolicited synopses and ideas for books are welcome provided they are of a high academic level.
Royalties paid annually.

Abacus

See **Sphere Books Ltd**

Abacus Kent

See **Gordon & Breach Science Publishers**

Abelard-Schuman Ltd

See **Blackie & Son Ltd**

Aberdeen University Press

Farmers Hall, Aberdeen AB9 2XT
☎ 0224 630724
Telex 739477 Fax 0224 643286

Managing Director *Colin Maclean*

FOUNDED 1840, the company was restricted to printing until 1979. Now owned by Pergamon Holdings. *Publishes* academic and general, principally Scottish with particular interest in dictionaries, Scottish history and Scottish literature. 33 titles in 1988.

Editorial Head *Colin Maclean* TITLES *Concise Scots Dictionary; A Linguistic Atlas of Late Mediaeval English; The History of Scottish Literature; The Waterfalls of Scotland; The Scottish Cat.* Unsolicited mss will be considered if they fall within AUP's categories of interest. Synopses and ideas for books welcome.
Royalties paid annually. *Overseas associates* Distribution overseas, as in the UK, by Pergamon.

Harry N. Abrams Inc.

43 High Street, Tunbridge Wells, Kent TN1 1XL
☎ 0892 45355
Telex 957565 Fax 0892 34905

Leading US Publisher of high-quality illustrated books, specialising in art, architecture, design and photography. About 80 titles a year.

Editorial office: **Harry N. Abrams Inc.,** New York.

Absolute Press

14 Widcombe Crescent, Bath, Avon BA2 6AH
☎ 0225 316013
Telex 449212 LANTEL G Fax 0225 69845

Managing Director *J. M. Croft*

FOUNDED 1980, the company brings out up to 10

titles a year. *Publishes* food- and wine-related subjects.

Editorial Director *J. M. Croft*

IMPRINT
Absolute Classics New play list. Publishing neglected world masterpieces in English translation. 10–15 titles annually. Unsolicited mss not welcome, though synopses and ideas for books are.
Royalties paid twice yearly.

Abson Books

Abson, Wick, Bristol, Avon BS15 5TT
☎ 0275822446

Partners *A. Bickerton, P. McCormack*

FOUNDED 1970, Abson publishes original paperbacks, but no fiction. National and European representation. 4 titles in 1988. *Publishes* English language glossaries, literary puzzle books, West Country, general information.

Editorial Head *A. Bickerton* TITLES *American English; Cockney Rhyming Slang; Jane Austen Quiz and Puzzle Book; Get Squash Straight; Job Hunters' Work Book; Correct Way to Speak Bristol; Resolving Rubik's Magic Cube; Into France with Ease.* Welcome unsolicited mss but require return postage.
Royalties either once or twice yearly.

Academic Press Inc. (London) Ltd

24–8 Oval Road, London NW1 7DX
☎ 01–267 4466
Telex 25775 Acpres G Fax 01–482 2293

Managing Director *Joan Fujimoto*

Part of **Harcourt Brace Jovanovich,** USA. Now also own **Holt Rinehart & Winston, W. B. Saunders Co.** and Ballière Tindall. *Publishes* academic, agriculture, animal care, archaeology, biology, chemistry, economics, educational, engineering, geography, geology, mathematics and statistics, medical, physics, psychology, reference books, scientific, technical, sociology, veterinary. 150 titles in 1988.

Editorial Director *Dr Conrad Guettler*

DIVISIONS
Academic Press, Medical Books
Mss, synopses and ideas welcome.
Royalties paid annually for Academic Press titles, twice yearly for **Ballière Tindall** titles.

Authors' Rating A good, solid list closely tied to the university market. A natural for academics who put reputation before earnings.

Academy Editions

7 Holland Street, London W8 4NA
☎ 01–937 6996
Telex 896928 Academ G Fax 01–723 9540

Managing Director *Dr Andreas C. Papadakis*

FOUNDED 1967. Belongs to the Academy Group Ltd. *Publishes* books and magazines on art and architecture: *Architectural Design Magazine, Art & Design Magazine, The Journal of Philosophy and the Visual Arts* and *The UIA Journal.* 28 titles in 1988. Owns The London Art Bookshop in Holland Street, London W8, and the Art Shop at the Royal College of Art (selling art objects and materials).

Editorial Director *Dr Andreas C. Papadakis*
TITLES *Leonidov* Andrei Gozak & Andrei Leonidov; *Alphonse Mucha: Life & Art* Giri Mucha; *What is Deconstruction?* Andrew Benjamin & Christopher Norris; *Deconstruction Omnibus* Andreas Papadakis, Andrew Benjamin & Catherine Cooke.
No unsolicited mss but welcome unsolicited synopses and ideas.
Royalties paid annually.

Acair Ltd

Unit 8A, 7 James Street, Stornaway, Isle of Lewis, Scotland
☎ 0851 3020

Manager/Editorial Director *Agnes Rennie*

Publishes academic, biography and autobiography, children's, educational and text books, Gaelic, history/antiquarian, military, music, poetry, reference books and dictionaries, religious, Scottish culture, sports and games, transport. Unsolicited mss welcome.
Royalties paid twice yearly.

Addison–Wesley Publishers Ltd

Finchampstead Road, Wokingham, Berks RG11 2NZ
☎ 0734 794000
Telex 836136 ADIWES G Fax 0734 794035

Vice-President International *Peter Hoenigsberg*
Chairman *Don Hammonds*
Director/General Manager *Roderick Bristow*

Together with its parent company, **A–W Publishing Co. Inc.,** Massachusetts, USA, the company was bought by Pearson Longman in 1988 making it part of one of the biggest book publishers in the western world. *Publishes* scientific, technical, academic and senior school books, and is one of the leading computer science publishers. Several series covering computer science, micro-electronics and international business, for the international market. 300 titles in 1988.

Head of Acquisitions *Sarah Mallen* Unsolicited mss, synopses and ideas for books welcome.
Royalties paid twice yearly, in April and October.

Authors' Rating As part of the Pearson Longman conglomerate, offers exciting prospects for education writers hoping to break into the American market.

Adlard Coles Ltd

See **Grafton Books Ltd**

Airlife Publishing Ltd

7 St John's Hill, Shrewsbury, Shropshire SY1 1JE
☎ 0743 235651
Telex 35161 HOGROB G   Fax 0743 232944

Chairman/Managing Director *A. D. R. Simpson*
Approx Annual Turnover *c.* £1.5 million

Established to publish specialist aviation titles. *Publishes* both technical and general titles for pilots, historians and enthusiasts. 24 titles in 1988.

Editorial Head *A. D. R. Simpson* TITLES *Open Season; Flying the Big Jets; Whittle – The True Story; The Trees of Shropshire.*

IMPRINT
Swan Hill Press launched early 1989 to handle gradually broadening list, specialising in areas of country sport, local interest, natural history, travel and adventure.
Unsolicited mss, synopses and ideas for books welcome.
Royalties paid annually, twice yearly by arrangement.

Albyn Press

See **Charles Skilton Publishing Group**

Alison Press

See **Secker & Warburg Ltd**

Ian Allan Ltd

Terminal House, Shepperton TW17 8AS
☎ 0932 228950
Telex 929806   Fax 0932 232366

Chairman *Norman Miles*
Managing Director *Michael Harris*

Publishes atlases and maps, aviation, biography and autobiography, hobbies, guide books, defence and militaria, nautical, reference and dictionaries, transport, travel and topography. Recently acquired the general list of Jane's Transport Press from **Jane's Information Group**. 80 titles in 1988.

Publishing Manager *A. Farrow* Unsolicited mss considered.

Philip Allan Publishers

Market Place, Deddington, Oxford OX5 4SE
☎ 0869 38652   Fax 0869 38803

Managing Director *Philip Allan*
Approx Annual Turnover £1.2 million

FOUNDED 1973. Specialist publishers of books in accounting, economics, finance, politics and business studies. Also publish a range of teaching magazines and journals, including the *Economic Review, Geography Review, Contemporary Record* and *MBA Review*. 30 titles in 1989.

DIVISIONS

Business *Philip Allan* TITLES *Strategy and Marketing* Kenneth Simmonds. **Economics** *Philip Allan* TITLES *Modern Economics* David Heathfield. **Finance** *Philip Allan* TITLES *Multinational Finance* Adrian Buckley. **Politics** *Philip Cross* TITLES *British Party Politics* Gillian Peele. Almost all titles are commissioned; do not welcome unsolicited mss. Unsolicited synopses and ideas for books are welcome.
Royalties paid annually.

Allardyce, Barnett, Publishers

14 Mount Street, Lewes, East Sussex BN7 1HL
☎ 0273 479393

Publisher *Fiona Allardyce*
Managing Editor *Anthony Barnett*

FOUNDED 1981. *Publishes* art, literature and music, with emphasis on substantial collections by contemporary English language poets. 2 titles in 1988.

Editorial Director *Anthony Barnett* TITLES *Collected Poems* Veronica Forrest-Thompson;

Selected Poems Tim Longville.

IMPRINT
Agneau 2
Unsolicited mss or synopses not encouraged.

J. A. Allen & Co. Ltd

1 Lower Grosvenor Place, Buckingham Palace Road, London SW1W 0EL
☎ 01–834 0090
Telex 28905/3810 Fax 01–831 9489 Ref 3810

Chairman/Managing Director *Joseph A. Allen*
Approx Annual Turnover £600,000

Inaugurated in 1926 as part of J. A. Allen & Co. (The Horseman's Bookshop) Ltd. A separate independent company since 1960. *Publishes* equine and equestrian non-fiction. Presented with the British Horse Society's Award of Merit in 1980. 10 titles in 1988.

Editorial Manager *Mrs Caroline Burt* TITLES *Hickman's Farriery, Horse Breeding & Stud Management* Wynmalen; *A Dressage Judge's Handbook* Albrecht; *The Endurance Horse* Hyland; *Baily's Hunting Directory*; *Training Show Jumpers* Paalman; *The Basic Training of the Young Horse* Reiner Klimke.
Unsolicited mss, synopses and ideas for books welcome.
Royalties paid twice yearly.

W. H. Allen & Co. plc

Sekforde House, 175–9 St John Street, London EC1V 4LL
☎ 01–490 1232
Telex 28117 Fax 01–608 3360

Chairman *Robert Devereux*
Managing Director *Tim Hailstone*
Approx Annual Turnover £7 million

FOUNDED early 1800s. Recently acquired **Virgin Books** and **Allison & Busby**, and has just signed a three-year deal with *The Observer* to publish up to ten books a year. *Publishes* art, ballet, biography and memoirs, current affairs, educational, fiction, films, general history, humour, practical handbooks, reference, sociology, television, theatre, travel.

DIVISIONS
W. H. Allen *Mike Bailey* General fiction and non-fiction hardbacks *Pat Hornsey* Illustrated books **Mercury** *Robert Postema* Business books **Star** *Chelsey Fox* Mass-market paperbacks **Virgin Books** *Cat Ledger* Humour, music and youth culture **Allison & Busby** *Clive Allison* Literary fiction and non-fiction. Unsolicited mss, synopses and ideas for books welcome.
Royalties paid twice yearly.

Authors' Rating Once the home of fast-formula showbusiness biographies, W. H. Allen has been given a new lease of life with an injection of Richard Branson money. A varied output allows plenty of room for new ideas but they have to be potential bestsellers. Latest development is the revival of the Allison & Busby list including star turn Jack Trevor Story and his first and best novel *The Trouble With Harry*, about a body which won't stay buried – which is what they used to say about A & B.

Allison & Busby

See **W. H. Allen & Co. plc**

Alphabooks

See **A. & C. Black (Publishers) Ltd**

Amber Lane Press Ltd

Cheorl House, Church Street, Charlbury, Oxon OX7 3PR
☎ 0608 810024

Chairman *Brian Clark*
Managing Director *Judith Scott*

FOUNDED 1979 to publish modern play texts. *Publishes* plays and books on the theatre. 12 titles in 1988.

Editorial Head *Judith Scott* TITLES *Children of a Lesser God; Whose Life is it Anyway; After Aida; The Best of Friends; The Dresser* (play texts); *Portrait of Ellen Terry* David Cheshire; *Sir Donald Wolfit* Ronald Harwood; *Playwrights' progress, Patterns of Postwar British Drama* Colin Chambers & Mike Prior.
No unsolicited mss. Synopses and ideas welcome.
Royalties paid twice yearly.

Amsco

See **Omnibus Press**

Andersen Press Ltd

62–5 Chandos Place, Covent Garden, London WC2N 4NW
☎ 01–240 8162
Telex 261212 Litldn G Fax 01–240 8636

Managing Director/Publisher *Klaus Flugge*

FOUNDED 1976 by Klaus Flugge and named after Hans Christian Andersen. *Publishes* children's hardcover fiction. Sixty per cent of their books are sold as co-productions abroad. 40 titles in 1988.

Editorial Director *Audrey Adams* TITLES Best sellers include *Not Now Bernard* David McKee; *A Dark, Dark Tale* Ruth Brown; *I Want my Potty* Tony Ross; *Badger's Parting Gift* Susan Varley. AUTHORS Louis Baum, Philip Curtis, Michael Foreman, Satoshi Kitmura, Ursula Moray-Williams, Christine Nostlinger, Hazel Townson, Jean Willis. Unsolicited mss are only welcome for picture books or young readers (up to 12).
Royalties paid twice yearly.

Angus & Robertson (UK)

16 Golden Square, London W1R 4BN
☎ 01–437 9602
Telex 897284

Managing Director *Barry Winkleman*

Bought by Bay Books in 1981. Part of **Times Books Ltd.** FOUNDED over 100 years ago in Australia. *Publishes* biography and autobiography, children's books, cookery, wines and spirits, humour, illustrated and fine editions, natural history, photography, travel and topography. 100 titles in 1988.

Editorial Director *Valerie Hudson* TITLES Theatre and Television: *Neighbours: Behind the Scenes* James Oram; *Slapstick!* Tony Staveacre. Humour: *The World's Best Jokes Series; Kenny Everett's Ultimate Loo Book; Coping with Helen Lederer; Golf Widows* Noel Ford; *Girl Chasing* Cathy Hopkins & Gray Jolliffe. General non-fiction: *Myra Hindley, The Leslie Grantham Story* Jean Ritchie; *The Second Little Book of Hugs* Kathleen Keating. Design: *The Designer's Guide to Colour series.* Children's non-fiction: *Activity Books series: Fold Your Own Dinosaurs, Hand Shadows, More Tricks and Games with Paper.* Health & Self-Help: *Dr Claire Weekes' Self-Help series; The Art of Breastfeeding.* Wine: *Halliday's Australian Wine Compendium* and annual *Wine Guides.*
Welcome unsolicited mss, synopses and ideas for books (other than adult fiction).
Royalties paid twice yearly.

Authors' Rating Mostly light entertainment books which sell as strongly in newsagents as in bookshops. Close links with Australian market.

Antique Collectors' Club

5 Church Street, Woodbridge, Suffolk IP12 1DS
☎ 0394 385501 Fax 0394 34434

Joint Managing Directors *John Steel, Diana Steel*

FOUNDED 1966. Has a five-figure membership spread throughout the world. It was in response to the demand for information on 'what to pay' that the price guide series was introduced in 1968 with the first edition of *The Price Guide to Antique Furniture.* Club membership costs about £15 per annum. Members buy the Club's publications at concessional rates. *Publishes* specialist books on antiques and collecting. Subject areas include furniture, silver/jewellery, metalwork, glass, textiles, art reference, ceramics, horology. Also books on architecture and gardening.

Editorial Head *John Steel* TITLES *The English Garden in Our Time* Jane Brown; *The Book of Wine Antiques* R. Butler & G. Walking; *The Price Guide to Antique Furniture* John Andrews; *English Country Houses* (3 vols) C. Hussey; *Popular 19th Century European Painting* Hook & Politmore; *The Dictionary of British Watercolour Artists* (2 vols) H. Mallalieu.
Unsolicited mss, synopses and ideas for books welcome.
Royalties paid quarterly as a rule, but can vary.

Antler Books Ltd/Berkswell Publishing Ltd

PO Box 420, Warminster, Wiltshire BA12 9XB
☎ 0985 40189

Chairman/Managing Director *John Stidolph*

Antler Books (FOUNDED 1979) and Berkswell (1974) merged to form this new company in 1985. There are now plans to form a new imprint to publish titles with a West Country flavour. *Publishes* illustrated books, royalty, heritage, country sports. 4 titles in 1988. Welcome unsolicited mss, synopses and ideas for books.
Royalties paid according to contract.

Anvil Press Poetry

69 King George Street, London SE10 8PX
☎ 01–858 2946

Managing Director *Peter Jay*

FOUNDED 1968 to promote contemporary English and foreign poetry (in translation). English list includes Peter Levi and Carol Ann Duffy, and has now developed to the point at which most of Anvil's new titles are new volumes by their regulars. Only one or two first collections by new writers a year.

Editorial Director *Peter Jay* Welcome unsolicited mss.

Authors' Rating Distancing himself from the

aggressive marketing tactics paraded by some other houses, Peter Jay is said to be 'the least likely of all publishers to sign a fashionable poet for merely commercial reasons!' But he has had a great success with younger poets.

Apple

See **Quarto Publishing plc (UK Packagers Section)**

Appletree Press Ltd

7 James Street South, Belfast, Co. Antrim BT2 8DL
☎ 0232 243074/246756 Telex 42094 Books G

Managing Director *John Murphy*

FOUNDED 1974. Currently have about 100 books in print. *Publishes* mainly Irish interest non-fiction.

Senior Editor *Douglas Marshall* TITLES *Ireland: The Complete Guide; Real Ireland; Northern Ireland: The Background to the Conflict.* Prefer initial letter or synopsis.
Royalties paid twice yearly.

Aquarian Press Ltd

See **Thorsons Publishing Group Ltd**

Aquila Publishing (UK) Ltd

See **Prospice Publishing Ltd**

The Architectural Press

9 Queen Anne's Gate, London SW1H 9BY
☎ 01–222 4333
Telex 8953505 Fax 01–222 5196

Managing Director *Leslie Fairweather*

The Architectural Press book titles were recently bought by **Butterworth Scientific.** Publications now consist of four magazines: *The Architects' Journal, The Architectural Review, Designers' Journal, A. J. Focus,* plus one annual called *Specification.* In addition, *The Architects' Journal* publishes two occasional supplements, *Renovation* and *Architech* (Information Technology.)

Argus Books Ltd

Boundary Way, Hemel Hempstead, Herts HP2 7ST
☎ 0442 66551

Managing Director *Peter Welham*
Publisher *Rab Macwilliam*
Approx Annual Turnover £750,000

The book-publishing division of Argus Specialist Publications, magazine publisher. *Publishes* crafts, field sports, leisure and hobbies, modelling, new technology, wine and beer making, woodwork. 40 titles in 1988. Prefer to see synopses rather than completed mss.
Royalties paid twice yearly.

Aris & Phillips Ltd

Teddington House, Warminster, Wiltshire BA12 8PQ
☎ 0985 213409

Managing/Editorial Director *Adrian Phillips*

FOUNDED 1972, publishing books on Egyptology. A family firm which has remained independent. *Publishes* academic, classical, oriental and hispanic classics. 21 titles in 1988.

Hispanic Classics Editor *Lucinda Phillips* With such a highly specialised list, unsolicited mss and synopses are not particularly welcome, although synopses will be looked at.
Royalties paid twice yearly.

Ark

See **Routledge**

Arlington Books, Publishers, Ltd

15–17 King Street, St James's, London SW1Y 6QU
☎ 01–930 0097 Fax 01–321 0190

Chairman *Desmond Elliott*

FOUNDED 1960 by Desmond Elliott. Has remained independent. *Publishes* biography and autobiography, general fiction and crime, cookery, wines and spirits, health and beauty, humour, illustrated and fine editions. 25 titles in 1988.

Editor *Peter Danckwerts* TITLES *Home Ecology* Karen Christensen; *The Assertive Woman* Phelps & Austin; *Overcoming Endometriosis* Mary Lou Ballwegg; *Ceremony of Innocence* Anthony Cassidy. Unsolicited mss will be looked at but prefer synopsis with covering letter, plus s.a.e., in first instance.
Royalties paid twice yearly.

Armada

See **Collins Publishers**

Arms & Armour Press Ltd

Artillery House, Artillery Row,
London SW1P 1RT
☎ 01–222 7676
Telex 9413701 Caspub G Fax 01–799 1514

Chairman/Managing Director *Philip Sturrock*

Part of **Cassell plc.** *Publishes* aviation, crafts and hobbies, military and war, nautical, politics and world affairs, transport. 50 titles in 1988.

Editorial Director *Rod Dymott* TITLES *War Games! Rehearsal for Battle* Meisner & Fowler; *Jungle Warfare: Experiences & Encounters* John Cross; *Terrorism in the 80s* Edgar O'Ballance; *Battles & Battlescenes of WW2* David Chandler. Unsolicited mss and synopses welcome.
Royalties paid annually.

Edward Arnold (Publishers) Ltd

See **Hodder & Stoughton Ltd**

E. J. Arnold Publishing

Lockwood Distribution Centre, Parkside Lane, Dewsbury Road, Leeds LS11 5TD
☎ 0532 772112 Telex 556347

Managing Director *David Adam*
Approx Annual Turnover £5.4 million

Owned by the **Pergamon Group.** *Publishes* atlases and maps, biology and zoology, chemistry, computer science, computer software (educational), economics, educational and textbooks, geography and geology, history and antiquarian, languages and linguistics, mathematics and statistics, music, and physics. 120 titles in 1988. Education division sold to Thomas Nelson for £17 million.

Publishing Director *Stan Sharp* Unsolicited mss considered.
Royalties paid annually.

Arrow Books Ltd

See **Century Hutchinson Ltd**

Artech House

28 Eaton Row, London SW1 0JA
☎ 01–235 8121 Telex 885744 MICSOL G

Managing Director (USA) *William Bazzy*

FOUNDED 1970. The European office of Artech House Inc., Boston. *Publishes* electronic engineering. 50 titles in 1988.

Editorial Head *Martin Bailey* Will consider unsolicited mss and synopses.
Royalties paid twice yearly.

Artist's House

See **Mitchell Beazley Ltd**

Ashford Press Publishing

1 Church Road, Shedfield, Hampshire SO3 2HW
☎ 0329 834265
Telex 859783 Fax 0329 834250

Chairman *Clive Martin*
Publishing Director *Richard Joseph*
Approx Annual Turnover £800,000

FOUNDED 1984 and taken over by Martins Printing Group in 1987. Now *publishes* about 40 books a year. Successful 1988 titles included *Groc's Candid Guides* series to the Greek Islands, *Shropshire Lad, Fair Game, Bridge is Still an Easy Game.* Specialises in non-fiction, nautical, field sports, travel, education and business.

Publishing Head *Richard Joseph* Unsolicited mss welcome if return postage included. Synopses and ideas for books considered.
Royalties paid twice yearly.

Authors' Rating An exciting young company with a strong sense of marketing and promotion.

Ashgrove Press Ltd

4 Brassmill Centre, Brassmill Lane, Bath, Avon BA1 3JN
☎ 0225 25539 Fax 0225 69845

Chairman/Managing Director *Robin Campbell*

FOUNDED 1980. Originally published local history but then moved more into 'alternative' life-styles. *Publishes* health, healing and diet, psychology, metaphysics, countryside, regional and local subjects. 7 titles in 1988. Unsolicited mss welcome, preferably after initial letter. Synopses and ideas for books welcome.
Royalties paid twice in the first year; thereafter annually.

Athlone Press

44 Bedford Row, London WC1R 4LY
☎ 01–405 9836 Telex 261507 ref 1334

Managing Director *Brian Southam*

FOUNDED 1950 as the publishing house of the University of London. Now wholly independent, but preserves links with the University via an academic advisory board. Anticipated developments in the near future: more emphasis on women's/feminist studies and environmental/ 'green' issues, including medicine. *Publishes* archaeology, architecture, art, economics, history, medical, music, Japan, oriental, philosophy, politics, religion, science, sociology, zoology, women's/feminist issues. 35 titles in 1988.

Editorial Head *Brian Southam* Unsolicited academic mss welcome. Synopses and ideas for books considered.
Royalties paid annually/twice yearly by arrangement. *Overseas associates* The Athlone Press, Atlantic, New Jersey, USA.

Atlantic Large Print

See **Chivers Press (Publishers)**

Attic Books

The Folly, Rhosgoch, Painscastle, Builth Wells, Powys LD2 3YJ
☎ 04975 205

Managing Director *Jack Bowyer*

FOUNDED 1984 by its architect owners. *Publishes* books on building crafts, architecture and engineering. Technical books for the industry dealing mainly with restoration and conservation. 3 titles in 1989.

Editorial Head *Jack Bowyer*

IMPRINT
Orion Books TITLES *A History of Buildings* Jago V. Swillerton & Toomer. Unsolicited mss, synopses and ideas for books welcome.
Royalties paid annually.

Aurum Press Ltd

33 Museum Street, London WC1A 1LD
☎ 01–631 4596
Telex 299557 AURUM G Fax 01–580 2469

Managing Director *Timothy J. M. Chadwick*

FOUNDED 1977. A member of The Really Useful Group plc. Committed to producing high quality illustrated non-fiction books, biographies, travel and health. 40 titles in 1988.

Publishing Directors *Michael Alcock* (adult books), *Sue Tarsky* (children's books) TITLES *A World Portrait of Golf* Brian Morgan; *Camille* Reine-Marie Paris; *Rock 'n' Roll Cuisine* Peggy-Sue Honeyman-Scott & Robin Le Mesurier; *G.O.S.H. ABC Book; Mrs Mary Malarky's Seven Cats* Judy Hindley & Denise Teasedale.

IMPRINT
Aurum Books for Children launched Autumn 1988, specialising in picture books for the under fives and classic story books.
Must see synopsis before considering completed mss.
Royalties paid twice yearly.

Authors' Rating Owned by the Really Useful Company which, in turn, is controlled by the Incredibly Successful Andrew Lloyd Webber, Aurum went through a period of uncertainty when its parent decided against further diversification into more theatrical enterprises. But rumours of a sale were hotly denied and with a reported strengthening of the bottom line, further expansion is promised.

Avebury

See **Gower Publishing Group**

Samuel Bagster & Sons Ltd

See **Marshall Pickering**

Bailey Bros & Swinfen Ltd

Warner House, Bowles Well Gardens, Folkestone, Kent CT19 6PH
☎ 0303 850501
Telex 96328 Bailey G Fax 0303 850162

Chairman/Managing Director *J. R. Bailey*

FOUNDED 1929. In 1967, to accommodate the expanding business in educational and trade publishing, they moved from London to Folkestone. Now cover distribution for book publishers, subscription processing for journal publishers, and a publicity mailing service for book publishers. Part of Bailey & Swinfen Holdings. *Publishes* general, children's and reference.

Editorial Director *J. R. Bailey* TITLES *The Data Book for Pipe Fitters and Pipe Welders* E. H. Williamson; *The Basic Gurkhali Dictionary; White Tie Tales* John Morecroft; *Act imaginatively* Stanley Blow; *The School Library* Keith Barker. Do not welcome unsolicited mss but will consider unsolicited synopses and ideas.
Overseas offices in Australia and New Zealand.

Howard Baker Press Ltd

27A Arterberry Road, Wimbledon, London SW10 8AF
☎ 01–947 5482

Chairman/Managing Director *W. Howard Baker*

FOUNDED 1968 in Bloomsbury and moved to Wimbledon in 1971. *Publishes* general non-fiction, political science, autobiography, de-luxe editions, biography, maps, reference books, specialist facsimile editions in volume form of pre-war magazines such as *Magnet, Gem,* etc.

IMPRINTS

Howard Baker, Greyfriars Press, Greyfriars Book Club No unsolicited mss. Synopses welcome if accompanied by s.a.e.
Royalties paid twice yearly.

Ballière Tindall

See **Academic Press Inc. (London) Ltd**

Bantam/Bantam Press

See **Transworld Publishers Ltd**

Arthur Barker Ltd

See **Weidenfeld & Nicolson Ltd**

Barny Books

The Cottage, Hough on the Hill, near Grantham, Lincs NG32 2BB
☏ 040050246

Managing Director *Molly Burkett*
Approx Annual Turnover £10,000

Founded with the aim of encouraging new writers and illustrators. *Publishes* children's books. Also offer an advisory service to writers to encourage own publication and ask for a £10 fee to cover costs/postage.

Editorial Head *Molly Burkett* Too small a concern to have the staff/resources to deal with unsolicited mss. Writers with strong ideas should approach Molly Burkett by letter in the first instance.
Royalties Division of profits 50/50.

Barracuda Books Ltd (Quotes Ltd)

Meadows House, Well Street, Buckingham, Bucks MK18 1EW
☏ 0280 814441/2

Managing Directors *Clive Birch* (Barracuda), *Carolyn Birch* (Quotes Ltd)

Barracuda was formed in 1974, and its sister company Quotes in 1985. The **Sporting and Leisure Press** imprint was launched in 1976, and **Saga** in 1987. Now developing co-ventures with industry and commercial organisations. *Publishes* local and natural history, country and sporting life, military, transport, church and genealogical histories. 41 titles in 1988.

DIVISIONS

Barracuda Books *Clive Birch* TITLES *Yesterday's Town: Dulwich; Lincolnshire Methodism.* **Quotes Ltd** *Carolyn Birch* TITLES *Chenies and Chorleywood in Camera; Methodism in Camera; Nottinghamshire Buses in Camera.* **Saga** Popular heritage TITLES *The Lumie Tree (Town and Thames in the '20s).* **Sporting & Leisure Press** *A Potter's Tale (Stoke City Football Club).* Unsolicited mss, synopses and ideas for books welcome.
Royalties paid annually.

Barrie & Jenkins Ltd

289 Westbourne Grove, London W11 2QA
☏ 01–727 9636
Telex 267009 Fax 01–229 4571

Managing Director *Julian Shuckburgh*

Part of **Century Hutchinson.** *Publishes* general non-fiction, including antiques, art, gardening, history. Now publishing fiction since mid-1989.

Editorial Directors *Anne Furniss, Euan Cameron, Sarah Molloy* TITLES *History of Cricket* Benny Green; *Paradise Lost* Christopher Wood. Will consider unsolicited mss but prefer initial introductory letter.
Royalties paid twice yearly.

Authors' Rating A welcome revival of a publishing name which dates back to Florence Nightingale (one of Barrie & Jenkins' first authors). Benefits from sales and marketing support from Century Hutchinson. After a ten year gap, the restarted fiction list is set to grow at a maximum of 24 new titles a year. Fiction editor Sarah Molloy describes her project as 'long-term' with 'a commitment to building authors'. Suiting action to words, the list was launched with three young writers.

John Bartholomew & Son Ltd

12 Duncan Street, Edinburgh EH9 1TA
☏ 031–667 9341
Telex 728134 Fax 031–662 4282

Chairman *George Barber*
Managing Director *David Ross Stewart*
Approx Annual Turnover £8.5 million

ESTABLISHED over 150 years ago. Produces everything from town plans to world atlases including the cartography for the *Times Atlas of the World* (**Times Books** is now its sister company). Family owned until ten years ago, when it was sold to

Reader's Digest. Bought by News International in 1985. 50 titles in 1988.

IMPRINTS
Bartholomew *Colin Kirkwood* TITLES *Road Atlas Britain; Walk the Cotswolds; Walk the Cornish coastal path 1:100,000 Leisure Maps; Road Atlas Europe; Tourist Route Maps; Whisky Map.* **Geographia** *Colin Kirkwood* Street maps and atlases TITLES *Greater London Street Atlas; 30 Miles Around London; Devon Tourist Maps.* **J & B Maps** *Colin Kirkwood* TITLES *Touring Map of Scotland; Irish Family Names Map.* **Clyde/ Bartholomew** Joint publications of leisure/ tourist maps of overseas countries and island groups.
No unsolicited mss. Letter essential in the first instance.
Royalties paid twice yearly.

B. T. Batsford Ltd

4 Fitzhardinge Street, London W1H 0AH
☎ 01–486 8484 Fax 01–487 4296
Telex 943763 CROCOM G Ref BAT

Managing Director *P. A. J. Kemmis Betty*
Editorial Director *T. Auger*
Approx Annual Turnover £5 million

FOUNDED 1843, as a bookseller; started publishing in 1874. An independent company which has become the world leader in books on chess and lacecraft. *Publishes* non-fiction: academic and scholarly, archaeology, architecture and design, cinema, crafts and hobbies, educational and textbooks, fashion and costume, history and antiquarian, literary criticism and linguistics, sports and games, theatre and drama, transport, travel and topography, vocational training/ careers. Generally publish 150 plus titles a year, with a backlist of 1200.

DIVISIONS
Academic/Educational (including Mitchell imprint) *Tony Seward* TITLES *Mitchell's Building Construction; The English Heritage Book of Avebury; Victorian Things.* **Special Interest** *Pauline Snelson* TITLES *Quinlan's Illustrated Directory of Film Stars; The Batsford Book of Chess Openings; Dress in Ireland; London Traveletter Guidebook; Rhododendrons of China.* **Arts and Crafts** *Timothy Auger* TITLES *Design Techniques for Modern Lace; The Crochet Workbook.* Welcomes unsolicited mss and synopses/ideas for books.
Royalties paid twice in first year, annually thereafter.

Authors' Rating A quietly thriving independent company which does well by sticking to what it knows best – mainly hobbies and intellectual games. A new series with English Heritage promises well.

BBC Books

80 Wood Lane, London W12 0TT
☎ 01–576 2000
Telex 934678 Fax 01–749 8766

Head of Book Publishing *Nicholas Chapman*
Senior Commissioning Editors *Sheila Ableman, Suzanne Webber*

BBC Books, a division of BBC Enterprises, is expanding its list to the extent that it now publishes books which, though linked with BBC television or radio, may not simply be the 'book of the series'. An example of this is the publishing of cookery books by past television cooks which no longer have series running. 100 titles in 1988.
TITLES *Reaching for the Skies* Ivan Rendell; *The Mind Machine* Colin Blakemore; *Out of the Doll's House* Angela Holdsworth; *At Home with The Roux Brothers* Michel & Albert Roux; *Floyd on Britain and Ireland* Keith Floyd; *Supersense* John Downer; *Allo 'Allo: The War Diaries of René Artois* John Haselden. Books with no BBC link are of no interest, and unsolicited mss (which come in at the rate of 15 weekly) are rarely even read. If books are not commissioned, they are packaged and devised in consultation with known writers, or through known agents. Having said that, strong ideas well expressed will always be considered, and promising letters stand a chance of further scrutiny.
Royalties paid twice yearly.

Authors' Rating After a long period of hibernation, BBC Books is shaping up to be a first-rank publisher. Home of bestsellers linked to popular television series. Plans to go into children's books in a big way.

Bedford Square Press

26 Bedford Square, London WC1B 3HU
☎ 01–636 4066 Fax 01–436 3188

Managing Director *Jonathan Croall*
Approx Annual Turnover £100,000

FOUNDED 1968. Publishing imprint of The National Council for Voluntary Organisations. Established to reflect the concerns of the NCVO in relation to the voluntary sector. In 1987 new policy led to wider brief to publish books on social issues for a wider audience, and representation by Troika. Now celebrating 21 years of social action publishing. *Publishes* social

action, community issues, directories, fundraising books. 13 titles in 1988.
TITLES *Voluntary Agencies Directory; The New Dissenters: The Non-Conformist Conscience in the Age of Thatcher; Shutdown – The Anatomy of a Shipyard Closure.* Unsolicited mss, synopses and ideas for books welcome, though most books are commissioned.
Royalties paid twice yearly.

Bellew Publishing Co. Ltd

Nightingale Centre, 8 Balham Hill,
London SW12 9EA
☎ 01–673 5611
Telex 8951182 GECOMS G Fax 01–675 3542

Chairman *Anthony Rainbird*
Managing Director *Ib Bellew*
Approx Annual Turnover £250,000

FOUNDED 1983 as a publisher/packager. *Publishes* craft, art and design, fiction, illustrated non-fiction, general interest, and politics. 12 titles in 1988. Welcomes unsolicited mss and synopses.
Royalties paid annually.

Berg Publishers Ltd

77 Morrell Avenue, Oxford OX4 1NQ
☎ 0865 245104 Fax 0865 791165

Chairman/Managing Director *Marion Berghahn*
Approx Annual Turnover £250,000

Publishes scholarly books in the fields of history, economics and other social sciences. Scholarly and general titles in literature and the arts, biography and current affairs published under the imprint **Oswald Wolff.** 60 titles in 1988.

Editorial Head *Justin Dyer* TITLES *Schopenhauer: Manuscript Remains* in 4 volumes; *Women of Theresienstadt* R. Schwertfeger.

IMPRINTS
Oswald Wolff Books TITLES *Leonard Bernstein* Gradenwitz; *Heinrich Böll* J. H. Reid. No unsolicited mss. Unsolicited synopses and ideas for books welcome.
Royalties paid annually.

BFI Publishing

British Film Institute, 21 Stephen Street,
London W1P 1PL
☎ 01–255 1444
Telex 27624 Fax 01–436 7950

Head of Publishing *Geoffrey Nowell-Smith*
Approx Annual Turnover £100,000

FOUNDED 1982. Part of the British Film Institute. *Publishes* film- or television-related academic books. 6 titles in 1988.

Editorial Head *Geoffrey Nowell-Smith* TITLES *Eisenstein Writings Volume 1: 1922-34* Richard Taylor; *The Last Picture Show: Britain's Changing Film Audience* David Docherty; *The Logic of the Absurd: On Film and Television Comedy* Jerry Palmer; *Ozu* David Bordwell; *Femininism and Film Theory* Constance Penely; *Film & TV The Way In: A Guide to Careers* Robert Angell; *Television and its Audience: International Research Perspectives* Phillip Drummond & Richard Paterson; *East of Dallas: The European Challenge to American Television* Allessandro Silj. Prefer unsolicited synopses and ideas rather than complete mss.
Royalties paid annually.

Bishopsgate Press Ltd

37 Union Street, London SE1 1SE
☎ 01–403 6544 Fax 01–403 5742

Chairman/Managing Director *Ian F. L. Straker*

FOUNDED 1800. Since then has been mainly producing financial books for the City but over the last five years has developed into general publishing. *Publishes* arts and crafts, biography, children's books, crafts, general books, non-fiction, poetry, religous books.

Publishing Director *Austen Smith* TITLES *Small Hand Big Ideas* Tony Hart; *Old Garden Flowers* Brian Halliwell; *Just Like You and Me* Johnny Morris; *Georgian Houses* Richard Reid; *Population: The Human Race* Eric McGraw; *The Book of Nature Reserves* Dennis Furnell; *Practical Guides* series. Unsolicited mss and synopses welcome.
Royalties paid twice yearly.

A. & C. Black (Publishers) Ltd

35 Bedford Row, London WC1R 4JH
☎ 01–242 0946 Telex 32524 Acblac

Chairman *Charles Black*
Joint Managing Directors *Charles Black and David Gadsby*
Approx Annual Turnover £4.8 million

Publishes academic, agriculture, antiques and collecting, archaeology, architecture and design, aviation, children's books, crafts and hobbies, educational and textbooks, fashion and costume, fine art and art history, geography and geology, guide books, history and antiquarian, medical, music, nautical, reference books, dictionaries, sports and games, theatre and drama, travel and topography, veterinary. 100 titles in 1988. TITLES *Writers' & Artists' Yearbook; The Blue Guides Travel series.*

IMPRINTS
Alphabooks, Nautical Publishing Co. Ltd. Welcome unsolicited mss, synopses and ideas for books.
Royalties payments vary according to each contract.

Authors' Rating With *Who's Who* on the list, how can a publisher go wrong? Well regarded in education and children's books. A new non-fiction list for children is planned and the famous Blue Guides list is set to expand.

Black Spring Press Ltd

46 Rodwell Road, East Dulwich,
London SE22 9LE
☎ 01–299 1514 Fax 01–299 4632

Managing Director *Simon Pettifar*

FOUNDED 1986. *Publishes* fiction, literary criticism, theatre and cinema studies, popular music. 5 titles in 1989.

Editor *Simon Pettifar* TITLES *The Paris Olympia Press: An Annotated Bibliography* Patrick J. Kearney; *D. H. Lawrence, An Unprofessional Study* Anaîs Nin; *King Ink* Nick Cave. Prefer to see a proposal rather than completed mss.
Royalties paid twice yearly.

Black Swan

See **Transworld Publishers Ltd**

Blackie & Son Ltd

Wester Cleddens Road, Bishopbriggs,
Glasgow G64 2NZ
☎ 041–772 2311
Telex 777283 BLACKI G Fax 041–762 0897

Chairman/Managing Director *R. Michael Miller*

FOUNDED 1809. Still independently owned. Educational and Academic divisions based in Glasgow. Children's division in London (see below). *Publishes* educational textbooks, children's books, academic and professional. 150 titles in 1988.

DIVISIONS
Academic *Dr A. G. Mackintosh* Biology, biochemistry, biotechnology, business studies, chemistry, concrete technology, earth sciences, ecology, engineering, food technology, materials technology, microbiology, packaging, physics, reference. **Children's** *A. D. Mitchell* located at 7 Leicester Place, London WC2H 7BP. Picture books for the very young/older children: *Topsy and Tim; Flower Fairies;* general fiction; fairy tales, folk tales and anthologies; non-fiction. **Educational** *A. Rosemary Wands* Textbooks; teachers' books and resource books covering all subjects across the curriculum for 5–18 years. Particular interest in mathematics, science, religious education, home economics.
Unsolicited mss, ideas and synopses welcome. Subsidiary company **Abelard-Schuman Ltd** (children's books).

Authors' Rating Mostly publish formula texts for the core curriculum and children's whimsy. Not exactly riveting but steady and reliable.

Blackstaff Press Ltd

3 Galway Park, Dundonald, Belfast BT16 0AN
☎ 021 387161

Directors *Michael Burns, Anne Tannahill*

FOUNDED 1971 by Jim and Diane Gracey and bought by Michael Burns in 1980. *Publishes* mainly but not exclusively Irish interest books, fiction, poetry, history, politics, natural history, and folklore. 17 titles in 1988.

Editorial Head *Anne Tannahill* Unsolicited mss, synopses and ideas welcome.
Royalties paid twice yearly.

Authors' Rating One of the best of the small publishers.

Basil Blackwell Ltd

108 Cowley Road, Oxford OX4 1JF
☎ 0865 791100 Fax 0865 791347

Chairman *Nigel Blackwell*
Managing Director *René Olivieri*

Part of the Blackwell Group, 50 Broad Street, Oxford. FOUNDED 1922 as an academic and educational publishing house; the early list included fiction, poetry and (curiously) Enid Blyton. Expanded into journals and now owns more than 50. Rapid growth in the 1970s and 1980s included the establishment of a wholly-owned distribution company, the takeover of Martin Robertson, and a joint venture company with **Polity Press.** In 1989 formed another joint venture company with National Computing Centre in Manchester. *Publishes* academic, economics, humanities, professional, social sciences, primary and secondary schoolbooks, books for teachers, general books. 300 titles in 1988.

DIVISIONS
Academic & General *John Davey*
Education *James Nash*
Journals *Sue Corbett*

IMPRINTS
Shakespeare Head Press *David Martin*
Raintree Press *James Nash* Unsolicited mss welcome, but prefer synopses with specimen chapter and table of contents.
Royalties paid annually. *Overseas associates* Basil Blackwell Inc., Cambridge, Massachusetts.

Authors' Rating Family-owned which at least guarantees shelf space in a certain leading bookseller. Comfortable relationships with authors. Strong in school publishing.

Blackwell Scientific Publications Ltd

Osney Mead, Oxford OX2 0EL
☎ 0865 240201
Telex 83355 Medbok G Fax 0865 721205

Chairman *Peter Saugman*
Managing Director *Robert Campbell*
Approx Annual turnover £27 million

FOUNDED 1939. Part of the Blackwell Group. Growth in the 1960s led to a move to Oxford. In 1987 the company broadened its base by buying **Collins'** professional list. *Publishes* medical, professional and science. 230 titles in 1988.

Editorial Director *Peter Saugman* TITLES *Textbook of Dermatology* edited by Rook *et al; Essential Immunology* Roitt; *Lecture Notes in Clinical Medicine* Rubenstein. Unsolicited mss and synopses welcomed.
Royalties paid annually. *Overseas associates* Blackwell Scientific Publications Inc., USA; Blackwell Scientific Publications Pty Ltd, Australia.

Authors' Rating A tightly organised, highly competent publisher. Rewards may not be madly generous but they do pay on time.

Blandford Publishing Ltd

Artillery House, Artillery Row,
London SW1P 1RT
☎ 01–222 7676
Telex 9413701 CASPUB G Fax 01–799 1514

Chairman/Managing Director *Philip Sturrock*

FOUNDED 1919, the company took its name from the location of its first office in London's West End. Taken over ten years ago by Link House and four years ago by United Newspapers. Acquired by **Cassell plc** who plan a rapid programme of expansion. *Publishes* animal care and breeding, acquaria, art and graphics, aviation, aviculture, bodybuilding and sport, crafts and hobbies, do-it-yourself, fashion and costume, fishing, gardening, history, humour, military and war, natural history, new age, photography, popular music, sports and games, theatre and drama, transport. 100 titles in 1988.

Editorial Director *Clare Howell*

DIVISIONS
Art & Graphics TITLES *Practical Chinese Painting* Jean Long. **Aviculture** TITLES *Popular Parrakeets* Dulcie & Freddie Cooke. **Crafts** TITLES *The Flower Arranger's Encyclopedia of Preserving and Drying* Maureen Foster. **Gardening** TITLES *The Fuchsia Grower's Handbook* Ron Ewart. **Military** TITLES *Soldier's War* Peter H. Liddle. **Natural History** *Turtles and Tortoises of the World* David Alderton.
Royalties paid twice yearly.

Bloodaxe Books Ltd

PO Box 1SN, Newcastle upon Tyne NE99 1SN
☎ 091–232 5988

Chairman *Simon Thirsk*
Managing Director *Neil Astley*

Publishes photography, poetry, literature and criticism, theatre and drama, women's studies. 21 titles in 1988. Ninety per cent of their list is poetry.

Editorial Director *Neil Astley* Unsolicited poetry mss welcome. Authors of other material should write first with details of their work.
Royalties paid annually.

Authors' Rating 'The liveliest and most innovative poetry house', according to the editor of *Poetry Review*. Strong on women's poetry and on translations.

Bloomsbury Publishing Ltd

2 Soho Square, London W1V 5DE
☎ 01–494 2111 Fax 01–434 0151

Chairman/Managing Director *Nigel Newton*

One of the three major new imprints set up in 1986, Bloomsbury was launched in a glare of publicity which made much of its radical manifesto: the attempt to bring authors into far greater involvement with the machinery of publishing, and the setting aside of a share of the company's equity for division among its authors. Bloomsbury was founded by Nigel Newton (ex-Sidgwick & Jackson) together with David Reynolds (ex-Shuckburgh Reynolds), who then headhunted Alan Wherry from Penguin (marketing) and Liz Calder from Cape (editorial). Less than 2 years after publication of their first titles, Bloomsbury had put 15 books onto *The Sunday Times* Bestseller list.

Publishing Directors *David Reynolds, Liz Calder* **Editorial Directors** *Kathy Rooney, Mike Petty* TITLES *When The Fighting is Over* John & Robert Lawrence; *Cat's Eye* Margaret Atwood; *No Time to Wave Goodbye* Ben Wicks; *A Case of Knives* Candida McWilliam; *Imagine* John Lennon; *Story of My Life* Jay McInerney; *Walking Tall* Simon Weston; *A Prayer for Owen Meany* John Irving.
Welcome unsolicited mss and synopses.
Royalties paid twice yearly (April/October).

Authors' Rating Notwithstanding all the Jeremiahs who said that Nigel Newton and his friends were biting off more than a mouthful, Bloomsbury can boast fiction and non-fiction lists which compare favourably with the output of bigger and older established rivals. The esteemed editor Liz Calder is as a magnet to top writers. Bloomsbury was among the first publishers to sign the Minimum Terms Agreement.

Bobcat

See **Omnibus Press**

The Bodley Head

30–32 Bedford Square, London WC1B 3SG
☎ 01–255 2393 Fax 01–255 1620

One of Britain's oldest publishing houses, The Bodley Head, is to close after several years of financial difficulties. The house will be absorbed by its sister company, Cape. Some books will be published by Cape under a Bodley Head imprint.

The Book Guild Ltd

Temple House, 25–6 High Street, Lewes, East Sussex BN7 2LU
☎ 0273 472534
Telex NOSLIP VIA 987562 COCHAS

Chairman *Gerald Konyn*
Managing Director *Carol Biss*
Approx Annual Turnover £500,000

FOUNDED 1982. *Publishes* fiction, general, juvenile, sport. 60 titles in 1988.

DIVISIONS
Fiction *Citizen Cocaine* Tony Walton; *Victorian Railway Days* Frances Bennion; *Sugar Cube in the Sky* Stephen Debenham; *The Heppelthwaite Mysteries* Michael McFall; *The Hannoverian Connection* Countess Althan; *The Longest Night* Hugh Franks. **General** *How Many Roads? A History and Guide to American Singer/Songwriters* Mike Swann; *What the Civilian Manager Isn't Taught* Colin Lyle; *Touring Days* Gavin Doyle; *Closest Correspondence* Evelyn King; *Tank Soldier* Norman Smith; *Seafaring in the Thirties* Capt McBrearty. **Religion and Philosophy** *Living As If: A View of Reincarnation* Ivor Morrish; *A Layman Considers His Faith* Dr Gurney-Smith; *Seeing Man Whole* Ted Moss. **Juvenile** *Leaving Mottram Park* Jill Chaney; *The Land of Tomorrow* Ben Maile.

IMPRINTS
Temple House Books *Carol Biss* TITLES *Breaking The Ice* Ian Crichton; *Selling: How to Succeed in the Sales Arena* David Baldwin; *Holiday Retreats for Cats and Dogs* Scarlett Tipping; *Weathervanes of Sussex* Brigid Chapman. No unsolicited mss. Ideas and synopses welcome.
Royalties paid twice yearly.

Authors' Rating Specialises in publishing books heavily subsidised by authors. Denies claims that it is a vanity publisher and prefers 'cooperative publishing' to describe an operation in which costs are divided between publisher and the author. But whichever way you say it, the author has to put money up front.

Bookmarks Publications

265 Seven Sisters Road, Finsbury Park, London N4 2DE
☎ 01–802 6145

Managing Director *Peter Marsden*
Approx Annual Turnover £75,000

FOUNDED 1979 to project the international socialist movement. Linked with the Socialist Workers Party and its internationally related organisations. 'Our aim is to build a list of socialist books and pamphlets which reaches across the spectrum of political issues.' *Publishes* politics, economics, labour history, trade unionism, international affairs. 7 titles in 1988.

DIVISIONS
General Publishing *Peter Marsden* **Revolutionary Classics** *Charles Hore* TITLES *The Fire Last Time: 1968 and After* Chris Harman; *The Labour Party: A Marxist History* Tony Cliff & Donny Gluckstein.
Unsolicited synopses and ideas welcome as long as they are compatible with existing policy. No unsolicited mss.

Royalties paid annually. *Overseas associates* Chicago, USA; Melbourne, Australia.

Bounty Books

Michelin House, 81 Fulham Road,
London SW3 6RB
☎ 01–581 9393
Telex 920191 Fax 01–589 8419

General Manager *Lanning Aldrich*

Part of **Paul Hamlyn Publishing** which is itself a part of the Octopus Publishing Group. FOUNDED 1981 as the Bargain Reprint Division of Octopus. *Publishes* out-of-print titles only: antiques, children's, cookery, facsimiles, fiction, gardening, general interest, humour, militaria, natural history, sport. No unsolicited mss, synopses or ideas for books.

Bowker–Saur Ltd

Borough Green, Sevenoaks, Kent TN15 8PJ
☎ 0732 884567
Telex 95678 Fax 0732 884079

Managing Director *Dr Shane O'Neill*

Part of **Butterworth & Co.** *Publishes* biography and library service; biography and autobiography, politics and world affairs.

Editorial Director *Shane O'Neill*. Editorial Office: Shropshire House, 2–10 Capper Street, London WC1E 6JA. Unsolicited mss considered. *Royalties* paid twice yearly.

Boxtree

36 Tavistock Street, London WC2E 7PB
☎ 01–379 4666 Fax 01–836 6741

Chairman *Hugh Campbell*
Managing Director *Sarah Mahaffy*
Senior Editor *Anna Selby*
Editor *Cheryl Brown*

FOUNDED April 1987, specialises in books linked to and about television programmes. Other areas of interest include books about collectables, leisure and children's non-fiction. Over 50 titles were planned for 1989. TITLES include *The Best of Treasure Hunt; Disappearing World; How they made Piece of Cake; Art of the Western World.* Ideas and synopses, especially from film, TV and production companies, are welcome.
Royalties paid twice yearly.

Authors' Rating Popular books linked to the best of commercial television. Boxtree is blessed with imagination and flair.

Marion Boyars Publishers Ltd

24 Lacy Road, London SW15 1NL
☎ 01–788 9522

Managing Director *Marion Boyars*

FOUNDED 1975. Formerly Calder and Boyars. *Publishes* academic and scholarly, architecture and design, biography and autobiography, business and industry, economics, fiction, health and beauty, law, literature and criticism, medical, music, philosophy, poetry, politics and world affairs, psychology, religion and theology, sociology and anthropology, theatre and drama, travel, women's studies. 30 titles in 1989.

Editorial Director *Marion Boyars* **Editor-in-Chief** *Arthur Boyars* **Non-fiction Editor** *Ken Hollings* **Iris Series Editor** *Stephanie Lewis* TITLES *State of the Art* Pauline Kael; *Collected Poems* Robert Creeley; *Stockhausen and Music* Karlheinz Stockhausen; *The Streetcleaners, The Yorkshire Ripper Case On Trial* Nicole Ward-Jouve; *The Devil and Dr Barnes, Portrait of an American Art Collector* Howard Greenfeld; *The Bathroom* Jean-Philippe Toussaint; *The Foreign Husband* Clive Collins.

Unsolicited mss not welcome for fiction; submissions from agents preferred. Unsolicited synopses and ideas welcome for non-fiction.
Royalties paid annually. *Overseas associates* Marion Boyars Publishers Inc., 26 East 33rd Street, New York, NY 10016, USA.

Authors' Rating A publisher with an eye for originality. A refuge for talent which others have failed to appreciate but can be offhand with lesser mortals.

Boydell & Brewer Ltd

PO Box 9, Woodbridge, Suffolk IP12 3DF
☎ 0394 411320

Publishes non-fiction only. All books commissioned. Most definitely do not welcome unsolicited material.

Authors' Rating A self-contained publisher best left to make their own decisions unhindered by authors or agents. Reports of confusing royalty statements.

BPS Books

St Andrews House, 48 Princess Road East, Leicester LE1 7DR
☎ 0533 549568 Fax 0533 470787

Publishing division of the British Psychological Society. *Publishes* psychology aimed at psychologists, other professional groups and the trade. 10-15 titles a year.

Editor *Cassy Spearing* TITLES *Learning to Talk: From Birth to Three* Louise T. Higgins; *Managing People at Work* Cary Cooper & Peter Makin; *Living with your Pain: A Self-Help Guide to Managing Pain* Annabel Broome & Helen Jellicoe; *So What is Psychology?* Anthony Gale.

Martin Brian & O'Keeffe Ltd

78 Coleraine Road, London SE3 7PE
☎ 01–858 5164

Chairman *Timothy O'Keeffe*
Approx Annual Turnover *c.*£10,000

FOUNDED 1971. *Publishes* general. No unsolicited mss but welcome synopses and ideas for books. 1 title in 1988.

Editorial Head *Timothy O'Keeffe* TITLES *Bogmail.*
Royalties paid twice yearly

Brimax Books Ltd

4–5 Studlands Park Industrial Estate, Exning Road, Newmarket, Suffolk CB8 7AU
☎ 0638 664611
Telex 817625 BRIMAX G Fax 0638 665220

Managing Director *Patricia Gillette*

Old established publisher specialising in children's books. Some educational: reading books for young children up to the age of 13, board books for the very young, and extensive casebound pre-school range for age group 3–5 years. All full colour and illustrated. Now part of the **Octopus Publishing Group**. Over 90 hardback titles in 1989. Unsolicited mss will be considered but would prefer to see synopses.
Royalties paid twice yearly.

Bristol Classic Press

226 North Street, Bristol BS3 1JD
☎ 0272 664093

Managing Director *T. A. G. Foss*
Approx Annual Turnover £225,000

Offshoot of Chapter & Verse Bookshops Ltd. FOUNDED 1977 to revive the study of classics in schools and colleges by producing cheap texts. *Publishes* academic and scholarly, archaeology, educational and textbooks, English literature, languages and linguistics, literature and criticism, philosophy, classics textbooks. 55 titles in 1989.

General Editor *John H. Betts* Unsolicited mss and synopses welcome.
Royalties paid annually.

The British Academy

20–21 Cornwall Terrace, London NW1 4QP
☎ 01–487 5966

Publications Officer *J. M. H. Rivington*
Approx Annual Turnover £115,000

FOUNDED 1901. The primary body for promoting scholarship in the humanities, the Academy publishes 10–15 titles a year, mostly in series of source material stemming from its own longstanding research projects. Main subjects include history, art and archaeology.

SERIES *Auctores Britannici Medii Aevi; Early English Church Music; Oriental Documents; Records of Social and Economic History.* Unsolicited proposals are forwarded to the relevant project committees. 'The British Academy does not publish for profit; *royalties* are paid only when titles have covered their costs.'

Brown, Son & Ferguson, Ltd

4–10 Darnley Street, Glasgow G41 2SD
☎ 041–429 1234

Chairman/Joint Managing Director *T. Nigel Brown*

FOUNDED 1850. Specialises in nautical text books, both technical and non-technical. Also *publishes* Boy Scout and Girl Guide books, and Scottish one-act and three-act plays.
Unsolicited mss, synopses and ideas for books welcome.
Royalties paid annually.

Brown Watson (Leicester) Ltd

55A London Road, Leicester LE2 0PE
☎ 0533 545008
Telex 342679 BWL GB Fax 0533 555782

Managing Director *Michael B. McDonald*

FOUNDED 1982. Part of **Peter Haddock Ltd.** *Publishes* children's books. 80 series in 1989. Most books are commissioned and therefore unsolicited mss and synopses are not welcome.

Authors' Rating Children's books for the cheaper end of the market. Authors must work fast to make money.

Buchan & Enright, Publishers (Fountain Press Ltd)

45 The Broadway, Tolworth, Surrey KT6 7DW
☎ 01–390 7768

FOUNDED 1982 in a spare bedroom by two ex-**Cassell** editors. Acquired by **Fountain Press Ltd** in 1988. *Publishes* biography, country pursuits, history and antiquarian, humour, military and war, sports and games. 10 titles in 1988.

Editor *Tony Buchan* TITLES *A–Z Self Employment* Sidney Bloch; *Egg on Your Face* Patrick Scrivenor; *Final Betrayal* Richard Garrett; *Histrionics* Mark Seaman. Prefer to see synopses and ideas rather than unsolicited mss.
Royalties paid twice yearly.

Burke Publishing Co. Ltd

Pegasus House, 116–20 Golden Lane, London EC1Y 0TL
☎ 01–253 2145
Telex 975573 Burke G

Chairman *Harold K. Starke*
Managing Director *Naomi Galinski*

FOUNDED 1935 to publish general books and children's fiction and non-fiction. Reconstituted in 1960 to concentrate on education. *Publishes* children's books, educational and textbooks (all levels), medical, reference books and dictionaries, the latter under the imprint of a wholly owned subsidiary, **Harold Starke Ltd.** 30 titles in 1988.

Editorial Director *Naomi Galinski* TITLES *Headstart Books; Read for Fun; Sparklers; Animals and their Environment; Encyclopaedia of Psychoactive Drugs; World Leaders; Young Specialist; Wake Up to the World of Science.* Welcome unsolicited mss, synopses and ideas but require return postage or s.a.e.
Royalties paid annually.

Graham Burn

9–13 Soulbury Road, Linslade, Leighton Buzzard, Beds LU7 2RL
☎ 0525 377963/376390 Fax 0525 382498
Telex 825562 Chacom G Burnpub

Publishes mainly for the overseas market. Current emphasis on total production services for other publishers.

Burns & Oates Ltd

See **Search Press Ltd**

Business Education Publishers

Leighton House, 17 Vine Place, Sunderland, Tyne & Wear SR1 3NA
☎ 091–567 4963

Joint Managing Directors *P. M. Callaghan, T. Harrison*
Approx Annual Turnover £250,000

FOUNDED 1981. Currently expanding into further and higher education, computing and books for the Health Service. *Publishes* business education, economics, law. 20 titles in 1988. TITLES *BTEC National Course Studies* Paul Callaghan, Tom Harrison & John Ellison; *Law for Housing Managers* Tom Harrison; *The Abbotsfield File* Paul Callaghan & John Ellison; *Computer Studies (for BTEC National)* Knott, Waites, Callaghan & Ellison; *Transferable Personal Skills (for BTEC)* D. Hind; *Getting Started with Information Technology* D. Eadson & K. Williams; *Marketing* A. Hill; *Travel and Tourism* P. Callaghan.
Unsolicited mss and synopses welcome.
Royalties paid annually.

Businessmates

See **Richard Drew Publishing Ltd**

Butterworth & Co. Ltd

Borough Green, near Sevenoaks, Kent TN15 8PH
☎ 0732 884567
Telex 95678 Fax 0732 882108

Chairman *W. Gordon Graham*
Chief Executive *G. R. N. Cusworth*
Approx Annual Turnover £90 million

FOUNDED 1818 by Henry Butterworth. Now part of Reed International. By the turn of the century Butterworth was publishing many of the legal titles familiar today. The Bond family bought the company at that time, and added to its list such classics as *Halsbury's Laws of England* and *Encyclopaedia of Forms and Precedents.* Recent acquisitions include K. G. Saur, the Munich-based publisher, **John Wright** and Professional Books. Acquired Australian publishers D. W. Thorpe Pty in 1988. *Publishes* legal, medical, scientific, technical, bibliographic books and journals. 267 titles in the UK in 1988.

DIVISIONS
British and Irish Legal *D. L. Summers* Located at 88 Kingsway, London WC2B 6AB Tel 01–405 6900. TITLES *All England Law Reports; Stones Justices Manual; Simon's Taxes;* plus full legal, tax, banking textbook lists. **Butterworth Scientific** *E. J. Newman, G. Burn* Located at Westbury House, Bury Street, Guildford, Surrey GU2 5AW Tel 0483 31261. TITLES *Operative Surgery; A History of British Architecture.* **Focal Press** TITLES *Techniques of TV Production; Basic Photography.* **Bowker–Saur** and **Architectural Press** (see separate entries).

Unsolicited mss welcome, but preliminary letter preferred. Synopses and ideas for books should be addressed to the relevant publishing director.
Royalties paid twice yearly.
Overseas associates in Australia, Ireland, Malaysia, New Zealand, Singapore, Canada, USA.

Authors' Rating Shares with **Sweet & Maxwell** the highly profitable market for law books. But while classics like *Halsbury's Laws of England* ensure a sound base income, the scientific and medical lists are coming up fast and further expansion can be expected.

Byway Books

Unit 7/8, Tweedbank Craft Centre, Haining Drive, Tweedbank, Selkirkshire TD1 3RU
☎ 0896 57869

Managing Director *W. F. Laughlan*

FOUNDED 1981. Small publishing house now concentrating on children's books. *Publishes* children's picture books in paperback series: *Byway Bairns.*
TITLES *The Enchanted Boy* Mollie Hunter; *Nancy & Barnaby* series Mary Lightbody; *Nursery Rhyme People* George Gilfillan; *Sam Sees Edinburgh, Sam Sees a Steam Train* Ann Scott. All books are full colour illustrated throughout. ILLUSTRATORS include Mahri Christopherson, Brigid Collins, Andrea Hellyar, Alison Johnston, Jennie McCall, Lesley McLaren, Ann Scott.
Prefer synopses to unsolicited mss.
Royalties paid twice yearly.

Cadogan Books Ltd

16 Lower Marsh, Waterloo, London SE1 7RJ
☎ 01–633 0525
Telex 917706 Fax 01–928 6539

Chairman *Tom Hempenstall*
Managing Director *Paula Levy*
Approx Annual Turnover £250,000

Part of Metal Bulletin plc. The company was once called Gentry Books, and published motor titles, anthologies and guide books. In 1985 they decided to concentrate solely on guide books. 15 titles in 1988.

Editorial Director *Rachel Fielding* TITLES *Cadogan Guides.* Unsolicited mss not welcome; introductory letter and synopsis essential. Unsolicited synopses and ideas for books welcome.
Royalties paid twice yearly.

John Calder (Publishers) Ltd

18 Brewer Street, London W1R 4AS
☎ 01–734 3786

Chairman/Managing Director *John Calder* A publishing company which has grown around the tastes and contacts of its proprietor/manager/editorial director John Calder, the iconoclast of the literary establishment. *Publishes* autobiography, biography, drama, fiction (literary), literary criticism, music, opera, poetry, politics, playscripts, sociology.

Editorial Head *John Calder* TITLES include all Beckett's prose and poetry. AUTHORS William Burroughs; Marguerite Duras; P. J. Kavanagh; Alain Robbe-Grillet; Nathalie Sarraute; Claude Simon; Howard Barker (plays); ENO and ROH opera guides. No unsolicited mss. Synopses and ideas for books welcome.
Royalties paid annually.
Overseas associates Riverrun Press, New York.

Author's Rating A brave publisher who has often ventured where others fear to tread. But the operation is of modest size and sometimes (as with occasional late payments) gives the impression of being run on a shoestring.

Caliban Books

17 South Hill Park Gardens, London NW3 2TD
☎ 01–435 0222

Chairman *P. E. Razzecc*

FOUNDED by P. E. Razzecc in 1975 and has been steadily expanding ever since. *Publishes* psychology and psychotherapy, sociology, history, working class biography, general. AUTHORS include Henry Mahew, George Sturt, Patrick Magick. 5 titles in 1988. No unsolicited mss; welcome synopses and ideas for books.
Royalties paid twice yearly.

University of California Press

Avonlea, 10 Watlington Road, Cowley,
Oxford OX4 5NF
☎ 0865 748405 Fax 0865 748401

Director *James Clark*

Became part of The University Presses of Columbia and Princeton in June 1987. *Publishes* academic, art, Asian studies, scholarly. 220 titles in 1988. Editorial work carried out in the USA.

Cambridge University Press

The Edinburgh Building, Shaftesbury Road,
Cambridge CB2 2RU
☎ 0223 312393
Telex 817256 Fax 0223 315052

Chief Executive *Geoffrey A. Cass*
Managing Director (Publishing Division) *A. K. Wilson*

The oldest press in the world, and part of Cambridge University. Recently the Press has diversified into reference publishing, ELT and software, and expanded its activities in Australia and the USA as well as establishing a joint publishing imprint for reference titles with **W. & R. Chambers**. *Publishes* academic and educational books for international English-language markets, at all levels from primary school to postgraduate. Also publishes bibles and academic journals. 950 titles in 1988.

DEPARTMENTS
Bibles *R. Coleman* **ELT** *C. J. F. Hayes* **Humanities/Social Science** *R. J. Mynott* **Journals** *R. L. Ziemacki* **Reference** *A. du Plessis* **Schoolbooks** *R. Davidson* **Science** *S. Mitton.*

Authors' Rating Smaller than its younger Oxford counterpart (no children's list, for example) but probably the best managed of all the academic presses. Latest of the impressive multi-volume series is the awe inspiring *History of Japan.*

Campbell Books Ltd

12A Golden Square, London W1R 4BA
☎ 01–437 0713

In November 1986 Rod Campbell, children's illustrator and author, set up with his principal publisher **Blackie & Son,** a jointly-owned publishing firm, Campbell Blackie Books Ltd. The venture concentrated on publishing for the under-fives. Turnover has trebled since and Rod Campbell's miniature edition of *Dear Zoo* has sold 250,000 copies. Mr Campbell has now bought Blackie's share and the new company Campbell Books Ltd, publishes under the Campbell Books imprint.

Canongate Publishing Ltd

17 Jeffrey Street, Edinburgh EH1 1DR
☎ 031–557 5888
Telex 72165 Canpub Fax 031–557 5665

Managing Director *Stephanie Wolfe Murray*
Approx Annual Turnover £400,000

FOUNDED 1973. Member of the Musterlin Group plc, owners of **Phaidon Press**. Maintained a healthy mix of newly published work and reprints both for *Canongate Classics* series of Paperbacks (adults) and the *Kelpie* series (children). Also introduced *Kelpie Picture Books*, full-colour illustrated books for young children. 49 titles in 1988.
Prefer to consider synopses rather than unsolicited mss.
Royalties paid twice yearly.

Authors' Rating One of the best of the small publishers. Especially good on children's books and Scottish literature. Recently launched an *International folklore* series and *Canongate Classics*, reprints of Scottish texts long out of print. Marketing arm strengthened by link with Dutch owned Musterlin.

Jonathan Cape Ltd

32 Bedford Square, London WC1B 3EL
☎ 01–255 2393
Telex 299080 Cvbcse G Fax 01–255 1620

Chairman *Tom Maschler*
Publishing Director *David Godwin*

Taken over by **Random House Inc.,** New York, in May 1987, along with its partners **Bodley Head** and **Chatto**, now part of the Random Century. *Publishes* academic and scholarly, archaeology, architecture and design, children's books, economics, fiction, fine art and art history, history and antiquarian, humour, illustrated and fine editions, literature and criticism, natural history, philosophy, poetry, politics and world affairs, psychology, reference books and dictionaries, sociology and anthropology, travel and topography. 100 titles in 1988.
TITLES Children's: *Cyril of the Apes* Jonathan Gathorne-Hardy; *Mathilda* Roald Dahl. Fiction: *The Bonfire of the Vanities* Tom Wolfe; *Love in the Time of Cholera* Gabriel Garcia Marquez; *The Fifth Child* Doris Lessing. Non-fiction: *Greetings From the Fast Lane – 32 postcards for the Post-*

Modern World Chic Pix Stanley Becker & Peta Copelans; *The Secrets of the Service* Anthony Glees; *The Life of R. A. Butler* Anthony Howard; *Whale Nation* Heathcote Williams.
Will consider unsolicited mss for fiction. Prefer synopsis with sample chapters for non-fiction.
Royalties paid twice yearly.

Authors' Rating Trying hard to re-establish its identity as leading fiction publisher after the recent vicissitudes of ownership and control and the loss of key personnel. An encouraging initiative is the promotion of emerging talent as 'Gilt Edged New Writers' including a free magazine format brochure containing author interviews and extracts from latest novels.

Carcanet Press Ltd

208 Corn Exchange Buildings,
Manchester M4 3BQ
☏ 01–834 8730 Fax 061–832 0084

Chairman *Robert Gavron*
Managing Director *Michael Schmidt*

Carcenet has grown since the mid 70s from an undergraduate hobby into a substantial venture. Anglo-European in orientation, they are Manchester-based. Robert Gavron bought the company in 1983. *Publishes* academic, biography, fiction, memoirs, and translations but mostly poetry. Success has led to tie-ins with **Grafton**. Some Carcanet titles now appear in Paladin editions, and **Grafton** launched its own poetry list in association with Carcanet. 40 titles in 1989 (and 6 issues of P.N. Review).

Editorial Director *Michael Schmidt* **Fiction Editor** *Michael Freeman* AUTHORS John Ashbery, Edwin Morgan, Elizabeth Jennings, Iain Crichton Smith, Natalia Ginzburg, Stuart Hood, Leonardo Sciascia, Christine Brooke-Rose, Pier Paolo Pasolini.
Royalties paid annually.

Authors' Rating A small publisher of high repute. Strong on poetry. Described by *The Times* as the 'last serious publisher in this country to pay more attention to its books than its balance sheet'. The cosmopolitan touch comes from Michael Schmidt whose family emigrated from Saxony to Mexico; hence his claim to be the only Mexican in UK publishing. Used to be criticised for dull production but lately more attention given to elegant design.

Cardinal

See **Sphere Books Ltd**

Carnival

See **Collins Publishers**

Frank Cass

Gainsborough House, 11 Gainsborough Road,
London E11 1RS
☏ 01–530 4226
Telex 987719 Fax 01–530 7795

Managing Director *Frank Cass*

Publishes Africa, development and strategic studies, education, history and antiquarian, literature, Middle East, politics and world affairs.

Editorial Head (books) *Margaret Goodare* TITLES *Looking Back on India* Hubert Evans; *Wilfred Owen – Anthem for a Doomed Youth* Simcox; *The Best of Enemies – Israel and Trans-Jordan in the War of 1948* Uri R. B. Joseph; *Strategic and Operational Deception in the Second World War* ed. Michael I. Handel; *An African Victorian Feminist: The Life and Times of Adelaide Smith Casely Hayford* Adelaide M. Cromwell; *Right-wing Extremism in Western Europe* Von Beyne; *Inside Terrorist Organisations* Rappoport; *Medical Negligence: A Plaintiff's Guide* Lewis; *Jabotinsky and the Revisionist Movement* Shavit; *Leaders and Intelligence* ed. Handel.

IMPRINT
Woburn Press *Margaret Goodare* *Publishes* educational. TITLES *The Study of Education* ed. Peter Gorden; *Educational Policy in England in the Twentieth Century* Peter Gorden, Richard Aldrich & Dennis Dean; *Special Needs in Ordinary Schools – A Teacher's Guide* Neville Jones; *Dictionary of British Educationalists* ed. Richard Aldrich & Peter Gorden.
Although unsolicited mss will be considered, a synopsis with covering letter is preferred.
Royalties paid annually.

Cassell plc

Artillery House, Artillery Row,
London SW1P 1RT
☏ 01–222 7676
Telex 9413701 CASPUB G Fax 01–799 1514

Chairman/Managing Director *Philip Sturrock*
Approx Annual Turnover £10 million

FOUNDED 1848 by John Cassell; bought by Collier Macmillan the same year, sold to CBS Publishing Europe in 1982, and finally achieved independence in 1986, as Cassell plc. In its first year of operations, Cassell acquired the book publishing division of Tycooly Publishing Ltd as well as Link House Books, since renamed **Blandford Publishing Ltd**. The part of Link dealing with railway books was since sold to **Haynes** in 1987. Also acquired **Mansell** in December 1987, then **Mowbray** in November 1988. Other imprints include **Arms & Armour Press, Javelin, Geoffrey Chapman** and New Orchard Editions. Latest acquisition is **Ward Lock**, famous for Mrs Beeton's cookery, which has been in print continuously since 1861. The purchase price remains secret. *Publishes* business, education, English language teaching, general non-fiction, primary and secondary school books, religious. 300 titles in 1989.

DIVISIONS

General Non-fiction (**Cassell, Blandford, Studio Vista, Wisley** imprints) **Editorial Director** *Clare Howell* Lead TITLES 1989 *The Art of the Picnic; Samurai Warlords.* **Educational** (**Cassell, Geoffrey Chapman, Mowbray** imprints) **Editorial Director** *Stephen Butcher* Lead TITLES 1989 *The Cassell Concise English Dictionary; Brewer's Dictionary of Phrase and Fable, 14th edition; Accurate English; The Jerome Biblical Commentary,* 2nd edition. **Reference** (**Mansell, Tycooly** imprints) **Editorial Director** *John Duncan* Lead TITLES 1989 *Index of English Literary manuscripts; Index Islamicus.*

Unsolicited mss welcome but only for non-fiction. Synopses preferred.
Royalties payment depends on sales potential.

Authors' Rating A mixed bag of publishers being given a new lease of life by strong management. A start towards forging a clear identity has been made with the new corporate logo. Development plans are concentrated on existing areas of strength, notably the reference list which is soon to have a new edition of Cassell's English Dictionary. The educational side boasts a strong ELT list.

Godfrey Cave Associates Ltd

42 Bloomsbury Street, London WC1B 3QJ
☎ 01–636 9177 Fax 01–636 9091

Managing Director *John Maxwell*
Deputy Managing Director *Geoffrey Howard*

Also own Omega Books Ltd and Benson Books (paperback remainders & reprints). No new books. The list consists entirely of reprints of illustrated books where rights have reverted, and the re-issue of out-of-print titles. 70 titles in 1989.

Centaur Press Ltd

Fontwell, Arundel, Sussex BN18 0TA
☎ 0243 543302

Chairman/Editorial Head *Jon Wynne-Tyson*

FOUNDED 1954. A one-man outfit publishing some 20 titles a year (literary, philosophical, classical, monographs) at its peak. Now adding only 1–3 to a list increasingly preoccupied with human education. TITLES *A Dictionary of Humane Thought; Animals' Rights; The Scientific Conscience, The Philosophy of Compassion; Victims of Science; Art as Revelation; Publishing Your Own Book.*

IMPRINT

Linden Press (no connection with **Simon & Schuster**'s later adoption).

No unsolicited mss, new titles tending to be commissioned, or resulting from Jon Wynne-Tyson's own extra-publishing pursuits.

Authors' Rating Given the limited range of its own output it may seem appropriate that Centaur offers a useful guide to Publishing Your Own Book (£2.50).

Central Books Ltd

14 The Leathermarket, London SE1 3ER
☎ 01–407 5447 Fax 01–378 1811

Managing Director *William Norris*
Approx Annual Turnover £1.25 million

FOUNDED 1939 principally as book distributors. Imports from Eastern Europe, USA and West Germany, as well as distributing books from small presses. Do originate some titles. *Publishes* children's books, economics, history, politics, scientific and technical. 300 titles (mostly imported) in 1987.

Editorial Director *William Norris* As (mainly) book importers they do not welcome unsolicited mss, but will consider synopses and ideas.
Royalties paid annually.

Century Hutchinson Ltd

Brookmount House, 62–5 Chandos Place, London WC2N 4NW
☎ 01–240 3411
Telex 261212 Litldn G Fax 01–836 1409

Chairman *Anthony Cheetham*
Group Finance Director *Peter Roche*
Managing Director (Hardcover Division) *Piet*

Snyman
Managing Director (Paperback Division) *David Attwool*
Approximate Annual Turnover £45 million

Publishes antiques and collecting, aviation, biography/autobiography, business and industry, children's books, cinema and video, cookery, crime, crafts and hobbies, DIY, fashion and costume, fiction, fine art and art history, gardening, guide books, health and beauty, humour, illustrated and fine editions, magic and the occult, military and war, natural history, photography, poetry, politics and world affairs, reference and dictionaries, sports and games, theatre and drama, travel and topography, wines and spirits. 600 titles in 1988.

DIVISIONS
Arrow Books *Jane Wood* **Children's** *Caroline Roberts* **Fiction** *Rosemary Cheetham* **Hutchinson** *Robyn Sisman* **Non-fiction** *Sarah Wallace* **Stanley Paul** *Roddy Bloomfield* **Frederick Muller** *Paul Sidey* **Radius** *Neil Belton* **Ebury Press** *Gail Rebuck.*

Century Hutchinson welcome unsolicited mss, synopses and ideas for books.
Royalties paid twice yearly.
Overseas subsidiaries Century Hutchinson Australia/New Zealand/South Africa. *Overseas associates* Little, Brown (Canada).

Authors' Rating A new chapter opens with the sale of Century Hutchinson to Random House for £64 million. Anthony Cheetham becomes chairman and chief executive of Random Century which suggests more imaginative marketing for the Random houses, Chatto and Jonathan Cape. Arrow paperbacks should benefit from an injection of new titles.

Ceolfrith Press

Northern Centre for Contemporary Art, 17 Grange Terrace, Sunderland, Tyne & Wear SR2 7DF
☎ 091–514 1214

Sunderland Arts Centre was founded by Chris Carrell whose original connection with the arts was a second-hand-bookshop. Premises were obtained at Grange Terrace and development has led to a concentration on visual arts and crafts exhibitions. *Publishes* visual arts and craft, criticism, design, general, and visual poetry. 5 titles in 1988. Do not welcome unsolicited mss; most books are commissioned or produced in-house.
Royalties paid twice yearly.

Chadwyck-Healey Ltd

Cambridge Place, Cambridge CB2 1NR

Chairman *Sir Charles Chadwyck-Healey*
Approx Annual Turnover £1.5 million

FOUNDED 1973. Chadwyck-Healey Inc, Washington DC, followed the next year, and Chadwyck-Healey France in 1985. *Publishes* mainly on microform with a few reference works and guides for microform collections. Occasionally publishes monographs on fine art and architecture. Winner of a 1987 Queen's Award for Exports. 50 titles in 1988.

Editorial Head *Alison Moss* TITLES *The English Satirical Print; Theatre in Focus; Index of Manuscripts in The British Library.* No unsolicited mss. Synopses and ideas for books welcome.
Royalties paid annually.

W & R Chambers

43–5 Annandale Street, Edinburgh EH7 4AZ
☎ 031–557 4571
Telex 727967 Fax 031–557 2936

Executive Chairman *W. G. Henderson*
Chief Executive *John Clement*
Managing Director *W. G. Henderson*
Editorial Director *R. S. R. Mair*
Approx Annual Turnover £1.75 million

The company was established in the early 1800s to publish self-education books, but soon diversified into dictionaries and other reference works. *Publishes* reference, school and college text books, Scottish non-fiction, self-help guides in medical, social, language subjects. 38 titles in 1988. Now commencing co-publication of major reference books in association with **Cambridge University Press**. Prefer synopsis accompanied by letter to unsolicited mss.
Royalties paid annually. *Overseas representation* by Cambridge University Press, among other agents/publishers.

Authors' Rating Recently taken over by Grange de la Cité. Core of the business is Chambers English Dictionary the official Scrabble dictionary.

Chameleon International Ltd

Chameleon House, Westlode Street, Spalding, Lincolnshire PE11 2AF
☏ 0775 4151 Fax 0775 710532

Chairman/Managing Director *I. K. B. Thorp*
Approx Annual Turnover £250,000

Comparatively small publisher, attached to a large design and printing company. *Publishes* children's, local history, philosophy and spiritual awareness. Books produced as perfect bound or fully case-bound hardbacks. Unique in that everything is carried out under one roof – which is certainly an advantage for the writer. First published in 1986 and expanding rapidly with 20 titles planned for 1989. 4 titles in 1988. Welcome unsolicited mss, synopses and ideas for books.
Royalties paid twice yearly.

Chapman and Hall Limited

11 New Fetter Lane, London EC4P 4EE
☏ 01–583 9855
Telex 263398 ABPLDN G Fax 01–583 0701

Managing Director *Paul Gardner*

FOUNDED 1830. Formerly part of Associated Book Publishers, now owned by International Thomson plc. Chapman and Hall embraces the old ABP companies, Chapman & Hall and E. & F. N. Spon, and has now been joined by **Van Nostrand Reinhold International** (see separate entry). *Publishes* scientific, technical and medical books. 250 titles in 1988.

Publishing Director *Anthony Watkinson* (**E. & F. N. Spon** *Phillip Read*). Unsolicited mss and synopses in science, technology and medicine are welcome.
Royalties paid twice yearly.

Paul Chapman Publishing Ltd

144 Liverpool Road, London N1 1LA
☏ 01–609 5315

Managing Director *Paul R. Chapman*
Editorial Director *Marianne Lagrange*

Publishes business, management accountancy and finance, education, geography and economics for the academic and professional market. A new list is being developed in information technology. Books are marketed world-wide. Unsolicited manuscripts and synopses welcome.
Royalties paid twice yearly.

Chatto, Bodley Head, Cape (CBC)

32 Bedford Square, London WC1B 3EL
☏ 01–255 2393
Telex 299080 CVBCSE G

Parent organisation for three publishers who, together with their former partner, **Virago**, met with crisis when their joint administration was publicly criticised by leading author Graham Greene. The crisis was resolved by **Random House Inc.,** New York, who came up with an attractive takeover bid but **Virago** staged a management buy-out. Simon Master, formerly managing director of **Pan**, was chosen to head the company. But the story goes on. Random House has now bought Century Hutchinson to form Random Century. Anthony Cheetham of Century Hutchinson becomes chairman and chief executive of the new company while Simon Master becomes group managing director. (See separate entries for **Chatto & Windus, The Bodley Head, Jonathan Cape, Century Hutchinson.**)

Chatto & Windus Ltd/The Hogarth Press Ltd

30 Bedford Square, London WC1B 3RP
☏ 01–255 2393
Telex 299080 CVBCSE G Fax 01–255 1620

Chairman *John Charlton*
Managing Director *Carmen Callil*

Taken over by **Random House Inc.,** New York in May 1987, and now part of Random Century. Formerly part of the Chatto, Virago, Bodley Head and Jonathan Cape group. The original Chatto was founded in 1855, and took over The Hogarth Press, which had been founded by Leonard and Virginia Woolf, in 1946. The Hogarth Press was relaunched as a paperback imprint in 1984, and again in 1989 to publish about 10 hardback and 10 paperback titles a year. First titles due January 1990. *Publishes* academic and scholarly, archaeology, architecture and design, autobiography, business and industry, cookery, crime, fiction, fine art and art history, gardening, health and beauty, history and antiquarian, humour, illustrated and fine editions, literature and criticism, music, natural history, philosophy, photography, poetry, politics and world affairs, psychology, science fiction, sociology and anthropology, theatre and drama, travel and topography, women's studies. 104 titles in 1988.

IMPRINTS
Chatto & Windus Editorial Director *Rupert Lancaster* **Consultant Director** *Andrew Motion* AUTHORS include Iris Murdoch; A. S. Byatt; Angela Carter; Timothy Mo; Blake Morrison; Michael Holroyd; Alan Hollinghurst; Marina Warner; Anthony Sher. **The Hogarth Press Ltd Editorial Director** *Rupert Lancaster* TITLES include works by Virginia Woolf, Sigmund Freud and others in the *International Psycho-Analytic Library*. The list also covers fiction, lives and letters, crime, travel, poetry, critics.

Unsolicited mss, synopses and ideas for books welcome if sent with return postage.
Royalties paid twice yearly.
Overseas associates Australasian Publishing Co., Sydney; Book Reps Ltd, New Zealand.

Authors' Rating Redisovering its identity after the Random House takeover with plenty of good ideas, not least *CounterBlasts*, a series of pamphlets in which leading writers express controversial views on topical social and political issues. A new hardback crime series was launched in mid '89.

Cherrytree Press
See **Chivers Press (Publishers)**

Chivers Press (Publishers)
Windsor Bridge Road, Bath, Avon BA2 3AX
☏ 0225 335336 Fax 0225 310771

Chairman *T. Scruby*
Managing Director *Roger H. Lewis*

Part of The Gieves Group. Originally part of Cedric Chivers; known as Chivers Press since 1979. *Publishes* mainly reprints for libraries – biography/autobiography; children's books; crime; fiction; large-print editions, complete and unabridged; spoken word cassettes. Launched a new children's information book imprint in 1988 – **Cherrytree Children's Books.** 700 titles in 1989.

IMPRINTS
Atlantic Large Print, Firecrest Books, Gunsmoke Westerns, Lythway Children's Large Print, Lythway Large Print, New Portway Facsimile Reprints, New Portway Large Print, Swift Children's Books, Cherrytree Press Children's Books (new children's informative imprint launched 1988), **Windsor Large Print.** Cassette Imprints: **Chivers Audio Books, Chivers Children's Audio, Cavalcade Story Cassettes, Moonlight Romance**.

Do not consider mss or synopses as are concentrating on reprinting for the time being.
Royalties paid twice yearly.

Churchill Livingstone
Robert Stevenson House, 1–3 Baxter's Place, Leith Walk, Edinburgh EH1 3AF
☏ 031–556 2424
Telex 727511 Fax 031–558 1278

Managing Director *Andrew Stevenson*

Part of the **Longman Group**. FOUNDED in the early 1970s from two originally private companies, E. & S. Livingstone and J. & A. Churchill, which had earlier become separate parts of **Longman**. *Publishes* medical and nursing books, medical journals. 140 titles in 1988.

Publishing Managers (books) *Timothy Horne, Mary Law, Peter Richardson;* (journals) *Sally Morris.* Do not welcome unsolicited mss. Welcome synopses and ideas.
Royalties paid annually.
Overseas associate Churchill Livingstone Inc., New York.

Authors' Rating The best of the medical publishers.

Churchman Publishing Ltd
117 Broomfield Avenue, Worthing, West Sussex BN14 7SF
☏ 0903 692430

Chairman/Managing Director *E. Peter Smith*

Publishes biography, history, psychology, religion and theology (ecumenical), social science and education, travel.

IMPRINTS
The Lantern Press *E. P. Smith* **Landmark Books** *E. P. Smith.* Unsolicited mss and synopses welcome in all non-fiction subjects. Very little poetry. No fiction.
Royalties paid annually.
Overseas associates in Canada, USA, Australia and New Zealand.

John Clare Books
34 Sydenham Road, London SE26 5QF
☏ 01–659 3788

Proprietor *Bryan Breed*

FOUNDED 1979. Started with a wide general list and became increasingly specialised.
Parent Company Interpress Features. *Publishes* non-fiction with an educational bias, social

education. TITLES *Music Therapy* Juliet Alving; *Social Drama* Bert Amies. Prefer synopses and ideas for books within their specialist field.
Royalties paid twice yearly.

Clarendon Press

See **Oxford University Press**

T. & T. Clark Ltd

59 George Street, Edinburgh EH2 2LQ
☎ 031–225 4703
Telex 728134 Fax 031–662 4282

Chairman *David Ross Stewart*
Managing Director *Geoffrey Green*
Approx Annual Turnover £750,000

FOUNDED 1821. Acquired by **John Bartholomew & Son Ltd** in 1984. *Publishes* religion, theology, law, philosophy (all academic). 24 titles in 1988.

Editorial Head *Geoffrey Green* TITLES *Church Dogmatics* Karl Barth; *A Textbook of Christian Ethics* ed. Robin Gill; *Scottish Law Directory; The Law of Arbitration in Scotland* R. L. C. Hunter. Unsolicited mss, synopses and ideas for books welcome.
Royalties paid annually.

Clematis Press Ltd

18 Old Church Street, London SW3 5DQ
☎ 01–352 8755

Chairman/Managing Director *Clara Waters*

Clematis Press act as distributors of imported books and have no editorial facilities. No unsolicited mss.

Clio Press Ltd

55 St Thomas' Street, Oxford OX1 1JG
☎ 0865 250333
Telex 83103 CLIO G Fax 0865 790358

Chairman/Managing Director *John Durrant*
Approx Annual Turnover £2.5 million

Part of ABC-Clio Inc., Santa Barbara, California. FOUNDED 1971 in Oxford to publish academic reference works. Now also publishes art reference and large print titles for both children and the elderly, and unabridged talking books for a wide audience. *Publishes* social sciences and humanities; general fiction and non-fiction in large print. 110 titles in 1988.

DIVISIONS
Isis Large Print *V. Babington Smith* TITLES *Know Your Medicine; Charles and Diana.* **Windrush Large Print** *V. Babington Smith* TITLES *Charlie and the Chocolate Factory* **Clio Press** *R. G. Neville* TITLES *World Bibliographical Series.* **Art Bibliographies** *J. Chibnall* TITLES *Artbibliographies Modern* **Isis Audio Books** *V. Babington Smith* TITLES *Oscar & Lucinda.*
Royalties paid twice yearly.

Clyde/Bartholomew

See **John Bartholomew & Son Ltd**

Frank Coleman Publishing

Maulden Road, Flitwick, Beds MK45 5BW
☎ 0525 712261
Telex 825115 Fax 0525 718205

Managing Director *Neil Goldman*
Approx Annual Turnover under £100,000

Publishes children's books. 12 titles in 1989. Unsolicited mss welcome. Synopses and ideas for books considered.
Royalties paid annually.

Collins Publishers

8 Grafton Street, London W1X 3LA
☎ 01–493 7070
Telex 25611 Colins G Fax 01–493 3061
PO Box, Glasgow G4 0NB
☎ 041–772 3200

Chairman *K. R. Murdoch*
Chief Executive *G. Craig*
Approx Annual Turnover £144 million

Following remarkable growth over the last decade and a steady 1200 plus titles a year, Collins was sold to News International (Rupert Murdoch) in January 1989, bringing about a number of new appointments, displacements and resignations.

DIVISIONS
Collins General Division incorporating **Collins** (general hardbacks) **Collins Harvill** (see below) **Crime Club Fontana Paperbacks** (IMPRINTS **Fontana, Flamingo, Fontana Press).** TITLES Non-fiction: *Making It Happen* John Harvey-Jones; *Reflect on Things Past* Lord Carrington; *On My Way to the Club* Ludovic Kennedy. Fiction: *All the Grey Cats* Craig Thomas; *A Season in Hell* Jack Higgins; *The Cardinal of the Kremlin* Tom Clancy. 427 titles in 1988. **Collins Children's Division** *L. Davis, R. Sandberg* TITLES Fiction: *Little Grey Rabbit* books; *Paddington Bear.* Classics: *Narnia* stories. Non-fiction: *Beginner* books, nature, history, prehistoric world, hobbies, dictionaries and lan-

guage; *Help Your Child* series. 386 titles in 1988.

IMPRINTS
Armada, Dinosaur, Lions, Collins, Carnival.

Collins Reference – Dictionaries & Reference (Glasgow) includes the major range of English and bilingual dictionaries with every combination of English, French, German, Italian and Spanish; Collins English Dictionary; Collins Robert-French dictionary. **Bilingual Reference** *Pierre Cousin* **English Dictionaries** *Patrick Hanks.* **General Reference** includes a new range of paperback subject dictionaries launched 1988 (mathematics, art & artists, economics, music, electronics, etc.) *Christopher Riches.* **Travel Reference** phrase books and holiday guides *Caroline McCreath.* **Natural History** Wide range of pocket and field guides and other books on the subject. *Crispin Fisher* – New Generation Guides *The Living Planet.* **Willow/Leisure** wide range of publications for special interests: DIY, Collins Aura Garden handbooks, Learn to Paint *Joan Clibbon.* 700 titles in 1989.

Collins Religious Books incorporating bibles *A. Watson* (Glasgow); **Liturgical** *S. Caldecott* Fount religious paperbacks. 737 titles in 1989. **Collins ELT** *R. H. Thomas* Courses, readers, grammars and dictionaries including Collins Cobuild. **Collins Educational Division** Textbook publishing for schools (5–18 years) – all subject areas for primary, with main strengths in secondary being English, history, geography, science and CDT. Proposals to *Roy Davey.*

Adlard Press sailing books only. **Collins Grafton** (see **Grafton**) **Collins Harvill** *Christopher MacLehose* **Maps & Atlases** *D. Thompson.*

Authors Rating It is difficult now to imagine how anyone could have possibly believed that Rupert Murdoch would *not* take over Collins. After gaining a substantial minority interest the urge to go for the full house must have been irresistible. He gained a thriving company at a bargain price. After loud protests from top authors, Ken Follett and Colin Forbes departed for Macmillan. But most seem to have accepted the new regime. Led by George Craig who prowled around Harper and Row on behalf of Mr Murdoch, Collins is expected to sharpen its commercial edge.

Columbus Books Ltd

See **Harrap Publishing Group Ltd**

Constable & Co Ltd

10 Orange Street, London WC2H 7EG
☎ 01–930 0801
Telex 27950 Fax 01–930 0802

Chairman/Managing Director *Benjamin Glazebrook*

In 1890 Archibald Constable, a grandson of Walter Scott's publisher, founded the publishing company of Archibald Constable which in 1909 became Constable & Co. Controlling interest was bought by Benjamin Glazebrook in 1967 with a minority interest owned by Random Century. *Publishes* archaeology, architecture and design, biography and autobiography, cookery, fiction, guide books, history and antiquarian, natural history, psychology, sociology and anthropology, travel and topography, wines and spirits. 75 titles in 1988.

Editorial Director *Robin Baird Smith* TITLES *Tomorrow is too Late* Ray Moore; *A Far Cry From Kensington* Muriel Spark; *Madrid, A Traveller's Companion* Hugh Thomas; *The Pursuit of Happiness* Peter Quennell; *A History of Parliament* Ronald Butt. Unsolicited mss, synopses and ideas for books welcome.
Royalties paid twice yearly.

Authors' Rating A major coup in attracting Muriel Spark from **Bodley Head**. Other eminent writers may soon be attracted by the personal style of management which emphasises the relationship between author and editor. Distinguished by paying to authors at least two thirds of income from the sale of paperback rights. The average is closer to 60%. Scored heavily with two recent bestsellers: Ray Moore's *Tomorrow is too Late* and Paul Sayer's *Comforts of Madness.*

Corgi

See **Transworld Publishers Ltd**

Cornwall Books

See **Golden Cockerel Press Ltd**

Coronet Books

See **Hodder & Stoughton Ltd**

Costello

43 High Street, Tunbridge Wells, Kent TN1 1XL
☏ 0892 45355 Fax 0892 34905

Chairman *Rosemary Costello*
Managing Director *David Costello*
Approx Annual Turnover £0.7 million

FOUNDED 1972 as agent for major US publishers. Began educational publishing in 1978 and general publishing in 1985. *Publishes* history, militaria, arts and crafts. 18 titles in 1988.

Arts, Crafts and Collectables *Rosemary Costello* **History and Militaria** *Anne Cree* **Jazz** *David Costello.*

Countryside Books

3 Catherine Road, Newbury, Berks RG14 7NA
☏ 0635 43816

Publisher *Nicholas Battle*

FOUNDED 1978. *Publishes* mainly paperbacks on regional subjects, generally by county. Local history, genealogy, walking and photographic, some transport. 31 new titles in 1988. Welcome unsolicited mss and synopses.
Royalties paid twice yearly.

Cressrelles Publishing Co. Ltd

311 Worcester Road, Malvern, Worcs WR14 1AN
☏ 0684 565045

Managing Director *Leslie Smith*

Publishes general children's books. Own **Kenyon-Deane** and J. Garnet Miller Ltd who publish theatre and drama. Also Actinic Press, specialising in books on chiropody.

The Crowood Press

Crowood House, Ramsbury, Marlborough, Wilts SN8 2HE
☏ 0672 20320
Telex 449703 Fax 0672 20134

Chairman/Publisher *John Dennis*
Managing Director *Ken Hathaway*

FOUNDED 1982 by John Dennis as a one-man concern, The Crowood Press has grown steadily to employ more than thirty people. *Publishes* sport and leisure including animal and land husbandry, climbing and mountaineering, country sports, equestrian, fishing and shooting. Also chess and bridge, cookery, crafts, dogs, gardening, health and social issues, military and motor. 100 titles in 1989. Preliminary letter preferred in all cases. Synopses and ideas for books welcome.
Royalties paid twice yearly for first year, annually thereafter.

Crucible

See **Thorsons Publishing Group Ltd**

Curzon Press Ltd

42 Gray's Inn Road, London WC1
☏ 01–242 8310

Managing Director *John F. Standish*

Scholarly and specialised publishing house with imprints on Asian and African studies. *Publishes* academic and scholarly, history and archaeology, languages and linguistics, Oriental and African studies, philosophy, religion and theology, sociology and anthropology. 17 titles in 1988. Unsolicited mss considered.
Royalties according to contract.

Dalesman Publishing Co. Ltd

Clapham, Lancaster LA2 8EB
☏ 04685 225

Managing Director *Dennis Bullock*

Also publishers of the famous country magazine of the same name. *Publishes* crafts and hobbies, geography and geology, guide books, history and antiquarian, humour, transport, travel and topography. 21 titles in 1988.

Editorial Director *David Joy* Unsolicited mss considered on all subjects.
Royalties paid twice yearly.

Darf Publishers Ltd

50 Hans Crescent, London SW1X 0NA
☏ 01–581 1805 Fax 01–581 8988

Chairman *M. Fergiani*
Managing Director *M. B. Fergiani*
Approx Annual Turnover £500,000

Formed in 1982 to publish and republish books on the Middle East, theology and travel. Strong emphasis on students' books. *Publishes* geography, history, language, literature, oriental, politics, theology, travel and sport. 50 titles in 1988.

Editorial Head *M. Fergiani* TITLES *The Historical Geography of Arabia, vols. 1 & 2; Spoken Arabic: Self Taught; The Elevens of England; Tales From the Tin Tabernacle.* Unsolicited mss, synopses and ideas for books welcome.

Royalties paid twice yearly. *Overseas associates* Dar Al-Fergiani, Cairo and Tripoli.

Darton, Longman & Todd Ltd

89 Lillie Road, London SW6 1UD
☏ 01–385 2341

Chairman *Derek Stevens* (non-executive)
Managing Director *Christopher Ward*
Approx Annual Turnover £750,000

FOUNDED by Michael Longman, who broke away from Longman Green in 1959 when that publisher decided to stop its religious list. First major publication was the *Jerusalem Bible*. The company is in the process of becoming a common ownership business. *Publishes* Christian books of all types. 40 titles in 1988. New imprint **Daybreak** launched March 1989.

Editorial Director *Sarah Baird-Smith* BEST SELLING TITLES *Jerusalem Bible; New Jerusalem Bible; God of Surprises*. Unsolicited mss, synopses and ideas for books welcome.
Royalties paid twice yearly.

David & Charles Publishers plc

Brunel House, Forde Road, Newton Abbott, Devon TQ12 4PU
☏ 0626 61121
Telex 42904 BOOKS G Fax 0626 64463

Chairman *David St John Thomas*
Approx Annual Turnover £13 million

FOUNDED 1960 as a specialist company. Still family controlled. Major subsidiary the Readers' Union Book Clubs for Enthusiasts. *Publishes* practical: crafts, gardening, military, hobbies, popular art, wide-ranging non-fiction. No fiction, poetry, memoirs or children's. 130 titles in 1988.

Editorial Head *Michael de Luca* TITLES *Knitting in Vogue; Great Days of the Country Railway; Complete Book of Microwave Cookery; Passion for Birds; Embroiderer's Garden; Battle Standards* military paperback series. Unsolicited mss, synopses and ideas welcome. *Author's Guide* available on receipt of a first class stamp.
Royalties paid annually; twice yearly in first two years on request.

Authors Rating No longer the high flyer but strong on leisure and hobby books. Can be tough on payments. Run like a cottage industry – but on a large scale. Readers' Union is among the leading non-fiction book clubs. Recently started a home study course for writers which guarantees money back if earnings from writing do not equal course fees.

Christopher Davies Publishers Limited

PO Box 403, Sketty, Swansea, West Glamorgan SA2 9BE
☏ 0792 648825

Managing Director *Christopher T. Davies*
Approx Annual Turnover *c.*£100,000

FOUNDED 1949 to increase the output of Welsh language publications. By the 1970s this had reached the level of over 50 titles a year. The drop in Welsh sales in that decade led to the establishment of a small English list, which has continued. *Publishes* biography, cookery, fiction, general sport, history and literature. About 12 titles a year.

Editorial Head *Christopher Davies* TITLES *English/Welsh Dictionaries; Wild Mushrooms; Minutes of Time; Rugby Wales '88; Castles of the Welsh Princes* Paul R. Davies; *John Morgan's Wales*. Unsolicited mss welcome only if relevant to their field. Synopses and ideas for books welcome.
Royalties paid twice yearly.

Authors' Rating A favourite for Celtic readers. Plans are in hand to beef up marketing and promotion.

Debrett's Peerage Ltd

73–7 Britannia Road, London SW6 2JR
☏ 01–736 6524/6 Fax 01–731 7768

Chairman *Ian McCorquodale*
Managing Director *R. M. Summers*

FOUNDED 1769. Main publication *Debrett's Peerage and Baronetage* every five years (next edition 1990) and *Debrett's Distinguished People of Today* annually. *Publishes* books on etiquette, modern manners and correct form, royalty, and sporting subjects. 5 titles in 1988.

General Manager *John Porter* Welcome unsolicited mss and synopses.
Royalties paid twice yearly.

Dennys Publications Ltd

2 Carthusian Street, London EC1M 6ED
☏ 01–253 5421

Chairman *P. P. Maher*

FOUNDED 1976. Part of the Dennys Group. *Publishes* academic books.

Editorial Director *A. Maher* TITLE *The Handbook of Mathematical Formulae For Scientists and Engineers.* Welcome unsolicited mss and synopses.
Royalty payments vary from contract to contract.

Dent Children's Books

See **Weidenfeld & Nicolson Ltd**

Dent General & Everyman

See **Weidenfeld & Nicolson Ltd**

André Deutsch Ltd

105–6 Great Russell Street, London WC1B 3LJ
☏ 01–580 2746
Telex 261026 Adlib G Fax 01–631 3253

Joint Chairman *André Deutsch*
Joint Chairman & Sole Managing Director *T. G. Rosenthal*
Approx annual turnover £3.55 million

FOUNDED 1950 by André Deutsch, the original list included *Books are Essential, To Live in Mankind* and *Jewish Cookery*. A major fiction list followed, with writers like V. S. Naipaul, Philip Roth and Norman Mailer. *Publishes* adult fiction, art illustrated, children's picture books, fiction and non-fiction, general books (particularly biography, current affairs, history, politics), photographic. 120 titles in 1988.

DIVISIONS
Adult books (and submissions) *Esther Whitby* AUTHORS John Updike, Paul Erdman, Penelope Lively, Carlos Fuentes, William Gaddis, Gore Vidal, Dan Jacobson, Gerald Priestland, Malcolm Bradbury, Dale Spender, Julian Critchley. **Children's books** (and submissions) *Pam Royds* TITLES *Postman Pat; You're Thinking about Doughnuts; Different Friends; The Tooth Ball; The Story of a High Street; House Inside Out.* Unsolicited mss, synopses and ideas for books welcome.
Royalties paid twice yearly.

Authors' Rating One of the last of the distinguished independents to resist takeover. Supported for years on André Deutsch's favourite maxims – low overheads and minimum borrowing – the company was given a new lease of life when Tom Rosenthal came over from Secker. Celebrated writers one and all. A fine children's list.

Dinosaur

See **Collins Publishers**

Dolphin Book Co. Ltd

Tredwr, Llangrannog, Llandysul, Dyfed SA44 6BA
☏ 023978 404

Managing Director *Martin L. Gili*
Approx Annual Turnover £5000

FOUNDED 1957. A small publishing house specialising in Spanish and South American academic books. Only one title in 1988, with 2 forecast for 1989. TITLE *The Late Poetry of Pablo Neruda* Christopher Perriam. Unsolicited mss not welcome. First approach by letter.
Royalties paid annually.

John Donald Publishers Ltd

138 St Stephen Street, Edinburgh EH3 5AA
☏ 031–225 1146

Managing Director *Donald Morrison*

Publishes academic and scholarly, agriculture, archaeology, architecture and design, business and industry, economics, educational and textbooks, guide books, history and antiquarian, languages and linguistics, military, music, religious, sociology and anthropology, sports and games, transport. 30 titles in 1988.

Editorial Director *John Tuckwell* Unsolicited mss considered.
Royalties paid annually.

Dorling Kindersley Ltd

9 Henrietta Street, London WC2E 8PS
☏ 01–836 5411
Telex 8954527 Deekay G Fax 01–836 7570

Chairman *Peter Kindersley*
Deputy Chairman *Christopher Davis*

FOUNDED 1974. Packagers for the international market and publishers in the UK. *Publishes* illustrated non-fiction on subjects such as children's cookery, crafts, gardening, health. Average 50 titles annually.

Editorial Director *Alan Buckingham* TITLES *Baby Care* Miriam Stoppard; *Sotheby's World Wine Encyclopaedia* Tom Stevenson; *The Way Things Work* David Macaulay; *Eyewitness Series.* Welcome unsolicited synopses and ideas for books.

Doubleday

See **Transworld Publishers Ltd**

Richard Drew Publishing Ltd

6 Clairmont Gardens, Glasgow G3 7LW
☎ 041–333 9341 Telex 777308

Managing Director *Richard Drew*

Publishes fiction, general non-fiction, art, travel, children's books, Scottish books. 30 titles in 1988.

Editorial Head *Richard Drew*

IMPRINTS (Paperback & Hardback)
Businessmates French and German **The Scottish Collection** TITLES *Walk Don't Walk* Gordon Williams, *Time Will Knit* Fred Urquhart. **Swallows** TITLES *The River Tree* Mairi Maclachlan; *The Third Eye* Mollie Hunter. **Travelmate** (New Edition) French, German, Greek, Italian, Spanish, Portuguese, *Euromate*. **Schoolmate** French and German.
Welcome unsolicited mss, synopses and ideas for books.
Royalties paid twice yearly.

Authors' Rating One of the big three of Scottish publishing. Much admired for close editor–author relationships.

Gerald Duckworth & Co. Ltd

The Old Piano Factory, 43 Gloucester Crescent, London NW1 7DY
☎ 01–485 3484

Chairman/Joint Managing Director *Colin Haycraft*

FOUNDED 1898. Authors on their early list included Hilaire Belloc, August Strindberg, Henry James and John Galsworthy. *Publishes* mainly academic with some fiction. Approximately 60 titles in 1988.

Editorial Head *Colin Haycraft* TITLES *Wittgenstein, A Life* Brian McGuinness; *East End 1888* W. J. Fishman; *Language Logic and Experience* Michael Luntley; *Matters, Space and Motion* Richard Sorabji; *Moving Pictures* Judy Carver; *Archaeology Explained* Keith Brannigan.

IMPRINT
Paperduck Paperbacks
Welcome unsolicited mss, synopses and ideas for books.
Royalties paid twice yearly at first, annually thereafter.

Authors' Rating Colin Haycraft believes in a business relationship with authors which excludes third parties. As he puts it, 'If you can't cope with life, write about it; if you can't write, publish; if you can't get a job in publishing, become a literary agent; if you are a failed literary agent – God help you.' A certain entrepreneurial style has been introduced by Roger Shasoua, himself a successful author, who recently bought a substantial stake in the company. Promised innovations include a growing list of financial deals with other companies in the UK and Europe, and backing for transforming novels into film scripts.

The Dunrod Press

8 Brown's Road, Newtonabbey,
Co. Antrim BT36 8RN
☎ 02313 2362

Managing Director *Ken Lindsay*

FOUNDED 1979. *Publishes* children's books, politics and world affairs. 3 titles in 1988.

Editorial Head *Ken Lindsay* Preliminary letter essential. Synopses and ideas for books welcome.
Royalties paid annually. *Overseas associates* The Dunrod Press, Irish Republic.

Ebury Press

Colquhoun House, 27–37 Broadwick Street, London W1V 1FR
☎ 01–439 7144
Telex 263879 NATMAG G Fax 01–439 0062

Publishing Director *Charles Merullo*
Approx Annual Turnover £3.5 million

Bought by **Century Hutchinson** from National Magazine Company in 1989. With the sale of Century Hutchinson to Random House, Ebury is now part of Random Century. *Publishes* illustrated reference books in subject areas ranging from biography to cookery, crafts, homecraft, humour and photography. 60 titles in 1988.

Editorial Director *Gail Rebuck* Unsolicited mss, synopses and ideas for books welcome.
Royalties paid twice yearly.

Authors' Rating Looks set for a more exciting future now that Century Hutchinson has taken over. With a five year licence to publish titles based on National Magazine journals such as *Good Housekeeping*, *Harpers & Queen* and

Cosmopolitan, the strongest development is likely to be in the area of illustrated books.

Economist Publications Ltd

40 Duke Street, London W1A 1DW
☎ 01–499 2278
Telex 266353 Fax 01–499 9767

Managing Director *Hugo Meynell*
Approx Annual Turnover £1.5 million

Owned by **The Economist**. *Publishes* business and finance, economics, educational and textbooks, guide books, politics and world affairs, reference books. 12 titles in 1988.

Editorial Director *Sarah Child* Unsolicited mss considered.
Royalties paid twice yearly.

Authors' Rating Powerful marketing via *The Economist* distribution network. Strong on direct sales.

Edinburgh University Press

22 George Square, Edinburgh EH8 9LF
☎ 031–667 1011
Telex 727442 Unived Fax 031–667 7938

Publishes academic and scholarly, archaeology, biology and zoology, computer science, history, Islamic studies, law, linguistics, literary criticism, philosophy, physics, social sciences. Acquired **Polygon** in 1988. 60 titles in 1989.

Chief Editor *Martin Spencer* Would prefer to be approached with a letter or synopsis rather than unsolicited mss.
Royalties paid annually.

Authors' Rating One of the smaller university publishers drawing mainly on local talent. Recently took over **Polygon Books** from the Edinburgh Student Union to add the quarterly *Edinburgh Review* and six first novels to the EUP list.

Element Books Ltd

The Old School House, The Courtyard, Bell Street, Shaftesbury, Dorset SP7 8BP
☎ 0747 51448 Fax 0747 51394

Chairman/Managing Director *Michael Mann*
Approx Annual Turnover £3 million

FOUNDED 1978 by John Moore and Michael Mann. Publish 40 of their own titles annually, and in addition represent and distribute for over 60 publishers from the UK, USA, Australia and Europe, bringing the present list to over 1000 titles. An increase of new titles to around 60 per year is anticipated. 50 titles in 1988. *Publishes* art, astrology, complementary medicine and therapies, esoteric traditions, mysticism, philosophy, psychology and religion.

DIVISIONS
Broadcast Books Ltd *David Porteous* **Element Books Ltd** *Michael Mann* Senior Commissioning Editor *Simon Franklin*.
Royalties paid twice yearly.

Authors' Rating Hitherto better known as a distributor than as a publisher, Element Books is now committed to expanding into general books.

Elliot Right Way Books

Kingswood Buildings, Lower Kingswood, Tadworth, Surrey KT20 6TD
☎ 0737 832202

Joint Managing Directors *Clive Elliot, Malcolm G. Elliot*

FOUNDED 1946 by Andrew G. Elliot. All the early books were entitled *The Right Way to . . .*, but this format became too restrictive. However, most books are still *How to* titles, instruction books illustrated with line drawings, published in **Paperfronts.** *Publishes How to* books on car repairs, cooking, DIY, family financial and legal matters, family health and fitness, fishing, looking after pets and horses, motoring, popular education, puzzles and jokes, quizzes. 13 titles in 1988.

IMPRINT
Paperfronts *Clive Elliot* Unsolicited mss, synopses and ideas for books welcome.
Royalties paid annually.

Aidan Ellis Publishing Ltd

Cobb House, Nuffield, Henley-on-Thames, Oxon RG9 5RT
☎ 0491 641496
Telex 449907 IOP DIS G Fax 0491 573649

Chairman *Lucinda Ellis*
Managing Director *Aidan Ellis*
Approx Annual turnover £250,000

FOUNDED in 1971 by Aidan Ellis, who was bored with being an accountant. *Publishes* fiction and general trade books. 14 titles in 1988.

Editorial Heads *Aidan Ellis, Lucinda Ellis* TITLES Fiction: *The Nationalists* (series vol. XI) Vivian Stuart; *Carn* Patrick McCabe; *The Summer Woods* Margaret Morley. Non-fiction: *Guide du Fromage; The Bodleian Library & Its Treasures;*

Collection of Essays by Marguerite Yourcenar. Unsolicited mss, synopses and ideas for books welcome.
Royalties paid twice yearly. *Overseas associates* in Australia and New Zealand, Europe, Far East, Africa, South America and South Africa.

Elm Tree Books

See **Hamish Hamilton Ltd**

Elsevier Science Publishers Ltd

Crown House, Linton Road, Barking,
Essex 1G11 8JU
☎ 01–594 7272 Fax 01–594 5942

Managing Director *Hans Gieskes*
Parent company *Elsevier Science Publishers, Amsterdam*

Publishes scientific and technical books, journals and magazines. 150 titles in 1988, and 80 journals.

DIVISIONS
Applied Science *Dr Norman Paskin* **Advanced Technology Group** *Chris Lloyd* **Elsevier Publications (Cambridge)** *David Bousfield*. Welcome unsolicited mss, synopses and ideas for books.
Royalties paid annually.

Authors' Rating An offshoot of the third largest Dutch publisher. Refreshingly open with authors in the tradition of northern European publishers – early news on print-runs and royalties paid promptly. Links with the UK are strengthened by having Pearson as a major shareholder. Moves towards a closer union are expected but likely to stop short of a full merger.

Elvendon Press

The Old Surgery, High Street, Goring on Thames, Reading RG8 9AW
☎ 0491 873003
Telex 849021 Fax 0491 32468

FOUNDED 1978. *Publishes* cookery, drink, food and nutrition, but is branching out into other areas and will consider all general subjects except fiction. Specialises in packaging for publishers and manufacturers.

Editorial Head *Mr R. Hurst* No unsolicited mss. Preliminary letter essential. Synopses and ideas for books welcome.

Emblem

See **Mitchell Beazley Ltd**

Enitharmon Press

40 Rushes Road, Petersfield,
Hampshire GU32 3BW
☎ 0730 62753

Director *S. J. A. Stuart-Smith*

FOUNDED in 1969. Enitharmon is one of the leaders in a specialised field, widely known for the excellence of the work it publishes and for its quality of production. *Publishes* literature, especially poetry. 25 titles in 1988/9. TITLES include first collections by Neil Curry, Michael Henry, Tessa Lund, Peter Armstrong, Alan Sharples and Deirdre Shanahan. Also new titles by already-established writers among them David Gascoyne, Jeremy Reed, Phoebe Hesketh (*Collected Poems*), John Heath-Stubbs, Jeremy Hooker, Duncan Forbes, John Moat. Unsolicited mss welcome, but only after introductory letter.
Royalties rare; payments vary according to contract. *Representation* by Password (Brooks) Ltd, 23 New Mount Street, Manchester M4 4DE.

Epworth Press

Room 195, Central Buildings, Westminster,
London SW1H 9NR
☎ 01–222 8010 ext 234

Chairman *John Stacey*

Publishes humour, philosophy, religion and theology. 14 titles in 1988.

Editorial Director *John Stacey* TITLES *Enquiring Within* J. Neville Ward; *A Coat of Many Colours* Michael Wilson; *A History of the Methodist Church in Great Britain* Rupert Davies, A. Raymond, George and Gordon Rupp. Unsolicited mss considered.
Royalties paid annually.

Equation

See **Thorsons Publishing Group Ltd**

Estamp

204 St Albans Avenue, London W4 5JU
☎ 01–994 2379

New publishing company set up to publish books specifically about the fine art of printmaking, papermaking, and bookmaking. Books are designed and written for people with special or professional interest in the inter-related crafts of papermaking, artists' books and original prints. First title 1989 with *A Printmaker's Handbook* ed. Silvie Turner. Best approach in writing in first instance. **Contact** *Silvie Turner.*

Evans Brothers Ltd

2A Portman Mansions, Chiltern Street, London W1M 1LE
☎ 01–935 7160
Telex 8811713 EVBOOK G Fax 01–487 5034

Managing Director *Stephen Pawley*
Approx Annual Turnover £2 million

FOUNDED 1908 by Robert and Edward Evans. Originally published educational journals, books for primary schools and teacher education. But after rapid expansion into popular fiction and drama, both lists were sacrificed to a major programme of educational books for schools in East and West Africa. A new UK programme launched in 1986. *Publishes* UK children's and educational books, adult travel, educational books for Africa, Caribbean and Far East. 25 titles in 1988.

Editorial Director *Brian Jones*

DIVISIONS
Overseas TITLES *Effective English for Junior/Secondary Schools.* **UK Publishing** TITLES *Ready Steady Go; Foundations of Geography; Kenya – A Visitor's Guide.* Unsolicited mss, synopses and ideas for books welcome.
Royalties paid annually. *Overseas associates* Kenya, Cameroon, Sierra Leone, Hong Kong & Pacific, Evans Bros (Nigeria Publishers) Ltd.

Authors' Rating A company which has suffered more than most from the vagaries of African currencies. From being one of the leaders in educational publishing in the 1960s, Evans all but disappeared in the late 1970s. Now well on its way on the long haul back to prosperity but publishing mostly for overseas education.

University of Exeter Publications

Publications Office, Reed Hall, Streatham Drive, Exeter EX4 4QR
☎ 0392 263061 Telex 42894

Publications Officer *Mrs B. V. Mennell*

FOUNDED 1956 as a publisher of scholarly books for members of staff and research students. *Publishes* academic books. 17 titles in 1988. Do not welcome unsolicited mss as the University only publishes works by members of staff and present or former research students.
No royalties paid.

Exley Publications

16 Chalk Hill, Watford, Herts WD1 4BN
☎ 0923 48328/50505
Telex 927500 Fax 0923 818733

Managing Director *Richard Exley*

FOUNDED 1976. *Publishes* general non-fiction, gift books, humour. Has a very substantial children's non-fiction list. 20 titles in 1988.

Editorial Director *Helen Exley* Do not welcome unsolicited mss but will consider synopses if accompanied by s.a.e.

Eyre & Spottiswoode Publishers Ltd

North Way, Andover, Hants SP10 5BE
☎ 0264 334202

Managing Director *A. Holder*

Division of **Octopus Publishing Group.** *Publishes* bibles, prayer books and religious books. No unsolicited mss. Will consider synopses and ideas for books.
Royalties paid twice yearly.

Faber & Faber Ltd

3 Queen Square, London WC1N 3AU
☎ 01–278 6881 Fax 01–278 3817

Chairman/Managing Director *Matthew Evans*

Geoffrey Faber and Richard de la Mare founded the company in the 1920s, with T.S. Eliot as an early recruit to the board. The original list was based on contemporary poetry and plays (the distinguished backlist includes Eliot, Auden and MacNeice). *Publishes* poetry and drama, art, children's, fiction, nursing and medical, music, specialist cookery, and a growing number of miscellaneous one-offs. The new blood of recent years has led to Faber looking to new areas, such as film/screenplays.

DIVISIONS
Art *Giles de la Mare* **Children's** *Janine Thomson* AUTHORS Gene Kemp, Helen Cresswell. **Cookery** *Tracey Scoffield* TITLES *The Vegan Cookbook; The Student Cookbook; Pastability.* **Fiction** *Robert McCrum* AUTHORS P.D. James, Lawrence Durrell, William Golding, Milan Kundera, Mario Vargas Llosa, Garrison Keillor, Paul Anster. **Music** *Helen Sprott* **Nursing & Medical** *Roger Osborne* Specialist titles and popular books. **Plays** *Frank Pike* AUTHORS Samuel Beckett, David Hare, Tom Stoppard.

Poetry *Craig Raine* AUTHORS Seamus Heaney, Ted Hughes, Douglas Dunn, Tom Paulin. **Non-fiction** *Will Sulkin* TITLES *Wine Snobbery; Live From Number 10; Shooting in the Dark.*

Unsolicited mss will be considered; synopses and ideas for books welcome.
Royalties paid twice yearly. *Overseas office* Boston.

Authors' Rating Applause for one of the original signatories of the Minimum Terms Agreement (MTA). Heavily dependent on its dealings with the literary establishment, and on backlist profits including royalties from the musical 'Cats'. New-style marketing is in evidence with bright, distinctive book jackets and a memorable logo. Poetry accounts for one sixth of total turnover and some bestsellers. The drama list has benefited from disarray at Methuen, gaining Harold Pinter and Simon Gray. Scores heavily in 'Books of the Year' features run by the posh newspapers.

Facts on File

Collins Street, Oxford OX4 1XJ
☏ 0865 728399 Fax 0865 244839

Chairman *Ed Knappman*
Managing Director *Alan Goodworth*
Approx Annual Turnover £0.5 million

Subsidiary of Facts on File Inc., New York. Specialises in information books on virtually any subject from antiques to zoology. Current growth trends promise much. Claim to be 'in an excellent position to adopt world English language rights in titles for simultaneous publication worldwide'. Publish up to 100 books per year with growing backlist (currently 600 titles).

DIVISIONS
Trade *Stephen Setford* **Reference/Academic/Professional** *Alan Goodworth* **Educational** *Stephen Setford* TITLES *Kingmakers & Usurpers; History of Space Flight; Home Economics on File.* Welcome unsolicited mss, synopses and ideas in non-fiction only.
Royalties paid twice yearly.

Falling Wall Press Ltd

11 Colston Yard, Colston Street, Bristol BS1 5BD
☏ 0272 225719

Managing Director *Jeremy Mulford*

FOUNDED 1971. *Publishes* autobiography, biography, history, non-fiction, politics.

Editorial Director *Jeremy Mulford* TITLES *Wonderful Adventures of Mrs Seacole in Many Lands; Black Women and the Peace Movement* Wilmette Brown; *Ask Any Woman – A London Enquiry into Rape and Sexual Assault; Educating Grandma* Winnie Bridges.

IMPRINT
Loxwood Stoneleigh High-quality new fiction and poetry. Prefer to see synopses and ideas for books, plus s.a.e.
Royalties paid twice yearly for the first year and then annually.

Falmer Press

Rankine Road, Basingstoke, Hants RG24 0PR
☏ 0256 840366 Telex 858540

Managing Director *Malcolm Clarkson*

Publishes educational: books about education, educational materials for all levels. Largely commissioned.

Editorial Director *Malcolm Clarkson* Unsolicited mss considered.
Royalties paid annually.

Firecrest Books

See **Chivers Press (Publishers)**

Flamingo

See **Collins Publishers**

Floris Books

21 Napier Road, Edinburgh EH10 5AZ
☏ 031–337 2372

Managing Director *Christian Maclean*
Approx Annual £150,000

Trading since 1977. Publishes books related to the Steiner movement including arts & crafts, children's, the Christian community, history, religious, science, social questions. 20 titles in 1988.

Editorial Head *Michael Jones*

IMPRINT
Floris Classics *Michael Jones* No unsolicited mss. Unsolicited synopses and ideas for books welcome.
Royalties paid annually.

Focal Press

See **Butterworth & Co. Ltd**

Fontana

See **Collins Publishers**

G. T. Foulis & Co Ltd

See **Haynes Publishing Group**

Fountain Press Ltd

45 The Broadway, Tolworth, Surrey KT6 7DW
☎ 01–390 7768 Fax 01–390 8062

Managing Director *Mr H. M. Ricketts*
Approx Annual Turnover £1 million

FOUNDED 1923 when it was part of the Rowntree Trust Group. Owned by the British Electric Traction Group until seven years ago when it was bought out by the present managing director. Acquired **Buchan & Enright, Publishers** (see separate entry) in 1988. *Publishes* architecture and design, British history, crafts and hobbies, do-it-yourself, medical, photography, veterinary. TITLES *Photography Year Book* and *An African Sketchbook* Ray Nestor. Unsolicited mss and synopses are welcome.
Royalties paid twice yearly.

Fourth Estate Ltd

Classic House, 113 Westbourne Grove, London W2 4UP
☎ 01–727 8993 Fax 01–727 9840

Chairman/Managing Director *Victoria Barnsley*
Approx Annual Turnover £500,000

FOUNDED 1984. Independent publishers with strong emphasis on literary fiction and well-designed upmarket non-fiction. Emphasis on high media profile books and design. Winner of 1987 **David Higham Prize**, 1988 **Time-Life Silver PEN Award**, and the first *Sunday Times* 'Best Small Publisher' award (1987). *Publishes* current affairs, design, fiction, humanities, humour, popular culture, reference (hardback and trade paperback). Approximately 30 titles a year.

DIVISIONS
Fiction *Giles O'Bryen* TITLES *The 13th House* Adam Zameenzad; *Milk Sulphate and Alby Starvation* Martin Millar. **Non-Fiction** *Victoria Barnsley* TITLES *Waugh on Wine* Auberon Waugh; *Blueprint Monographs* series ed. Deyan Sndjic; *Design Museum Books* series ed. Stephen Bayley. Unsolicited mss, synopses and ideas for books welcome.
Royalties paid twice yearly.

Authors' Rating Awarded *The Sunday Times* accolade of 'Best Small Publisher of 1987', Fourth Estate is attracting new and exciting writers. If there was a prize for the most memorable catalogue, Fourth Estate would win that too. A co-publishing deal with the new Design Museum promises another area for expansion.

W. H. Freeman & Co. Ltd

20 Beaumont Street, Oxford OX1 2NQ
☎ 0865 726975 Telex 83677

President *Linda Chaput* (New York Office)
Managing Director *Graham Voaden* (Oxford)

Part of W. H. Freeman & Co., USA. *Publishes* academic, agriculture, animal care and breeding, archaeology, artificial intelligence, biochemistry, biology and zoology, chemistry, computer science, economics, educational and textbooks, engineering, geography and geology, mathematics and statistics, medical, natural history, neuroscience, paleontology, physics, politics and world affairs, psychology, *Scientific American Library*, sociology and anthropology, and veterinary. 50 titles in 1988 (both UK and USA).
Editorial office in New York (Oxford is a sales and marketing office only) but unsolicited mss can go through *Graham Voaden*, who filters out the obviously unsuitable and passes on the rest to New York.
Royalties paid annually.

Freeway

See **Transworld Publishers Ltd**

Samuel French Ltd

52 Fitzroy Street, London W1P 6JR
☎ 01–387 9373

Chairman *M. A. Van Nostrand*
Managing Director *John L. Hughes*

FOUNDED 1830 with the object of acquiring acting rights and publishing plays. Part of Samuel French Inc., New York. *Publishes* plays only. 50 titles in 1988. Unsolicited mss welcome and should be addressed to The Performing Rights Department. No synopses or ideas.
Royalties paid twice yearly.

Author's Rating Unlike some drama publishers who limit themselves to critically approved plays, Samuel French takes a more liberal view of what makes a publishable text. A boon to playwrights and amateur dramatic societies alike.

Futura

See **Macdonald & Co. Ltd**

The Gay Men's Press (GMP Publishers Ltd)

PO Box 247, London N17 9QR
☎ 01–365 1545 Fax 01–365 1252

Managing Director *Aubrey Walter*

Publishes primarily books by gay authors about gay-related issues; art: painting and drawing; biography and autobiography, fiction: literary and popular (historical romance to crime and science fiction); health and leisure. Works must be submitted by the author on disc.

Editors *Richard Dipple* (fiction and rights), *Aubrey Walter* (art and photography), *David Fernbach* (non-fiction) TITLES *Private: The Erotic Art of Duncan Grant; Aubade* Kenneth Martin; *The Novice* Timothy Ireland; *Because We're Queers* Simon Shepherd. One-off payments rather than royalties. Terms open to negotiation.

Geographia

See **John Bartholomew & Son Ltd**

Ginn & Company Ltd

Prebendal House, Parson's Fee, Aylesbury, Bucks HP20 2QZ
☎ 0296 88411
Telex 83535 GINN G Fax 0296 25487

Chairman *Nicholas Thompson*
Managing Director *William Shepherd*

Part of the Educational and Professional Division of **Octopus Publishing Group**. Though started in Boston, USA, in 1867, Ginn now has no US connections. *Publishes* educational books for primary schools. 800 titles in 1988.

Editorial Director *Olga Norris* Almost all titles are commissioned and unsolicited mss are generally not considered. Synopses and ideas for books are welcome largely as a means of introduction to potential authors.
Royalties paid annually. *Overseas* various agency and representative arrangements.

Authors' Rating With the decline of the *Janet and John* readers, Ginn was a sad little company when it was bought by **Heinemann**. It is now busily trying to re-establish its credentials in the educational market.

Mary Glasgow Publications Ltd

Avenue House, 131–3 Holland Park Avenue, London W11 4UT
☎ 01–603 4688 Fax 01–602 5197

Managing Director *Paul St. C. Proctor*

Part of the Wolters Kluwer Group. Mary Glasgow founded Mary Glasgow & Baker Ltd in 1956 with the publication of her first French magazine, *Bonjour*. Her objective was to provide a service for teachers and students of languages, aiming to make their work more effective and more enjoyable. The company changed its name in January 1970 to Mary Glasgow Publications Ltd. Apart from a regular output of magazines, there is an established and continually expanding list of secondary school main course, text and teacher-support materials in foreign languages, geography, music and media studies and a rapidly growing list of primary school materials for reading, science and cross-curricular work. *Publishes* mainly language magazines, books and teacher-support material.

DIVISIONS
Books *Nick Hutchins* **Magazines** *Sally Gray* No unsolicited mss but will consider synopses and ideas for books.

Golden Cockerel Press Ltd

25 Sicilian Avenue, London WC1A 2QH
☎ 01–405 7979 Telex 23565

Chairman/Managing Director *Thomas Yoseloff*

Set up in London in 1980 to distribute the books published by its overseas associate company, Associated University Presses Inc., New Jersey. Now acts as a full publishing house, with its own editorial function. *Publishes* art, collecting, film, history, Judaica, literary criticism, music, philosophy, sociology, special interest. 80–100 titles in 1988.

Editorial Head *Michael Wright*

IMPRINTS
AUP member presses: **Bucknell, Delaware, Fairleigh Dickinson, Folger Shakespeare Library** *Publishes* scholarly and academic. **Cornwall Books** *Publishes* trade hardbacks. **Lehigh University Press, Susquehanna University Press.**

Unsolicited mss, synopses and ideas for books

welcome.
Royalties paid annually.

Victor Gollancz Ltd

14 Henrietta Street, London WC2E 8QJ
☎ 01–836 2006
Telex 265003 Fax 01–379 0934

Chairman *Livia Gollancz*
Managing Director *Stephen Bray*

FOUNDED 1928 by Victor Gollancz as a general publishing company, and famous for its political books during the 1930s and 1940s (*Left Book Club*). After sixty years of independence, Gollancz is now 'looking for a new owner who will fully retain the firm's literary traditions and standing'. *Publishes* biography and memoirs, bridge, children's cookery, current affairs, detective stories and thrillers, general fiction, history, mountaineering, music, science fiction, travel, vernacular architecture. Wholly owned subsidiary: **H. F. & G. Witherby Ltd** which publishes angling, natural history, ornithology, travel and wine.

Editors *Chris Kloet* (Children's), *Joanna Goldsworthy* (Fiction and general non-fiction), *Livia Gollancz* (Music and Mountaineering), *Julia Wisdom* Thrillers, *Liz Knight* (Paperbacks), *Peter Crawley* (Vernacular architecture and bridge), *David Burnett* (**H. F. & G. Witherby**). Prefer typescripts to be preceded by descriptive letter. Unsolicited synopses and ideas for books welcome.
Royalties paid twice yearly.

Authors' Rating Changes to be expected now that 'a decision has been taken that a new owner must be found for the Company'. But Gollancz has come a long way from the somewhat eccentric ideals of their founder ... Prompt and, in some ways, generous payers. For example, Gollancz offers a standard 15% on overseas sales, a third higher than most publishers. Now moving into paperback crime.

Gordon & Breach Science Publishers

1 Bedford Street, London WC2E 9PP
☎ 01–836 5125
Telex 23258 SCIPUB G Fax 01–379 0800

Chairman *Martin Gordon*
Managing Director *Alan Davies*
Editor-in-Chief (London) *John Gillman*
Editorial Director (New York) *Philip Manor*

FOUNDED 1961. *Publishes* books and journals across a range of disciplines including engineering and technology, mathematics and computer science, physics, chemistry, biomedicine, psychology, social science, economics, music and dance. 200+ titles in 1988.

IMPRINT
Harwood Academic Publishers *Publishes* biomedical, medical science and social science books and journals. **Abacus Kent** *Publishes* science, technical, and medical. Unsolicited mss and synopses welcome.
Royalties paid annually. *Overseas office* Gordon & Breach Publishers Inc., New York.

Gowan Publishing Ltd

24 Fremount Drive, Beechdale,
Nottingham NG8 3GL
☎ 0602 292995

Managing Director *Joan Wallace*

FOUNDED 1983, initially to help and encourage new writers. *Publishes* fiction. Particularly interested in showbiz books, both fiction and non-fiction. Published 4 books since 1983.

Editorial Head *Shirley Herbert* TITLES *Two of Clubs, Independent Street* and *Independent Street At War* Joan Wallace; *The Mystery of Shalbury Manor* Graham Radford. Regret no uncommissioned work at present.

Gower Medical Publishing

See **Harper & Row Ltd**

Gower Publishing Group

Gower House, Croft Road, Aldershot,
Hants GU11 3HR
☎ 0252 331551 Telex 858001

Chairman/Managing Director *Nigel Farrow*

FOUNDED 1967. *Publishes* professional and academic books in business, humanities, professions, social sciences, and technology. Over 300 titles in 1988.

DIVISIONS
Avebury *Sarah Sutton* Research monographs on the social sciences. **Elgar** *Edward Elgar* Academic books on economics and other social sciences. **Dartmouth** *John Irwin* New imprint specialising in international relations and international law. **Gower** *Malcolm Stern* Business, professional and academic books and journals. **Scolar** *Brian Last* Quality-produced hardbacks on art, architecture, biography, books and illustration, cinema/photography, history, liter-

ature, mediaeval studies, music. **Technical Press** *Jill Pearce* Books on applied technology and industrial process, especially in the areas of construction and building technology, project management and quality management. **Wildwood House** *Christopher Simpson* The paperback imprint of the group.

Unsolicited mss welcome. Unsolicited synopses and ideas for books considered.
Royalties paid as per contract. *Overseas associates* USA, Australia, Hong Kong, Singapore.

Authors' Rating Growing fast in the area of quality non-fiction for the general reader. The purchase of its US distributor, Brookfield Publishing of Vermont, could well be the preliminary to expansion in the States. Some complaints of confused royalty statements and slow payments.

Grafton Books Ltd

8 Crafton Street, London W1X 3LA
☎ 01–493 7070
Telex 21343 Fax 01-493 1916

Managing Director *Jonathan Lloyd*

Part of **Collins**. Formerly known as Granada Publishing, the company was sold by the Granada Group in 1983. Name changed to Grafton Books in 1985. *Publishes* general trade hardbacks, fiction, non-fiction, paperbacks, sailing books. 500 titles in 1988. No unsolicited mss.

DIVISIONS
Adlard Coles *Janet Murphy* Sailing books on technical, instructional, building and design, travel subjects. **Grafton Hardbacks** *John W. Boothe* TITLES Non-fiction: *Inside the Brotherhood* Martin Short; *Modern Mysteries of the World* Janet & Colin Bord; *Articles of War: The Spectator Book of WW2; One Summer's Grace* Libby Purvis; *The Secret Lore of the Cat* Fred Gittings; *Pick of the Punch* ed. David Thomas; *One Day in the Life of Television* ed. Sean Day-Lewis; *Inside the House of Commons* John Biffin MP. Fiction: *Devils for a Change* Wendy Perriam; *French Kiss* Eric Van Lustbader; *The Ancient Solitary Reign* Martin Hocke; *In Love & War* Eileen Townsend; *Trevayne* Robert Ludlum; *Day of the Cheetah* Dale Brown. **Grafton Paperbacks** *Nick Austin* TITLES *To be the Best* Barbara Taylor Bradford; *The Icarus Agenda* Robert Ludlum; *Latecomers* Anita Brookner; *Spy Hook* Len Deighton. **Paladin** *Nick Austin*.
Royalties paid twice yearly. *Overseas associates* see **Collins**.

Authors' Rating Still trying to establish a clear identity after abandoning the Granada label four years ago. A tightly-organised, commercially sharp company, aiming fair and square at the mass market.

Graham & Trotman Ltd

Sterling House, 66 Wilton Road,
London SW1V 1DE
☎ 01–821 1123
Telex 298878 GRAMCO G Fax 01–630 5229

Managing Director *Alastair M. W. Graham*

FOUNDED 1974. Part of the Kluwer UK Group from 1986. *Publishes* books, directories, journals and looseleaf in the fields of earth sciences, environmental sciences, finance, international business and law. There are plans to increase output. 60 titles in 1988.

DIVISIONS
Business Law *A. M. W. Graham* **Technical** *H. van Dorssen.* Unsolicited mss, synopses and ideas for books welcome.
Royalties paid twice yearly. *Overseas sister company* Kluwer Inc., Boston.

Graham-Cameron Publishing

10 Church Street, Willingham,
Cambridge CB4 5HT
☎ 0954 60444

Editorial Director *Mike Graham-Cameron*
Art Director *Helen Graham-Cameron*

FOUNDED 1984 mainly as a packaging operation. *Publishes* illustrated books for children and for institutional and business customers. Also publishes biography, educational materials and social history. 10 titles in 1988. TITLES *Up From the Country* (children's); *Anglo-Saxon Households* (educational); *In All Directions* (biography). No unsolicited mss.
Royalties paid annually.

Granville Publishing

102 Islington High Street, London N1 8EG
☎ 01–226 2904

Managing Director *John Murray-Browne*
Approx Annual Turnover 'very small'

FOUNDED 1983. Part of a bookshop. *Publishes* literature reprints.

Grapevine

See **Thorsons Publishing Group Ltd**

Green Books

Ford House, Hartland, Bideford,
Devon EX39 6EE
☎ 02374 621

Chairman *Satish Kumar*
Approx Annual Turnover £30,000

FOUNDED in 1986 and supported by the Schumacher Society, Friends of the Earth, The Council for the Protection of Rural England, the Dartington Hall Trust, *Resurgence* magazine and other environmental organisations. Established to meet the increased interest in and demand for environmental literature. *Publishes* high-quality paperbacks on recycled paper covering a wide range of environmental topics. 14 titles in 1988.

Managing Editor *Elizabeth Saxby* TITLES *High Horse Riderless* L. T. C. Rolt; *Good Neighbours* Walter Rose; *Our Fragmented World* Ronald Harvey. Welcome unsolicited mss but prefer introductory letter and outline in the first instance. Welcome unsolicited synopses and ideas.
Royalties paid twice yearly.

Gresham Books

PO Box 61, Henley-on-Thames, Oxon RG9 3LQ
☎ 0735 22 3789

Managing Director *Mary V. Green*
Approx Annual Turnover £80,000

Bought by Mary Green in 1980 from Martins Publishing Group. A small specialist one-woman publishing house. *Publishes* hymn and service books for schools; *The Headmasters' Conference Hymnbook.* No unsolicited material or ideas. Only deals with schools and music publishers.

Grevatt & Grevatt

9 Rectory Drive, Newcastle-upon-Tyne NE3 1XT

Chairman *Dr S. Y. Killingley*

Part-time business started in 1981 as an alternative publisher of works not normally commercially viable. Authors waive royalties on the first 500 copies. Three books have appeared with financial backing from professional bodies. *Publishes* academic books, especially on language, linguistics and religious studies. Some poetry. 1987 TITLES included *Prosodic Phonology: The Theory and its Application to Language Acquisition and Speech Processing* and *Views of Durham Cathedral*, the latter compiled by Dr Killingley. In 1988 launched a new programme: a series of rewritten conference proceedings at the University of Newcastle, entitled *The Sanskrit Tradition in the Modern World (STIMW) Papers.* First paper of the series *Aurobindo and Zaehner on the Bhagavad-Gítá* by Yvonne Williams & Michael McElvaney.

Editorial Head *Dr S. Y. Killingley*
No unsolicited mss. Synopses and ideas should be accompanied by an s.a.e.
Royalties annually after the initial 500 copies.

Authors' Rating since print-runs are invariably low, the prospect of receiving royalties are limited.

Grosvenor Books

54 Lyford Road, Wandsworth, London SW18 3JJ
☎ 01–870 2124

Managing Director *J. H. V. Nowell*

FOUNDED 1964. Part of The Good Road Ltd. Publishers for Moral Rearmament. *Publishes* biographies, children's books, contemporary issues, educational and religious. 1 title only in 1988.
TITLES *Listen for a Change; Making Marriage Work* Annejet Campbell; *For the Love of Tomorrow* Jacqueline Piguet; *On History's Coat-tails* Michael Henderson; *The Return of the Indian Spirit* Phyllis Johnson. Do not welcome unsolicited mss but will consider synopses.
Royalties paid yearly. *Overseas associates* in Australia, New Zealand, USA, Canada.

Grotius Publications

PO Box 115, Cambridge CB3 9BP
☎ 0223 323410 Fax 0223 313545

Managing Director *C. J. Daly*

FOUNDED 1979 for the publication of the *International Law Reports* and other related titles in the international law sphere. 20 titles in 1988.

Editorial Director *S. R. Pirrie* TITLES *International Law Reports* ed. E. Lauterpacht QC; *International Law* Dr M. N. Shaw; *International Wildlife Law* Simon Lyster; *Chernobyl: Law and Communication* ed. P. J. Sands; *War, Aggression and Self-Defence* Professor Yoram Dinstein. Welcome unsolicited mss, synopses, and ideas

for books if within specialist framework.
Royalties paid annually.

Guinness Publishing Ltd

33 London Road, Enfield, Middlesex EN2 6DJ
☎ 01–367 4567
Telex 23573 Fax 01–367 5912

Chairman *Shaun C. Dowling*
Managing Director *David F. Hoy*
Approx Annual Turnover £6 million

FOUNDED 1954 to publish *The Guinness Book of Records*, now the highest-selling copyright book in the world, published in 35 languages. In the late 1960s the company set about expanding its list with a wider range of titles linked mostly to records and record-breaking. 30 titles in 1989.

Editorial Director *Donald F. Sommerville* TITLES *The Guinness Book of Records; British Hit Singles; Guinness Book of Answers.* Welcome ideas and synopses for books if they come within their fields of sport, human achievement, travel, and family reference.

Authors' Rating Any idea must seem inferior to the first book – in itself a record breaker. However the company does want to broaden its base and it has the resources to achieve its aim.

Peter Haddock Ltd

Pinfold Lane, Bridlington, E. Yorks YO9 5BT
☎ 0262 678121
Telex 52180 Fax 0262 400043

Managing Director *Peter Haddock*
Contact *P. Hornby*

FOUNDED 1952. *Publishes* children's picture story books, activity books. Published 200 series in 1988. Welcomes ideas for picture books.
Royalties payments vary according to each contract.

Authors' Rating Cheap end of the market. Writers need to work fast to make a living.

Robert Hale Ltd

Clerkenwell House, 45–7 Clerkenwell Green, London EC1R 0HT
☎ 01–251 2661
Telex 23353 NURBKS G Fax 01–251 0584

Chairman/Managing Director *John Hale*

FOUNDED 1936, and still a family company. *Publishes* most types of adult fiction; every kind of adult non-fiction, excluding specialist areas (such as educational/legal/medical and scientific). 347 titles in 1988.

Commissioning Editors *John Hale* (Fiction) TITLES *A Demon Close Behind* Leslie Halliwell; *Nothing Larger Than Life* David Holbrook; *Never Laugh at Love* Barbara Cartland; *Personal Relations* Pamela Street. *Rachel Wright* (Non-fiction) *Elvis in Private* Peter Haining; *The People in Britain* Roy Kerridge; *Psychic Animals* Dennis Bardens. Unsolicited mss, synopses and ideas for book welcome.
Royalties paid twice yearly.

Authors' Rating Takes good care of authors but can be tough on advances. Favours the popular end of the fiction market.

The Hambledon Press

102 Gloucester Avenue, London NW1 8HX
☎ 01–586 0817

Chairman/Managing Director *Martin Sheppard*
Approx Annual Turnover £120,000

FOUNDED 1980 when cricket books were top of the list. These have now been dropped. *Publishes* academic history, some academic literature, history – English and European, post-classical to modern. 10–15 titles annually.

Editorial Head *Martin Sheppard* TITLES *Studies in Mediaeval Thought from Abelard to Wyclif* Beryl Smalley; *Godly People: Essays on English Protestantism and Puritanism* Patrick Collinson. No unsolicited mss. Preliminary letter. Synopses and ideas for books welcome.
Royalties paid annually. *Overseas associates* The Hambledon Press (USA), West Virginia.

Hamish Hamilton Ltd

27 Wright's Lane, London W8 5TZ
☎ 01–938 3388 Telex 917181
fax 01–937 8704 (general)
fax 01–937 8783 (production)

Publishing Director *Andrew Franklin*
Approx Annual Turnover £6.5 million

FOUNDED 1931, subsequently bought by the Thomson Organisation and taken over by **Penguin** in 1985. *Publishes* Africana and natural history, biography, children's books, current affairs, fiction, film history, literature, music, politics, theatre, travel.

DIVISIONS
Elm Tree *Penelope Hoare* AUTHORS Susan Hampshire, Roger Phillips, John Reader, Jonathan Scott. **Hamish Hamilton** *Penelope Hoare* AUTHORS Peter Ackroyd, Isabel Allende, Sybille

Bedford, William Boyd, Germaine Greer, Francis King, Bernice Rubens, Paul Theroux, Rose Tremain. **Hamish Hamilton Children's** *Jane Nissen* AUTHORS Raymond Briggs, Anthony Browne, Eric Carle, Anne Fine, Susan Hill, Mollie Hunter, Joan Lingard.

IMPRINTS
Hamish Hamilton Trade Paperbacks *Penelope Hoare* AUTHORS Harold Acton, Kenneth Clark, Sir Peter Hall, Nancy Mitford, Marina Warner.

Unsolicited mss, synopses and ideas for books welcome.
Royalties paid twice yearly. *Overseas associates* see **Penguin.**

Authors' Rating Future uncertain as Penguin begin a major shakeup of their subsidiaries. Company likely to be slimmed down with editors reporting directly to Penguin executives. At time of writing, former MD Christopher Sinclair-Stevenson looks set to go independent.

Hamlyn Publishing

Michelin House, 81 Fulham Road,
London SW3 6RB
☎ 01–581 9393
Telex 920191 Fax 01–589 8419

FORMED 1987 out of Octopus Books Ltd and the Hamlyn Publishing Group. It is a major international illustrated popular reference and information publisher with a worldwide reputation for quality and value. *Publishes* atlases, aviation, children's, cookery, fashion, gardening, general interest, life-style, natural history, reference, and sport. It is the main supplier of own-brand books to Marks & Spencer, Tesco and Sainsbury.

DIVISIONS
Adult *Jonathan Goodman* TITLES *Larousse Gastronomique; Michelin Road Atlas of Europe; The Hollywood Story; Beatles Recording Session.* **Children's** *Derek Hall* TITLES *Wizzpax; Pink Flamingoes; The Parent and Child Programme; Colour Fax.* **New Editions** *Terence Cross* TITLES *Bounty Bargain Books; Filofiction; Hamlyn Books on Tape.*

Prefer to see synopses and ideas for books.
Royalties paid twice yearly.

Harcourt Brace Jovanovich Ltd

24–8 Oval Road, London NW1 7DX
☎ 01–267 4466

Managing Director *Joan Fujimoto*

Harcourt Brace Jovanovich Inc., New York, owns **Academic Press** (see separate entry). *Publishes* academic, accountancy and taxation, archaeology, biology and zoology, business and industry, chemistry, children's, cinema and video, computer science and business software, economics, educational and textbooks, EFL, fiction, fine art, geography and geology, history, antiquarian, languages and linguistics, law, literature and criticism, mathematics and statistics, medical, music, philosophy, physics, poetry, politics, psychology, religious, sociology and anthropology, theatre and drama, training and careers, women's studies.

Editorial Director *Dr Conrad Guettler*
Unsolicited mss welcome.
Royalties paid twice yearly.

Harper & Row Ltd

Middlesex House, 34–42 Cleveland Street,
London W1P 5FB
☎ 01–636 8300
Telex 21736 Fax 01–631 3594

Offshoot of the American company now jointly owned by **Collins** and News International. Chief executive George Craig, formerly vice chairman of Collins. *Publishes* academic, non-fiction, professional, medical and nursing, trade books. Unsolicited mss welcome.

IMPRINT
Gower Medical Publishing
Royalties paid twice yearly.

Harrap Columbus

See **Columbus Books**

Harrap Publishing Group Ltd

19-23 Ludgate Hill, London EC4M 7PD
☎ 01–248 6444 Fax 01–248 3357

Chairman *N. W. Berry*
Managing Director *Eric R. Dobby*
Publisher *Jean-Luc Barbanneau*

Publishes biography and autobiography, cinema and video, costume, some crime, fine art and art history, guide books, history, humour, illustrated and fine editions, magic and the occult, military and war, photography, political and world affairs, reference and dictionaries, sports and games, theatre and drama, travel and topography. 180 titles in 1988.

DIVISIONS
Columbus Books *Gill Gibbins* TITLES *A Nice Girl Like Me* Gloria Lovatt; *Unholy Matrimony* Liz Hodgkinson. **Dictionaries and Reference** *David Skinner* TITLES *Harrap's Illustrated Diction-*

ary of Music & Musicians; Harrap's Book of 1000 Plays. **Harrap General Books** *Susanne McDadd* TITLES *Inside Time* Ken Smith; *The Blake Escape* Michael Randle & Pat Pottle. **Impact Books/Olive Press** *Jean-Luc Barbanneau* TITLES *A Winter in Tibet* Charles & Jill Hadfield; *Street Food* Rose Grant. **Self Study** *David Skinner.*

Unsolicited mss and synopses welcome.
Royalties paid twice yearly.

Authors' Rating Solid foundation of reference books with a list of middle-of-the-road non-fiction which is beginning to make incursions into the bestseller lists.

Haynes Publishing Group

Sparkford, near Yeovil, Somerset BA22 7JJ
☎ 0963 40635 Fax 0963 40825

Chairman *John H. Haynes*
Managing Director *Jim Scott*
Approx Annual Turnover £8.5 million

FOUNDED 1960 by John H. Haynes. In the mid-sixties produced the first *Owners' Workshop Manual*, now the mainstay of the programme. A family-run business which does its own typesetting and printing on the premises. *Publishes* DIY workshop manuals for cars and motorbikes. Now branching out into wider areas but keeping a strong bias towards motoring and transport.

IMPRINTS
G. T. Foulis & Co. Ltd *R. Grainger* Cars and motoring-related books. **J. H. Haynes & Co. Ltd** *J. R. Clew, P. Ward* **Oxford Illustrated Press** *Jane Marshall* General titles: photography; sports and games; gardening; travel and guide books. **Oxford Publishing Co.** *R. Grainger* Railway titles. Welcome unsolicited mss if they come within the subject areas covered.
Royalties paid annually. *Overseas associates* Haynes Publications Inc., California, USA.

Authors' Rating Making a strong impact in its specialist market. Recently bought the Oxford Publishing Co. (railway books) from Cassell.

Headline Book Publishing plc

Headline House, 79 Great Tichfield Street,
London W1P 7FN
☎ 01–631 1687
Telex 268326 HEADLN G Fax 01–631 1958

Managing Director *Tim Hely-Hutchinson*

FOUNDED 1986 with substantial City funding, Headline specialises in commercial fiction, both hardback and paperback, and also publishes non-fiction, particularly in the areas of biography, cinema, design and film, food and wine, and TV tie-ins. The company is a signatory of a Minimum Terms Agreement with the **Society of Authors** and **The Writers' Guild of Great Britain**. 200 titles planned for 1989.

Editorial Director *Sue Fletcher* TITLES *Heretic's Apprentice* Ellis Peters; *Midnight* Dean R. Koontz; *Tuppence to Tooley Street* Harry Bowling; *Shark* Jeremy Stafford-Deitsch; *Dicken's London* Peter Ackroyd; *I Am the Only Running Footman* Martha Grimes; *Encounters* Isaac Asimov; *Professional Illustration & Design* Simon Jennings; *The Rose & The Vine* Unity Hall; *Talent* Nigel Rees; *Scandals* Una-Mary Parker; *It's Only a Movie Ingrid* Alexander Walker; *The Sight* Katherine Neville; *Succession* Andrew MacAllan; *The Art of Sensual Loving* Dr Andrew Stanway; *Child Star* Shirley Temple Black; *Richard Branson* Mick Brown.

Welcome unsolicited mss and synopses.
Royalties paid twice yearly.

Authors' Rating One of the most existing of the young publishing houses, Headline is forging ahead. Much praised by authors who feel that editors actually care about them. Open to ideas for commercial fiction and popular non-fiction.

Heinemann Educational Books Ltd

Halley Court, Jordan Hill, Oxford OX2 8EJ
☎ 0865 311366 Fax 0865 310043

Chairman *Nicholas Thompson*
Managing Director *David Fothergill*

Parent Company **Octopus Publishing Group**. *Publishes* textbooks, readers drama and other educational resources for primary and secondary education and for English language teaching; textbooks and literature for overseas markets, principally in Africa and the Caribbean.

DIVISIONS
International Publishing *Mike Esplen* (**African & Caribbean** *Vicky Unwin*) TITLES *African & Caribbean Writers Series; Heinemann Guided Readers; New Generation; Snap.* **Schools Publishing** *Bob Osborne* (**Humanities** *Kay Symons,* **Science and Maths** *Stephen Ashton*) TITLES *The New Windmill Series; Hereford Plays; Scottish Primary Maths; Sunshine.*

Unsolicited mss, synopses and ideas for books welcome.
Royalties paid twice yearly. *Offices* in Oxford, London, Edinburgh, Melbourne, Sydney, Auckland, Singapore, Madrid, Athens, Ibadan, Nairobi, Gaborone, Harare, Kingston,

Portsmouth NH.

Authors' Rating though part of the all-embracing **Octopus**, Heinemann Educational has managed to keep a distinct identity, an achievement endorsed by an office move to the Oxford Business Park. Strong on African and Caribbean books.

William Heinemann Ltd

Michelin House, 81 Fulham Road,
London SW3 6RB
☎ 01–581 9393
Telex 920191 Fax 01–589 8437

Publisher *Helen Fraser*

FOUNDED 1890 by William Heinemann, whose policy of publishing a broad range of literary and popular fiction, non-fiction, children's illustrated and information books has, despite many changes and the development of specialised divisions of the list, remained the characteristic publishing style. In 1985 the Heinemann Group became part of the **Octopus Publishing Group.** *Publishes* adult fiction and general non-fiction, popular psychology, inspirational.

Editorial Directors *Laura Longrigg, Amanda Conquy, Roger Smith* **Fiction & General** TITLES *Rock Star* Jackie Collins; *Never Despair* Martin Gilbert; *Long Dark Teatime of the Soul* Douglas Adams; *Baumgartner's Bombay* Anita Desai; *Grace* Maggie Gee; *In Search of Salinger* Ian Hamilton.

IMPRINTS

Heinemann Young Books (see entry).

Unsolicited mss, if preceded by a preliminary enquiry, and synopses/ideas for books welcome.
Royalties paid twice yearly. *Overseas associates* Heinemann Books Australia (Pty); Heinemann Publishers (NZ) Ltd, New Zealand; Heinemann Publishers South Africa (Pty).

Authors' Rating After a period of traumatic change, has re-emerged as a powerful contender for shop space. Now has its own paperback list.

Heinemann Young Books

Michelin House, 81 Fulham Road,
London SW3 6RB
☎ 01–581 9393
Telex 920191 Fax 01–589 8421

Publisher *Ingrid Selberg*
Executive Editor *Jane Fior*
Rights *Victoria Birkett*

An imprint of **William Heinemann Ltd**, part of the **Octopus Publishing Group**. *Publishes* quality picture books, novels, anthologies and TV tie-ins.
TITLES *Thomas the Tank Engine* Rev. Awdry; *The Jolly Postman* Janet & Allan Ahlberg; *Spot* Eric Hill; *Christmas, Easter* Jan Piénkowski; *Why the Whales Came* Michael Morpurgo. Unsolicited mss, if preceded by a preliminary enquiry, and synopses/ideas for books welcome.
Royalties paid twice yearly. *Overseas associates* Heinemann Books Australia (Pty), Heinemann Publishers (NZ) Ltd.

Christopher Helm Publishers Ltd

21–5 North Street, Bromley, Kent BR1 1SD
☎ 01–466 6622 Fax 01–290 0281

Chairman *Christopher Helm*
Approx Annual Turnover £1.2 million

FOUNDED 1986 from the general book division of Croom Helm. *Publishes* specialist non-fiction, including food and wine, ornithology, gardening and travel, sport, natural history and current affairs. 60 titles in 1988. No unsolicited mss but welcome synopses and ideas for books.

Contact *Malcolm Mayer, Robert Kirk.*

DIVISIONS

Natural History/Gardening *Jo Hemming* **Travel/Current Affairs** and **Music** *Alison Starling* TITLES *Shorebirds: An Identification Guide to Waders of the World; The Genius Pleione: A Kew magazine Monograph; The Eperon Regional Guides to France; The Education Crisis.*
Royalties paid by arrangement.

The Herbert Press Ltd

46 Northchurch Road, London N1 4EJ
☎ 01–254 4379
Telex 8952022 Fax 01–249 5731

Managing Director *David Herbert*

Publishes archaeology, architecture and design, biography and autobiography, crafts and hobbies, fashion and costume, fine art and art history, natural history, photography, travel and topography. 12 titles in 1988.

Editorial Director *David Herbert* Unsolicited mss welcome.
Royalties paid twice yearly.

Heretic Books

PO Box 247, London N17 9QR

Managing Director *David Fernbach*

Publishes books relevant to the growing Green movements: animal liberation, deep-ecology, Green politics and philosophy, how-to, vegetarianism. Work submitted for publication must be on author's disc.

Editorial Directors *David Fernbach, Aubrey Walter.*
One-off payments rather than royalties. Terms open to negotiation.

Nick Hern Books

See **Walker Books Limited**

Heywood Books Ltd

55 Clissold Crescent, London N16 9AR
☏ 01–241 3861 Fax 01–241 3867

Managing Director *Derek Searle*

Set up in August 1988 to publish low-cost paperbacks; the first list came out in March 1989, with 6 titles a month planned thereafter. Concentrates on popular fiction with a female bias but also includes thrillers, horror and crime. Books must have been previously published and there must be a setting that can be used to offset. Maximum length 320 pages. *Publishes* paperback fiction reprints, particularly women's. No unsolicited mss, synopses or ideas for books.

Editorial Head *Chris Holifield* TITLES *Muckle Annie* Jan Webster; *Hammerstrike* Walter Winward; *The Windmill Years* Vicky Martin.
Royalties paid twice yearly.

Hippo Children's Paperbacks

See **Scholastic Publications Ltd**

Hippopotamus Press

PO Box 120, Sutton, Surrey SM2 5WG
☏ 01–643 1470
Approx Annual Turnover £20,000

FOUNDED 1974 as a poetry press. In 1986 took over the UK's oldest, independent poetry magazine, *Outposts Poetry Quarterly*. Receives financial assistance from the Arts Council. *Publishes* poetry. 6 titles in 1988. TITLES *Images of Summer* Roy Bennett; *The Hollow Landscapes* William Bedford. Welcome unsolicited mss.
Royalties paid quarterly.

Hobsons Publishing plc

Bateman Street, Cambridge CB2 1LZ
☏ 0223 354551
Telex 81546 HOBCAM Fax 0223 323154

Managing Director *Adrian A. Bridgewater*
Approx Annual Turnover £4.7 million

FOUNDED 1973 by Adrian Bridgewater. Went public in 1987. *Publishes* textbooks, career guides, computer software; particular successful in the directories market, with comprehensive listings and advertisements giving job and product information. Consultancy publishing work for employers and government departments. Bought Johansen Publications Ltd, publishers of *Recommended Hotels in UK* in 1987, and then in 1988 acquired Health and Technical Publications, Health and Technical Exhibitions, and Doverlodge. 360 titles in 1989.

Editorial Head *Julie Horne*

Authors' Rating Formula publishing based on a close and shrewd analysis of the education and business markets.

Hodder & Stoughton Ltd

47 Bedford Square, London WC1B 3DP
☏ 01–636 9851 Telex 885887

Joint Managing Directors *Michael Attenborough, Richard Morris*
Approx Annual Turnover £55.32 million

FOUNDED 1868. An independent company which engages in a diverse range of publishing. *Publishes* academic, children's books, fiction, medical, non-fiction, religious. Also paperbacks (see imprints list below). 750 titles in 1988.

Publishing Director *Michael Attenborough*

DIVISIONS
Children's *David Grant* AUTHORS R. Goscinny/A. Uderzo (*Asterix*), Eric Carle. **Educational** Now fully merged with Edward Arnold (see below). **General** *Eric Major/Ion Trewin* AUTHORS John le Carré, Jeffrey Archer, James Clavell, Thomas Keneally, Gavin Lyall, Mary Stewart. **New English Library** *Clare Bristow* AUTHORS Stephen King, Rosamunde Pilcher, James Herbert. **Religious** *David Wavre* AUTHORS Catherine Marshall, John Wimber, Michael Green. Also publish the *NIV Bible*.

IMPRINTS
Edward Arnold *Richard Morris* (Managing

Director) *Brian Steven* (Managing Director – school books) *Richard Stileman* (Managing Director – tertiary publishing). *Publishes* secondary education, further education, *Teach Yourself* series, colleges of education books, academic, scientific, medical, ELT. Paperbacks: **Coronet Books** and **Sceptre Books** *Adrian Bourne* (Managing Director) *Amanda Stewart* (Editorial Director); **Knight Books** *Elizabeth Roy* AUTHORS as for **General, New English Library** and **Children's** lists.

Hodder & Stoughton actively discourage the submission of unsolicited mss, though 'the company is very willing to assess synopses and sample chapters.'
Royalties paid twice yearly. *Overseas associates* Australia, New Zealand and a wide-spread network of other overseas companies and agencies.

Authors' Rating The sixth publisher to sign the Minimum Terms Agreement (Feb 89), Hodder is said by Mark Le Fanu of the **Society of Authors** to have 'one of the best house contracts around'. A welcome component is the right of authors to buy copies of their books at 50% discount. Signs of more energetic marketing include an intensive promotional campaign for the *Teach Yourself* series and the signing up of Saatchi and Saatchi to advertise John Le Carré's latest book.

The Hogarth Press Ltd

See **Chatto & Windus Ltd**

Holmes McDougall Ltd

Allander House, 137–41 Leith Walk, Edinburgh EH6 8NS
☎ 031–554 9444 Fax 031–554 4051

Chief Executive *F. J. Baillie*
Approx Annual Turnover £1.5 million

FOUNDED 1962. *Publishes* educational and textbooks (primary and secondary). 50 titles in 1988.

Editorial Director *E. Ketley* TITLES *Schools Council History; Link-Up Reading Scheme Primary English; Science and Creative Technology.* Welcome unsolicited mss and synopses.
Royalties paid twice yearly.

Holt Rinehart & Winston

24–8 Oval Road, London NW1 7DX
☎ 01–267 4466

Owned by CBS Inc., USA, until bought by **Academic Press** in 1987. *Publishes* academic, accountancy and taxation, biology and zoology, business and industry, chemistry, computer science, computer software (business and educational), economic, educational and textbooks, engineering, languages and linguistics, mathematics and statistics, physics, reference books and dictionaries, scientific and technical, sociology and anthropology.

Human Horizons

See **Souvenir Press Ltd**

C. Hurst & Co.

38 King Street, London WC2E 8JT
☎ 01–240 2666

Chairman/Managing Director *Christopher Hurst*

FOUNDED 1967. Independent, and active in the **Publishers Association**. Aims to cultivate a small publisher's concern for literacy, detail and the visual aspects of the product. *Publishes* autobiography, contemporary history, political science, religion. 12 titles in 1988.

Editorial Head *Christopher Hurst* with *Michael Dwyer* TITLES *The Break-up of Sri Lanka; The State in Burma; U. Thant in New York 1961-1971; Modernist Conjectures (A Movement in European Literature, 1910-1940; The Improbable Survivor (Yugoslavia and its Problems 1918-1988); The Northern Ireland Assembly: a Constitutional Experiment.* No unsolicited mss but unsolicited synopses and ideas for books welcome.
Royalties paid twice yearly twice after publication and annually thereafter.

Hutchinson Academic

See **Unwin Hyman Ltd**

IBC Financial Publishing Ltd

57–61 Mortimer Street, London W1N 7TD
☎ 01–637 4383 Fax 01–631 3214

Chairman *Michael Bell*
Managing Director *Jenny Ireland*
Approx Annual Turnover £29 million

Part of International Business Communications (Holdings) plc. *Publishes Banking Technology* magazine and a range of business to business books, newsletters and directories aimed at senior management. 5 titles in 1988.

DIVISIONS
IBC Financial Books Ltd *Karen Hindle* TITLES *Retail Banking Technology; Electronic Banking*

and The Law. **IBC Financial Publishing Ltd – Directories** *Diane Holyoak* TITLES *Insurance Computer Systems 1989; Planning for Disaster Recovery.*
Welcome unsolicited synopses and ideas. Best approach by phone in first instance.
Royalties paid twice yearly. *Overseas subsidiaries* Euroforum BC, The Netherlands; Donogue Organisation Inc, USA; IBC Pty Ltd, Australia; IBC (Holdings) USA Inc.

Impact Books

See **Harrap Publishing Group Ltd**

J & B Maps

See **John Bartholomew & Son Ltd**

Arthur James Ltd

1 Cranbourne Road, London N10 2BT
☎ 01–883 1831/2201/8307 Fax 0386 6566

Managing Director *Denis Duncan*
Approx Annual Turnover £100,000

FOUNDED 1944 by A. J. Russell, a Fleet Street journalist. *Publishes* day books, devotional, psychological, religious, social work, New Testament translation.

Editorial Head *Denis Duncan* TITLES *God Calling; God at Eventide.* No unsolicited mss.
Royalties paid annually. *Overseas associates* Buchanan, Australia.

Jane's Information Group

163 Brighton Road, Coulsdon, Surrey CR3 2NX
☎ 01–763 1030
Telex 916907 Fax 10–763 1005

Managing Director *Michael Goldsmith*
Approx Annual Turnover £25 million

FOUNDED 1898 by Fred T. Jane with publication of *All The World's Fighting Ships.* Since then the company has grown to produce, in 1989, 21 yearbooks, a number of subscription services, and the leading international weekly defence magazine, *Jane's Defence Weekly.* In 1985, Jane's acquired DMS Inc. of the USA, a market research company, and in 1987 purchased Interavia Publishing Group of Switzerland. Jane's is a subsidiary of Thomson Information Services Ltd and is part of the International Thomson Organisation. *Publishes* defence, aerospace and transport topics, including yearbooks which give details of equipment and systems; directories and strategic studies. Planning publication of a number of new yearbooks including *Jane's Radar & Electronic Warfare,* and *Jane's Strategic Weapons* (looseleaf binder/subscription service). Also launched in 1989 a new monthly subscription magazine, *Jane's Soviet Intelligence Review.*

DIVISIONS
Jane's Defence Weekly *Peter Howard.* **DMS Inc.** *Grant Stockdale* TITLES *World Armoured Vehicle Forecast.* **Interavia Publishing Group** *Pierre Condom* TITLES *Interavia Aerospace Review; International Defense Review.* **Jane's Defence Data** *Bob Hutchinson* TITLES *Soviet High Command; Red Banner; Jane's All the World's Aircraft.* **Jane's Air Data and Transport Data** *Ken Harris* TITLES *Jane's Airport Review; Jane's World Railways.*

Welcome unsolicited mss, synopses and ideas for books.
Royalties paid twice yearly. *Overseas associates* Jane's Information Group Inc., USA; DMS Inc., USA; Interavia Publishing Group SA, Switzerland.

Michael Joseph Ltd

27 Wright's Lane, London W8 5TZ
☎ 01–937 7255
Telex 917181/2 Fax 01–937 8704

Publishing Director *Susan Watt*

FOUNDED 1936. Parent company **Penguin Books Ltd**. *Publishes* belles-lettres, biography and memoirs, current affairs, fiction, general, history, humour, travel. 112 titles in 1988. TITLES include bestsellers by Dick Francis and A. Wainwright. Unsolicited manuscripts welcome.

IMPRINT
Mermaid Books Paperback *Publishes* nonfiction illustrated.
Royalties paid twice yearly. *Overseas associates* Penguin Overseas.

Authors' Rating Future uncertain as Penguin embarks on a major shapeup of its subsidiaries. MD Alan Brooke has departed. Tighter control of editorial policy anticipated.

Kahn & Averill

9 Harrington Road, London SW7
☎ 01–743 3278

Managing Director *M. Kahn*

FOUNDED 1967. Originally published juvenile titles but gradually changed to music titles. A small independent publishing house. *Publishes* mainly music titles with some general nonfiction. Do not welcome unsolicited mss but will

consider synopses and ideas for books.
Royalties paid twice yearly.

The Kensal Press

Riverview, Headington Hill, Oxford OX3 0BT
☎ 0865 750302 Telex 849462 Telfac G

Managing Director *Mrs Betty Millan*

FOUNDED 1982. *Publishes* historial biographies. 3 titles in 1988.

General Manager *Miss Georgina Shomroni* TITLES *A Lady of Extraordinary Beauty* Madeleine Rogers; *Sir Bernard Bourdillon* Robert D. Pearce; *The Share Game* Martin Braune; *The Musical Peacemaker, The Life and Music of Sir Edward German* Brian Rees; *My Brother Benjamin* Beth Britten; *The Harlot and the Statesman, The Story of Elizabeth Armitstead and Charles James Fox* I. M. Davis. Prefer to see a synopsis rather than completed mss.
Royalties paid twice yearly for the first year and annually thereafter.

Kenyon-Deane

See **Cressrelles Publishing Co. Ltd**

William Kimber Ltd

See **Thorsons Publishing Group Ltd**

Kime Publishing

PO Box 1, Hunstanton, Norfolk PE36 5JY
☎ 048525 347

Owner *Dr Clive Layton*

FOUNDED August 1988. First publication November 1988. *Publishes* martial arts, sports psychology. 1 title in 1988. Welcome unsolicited mss, synopses and ideas for books.

Kingfisher Books

Elsley House, 24–30 Great Titchfield Street, London W1P 7AD
☎ 01–631 0878
Telex 27725 Gridem G Fax 01–323 4694

Managing Director *Daniel Grisewood*

The publishing imprint of Grisewood and Dempsey Ltd. *Publishes* children's books (poetry and fiction, history, general reference, paperbacks, young readers, picture books), dictionaries, natural history and reference books. 80 plus titles in 1988.

Editorial Head *Jane Olliver* CHILDREN'S TITLES Reference: *Picture Encyclopedia of Our World; Astronomy Today; Kingpin Superbooks/Factbooks.* Science & Nature: *Exploring the Countryside; Dictionary of Animals.* Poetry/Fiction: *A Spider Bought a Bicycle; The Odyssey.* ADULT TITLES *Coastline: Britain's Threatened Heritage; Guide to Birds/Mushrooms/Herbs; Field Guide to Wild Flowers/Wildlife/Plantlife/Birds of Britain and Europe.* Welcome unsolicited mss.
Royalties paid twice yearly.

Kluwer Academic Press

PO Box 55, Lancaster LA1 1PE
☎ 0524 34996 Fax 0524 32144

Managing Director *Dr F. W. B. van Eysinga*
Publishing Director *Peter Clarke*
Approx Annual Turnover £1.5 million

Specialises in medical and scientific publishing at the postgraduate level. Recently acquired Hutchinson Education, a list of some 700 titles with an annual turnover of £3 million. *Publishes* research monographs, postgraduate textbooks, colour atlases and texts for family physicians. Particular areas of specialisation include cardiology, nephrology, radiology, oncology, pathology, neurosciences and immunology. 55 titles in 1988.
TITLES *AIDS* (second edition) Dr V. Daniels; *The Inner Consultation* Dr R. Neighbour; *Current Histopathology* series A Gresham (series ed.); *Immunology and Medicine* K. Whaley (series ed.); *Developments in Cardiology* series; *Replacement of Renal Function by Renal Dialysis* (third edition) Maher; *Peritoneal Dialysis* Nolph.

Knight Books

See **Hodder & Stoughton Ltd**

Kogan Page Ltd

120 Pentonville Road, London N1 9JN
☎ 01–278 0433
Telex 263088 KOGAN G Fax 01–837 3768

Managing Director *Philip Kogan*
Approx Annual Turnover £3.4 million

FOUNDED 1967 by Philip Kogan, the company originally published only one title: *The Industrial Training Yearbook.* Now *publishes* business and management, education and careers, marketing, personal finance, personnel, science and technology, small businesses, training and industrial relations, transport, plus journals. Continuing to expand, particularly in the professional, and technical areas. 180 titles in 1988.

DIVISIONS
Kogan Page *Piers Burnett, Pauline Goodwin, June Lines* TITLES *New Technology Modular* series; *New Generation computing* series; *Working for Yourself* series; BIM books; *Professional* paperbacks; *Careers* series; *Stoy Hayward Business Tax Guide.* **North Oxford Academic Publishers** *Piers Burnett* TITLES *World Yearbook of New Generation Computing. Publishes* computer science.

Unsolicted mss, synopses and ideas for books welcome.
Royalties paid twice yearly.

Authors' Rating An object lesson on how to succeed in publishing by carving out a section of the market. Thriving on the boom in business education, Kogan Page is king of the airport bookstalls.

K. T. Group Publishing

1 St Anne's Road, Eastbourne,
East Sussex BN21 3UN
☎ 0323 410930 Fax 0323 411970

Chairman *Rev. Gilbert Kirby*
Managing Director *Geoffrey Ridsdale*
Approx Annual Turnover £1.5 million

Part of the Kingsway Trust Group, owned by a charitable trust with Christian objectives. *Publishes* Christian literature, fiction, the arts, humour. 103 titles in 1988.

DIVISIONS
Kingsway Publications *Richard Herkes* TITLES *The Truth About AIDS* Patrick Dixon; *Pathway Through Pain* Jane Grayshon; *Battered Bride?* David Winter; *Ten Inner-City Churches* ed. Michael Eastman.

IMPRINTS
Monarch Publications, Minstrel, Marc *Anthony Collins* Welcome unsolicited mss but partial submission/synopsis preferred.
Royalties paid annually.

Ladybird Books Ltd

Beeches Road, Loughborough, Leics LE11 2NQ
☎ 0509 268021
Telex 341347 Fax 0509 234572

Chairman *T. J. Rix*
Managing Director *M. P. Kelley*
Approx Annual Turnover £15 million

FOUNDED 1860s. Part of the **Longman Group**. The Ladybird name and format was established as a result of the development of a children's list during World War 1. In the early 1960s the print side of the operation was abandoned in favour of publishing and in 1971 the company was bought by the Pearson Longman Group. *Publishes* children's trade titles only. 80 titles in 1988.

Editorial Head *M. H. Gabb* TITLES *Well Loved Tales; Puddle Lane* series; *Activity Books and Packs; Learning to Read; Read it Yourself; Thomas the Tank Engine; Transformers; Rupert; Disney; Beatrix Potter;* Ladybird *Tell-a-Tale* cassette/book, and video packs. Very rarely able to make use of unsolicited mss as material is generally commissioned once publication programme has been determined. *Overseas Associates* Ladybird Books, Auburn, Maine, USA.

Authors' Rating Good simple stuff for kiddies of a sentimental turn of mind. Criticised for perpetuating the image of female subservience. But popular in the bookshops. One of the few imprints everyone has heard of. Now expanding into book cassette packs, stationery and videos.

Lakeland Paperbacks

See **Marshall Pickering Holdings Ltd**

Allen Lane The Penguin Press

See **Viking**

Lawrence & Wishart Ltd

144A Old South Lambeth Road,
London SW8 1XX
☎ 01–820 9281

Chairman *R. Simon*
Managing Director *Sally Davison*

FOUNDED 1936 in its present form. *Publishes* cultural politics, economics, history, politics, and sociology. 13–20 titles a year.

Editor *Stephen Hayward* TITLES *Bending the Rules: Education After Baker; Gramsci Reader; Unbroken: Resistance and Survival in the Concentration Camps; Male Order: Unwrapping Masculinity; Sweet Dreams.* Unsolicited mss welcome if in keeping with the character of the list. Synopses preferred to complete mss. Ideas welcome.
Royalties paid annually, unless by arrangement.

Authors' Rating One of the few genuine left-wing publishers. Authors should expect to surrender profit to principles.

Leicester University Press

Fielding Johnson Building, University of Leicester, University Road, Leicester LE1 7RH
☎ 0533 523333
Telex 341198 Fax 0533 522200

Publisher *Alec McAulay*

Now part of Pinter Publishers Ltd but remains a university press. *Publishes* academic books in archaeology, defence studies, history, literature, politics and international relations. A new science list is currently being developed. 15 titles in 1988. Unsolicited mss considered if on appropriate subjects. Synopses and ideas for books welcome.
Royalties paid annually.

Authors' Rating Strong but small academic list which was under threat until Pinter Publishers injected some urgently needed funds.

Lennard Publishing

Musterlin House, Jordan Hill Road, Oxford OX2 8DP
☎ 0865 311075 Fax 0865 310562

Chairman *George Riches*
Managing Director *Adrian Stephenson*
Approx Annual Turnover £1.5 million

A division of Lennard Books Ltd. FOUNDED 1986 by Adrian Stephenson. Became part of the Musterlin Group in Nov 1988. First publishing list appeared in 1987 with titles such as *The World's Worst Golf Club* Bill Tidy and *Unexplored London* Paul Barkshire. 30 titles in 1989.

Editorial Head *Roderick Brown* TITLES *Astride The Wall* Ursula Wyndham; *E. F. Benson* Geoffrey Palmer & Noel Lloyd; *Body Styles* Ted Polhemus. Unsolicited mss, synopses and ideas for books welcome.
Royalties paid twice yearly.

Lewis Brooks Ltd

2 Blagdon Road, New Malden, Surrey KT3 4AD
☎ 01–949 4699 Telex 24667 Impemp G

Chairman/Editorial Director *John M. Verge*

Publishes academic and scholarly, architecture & design, engineering, reference books and dictionaries, scientific and technical.

Lion Publishing plc

Peter's Way, Sandy Lane West, Littlemore, Oxford OX4 5HG
☎ 0865 747550
Telex 837161 Fax 0865 747568

Approx Annual Turnover £6 million

FOUNDED 1971. Went public 1975. A Christian book publisher strong on illustrated books for a popular readership. International market, with rights sold in 56 languages worldwide. Set up US subsidiary in 1984. *Publishes* diverse list with Christian viewpoint the common denominator. All ages, from board books for children to multi-contributor adult reference. Children's fiction and non-fiction, educational, paperbacks, and colour co-edition. 60 titles in 1988.

Contacts Unsolicited adult mss: *Vernon Blackmore*; unsolicited children's mss: *Ms Su Box*. Unsolicited mss welcome providing they have a positive Christian viewpoint intended for a wide general and international readership. No books on academic theology, or books intended expressly for the Church. Unsolicited synopses and ideas for books also welcome.
Royalties paid twice yearly. *Overseas associates* Lion Publishing Corp., USA.

Authors' Rating Came out ahead in the 1988 **Society of Authors** survey of author-publisher relationships. Much praised for straight dealing and for taking care of authors.

Lions

See **Collins Publishers**

Liverpool University Press

PO Box 147, Liverpool L69 3BX
☎ 051–794 2232/37 Telex 627095

Managing Director (Acting) *Robin Bloxsidge*

FOUNDED 1899 as the publishing arm of the university, LUP has made its mark in the social sciences and humanities. In the 1980s the list has expanded to take in medicine and veterinary science. *Publishes* academic and scholarly, hardback and paperback books in the fields of archaeology, commerce, economics, education, geography, ancient and modern history, English literature, philosophy, sociology, town planning, veterinary science and medicine. 11 titles in 1988.

Acting Publisher/Editorial Head *Robin Bloxsidge* TITLES *Luso – Brazilian Studies; Byron and the Limits of Fiction; Pedro Calderón de la Barca: El Purgatorio de San Patricio; The Merchant Taylors' School for Girls; Crosby: One Hundred Years of Achievement, 1888–1988; The Public's Schools in the 1990s; A Guide to Port Sunlight Village; Gregory of Tours: Glory of the Martyrs* and *Glory of the Confessors; so Much for So Few: A View of Sheltered Housing.* Unsoli-

cited mss, synopses and ideas for books welcome.
Royalties paid annually.

Livewire

See **The Women's Press**

Longman Group UK Limited

Longman House, Burnt Mill, Harlow, Essex CM20 2JE
☎ 0279 26721
Telex 81259 Fax 0279 31059

Chairman *Tim Rix*
Chief Executive (Publishing) *Paula Kahn*

FOUNDED 1724 by Thomas Longman. Now the largest educational publishing house in the English-speaking world (outside the United States). Part of Pearson plc. Acquired Kluwer's law publishing list through Longman Law Tax and Finance in March 1989. *Publishes* educational, medical books and journals, professional and reference, ELT, dictionaries and general.

DIVISIONS
Academic Scientific & Medical *Robert Duncan* **Business & Professional** *Peter Warwick* **International** *Paula Kahn* **UK Schools** *Roger Watson*

MAIN IMPRINTS
Churchill Livingstone, Longman, ELT, Longman Professional, Longman Scientific & Technical, Oliver & Boyd, Pitman. All unsolicited mss should be addressed to **Contracts & Copyright Manager** *David Lea.*
Royalties paid annually. *Overseas associates* in 23 countries around the world.

Authors' Rating Spearhead for the Pearson assault on the American education market. The recent purchase of **Addison-Wesley** was a big advance on this front. Longman is responsible for much formula publishing for the education market. Not especially exciting but always profitable. Now there are signs of development in general publishing where Longman have scored top marks for *Chronicle of the Twentieth Century* – 'a report or news item for over half the days of the century' elevated to a bestseller. The idea has been around for years, ever since the days of the early partworks, but no other publisher has had the sense or courage to take on the project. Expansion also in law and finance with the purchase of the Kluwer law and finance list. The aim is to be 'the fastest growing law publisher'.

Loxwood Stoneleigh

See **Falling Wall Press Ltd**

Lund Humphries Publishers Ltd

16 Pembridge Road, London W11 3HL
☎ 01–229 1825 Telex 2187 GTLXGGHB

Chairman *Lionel Leventhal*
Managing Director *Clive Bingley*

Part of Book Publishing Development plc (same address). Founded to publish fine art books, the first Lund Humphries titles appeared in 1895. The company became Percy, Lund Humphries in the 1930s, and achieved its present identity in 1969. *Publishes* art and architecture, design, graphics and language guides. 16 titles in 1988. There are plans to expand the graphic arts and design list in the years to come. Unsolicited mss welcome but prefer initial introductory letter. Synopses and ideas for books considered.
Royalties paid twice yearly.

Lutterworth Press

PO Box 60, Cambridge CB1 2NT
☎ 0223 350865 Fax 0223 66951

Managing Director *Adrian Brink*

Lutterworth Press dates back to the 18th century when it was founded by the Religious Tract Society. In the 19th century it was best known for its children's books, both religious and secular, including *The Boys' Own Paper.* Bought by the Cambridge publishing house, James Clarke & Co. Ltd in 1984 and absorbed the Patrick Hardy Books. *Publishes* general non-fiction: antiques and collecting, architecture and design, children's books, crafts and hobbies, educational and textbooks, fine art and art history, gardening, natural history, religion and theology, sports and games, theatre and drama. 27 titles in 1988.

Senior Editor *Linda Yeatman* TITLES *Ransom and Murder in Greece, Lord Muncaster's Journal 1870* Crosby Stevens; *Witness in a Pagan World, A Study of Mark's Gospel* Eric Johns & David Major; *Tenrec's Twigs* Bert Kitchen; *The Magic of Dolphins* Horace Dobbs; *Biotechnology A Brave New World?* ed. Stephanie Yanchinski. Unsolicited mss and synopses are welcome.
Royalties paid both annually and bi-annually.

Authors' Rating The list is expanding but it still

has its anchor in evangelical publishing. Imaginative children's list.

Lythway Large Print

See **Chivers Press (Publishers)**

Macdonald & Co. Ltd

Headway House, 66-73 Shoe Lane,
London EC4P 4AB
☎ 01-377 4600 Telex 885233

Managing Director *James Mann*
Approx Annual Turnover £30 million

FOUNDED in the 1930s. Part of BPCC since the 1960s and now part of Maxwell Communications. Recently announced the run down of their Orbis division which specialises in highly illustrated books. *Publishes* architecture and design, biography and autobiography, cinema, cookery, crafts and hobbies, DIY, fiction, gardening, geography/geology, guide books, history, humour, illustrated editions, medical, natural history, nautical, photography, poetry, reference, sports/games, theatre and drama, travel and topography, wines and spirits. 810 titles in 1986. Welcome unsolicited mss.
Royalties paid twice yearly

DIVISIONS
Macdonald fiction, non-fiction. **Queen Anne Press** sporting annuals, autobiographies, and leisure. **Macdonald Orbis** cooking, gardening, interiors, graphic design, and fine arts.

IMPRINTS
Futura *Alan Samson/Marion Donaldson* Mass-market fiction and non-fiction TITLES *Eyes of the Dragon* Stephen King; *The Dandelion Seed* Lena Kennedy; *Over the Edge* Jonathan Kellerman; *The Hermit of Eyton Forest* Ellis Peters; all in paperback, plus a literary B–format list. **Optima** *Alan Samson/Harriet Griffey* Alternative books on health/women's interest/popular psychology including the bestselling series of *Positive Health Guides*; all in B–format paperback. **Macdonald** *Alan Samson/Marion Donaldson* Mass-market fiction and non-fiction in hardback TITLES *The Inn on the Marsh* Lena Kennedy; *The Butcher's Theatre* Jonathan Kellerman; *An Imperfect Lady* Sarah Harrison; *Woman in the Mists* Farley Mowat. **Macdonald Orbis** *Sarah Snape* Illustrated books in hardback TITLES *Le Manoir aux Quat' Saisons* Raymond Blanc; *The Macdonald Guide to French Wines; William Morris By Himself.* **Queen Anne Press** *Alan Samson/Celia Kent* Sporting and leisure pursuits TITLES *Rothmans Football Yearbook; Leading From the Front* Mike Gatting; *American Football Yearbook; Racing Characters.*

Authors' Rating Bereft of its children's and educational list (all sold to **Simon & Schuster** in early '89), the future of Macdonald as a hardback trade publisher is confused. The purchase of the Sphere paperback list from Penguin adds to the confusion. But whoever said that working for Robert Maxwell was easy?

McGraw-Hill Book Co. (UK) Ltd

McGraw-Hill House, Shoppenhangers Road,
Maidenhead, Berks SL6 2QL
☎ 0628 23432
Telex 848484 Fax 0628 35895

Managing Director *Stephen White*

FOUNDED 1899 in London and moved to Maidenhead in 1963. Parent company McGraw-Hill Inc., New York. The British publishing programme started in 1965. *Publishes* high-level textbooks, academic books in the fields of science and chemistry, educational and reference books for the professions and management. 60 titles in 1988.

DIVISIONS
Education *Stephen White* **Professional** *Roland Elgey* Unsolicited mss, synopses and ideas for books welcome.
Royalties paid twice yearly.

Authors' Rating Plans to pool educational publishing with Maxwell Macmillan could lead to more aggressive marketing here and in the States.

Macmillan Children's Books Ltd

4 Little Essex Street, London WC2R 3LF
☎ 01-836 6633 Fax 01-370 4204

Publishing Director *Michael Wace*

Publishes children's fiction and non-fiction. 165 titles in 1988. Mss and synopses welcome.
Royalties paid twice yearly.

Authors' Rating A popular list overseen by one of the pioneers of imaginative children's publishing.

Macmillan Education Ltd

Houndmills, Basingstoke,
Hampshire RG21 2XS
☎ 0256 29242 Fax 0256 479476

Chairman *A. Soar*
Managing Director *J. E. Jackman*

Publishes primary and secondary school textbooks across the curriculum, including resource guides for teachers, and assessment material. At tertiary level biology and zoology, business and industry, computer science, computer software (educational), economics, educational and textbooks, engineering, geography and geology, history and antiquarian, languages and linguistics, law, literature and criticism, mathematics and statistics, medical, music, natural history, philosophy, physics, politics and world affairs, psychology, reference and dictionaries, religion and theology, scientific and technical, sociology and anthropology, theatre and drama, vocational training and careers, women's studies.

Publishing Directors: (School Curriculum) *P. Murby*, (School Library & Reference) *I. Dawson*, (Further Education) *J. Winndaw*, (Higher Education) *S. Kennedy*, (Higher Education, Science) *R. Parry*. TITLES *New Way Reading Scheme; Macmillan Master Series; Macmillan Work Out Study Aids*. Unsolicted mss welcome.
Royalties paid annually.

Authors' Rating After a rocky few years when school budgets were tight, the company is now restored as a major force in the market. The *Master* series has emerged as a strong competitor to *Teach Yourself*. Strong on overseas sales.

Macmillan London Ltd

4 Little Essex Street, London WC2R 3LF
☎ 01–836 6633 Fax 01–370 4204

Chairman *Nicholas Byam Shaw*
Managing Director *Felicity Rubenstein*

Publishes biography and autobiography, cookery, crime, fashion and costume, fiction, fine art and art history, gardening, guide books, health and beauty, history and antiquarian, humour, literature and criticism, music, natural history, photography, poetry, politics and world affairs, psychology, sports and games, theatre and drama, wines and spirits.

Editorial Directors: *Hilary Hale* AUTHORS Simon Brett, Colin Dexter, Sue Grafton, Paula Gosling, Julian Symons, Loren D. Estleman. *Fanny Blake* AUTHORS Joseph Heller, E. L. Doctorow, Barry Humphries, Joyce Carol Oates, E. V. Thompson, Hilary Bailey, Roy Hattersley, Iain Banks. *Adam Sisman* AUTHORS Alistair Horne, Hugo Young, Tom Peters, John Pearson. *Kyle Cathie* AUTHORS Peter Gay, Duchess of Devonshire, Barrie Pitt, Jane Lapotaire, Anton Mosiman, Les Dawson, Peter Levi. Unsolicited mss and synopses welcome.
Royalties paid twice yearly.

Authors' Rating Yet another revolution as Philippa Harrison gives way to Felicity Rubenstein, one of the youngest MDs in the business. All seems to be working well, however, with the new marketing set-up covering Pan, Sidgwick, Macmillan London and Macmillan Children's Books (the rationalisation which prompted Ms Harrison's resignation) adding credibility to Macmillan's declared aim to go for the big sellers.

The Macmillan Press Ltd

Stockton House, 1 Melbourne Place,
London WC2B 4LF
☎ 01–836 6633 Fax 01–379 4980

Chairman *A. Soar*
Managing Director *C. J. Paterson*

Publishes academic and scholarly, and works of reference in: accountancy and taxation, agriculture, animal care and breeding, archaeology, architecture and design, bibliography and library service, biography and autobiography, biology and zoology, business and industry, chemistry, cinema and video, computer science, economics, engineering, art history, geography and geology, guide books, history and antiquarian, languages and linguistics, law, literature and criticism, mathematics and statistics, medical, military and war, music, natural history, philosophy, physics, politics and world affairs, psychology, dictionaries, religion and theology, scientific and technical, sociology and anthropology, theatre and drama, transport, travel and topography, business reference and directories, biotechnical reference, telecommunications, vocational training and careers, women's studies. 400 titles in 1988.

DIVISIONS
Medical & Scientific Books & Journals *H. Holt* **Postgraduate & Scholarly** *T. M. Farmiloe* **Reference, Professional & Music** *J. F. K. Ashby* Unsolicited mss welcome.
Royalties paid annually.

Authors' Rating Renowned for blockbuster reference and eclectic range of academic books, which seems to belie the stories of cutbacks in library publishing. Recently signed a deal with *The Telegraph* to publish a major series of books.

Macmillan Publishers Ltd

4 Little Essex Street, London WC2R 3LF
☎ 01–836 6633 Fax 01–370 4204

Chairman *Earl of Stockton*

Managing Director *N. G. Byam Shaw*
Approx Annual Turnover £176 million

DIVISIONS
Parent Company of **BASW Macmillan Ltd, Macmillan Children's Books Ltd, Macmillan Education Ltd, Macmillan Intek Ltd, Macmillan London Ltd, Macmillan Magazines Ltd, Macmillan Publishers (Overseas) Ltd, The Macmillan Press Ltd, Pan Books Ltd, Sidgwick & Jackson Ltd.**

Overseas associates Gill & Macmillan (Eire), Macmillan India Ltd, The Macmillan Co. of Australia Pty Ltd, Macmillan Shuppan KK Ltd (Japan), Macmillan South-East Asia Pty Ltd (Singapore), Macmillan Publishers (Overseas) Ltd, Macmillan Publishers (China) Ltd, Macmillan Kenya (Publishers) Ltd, The Macmillan Co. of New Zealand Ltd, Macmillan Boleswa Publishers Ltd, Macmillan Nigeria Publishers Ltd, **St Martin's Press Inc.** (New York), The College Press Ltd (Zimbabwe), Editorial Macmillan de Mexico SB de CV, Macmillan Publishers (Malaysia), Grove's Dictionary of Music Inc. (New York), Stockton Press Inc. (New York), Nature America Inc. (New York), Nature Japan KK, The Macmillan Language House Ltd, Japan, Bookmark Associates Ltd (Hong Kong).

Authors' Rating Still a family company (the chairman is the second Earl of Stockton), Macmillan has self-financed its way to the top. Said to be one of the country's largest and most profitable publishers, which may tell us as much about tight accounting procedures as about the art of turning out good books.

Julia MacRae Books

87 Vauxhall Walk, London SE11 5HJ
☎ 01-793 0909
Telex 8955572 Fax 01–587 1123

Managing Director *Julia MacRae*

FOUNDED 1979 by Julia MacRae (previously with **Hamish Hamilton**). A division of **Walker Books**. *Publishes* children's books, mostly fiction with some non-fiction. Also some general books. About 45 titles each year.
TITLES *Gorilla, Alice's Adventures in Wonderland* Anthony Brown; *Through the Dolls' House Door* Jane Gardam; *The Nature of the Beast* Janni Howker; *Running Scared* Bernard Ashley. Welcome unsolicited mss, synopses and ideas for books.
Royalties paid twice yearly.

Magnet

See **Mammoth & Teen Paperbacks**

Mainstream Publishing Co. (Edinburgh) Ltd

7 Albany Street, Edinburgh EH1 3UG
☎ 031–557 2959 Fax 031–556 8720

Directors *Peter MacKenzie, Bill Campbell*
Approx Annual Turnover £1 million

Publishes autobiography, biography, current affairs, fiction, health, history, illustrated and fine editions, literature and criticism, military and war, photography and sport, politics and world affairs, popular paperbacks. 63 titles in 1988.

Editorial Director *Bill Campbell* Unsolicited mss welcome.
Royalties paid twice yearly.

Authors Rating One of the leaders in the revival of Scottish publishing. Well regarded by authors.

Mammoth and Teens Paperbacks

Michelin House, 81 Fulham Road,
London SW3 6RB
☎ 01–581 9393 ext 2093 Fax 01–589 8419

Publisher *Rosemary Canter*

A new division (the Children's Paperback list) of the **Octopus Publishing Group.** *Publishes* children's books (picture, fiction, non-fiction, for babies to early teens). Incorporates titles formerly under **Magnet** list. 120 titles in 1989. Welcome unsolicited manuscripts, synopses and ideas for books.
Royalties paid twice yearly.

Manchester University Press

Oxford Road, Manchester M13 9PL
☎ 061–273 5539
Telex 668932 MCHRUL Fax 061–274 3346

Publisher/Chief Executive *Francis Brooke*
Approx annual turnover £1 million

A department of Manchester University founded early this century. The list remained largely history-based until after the war, when it took up anthropology with great success. Now Britain's third-largest university press. *Publishes* academic and educational books in the areas of anthropology, biomedical science and nonlinear dynamics, history, law (especially international), literature, modern languages, politics, sociology. 90 titles in 1988. It also publishes 5 journals.

DIVISIONS
Humanities *John Banks* **History** *Ray Offord* **Politics** *Richard Purslow* **Science** *Alec McAulay* Unsolicited mss welcome.
Royalties paid annually.

Authors' Rating Not usually associated with publishing controversy, MUP was in the news last year after a decision to reject a commissioned book on gay politics partly on the grounds that the tone of the writing was 'much more polemical than we were led to believe'. There would seem to be a message for other MUP authors.

Mandala
See **Unwin Hyman Ltd**

Mandarin
See **Octopus Publishing Group**

George Mann Books
PO Box 22, Maidstone, Kent ME14 1AH
☎ 0622 595591

Chairman/Managing Director *John Arne*

FOUNDED 1972 originally as library reprint publishers but with the collapse of the library market moved on to other things. *Publishes* selected reprints with some original non-fiction: autobiography, militaria, the occult and prophecy. No new fiction. Must have synopsis with preliminary letter, and must enclose by-return postage/s.a.e. if by-return response is wanted.

On line for 1989: new imprint, Recollections, to cater for non-commercial, prestigious publications of short-run, strictly limited editions of true books of adventure and experience of a biographical/autobiographic nature. Unlimited editorial advice and assistance provided for this. Send preliminary letter enclosing large s.a.e.
Royalties paid twice yearly.

Marshall Pickering
Middlesex House, 34–42 Cleveland Street, London W1P 5FB
☎ 01–636 8300 Fax 01–631 3594

Managing Director *Ron Chopping*

Bought by **Harper & Row,** making it part of the Murdoch empire, and **Collins Religious**. One of the biggest Christian paperback publishers. *Publishes* academic and scholarly, biography and autobiography, children's, fiction, music, poetry, reference books and dictionaries, religion and theology. About 100 titles a year.

Publishing Manager *Christine Whitell*

IMPRINTS
Marshall, Morgan & Scott, Marshall Pickering, Pickering & Inglis, Samuel Bagster & Sons.
Unsolicited mss welcome.
Royalties paid twice yearly.

Mercury
See **W. H. Allen & Co plc**

Merlin Press Ltd
10 Malden Road, London NW5 3HR
☎ 01–267 3399

Managing Directors *Martin Eve, Norman Franklin, Jon Carpenter*
Approx Annual Turnover £100,000

FOUNDED 1956 by Martin Eve. *Publishes* ecology, economics, history, philosophy, left wing politics. 10 titles in 1987.

AUTHORS Georg Lukacs, Ernest Mandel, Istvan Meszaros, Ralph Miliband, E. P. Thompson. No unsolicited mss; letter essential before sending either finished mss or synopses.

IMPRINTS
Green Print, Seafarer
Royalties paid twice yearly.

Mermaid Books
See **Michael Joseph Ltd**

Merrill Publishing Company
Holywell House, Osney Mead, Oxford OX2 0ES
☎ 0865 791497 Fax 0865 727830

Manager *Michael Brightmore*

Part of Bell & Howell Inc, USA. *Publishes* academic and scholarly, business and industry, computer science, educational and textbooks, engineering, geography and geology, psychology, scientific and technical. 120 titles in 1988. Editorial office is in America (sales and marketing function only in UK) but all mss and queries should go through Michael Brightmore in Oxford. Unsolicited mss will be passed on to

Merrill Publishing Co., 1300 Alum Creek Road, Columbus, Ohio 43216, USA.

Methuen Children's Books

Michelin House, 81 Fulham Road,
London SW3 6RB
☎ 01–581 9393/ext. 2093
Telex 290191 Fax 01–589 8419

Publisher *Rona Selby*

A division of the **Octopus Publishing Group.** *Publishes* children's books (picture, fiction, non-fiction for babies to early teens). Children's paperbacks formerly under the **Magnet** imprint, now transferred to **Mammoth and Teens Paperbacks** (see separate entry). 100 titles in 1988. Welcome unsolicited mss, synopses and ideas for books.
Royalties paid twice yearly.

Methuen London

Michelin House, 81 Fulham Road,
London SW3 6RB
☎ 01–581 9393
Telex 280191 Fax 01–589 8419

Publishing Director *Geoffrey Strachan*

A division of **Octopus.** *Publishes* general (adult fiction and non-fiction). 200 titles in 1988. Send synopsis in the first instance.
Royalties paid twice yearly.

Authors' Rating Still shell-shocked from recent changes of ownership – from Associated Book publishers to Thomson International to Octopus – not to mention a move across London, Methuen is fighting hard to retain its identity. A fair example of the problems they are facing is the departure of drama editor Nick Hern to **Walker Books,** taking with him some top writers. Methuen is the latest publisher to sign the Minimum Terms Agreement.

Milestone Publications

62 Murray Road, Horndean, Hants PO8 9JL
☎ 0705 597440 Fax 0705 591975

Managing/Editorial Director *Nicholas J. Pine*

Publishes antiques and collecting, business, economics military and war, and reference. Unsolicited mss not welcome. Approach in writing essential in first instance.
Royalties paid twice yearly.

Miller's Publishing

See **Mitchell Beazley Ltd**

Mills & Boon Ltd

Eton House, 18–24 Paradise Road, Richmond, Surrey TW9 1SR
☎ 01–948 0444
Telex 24420 Milbon G Fax 01–940 5899

Chairman *John T. Boon*
Managing Director *R. J. Williams*

FOUNDED 1908. *Publishes* fiction only. Over 500 titles in 1988.

Editorial Director *Frances Whitehead*

IMPRINTS
Mills & Boon Romances Traditional love stories, with happy endings assured. **Mills & Boon Temptation** *Linda Fildew* Modern storylines aimed at younger and more affluent readers; temptation and choices with satisfying resolutions. **Doctor Nurse & Masquerade** *Elizabeth Johnson* Established in the 1950s, and still very popular. **Doctor Nurse** romances are love stories set in a realistic medical world; *Masquerade* are historical romances, slightly longer than usual. **Worldwide** *Linda Fildew* Individual women's fiction titles, minimum of 100,000 words. **Silhouette Desire, Special Edition** and **Sensation** are considered by Silhouette Books, 300 E. 42nd St, 6th Floor, New York, NY 10017, USA. (No unsolicited mss; query letter in first instance. Tip sheets available from this address.)
Unsolicited mss very welcome except as outlined above in the case of Silhouette.
Royalties paid twice yearly.

Authors' Rating Not so much a company, more a national institution. So overwhelmed are they by writers dreaming of becoming romantic novelists (2000 unsolicited mss arrive over a year). Mills & Boon have produced a forty-minute cassette tape, *And Then He Kissed Her*, which gives advice on how to construct a novel for this highly specialist market (£2.99 from PO Box 236, Croydon, Surrey). While unsolicited mss are welcome for most series, Silhouette Books require a query letter in the first instance (see above). Writing for Mills & Boon is nowhere as easy as it looks but for those who can work the formula, the rewards are great. Mills & Boon take the public relations prize of the year with their promotion of *Britains Most Romantic Politician*, a story which was given wide coverage in nearly all the papers.

The MIT Press Ltd

126 Buckingham Palace Road,
London SW1W 9SD
☎ 01–730 9208
Telex 23993 Fax 01–730 8728

Chairman *F. Urbanowski*
Managing Director *N. C. Gosling*

Part of **MIT Press,** USA. *Publishes* academic, architecture and design, bibliography, biography and autobiography, biology and zoology, business and industry, chemistry, cinema and video, computer science, economics, educational and textbooks, engineering, fine art and art history, geography and geology, history and antiquarian, languages and linguistics, law, mathematics and statistics, medical, music, natural history, philosophy, photography, physics, politics and world affairs, psychology, reference, scientific and technical, sociology and anthropology, transport, travel and topography. All mss should go to the American office: 55 Hayward Street, Cambridge, Mass. 02142.

Mitchell Beazley Ltd

Artists' House, 14–15 Manette Street,
London W1V 5LB
☎ 01–439 7211
Telex 24892 Mbbook G Fax 01–734 0389

Chairman *Nicolas Thompson*
Managing Director *Duncan Baird*
Approx Annual Turnover £10 million

FOUNDED 1969 by James Mitchell and John Beazley. Bought by the **Octopus Publishing Group,** May 1987 for £4.85 million. *Publishes* illustrated non-fiction only, in general and leisure subjects: antiques, archaeology, astrology, cinema, cookery, crafts, fine art, gardening, geography and geology, guide books, health and beauty, history, medical, music, natural history, photography, reference and dictionaries, religion and theology, travel and topography, wines. 35 titles in 1988.

DIVISIONS
Antiques *Judith Miller* TITLES *Introduction to Antiques; The Antiques Directory.* **Gardening & Interiors** *Bob Saxton* TITLES *R. H. S. Gardening Guides; Period Details, Contemporary Stained Glass.* **General Reference** *James Hughes* TITLES *World Atlas of Archaeology; Atlas of the Universe; Atlas of Warfare; Ribbons of Time.* **Mitchell Beazley Encyclopaedias** *Frank Wallis* TITLES *The Joy of Knowledge; Lands and People.* **Photography** *Bob Saxton* TITLES *Kodak Encyclopaedia of Creative Photography; 35mm Source Book.*
Travel *Chris Foulkes* TITLES *American Express Travel Series.* **Wine** *Chris Foulkes* TITLES *World Atlas of Wine.*

IMPRINTS
Artist's House *Sue Egerton-Jones* TITLES *Men of the Stars* Patrick Moore; *Stitch Directory.* **Emblem** Trade paperbacks. **Miller's Publishing** *Judith Miller* TITLES *Miller's Antiques Price Guide Yearbook; Miller's Collectables Price Guide.*

Welcome unsolicited mss, synopses and ideas for books within subject areas listed.
Royalties paid twice yearly.

Moorland Publishing Co Ltd

Moorfarm Road, Airfield Estate, Ashbourne,
Derbyshire DE6 1HD
☎ 0335 44486 Fax 0335 46397
Telex 377106 Chacom G MPC

Managing Director *Mr C. L. M. Porter*
Approx Annual Turnover £1 million

FOUNDED 1971. Represented by **David & Charles** since 1986. Rapidly expanding; the main thrust still being the production of travel guides, namely *Visitor's Guide* series. *Publishes* travel guides, history of transport, collecting, and countryside guides. 59 titles in 1989.

Editorial Head *Dr J. Robey* Unsolicited mss will be considered, but synopses accompanied by letters of introduction preferred.
Royalties paid annually.

Motor Racing Publications

Unit 6, The Pilton Estate, 46 Pitlake, Croydon,
Surrey CR0 3RY
☎ 01–681 3363 Fax 01–760 5117

Chairman *John Blunsden*
Approx Annual Turnover £0.5 million

FORMED soon after the end of World War Two to concentrate on motor racing titles. Went into something of a 'limbo' in the mid 60s but was reactivated in 1968 with new shareholding structure. Present Chairman acquired majority shareholding soon after and major expansion of titles followed in the 70s. Introduced a second imprint (Fitzjames Press) in 1987 and acquired Speedsport Motobooks around the same time. Nearly 100 titles, with 6 in 1988. *Publishes* motorsporting history, classic car collection and restoration, road transport, motorcycles, off-road driving and related subjects.

Editorial Head *J. B. Blunsden* TITLES *The Jaguar E-Type, A Collector's Guide; Triumph Cars: The Complete Story; The Monaco Grand Prix; Tuning SU Carburettors.*

IMPRINT
Fitzjames Press TITLES *The Supertrucks of Scammell; Classic Hauliers.* Welcome unsolicited mss, synopses and ideas in specified subject area.
Royalties paid twice yearly.

Mowbray

Artillery House, Artillery Row,
London SW1P 1RT
☏ 01–222 7676
Telex 9413701 CASPUB G Fax 01–799 1514

Chief Executive *Dennis Edwards*
Managing Director (Publishing Division) *Kenneth Baker*
Approx Annual Turnover £400,000

FOUNDED 1858. Bought by **Cassell plc** in Nov 1988. Member of the **Publishers' Association** since 1899. *Publishes* theology, Christian paperbacks, handbooks for clergy and laity. 30 titles in 1988.

Editorial Head *Ruth McCurry* Unsolicited mss welcome if accompanied by postage. Synopses and ideas for books considered.
Royalties paid twice yearly (unless under £10 is due).

Frederick Muller

See **Century Hutchinson Ltd**

John Murray (Publishers) Ltd

50 Albemarle Street, London W1X 4BD
☏ 01–493 4361
Telex 21312 Murray G Fax 01–499 1792

Chairman *John R. Murray*
Managing Director *Nicholas Perren*

FOUNDED 1768 and continuously independent since then with its own distribution operation. Original publishers of Lord Byron, Jane Austen, Charles Darwin, Sir Arthur Conan Doyle, Freya Stark, Kenneth Clark and John Betjeman. *Publishes* general trade books, educational (secondary school and college textbooks), success studybooks. 65 titles in 1988.

DIVISIONS
General Books *Grant McIntyre* **Educational Books** *Keith Nettle* **Success Study books** *Bob Davenport.* Welcome unsolicited mss or synopses.
Royalties paid annually.

Authors' Rating One of the old school of publishers. High quality non-fiction for the erudite reader. Sensitive to authors and reliable on payments.

Nautical Publishing Co Ltd

See **A. & C. Black (Publishers) Ltd**

Thomas Nelson & Sons Ltd

Nelson House, Mayfield Road, Walton-on-Thames, Surrey KT12 5PL
☏ 0932 246133
Telex 929365 Nelson G Fax 0932 246109

Managing Director *Michael Thompson*
Approx Annual Turnover £12 million

FOUNDED in 1798. Part of the International Thomson Organisation. *Publishes* educational (infant, primary, secondary); school atlases and dictionaries, English language teaching worldwide, educational books for Caribbean.

Divisional Directors *Pamela Bowen* (Primary), *Graham Taylor* (Secondary & Caribbean), *John Tuttle* (ELT) TITLES *Vayal!; Nelson Handwriting; Counterpoint; The World; Progress Papers; Biology, A Functional Approach.* Unsolicited mss and synopses are welcome.
Royalties paid twice yearly.

Authors' Rating Coming back to life after a long period in the doldrums. Open to ideas for books on the practical side of education.

New Editions

See **Octopus Publishing Group**

New English Library

See **Hodder & Stoughton Ltd**

New Portway Large Print

See **Chivers Press (Publishers)**

NFER-NELSON Publishing Co Ltd

Darville House, 2 Oxford Road East, Windsor, Berks SL4 1DF
☏ 0753 858961
Telex 937400 Fax 0753 856830

Managing Director *Michael Jackson*

FOUNDED 1981. Jointly owned by **Thomas Nelson & Sons** and the National Foundation for Educational Research. *Publishes* educational and psychological tests, educational books and journals. 45 titles in 1988.

Editorial Head *Tim Cornford* Some books and tests are commissioned, but unsolicited material is welcomed.
Royalties vary according to each contract.

Nonesuch Press

See **Reinhardt Books Ltd**

North Oxford Academic Publishers

See **Kogan Page Ltd**

Northcote House Publishers Ltd

Harper & Row House, Estover Road,
Plymouth PL6 7PZ
☎ 0752 705251
Telex 45635 Fax 0752 777603

Managing Director *Roger Ferneyhough* (Editorial)

FOUNDED 1985 by Roger Ferneyhough and Brian Hulme following the purchase of 100 titles from **Longman** and **Mitchell Beazley.** Distributed by **Harper & Row,** it was formed to develop trade paperbacks, business, student and other titles designed to meet the needs of a young and forward-looking readership. *Publishes* self-help paperbacks, including *How to* books, also textbooks and revision aids for students; business, professional and reference, and travel books. 22 titles in 1988.

Editorial Director *Roger Ferneyhough* 'Well thought out proposals with marketing arguments welcome.'
Royalties paid annually

Nutshell Publishing Co Ltd

12 Dene Way, Speldhurst, near Tunbridge Wells, Kent TN3 0NX
☎ 0892 86 2860

Managing Director *Bryan Smithers*
Approx Annual Turnover £70,000

FOUNDED 1989. Jointly owned by Bryan Smithers and Ian Morley-Clarke (of **Spellmount Ltd).** *Publishes* non-fiction hardback titles, militaria, *Clash of Arms* series, and biographies. No unsolicited mss.

Oak

See **Omnibus Press**

Oberon Books

Mill Street, Aston, Birmingham B6 4BS
☎ 021–359 2088

Managing Director *James Hogan*

Publishes Oberon's Theatre Directory and play texts.

Octopus Publishing Group

Michelin House, 81 Fulham Road,
London SW3 6RB
☎ 01–581 9393
Telex 920191 Fax 01–589 8419

Chairman *Paul Hamlyn*
Chief Executive *Ian Irvine*
Director of Publishing Development *Paul Richardson*

FOUNDED 1971. Launched its first list in 1972 with 55 titles. Went public in 1983. The Octopus Group acquired Bookwise Service Ltd in 1984 and then Brimax Books; and the Heinemann Group merged with Octopus in September 1985. Acquired Hamlyn Publishing Group in March 1986 and half of the Collins share of **Pan Books** in September 1986. **Pan** interest sold to **Macmillan** in 1987. Bought **Methuen London, Methuen Children's Books, Eyre and Spottiswoode** and **Pitkin Pictorials** December 1987. Acquired **Mitchell Beazley** in May 1987, **George Philip** in March 1988, Rigby and Budget Books, Australia, in April 1988, and bought a half share in Book Club Associates in October 1988. Launched Mandarin (paperbacks) in 1989 with *Richard Charkin* as managing director. Now owned by Reed International.

DIVISIONS
Children's: **Heinemann Young Books, Methuen Children's Books, Octopus Children's Publishing, Parent & Child.** Trade: **Leo Cooper, Eyre and Spottiswoode, William Heinemann, Mandarin Paperbacks, Methuen London, Secker & Warburg.** Illustrated: **Conran Octopus, Paul Hamlyn Publishing, New Editions, Bounty Books, Pitkin Pictorials, Octopus Books, Spring Books.** Heinemann Educational & Professional: **Heinemann Educational Books,**

Heinemann International, Heinemann Professional Publishing, Mitchell Beazley, George Philip.

Authors' Rating Paul Hamlyn is one of the great publishing buccaneers who seems to gain energy with the years. Having sold his group to Reed International for 540 million, he remains the man in charge, resisting all unsolicited invitations to move on to a quieter life. Said to be more interested in marketing than in books. His various imprints are still in the resettling period (giving some anguish to authors) after the move to Michelin House. Mandarin, the latest in mass marketing paperback houses, is still settling in after an April launch with Michael Jackson's *Moonwalk* leading the list. Created to fill a gap at Octopus after the sale to Macmillan of their share of Pan, Mandarin can feed off the Octopus backlist but is also keen to buy in titles. Given that Octopus is the largest children's publisher in the UK, writers for young people are likely to benefit. A strong spend on promotion is budgeted.

Olive Press

See **Harrap Publishing Group Ltd**

Omnibus Press

8–9 Frith Street, London W1V 5TX
☏ 01–434 0066
Telex 21892 Fax 01–439 2848

Director *Frank Warren*

FOUNDED 1971 by Robert Wise and remains independent. Produces books, song sheets, songbooks, educational tutors, cassettes, videos and software. *Publishes* music books and rock and pop biographies. 50 titles in 1988.

Editorial Head *Chris Charlesworth*

IMPRINTS
Amsco, Bobcat, Oak, Omnibus, Proteus, Wise, Zomba. Welcome unsolicited mss, synopses and ideas for books.
Royalties paid twice yearly. *Overseas associates* Music Sales Corporation, New York; Music Sales Pty, Sydney.

Open Books Publishing Ltd

Beaumont House, Wells, Somerset BA5 2LD
☏ 0749 77276

Managing Director *Patrick Taylor*

FOUNDED 1974. *Publishes* academic and general. 6 titles in 1988. All books are commissioned so do not welcome unsolicited mss and synopses.
Royalties paid twice yearly. *Overseas associates* Cambridge University Press, Australia; Century Hutchinson, South Africa.

Optima

See **Macdonald & Co Ltd**

Orbis

See **Macdonald & Co Ltd**

Orchard Books

10 Golden Square, London W1R 3AF
☏ 01–734 8738
Telex 262655 GROLOK G Fax 01–439 1440

Managing Director *Judith Elliott*

FOUNDED 1985. Part of **The Watts Group** (see entry). *Publishes* children's hardbacks. 42 titles in 1988. Unsolicited mss, synopses and ideas for books welcome.
Royalties paid twice yearly. *Overseas associates* Franklin Watts, Australia; Orchard Books, New York.

Orion Books

See **Attic Books**

Osprey

See **George Philip Ltd**

Peter Owen Ltd

73 Kenway Road, London SW5 0RE
☏ 01–373 5628/370 6093

Chairman *Peter Owen*
Senior Editor *Michael Levien*

FOUNDED 1951. Known for its literary fiction, both English and translated. AUTHORS include Shusako Endo, Paul Bowles, Anais Nin, Jane Bowles, Anna Kavan, Peter Vansittart. *Publishes* biography, general books, literary fiction, sociology. No middlebrow romance, thrillers, or children's books. 30 titles in 1988. Unsolicited synopses welcome; mss should be preceded by a descriptive letter or synopsis with s.a.e.
Royalties paid annually. *Overseas associates* 'Represented throughout the world'.

Authors' Rating Publishes very good books which are not strong sellers. One of the few publishers willing to risk new fiction. Good on translations. Sometimes slow on payments.

Oxford Illustrated Press

See **Haynes Publishing Group**

Oxford Publishing Co.

See **Haynes Publishing Group**

Oxford University Press

Walton Street, Oxford OX2 6DP
☎ 0865 56767 Telex 837330

Chief Executive *Professor Sir Roger Elliot*
Approx Annual Turnover £110 million

A department of the university for several hundred years, the company grew out of the university's printing works and developed into a major publishing business in the nineteenth century, concentrating on bibles and education. *Publishes* academic books in all categories, student texts, scholarly journals, schoolbooks, ELT material, dictionaries, reference books, music, bibles, imported titles from the USA and beyond, as well as paperbacks, general non-fiction and children's books. Approximately 1200 titles per year.

DIVISIONS
Arts and Reference *I. S. Asquith* TITLES include the *Concise Oxford Dictionary.* **Education** *P. R. Mothersole* GCSE titles. **ELT** *G. P. Lewis* Streamline ELT course. **Science, Medical and Journals** *J. R. Manger* TITLES include the *Oxford Textbook of Medicine.*

IMPRINTS
Clarendon Press *I. S. Asquith* Monographs in sciences, humanities, and social sciences. **Oxford Paperbacks** The trade paperback list.

OUP welcomes first-class academic material in the form of proposals or accepted theses.
Royalties paid once/twice yearly. *Overseas subsidiaries* branches in Australia, India, Canada, Singapore, Hong Kong, Japan, East Africa, South Africa, New Zealand, plus sister company in New York.

Authors' Rating Inhibited for many years by its ties with the university and by the fanciful notion that academics know all there is to know about publishing, OUP has lately streamlined its administration and editorial services for a belated leap into the second half of the twentieth century. Can safely claim one of the finest academic lists in the world. Publishing policy allows for the acceptance of some unremunerative but worthy titles. Authors who still complain of production delays and unanswered correspondence agree that OUP are at least good payers. Now the proud parent of the second edition of the *Oxford English Dictionary,* a ten million pound investment described by Anthony Burgess as the greatest publishing event of this century and prompting a wag to ask if they have a word for someone who can afford fifteen hundred pounds for a dictionary.

Pagoda Books

79 Great Titchfield Street, London W1P 7FN
☎ 01–637 0890
Telex 23539 VISION G Fax 01–631 0043

Managing Director *David Alexander*
Publisher *Susan Pinkus*

FOUNDED 1983. *Publishes* astrology, highly illustrated fiction, illustrated non-fiction, fine art, health, humour, juvenile, music, parenting. 20 titles in 1988.
TITLES *The Bible in Twentieth Century Art;* Series of Illustrated Opera Libretti; *The Dream – A Rebus; Gottle O' Geer* Ray Alan; *Ming Shu – The Art and Practice of Chinese Astrology, Feng Shui – Perfect Placing for your Happiness and Prosperity* Derek Walters; *The Lord Charles Wine Guide; Amazing Cakes* David MacCarfrae.
Welcome unsolicited mss, synopses and ideas for books.
Royalties paid twice yearly.

Pan Books Ltd

18–21 Cavaye Place, London SW10 9PG
☎ 01–373 6070
Telex 917466 Fax 01–370 0746

Managing Director *Alan Gordon Walker*
Publishing Director *Ian S. Chapman*
Approx Annual Turnover £30 million

Mass-market paperback house. FOUNDED 1944. Published its first list in 1947. In 1961 had its first million-selling title, *The Dam Busters.* In 1961 published *Dr No* which went on to sell over 2 million copies. In 1964 instituted the Golden Pan Award for authors whose titles sold a million. The first winner was Alan Sillitoe for *Saturday Night, Sunday Morning.* **Piccolo**, the children's imprint, was set up in 1971. **Picador,** international modern fiction and non-fiction, started in 1972. The first Pan bookshop opened in the Fulham Road in 1975. **Macmillan** took over warehousing and distribution in 1981. Jointly owned by Macmillan and **Octopus** until 1987 when Macmillan bought out its co-owner. (The third founding partner, **Collins,** sold out to

Macmillan and Octopus in 1986.) **Piper,** children's fiction, launched in Jan 1988.

Publishes archaeology, architecture and design, atlases and maps, biography and autobiography, business and industry, children's, cinema and video, cookery, crafts and hobbies, economics, fiction, gardening, guide books history and antiquarian, humour, languages and linguistics, literature and criticism, medical, military and war, natural history, philosophy, photography, politics and world affairs, psychology, reference books and dictionaries, sports and games, theatre and drama, travel and topography, wines and spirits. Approximately 300 titles in 1988.

IMPRINTS
Pan *Ian S. Chapman* AUTHORS Douglas Adams, Jackie Collins, Daphne du Maurier, Colin Forbes, Dick Francis, Arthur Hailey, Georgette Heyer, Jack Higgins, Susan Howarth, John Le Carré, Somerset Maugham, Jean Plaidy, Tom Sharpe, Sidney Sheldon, Nevil Shute, Wilbur Smith, John Steinbeck. *Suzanne Baboneau* (Fiction) AUTHORS Renata Adler, Hilary Bailey, Joan Didion, Gail Godwin, Alice Hoffman, Sara Maitland, Bel Mooney, Joyce Carol Oates, Lisa St Aubin de Teran, Susan Fromberg Schaeffer, Jill Tweedie, Fay Weldon. *Kathy Gale* (Fiction) AUTHORS Stephen Brust, Chris Claremont, Sean Costello, Julian May, Rex Miller, Pamela Sargeant, Susan Schwartz, Robert Silverberg, Brian Stableford, Chris Stasheff, Judith Tarr, Vernon Vinge. *Hilary Davies* (Non-fiction) AUTHORS Gordon Burn, Heather Couper, Arthur Eperon, Frances Edmunds, Keith Floyd, Linda Goodman, Max Hastings, James Herriott, Madhur Jaffrey, Jack Nicklaus, Christopher Nolan, Roger Phillips. **Picador** *Geoffrey Mulligan* AUTHORS Julian Barnes, Samuel Beckett, William Burroughs, Italo Calvino, Angela Carter, Bruce Chatwin, Umberto Eco, Germaine Greer, Gabriel Garcia-Marquez, Knut Hamsum, Russell Hoban, Clive James, Ken Kesey, Doris Lessing, IanMcEwan, Mario Vargas Llosa, Vladimir Nabokov, Thomas Pynchon, Jonathan Raban, Salman Rushdie, Edmund White, Tom Wolfe. **Piccolo** (children's non-fiction) **Piper** (children's fiction) *Marion Lloyd* AUTHORS Enid Bagnold, Judy Blume, Enid Blyton, Stephen Bowkett, Paula Danziger, Rudyard Kipling, Thomas Rockwell, Robert Westall, David Henry Wilson, Aliki and Franz Brandenburg, Michael Bond.
Welcome unsolicited mss, synopses and ideas for books.
Royalties paid twice yearly. *Overseas associates* Pan Books Australia (Pty) Ltd.

Authors' Rating Now entirely owned by Macmillan, this leading paperback house has a marketing linkup with the rest of Macmillan's general publishing. A huge range of titles benefits from skilful presentation and sales but there is a worry that the quality end of the market may be under pressure.

Pandora Press
See **Unwin Hyman Ltd**

Paperduck
See **Gerald Duckworth & Co Ltd**

Paperfronts
See **Elliot Right Way Books**

Partridge Press
See **Transworld Publishers Ltd**

Stanley Paul
See **Century Hutchinson Ltd**

Pavilion Books Ltd
196 Shaftesbury Avenue, London WC2H 8HL
☏ 01–836 1306
Telex 268369 Fax 01–240 7684

Joint Chairmen *Tim Rice, Michael Parkinson*
Managing Director *Colin Webb*

Publishes biography, some children's, cinema and video, cookery, gardening, humour, knitting, popular art, sport, travel. 56 titles in 1988.

Editorial Director *Vivien Bowler* TITLES *Painted Gardens,* Penelope Hobhouse & Christopher Wood; *Elizabeth Taylor* Sheridan Morley; *Landscape in Spain* photographs by Michael Busselle, text by Nicholas Luard; *A Taste of Provence* Julian & Carey More; *The Taste of Thailand* Vatcharin Bhumichitr; *A Victorian Posy* ed. Sheila Pickles. Unsolicited mss not welcome. Non-fiction synopses and ideas considered but not for children's books.
Royalties paid twice yearly.

PBI Publications
Britannica House, High Street, Waltham Cross, Herts EN8 7DY
☏ 0992 23691
Telex 23957 Fax 0992 26452

Chairman/Managing Director *Dr D. G. Hessayon*

Part of the Tennant Group. Paperback publisher

of gardening and agriculture books by Dr D. G. Hessayon. TITLES *The Armchair Book of the Garden; The Gold Plated House Plant Expert; Rose Jotter; House Plant Jotter; Vegetable Jotter* D. G. Hessayon. Do not consider unsolicited material.

Pelham Books

27 Wright's Lane, London W8 5TZ
☎ 01–937 7255 Telex 917181/2

Publisher *Roger Houghton*

FOUNDED 1960 specifically to publish *Pears Cyclopaedia* when the rights were brought from Lever Bros. The general imprint of **Michael Joseph;** parent company, **Penguin Books Ltd.** *Publishes* crafts, cookery, DIY, handbooks, sports biographies, sport and some leisure. 50 titles in 1988.

Chief Editor *John Beaton* TITLES *Pears Cyclopaedia; Benson & Hedges Cricket Year; Benson & Hedges Snooker Year; Children's Parties* Jane Asher; *Fatima: The Autobiography of Fatima Whitbread; The Teeny Weeny Cat Book* Martin Leman. Welcome unsolicited mss, synopses and ideas for books.
Royalties paid twice yearly. *Overseas associates* Penguin Overseas.

Authors' Rating More muscle for Pelham's marketing arm following a deal with the Stephen Greene Press of Lexington, another Penguin owned company specialising in sports and leisure. Both now carry dual imprints.

Pelican

See **Penguin Books Ltd**

Penguin Books Ltd

27 Wright Lane, London W8 5TZ
☎ 01–938 2200
Telex 917181/2 Fax 01–938 8704

Chief Executive *Peter Mayer*
Managing Director *Trevor Glover*
Approx Annual Turnover £225 million (Penguin Group worldwide)

Owned by Pearson. *Publishes* general and academic books of all kinds; atlases and maps, biography and autobiography, business, children's, classics, crime, ELT, fiction, guide books, health, literature and criticism, poetry, reference and dictionaries, sports, travel, women's studies. Parent company of **Michael Joseph, Hamish Hamilton and Sphere.**

Publishing Director *Peter Carson* Responsible for Penguin's adult publishing.

IMPRINTS
Pelican High-quality paperback non-fiction largely in the fields of the humanities and social sciences. **Peregrine** Academic paperbacks of lasting cultural or intellectual significance. **Puffin** *Elizabeth Attenborough* The leading children's paperback list in the UK, publishing in virtually all general fields, fiction, non-fiction, picture books, poetry. **Viking** (see separate entry). **Viking Kestrel** (see **Viking** entry). **Frederick Warne** (see separate entry).

Unsolicited mss generally welcome but preliminary letter essential for **Frederick Warne.** *Royalties* paid twice yearly. *Overseas associates* in Australia, New Zealand, and USA. Associate companies throughout the world including **New American Library,** Dutton and Dial.

Author's Rating One of the great names of publishing which nearly disappeared under a surfeit of self satisfaction. Recovery began with the appointment of Peter Mayer who managed to inject American enterprise without destroying the character of an essentially British institution. 75% of Penguin's sales come from the backlist, a uniquely high figure in paperback publishing. Links with **New American Library** have improved chances of British writers crossing the water. Latest innovation: *Twentieth Century Classics* which takes over from the somewhat idiosyncratic list known as *Modern Classics,* and a new series for mystics called *Arkana.*

Peregrine

See **Penguin Books Ltd**

Pergamon Press plc

Headington Hill Hall, Oxford OX3 0BW
☎ 0865 64881
Telex 83177 Pergap G Fax 0865 60285

Joint Managing Directors *G. F. Richards, Dr P. S. H. Bolman*

FOUNDED 1948. Owned by Maxwell Communications Corporation. *Publishes* academic and professional text and reference books and journals in agriculture, bibliography and library service, biology and zoology, business and industry, chemistry, computer science, economics, education, engineering, geography and geology, languages and linguistics, mathematics and statistics, medical, open learning, philosophy, physics, politics and world affairs, psychology, sociology and anthropology, vocational training and careers, women's studies. 300 titles in 1988. Also publishes *Chess* magazine and chess books.

Chief Executive *Ian Maxwell* **Associate Publisher** (Books) *Alan J. Steel* **Editorial Directors** *Barbara Barrett* (Social & Life Sciences), *Dr Colin Drayton* (Major Reference Works), *Jim Gilgunn-Jones* (Physical Sciences & Engineering). Welcome unsolicited mss if within specialist range.
Royalties paid annually. *Overseas associates* in USA, Australia, Japan, China, Germany and France.

Authors' Rating Factory publishing true to the ideals of Robert Maxwell. Impersonal but efficient as long as the author is prepared to do his own editing.

Phaidon Press Ltd

Musterlin House, Jordan Hill Road,
Oxford OX2 8DP
☎ 0865 310664
Telex 83308 Fax 0865 310662

Chairman *George J. Riches*
Managing Director *Geoff Cowen*

Publishes antiques and collecting, archaeology, architecture and design, crafts and hobbies, fine art and art history, guide books, photography, theatre and drama. 60 titles in 1989.

Editorial Head *Roger Sears* Major TITLES 1989: *Pierre Deux's Normandy; Ashmolean Handbooks, British Impressionism; Contemporary Russian Art; Van Gogh Flowers; History of Banking; Atlas of Russia; Inside London/Paris.* Welcome unsolicited mss although 'only a small amount of unsolicited material gets published'. *Royalties* paid quarterly.

Authors' Rating One of the two leading art publishers (the other is **Thames and Hudson**). Beautiful books on esoteric subjects.

George Philip Ltd

59 Grosvenor Street, London W1X 9DA
☎ 01–493 5841
Telex 27278 Fax 01–491 3803

Managing Director *M. A. Bovill*
Approx Annual Turnover £10 million

Part of **Octopus Group** since April 1988. One of the world's leading map and atlas publishers, Philip also specialise in travel, astronomy, and Britain's countryside and heritage. The thriving **Osprey** imprint has specialist aviation, military and motoring lists. *Publishes* aerospace, astronomy, atlases, automotive, countryside, maps, military, road atlases, sailing, travel.

DIVISIONS
George Philip *John Gaisford* TITLES *Great World Atlas; RAC Road Atlases of Britain & Europe; Charlie Waite's Venice, Dordogne, Provence,* etc. **Osprey** *John Gaisford* TITLES *Men at Arms; Car Restoration; Air Combat.* Welcome unsolicited mss, synopses and ideas for books.
Royalties paid twice yearly.

Piatkus Books

5 Windmill Street, London W1P 1HF
☎ 01–631 0710
Telex 266082 PIATKS G Fax 01–436 7137

Managing Director *Judy Piatkus*
Approx Annual Turnover £2 million

FOUNDED 1979. *Publishes* astrology and paranormal, business, childcare and parenting, cookery, fiction, gift, health, practical, women's interests. Also have a separate company Diamond Books, producing attractive titles for stationery/gift markets. 100 titles in 1989.

Fiction *Judy Piatkus* TITLES *Rowan's Mill* Elizabeth Walker. **Non-fiction** *Gill Cormode* TITLES *Colour Me Beautiful Make Up Book.* Welcome unsolicited mss, synopses and ideas for books.
Royalties paid twice yearly.

Authors' Rating Piatkus Books has grown from a one-room band to a thriving independent list. The company claims to give commitment to each book they take on and to treat every non-fiction title as a lead.

Picador

See **Pan Books Ltd**

Piccadilly Press

5 Canfield Place, London NW6 3BT
☎ 01–625 9582
Telex 295441 Fax 01–328 8256

Managing Director *Brenda Gardner*
Approx Annual Turnover £500,000

FOUNDED 1983 by Brenda Gardner. First titles published February 1984. Piccadilly plans to stay small, publishing between 25 and 30 titles per year. A total staff of three. *Publishes* children's hardbacks, picture and story books, some teenage non-fiction. Just moving into teenage fiction. Unsolicited synopses and ideas for

books welcome with s.a.e.
Royalties paid twice yearly.

Piccolo
See **Pan Books Ltd**

Piper
See **Pan Books Ltd**

Pitkin Pictorials Ltd
See **Octopus Publishing Group**

Pitman Publishing
128 Long Acre, London WC2E 9AN
☎ 01–379 7383
Telex 261367 Pitman G Fax 01–240 5771

Managing Director *Peter Warwick*
Approx Annual Turnover £6.5 million

Part of the **Longman Group.** FOUNDED 1837 as the publisher of the Pitman Shorthand System. Pitman has now joined Longman as its specialist Business Education and Information Technology publishing house. *Publishes* textbooks, reference and dictionaries in business education, including secretarial, business studies, management and professional studies. Professional and textbook publishers in all areas of information technology, including computers, microelectronics and telecommunications. 120 titles in 1988.

DIVISIONS
Business Education *Liz Hartley* TITLES *Business A/Cs 1 & 2* Frank Wood. **Business Management** *Soraya Romano* TITLES *English Law; Accounting Theory and Practice.* **Information Technology** *John Cushion* TITLES *Research Notes in Artificial Intelligence; Systems Design with Advanced Microprocessors.* **Professional Studies** *Pat Bond* TITLES *M & E Handbooks.* **Secretarial Studies** *Ann Webster* TITLES *Universal typing.*

IMPRINTS
Pitman *Peter Warwick*, **M & E.** Unsolicited mss, synopses and ideas for books welcome.
Royalties paid annually.

Authors' Rating Formerly a medical publisher of note, some authors were unhappy when they were hived off to other parts of the **Longman** empire. But Pitman are reasserting themselves with a growing reputation for good quality business books.

Plenum Publishing Ltd
88–90 Middlesex Street, London E1 7EZ
☎ 01–377 0686

Chairman *Martin E. Tash* (USA)
Managing Director *Dr Ken Derham*

FOUNDED 1940. Part of **Plenum Publishing** New York. The London office is the editorial and marketing base for the UK and Europe. *Publishes* postgraduate, professional and research level scientific, technical and medical monographs, conference proceedings, reference books. Approximately 325 new titles (world-wide) per year.

Editorial Head *Dr Ken Derham* (UK and Europe)

IMPRINTS
Consultants Bureau, IFI Plenum Data Company, Plenum Medical Company, Plenum Press.
Prefer synopses rather than finished mss.
Royalties paid annually.

Plexus Publishing Ltd
26 Dafforne Road, London SW17 8TZ
☎ 01–672 6067 Telex 947157 PLEXUS G

Chairman *T. C. Porter*
Managing Director *S. M. Wake*

FOUNDED 1973. *Publishes* high quality illustrated books, specialising in international co-editions with an emphasis on art and cinema, biography, popular culture, popular music. 6 titles in 1988.

Editor *Helen Gummer* Lead titles in 1989 *The Wit and Wisdom of the Royals; Jimmy Dean: The First American Teenager; The Psychotronic Encyclopaedia of Film.*
Unsolicited mss, synopses and ideas welcome.
Royalties paid twice yearly.

Pluto Press Ltd
11–21 Northdown Street, London N1 9BN
☎ 01–837 3322

FOUNDED 1970. Developed a reputation for innovatory publishing in the field of non-fiction. Bought by Zwan Publishers in 1987. *Publishes* academic and scholarly books, cultural studies, general theory and ideology, politics and world affairs, social sciences, socialist, feminist and Marxist books, socialist reprints. 50 titles planned in 1989.

Authors' Rating Zwan takeover led to a radical editorial rethink. Now less cultural (no more theatre, cinema, literary criticism), much more political.

Polity Press

Dales Brewery, Gwydir Street,
Cambridge CB1 2LJ
☏ 0223 324315 Fax 0223 461385

FOUNDED 1984. All books are published in association with **Basil Blackwell Ltd.** *Publishes* archaeology and anthropology, criminology, economics, feminism, general interest, history, human geography, literature, media and cultural studies, medicine and society, philosophy, politics, psychology, religion and theology, social and political theory, sociology. 55 titles in 1988. Welcome unsolicited mss, synopses and ideas for books.
Royalties paid annually.

Polygon

22 George Square, Edinburgh EH8 9LF
☏ 031–667 1011 ext. 2412 Fax 031–667 7938

Owned by **Edinburgh University Press** since 1988. *Publishes* international fiction and poetry. Is especially interested in receiving ideas for translations. SERIES include *Sigma* (for aphorisms, anarchisms and surreal material), *Determinations* (Scottish cultural polemics) and *Living Memory* (Oral History).

Princeton University Press

Avonlea, 10 Watlington Road, Cowley,
Oxford OX4 5NF
☏ 0865 748405 Fax 0865 748401

Director *Walter Lippincott* (USA)

Wide range of academic books, especially on biology, history and literature. 220 titles in 1988. Editorial department in the USA.

Prism Press Book Publishers Ltd

2 South Street, Bridport, Dorset DT6 3NQ
☏ 0308 27022 Fax 0308 27376
Telex 265871 MONREF G 84 MNU 247

Managing Director *Julian King*

FOUNDED 1974 by Julian King and Colin Spooner. *Publishes* alternative medicine, architecture, building, conservation, environment, farming, feminism, health, law, mysticism, occult, philosophy, politics and wholefood cookery. 20 titles in 1988.

TITLES *Our Drowning World* Antony Milne; *Sentics* Manfred Clynes; *Exploring The Paranormal (Reader); Peace of Mind* Ian Gawler. Unsolicited mss, synopses and ideas welcome. *Royalties* paid twice yearly. *Overseas associates* Prism Press, USA.

Prospice Publishing Ltd

PO Box 18, Buxton, Derbyshire SK17 6YP
☏ 0298 72471 Fax 0298 72402

Chairman/Managing Director *J. C. R. Green*

FOUNDED 1968 in Glasgow by J. C. R. Green. Became part of the Johnston Green group in the latter half of the 1970s. James and Anne Green 'bought out' the company from Johnston Green in 1986 and have since moved to Derbyshire where Aquila now operates as a wholly independent concern. *Publishes* literary biography, critical studies, drama, essays, fiction, poetry. Particularly well known for its list of translation titles. Also publishes the literary quarterly, *Prospice,* as well recently as more and more books (by both British and overseas authors) as co-publications with North American/Australasian publishers. 100 titles in 1989.

IMPRINTS
Aquila Books; Aquila Critical Studies; Aquila Drama; Aquila Fiction; Aquila Guides; Aquila Pamphlets; Aquila Pamphlet Poetry; Aquila Poetry; Iolaire Selection. Enquiries preferred to unsolicited mss. Unsolicited synopses and ideas for books welcome. 'We often commission books from ideas, and indeed from essays submitted to our magazine, *Prospice,* but we do need to know that a writer has a track record and the ability to follow through a commission.' (J. C. R. Green)
Royalties paid twice yearly. *Overseas associates* Aquila Publishing (Ireland) Ltd, Dublin; Aquila America Inc., Washington State, USA.

Proteus

See **Omnibus Press**

Puffin

See **Penguin Books Ltd**

Quartet Books

27–9 Goodge Street, London W1P 1FD
☏ 01–636 3992
Telex 919034 Fax 01–439 6489

Chairman *Naim Attallah*
Approx Annual Turnover £1.4 million

FOUNDED 1972 by four ex-Granada employees, the company was acquired by Naim Attallah in 1976. Part of the Namara Group which includes **The Women's Press** (1977) and Robin Clark Ltd, (bought in 1980, now an imprint of Quartet Books). *Publishes* classical music books, fiction, jazz, literary biography, literature in translation (including French, Spanish, Russian, German, Swedish and Arabic), photographic, politics, popular non-fiction. 85 titles in 1988.

Editorial Director *Stephen Pickles*

DIVISIONS
Anthony Blond, Robin Clark, Quartet Encounters (a series of European literature in translation, prose only) TITLES *Old Masters* Thomas Bernhard; *Palinuro of Mexico* Fernando del Paso; *In the Fast Lane* Alexandre Jardin; *Hard Pressed* Glenys Roberts; *My Companions in the Bleak House* Eva Kantuårková; *The Sacred Night* Tahar Ben Jelloun; *Heartsnatcher* Boris Vian; *The Demons* Heimito von Doderer; *Notebooks 1924–54.* Wilhelm Furtwängler.
Welcome unsolicited mss, synopses and ideas for books.
Royalties paid twice yearly.

Authors' Rating A high-profile company riding on the flamboyant reputation of its owner, Naim Attallah, a wealthy Palestinian-born entrepreneur whose other publishing interests include the best of the book journals, *The Literary Review.* Owns Pipeline, one of the most efficient of the paperback wholesalers. Writers are encouraged to think big but payments can be erratic.

Queen Anne Press

See **Macdonald & Co. Ltd**

Quiller Press

46 Lillie Road, London SW6 1TN
☏ 01–499 6529
Telex 21120 Fax 01–381 8941

Managing Director *Jeremy Greenwood*

Quiller specialise in sponsored books and publications sold through non-book trade channels as well as bookshops through **Century Hutchinson.** But not vanity publishing. *Publishes* architecture, biography, business and industry, children's, cookery, crafts and hobbies, DIY, gardening, guide books, humour, reference, sports, travel, wine and spirits. 15 titles in 1988.

Editorial Director *Jeremy Greenwood* Unsolicited mss not welcome, as ideas nearly always originate in-house.
Royalties paid twice yearly.

Radius

See **Century Hutchinson Ltd**

Raintree Press

See **Basil Blackwell Ltd**

The Ramsay Head Press

15 Gloucester Place, Edinburgh EH3 6EE
☏ 031–225 5646

Joint Managing Directors *Conrad Wilson, Mrs Christine Wilson*

A small independent family publisher. FOUNDED 1968 by Norman Wilson OBE. *Publishes* biographies, cookery, Scottish fiction and non-fiction. 5 titles in 1988.
TITLES *Dry Stone Days; Reminiscences of Growing Up in Buchan* David Ogston; *John Donne, You Were Wrong* Janet Caird; *A Handy Guide to Scots* William Graham; *The Autobiography of a Poet* Duncan Glen; *Shadows from the Greater Hill* Tessa Ransford.
Welcome synopses and ideas for books if they come within their range (Scottish).
Royalties paid twice yearly.

Reader's Digest Association Ltd

25 Berkeley Square, London W1
☏ 01–629 8144 Fax 01–236 5956

Managing Director *Neil McRae*
Approx Annual Turnover £90 million

Publishes reference: gardening, natural history, cookery, DIY, travel and word books. 4 titles in 1988.

DIVISIONS
Reader's Digest, Special Books Editorial Head *Robin Hozie* TITLES *Family Medical Adviser; The Gardening Year; Nature Lover's Library; New DIY Manual; The Repair Manual.*
Welcome unsolicited mss, synopses and ideas for books.
Royalties paid according to contract.

Reinhardt Books Ltd

27 Wright's Lane, London W8 5TZ
☏ 01–938 1253

Chairman/Managing Director *Max Reinhardt*

FOUNDED 1987 by Max Reinhardt after resigning from the **Chatto, Bodley Head, Cape** group. 'A team of friends and colleagues publishing for pleasure.' With authors Graham Greene, Alistair Cooke and Maurice Sendak under their wing, plan to publish biography, children's books and fiction. First publication in September 1988, Graham Greene's new novel, *The Captain and the Enemy*. Also own **Nonesuch Press,** and plan to start republishing in 1989, with limited editions of Greene's *Why The Epigraph,* and the definitive edition of Robert Louis Stevenson's *The Wrong Box*.

Assistant Publisher *Elizabeth Bowes Lyon* **Editorial Consultants** *Joan Reinhardt, Judy Taylor* **Typographical Consultant** *John Ryder*.

Authors' Rating The grand old man of publishing sets out on his own – with a little help from Graham Greene and other devotees. Max Reinhardt believes there is a niche for publishers 'who are small, personal and more attentive to their authors'. He is right. But he admits the need for accommodation and a distribution service – provided by big brother **Penguin.** Children's book list launched in early 1989 with Maurice Sendak (previously of Bodley Head) leading the way.

Robinson Publishing

11 Shepherd House, Shepherd Street,
London W1Y 7LD
☎ 01–493 1064 Telex 28905 Ref 778
fax 01–629 0316 Ref ROB PUB

Managing Director *Nick Robinson*

FOUNDED 1983. *Publishes* general fiction and non-fiction trade paperbacks, some hardbacks. Specialist areas include cookery, crime, fantasy, health, film, general, and science fiction. SERIES include *Mammoth Books, Dark Fantasy,* and *Classic Authors*. 35 titles in 1989.

Editorial Head *Nick Robinson* No unsolicited mss. Synopses and ideas for books welcome.
Royalties paid twice yearly.

Robson Books Ltd

Bolsover House, 5–6 Clipstone Street,
London W1P 7EB
☎ 01–323 1223 Fax 01–636 0798

Managing Director *Jeremy Robson*

FOUNDED 1973 by Jeremy Robson. *Publishes* mainly general non-fiction including biography, cinema, cookery, gardening, guide books, health and beauty, humour, sports and games, theatre and drama, travel and topography. 60 titles in 1988.

Editorial Head *Anthea Matthison* Unsolicited mss (accompanied by s.a.e), synopses and ideas for books welcome.
Royalties paid twice yearly.

Authors' Rating Sensitive to authors but decisions take time to filter through.

Routledge

11 New Fetter Lane, London EC4P 4EE
☎ 01–583 9855
Telex 263398 ABPLDN G Fax 01–583 0701

Managing Director *David Croom*
Approx Annual Turnover £10 million

A division of **Routledge, Chapman & Hall,** part of Thomson Information Services Ltd. George Routledge set up business as a bookseller in 1836 and published his first book in that year. In 1911 Routledge took over the management of Kegan Paul, Trench, Trübner, a soundly-based academic company. At the beginning of the war it published a mixture of trade books, political books and an increasing academic list. Became Routledge & Kegan Paul in 1977 and in 1979 published their first bestseller since *Uncle Tom's Cabin* – Stephen Pile's *Book of Heroic Failures*. Bought by Associated Book Publishers in 1985 and now owned by International Thomson plc. The new Routledge comprises Routledge & Kegan Paul, Tavistock, Croom Helm and Methuen Academic.
Publishes archaeology, anthropology, business and management, classical studies, criminology, dictionaries, economics, education, geography, history, linguistics, literature and literary criticism, library science, media and cultural, Middle East, philosophy, political economy, psychology, reference, religion, social studies/sociology, women's studies. Also, academic journals. 600 titles in 1988.

DIVISIONS
Economics/Education/Politics/Geography/Middle East/Soviet/Critical Assessments *Peter Sowden* TITLES *Sigmund Freud: Critical Assessments; Soviet politics: An Introduction.* **Social & Behavioural** *Gill Davies* TITLES *Women, Policing & Male Violence; Growing Old in the 20th Century.* **Humanities** *Janice Price* TITLES *Chronicles of Darkness; Derrida & Deconstruction. Reference & Linguistics Wendy Morris* TITLES *Dictionary of British Women Writers; Colloquial* series.

IMPRINTS
Ark *Elizabeth White*

Prefer to see synopses with sample chapter and

c.v. rather than complete mss.
Royalties paid annually.

Routledge, Chapman & Hall Ltd

11 New Fetter Lane, London EC4P 4EE
☎ 01–583 9855
Telex 263398 ABPLDN G Fax 01–583 0701

Managing Director *Robert Kiernan*

The new trading company for two publishers, **Routledge** and **Chapman & Hall Ltd** (see separate entries). Formed following the acquisition of Associated Book Publishers by International Thomson in 1987. Since this major reorganisation the following companies have ceased publishing: Croom Helm, Methuen and Co., Routledge and Kegan Paul, and Tavistock Publications. All of these have been incorporated in the new **Routledge. Chapman & Hall Ltd** embraces the old ABP companies Chapman & Hall and **E & F. N. Spon,** together with **Van Nostrand Reinhold International** of New York. *Overseas associates* Routledge, Chapman & Hall Inc., New York.

Authors' Rating A formidable combination of talents in academic publishing who needed to come together and rationalise to survive. Improvements in marketing are expected to achieve more satisfactory sales figures and, hopefully, less confusing royalty statements.

Sackville Books Ltd

Hales Barn, Stradbroke, near Eye,
Suffolk IP21 5JG
☎ 0379 848213 Fax 0379 84797

Managing Directors *Al Rockall, Heather Thomas*

FOUNDED 1986. Part of the same group as Sackville Design, the successful packaging operation. *Publishes* illustrated cookery, home, leisure and sports titles. TITLES *Sackville Golf Clinic; Sackville Sports Clinic; Golf for Women; Golf: Is it only a Game?* Bruce Forsyth. Prefer synopses and ideas for books.
Royalties usually twice yearly but can vary according to contract.

Sage Publications Ltd

28 Banner Street, London EC1Y 8QE
☎ 01–253 1516 Fax 01–253 5206

Managing Director *David Hill*

FOUNDED 1967 in California. *Publishes* academic and scholarly.

Editorial Director *Stephen Barr* TITLES *Robert Colquhoun* Raymond Arron. Welcome unsolicited mss and synopses.
Royalties paid quarterly.

Salamander Books Ltd

52 Bedford Row, London WC1R 4LR
☎ 01–242 6693 Fax 01–404 4926

Managing Director *Malcolm H. Little*

FOUNDED 1973. Independent publishing house. *Publishes* collecting, cookery and wine, knitting and craft, military and aviation, pet care, sport, technical books. 55 titles in 1988.

Editorial Directors *Ray Bond, Philip de Ste Croix* TITLES *Creative Cookery Series; Creative Craft Series; Fishkeepers' Guides; The Intelligence War.* Welcome unsolicited synopses and ideas for books.
Royalties pay an outright fee instead of royalties.

Sangam Books Ltd

57 London Fruit Exchange, Brushfield Street,
London E1 6EP
☎ 01–377 6399

Executive-In-Charge *Anthony de Souza*

Traditionally educational publishers at school and college levels but also publishes books on art, India, medicine, science and technology, and social sciences. Some fiction in paperback list. Unsolicited mss and synopses welcome.

W. B. Saunders Co.

See **Academic Press Inc. (London) Ltd**

Sceptre Books

See **Hodder & Stoughton Ltd**

Scholastic Publications Ltd

Marlborough House, Holly Walk, Leamington
Spa, Warwickshire CV32 4LS
☎ 0926 813910
Telex 312138 SPLSG Fax 0926 883331

Chairman *M. R. Robinson*
Managing Director *John Cox*
Approx Annual Turnover £8.5 million

FOUNDED 1964 as a subsidiary of **Scholastic Inc.** of New York, Scholastic is the largest school-based book club operator in the UK. The Hippo children's paperbacks imprint was launched in 1980, and educational books were added to the list in 1984. A major expansion of the educational book publishing programme is planned for the near future. *Publishes* teachers' magazines including *Child Education* and *Junior Education,* children's paperbacks, professional reference books for primary school teachers, primary school pupil materials. 110 titles in 1988.

DIVISIONS
Hippo Children's Paperbacks *Anne Finnis* TITLES *Postman Pat; Cheerleaders; Hauntings; 101 Dalmatians* and other Disney Classics; *Conrad's War.* **Scholastic Educational Books** *Peter Osborn, Priscilla Chambers* TITLES *Bright Ideas* series *Teacher Handbooks; Management Series; Photocopiables.*

Unsolicited mss, synopses and ideas for books welcome.
Royalties paid twice yearly.

Authors' Rating Has been described as the Heineken of the book trade – reaching parts other publishers cannot reach. Books on offer come from a variety of sources with about a quarter of all titles from the Scholastic imprint, Hippo. A skilful and fast-growing marketing operation bringing welcome rewards to education writers.

Schoolmate
See **Richard Drew Publishing Ltd**

SCM Press Ltd
26–30 Tottenham Road, London N1 4BZ
☏ 01–249 7262/5
Telex 295068 THEOLO G Fax 01–249 3776

Managing Director *Rev. Dr John Bowden*
Approx Annual Turnover £1 million

Publishes mainly religion and theology with some ethics and philosophy. 44 titles in 1988. Will consider unsolicited mss and synopses if sent with s.a.e.
Royalties paid annually.

Authors' Rating Leading publisher of religious ideas with well-deserved reputation for fresh thinking. At SCM, 'questioning theology is the norm'. A recent deal with Trinity Press of New York requiring both to work as a single organisation publishing under both imprints means that SCM authors can now be published worldwide.

Scolar
See **Gower Publishing Group**

Scope Books Ltd
62 Murray Road, Horndean, Hants PO8 9JL
☏ 0705 597440 Fax 0705 591975

Managing/Editorial Director *Tim Harland*

Sister company of **Milestone Publications.** *Publishes* business, finance, specialist and exclusive personal management. Unsolicited mss not welcome. Approach in writing essential in first instance.
Royalties paid twice yearly.

Scorpion Publishing Ltd
Victoria House, Victoria Road, Buckhurst Hill, Essex IG9 5ES
☏ 01–506 0606 Fax 01–506 0553

Managing Director *Leonard Harrow*

FOUNDED 1976. Part of the Scorpion Group. *Publishes* Islamic art, history and culture plus a socialist list.

Editorial Director *Leonard Harrow* Welcome unsolicited mss and synopses if they come within their subject areas.
Royalties vary according to contract.

Scottish Academic Press
33 Montgomery Street, Edinburgh EH7 5JX
☏ 031–556 2796

Managing Director *Dr Douglas Grant*

FOUNDED 1969. *Publishes* academic: architecture, education, geology, history, journals, literature, social sciences, theology. Work in conjunction with Handsel Press (theology). Distribute titles for **Sussex University Press.** 40 titles in 1988. Most of the books are commissioned but will consider unsolicited mss and synopses.
Royalties paid annually.

Search Press Ltd/Burns & Oates Ltd
Wellwood, North Farm Road, Tunbridge Wells, Kent TN2 3DR
☏ 0892 510850
Telex 957258 Fax 0892 515903

Managing Director *Countess de la Bédoyère*

Burns & Oates were founded in 1847 and are publishers to the Holy See. Search Press *publishes* full colour arts and craft, cookery, needlecrafts, etc. Burns & Oates *publish* philosophy, reference, social sciences, theology, literary criticism, history, spirituality, educational and Third World.

DIVISIONS
Academic *Paul Burns* TITLES include the *Liberation & Theology* series; three books already published and four scheduled for 1989. **Craft etc.** *Rosalind Dace* Major TITLES for 1989 include *Wool 'n Magic* Jan Messent, and *The Art of Painting on Silk Vol 3.* Unsolicited mss, synopses and ideas for books welcome.
Royalties paid annually.

Secker & Warburg Ltd

Michelin House, 81 Fulham Road,
London SW3 6RB
☎ 01–581 9393
Telex 920191 Fax 01–589 8419

Publisher *Dan Franklin*

Part of the **Octopus Publishing Group.** FOUNDED 1936 by Fred Warburg when he bought out Martin Secker. *Publishes* autobiography and biography, cinema, fiction, history, humour, illustrated and fine editions, literature and criticism, photography, poetry, politics and world affairs, theatre and drama. 45 titles in 1988.
TITLES *The Modern World* Malcolm Bradbury; *Nice Work* David Lodge; *Inflagrante* Chris Killip; *Mother London* Michael Moorcock; *Whitehall* Peter Hennessy.

IMPRINT
Alison Press *Barley Alison* (Publisher) TITLES *More Die of Hearbreak* Saul Bellow. Welcome unsolicited mss and synopses.
Royalties paid twice yearly.

Authors' Rating The odd-man out of the Octopus group. Quality books appealing to the literary establishment. Currently unsettled by dramatic changes at the top and a move into new offices said by one author to be 'the size of a railway carriage'.

Serpent's Tail

Unit 4, Blackstock Mews, 100 Blackstock Road,
London N4 2DR
☎ 01–354 1949 Fax 01–354 5372
Approx Annual Turnover £70,000

FOUNDED 1986. 'Serpent's Tail has introduced to British audiences a number of major internationally-known writers who have been otherwise neglected by UK publishers.' A strong emphasis on design – including flaps on paperback covers in the continental style – and an eye for the unusual. *Publishes* contemporary fiction, including works in translation; related fields, including autobiography. 20 titles in 1988.

IMPRINTS
Masks *Peter Ayrton/Marsha Rowe* TITLES *The Seven Deadly Sins* ed. Alison Fell; *Who Was That Man?* Neil Bartlett. **Serpent's Tail** *Peter Ayrton/Marsha Rowe* TITLES *The Variety Artistes* Tom Wakefield. Unsolicited synopses and ideas for books welcome.
Royalties normally paid twice yearly.

Author's Rating Winner of the 1989 *Sunday Times* small publisher of the year award, Serpent's Tail was praised for their 'daring, sophisticated and good-looking books'. Strong on translated fiction.

Severn House Publishers

35 Manor Road, Wallington, Surrey SM6 0BW
☎ 01–773 4161
Telex 295041 Severn G Fax 01–773 4143

Chairman *Edwin Buckhalter*

FOUNDED 1974, a leader in library fiction publishing. Several bestsellers both in the UK and overseas. *Publishes* mainly hardcover fiction, with a growing paperback, non-fiction list plus some mass-market titles. 135 titles in 1987.

DIVISIONS
Fiction *Stephanie Townsend* **Non-Fiction** *Julie Briscoe* Welcome unsolicited mss but all unsolicited mss should be sent to *Hilary Gibb.* Synopses/proposals only through bona fide literary agents.
Royalties paid twice yearly. *Overseas associates* Severn House Publishers Inc., New York.

Shakespeare Head Press

See **Basil Blackwell Ltd**

Shepheard-Walwyn (Publishers) Ltd

Suite 34, 26 Charing Cross Road,
London WC2H 0DH
☎ 01–240 5992

Managing Director *Anthony Werner*
Approx Annual Turnover £100,000+

FOUNDED 1972 and publishes on average 4–6 titles a year. 'We are more interested in original ideas than in re-hashes of previous books, unless in the form of a good anthology.' *Publishes* general non-fiction in three main areas: Scottish interest; gift books in calligraphy and/or illustrated; and history, political economy, philosophy/religion. 5 titles in 1988. Welcome synopses and ideas for

books.
Royalties paid twice yearly.

Shire Publications Ltd

Cromwell House, Church Street, Princes Risborough, Aylesbury, Bucks HP17 9AJ

Managing Director *John Rotheroe*

FOUNDED 1967. *Publishes* original non-fiction paperbacks. 60 titles in 1988. No unsolicited material. Prefer introductory letter with detailed outline of idea.
Royalties paid annually.

Sidgwick & Jackson Ltd

1 Tavistock Chambers, Bloomsbury Way, London WC1A 3AA
☎ 01–242 6081
Telex 8952953 SIDJAK G Fax 01–831 0874

Chairman *The Earl of Stockton*
Managing Director *William Armstrong*
Approx Annual Turnover £4.5 million

FOUNDED 1908, the company was controlled by Lord Forte from the early 1960s until its sale to **Macmillan** in 1986. Lord Stockton took over from Lord Rees-Mogg as Chairman at the end of 1988. *Publishes* astronomy, autobiography, cinema and theatre, cookery, craft, current affairs, humour, illustrated classics, illustrated gift books, management and business, military history, pop/rock, popular fiction, religion, sport. 100 titles in 1988. Introduced a new trade paperback list (Sidgwick Softcovers) in 1988.

Editorial Director *Robert Smith* **Director/ Senior Editor** *Susan Hill* **Fiction Editor** *Oliver Johnson* **Editor** *Carey Smith* Bestselling TITLES include *Superwoman; The Third World War* General Sir John Hackett; Lee Iacocca's autobiography; *Is That It?* Bob Geldof; *Our Story* Reg & Ron Kray. Unsolicited mss are always welcome but rarely published. Prefer to see a synopsis and sample chapter. Most of the titles published are as a result of commissioned ideas (such as the Geldof autobiography), submissions from agents, or from staff contacts.
Royalties paid twice yearly.

Authors' Rating Settling in quite happily under the Macmillan umbrella. Strong on middle-brow non-fiction.

Simon & Schuster Ltd

West Garden Place, Kendal Street, London W2 2AQ
☎ 01–724 7577
Telex 21702 Fax 01–402 0639

Publisher *Clyde Hunter*

FOUNDED 1986. Offshoot of the leading American publisher, **Simon & Schuster,** New York. *Publishes* general books (no academic or technical), specialising in trade books – children's fiction, sport, and travel. 50 titles in 1988.

Children's Books Editor *Denise Johnstone-Burt* **Fiction Editor** *Robyn Sisman* **Non-fiction Editor** *Nicholas Brealey* **Sport, Travel & Arts Editor** *Richard Wigmore* TITLES *The Spy in Question* Tim Sebastian; *Jericho Falls* Christopher Hyde; *Yamani, The Inside Story* Jeffrey Robinson; *Gershwin* Edward Jablonski; *Power Golf* Ben Hogan; *Webster's Wine Tours; Edward Loses His Teddy* Michaela Morgan & Sue Porter. Welcome unsolicited mss and synopses.

IMPRINTS
Harvester Wheatsheaf
Royalties paid twice yearly.

Authors' Rating A breath of fresh air on the UK publishing scene. Exciting new fiction including first-time authors. Eager for product and open to ideas. Much praised for imaginative promotion of young writers. A paperback called *New Fiction* containing extracts from five spring novels was given out free in bookshops. A big expansion to the list follows the purchase of some 1500 titles from Macdonald Children's Books and Macdonald Educational.

Charles Skilton Publishing Group

2 Caversham Street, London SW3
☎ 01–351 4995

Chairman/Managing Director *Charles Skilton*

FOUNDED 1945. Independent publisher with offices in London and Scotland. *Publishes* general books including art, architecture, memoirs, poetry and fiction, all Scottish subjects. 50 titles in 1988.

DIVISIONS
Charles Skilton Ltd *Leonard Holdsworth* TITLES *Collected Poems of Randle Manwaring; Watermills of London Countryside.* **Charles Skilton – Albyn Press** *Leonard Holdsworth* TITLES *Historic South Edinburgh Vol 4; Essex Mills Vols 1–5; Glasgow Forever.*
Unsolicited mss, synopses and ideas for books

welcome.
Royalties paid twice yearly.

Authors' Rating A tendency towards vanity publishing. The usual warnings apply.

Society for Promoting Christian Knowledge (SPCK)

Holy Trinity Church, Marylebone Road, London NW1 4DU
☏ 01–387 5282

Chairman *Mr Lionel Scott*
Gen. Secretary *Mr P. N. G. Gilbert*
Approx Annual Turnover £1.5 million

FOUNDED 1698, SPCK is the oldest religious publisher in England. *Publishes* academic theology, general religious titles and pastoral books including popular self-help. 80 titles in 1988.

Editorial Director *Judith Longman*

IMPRINTS
SPCK *Philip Law* TITLES *The Study of Spirituality; Science and Creation; Dictionary of Pastoral Care; Clergy Stress.* **Triangle** *Rachel Boulding* TITLES *Living by the Book; Praying with St Augustine.* **Sheldon Press** *Joanna Moriarty* TITLES *Helping Children Cope with Grief; Body Language; Curing Arthritis – The Drug-Free Way.* Unsolicited synopses/ideas for books welcome.
Royalties paid annually.

Authors' Rating Religion with a strong social edge.

Souvenir Press Ltd

43 Great Russell Street, London WC1B 3PA
☏ 01–580 9307/8 & 637 5711/2/3
fax 01–580 5064

Chairman/Managing Director *Ernest Hecht*

Publishes academic and scholarly, animal care and breeding, antiques and collecting, archaeology, autobiography and biography, business and industry, children's, cookery, crime, crafts and hobbies, educational, fiction, gardening, health and beauty, history and antiquarian, humour, illustrated and fine editions, magic and the occult, medical, military, music, natural history, philosophy, psychology, religious, sociology, sports, theatre and women's studies. 75 titles in 1989.

Senior Editor *Tessa Harrow* TITLES *The Dissent of Woman* Elaine Morgan; *Essential Cat* Thomas Wester; *Slightly Foxed – But Still Desirable, Ronald Searle's Wicked World of Book Collecting.*

IMPRINTS
Condor, Pictorial, Presentations, Pop Universal, Human Horizons (books for the disabled and those who care for them). Unsolicited mss welcome; initial letter of enquiry preferred though.
Royalties paid twice yearly.

Authors' Rating One of the best independent publishers in London. Since there are now so few independents left, this may not seem much of a compliment. But Ernest Hecht does manage to combine sensitivity towards authors with commercial acumen – a rare combination.

Spellmount Ltd

12 Dene Way, Speldhurst, near Tunbridge Wells, Kent TN3 0NX
☏ 0892 86 2860

Managing Director *Ian Morley-Clarke*
Approx Annual Turnover £300,000

FOUNDED 1983. Jointly owned by Ian and Kathleen Morley-Clarke and Vale Packaging Ltd, of Tonbridge. *Publishes* non-fiction hardback titles; biographies of composers, popular musicians, jazz, cricketers, militaria, companion guides to music and the arts. 18 titles in 1988.

DIVISIONS
Composers' biographies/Militaria *Kathleen Morley-Clarke* **Cricket biographies** *John Bright-Holmes* **Jazz biographies** *Alyn Shipton* **London Guides** *Robert Hardcastle.* No unsolicited mss. Synopses/ideas for books in Spellmount's specialist fields only.
Royalties paid annually.

Sphere Books Ltd

66–73 Shoe Lane, London EC4P 4AB
☏ 01–377 4600
Telex 885233 Fax 01–583 4407/8

Managing Director *Nicholas Webb*
Publishing Director *Barbara Boote*
Abacus *Julian Evans* (Director)

FOUNDED 1967. A medium-sized paperback house, formerly belonging to Penguin and now part of Robert Maxwell's Macdonald Futura Group. Remaining chiefly mass market, it has also successfully diversified into Management and Reference publishing. The trade paperback imprints, **Abacus** and **Cardinal**, are covered by the Sphere umbrella. *Publishes* paperback fiction and non-fiction of all kinds, except children's books. Particularly strong on literary/popular fiction and non-fiction, reference and management titles. 230 titles in 1988.

DIVISIONS
Abacus *Julian Evans* TITLES *Chatterton* Peter Ackroyd. **Cardinal** *Chris Potter* TITLES *Byron* Frederic Raphael. **Sphere** *Barbara Boote* TITLES *Kingdom of Shadows* Barbara Erskine.

Unsolicited mss are tolerated, 'despite being time-consuming and rarely bringing to light a commercially appealing book.' A qualified welcome for synopses. These should be accompanied by a sample chapter: 'execution is all'. Similarly, authors of ideas must show some evidence of their ability to deliver a publishable finished book. Buys on a volume-rights basis with **Macdonald, Hamish Hamilton** and **Michael Joseph.**
Royalties paid twice yearly.

Authors' Rating After an unsettled period in which persistent rumours of a sale have been denied by Penguin, Sphere has at last been sold to Robert Maxwell, to become part of the Macdonald Futura group. There is promise of investment and growth, both badly needed by a paperback house more accustomed of late to losing instead of gaining top writers.

John Spiers Publishing Ltd

52 Carlisle Road, Hove, East Sussex BN3 4FS
☎ 0273 26611
Telex 878380 HILTON G Fax 0273 23983

Chairman/Managing Director *John Spiers*
Approx Annual Turnover £200,000

FOUNDED 1988 by John Spiers after he sold his interests in three other international companies, successfully developed by him over 20 years: The Harvester Press Ltd, and Wheatsheaf Books Ltd (both sold to **Simon & Schuster**) and Harvester Press Microform Publications Ltd, subsequently sold to the International Thomson Organisation. Specialises in scholarly and trade books in Soviet studies, defence studies, strategic studies, intelligence, disinformation and terrorism. 12 titles in first year.
TITLES *The Soviet Propoganda Network: A Directory of Organisations Serving Soviet Foreign Policy* Sir Clive Rose; *Key Facts in Soviet History: A Directory and Chronology of Major Events Since 1971* Stephen de Mowbray; *The KGB In Britain* Peter Shipley; *Gorbachev: The New Russian Revolution?* T. P. McNeill; *The Soviet Approach to Arms Control* James Sherr.
Prefer initial letter with outline in the first instance. Welcome synopses and ideas for books if they come within their specialist subjects. In the market for ideas and authors.
Royalties paid twice yearly.

E. & F. N. Spon

See **Chapman & Hall Limited**

Spring Books

See **Octopus Publishing Group**

Springwood Books Ltd

Springwood House, The Avenue, Ascot, Berks SL5 7LY
☎ 0990 24053 Telex 8813271 GECOMS G

Chairman/Managing Director *Christopher K. Foster*

FOUNDED 1977. *Publishes* general non-fiction: astrology, autobiographies, children's books, company histories, sports. No unsolicited mss. Will consider synopses and ideas for books.
Royalties vary from contract to contract.

Stainer & Bell Ltd

PO Box 110, 82 High Road, London N2 9PW
☎ 01–444 9135

Chairman *Allen Dain Percival*
Managing Directors *Carol Y. Wakefield, Keith M. Wakefield*
Approx Annual Turnover £470,000

FOUNDED 1907 to publish sheet music. Now *publishes* music and religious subjects, mainly related to hymnody. 3 titles in 1988.

Editorial Director *A. D. Percival* TITLES *Practical Jazz* Lionel Engson; *Hymns & Congregational Songs Vol 1, Nos. 1 & 2.* Mss welcome only if preceded by letter enclosing brief précis. Unsolicited synopses/ideas for books welcome.
Royalties paid annually.

Star

See **W.H. Allen & Co. plc**

Harold Starke Ltd

Pegasus House, 116–20 Golden Lane, London EC1Y 0TL
☎ 01–253 2145

Chairman *Harold K. Starke*
Managing Director *Naomi Galinski*

Part of Burke Publishing Company Ltd. *Publishes* adult non-fiction, medical, reference. Welcome unsolicited mss, synopses and ideas

but return postage must be included.
Royalties paid annually.

Patrick Stephens Ltd

See **Thorsons Publishing Group Ltd**

Studio Publications (Ipswich) Ltd

The Drift, Nacton Road, Ipswich,
Suffolk IP3 9QR
☎ 0473 270880 Fax 0473 270113
Telex 98551 STUDIO G

Chairman *Mr M. Kelley*
Managing Director *Mr B. J. Henderson*
Approx Annual Turnover £1.5 million

FOUNDED 1973. Part of **Ladybird Books** (which is part of the **Longman Group**). Initially published sports books, but soon branched out into children's titles. Acquired by Ladybird in 1986. Studio Publications intend to broaden their range of titles to cater for older children, but will remain mass-market publishers. *Publishes* picture story books, board books, early educational, novelty and activity books; age range 0–10 years. Also television character series and short stories. 90 titles in 1988.

Editorial Head *R. Preston*

IMPRINTS
Playskool (pre-school range); **Stick-a-Tale** (sticker story books); **Balloon Heads** (3-D novelty story books) **Munch Bunch.** Unsolicited mss welcome if illustrated; otherwise submit synopses/ideas only.
Royalties paid twice yearly.

Surrey University Press

Bishopbriggs, Glasgow G64 2NZ
☎ 041–772 2311
Telex 777283 BLACKI G Fax 041–762 0897

Chairman/Managing Director *R. Michael Miller*

An imprint of **Blackie & Son Ltd**. *Publishes* academic, scientific and technical, and professional books.

Editorial Head *A. Graeme Mackintosh* Prefer synopses rather than complete mss.
Royalties paid annually and twice yearly.

Sussex University Press

No longer publishes. Distribution by **Scottish Academic Press.**

Alan Sutton Publishing Ltd

30 Brunswick Road, Gloucester GL1 1JJ
☎ 0452 419575 Fax 0452 302791

Managing Director *Alan Sutton*

FOUNDED 1979. *Publishes* academic, archaeology, biography, countryside, history, local history, pocket classics – lesser known novels by classic authors, topography. 130 titles in 1988.

Publishing Director *Peter Clifford* Prefer to see synopses rather than complete mss.
Royalties paid twice yearly.

Swallows

See **Richard Drew Publishing Ltd**

Sweet & Maxwell Ltd

South Quay Plaza, 183 Marsh Wall,
London E14 9FT
☎ 01–538 8686 Fax 01–538 9505

Managing Director *David Evans*

Part of International Thomson Professional Information Ltd. *Publishes* law books. 120 titles in 1988.

Publishing Directors *Robert McKay, Hugh Jones* TITLES (for the practitioner) *Company Accounts; Encyclopedia of Professional Partnerships; Planning Decisions Digest.* (For the student) *Litigation for the Law Society Finals; Administrative Law; ILEX: Introduction to Law.* Although mss will be considered it is unlikely they will be published due to the highly specialised nature of the list. Synopses and outlines welcome.
Royalties vary according to contract.

Swift Children's Books

See **Chivers Press (Publishers)**

I. B. Tauris & Co Ltd

110 Gloucester Avenue, London NW1 8JA
☎ 01–483 2681 Fax 01–483 4541

Chairman *Iradj Bagherzade*
Managing Director *Michael Cass*

Independent publisher FOUNDED 1984 and described by *The Observer* as 'tipped to be the Publisher of the Nineties'. *Publishes* general non-fiction and academic in the fields of international relations, current affairs, history,

Middle East, East-West relations and Soviet studies. 40 titles in 1988.
TITLES *Invisible Bomb* Frank Barnaby; *Beyond the Mother Country* Edward Pilkington; *Conspiracy in Jerusalem* Kamal Salibi; *Hungary: Art of Survival* Paul Lendvai; *Soviet Grassroots* J. W. Hahn; *Iran & Iraq at War* S. Chubin & C. Tripp. Welcome unsolicited mss, synopses and ideas for books.
Royalties paid twice yearly.

Technical Press

See **Gower Publishing Group**

Temple House Books

See **The Book Guild Ltd**

Thames and Hudson Ltd

30–4 Bloomsbury Street, London WC1B 3QP
☎ 01–636 5488
Telex 25992 Fax 01–636 4799

Managing Director *Thomas Neurath*

Publishes art books. Also archaeology, architecture and design, biography, crafts, fashion, history and antiquarian, illustrated and fine editions, mythology, music, photography, psychology, popular culture, travel and topography. 160 titles in 1988.

Editorial Head *Jamie Camplin* TITLES *World of Art series; The International Design Yearbook; David Hockney: A Retrospective; Design After Modernism; Fashion Illustration Today; Henri Cartier-Bresson in India; Exploring the World of the Pharaohs; Akhenaten: King of Egypt; Thames and Hudson Literary Lives; 1791 – Mozart's Last Year; How to Identify Prints; Beauty in History; The English Country Town; Russian and Soviet Theatre.*
Preliminary letter and outline before mss.
Royalties paid twice yearly.

Authors' Rating One of the two leading art publishers (the other is **Phaidon Press Ltd).** High-quality books which make you proud to be an author.

Stanley Thornes (Publishers) Ltd

Old Station Drive, Leckhampton, Cheltenham, Gloucestershire GL53 0DN
☎ 0242 584429
Telex 43592 Fax 0242 221914

Managing Director *Roy Kendall*
Approx Annual Turnover £5.2 million

FOUNDED 1972 by Stanley Thornes. Merger with Kluwer NV of the Netherlands in 1976. Now part of the Wolters-Kluwer Group. Original aims were to publish in maths/science for GCE O- and A-Level, and CSE and Technical education. Now publishes across the whole secondary and NAFE curriculum and, with the acquisition of Hulton Educational list, covers complete school range from age five upwards. 110 titles in 1988.

Publishing Director *Mike Rigby* TITLES *A Complete GCSE Maths* Greer; *A Practical Guide to Child Development* Reynolds; *British Economic and Social History* Sauvain; *Office Skills* Foster; *Bookshelf* – Primary reading scheme. Welcome unsolicited mss, synopses and ideas for books if appropriate to specialised list.

IMPRINTS
Hulton Educational Primary. **Stam Press** Technical.
Royalties paid annually.

Thornhill Press

24 Moorend Road, Cheltenham, Gloucestershire GL53 0EU
☎ 0242 519137

Managing Director *Desmond Badham-Thornhill*
Approx Annual Turnover £50,000

FOUNDED 1972. *Publishes* mainly walking and touring guides, sport, plus some general titles (no fiction or poetry). 6 titles in 1988.

Editorial Head *Desmond Badham-Thornhill* Unsolicited mss, synopses and ideas for books welcome.
Royalties paid quarterly.

Thorsons Publishing Group Ltd

Denington Estate, Wellingborough, Northants NN8 2RQ
☎ 0933 440033 Fax 0933 440512
Telex 311072 THOPUB G/312511 TPGBKS

Managing Director *David Young*
Approx Annual Turnover £11 million

FOUNDED 1930, acquired the **Aquarian Press** in 1955, and added **Patrick Stephens** to the group in 1984. The **Crucible** imprint was launched in 1986, the **Equation** imprint in March 1988. The **Grapevine** sub-imprint in May 1988, and **William Kimber Ltd** acquired in June 1988. Financial strain over the last couple of years, though, has led to the US co-venture company being wound down, and ultimately to loss of independence with the purchase of Thorsons by

Collins in 1989. 270 titles in 1988. Preferred approach is by preliminary letter with synopsis.

IMPRINTS
Thorsons *Annie Turrell* Complementary medical, health, special diets, positive thinking, business, crafts, parenting, organic gardening and conservation, pets and animal rights. TITLES *Medicine Chest; M. E. and You; Making Your Own Teddy Bear; Month by Month Organic Gardening.* **Grapevine** *Annie Turrell* Women's non-fiction: health, business, women's issues and lifestyle, sex and relationships. TITLES *The Independent Woman's Money Guide; Cervical Cancer; Do I Have to Give up Me to be Loved by You?* **Aquarian** *Eileen Campbell* Astrology, divination, esoteric teachings, healing, mythology, occultism, paranormal, self-development, tarot. TITLES *Relations; Astrology & Karma; Celtic Mythology; Life After Death.* **Crucible** *Eileen Campbell* Philosophy and esoteric thought, psychology and psychotherapy, religion and spirituality.TITLES *William Blake; Self-Therapy; Introduction to Sufism.* **Patrick Stephens Ltd** *Darryl Reach* Aviation, maritime, military and wargaming, model making and model engineering, motor cycling, motoring and motor racing, naval, railways, railway modelling sports and pastimes. TITLES *Titanic: Triumph and Tragedy; Power & Glory; Encyclopaedia of the World's Air Forces.* **William Kimber Ltd** *Darryl Reach* Aviation, military and naval biography and memoirs, fiction (including historical romance). TITLES *Nigel Mansell, The Makings of a Champion; Colditz Last Stop; One Man's SAS.* **Equation** *Michael Cox* Travel, performing arts, TV and cinema, historical and literary biography, social history, food and wine, true crime, supernatural fiction. TITLES *The Wine Roads of France; Nijinsky, 60 years of the Oscar; The English Country House Party.*

Authors' Rating Market leader in health, lifestyle and new age books. Powerful drive for expansion led to financial strain now eased somewhat by sales to **Collins.** Other changes may follow.

Times Books Ltd

16 Golden Square, London W1R 4BN
☎ 01–437 9602
Telex 897284 ARPUB G Fax 01–434 2080

Managing Director *Barry Winkleman*

Part of News International. *Publishes* mainly atlases with some reference and non-fiction. 31 titles in 1988.

Editorial Director *Paul Middleton* Unsolicited mss should be preceded by letter with outline. *Royalties* paid twice yearly.

Titan Books

58 St Giles High Street, London WC2H 8LH
☎ 01–836 4056 Fax 01–836 0853

Managing Director *Nick Landau*

FOUNDED 1981 by Nick Landau and has grown 'incredibly' in the last eight years to become the largest publisher of graphic novels and graphic albums in the UK. Moving into mass-market paperbacks with a range of *Star Trek* novels. *Publishes* film and television fantasy, comic strip. 90 titles in 1989.

Managing Editor *Katy Wild* TITLES *Batman; Judge Dread; Best of 2000 AD; Star Trek,* and *Star Trek: The Next Generation; Doctor Who; Gerry Anderson* ranges. Although they do not originate a lot of new material unsolicited ideas will be considered.
Royalties paid twice yearly.

Transworld Publishers Ltd

61–3 Uxbridge Road, London W5 5SA
☎ 01–579 2652
Telex 267974 Fax 01–579 5479

Managing Director *Paul Scherer*

FOUNDED 1950. A subsidiary of Bantam, Doubleday, Dell Inc., New York, which is a wholly owned subsidiary of Bertelsmann in Germany. *Publishes* general fiction and non-fiction, children's books, sports and leisure.

IMPRINTS
Bantam *Anthony Mott* AUTHORS Charlotte Bingham, Pat Conroy, Bill Cosby, Erica Jong, Louis L'Amour, Erich Segal. Young Adult series: *Sweet Dreams; Sweet Valley High; Satin Slippers.* **Bantam Press** *Mark Barty-King* AUTHORS Sally Beauman, Catherine Cookson, Jilly Cooper, Frederick Forsyth, Judith Krantz, Shirley MacLaine, Danielle Steel. **Black Swan** *Patrick Janson-Smith* AUTHORS Isabel Allende, Joseph Heller, John Irving, Howard Jacobson, Mary Wesley. **Corgi** *Patrick Janson-Smith* AUTHORS Catherine Cookson, Jilly Cooper, David Eddings, Ken Follett, Frederick Forsyth, Sven Hassel, Terry Pratchett, Elvi Rhodes. **Doubleday** *Marianne Velmans* AUTHORS Isaac Asimov, Stephen Coonts, Bill Cosby, Alex Haley, Leon Uris. In 1989 *A Vision of Britain* by H.R.H. The Prince of Wales. **Partridge Press** *Debbie Beckerman* AUTHORS Peter Alliss, Zola Budd, Frank Callan, Chris Cowdrey. **Children's & Young Adults Books** *Philippa Dickinson* **Corgi Hardcover**

AUTHORS Ian Beck, K. M. Peyton, Terry Pratchett. **Picture Corgi** AUTHORS/ARTISTS Frank Asch, Emilie Boon, Shirley Muir. **Young Corgi Paperback** AUTHORS Terence Dicks, Catherine Sefton. **Yearling** AUTHORS June Counsel, Helen Cresswell, John Cunliffe. **Corgi Paperback** AUTHORS Catherine Cookson, David Wiseman. **Freeway** AUTHORS Jean Ure, Robert Swindells.

Unsolicited mss welcome only if preceded by preliminary letter.
Royalties paid twice yearly. *Overseas associates* Transworld Australia/New Zealand, Trans-South Africa Book Distributors.

Authors' Rating Paying out big money to create a list of bestsellers. Recent recruits include Frederick Forsyth from Hutchinson, Catherine Cookson from Heinemann and Danielle Steel from Sphere. Transworld pays well and on time.

Travelmate

See **Richard Drew Publishing Ltd**

Unwin Hyman Ltd

15–17 Broadwick Street, London W1V 1FP
☎ 01–439 3126
Telex 886245 Fax 01–734 3884

Chairman/Chief Executive *Robin Hyman*
Approx Annual Turnover £16 million

Allen & Unwin and Bell & Hyman merged in 1986 to form Unwin Hyman Limited. The Group now publishes about 500 books a year in the UK, Australia, USA and New Zealand. Unwin Hyman have over 3000 titles in print with Tolkien, Pepys and Bertrand Russell the most prominent names on the reprint list. The trade side publishes general interest non-fiction, fantasy fiction, feminist publishing (**Pandora**), New Age (**Mandala** imprint) and health. These subjects are published both in hardback and Unwin Paperbacks. In 1988 Unwin Hyman acquired **Hutchinson Academic** from Century Hutchinson.

TRADE DIVISION
Managing Director *Mary Butler* **Editorial Director** *Michael Pountney* TITLES *The Rise and Fall of the Great Powers* Paul Kennedy; *Hunter's Moon* Garry Kilworth; *What Do You Care What Other People Think* Richard Feynman. **Pandora Press – Publishing Director** *Philippa Brewster.*

OTHER DIVISIONS
Academic – Managing Director *Nigel Britten*
Education – Managing Director *Christopher Kington.*

Welcome unsolicited mss, synopses and ideas for books.
Royalties vary according to contract.

Authors' Rating Rationalisation is beginning to prove its value with a successful mix of academic and general non-fiction. Firmer lead at the top as Robin Hyman takes over as chairman and chief executive.

Usborne Publishing Ltd

20 Garrick Street, London WC2E 9BJ
☎ 01–379 3535 Fax 01–836 0705

Managing Director *T. Peter Usborne*
Approx Annual Turnover £7.5 million

FOUNDED 1975. *Publishes* primarily non-fiction books for children, young adults and parents. 60 titles in 1988.

Editorial Director *Jenny Tyler*

DIVISIONS
Usborne Books at Home Oasis Park, Eynsham, Oxford OX8 1TP. Books are written in-house to a specific format and therefore do not welcome unsolicited mss. Will consider ideas which may then be developed in-house. Always very keen to hear from new illustrators and designers.
Royalties paid twice yearly.

Authors' Rating One of the best publishers of information books for children. Potential authors must believe that knowledge can be fun.

Van Nostrand Reinhold International

11 New Fetter Lane, London EC4P 4EE
☎ 01–583 9855
Telex 263398 Fax 01–583 0701

Managing Director *Paul Gardner*

VNR has been owned by the International Thomson Organisation since 1981. *Publishes* academic, professional and reference titles, and is responsible for the distribution of all Thomson books into the UK, Europe, the Middle East and Africa. It has worldwide agreements/agencies, mainly in the States, Canada, Australia and the Far East. 40 titles in 1988.

Publishing Director *Dominic Recaldin*

DIVISIONS
University & Professional *S. Wellings.*

IMPRINTS
Brooks Cole/Boyd & Fraser/Jones & Bartlet/PWS Kent/Wadsworth *R. Taylor,* **Gee** *Dr D.*

Recaldin, **Delmar** *A. Taylor* **VNR (US)** *J. Anthony.*

Unsolicited mss welcome if fall within subject areas. Unsolicited synopses and ideas for books considered.
Royalties paid twice yearly.

Verso

6 Meard Street, London W1V 3HR
☎ 01–434 1704/437 3546 Fax 01–734 0059

Chairman *Robin Blackburn*
Managing Director *Colin Robinson*
Directors *Tariq Ali, Robin Blackburn, Colin Robinson, Ellen Wood*

Formerly New Left Books which grew out of the magazine *New Left Review. Publishes* politics, history, sociology, economics, philosophy, cultural studies, plus *Questions for Feminism* series. 1989 sees the launch of a *Critical Studies in Latin American Culture* series. 35 new titles in 1988.
TITLES *The Freud Scenario* Jean-Paul Sartre; *Resources of Hope, Problems of Materialism and Culture, Writing in Society* Raymond Williams; *Sea Changes* Cora Kaplan. Unsolicited synopses and ideas for books welcome; no unsolicited mss.
Royalties paid annually. *Overseas office* in New York.

Viking

27 Wright's Lane, London W8 5TZ
☎ 01–938 2200
Telex 917181/2 Fax 01–937 8704
Approx Annual Turnover £5 million

FOUNDED 1983 as the 'hardback imprint' of **Penguin Books,** Viking has developed a distinct identity in the course of six years. AUTHORS include John Mortimer, Salman Rushdie, Dirk Bogarde, Barbara Vine (Ruth Rendell), Graham Swift, Robertson Davies, Joseph Brodsky, Christopher Hibbert. *Publishes* biography, gardening, highly illustrated art books, history, literary and commercial fiction, poetry, thrillers, and all kinds of general non-fiction.

Editorial Director *Tony Lacey*

IMPRINTS
Allen Lane The Penguin Press A new imprint (or rather a revival of an old), launched in April 1988, to publish a small range of significant academic books. Early titles include *Modern Ireland 1600-1972* Roy Foster, and *AIDS and its Metaphors* by Susan Sontag. **Viking Kestrel** The children's hardcover imprint of Penguin, mirroring much of **Puffin's** range, with a particular emphasis on quality children's fiction.

Editorial Director *Elizabeth Attenborough*

Authors' Rating An exciting list of big sellers including several million plus titles. Prepared to pay over the market rate for authors approaching their breakthrough book. Among established writers Margaret Drabble has come over from Weidenfeld and Caryl Phillips from Faber. But must be regretting just a tiny bit – the half million paid to Salman Rushdie to woo him from Cape. The **Allen Lane** imprint embraces 'works of outstanding culture and academic importance'.

Virago Press Ltd

20–23 Mandela Street, London NW1 0HQ
☎ 01–383 5150 Telex 927560

Chairman *Carmen Callil*
Joint Managing Directors *Ursula Owen, Harriet Spicer*
Approx Annual Turnover £2.5 million

Escaped from the Cape, Virago, Bodley Head and Chatto group just before the latter was taken over by **Random House.** FOUNDED 1973 by Carmen Callil, with the aim of publishing a wide range of books – education, fiction, health, history and literature – which illuminate and celebrate all aspects of women's lives. Nearly all titles are published in paperback; a distinguished reprint list makes up two thirds of these, with one third original titles commissioned across a wide area of interest. These areas currently include: biography, educational, fiction, health, history, non-fiction, philosophy, poetry, politics, reference, women's studies, young adults. 105 titles in 1989.

Editorial Director *Ursula Owen* TITLES Fiction: *The Handmaid's Tale* Margaret Atwood; *On the Golden Porch* Tatyana Tolstaya; *Indiscreet Journeys* Lisa St Aubin de Terán. Politics: *Is the Future Female?* Lynn Segal; *Insiders: Women's Experience of Prison* Prue Stevenson & Una Padel; *Let it Be Told Essays by Black Women Writers in Britain* ed. Lauretta Ngcobo. Psychology: *The Drama of Being a Child* Alice Miller; *A Life of One's Own* Marion Milner. Autobiography: *I Know Why The Caged Bird Sings* Maya Angelou; *All My Days* Kathleen Dayus.

Unsolicited mss welcome. Prefer to see a synopsis and a few sample chapters in the first instance in the case of non-fiction; for fiction prefer to see whole mss.
Royalties paid twice yearly. *Overseas associates*

Australasian Publishing Company, Australia Book Reps., New Zealand, Random House Canada.

Authors' Rating Broadening out from strictly feminist literature towards illustrated books, and titles on international and Third World subjects. At present the reprint list tends to dominate. The 'first and most famous feminist publishing house' is best known for reprinting neglected classics. But the search for new women writers is on with the emphasis on ethnic minorities. Virago is a company of high ideals but low advances.

Virgin Books

See **W. H. Allen & Co. plc**

Vision Press Ltd

28 Phillimore Walk, London W8 7SA
☎ 01–938 2929

Managing Director *Alan Moore*

FOUNDED 1947. *Publishes* academic and educational. 5 titles in 1988.

IMPRINTS
Artemis Press TITLES *GCSE Guidance & Answers* series. No unsolicited mss but welcome synopses and ideas for books.
Royalties paid annually.

University of Wales Press

6 Gwennyth Street, Cathays, Cardiff CF2 4YD
☎ 0222 231919 Fax 0222 396040

Director *John Rhys*
Approx Annual Turnover £250,000

Set up as an extension of the university in 1922. *Publishes* academic and scholarly books, mainly within the humanities and social sciences. Also works of Celtic scholarship. Occasionally publishes on behalf of learned bodies, such as the National Museum of Wales. 36 titles in 1988.

DIVISIONS
GPC Books *John Rhys* **Gwasg Prifysgol Cymru** *John Rhys* **University of Wales Press** *John Rhys* TITLES *Politics and Society in Wales, 1840–1922* ed. Geraint H. Jenkins & J. Beverly Smith; *The Welsh Spirit of Gwent* Mair Elvet Jones; *Y Gair ar Naith* G. R. Geraint Gruffydd. Unsolicited mss considered.
Royalties paid annually; more frequently by negotiation.

Walker Books Limited

87 Vauxhall Walk, London SE11 5HJ
☎ 01–793 0909 Fax 01–587 1123

Managing Director *Kate Mortimer*

FOUNDED 1979. *Publishes* illustrated children's books and teenage fiction. 200 titles in 1988.

Editor *Wendy Boase* TITLES *Pop Goes the Weasel!* Robert Crowther; *Where's Wally?* Martin Handford; *Vampire Master* Virginia Ironside; *All in One Piece* Jill Murphy; *There's an Awful Lot of Weirdos in our Neighbourhood.*

IMPRINT
Nick Hern Books Drama and adult fiction *Nick Hern* TITLES *Diving for Pearls* Howard Brenton. Welcome unsolicited mss and synopses.
Royalties paid twice yearly.

Authors' Rating An extraordinary success story based on adventurous marketing and on the principle that co-editions keep sales high and unit costs low. Walker Books publish more original children's books than any other British firm. One third of total sales goes through Sainsbury's supermarkets. Good terms including generous advances for quality writers and illustrators. Close relationships between editor and authors which probably accounts for the high rating achieved by Walker Books in the 1988 **Society of Authors** survey. Walker's latest imprint, **Nick Hern Books,** started up by the former drama editor at Methuen, has got off to an excellent start. Nick Hern's declared aim is 'to give attention to new writing'.

Ward Lock Educational

T. R. House, 1 Christopher Road, East Grinstead, W. Sussex RH19 3BT
☎ 0342 313844 Fax 0342 410471

Editorial Director *Martin Marix Evans*

FOUNDED 1952. Owned by Ling Kee, Hong Kong. Formerly part of **Ward Lock Ltd** but now completely independent. *Publishes* educational books (primary, middle, some secondary, teaching manuals) for English, mathematics and science subjects.
Royalties paid twice yearly.

Ward Lock Ltd

8 Clifford Street, London W1X 1RB
☎ 01–439 3100
Telex 262364 WARLOK G Fax 01–439 1582

Chairman *Robin H. D. Wood*
Managing Director *Chris Weller*

Approx Annual Turnover £3 million

FOUNDED 1854. Acquired by **Cassell** in 1989 for a price which remains secret. The original list consisted of popular information and general education, supplemented by Mrs Beeton. A magazine interest was also developed late last century. The now defunct list was founded on Conan Doyle, Edgar Wallace and Leslie Charteris, with children's information books, most notably the *Wonder Books*, coming later. *Publishes* general non-fiction, including crafts, cookery, decorating and design, and gardening. 100 titles in 1988.

Publishing Director *David Holmes*

IMPRINTS
Ward Lock *David Holmes* TITLES *Shorter Mrs Beeton; The Complete Man; Pergolas, Arbour, Gazebos and Follies.* **Warwick Press** *David Holmes* TITLES *Bible Stories; Creative Cooking.* Proposals welcome; send letter in the first instance.
Royalties paid twice yearly.

Frederick Warne

27 Wright's Lane, London W8 5TZ
☎ 01–938 2200
Telex 917181/2 Fax 01–938 8704
Approx Annual Turnover £10 million

Publishes children's books including Beatrix Potter; also Beatrix Potter non-fiction books for adults; general books, including walking guides and the *Observer* series (transport, hobbies, natural history, pets). Around 45 titles in 1988. (Also see **Penguin.**)

Editorial Director *Sally Floyer* TITLES include *Huxley Pig; Orlando The Marmalade Cat.* No unsolicited mss. Letter essential – many books are commissioned.
Royalties paid twice yearly.

Authors' Rating An astute takeover by **Penguin** has led to intensive exploitation of Beatrix Potter books. Not too much room for other titles.

Warner Chappell Plays Ltd (formerly English Theatre Guild)

129 Park Street, London W1Y 3FA
☎ 01–629 7600
Telex 268403 Fax 01–499 9718

General Manager *Michael Callahan*

Part of the Warner Chappell group which includes the literary agency of the same name (see *UK Agents*). *Publishes* theatre playscripts in paperback form. TITLES *Raping the Gold* Lucy Gannon; *Asylum* Paul Kember; *The Musical Comedy Murders of 1940* John Bishop; *The Light of Day* Graham Swannell; *Scales of Justice* Peter Saunders. Preliminary letter essential.
Royalties paid twice yearly.

Warwick Press

See **Ward Lock Ltd**

The Watts Group

12A Golden Square, London W1R 4BA
☎ 01–437 0713
Telex 262655 GROLUK G Fax 01–439 1440

Managing Director *David Kewley*

A division of the Franklin Watts Group, New York. *Publishes* general non-fiction, information and fiction books for children. 300 titles in 1989.

DIVISIONS
Franklin Watts *Chester Fisher* TITLES *Making Pencils* Ruth Thomson. **Orchard Books** *Judith Elliott* TITLES *Little Monsters* Jan Piénkowski. Unsolicited mss, synopses and ideas for books welcome.
Royalties paid twice yearly. *Overseas associates* in India, Caribbean, Scandinavia, Germany, France, Japan, South Korea, N. Ireland, Eire, S. Africa, Australia and New Zealand, US and Canada.

Wayland (Publishers) Ltd

61 Western Road, Hove, East Sussex BN3 1JD
☎ 0273 722561
Telex 878170 Waylan G Fax 0273 29314

Managing Director *John Lewis*
Approx Annual Turnover £5 million

Part of the Wolters Kluwer Group, Zwolle. FOUNDED 1969. Specialised in history in those days but now publish a broad range of subjects in approximately 23 subject areas – illustrated almost entirely in colour. *Publishes* illustrated non-fiction for children of 7 years and upwards. 200 titles in 1988.

Editorial Director *Paul Humphrey* Do not welcome unsolicited mss or synopses as all books are commissioned.
Royalties paid annually. *Overseas associates* Bookright Press Inc., USA.

Webb & Bower (Publishers) Ltd

5 Cathedral Close, Exeter, Devon EX1 1EZ
☎ 0392 435362 Fax 0392 211652

Managing Director *Richard Webb*

Publishes general interest illustrated books for the UK, US and international markets. 30 titles in 1988.

Editorial Head *Delian Bower* TITLES *AA Visitors' Guide; County Diary* titles; *V & A Colour Books; Countryside Commission; National Parks* series. Unsolicited mss, synopses and ideas for books welcome so long as they conform to type.
Royalties paid twice yearly.

Authors' Rating Small publisher noted for high standard of book production.

Weidenfeld & Nicolson Ltd

91 Clapham High Street, London SW4 7TA
☎ 01–622 9933 Telex 918066

Chairman *Lord Weidenfeld*
Publishing Director *Christopher Falkus*
Joint Managing Directors *Alan Miles, Richard Hussey*
Approx Annual Turnover £8.72 million

FOUNDED 1949 by George W. and Nigel N., the original list revolved around biography, history, memoirs, politics and quality fiction. Ten years later the sports/leisure publishers **Arthur Barker** was acquired; art and illustrated books followed, and the company developed the *Great* series – houses, gardens, rivers and so on. Today the reputation of the company rests in part on superbly produced and illustrated volumes on art, architecture, history and nature. Also publishes academic, archaeology, atlases and maps, autobiography and biography, business, cinema, health and beauty, humour, law, literature and criticism, philosophy, politics and sports. The publishing side of J. M. Dent was acquired in 1987 enlarging the company activities with Everyman and children's lists. 208 titles in 1988.

DIVISIONS
Academic *Christopher Falkus* TITLES *Introduction to Positive Economics; Law in Context; Voltaire; Social History of Rural England; Beginning Psychology; Global Economy; Market Economy.* **Art/Illustrated** *Michael Dover* TITLES *Royal Academy Catalogues; National Trust* titles; *Westminster Abbey; Gardens; Britain/London/Italy/Holy Land From the Air; Stills by Snowdon; Laura Ashley* titles. **Fiction** *David Roberts* TITLES *Jemima Shore* stories, Antonia Fraser; *The Radiant Way* Margaret Drabble; *Illusions* Charlotte Vale Allen; Claire Rayner titles; *Levant Trilogy* Olivia Manning. **General Non-fiction** *David Roberts* TITLES *Under the Eye of the Clock; Life of Kenneth Tynan; Vivien Leigh; Harold Wilson Memoirs; Kissinger Memoirs; Olivier Memoirs; Marcus Sieff Memoirs.* **Humour/Sport/Business** *David Roberts* TITLES *Bunbury Series; Brookside/The Archers Companions; Geoff Boycott; Ali Ross on Skiing; Steve Davis; Alan Border; Lloyd's; Saatchi & Saatchi Story.*

IMPRINTS
Arthur Barker & Weidenfeld Special Books, Dent Children's Books *Christopher Falkus* **Dent General & Everyman** Malcolm Gerratt.

Unsolicited mss welcome if legible; however, 'most publications come from selected authors'. Synopses and ideas for books welcome.
Royalties paid twice yearly for first two years, annually thereafter. *Overseas associates* Weidenfeld & Nicolson, New York.

Authors' Rating After a few dodgy years made secure by Getty money, a publishing house dominated by a single, charismatic personality. Big-name authors do well. Growth potential boosted by recent purchase of J. M. Dent but the company operates on a narrow profit margin. Sometimes slow on royalty statements and payments.

Wildwood House

See **Gower Publishing Group**

John Wiley & Sons Ltd

Baffins Lane, Chichester, Sussex PO19 1UD
☎ 0243 770234
Telex 86290 WIBOOKG Fax 0243 531058

Chairman *Mr W. Bradford Wiley* (USA)
Managing Director *Michael Foyle*

Part of John Wiley & Sons, New York, which dates from 1807. The London Office was opened in 1960. *Publishes* professional, reference and textbooks, scientific, technical and biomedical. 250 titles in 1988 (UK) and 75 periodicals.

Editorial Director *Dr John Jarvis*

DIVISIONS
Behavioural Sciences and Management *Michael Coombs* **Chemistry and Earth Sciences** *Dr Ernest Kirkwood* **Biomedical Sciences** *Dr Michael Dixon* **Maths, Computing and Engineering** *Ian McIntosh.*

Unsolicited mss welcome, as are synopses and ideas for books.
Royalties paid annually.

Authors' Rating A strong publisher in medicine and the sciences with good overseas marketing. Recently bought Alan Liss Inc., a fast growing New York publishers of life sciences books and journals.

The Windrush Press

Windrush House, 12 Main Street, Adlestrop, Moreton-in-Marsh, Gloucestershire GL56 0YN
☎ 0608718075 Fax 0608718860

Managing Director *Geoffrey Smith*

Independent company set up in 1987. *Publishes* travel, biography, memoirs, history, general, local history. 10 titles in 1988.

Editorial Head *Victoria Huxley* TITLES *Lady Colin Campbell: Victorian Sex Goddess; Lanzarote: A Windrush Island Guide; A Traveller's History of Greece.* Send synopsis and letter in first instance.
Royalties paid twice yearly.

Windsor Large Print

See **Chivers Press (Publishers)**

Wise

See **Omnibus Press**

Wisley Handbooks

See **Cassell plc**

Woburn Press

See **Frank Cass**

Wolfe Publishing Ltd

Brook House, 2–16 Torrington Place, London WC1E 7LT
☎ 01–636 4622
Telex 8814230 Fax 01–637 3021

Chairman *John F. Dill*
Managing Director *Michael Manson*
Approx Annual Turnover £5 million

Part of Times Mirror Group, USA. FOUNDED 1962 by Peter Wolfe, Sold to Year Book Medical Publishers of Chicago in 1985. *Publishes* dental, medical, scientific, technical and veterinary. 35 titles in 1988.

Editorial Director *Patrick Daly* TITLES *A Colour Atlas of Human Anatomy* R. M. H. McMinn & R. T. Hutchings; *A Colour Atlas of Endodontics J. J. Messing & C. J. R. Stock; A Colour Atlas of Surgical Anatomy of the Abdomen* R. Y. Calne; *A Colour Atlas of the Digestive System* R. E. Pounder, M. C. Allison & A. P. Dhillon; *A Colour Atlas of Comparative Veterinary Haematology* C. Hawkey & T. B. Dennett; *The Catalyst Handbook* M. V. Twigg.

No unsolicited mss. Welcome synopses and ideas for books.
Royalties paid twice yearly.

Oswald Wolff Books

See **Berg Publishers Ltd**

The Women's Press

34 Great Sutton Street, London EC1V 0DX
☎ 01–251 3007 Telex 919034 NAMARA G

Managing Director *Ros De Lanerolle*
Approx Annual Turnover £1 million

Part of the Namara Group (who also own **Quartet**). First titles appeared in 1978; expanded to 60 titles in 1987. The Women's Press also publish a Women Artists' Diary annually and feminist postcards. *Publishes* feminist fiction and non-fiction. Fiction usually has a female protagonist and a woman-centred theme. International writers and subject matter encouraged; some novels appear in translation and considerable emphasis is placed on the work of Third World and black women. Non-fiction: general subjects of interest to feminists, both practical and theoretical, and to women generally; art books, feminist theory, health and psychology, literary criticism. 60 titles in 1988.

DIVISIONS
Women's Press Crime *Jen Green* **Women's Press Science Fiction** *Sarah Lefanu* **Handbook series** *Hannah Kauter.*

IMPRINTS
Livewire *Carole Spedding/Christina Dunhill* Fiction and non-fiction for the teenage market.

Unsolicited mss, synopses and ideas for books welcome.
Royalties paid twice yearly, in September and March.

Authors' Rating Energetic devotion to the feminist cause. Budgets are tight and payments are sometimes slow.

John Wright

See **Butterworth & Co. Ltd**

Yale University Press (London)

23 Pond Street, London NW3 2PN
☏ 01–431 4422
Telex 896075 YUPLDN G Fax 01–431 3755

Managing Director *John Nicoll*

The UK company of **Yale University Press**, New Haven, Connecticut, USA. FOUNDED 1961. *Publishes* academic and humanities. 160 titles (jointly with the US company) in 1988.

Editorial Director *John Nicoll* TITLES *Impressionism: Art, Leisure and Parisian Society* Robert Herbert; *The Book of God* Gabriel Josipovici. Unsolicited mss and synopses welcome if within specialised subject areas.
Royalties paid annually.

Yearling

See **Transworld Publishers Ltd**

Zomba

See **Omnibus Press**

A Poetry Boom?

John Finch

So the publicists keep saying. In the last thirty years poetry has managed to have at least two. In the Sixties, with energy, humour and excitement, the Liverpool Poets re-invented poetry reading and sales shot up. Beatle fans scribbled verse in notebooks, literary mavericks took over **The Poetry Society**, and poets built themselves a huge new public for their visions of Albion. Poetry was paperbacked, mass-marketed, and sold in copious quantities. But by the time Punk emerged in the mid-Seventies, the whole thing had collapsed. Like the books themselves, sales were once again slim. A decade later and another boom: Martian poets; reading tours by helicopter; Kingsley Amis expounding the virtues of verse in the *Daily Mirror*; and a poet's poet, Ted Hughes, made laureate. Poetry was popular: new books, new writers, buoyant sales. Publishers spoke of commendable growth. Today, at the start of the Nineties, things are back to normal. Paperback novels regularly sell 25,000 copies; books of poems do well to shift 600. This, though, doesn't discourage people from writing poetry; far from it, the march of new poets goes on and on.

The situation is really one of inverted supply and demand. The number of readers available for new poetry is actually very small. Despite relatively good sales from market leaders such as Seamus Heaney, Ted Hughes, Philip Larkin, Fiona Pitt Kethley (on sex), Heathcote Williams (on dolphins and whales), and the doyenne of greeting card versifiers, Helen Steiner Rice, poetry in general fares pretty badly. Judge for yourself – check the shelves of your local library for proof. You'll find a lot of biography, but little verse. Even so, there are *so many* new writers around seeking publication that presses and periodicals have been forced to emerge specifically to serve them. For the first time in history we apparently have more writers of poetry than we have readers. It is quite an amazing situation. The Victorians kept diaries; we write poetry. Nearly all of the present day population is literate so in our spare time it's either creativity or graffiti. Judge for yourself which is coming in first.

The Traditional Outlets

There is a small, traditional market for new verse – *The TLS*, *The Listener*, now and again the quality Sunday papers, *London Magazine*, *The Spectator*, and the occasional poem in magazines like *The Lady*, *Encounter* and *The Countryman*. All of these are paying outlets, which is quite reassuring. But the sad truth is that if poetry were to cease to exist overnight, these periodicals would continue to publish without a flicker. And who, other than the poets, would notice? Book publishers like **Faber & Faber**, **Chatto & Windus**, **Century Hutchinson**, **OUP** and **Secker & Warburg** all have small but healthy poetry lists, but these are hardly central to their business operations. A little decoration for their catalogues perhaps? Poetry implies quality – unless it's Roger McGough, it rarely means money.

The Trailblazers

A number of companies at the cutting edge of publishing have recently shown an interest in original volumes of new poetry. Notable are **Penguin**, who have always published verse of some sort, and this year **Paladin**, who have a reputation for upmarket paperbacks. Both are trying for a commercial return from the kind of material everyone else regards as too difficult to market. Their lists show considerable innovation for mass-market houses, with Paladin breaking ground to bring out genuinely alternative poetry, and Penguin, with its long history of selling mainstream English Literature, now concentrating on substantially produced books by readable contemporary poets. Iain Sinclair, Tony Harrison, Jeremy Reed and Peter Redgrove are among those who have benefitted. Women's presses like **Virago** and **The Women's Press** are also using economic muscle now to push poetry as part of their overall strategy. It is an invigorating departure. How long these trailblazers keep at it will, of course, depend ultimately on the buyers, and I'm pretty sure there are not enough of those.

The Specialists

The real growth has been among the specialist presses. **Carcanet**, **Anvil**, **Bloodaxe** and **Seren Books** began as small operations, often the burning interest of one individual, but these apparently non-commercial literary ventures have now acquired staff, offices, and even national distribution. They stand apart from their trade cohorts, however, by continuing to put art before cash. They remain open to new writers and to new ideas. They are not afraid to experiment. Their titles are well designed and withstand comparison with anything else the booktrade has to offer. They are able to continue publishing mainly by the support of public money channelled via the Arts Council and regional arts associations. They are models of what poetry publishing should be – active, alert, exciting. The problem still is that they are too few.

The Small Press and the Little Magazine

Most poetry in this country actually sees the light of day through the small presses and little magazines. These have been the backbone of literary publishing here since the Second World War. The advance of printing technology – the advent of cheap duplicating, desktop litho, photocopying and now home wordprocessing – has brought the once arcane art of publishing within everybody's reach. Small presses, usually one person operations run from back bedrooms, have flourished. Little magazines published on a shoestring by enthusiasts have sprung up everywhere from Cardiff to Caithness. Don't expect printing perfection. Many of these spare time operations produce home-stapled pamphlets set on typewriters, and magazines with hand-coloured covers. But standards, though, are rising. From **Actual Size Press** publications to **Writers Forum** and **Acumen** magazine to **The Wide Skirt**, text is now being typeset and pages professionally bound. Gone are the spirit-duplicated, wastepaper swatches of yesteryear. Today it is colour, texture and quality. Small presses may not yet be the mirror image of their commercial rivals but they *are* a respectable alternative. For the new writer they are the obvious place to begin. Indeed some writers see little point in publishing elsewhere. This is where literature has its cutting edge.

Cash

A lot of writers new to the business are surprised to learn that their poetry will not make them much money. Being a poet is not really much of an occupation. You get better wages delivering papers. There's always the odd pound from the better-heeled magazine, perhaps even as much as £20 or so from those periodicals lucky enough to receive grants, but generally it will amount to free copies of the issue concerned, a thank-you letter, and little more. Those with collections published by a subsidised specialist publisher can expect £100 or so as an advance on royalties. Those using the small presses can look forward to a few dozen complimentary copies. The truth is that poetry *itself* is undervalued. You can earn money writing about it, reviewing it, lecturing on it and giving public recitations of it. In fact most things in the poetry business will earn better money than the verse itself. Expect to spend a lot on stamps and a fair bit on sample copies. Most of the time all you'll get in return is used envelopes.

Competitions

Poetry competitions have been the vogue of the '80s with the most unlikely organisations sponsoring them. The notion here is that anonymity ensures fairness. Entries are made under pseudonyms so that if your name does happen to be Seamus Heaney it won't help you much. Results seem to bear this out. The big competitions such as the **Arvon Foundation International** or the **Poetry Society's National**, attract an enormous response and usually throw up quite a number of complete unknowns among the winners. The money prizes can be large – thousands of pounds even – but it costs at least £2 a poem to enter in the first place. If it is cash you want, then horses are a better bet. There has been a recent trend for winners to come from places like Cape Girardeau, Missouri and Tibooburra, Australia. The odds are getting longer. Who won the 1986 Arvon? But if you do fancy a try then it is a pretty straightforward activity. You spend a couple of pounds and tie up a poem for a few months. Watch the small magazines for competition details, write to your local regional arts association, and check the entries under **Prizes** towards the back of *Writer's Handbook*.

Where to start

Probably the best place for the new poet to start is locally. Find out through the library or the nearest arts association which writers' groups meet in your area and attend a few. There you will meet others of a like mind, encounter whatever locally produced magazines there might be, and get a little direct feedback on your work.

'How am I doing' is a big question for the emerging poet and although criticism is not all that hard to come by, do not expect useful criticism from all sources. Magazine editors, for example, will rarely have the time to offer advice. It is best, too, to be a little suspicious of that offered by friends and relatives, who may only be trying to please. Writers' groups present the best chance for poets to engage in honest mutual criticism. But if you'd prefer a more detailed, written analysis of your efforts and are willing to pay a small sum, you could apply to the reading service operated nationally by the **Poetry Society** (21 Earl's Court Square, London SW5) and by local regional arts associations (see listing).

If you have made the decision to publish your work, the first thing to do is a little market research. I've already indicated how overstocked the business is with periodicals and publications but surprisingly you will not find many of these in your local W.H. Smith. Most poetry still reaches its public via the specialist. Begin, though, by reading a few newly published mainstream books, and ask your bookseller for recommendations. Enquire at the library. Try selecting a recent anthology of *contemporary* verse. Progress to the literary magazine. Write off to a number of the addresses which follow this article and ask for sample copies. Enquire about subscriptions. Expect to pay a little but inevitably not a lot. It is important that poets read not only to familiarise themselves with what is currently fashionable and to increase their own facility for self-criticism but also to help support the activity in which they wish to participate. Buy, read, and then, if appropriate, think about submitting your work.

How To Do It

Increase your chances of acceptance by following simple standard procedure:

- Type, single side of the paper, A4-size, single-spacing with double between stanzas, *exactly* as you'd wish your poem to appear when printed.
- Give the poem a title, clip multi-page works together, include your name and address at the foot of the final sheet.
- Keep a copy, make a record of what you send where and when, leave a space to note reaction.
- Send in small batches, 6 is a good number, include a brief covering letter saying who you are. Leave justification, apology and explanation for the writers' circle.
- Include an s.a.e. of sufficient size for reply and/or return of your work.
- Be prepared to wait some weeks for a response. Don't pester. Be patient. Most magazines will reply in the end.
- Never send the same poem to two places at the same time.
- Send your best – work which fails to fully satisfy even the author is unlikely to impress anyone else.

Where?

Try the list which follows, sending for samples as I've suggested. The total market is vast – 200 or so addresses here – more than 900 in *Small Presses and Little Magazines of the UK & Ireland* (£1.95 from Oriel, The Friary, Cardiff), literally thousands and thousands worldwide in the two main American directories: Judson Jerome's *Poet's Market* (Writer's Digest Books) and Len Fulton's *Directory of Poetry Publishers* (Dustbooks).

The Next Step

Once you have placed a few poems you may like to consider publishing a booklet. There are as many small presses around as there are magazines. Start with the upmarket professionals by all means – Secker & Warburg, OUP, Chatto & Windus, Century Hutchinson, Faber & Faber, Virago (see listing **UK Publishers**) – but be prepared for compromise. The specialists and the small presses are swifter and more receptive to new work.

If all else fails you could do it yourself. Blake did, so did Ezra Pound. Modern technology puts the process within the reach of us all and the business is not that difficult. Read my *How To Publish Yourself* (Allison and Busby) for more information.

What to Avoid – The Vanity Presses

Requests which should make you suspicious:

- Poems Wanted for new anthology.
- Publisher seeks new authors and poets for well-established list.
- Authors Wanted. Publisher seeks new material. Special interest in autobiography, war memoirs and poetry.

You'll find these small ads scattered through the classifieds of Sunday papers and in the Personal Sections of large circulation magazines. You can tell that something is wrong by the fact that they are there at all. No reputable publisher need advertise a need for poetry. The natural state of things is that there is always too much.

Vanity presses are shady businesses run by sharks interested in fleecing the unsuspecting. Considerations of literary worth do not come into it. The system works by making the amateur writer feel significant. You send in your work and receive a glowing response by return. 'The editor has read your poems with interest and is pleased to report that they show considerable talent. We would like to include them in our forthcoming anthology *Pageant of the British Muse*. This important anthology of new verse will be circulated among the editors of national newspapers such as the *Daily Mirror*, *Daily Express* and *Daily Mail* as well as being put on the shelves of the libraries of Oxford University, Cambridge University, Trinity College Dublin, The National Library of Wales and the British Library, London. Leading critics use our anthologies as touchstones. Inclusion is a considerable achievement.' It sounds terrific. You are dancing round the room. What follows is a lot of hoo-hah about copyright, assignment of author's rights, royalties, etc., all bound up in the form of a legal-sounding document – 'upon this day... the... of... witnessed the undersigned...' and so forth. The importance of the deal is made abundantly clear. The sting is in the small print at the bottom. 'In order to help defray publisher's overheads in this period of escalating printing costs, we are asking you for a small contribution of £40 per poem printed...' But by the time you get to this you are so enraptured with the success of your 'considerable talent' that you pay up without a murmur.

It is a deception, of course. Hundreds of others have received the same letter. The anthology, when it finally arrives, will be badly set with the poems crammed in like sardines. It will not be sold in bookshops either (no shop owners will stock it), not bought by libraries (those mentioned are copyright libraries and by law need to receive a copy of everything printed). It will be ignored by newspapers (those listed never review poetry anyway). In fact it will be bought and read by no-one bar the contributors themselves.

Criticise the presses for this piece of bamboozlery and they will tell you that they are doing no more than providing a service; people want their names in print and are willing to pay to see that happen. The establishment of vanity presses is the inevitable consequence. The immorality is that those who participate are always the inexperienced – often the young and the very old – generally those least able to pay. It is not that the vanity presses provide any value judgement on work submitted either. There is no discrimination – they print everything they receive. As a test one press was sent a poem by Gerard Manley Hopkins, a cut-up of the *Daily Star*, jottings by a 7-year-old and a piece assembled from overheard conversations in a launderette. 'Obvious talent' was clearly on display. They accepted the lot!

Variations and embellishments on the vanity press theme include offers to put your poetry to music, setting you off on the road to stardom; readings of your verse by actors with deep voices to help you break into the local radio market (there isn't one); and further requests for cash to help pay for your collected poems to appear in book form, preferably bound in expensive leather with your name gold-blocked on the front. Do not pay one single penny. If a publisher asks you for money, forget them. It is not the way things should be done.

Subsidy Publishing

This is the half-legitimate brother of the vanity press. Here authors of completed books, often poets, help out the publisher by providing some (or all) of the initiation costs with the idea that they will subsequently share any profits. The system has a long history. Dickens did it, as did Jane Austen, and so too poets like T.S. Eliot and R.S. Thomas. In the world of small presses it is common practice but potential participants should take care.

There are a number of houses masquerading as genuine publishers who actually do nothing but subsidy publication. They bring your book out because you have paid them to, not because there is a market for it or because they think you are of literary worth. You are also expected to do all the marketing and selling yourself. The help they will offer is minimal. Charges are high. Booksellers and reviewers will ignore you. You are lost before you start.

If you are approached for money in this context it is imperative to check the publisher's credentials carefully. Look at their list and get in touch with one or more of their authors. Find out how the deal worked for them. Ask about reputations at your local library and bookshop. The kind of money involved can run into thousands. Is it a real publisher you are dealing with here? Or a vanity operation in disguise? Be sure.

The Listings

None of the lists of addresses which follow are exhaustive. Publishers come and go with amazing frequency. There will always be the brand new press on the look-out for talent and the projected magazine desperate for contributions. For up-to-the-minute information check some of the 'Organisations of Interest to Poets' in the lists which follow. Poetry has a huge market. It pays to keep your ear to the ground.

Major Imprints which publish poetry

(Those with a substantial interest are preceded by * For addresses, see *UK Publishers* section)

Aberdeen University Press
Allison & Busby
Angus & Robertson Ltd
The Bodley Head
Marion Boyars Publishers Ltd
John Calder (Publishers) Ltd
Cambridge University Press
Canongate Publishing Ltd
Jonathan Cape Ltd
Cassell plc
***Century Hutchinson Ltd**
W & R Chambers
***Chatto & Windus Ltd/The Hogarth Press Ltd**
Collins, including **Grafton Books Ltd/Paladin**

Dent General & Everyman
André Deutsch Ltd
Gerald Duckworth & Co. Ltd
***Faber & Faber Ltd**
The Gay Men's Press (GMP) Ltd
Robert Hale Ltd
Hamish Hamilton Ltd
Hodder & Stoughton Ltd
Macdonald & Co. Ltd
Macmillan London Ltd
Onlywoman Press
***Oxford University Press**
***Penguin Books Ltd**
Quartet Books
Routledge
Scottish Academic Press
***Secker & Warburg Ltd**
Sidgwick & Jackson Ltd
Souvenir Press Ltd
Viking
Virago Press Ltd
Weidenfeld & Nicholson Ltd
The Women's Press

The Specialists

Anvil Press Poetry (press/magazine) *Peter Jay*, see **UK Publishers** section

Blackstaff Press (press) *Michael Burns*, see **UK Publishers** section

Bloodaxe Books (press) *Neil Astley*, see **UK Publishers** section

Carcanet Press (press/magazine) *Michael Schmidt*, see **UK Publishers** section

Seren Books (formerly Poetry Wales Press) (press/magazine) *Cary Archard* and *Mick Felton*, Andmor House, Trewsfield Industrial Estate, Tondu Road, Bridgend CF3 4LJ

Small Presses

Actual Size Press *Paul Brown*, 40 Elm Grove, Peckham, London SE15 5DE

The Ada Press *Andrew Hale*, 31 Ada Road, Canterbury, Kent CT1 3TS

Agenda & Editions Charitable Trust (press/magazine) *William Cookson*, 5 Cranbourne Court, Albert Bridge Road, London SW11 4PE

Allardyce, Barnett, Publishers *Anthony Barnett*, see **UK Publishers** section

Alun Books *Sally Jones*, 3 Crown Street, Port Talbot, West Glamorgan

Atlas Press *Alastair Brotchie*, 10 Park Street, London SE1 9AB

BB Books/Global Tapestry Journal (press/magazine) *Dave Cunliffe*, 1 Springbank, Longsight Road, Salebury, Blackburn, Lancashire BB1 9EU

Bedlam Press *David Moody*, Church Green House, Old Church Lane, Pateley Bridge, Harrogate HG3 5LZ

Big Little Poem Books *Robert Richardson*, 42 Peaksfield Avenue, Grimsby, South Humberside DN32 9QF

Blind Serpent Press 18 Ireland Street, Carnoustie, Dundee DD7 6AT

Blue Bridge Press *David Tipton*, 24 Aireville Road, Frizinhall, Bradford BD9 4HH

Bradgate Press 28 Stainsdale Green, Whitwick, Leicestershire LE6 3PW

Curlew Press Hare Cottage, Kettlesing, Harrogate HG3 2LB

Dangaroo Books PO Box 186, Coventry CV4 7HG

Christopher Davies Publishers Ltd *Christopher Davies*, see **UK Publishers** section

Dedalus Poetry Press *John F. Deane*, 46 Seabury, Sydney Parade Avenue, Sandymount, Dublin 4

Diamond Press *Geoffrey Godbert*, 5 Berners Mansions, 34–6 Berners Street, London W1

Dollar of Soul/Chicken Sigh Press *Owen Davis*, 15 Argyle Road, Swanage, Dorset BH19 1HZ

Downlander Publishing *Derek Bourne-Jones*, 88 Oxenden Gardens, Lower Willingdon, Eastbourne, East Sussex BN22 0RS

Echo Room Press (press/magazine) *Brendan Cleary*, 45 Bewick Court, Princess Street, Newcastle upon Tyne NE1 8EG

Enitharmon Press *Stephen Stuart-Smith*, see **UK Publishers** section

Equofinality (press/magazine) *Red Mengham*, 147 Selly Oak Road, Bournville, Birmingham B30 1HN

Ferry Press Bridges Farmhouse, Laughton, Lewes, East Sussex

Fleeting Monolith Enterprises 35 Dresden Road, London N19 3BE

Forest Books *Brenda Walker*, 20 Forest View, Chingford, London E4 7AY

Four Eyes Press (press/magazine) 510 Wilmslow Road, Withington, Manchester M20 9BT

Gallery Press *Peter Fallon*, 19 Oakdown Road, Dublin 14

Galloping Dog Press *Peter Hodgkiss*, 45 Salisbury Gardens, Newcastle upon Tyne NE2 1HP

Genera Editions/Shadowcat *Colin Simms*, Low Woodhead North, near Bellingham, Hexham, Northumberland NE48 2HX

Gild of St George 17 Hadassah Grove, Liverpool L17 8XH

Gomer Press *John Lewis*, Llandysul, Dyfed SA44 4BQ

Grevile Press Emscote Lawn, Warwick CV34 5QD

Hangman Books *Billy Childish*, 2 May Road, Rochester, Kent

Hard Pressed Poetry *Billy Mills*, 1 New Ireland Road, Rialto, Dublin 8

Hearing Eye *John Rety*, Box 1, 99 Torriano Avenue, London NW5

Hippopotamus Press *Roland John*, see **UK Publishers** section

Honno Ailsa Craig, Heol Y Cawl, Dinas Powys, South Glamorgan

International Concrete Poetry Archive *Paula Claire*, 11 Dale Close, Thames Street, Oxford OX1 1TU

Iron Press (press/magazine) *Peter Mortimer*, 5 Marden Terrace, Cullercoats, North Shields, Tyne and Wear NE30 4PD

Itinerant Publications 13 Albert Road, Gourock, Scotland

Jackson's Arm Press *Michael Blackburn*, 117 Newland Street West, Lincoln LN1 1QD

Jezebel Tapes & Books *Gillian Hanscombe*, PO Box 12, Seaton, Devon EX12 2XH

Johnson Green Publishing (UK) Ltd/Aquila (press/magazine) *J.C.R. Green*, PO Box 19, Buxton, Derbyshire SK17 6YD

Keepsake Press *Roy Lewis*, 2 Park House Gardens, East Twickenham TW1 2DE

KQBX *James Sale*, 30 Fitzroy Avenue, Luton LU3 1RS

Lobby Press (press/magazine) *Richard Tabor*, 1 Dairy Cottages, Compton Road, Yeovil, Somerset BA22 7EW

Lokamaya (Press) Book Publishing *Bahauddeen Latif*, 8 Batoum Gardens, London W6 7QD

Loxwood-Stoneleigh see **UK Publishers** section

Lucas Publications 85 Brasenose Road, Liverpool L20 8QA

Magenta Press *Maggie O'Sullivan*, Middle Fold Farm, Colden, Heptonstall, West Yorkshire HX7 7PG

Mammon Press/Poet's Voice (press/magazine) *Fred Beake*, 12 Dartmouth Avenue, Bath, Avon

Manderville Press *Peter Scupham*, *John Mole*, 2 Taylor's Hill, Hitchin, Hertfordshire

The Many Press (press/magazine) *John Welch*, 15 Northcott Road, London N16 7BJ

Mariscat Press *Hamish Whyte*, 3 Mariscat Road, Glasgow G41 4ND

Menard Press *Anthony Rudolf*, 8 The Oaks, Woodside Avenue, London N12 8AR

Microbridgade *Ulli Freer*, 74 Lodge Lane, Finchley Park, London N12 8JJ

Midnag Publications Northumberland Technical College, College Road, Ashington, Northumberland NE63 9RG

Keith Murray Publications 46 Portal Crescent, Tillydrone, Aberdeen AB2 2SP

Nanholme Press (formerly Littlewood Press and Giant Steps) Nanholme Centre, Shaw Wood Road, Todmorden, Lancashire OL14 6DA

Nether Halse Books *John Crisford*, Winsford, Minehead, Somerset TA24 7JE

New Beacon Books 76 Stroud Green Road, London N7 5EN

New Broom Private Press *Toni Savage*, 78 Cambridge Street, Leicester LE3 0JP

New River Project Unit P8, Metropolitan College of Craftsmen, Enfield Road, London N1 5AZ

North and South *Peterjon Skelt*, 23 Egerton Road, Twickenham, Middlesex TW2 7SL

Northern House 19 Haldane Terrace, Newcastle upon Tyne NE2 3AN

Northern Lights 66 Belsize Park, London NW3 4NE

Oasis Books *Ian Robinson*, 12 Stevenage Road, London SW6 6ES

Oleander Press *Philip Ward*, 17 Stansgate Avenue, Cambridge CB2 2QZ

Open Township/Folded Sheets (press/magazine) *Michael Haslam*, 14 Foster Clough, Heights Road, Hebden Bridge, West Yorkshire HX7 5QZ

Oracle *George Dowden*, PO Box 830, Brighton, East Sussex BN2 1BD

Oscars Press BM Oscars, London WC1N 3XX

Overdue Books *Jan Maloney*, 37 Melbourne Street, Hebden Bridge, West Yorkshire HX7 6AS

Peterloo Poets (press/magazine) *Harry Chambers*, 2 Kelly Gardens, Calstock, Cornwall PL18 9SA

Pig Press (press) *Ric Caddel*, 7 Cross View Terrace, Neville's Cross, Durham DH1 4JY

Poetical Histories 27 Sturton Street, Cambridge

Polygon Press *Peter Kravitz*, see **UK Publishers** section

Prebendal Press (press/magazine) PO Box 30, Thame, Oxon OX9 3AD

Prest Roots Press *P.E. Larkin*, 34 Alpine Court, Kenilworth CV8 2GP

Priapus Press *John Cotton*, 37 Lombardy Drive, Berkhamsted, Hertfordshire HP4 2LQ

Primitive Poetry Press *Ruskin Watts*, The Cottage, Longnor, near Buxton SK17 0LA

Purple Heather Publications *Richard Mason*, Flat 7, 4 Chestnut Avenue, Headingley, Leeds LS6 1BA

Raven Arts *Dermot Bolger*, PO Box 1430, Finglas, Dublin 11

Reality Studios 4 Howard Court, Peckham Rye, London SE15 3PH

Red Sharks Press *Christopher Mills*, 122 Clive Street, Grangetown, Cardiff CF1 7JE

Redbeck Press *David Tipton*, 24 Aireville Road, Frizinghall, Bradford BD9 4HH

Rivelin Grapheme Press *Snowdon Barnett*, The Annex, Kennet House, 19 High Street, Hungerford, Berkshire RG17 0NL

Sea Dream Music *Simon Law*, 236 Sebert Road, Forest Gate, London E7 0NP

Shearsman Books *Tony Fraser*, 47 Dayton Close, Plymouth PL6 5DX

Ship of Fools *Robert Sheppard*, 15 Oakapple Road, Southwick, Sussex

Slow Dancer Press (press/magazine) *John Harvey*, Flat 4, 1 Park Valley, Nottingham NG7 1BS

Smith/Doorstop/The North (press/magazine) *Peter Sansom*, Floor 4, Byram Arcade, Westgate, Huddersfield HD1 1ND

Spanner (press/magazine) *Allen Fisher*, 64 Lanercost Road, London SW2 3DN

Spectacular Diseases (press/magazine) *Paul Green*, 83B London Road, Peterborough PE2 9BS

Spectrum *Chris Bendon*, 14 Maes y Deri, Lampeter, Dyfed SA48 7EP

Stingy Artist/Last Straw Press 8 Chelmsford Street, Weymouth, Dorset DT4 7HR

Stone Lantern Press *Phil Maillard*, 10 Severn Road, Canton, Cardiff CF1 9EB

Street Editions 31 Panton Street, Cambridge CB2 1HL

Stride Publications (incorporating **Taxus Press**) (press/magazine) *Rupert Loydell*, 37 Portland Street, Newtown, Exeter, Devon EX1 2EG

Sub-Voicive 21 Cecile Park, London N8

Swan Books and Educational Services *E.O. Evans*, 13 Henrietta Street, Swansea

Taurus Press of Willow Dene *Paul Peter Piech*, 11 Limetree Way, Danygraig, Porthcawl, Mid Glamorgan CF36 5AU

Tiger Bay Press *Olly Rees*, 34 Cedarville Gardens, London SW16 3DA

Toad's Damp Press *Patricia Farrell*, 6 Montrose Walk, Weybridge, Surrey

Tuba Press (press/magazine) *Peter Ellison*, 23 Kinfauns Avenue, Eastbourne, East Sussex BN22 8SS

Turret Books *Bernard Stone*, 42 Lamb's Conduit Street, London WC1N 3LJ

Ver Poets *May Badman*, Haycroft, 61–3 Chiswell Green Lane, St Albans, Hertfordshire AL2 3AG

Vigil Publications *John Howard*, Suite 5, Somdor House, Station Road, Gillingham, Dorset SP8 4QA

Wellsweep Press/Nodding Donkey (press/magazine) *John Cayley*, 719 Fulham Road, London SW6 5UL

The Wide Skirt Press (press/magazine) *Geoff Hattersley*, 93 Blackhouse Road, Fartown, Huddersfield, West Yorkshire HD2 1AP

Womenwrite Press *Luana Dee*, PO Box 77, Cardiff CF2 4XX

Word and Action (Dorset) Ltd (press/magazine) 43 Avenue Road, Wimborne, Dorset BH21 1BS

Words Press Hod House, Child Okeford, Dorset DT11 8EH

Writers Forum/Kroklok (press/magazine) *Bob Cobbing*, 89A Petherton Road, London N5 2QT

Yew Tree Books *Mollie Rallings*, Skipton Office Services, 2 Otley Street, Skipton BD23 3NT

Zora Press PO Box 33, Kingsland High Street, London E8 2NF

Little Magazines

Acumen (press/magazine) *Patricia Oxley*, 6 The Mount, Furzeham, Brixham, Devon TQ5 8QY

Agenda (press/magazine) *William Cookson*, 5 Cranbourne Court, Albert Bridge Road, London SW11 4PE

Agog *Ed Jewasinski*, 116 Eswyn Road, Tooting, London SW17 8JN

Ambit *Martin Bax*, 17 Priory Gardens, London N6 5QY

Anthem (press/magazine) *Martin Tatham*, 57 Cyril Avenue, Bobbers' Mill, Derbyshire

Aquarius *Eddie S. Linden*, Flat 3, 116 Sutherland Avenue, London W9

Argo Museum of Modern Art, 30 Pembroke Street, Oxford OX1 1BP

The Bad Seed Review (press/magazine) *Martin Myers*, 2 Ashleigh Grove, West Jesmond, Newcastle upon Tyne NE2 3DL

Bête Noire *John Osborne*, Dept of American Studies, The University of Hull, Cottingham Road, Hull HU6 7RX

Bogg *George Cairncross*, 31 Belle Vue Street, Filey, Yorkshire YO14 9HU

Borderlines *Andrew Morrison*, Anglo-Welsh Poetry Society, The Flat, Cronkhill, Crosshouses, Shrewsbury SY5 6JP

The Bound Spiral Open Poetry Conventicle, 72 First Avenue, Bush Hill Park, Enfield EN1 1BW

Bradford Poetry Quarterly *Clare Chapman*, 9 Woodvale Road, Bradford BD7 2SJ

Briggistane *Shetland Arts Trust*, 22–4 North Road, Lerwick, Shetland

Celtic Dawn PO Box 271, Oxford OX2 6DU

Chapman (press/magazine) *Joy M. Hendry*, 15 Nelson Street, Edinburgh

Contra Flow Lobby Press, 104 Glenthorne Avenue, Yeovil, Somerset

Core *Mevlut Ceylan*, 37B Packingham Square, Islington, London N1 7UJ

Corpus *Pat Khan*, 76 Iveson Drive, Leeds LS16 6NL

Cyphers *Pearse Hutchinson*, 3 Selskar Tee, Ranelagh, Dublin 6

Dada Dance *Dee Rimbaud*, 12 Blairhall Avenue, Glasgow G41 3BA

Distaff *Jennifer Brice*, c/o London Women's Centre, Wesley House, 4 Wild Court, Kingsway, London WC2

A Doctor's Dilemma *Peter Godfrey*, Flat 3, 32 Brunswick Terrace, Hove, East Sussex BN3 1JH

Eavesdropper *Philip Woodrow*, 15 Mount Pleasant Crescent, London N4 4HP

The Echo Room (press/magazine) *Brendan Cleary*, 45 Bewick Court, Princess Street, Newcastle upon Tyne NE1 8EG

Ecutorial *Will Rowe*, Dept of Spanish, Kings College, Strand, London WC2

Edinburgh Review (press/magazine) *Peter Kravitz*, 48 Pleasance, Edinburgh EH8 9TJ

Envoi (press/magazine) *Anne Lewis Smith*, Penffordd, Newport, Dyfed SA42 0QT

Exe-Calibre (press/magazine) *Ken Taylor*, Flat 1, 33 Knowle Road, Totterdown, Bristol BS4 2EB

Exile *Herbert Marr*, 38 Melrose Avenue, Billingham, Cleveland TS23 2UW

Expressions 10 Turfpits Lane, Erdington, Birmingham B23 5DP

Figs (press/magazine) *Tony Baker*, Mews Cottage, Winster, Derbyshire DE4 2DJ

First Offence *Tim Fletcher*, Syringa, The Street, Stodmarsh, Canterbury, Kent CT3 4BA

First Time (press/magazine) *Josephine Austin*, 4 Burdett Place, George Street, Hastings TN34 3ED

Five Leaves Left Flat 7, 4 Chestnut Avenue, Headingley, Leeds LS6 1BA

Flint *David Orme*, 27 Pennington Close, Colden Common, Winchester SO21 1UR

Folded Sheets 14 Foster Clough, Heights Road, Hebden Bridge, West Yorkshire HX7 5QZ

Footnotes (press/magazine) *James Sale*, Schools' Poetry Association, 30 Fitzroy Avenue, Luton, Bedfordshire

The Frogmore Papers *Jeremy Page*, 28 Welta House, Hazellville Road, Highgate, London N19 3LZ

Gallery *Valerie Sinason*, 3 Honeybourne Road, London NW6 1HH

Global Tapestry Journal *Dave Cunliffe*, 1 Springbank, Longsight Road, Salebury, Blackburn, Lancashire BB1 9EU

Groundworks Fen Poetry Centre, The Fish, Sutton Gault, near Ely, Cambridgeshire CB6 2BE

Hat *Ian Hogg*, 1A Church Lane, Croft, near Skegness, Lincolnshire

The Honest Ulsterman *Frank Ormsby*, 70 Eglantine Avenue, Belfast BT9 6DY

Illuminations/First Writes *Simon Lewis*, Radley College, Abingdon, Oxon OX14 2HR

Impressions 84 Colwyn Road, Northampton NN1 3PX

Inkshed *Anthony Smith*, Flat 4, 387 Beverly Road, Hull HU5 1LF

Inverse *George Wickes*, 41 Finborough Road, Stowmarket, Suffolk IP14 1PS

Iota *David Holliday*, 67 Hady Crescent, Chesterfield, Derbyshire SH1 0EB

Irish Review *Kevin Barry*, Cork University Press, University College, Cork, Eire

Iron (press/magazine) *Peter Mortimer*, 5 Marden Terrace, Cullercoats, North Shields, Tyne and Wear NE30 4PD

Issue One (press/magazine) *Ian Brocklebank*, 2 Tewkesbury Drive, Grimsby, South Humberside DN34 4TL

Joe Soap's Canoe (press/magazine) *Martin Stannard*, 90 Ranelagh Road, Felixstowe, Suffolk IP11 7HY

Krax *Andy Robson*, 63 Dixon Lane, Leeds LS12 4RR

Krino Glenrevagh, Corrandulla, Co. Galway, Eire

Label *Paul Beasley*, 57 Effingham Road, Lee Green, London SE12 8NT

Lines Review Macdonald Publishing, Edgefield Road, Loanhead, Midlothian EH20 9SY

Litmus *Laurie Smith*, The City Lit, Stukeley Street, Drury Lane, London WC2B 5ZJ

London Magazine (press/magazine) *Alan Ross*, 30 Thurloe Place, London SW7 2HQ

Longstone Magazine *A. J. Noctor*, 37 Lowtherville Road, Ventnor, Isle of Wight

Magazing *Chris Mitchell*, 6 Athole Gardens, Glasgow G12 9AY

Mar Flat 1, 81 Back Road East, St Ives, Cornwall

Margin *Robin Magowan*, 20 Brook Green, London W6 7BL

Momentum *Jeff Bell*, Glan Lynn, Glyn Ceiriog, Llangollen, Clwyd LL20 7AB

Network of Women Writers *Melissa Mitcheson-Lee*, 8 The Broadway, Woking, Surrey GU21 5AP

New Departures (press/magazine) *Mike Horovitz*, Piedmont, Bisley, Stroud, Gloucestershire GL6 7BU

New Hope International *Gerald England*, 23 Gambrel Bank Road, Ashton under Lyme OL6 8TW

New Welsh Review *Belinda Humfrey*, Dept of English, St David's University College, Lampeter SA48 7ED

Ninth Decade *Robert Vas Dias*, 108 Hemingford Road, London N1 1DE

The North (press/magazine) *Peter Sansom*, Floor 4, Byram Arcade, Westgate, Huddersfield HD1 1ND

North Magazine *John Hughes*, 10 Stranmillis Park, Belfast BT9 5AY

Numbers *John Alexander*, 6 Kingston Street, Cambridge CB1 2NU

Nutshell *Jeff Phelps*, 21 Vicarage Road, Kings Heath, Birmingham B14 7QA

Orbis *Mike Shields*, 199 The Long Shoot, Nuneaton, Warwickshire CV11 6JQ

Ore *Eric Ratcliffe*, 7 The Towers, Stevenage, Hertfordshire SG1 1HE

Ostinato PO Box 522, London N8 7SZ

Other Poetry *Evangeline Paterson*, 2 Stoneygate Avenue, Leicester

Otter Parford Cottage, Chegford, Newton Abbot, Devon

Outposts *Roland John*, 22 Whitewell Road, Frome, Somerset BA11 4EL

Oxford Poetry Magdalen College, Oxford OX1 4AU

Pages (press/magazine) *Robert Sheppard*, 15 Oakapple Road, Southwick, Sussex BN4 4YL

Paraphernalia *Harvey Doctors*, 41 Maynard Road, Walthamstow, London E17 9JE

Pennine Ink *J. McEvoy*, c/o MPAA, The Gallery Downstairs, Yorke Street, Burnley, Lancashire

Pennine Platform *Brian Merrikin Hill*, Ingmanthorpe Hall Farm Cottage, Wetherby, West Yorkshire LS22 5EQ

People to People West Midlands Arts, 82 Granville Street, Birmingham B1 2LH

Planet *Ned Thomas*, PO Box 44, Aberystwyth, Dyfed

PN Review (press/magazine) *Michael Schmidt*, 208–212 Corn Exchange Buildings, Manchester M4 3BQ

Poetry and Audience *Jonathan Ward*, School of English, University of Leeds, Leeds, West Yorkshire LS2 9JT

Poetry Durham *Michael O'Neill*, Dept of English, University of Durham, Elvet Riverside, New Elvet, Durham DH1 3JT

Poetry Express *David Orme*, Schools' Poetry Association, 27 Pennington Close, Colden Common, near Winchester, Hampshire SO21 1UR

Poetry Ireland Review *John Ennis*, 44 Upper Mount Street, Dublin 2, Eire

Poetry Nottingham *Howard Atkinson*, 21 Duncombe Close, Nottingham NG3 3PH

Poetry Review The Poetry Society, 21 Earl's Court Square, London SW5 9DE

Poetry Voice *George Robinson*, 32 Ridgemere Road, Pensby, Wirral L61 8RL

Poetry Wales *Mike Jenkins*, 26 Andrew's Close, Heolgerrig, Mid-Glamorgan CF48 1SS

Poets Voice (press/magazine) *Fred Beake*, 12 Dartmouth Avenue, Bath, Avon BA2 1AT

Promotion *Geoff Stevens*, 8 Beaconsview House, Charlemore Farm, West Bromwich B71 3PL

Prospice *J. C. R. Green*, PO Box 19, Buxton, Derbyshire SK17 6YD

Psychopoetica *Geoff Lowe*, Dept of Psychology, University of Hull, Hull HU6 7RX

Rhinoceros 121 Sondan Street, Belfast BT1 6LD

The Rialto *John Wakeman*, 32 Grosvenor Road, Norwich NR2 2PZ

Roads 49 Meynell Heights, Leeds LS11 9PY

RSVP 29 Calversyke Street, Keighley BD21 1PA

Salmon Literary Magazine Anborn House, Upper Fairhill, Galway, Eire

Scribble *Graham Kendall*, 28 Westwood Avenue, Timperley, Altrincham, Cheshire WA15 6QF

Slow Dancer (press/magazine) *John Harvey*, Flat 4, 1 Park Valley, Nottingham NG7 1BS

Smoke (press/magazine) *Dave Ward*, 38 Canning Street, Liverpool L8 7NP

Sol 44 Station Road, Rayleigh, Essex SS6 7HL

Spectacular Diseases *Paul Green*, 83B London Road, Peterborough, Cambridge PE2 9BS

Spokes *Micky Hendricks*, 7 Park Hill, Toddington, Dunstable, Bedfordshire LU5 6AW

Stand (press/magazine) *Jon Silkin*, 19 Haldane Terrace, Newcastle upon Tyne NE2 3AN

Staple Magazine *Don Measham*, c/o School of Humanities, Derbyshire College of Further Education, Matlock, Derbyshire DE4 3FW

Start *Paul Smith*, Burslem Leisure Centre, 24A Market Place, Burslem, Stoke on Trent

Strength Beyond Bingo *Jeremy Tattersall*, 112 Sandock Road, Lewisham, London SE13

Stride (press/magazine) *Rupert Loydell*, 37 Portland Street, Newtown, Exeter, Devon EX1 2EG

Success *Kate Dean*, 17 Andrew's Crescent, Peterborough PE1 6XL

Sunk Island Review 117 Newland Street West, Lincoln LN1 1QD

Super Trouper/The Big Mouse *Andrew Savage*, 77 Thompson Street, Padiham, Burnley, Lancashire BB12 7BG

Talus *Hanne Bramness*, c/o Dept of English, Kings College, The Strand, London WC2R 2LS

Tears in the Fence *David Caddy*, 38 Hod View, Stourpaine, near Blandford Forum, Dorset DT11 8TN

The Third Half/K.T. Publications *Kevin Troop*, 16 Fane Close, Stamford, Lincolnshire PE9 1HG

Thursdays (press/magazine) *John Denny*, 70 Poplar Road, Bearwood, Warley, West Midlands B66 4AN

Tops *Anthony Cooney*, The Old Police Station, 80 Lark Lane, Toxteth Park, Liverpool L17 8XH

Tremenos *Kathleen Raine*, 47 Paultons Square, London SW3 5DT

Verse St Hugh's College, Oxford OX2 6LE

Verse Dept of English Literature, University of Glasgow G12 8QQ

Vision *Louis Foley*, 32 Gilchrist Avenue, Corby, Northamptonshire NN17 1BA

Westwords *Dave Woolley*, 15 Trelawney Road, Peverell, Plymouth, Devon PL3 4JS

Weyfarers *Margaret Pain*, 9 Whiterose Lane, Woking, Surrey GU22 7JA

The White Rose Literary Magazine *Nancy Whybrow*, 14 Browning Road, Temple Hill, Dartford, Kent DA1 5ET

The Wide Skirt (press/magazine) *Geoff Hattersley*, 8 Belbeck Court, Chapeltown, Sheffield, Yorkshire

Words International *Jean Shelley*, Bird-in-Eye, Uckfield, East Sussex TN22 5HA

The Works *Christopher Mills*, 122 Clive Street, Grangetown, Cardiff CF1 7JE

Writers' Own Magazine (press/magazine) *Eileen M. Pickering*, 121 Highbury Grove, Clapham, Bedford MK41 6DU

Writing *Barbara Horsfall*, 87 Brookhouse Road, Farnborough, Hampshire GU14 0BU

Writing Women 10 Mistletoe Road, Newcastle upon Tyne NE2 2DX

Z *Victoria Hurst*, 6A Switzerland Terrace, Douglas, Isle of Man

Zenos *Danielle Hope*, 59B Ilkerston Road, Nottingham NG7 3GR

Zip *Darren Poyzer*, 8 West Drive, Tinwistle, nr Hyde, Cheshire

ZLR *Neil Cross*, 23 Netherfield Road, Sandiacre, Nottingham NG10 5LP

Organisations of Interest to Poets

Apples & Snakes Room 2, Peter Pan Block, 23 Ladywell Lodge, Slagrove Place, London SE13 7HT (Tel: 01–690 9368). Grand Ole Opry of performance poetry, now an independent promoter and booking agency for alternative, ethnic and cabaret poets. **Contacts** *Paul Beasley & Ruth Harrison*, spokespersons for the collective.

The Association of Little Presses Founded in 1966. Represents some 300 publishers and associates throughout Britain. Strong bias towards poetry and creative writing. ALP produces an annual *Catalogue of Small Press Books in Print*, a quarterly magazine *PALPI* (Poetry And Little Press Information), an ALP *Newsletter* of printing and distribution tips, and *Getting Your Poetry Published*, a pamphlet of basic advice. ALP regularly organises bookfairs and exhibitions around the country and offers an unrivalled service of advice by post and telephone. Memership at £7.50 p.a. is open to publisher and non-publisher alike. Poets can purchase ALP publications by writing (with s.a.e.) to *Bob Cobbing*, ALP President, 89A Petherton Road, London N5 2QT.

The Arvon Foundation Founded by Ted Hughes, John Moat and John Fairfax. Runs five-day residential courses for people of all ages over 17, where a chance is given to meet and work with practising writers. At present there are two rural centres – Totleigh Barton near Okehampton; Devon & Lumb Bank in the Pennines. There is a strong emphasis on poetry. Recent courses have been tutored by Alan Brownjohn, Anthony Thwaite, Liz Lochhead, Paul Hyland, James Lasdun, Jeni Couzyn, Fleur Adcock, and others. Fees are currently £145 p.w. with reductions available in many cases. The Arvon Poetry Competition, run at three-year intervals, is the biggest of its kind with a first prize of £5000. Details of this and other activities appear in the *Friends of Arvon* quarterly newsletter. Write to either Totleigh Barton, Sheepwash, Beaworthy, Devon EX21 5NS, or Lumb Bank, Hebden Bridge, West Yorkshire HX7 6DF.

The National Convention of Poets and Small Presses An accessible – some might say disorganised – weekend jamboree of writers and poetry publishers held at a different venue each year. The amateur status of the event is undisputed but it can be good fun for those with enough stamina to last out the marathon readings. There is no central organising committee – bids to host future conventions being made in person at the event itself. So far it has visited Liverpool, Hastings, Corby, Dartford and Stamford. For information on the 1990 Convention **contact** *Kevin Troop*, The Third Half, 16 Fane Close, Stamford, Lincolnshire PE9 1HG.

Oriel Bookshop The Friary, Cardiff. Owned and run by the Welsh Arts Council. Publishes at regular intervals *Small Presses and Little Magazines of the UK and Ireland – An Address List*; specialises in twentieth-century poetry; operates a mail-order service; runs a critical service for writers; hosts poetry readings; and provides information on local competitions, workshops, groups and literary activities.

The Poetry Association of Scotland Formerly the Scottish Association for the Speaking of Verse. Promotes poetry through readings and related activities from its headquarters at 38 Dovecot Road, Edinburgh EH12 7LE.

The Poetry Library Formerly run by the Arts Council, now part of the South Bank Centre, and is located in the Royal Festival Hall, Level 5, Red Side, London SE1 8XX (Tel: 01–921 0943/0921). The library has 45,000 English language titles representing, in democratic order, the vast majority of poets published since 1912. There is an information service and a collection of poetry on video and audio cassette, as well as a retail stock of current literary magazines. **Librarian** *Mary Enright*. Membership free.

Poetry Listing Compiled by David Hart. An irregular publication which attempts with admirable success to list and comment on the whole panoply of available contemporary English language poetry worldwide. The survey is total, not limiting itself to the recently published. The result is doubly useful. Copies cost £2.55 from Wood Wind Publications, 52 All Saints Road, Kings Heath, Birmingham B14 7LL.

Poetry London Newsletter A publication for and about poetry activity in the Capital. Quarterly, it surveys all current poetry groups, listing specialisms; provides bibliographies; runs articles on funding, how to start your own group, how to put on a reading, etc. Invaluable at £3.50 p.a. Write to 26 Clacton Road, London E17 8AR.

The Poetry Society National Poetry Centre, 21 Earl's Court Square, London SW5 9DE (Tel: 01–373 7861). Founded 1909, which ought to make it venerable. Centre of the poetry universe for some, a total anathema for others. The PoSoc is the poetry world's equivalent of Covent Garden, although you wouldn't think so to judge by the look of its five-storey Victorian premises. In the UK we value our verse far less than our orchestras – the Society has to scrape its way by. Nonetheless, it does sterling work. Current activities include:

- Weekly readings and workshops at the National Poetry Centre, and occasionally at other venues.
- A quarterly magazine of new verse, views and criticisms, *The Poetry Review*, ed. Peter Forbes, and supplemented by a members' information bulletin.
- The National Poetry Secretariat – a poets' booking agency which helps finance readings and literature festivals up and down the country.
- The Poets in Schools Scheme, sponsored by W.H. Smith, to encourage young poeple

to write and enjoy poetry.

- A critical service which provides detailed reports on submitted work. Current charges £23 per 200 lines (discount for members).
- A specialist poetry bookshop and mail-order service.
- Spoken poetry and prose examinations taken by 1000s of young people annually.
- Competitions and awards including the annual National Poetry Competition with a first prize of £1000 (See entry **Prizes** section).

Society President *Dannie Abse* **Chairman** *Sebastian Barker*. Membership £15 (London); £12 (elsewhere).

Quartos Magazine 'Bi-monthly writers' forum and competition news'. Subscription £8 from BCM–Writer, London WC1N 3XX. On the weak side as a forum, but the best single source of information on poetry competitions anywhere.

Regional Arts Associations Most are of invaluable interest to poets as a source of information on local activities, poetry groups, competitions, publications, readings and creative writing weekends. Many publish a magazine of their own, a number run critical services for writers. Some provide fellowships for poets, paying for school visits, or for poets' workshops to be established. Service varies from region to region depending on demand and the influence and interest of the local literature officer. For more information see **Regional Arts Associations** section towards the back of *The Writer's Handbook*.

Scottish Poetry Library Houses mainly 20th-century poetry written in Scotland. Loans are free, available in person or by post. The library has a mobile unit called *Poetry Travels* in the form of a converted Post Office van, and publishes a regular newsletter and an annual bibliography of new poetry in Scotland. Membership £7.50. Tweedale Court, 14 High Street, Edinburgh EH1 1TE.

Small Press Group of Britain Founded in 1988. Represents small publishing in its broadest terms to a wide audience via bookfairs, exhibitions and trade fairs. Publishes a regular newsletter *Small Press Monthly* and an excellent *Small Press Yearbook* packed with information on members, together with an A–Z of advice on small publishing. Copies are available from the group at £6.69. Poetry has a fair coverage without being a central activity. More information from SPG, Andrew Hopton, Secretary, Counter Productions, 308C Camberwell New Road, London SE5 0RQ (Tel: 01–274 9009).

Yorkshire Federation of Small Presses Founded in 1984. Aims to provide a grassroots platform for writers with innovative ideas, especially those experiencing difficulty with commercial markets. The group is an amalgam of some two dozen presses and magazines, nearly all of whom publish poetry. Descriptive catalogue available from Richard Mason, Promotions and Distribution Officer, Flat 7, 4 Chestnut Avenue, Leeds LS6 1BA.

The Economics of Packaging

The packager deals in bestsellers. Having come up with an idea, typically a highly illustrated work of general reference such as *How to Care for Your Pets* or *The Wonderland of Knowledge,* he commissions a designer to show him how his book might look on a display shelf. If he likes what he sees he will invest a few hundred, or maybe a few thousand pounds on a visual representation of his idea, and set off on a selling tour of publishers at home and abroad. He needs at least one of them to add commercial muscle to his scheme: some money in advance, enough to keep the printer happy, and a commitment to buy a minimum number of copies for selling on to the trade. It is only when the deal is struck between packager and publisher that the editorial headhunting begins and writers are hired.

Warnings against packagers are loud and frequent. Financial insecurity, it is said, is endemic to businesses which operate on such narrow margins. But while it is undeniable that most packagers have fewer resources than publishers – why else would they be packagers? – there is no reason why they should not be run profitably. It is all a question of managing a tightly organised team of equals. What the writer must decide, once he has established that he is dealing with a packager of good repute, is whether he can work to order, suppressing individuality (normally the writer's strongest suit) to the needs of a genuinely cooperative venture.

Since deadlines are sacrosanct – if the packager cannot supply copies to the publisher by the contract date he is in deep financial trouble – the writer must be able to deliver copy as and when requested. Eight hundred words next Wednesday means just that. Seven hundred and fifty words on Friday will not do. But the writer is no mere lackey. The packager who cares about the quality of his product will involve the writer in every stage of the creative process. This can mean attending a lot of meetings where illustrations are chosen and layout discussed.

The rewards for the job are variable but average out at about £100 a thousand words. Much less than this suggests that the packager is being screwed too tightly by his publisher client, or that he is trying it on.

Where packagers are often misjudged is on their preference for paying a flat fee, or a combination of fee and a small royalty. A flat fee agreement makes sense when there are several contributors to a book. It may seem to offer less than a royalty deal with a conventional publisher but the comparison is not really a fair one. For a start, a publisher's royalty is a percentage of shop price, whereas the packager's royalty is based on the price per copy he gets from the publisher, a quarter or less of the retail price.

Another factor worth considering is the speed of payment. Fees are settled soon after delivery of copy; with royalties a writer may have to wait up to two years before receiving his due. This point takes on added significance when the writer has to work intensively to produce a substantial number of words. A fee payment of several thousand pounds is a great consolation for a hard slog.

The only proviso is that copyright should not be surrendered. In other words, a flat fee should be related to the sale of a certain number of copies of the book. Otherwise, years later, the writer can feel a sense of injustice when his words, modified and updated perhaps, but still *his* words, are bringing in income for packager and publisher but not for him. Contributors to the partwork magazines of the sixties and seventies, most of which continue to sell in packaged book form, are among those who lament their disregard for subsidiary rights.

At the same time, the advantages of flat fees, properly negotiated, are coming to be recognised in other areas of publishing, notably where advances are modest. Education writers in particular see the virtue of short cutting their invariably lengthy journey from completed manuscript to publication to first royalty cheque. The author who can persuade a publisher to put up a large sum of money just for his signature on a contract may be more favourably inclined towards royalties. But he is still a rarity.

UK Packagers

The Albion Press Ltd

P.O. Box 52, Princes Risborough, Aylesbury, Bucks HP17 9PR
☎ 084444018 Fax 084443358

Chairman/Managing Director *Emma Bradford*

FOUNDED 1984 to produce high quality illustrated titles. Client publishers in the UK include **Collins, Bloomsbury Publishing, Cassell, Macdonald, Michael Joseph, Heinemann.** Commissions illustrated trade titles, particularly English literature, social history, art, cookery, children's. 8 titles in 1988.
TITLES *Wessex Heights* Thomas Hardy; *The Art of the Picnic* Pamela Kay; *Step by Step* series, Diane Wilmer and Nicola Smee. Unsolicited synopses and ideas for books not generally welcome.
Royalties paid and fees paid for introductions and partial contributions.

Alphabet & Image Ltd

Alpha House, South Street, Sherborne, Dorset
☎ 0935 814944 Fax 0935 816717

Chairman/Managing Director *Anthony Birks-Hay*
Approx Annual Turnover £150,000

FORMED 1968. Founded Alpha Books imprint which was subsequently sold to A. & C. Black in 1987, following which Mr Birks-Hay resumed his book packaging activities in 1989. *Commissions* horticulture, horology, architecture, ceramics. 6 titles in 1988.

Editorial Head *Leslie Birks-Hay* Welcome unsolicited synopses and ideas for books.
Royalties paid twice yearly, or flat fee in lieu of royalties.

Amanuensis Books Ltd

12 Station Road, Didcot, Oxon OX11 7LL
☎ 0235 811066 Fax 0235 510134

Chairman *Kit Maunsell*
Managing Director *Loraine Fergusson*
Approx Annual Turnover £250,000

FOUNDED 1986. Commissions children's, crafts, medicine for the layperson, sport, travel. 18 titles planned for 1988. Co-editions sold in the US, Finland and Holland.

Editorial Head *Lynne Gregory* TITLES *Sports Injuries Handbook; Handtinting Photographs; China Journey; Childhood Illnesses Handbook.* Unsolicited synopses and ideas for books welcome.
Royalties paid twice yearly. Fees also paid on occasions, depending on contract.

AS Publishing

89 Woodstock Avenue, London NW11 9RH
☎ 01–458 3552

Managing Director *Angela Sheehan*

FOUNDED 1987. Commissions children's illustrated non-fiction. Do not welcome unsolicited synopses and ideas for books. Fees paid.

Autumn Publishing Ltd

10 Eastgate Square, Chichester, West Sussex PO19 1JH
☎ 0243 783587 Fax 0243 774433

Managing Director *Campbell Goldsmid*

FOUNDED 1976. Highly illustrated non-fiction: mainly children's, some cookery and books with a sporting slant. 10 titles in 1988.

Editorial Director *Ingrid Goldsmid* TITLES *365 Questions & Answers; My Book of Animals; Some Facts & Records.* Unsolicited synopses and ideas for books welcome if they come within relevant subject areas.
Usually pay a flat fee.

Beanstalk Books Ltd

The Gardens House, Hever Castle Gardens, near Edenbridge, Kent TN8 7ND
☎ 0892 870912
Telex 957320 TELEXUS G Fax 0732 863550

Directors *Shona McKellar, Penny Kitchenham*

FOUNDED 1983. Beanstalk Books work in three main areas: for publishers, for own brand retailers, and for commercial firms who want a book geared up to their own company and marketing. Commissions adult highly illustrated non-fiction and children's illustrated fiction and non-fiction. 10 titles in 1988. Welcome unsolicited synopses and ideas for books, particularly adult fine arts and travel. Also children's activity books, novelties, poetry and very interested in seeing writers and artists from ethnic minorities and third world countries.
Royalties paid twice yearly and/or fees.

Belitha Press Ltd

31 Newington Green, London N16 9PU
☏ 01–241 5566 Fax 01–254 5325

Chairman/Managing Director *Martin Pick*

FOUNDED 1980. Books packaged for **Franklin Watts, Methuen, Macdonald, André Deutsch, Hamish Hamilton** and **Collins.** Belitha have a joint venture with Collins which now has 60 books in its backlist. Now publishing independently with their own educational selling operation. Strong natural history/environmental interests. Commissions mostly children's books with occasional general books. 23 titles in 1988. TITLES (Packaged) *People of the Bible* (24 titles); *Great Tales from Long Ago* (25 titles); *Animals in the Wild* (16 titles); *Animal Habitats* (16 titles); *Let's Read Together* (8 titles) *Toppers* (6 titles); *Growing Up.*

IMPRINT
Belitha/Collins TITLES *Now I can Write/Spell/Count; Getting on with Writing/Spelling/Counting; Let's Draw; Match Them; Match and Sort.* **Belitha** 1989 TITLES *Today I am* SERIES; *Old Tree Stories; Animal Activities; Secret World; Belitha Information Library; Belitha Activity Atlas.*
No unsolicited mss. Welcome unsolicited synopses and ideas for books from experienced children's writers.

Bison Books Ltd

Kimbolton House, 117A Fulham Road,
London SW3 6RL
☏ 01–823 9222
Telex 888014 Fax 01–244 7139

Chairman *S. L. Mayer*

Part of Bison Group, Connecticut, USA; 'the world's largest book packager'. *Publishes* large format, illustrated books on art, cookery, history, militaria, transport and travel. 67 new titles and about 200 reprint and foreign editions.

Editorial Head *Jane Laslett* TITLES (History) *History of the World; Rise & Fall of the Third Reich,* William L. Shirer; (Transport) *Encyclopaedia of Sports Cars;* (Art) *Picasso, and Masterpieces of American Painting,* Leonard Everett Fisher. Unsolicited mss not welcome. The vast majority of titles originate by commission but synopses/ideas are considered.
Royalties by arrangement.

BLA Publishing Ltd

T. R. House, 1 Christopher Road, East Grinstead, West Sussex RH19 3BT
☏ 0342 313844
Telex 94011210 BLAP G Fax 0342 410471

Owner *Ling Kee,* Hong Kong

Editorial Director/Chief Operating Officer *Martin F. Marix Evans*

Commissions multi-volume encyclopedias for younger readers; information book series on various topics including science and natural history for primary school children. 40–50 titles annually. TITLES *Into Science* **(Oxford University Press)**

DIVISION
Thames Head Illustrated general non-fiction. TITLES *The Frampton Flora; War at Sea.* Will consider unsolicited synopses and ideas for books if they have good translation potential.
Payment varies according to contract (reference books tend to be flat fees; royalties for single author or illustrator).

Breslich & Foss

Golden House, 28–31 Great Pulteney Street,
London W1R 3DD
☏ 01–734 0706
Telex 264188 Bresl G Fax 01–494 0854

Director *Paula Breslich*
Approx Annual Turnover £750,000

Packagers of a wide variety of non-fiction subjects including art, children's, crafts, gardening, sport and health. Unsolicited mss welcome although synopses preferred. Always include s.a.e. with submissions.
Royalties paid twice yearly.

Brown Wells and Jacobs Ltd

2 Vermont Road, London SE19 3SR
☎ 01–653 7670
Telex 21685 FOTOGR Fax 01–771 1765

Managing Director *Graham Brown*

FOUNDED 1979. Commissions non-fiction, novelty, pre-school, natural history, science, first readers, character licence. 55 titles in 1988. Unsolicited synopses and ideas for books welcome.
Fees paid.

John Calmann & King Ltd

71 Great Russell Street, London WC1B 3BN
☎ 01–831 6351
Telex 29846 OWLS G Fax 01–831 8356

Chairman *Marianne Calmann*
Managing Director *Laurence King*
Approx Annual Turnover £2 million

FOUNDED 1976. Commissions books on art, design and nature. 18 titles in 1988. Unsolicited synopses and ideas for books welcome.
Royalties paid twice yearly.

Cameron Books (Production) Ltd

2A Roman Way, London N7 8XG

Directors *Ian A. Cameron, Jill Hollis*
Approx Annual Turnover £350,000

Commissions natural history, social history, decorative arts, fine arts, collectors' reference, gardening, cookery, conservation, film, design. About 6 titles a year. Welcome unsolicited synopses and ideas for books.
Payment varies with each contract. 'Sometimes royalties; sometimes percentage of receipts from publishers'.

Chancerel Publishers Ltd

40 Tavistock Street, London WC2E 7PB
☎ 01–240 2811
Telex 265871 Ref. SJJ130 Fax 01–836 4186

Managing Director *W. D. B. Prowse*

FOUNDED 1976. Commissions educational books. 10 titles in 1988. Welcomes unsolicited synopses and ideas for books, particularly language teaching materials.
Payment generally by flat fee but royalties sometimes.

Philip Clark Ltd

53 Carlton Avenue, Dulwich, London SE21 7DF
☎ 01–693 5605
Telex 8813433 MARINE G Fax 01–737 7881

Managing Director *Philip Clark*

Changed its name from Holland & Clark in 1988. A founder member of the Book Packagers Association. Philip Clark's first title, *The Industrial Heritage of Britain,* was published by **Ebury Press** in 1982. Since then the company has produced heavily illustrated books on a variety of subjects for some thirty publishers in the UK and overseas. Among its most successful ventures is *the Complete Guide to Windsurfing* (**Unwin Hyman**), which sold over 100,000 copies worldwide. Lead TITLES for 1989 include *France/Germany/Italy/Spain* in the *Travellers' Wine Guide* series. Unsolicited synopses and ideas for books, particularly on international subjects, welcome.
Fees paid.

Creative Comics

80 Silverdale, Sydenham, London SE26 4SJ
☎ 01–699 7725

Proprietor *Denis Gifford*

Specialises in children's comic strips and produce custom-made single strips or complete comics, cartoon booklets, paperbacks, etc., especially promotional and giveaway comics. Past projects include a weekly comic supplement in *Reveille* and a full colour comic for National Savings. No unsolicited material. Have 100 freelance cartoonists on their books.

Curtis Garratt Ltd

The Old Vicarage, Horton cum Studley, Oxon OX9 1BT
☎ 086735 536 Fax 086735 8844

Directors *Neil Curtis* (Editorial), *Richard Garratt* (Design)

FOUNDED 1983. General illustrated non-fiction trade books. 20 titles in 1988.
TITLES *Walking through History* **(Queen Anne Press);** *Oldhams Animal World* (Odhams Leisure Group). Will consider synopses and ideas for books though most of the works stems from their own ideas or from publishers.
Payments both royalties and fees.

Diagram Visual Information Ltd

195 Kentish Town Road, London NW5 8SY
☏ 01–482 3633 Fax 01–482 4932

Managing Director *Bruce Robertson*

FOUNDED 1967. Library, school, academic and trade reference books. 18 titles in 1988. Welcome unsolicited synopses and ideas for books without obligation to pay for sample material.
Fees paid.

Eddison Sadd Editions

St Chad's Court, 146B Kings Cross Road, London WC1X 9DH
☏ 01–837 1968
Telex 929879 Fax 01–837 2025

Managing Director *Nick Eddison*
Editorial Director *Ian Jackson*
Approx Annual Turnover £1.4 million

FOUNDED in 1982, Eddison Sadd now produces a wide range of popular illustrated non-fiction titles for an ever-increasing range of publishers around the world, with books published in 25 countries. Ideas and synopses are welcomed but must have international appeal. Catalogue available on request.
Royalties paid twice yearly; flat fees paid when appropriate.

Equinox (Oxford) Ltd

Musterlin House, Jordan Hill Road, Oxford OX2 8DP
☏ 0865 310665
Telex 83308 Fax 0865 310662

Chairman *G. J. Riches*
Managing Director *B. T. Lenthall*
Approx Annual Turnover £3.5 million

FOUNDED 1981. Sister company to **Phaidon Press.** Part of the Musterlin Group plc. Commissions international illustrated reference, single volumes and series. 10 titles in 1988.

Editorial Directors *Lawrence Clarke, Graham Bateman* TITLES *World of Science; Encyclopedia of Animals; Encyclopedia of Geography; Encyclopedia of the 20th Century;* cultural atlases, and *Junior Series,* including science, history and animals. Recommend letter in the first instance.
Royalties paid annually. Fees paid in addition to or instead of royalties.

Facer Publishing Ltd

7–9 Colleton Crescent, Exeter, Devon EX2 4DG
☏ 0392 50188 Fax 0392 420128

Chairman *Nick Facer*

FOUNDED 1983 by Nick Facer as a Book Production Consultancy. Began packaging in 1986 with *Judo* for **Guinness Books,** followed by *Modern Gym Fitness.* In 1987 was awarded contract to publish annually *The Official Football League Yearbook.* This was followed by *The European Football Yearbook* in 1988 with second edition in 1989. General leisure interest and sport. 5 titles in 1989. Still offer a comprehensive book production consultancy for writers, with computerised estimations, scheduling and cost control. CLIENTS include Webb & Bower.

Editorial Director *Rob Kendrew* TITLES *Flywheel; Self Defence.* Unsolicited synopses and ideas for books welcome.
Royalties paid twice yearly. Fees paid in addition to royalties.

Sadie Fields Productions Ltd

8 Pembridge Studios, 27A Pembridge Villas, London W11 3EP
☏ 01–221 3355
Telex 262284 Ref 1255 Fax 01–229 9651

Directors *David Fielder, Sheri Safran*
Approx Annual Turnover £1 million

FOUNDED 1981. Quality children's books. Conceive, design and produce pop-ups, three-dimensional, novelty, picture and board books. Several books have won awards in the UK and USA. Concentrate on books with international co-edition potential. About 20 titles a year. Approach with preliminary letter and sample material in the first instance.
Royalties based on a per copy sold rate and paid in stages.

Gaia Books Ltd

12 Trundle Street, London SE1 1QT
☏ 01–407 9003
Telex 914074 Fax 01–378 0258

Managing Director *Joss Pearson*

FOUNDED 1983. Natural living, health and ecology. 4 titles in 1988.
TITLES *Book of Massage; The Gaia Atlas of Planet Management.* No unsolicited mss, but outlines

accepted. Most projects conceived in-house.
Royalties paid.

Hamilton House

17 Staveley Way, Brixworth Industrial Estate, Northampton NN6 9EL
☎ 0604 881889 Fax 0604 880735

Managing Partner *Tony Attwood*
Approx Annual Turnover £350,000

FOUNDED 1979. Often works in collaboration with inexperienced authors, repackaging material, clearing copyright, etc., before selling the infant product on. *Publishes* business, employment, careers. Also book packagers for educational (secondary school), TV and radio tie-ins, directory and diary titles. 10 titles in 1988. Letter first. Mss should enclose s.a.e. Synopses and ideas for books also considered if accompanied by s.a.e.
Royalties paid annually.

Ilex Publishers Ltd

29–31 George Street, Oxford OX1 2AJ
☎ 0865 723148
Telex 837709 ILEX G Fax 0865 791267

Managing Director *Peter Sackett*

FOUNDED 1986. Highly illustrated colour information books for children and adults covering the whole information spectrum. 20 titles in 1988. TITLES *Children's Animal Atlas* **(Macmillan);** *Daily Telegraph Atlas of the World Today; Atlas of World Issues, Atlas of Environmental Issues* **(Oxford University Press).** No unsolicited material. All ideas are generated in-house.
Payment Outright fee or fee plus 5%–10% royalty against gross profit.

Johnson Editions Ltd

15 Grafton Square, London SW4 0DQ
☎ 01–622 1720 Fax 01–720 9114

Managing Director *Lorraine Johnson*
Approx Annual Turnover £350,000

Commissions practical and art-related books on fashion, gardening, interior design, architecture, cookery. 6 titles in 1988.

Knitwear *Louisa McDonnell;* **Interior Design** *Gabrielle Townsend;* **Gardening** *Georgina Harding* TITLES *A Table in Tuscany; A Table in Provence.* Unsolicited synopses and ideas for books welcome.
Royalties paid 'as agreed'. Fees paid in addition to or instead of royalties.

Justin Knowles Publishing Group

9 Colleton Crescent, Exeter EX2 4BY
☎ 0392 55467
Telex 42833 JKPUB G Fax 0392 420032

Managing Director *Justin Knowles*

Commissions highly illustrated non-fiction, including Disney books, gardening, knitting, collectables. Unsolicited synopses and ideas for books welcome.
Payment both fees and royalties paid (by arrangement).

Lexus Ltd

181 Pitt Street, Glasgow G2 4DR
☎ 041–221 5266
Telex 777308 Fax 041–226 3139

Managing Director *P. M. Terrell*

FOUNDED 1980. Language reference, bi-lingual books. 20 titles in 1988.

Editorial Director *P. M. Terrell* TITLES *Collins Italian Concise Dictionary; Harrap Study Aids; Hugo's Phrase Books; Hamlyn Phrase Books.* No unsolicited material. Books are mostly commissioned.
Flat fee paid.

Frances Lincoln Ltd

Apollo Works, 5 Charlton Kings Road, London NW5 2SB
☎ 01–482 3302
Telex 21376 Fax 01–485 0490

Managing Director *Frances Lincoln*

FOUNDED 1977. Commissions highly illustrated books on gardening, craft, interiors and health, as well as children's books. 21 titles in 1988.

Editorial Directors *Erica Hunningher* (Adult non-fiction), *Janetta Otter Barry* (Children's) TITLES *Garden Style* Penelope Hobhouse; *Bellamy's Changing World* David Bellamy; *Foliage Garden* John Kelly; *100 First Words* Edwina Riddell. Will consider synopses and ideas for books.
Royalties paid twice yearly.

Lionheart Books

10 Chelmsford Square, London NW10 3AR
☎ 01–459 0453

Senior Partner *Lionel Bender*

Approx Annual Turnover £150,000

A design/editorial packaging team that has been in successful operation for four years. Clients include most of the major children's books publishers. 'Packages' include titles conceived by the partnership and commissioned work from publishers. Highly illustrated non-fiction for children aged 8–14, mostly natural history and general science. 18 titles in 1988. Senior partner, Lionel Bender, is a writer of children's science books, with 25 titles to date. Welcomes unsolicited synopses and ideas only if conceived as illustrated works within special subject areas.
Normally flat fees paid; additional royalties negotiable.

Market House Books Ltd

2 Market House, Market Square, Aylesbury, Bucks HP20 1TN
☎ 0296 84911 Fax 0296 437073

Managing Director *Dr Alan Isaacs*

FOUNDED (as Laurence Urdang Associates) in 1970. Dictionaries, encyclopedias and reference. 15 titles in 1988.

Editorial Director *Dr John Daintith* TITLES *The Collins English Dictionary; The Macmillan Encyclopedia; Encyclopedia of the Renaissance; Concise Medical Dictionary, Concise Science Dictionary* (**Oxford University Press**). Unsolicited material not welcome as most books compiled in-house.
Fees paid.

Marshall Cavendish Books Ltd

58 Old Compton Street, London W1V 5PA
☎ 01–734 6710 Fax 01–734 6221

Chairman *Frank Yung* (Singapore)
Approx Annual Turnover £10 million

Part of the Marshall Cavendish Group of companies founded in 1968, primarily to exploit partwork material in book form; now, however, said to originate about 60% of their material. *Commissions* illustrated non-fiction. Approx. 100 titles in 1988. Welcome unsolicited synopses and ideas for books.
Fees paid, not royalties.

Marshall Editions Ltd

170 Piccadilly, London W1V 9DD
☎ 01–629 0079
Telex 22847 Fax 01–834 0785

Managing Director *Bruce Marshall*

FOUNDED 1977. Non-fiction subjects including thematic atlases, leisure interests, self-improvement. 8 titles in 1988.

Manager Editor *Ruth Binney* TITLES *The Atlas of Mysterious Places; The 35mm Photographer's Handbook; Contemporary Atlas of China.*

Merehurst Ltd

Ferry House, 51–7 Lacy Road, Putney, London SW15 1PR
☎ 01–780 1177
Telex 296616 Fax 01–780 1714

Managing Director *Carole Saunders*

Commissions books on cake decorating, cookery, travel, crafts and hobbies, pet care and aviculture, natural history, graphic arts and business.

MM Productions Ltd

8B East Street, Ware, Herts SG12 9HJ
☎ 0920 466003
Telex 818369 WORDS G Fax 0920 462267

Chairman/Managing Director *Mike Moran*
Approx Annual Turnover £1.5 million

Started as a packager for publishers seven years ago, now also in mainstream publishing. Fiction, educational, technical & scientific, medical, naval & military, dictionaries, art & architecture, children's, sports, games, pastimes, travel & adventure, directories & guide books. Electronic (database) publishing. 12 titles in 1988. Unsolicited synopses and ideas for books welcome.
Fees paid to authors in addition to royalties which are paid twice yearly.

Neil & Ting Morris

27 Riverview Grove, London W4 3QL
☎ 01–994 1874

Partners *Neil Morris, Ting Morris*

FOUNDED 1979. Mainly children's fiction and non-fiction. 20 titles in 1988. No unsolicited mss but interested in seeing examples of illustrators' work.
Royalties usually paid.

Phoebe Phillips Editions

6 Berners Mews, London W1P 3DG
☎ 01–637 1673/7933 Fax 01–436 4819
Telex 912881 Telex G (Attn PPE)

Managing Director *Phoebe Phillips*

Approx Annual Turnover £900,000

FOUNDED 1982. Commissions medieval history, gardening, cookery, crafts, decorative arts, illustrated poetry. Publishers include **Weidenfeld & Nicolson, Collins, Thames & Hudson, Bantam, Century Hutchinson, Boydell & Brewer.** Are expanding operations in 1989. 10 titles in 1988. Welcome unsolicited synopses and ideas for books.
Payment both fees and royalties paid (by arrangement).

Playne Books

New Inn Lane, Avening, Tetbury,
Gloucestershire GL8 8NB
☎ 0453 835155 Fax 0453 835590

Chairman *David Playne*

FOUNDED 1987 as a sister company to Playne Design and Playne Photographic to look after the book packaging and commercial book side of the business. Commissions highly illustrated books on any subject and practical books. 4 titles in 1988.
TITLES *Battlefields of Northern France and the Low Countries.* Welcome unsolicited synopses and ideas for books.
Royalties paid 'on payment from publishers'. Fees sometimes paid instead of royalties.

Mathew Price Ltd

Old Rectory House, Marston Magna, Yeovil,
Somerset BA22 8DT
☎ 0935 851158
Telex 46720 MPRICE G Fax 0935 851285

Chairman/Managing Director *Mathew Price*
Approx Annual Turnover £700,000

Commissions high quality, full colour picture books, fiction for young children, novelty books and non-fiction. 15 titles in 1988. Unsolicited synopses and ideas for books welcome.
Fees sometimes paid instead of royalties.

Quarto Publishing plc

The Old Brewery, 6 Blundell Street,
London N7 9BH
☎ 01–700 6700
Telex 298844 Fax 01–700 4191

Chairman *Laurence Orbach*
Approx Annual Turnover £12 million

FOUNDED 1976 and now Britain's largest book packaging company. Since 1986, Quarto has also published under the **Apple** imprint. USM flotation in 1986. Also magazine publishers since 1987. Illustrated non-fiction, including painting, graphic design, visual arts, history, cookery, gardening, crafts. 90 titles in 1988 published under the Apple imprint and packaged for other publishers. Unsolicited synopses and ideas for books welcome.
Payment flat fees paid.

Roxby Press Ltd

126 Victoria Rise, London SW4 0NW
☎ 01–720 8872
Telex 2918929 TLXG Fax 01–622 9528

Chairman/Managing Director *Hugh Elwes*
Approx Annual Turnover £1 million

FOUNDED 1974. Part of Roxby & Lindsey Holdings Ltd. Commissions illustrated non-fiction titles for international co-edition market. 6 titles in 1988. Unsolicited synopses and ideas for books welcome 'provided the author is prepared to work with the editors to prepare any material submitted for the international markets'.
Royalties paid annually. Fees paid only for books with many different contributors.

Sackville Design Group Ltd/ Sackville Books

Hales Barn, Stradbroke, Suffolk
☎ 0379 848213 Fax 0379 84797

Managing Director *A. F. Rockall*

FOUNDED 1973. Highly illustrated books in the fields of home, leisure and sports. About 20 titles a year.

Editorial Director *Philippa Algeo* TITLES *Improve Your Sports* series for **Collins.** No unsolicited mss. Will consider synopses and ideas for books if they come within their subject area.
Fees usually paid rather than royalties.

Savitri Books Ltd

Southbank House, Suite 106, Black Prince Road,
London SE1 7SJ
☎ 01–587 1590
Telex 295555 Fax 01–735 1555

Managing Director *Mrinalini S. Srivastava*
Approx Annual Turnover £200,000

FOUNDED 1983. Consider it important to work 'very closely with authors/illustrators and try to establish long-term relationships with them, and doing more books with the same team of people.' Commissions books on nature, natural

history and craft. Any subject which comes under the heading of 'high quality illustrated non-fiction'. 4 titles in 1988. Unsolicited synopses and ideas for books 'very welcome'.
Royalties between 10–15% of the total price paid by the publisher. 'Rarely work on a flat fee basis except in the case of some books for which the text would be compiled in-house and an illustrator was commissioned to do a series of pictures. In such a case, and should the illustrator's contribution to the book have been of great importance, a small royalty may be paid on subsequent editions.'

Sceptre Books

Time–Life Building, New Bond Street, London W1Y OAA
☏ 01–499 4080 Fax 01–499 9377

Managing Director *David Owen*

FOUNDED 1976. Wholly owned by Time-Life. High-quality illustrated books. Non-fiction only. TITLES *The Family Book of Games; National Parks.* No unsolicited mss. Will consider synopses and ideas for books.
Royalties or fees paid according to contract.

Sheldrake Press Ltd

188 Cavendish Road, London SW12 0DA
☏ 01–675 1767 Fax 01–675 7736

Managing Director *Simon Rigge*
Approx Annual Turnover £600,000

Controlling company is Sheldrake Publishing. Commissions illustrated non-fiction: cookery, travel, style, and history of technology. 9 titles in 1988. Unsolicited synopses and ideas for books welcome.
Fees paid.

Swallow Books

260 Pentonville Road, London N1 9JY
☏ 01–278 1483
Telex 8954111 Fax 01–278 7277

Managing Director *Michael Edwards*
Approx Annual Turnover £1 million

Majority share owned by Imago Group. Started trading in 1981. Steady growth since then as packagers of international co-editions. Commissions illustrated non-fiction. 25 titles in 1988.

Editorial Head *Stephen Adamson* TITLES *Garden Trees Handbook; At Home with Flowers; Art Class; Natural History of China; Shell Guide to Ireland.* Unsolicited synopses and ideas for books welcome.
Royalties paid annually. Fees paid in addition to royalties.

Victoria House Publishing Ltd

4 North Parade, Bath BA1 1QF
☏ 0225 463401 Fax 0225 460942

Managing Director *David Bailey*
Approx Annual Turnover £4 million

Part of Joshua Morris Publishing Inc., Connecticut, USA. *Commissions* children's novelty, pop-up, jigsaw books, plastic bath books. 200 titles in 1988.
Royalties or flat fee according to contract.

The Literary Agent

Friend or Foe?

Agents come in all shapes and sizes. Sadly, it is impossible to judge them by their appearance though plenty of authors are prepared to try.

'How did I choose my agent? Well, he looked a decent enough sort of chap.' Pause. 'At the time.'

The punch line is worth waiting for. One writer's mistake is another writer's warning signal. In fact, this is the only reliable way of finding an agent, by quizzing other authors and by learning from their experiences.

To help in the interrogation, a valuable plus and minus check list comes from William Armstrong, managing director of **Sidgwick & Jackson**, in a recent speech to **The Writers' Guild**.

First the minus points. Avoid the agent who:

1. Puts short term interests first, such as going for a large advance. A lot of money up front need not be in the best interests of the author, who may do better with a publisher who puts more emphasis on, say, long-term promotion and marketing. But a big advance is attractive to the type of agent who thinks solely of making his return on a deal as quickly as possible.
2. Takes the line of least resistance – grabbing the first offer that comes along. At least the deal is consummated – but is it the best deal?
3. Indulges in cronyism. It is easier and more pleasurable for a literary agent to sell to his friends, but is this in the best interest of the author?
4. Shows signs of laziness, such as not bothering to read the author's manuscript, or not reading it with sufficient attention. The author can benefit from the advice of a literary agent before – and after – the completion of the book: maybe in defending the book against the publisher's intemperate or ill-informed judgement or persuading the author to accept the publisher's wise council.
5. Washes his hands of a book once it has been delivered and paid for. There may be disputes with publishers about emphasis, technique or quality of the manuscript, or the best method of publishing it, and a third opinion is useful and often influential.

Now the plus points:

1. Help in submission. A good agent knows where to submit a book and knows the points which will appeal to a particular publisher. A publisher will always give special consideration to a book coming from a good agent.
2. Terms. A good agent knows what the market will bear, and the best terms that can be extracted.
3. Consultation. The good agent should be available for author consultation, on

short-term problems and long-term perspectives. He should read the book and be able to give an objective and convincing opinion on it.

4. Creativity. The good agent should be in contact with publishers, seeing if any of the publisher's ideas can be 'married' to his authors.
5. Watching brief. A reputable agent is often an insurance policy for the publisher's good behaviour. There are certainly knaves and fools among the ranks of publishers. If they know that a powerful agent is observing their activities, they may curb their knavery and foolery. A good agent will be watching the publishing process very closely and should not hesitate to challenge or encourage the publisher to do better on behalf of his author.

First Moves

Having decided on a likely prospect, the best approach to an agent is to send an example of work in hand with a background letter and samples of published material. As with any business correspondence which calls for a personal response, it is bad practice to send out a duplicated letter to all and sundry. It is a strict rule of the agency business that round robins plummet straight into the waste bin.

When submitting a completed manuscript, state openly if any publishers have already turned it down. Make sure you direct your sales pitch at an agent who covers your area of interest. Some agencies do not deal directly with plays or television scripts, for example, though they may well have outside associates who handle this side of the business.

Most agents do not charge reading fees but a writer who sends a stamped addressed envelope with his material will be off to a good start. It has been argued, by writers as well as agents, that a reading fee is a guarantee of serious intent; that if an agent is paid to assess the value of a manuscript, he is bound to give it professional attention. Sadly, this is not necessarily the case. While there are respectable agents who deserve a reading fee, they are outnumbered by the charlatans who take the money and run.

Do not be disappointed if an agent, or even several agents, turn you down. All writing is in the realm of value judgement. Where one agent fails to see talent, another may be more perceptive. The best advice is to keep trying.

When you do strike lucky, the first priority is to arrive at a clear understanding as to the scope of your mutual commitment. Do you want your agent to handle all freelance work including, for example, journalism, personal appearances on radio and television, and lecturing – or just plays and scripts – or just books? Are you prepared to let the agent take a percentage of all earnings including those he does not negotiate? This is a touchy subject. Some writers think of their agency as an employment exchange. Any work they find themselves should not be subject to commission. But this is to assume a clear dividing line between what the agent does and what the writer achieves on his own account. In reality the distinction is not always apparent.

Understanding the market, what subjects are needed, by whom, in what form and in which media is all part of an agent's job. Once he knows what you can do, he is able to promote your talents to the people most likely to want to buy. Eventually, when your reputation is established, offers will come out of the blue – an invitation to write for a newspaper, say, or an editing job or a chance to present a television programme. It is at this point that the writer is tempted to bypass his agent. 'Why should I pay him, he didn't get me the work?' But the chances are he did, by making you into a saleable property in the first place.

An agent negotiates contracts, often a fiddly and worrying business if handled without professional advice, and secures the best possible financial terms. Writers are generally inhibited when it comes to arguing money. It is a brave man who can say 'This is the figure I want because this is what I believe I am worth'. But an agent who has the full range of market rates at his fingertips, can more easily assert the incomparable talents of his client and press for a reward that is commensurate with his ability. Moreover, when it is time for money to be paid to the writer, the agent is usually in the best position to put the squeeze on recalcitrant bookkeepers.

A growth area of agents' responsibility is the sale of subsidiary rights. These can include paperback and serial rights; TV, film and radio adaptations; US and other overseas rights outside the publisher's declared market and translation rights. A book does not have to be a bestseller to earn advances and royalties in several countries, languages and formats, sums which in themselves may be quite small but which can add up to a healthy income. A writer acting on his own behalf is unlikely to realise all the possibilities.

If asked to provide his own job definition, an agent would probably call himself a professional adviser. (Not, he would hasten to add, a teacher. An agent does not expect to tell anyone *how* to write.)

Yet another way of defining an agent is to think of him as a partner. The relationship between writer and agent, assuming they get on well together, invariably lasts longer than any connection with individual editors, publishers, producers or directors.

To a confused world, the agent brings a welcome note of stability.

UK Agents

A. & B. Personal Management Ltd

5th Floor, Plaza Suite, 114 Jermyn Street, London SW1Y 6HJ
☎ 01–839 4433
Telex 21901 JWPPLG Fax 01–839 6075

Contact *Bill Ellis*

FOUNDED 1982. Interested in anything that has the potential to become a film or play. TV/radio and theatre scripts. No unsolicited mss. Prefer preliminary letter with synopsis, with s.a.e. Reading fee: £25 including VAT for full mss.
Commission Home 12½%; US 15%; Translation either 12½% or 15%.

Aitken & Stone Ltd

29 Fernshaw Road, London SW10 0TG
☎ 01–351 7561
Telex 298391 Fax 01–376 3594

Contact *Gillon Aitken, Brian Stone, Antony Harwood*

Gillon Aitken joined up with Hughes Massie in 1984. *Handles* fiction and non-fiction. No plays or scripts unless by existing clients. Require a preliminary letter, synopsis and return postage in the first instance. No reading fee. CLIENTS include Bruce Chatwin, Agatha Christie, Germaine Greer, V. S. Naipaul, Piers Paul Read, Salman Rushdie, Paul Theroux.
Commission Home 10%; US 15%; Translation 20%. *Overseas office* Wylie, Aitken & Stone Inc., 250 West 57th Street, New York, NY 10107, USA.

Jacintha Alexander Associates

47 Emperor's Gate, London SW7 4HJ
☎ 01–373 9258

Contact *Jacintha Alexander, Julian Alexander*

FOUNDED 1981. Jacintha Alexander was previously with **A. M. Heath & Co.** *Handle* fiction and non-fiction of all kinds. Scripts handled for established clients only. No romantic fiction or academic books. Mss should be preceded by a letter with s.a.e. No reading fee.
Commission Home 15%; US 20%; Translation 20%.

Darley Anderson

Estelle House, 11 Eustace Road, London SW6 1JB
☎ 01–385 6652 Fax 01–386 5571

Contact *Darley Anderson*

Handle commercial fiction & non-fiction; also scripts for TV/radio and theatre. No academic books. *Special interests* Fiction: family sagas; glitzy women's; thrillers; crime and comedy. Non-fiction: popular psychology; biography; health; gardening; cookery; religious. Send letter and outline with 1–3 chapters, plus return postage. Brief synopsis and first chapter giving a strong flavour of the book preferred. CLIENTS Dr Vernon Coleman; Beryl Kingston; Adrian Plass; Fred Secombe; Valerie Singleton. TITLES include Allan Pease's *Body Language* with over one million copies in print and *A Time to Love* Beryl Kingston.
Commission Home 15%; US 15–20%; Translation 20%. *Overseas associates* 'too numerous' to list – works with major foreign agents worldwide.

Badcock & Rozycki

12 Flitcroft Street, London WC2H 8DJ
☎ 01–836 0782 Telex 923995

Contact *June Badcock, Barbara Rozycki*

Not literary agents in the usual sense; Badcock & Rozycki are scouts representing ten international publishers. They seek out suitable books for translation, and deal only with other agents and publishers. Do not send mss of any kind to them direct.

Blake Friedmann Literary Agency Ltd

37–41 Gower Street, London WC1E 6HH
☎ 01–631 4331
Telex 9312102498 BFG Fax 01–323 1274

Contact *Carole Blake* (books), *Julian Friedmann* (film/TV), *Conrad Williams* (original scripts/radio), *Marisa Lesser* (short stories/journalism)

FOUNDED 1977. *Handle* all kinds of fiction, from genre to literary; a varied range of specialised and general non-fiction; some juvenile titles, plus scripts. No poetry. *Special interests* thrillers, commercial women's fiction. Unsolicited mss welcome, but should be preceded by a letter with synopsis and first two chapters. Letters should contain as much information as possible on previous writing experience, aims for the future, etc. No reading fee. CLIENTS include Ted Allbeury, Barbara Erskine, John Trenhaile, Pamela Vandyke Price.
Commission Books: Home 15%; US 20%; Translation 20%; Radio/TV/film: 15%; Journalism/short stories: 25%. *Overseas associates* throughout Europe and USA.

David Bolt Associates

12 Heath Drive, Send, Surrey GU23 7EP
☎ 0486 221118

Contact *David Bolt*

FOUNDED 1983. Ex-**David Higham.** *Handle* fiction, general non-fiction. No books for small children, or verse (except in special circumstances). No scripts. *Special interests* fiction, African writers, biography, history, military, theology. Preliminary letter with s.a.e. essential. £25 reading fee except for published writers. CLIENTS include Chinua Achebe, Ellis Dillon, Arthur Jacobs, Colin Wilson.
Commission Home 10%; US 19%; Translation 19%.

Rosemary Bromley Literary Agency

Avington, near Winchester,
Hampshire SO21 1DB
☎ 0962 78656 Fax 0962 64649

Contact *Rosemary Bromley*

FOUNDED 1981. *Handle* fiction and non-fiction. Also scripts for TV and radio. No poetry or short stories. *Special interests* natural history, leisure, biography and cookery. No unsolicited mss. Preliminary letter with full details and s.a.e. essential in first instance. CLIENTS include Fanny Cradock, Christine Franklin, Jacynth Hope-Simpson, Ron Wilson.
Commission Home 10%; US 15%; Translation 20%.

Curtis Brown Group Ltd

162–8 Regent Street, London W1R 5TB
☎ 01–872 0331
Telex 920379 BRNSPK G Fax 01–872 0332

Material should be addressed to the company. It is then dealt with by the appropriate agent.

Long established literary agency. First sales were made in 1899. Merged with **John Farquharson,** forming Curtis Brown Group Ltd, in January 1989. *Handle* a wide range of subjects including fiction, general non-fiction, children's, professional and specialist, scripts for TV/radio. 'Being a large agency we will consider anything.' Prefer synopsis with covering letter and c.v. rather than complete mss. No reading fee.
Commission Home 10%; US 15%; Translation 20%. *Overseas offices* Curtis Brown (Australia) Pty Ltd; Curtis Brown Ltd, New York; Curtis Brown, Toronto, Canada.

Peter Bryant (Writers)

51 Allerton Road, London N16 5UF
☎ 01–802 0798

Contact *Peter Bryant*

FOUNDED 1980. Mostly fiction, but also handles scripts of all kinds, with drama the agency's special interest. Unsolicited mss welcome, and no one should write unless they also send 'something to read'. No reading fee. CLIENTS include Roy Apps, Gwen Cherrell, Gerald Frow, Owen Holder.
Commission Home 10%; US 10%. *Overseas associates* James Brookes & Associates, New South Wales, Australia.

Diane Burston Literary Agency

46 Cromwell Avenue, Highgate, London N6 5HL
☎ 01–340 6130

Contact *Diane Burston*

FOUNDED 1984. *Handle* fiction, non-fiction and short stories. No scripts. Particularly interested in short stories suitable for women's magazines, middle of the road fiction, and adventure non-fiction. For full-length mss, send synopsis along with first three chapters in first instance. S.a.e. essential.

Commission Home 10%; US 15%; Translation 20%.

Campbell Thomson & McLaughlin Limited

31 Newington Green, London N16 9PU
☎ 01–249 2971 Fax 01–923 1375

Contact *John McLaughlin, John Richard Parker, Charlotte Bruton*

FOUNDED 1931. *Handle* all mss except plays, film scripts, articles or poetry. Short stories from existing clients only. No reading fee.
Overseas associates Fox Chase Agency (Philadelphia) and **Raines & Raines** (New York).

Carnell Literary Agency

Danescroft, Goose Lane, Little Hallingbury, Herts CM22 7RG
☎ 0279 723626

Contact *Pamela Buckmaster*

FOUNDED 1951. *Handle* fiction and general non-fiction, specialising in science fiction and fantasy books. No poetry, and no scripts except from published authors. No unsolicited mss. Preliminary letter and s.a.e. essential in first instance. No reading fee.
Commission Home 10%; US and Translation 19%. Works in conjunction with agencies worldwide.

Serafina Clarke

98 Tunis Road, London W12 7EY
☎ 01–749 6979

Contact *Serafina Clarke, Jan Ward* (children's)

FOUNDED 1980. Fiction: romance, horror, thrillers, literary. Non-fiction: travel, humour, cookery, gardening and biography. No science fiction. Only deal in scripts by authors already on the books. *Special interests* gardening, history, country pursuits. Unsolicited mss welcome, though introductory letter with synopsis (and return postage) preferred. No reading fee. CLIENTS include Leonid Borodin, Christopher Fowler, Peter Hudson, Deborah Kellaway, Elizabeth Walker.
Commission Home 10%; US 20%; Translation 20%.
Represents Permanent Press (USA), Second Chance Press (USA), James Fox Associates (USA), Possev Verlag (Germany).

Jonathan Clowes Ltd

22 Prince Albert Road, London NW1 7ST
☎ 01–722 7674
Telex 23973 Fax 01–722 7677

Contact *Jonathan Clowes, Ann Evans, Brie Burkeman*

FOUNDED 1960. Pronounced Clewes. Now one of the biggest fish in the pond, and not really for the untried unless they are true high-flyers. Fiction and non-fiction, plus scripts. No textbooks or children's. *Special interests* situation comedy, film and television rights. No unsolicited mss; authors come by recommendation or by successful follow-ups to preliminary letters. CLIENTS include Kingsley Amis, David Bellamy, Len Deighton, Carla Lane, Doris Lessing.
Commission Home 10%; US 15%; Translation 19%. *Overseas associates* Andrew Nurnberg Associates; Lennart Sane Agency, Sweden; Tuttle Mori Agency, Japan.

Elspeth Cochrane Agency

11–13 Orlando Road, London SW4 0LE
☎ 01–622 0314

Contact *Elspeth Cochrane, Donald Baker*

FOUNDED 1960. *Handle* fiction, biography and autobiography, children's books, picture books. Books tend to be a spin-off from show business deals. Subjects include Lord Olivier, Leonard Rossiter, Sir Ralph Richardson, Shakespeare, Sir John Gielgud, Dame Peggy Ashcroft, Dirk Bogarde, John Mills, Marlon Brando. Also handle scripts for all media. *Special interest* drama. No unsolicited mss. Preliminary letter with a description of the work, a brief outline, plus s.a.e. essential in first instance. No reading fee. CLIENTS include John Charters, David Pinner, Robert Tanitch.
Commission Home 10%; US 10%; Translation 10% ('but this can change – the % is negotiable, as is the sum paid to the writer').

Dianne Coles Literary Agency

The Old Forge House, Sulgrave, Banbury, Oxon OX17 2RP
☎ 0295 76692/50731

FOUNDED 1980. Full-length manuscripts. Non-fiction, especially craft, leisure, women's, biography. Literary fiction. Preliminary letter and

return postage essential.
Commission Home & TV 10%; Overseas 20%.

Rosica Colin Ltd

1 Clareville Grove Mews, London SW7 5AH
☏ 01–370 1080

Contact *Joanna Marston*

FOUNDED 1949. *Handle* all full length mss, plus theatre, film, television and sound broadcasting. Preliminary letter with return postage essential; writers should outline where their mss have previously been submitted. Takes 3–4 months to consider full mss; prefer to see synopsis in first instance. No reading fee.
Commission Home 10%; US 15%; Translation 20%.

Jane Conway-Gordon

213 Westbourne Grove, London W11 2SE
☏ 01–229 4451

Contact *Jane Conway-Gordon*

FOUNDED 1982. *Handle* fiction and self-help books. TITLES *Conversations with Lord Byron* (Cape), *Talleyman* (Gollancz), *The Working Mother's Survival Guide* (Simon & Schuster), *Women Who Love Too Much* (Arrow). Occasionally handle scripts for TV/radio/theatre. No poetry or science fiction. Unsolicited mss welcome; preliminary letter and return postage preferred. No reading fee. CLIENTS include Juliet Dymoke, John James, Amanda Prantera, Dr Brian Roet.
Commission Home 10%; US 20%; Translation 20%. *Overseas associates* **McIntosh & Otis Inc.,** New York; plus agencies throughout Europe and Japan.

Vernon Conway Ltd

19 London Street, Paddington, London W2 1HL
☏ 01–262 5506/7

Contact *Vernon Conway*

FOUNDED 1977. *Special interests* novels, biographies, plays. No textbooks or academic. Welcome unsolicited mss, preceded by an introductory letter, plus return postage. No reading fee. CLIENTS include Anne Born, Ian Grimble, David Halliwell, Monty Haltrecht, Thomas Marty, Elizabeth Morgan, Hilary Patel, Aled Vaughan.
Commission 10% on all sales.

Rupert Crew Ltd

King's Mews, London WC1N 2JA
☏ 01–242 8586 Fax 01–831 7914

Contact *Doreen Montgomery, Shirley Russell*

FOUNDED 1927 by Rupert Crew. *Handle* fiction and non-fiction, primarily for books but major newspaper/magazine feature/series, and specialist short fiction negotiated. No plays or poetry. No unsolicited mss. Preliminary letter essential. No reading fee.
Commission Home (books) 10%, (short material) 15%; US and Translation 20%.

Cruickshank Cazenove Ltd

97 Old South Lambert Road, London SW8 1XU
☏ 01–735 2933 Fax 01–820 1081

Contact *Harriet Cruickshank*

FOUNDED 1983. Fiction, general non-fiction, scripts for TV/radio/film. No unsolicited mss. Preliminary letter with synopsis and s.a.e. essential. Works with foreign agents abroad.
Commission Home 10%; US and Translation varies according to contract.

Judy Daish Associates Ltd

83 Eastbourne Mews, London W2 6LQ
☏ 01–262 1101
Telex 916824 DAISH G Fax 01–706 1027

Contact *Judy Daish, Louise Cooper, Sara Stroud*

FOUNDED 1978. Theatrical literary agent only. Scripts for film/TV/theatre/radio. No books. Preliminary letter essential. No unsolicited mss.

Reg Davis-Poynter

118 St Pancras, Chichester,
West Sussex PO19 4LH
11 Bolt Court, Fleet Street, London EC4A 3DU
☏ 0243 779047/01–353 9365

Contact *R. G. Davis-Poynter*

Handle books and scripts (TV, radio, theatre, film). *Special interests* autobiography, biography, history, politics, sociology, theatre. No children's or religious. Unsolicited mss welcome if accompanied by letter, synopsis, sample chapter and return postage. Prefer that writers approach with preliminary letter and return postage in first instance. No reading fee.
Commission Home 15%, US 20%; Translation 15%; Theatre, films, television and radio 10%.

Overseas associates in Germany, Scandinavia, Japan, Italy, France and USA.

Felix de Wolfe

Manfield House, 376–8 The Strand,
London WC2R 0LR
☎ 01–379 5767 Telex 931770 A/B WIBU G

Contact *Felix de Wolfe*

FOUNDED 1938. *Handle* quality fiction and scripts only. No non-fiction or children's. No unsolicited mss; approach by letter in first instance. No reading fee. CLIENTS include S. Campbell-Jones, Brian Glover, Jennifer Johnston, John Kershaw, Bill MacIlwraith, Braham Murray, Uliek O'Connor, Charles Savage, Alan Sievewright, Julian Slade, David Thompson and Dolores Walsh.
Commission Home 10%; US 20%.

John Dorman

20 Mill Street, Shipston-on-Stour,
Warwickshire CV36 4AW
☎ 0608 63435 Telex 418253

Contact *John Dorman*

FOUNDED 1983. *Handle* sport (autobiography and instructional) and sports-related subjects, leisure activities. Autobiographies of Geoff Boycott, Graham Dilley, Steve Smith Eccles, John Francome, Bob Willis. No scripts, no fiction, no children's. *Special interests* cricket, horse racing, rugby union, soccer. No unsolicited mss; initial letter and typed synopsis essential. No reading fee. CLIENTS include Gee Armytage, Pat Eddery, John Emburey, Pat Gibson (*Sunday Express* cricket correspondent), Graham Gooch, Alan Lee, Clive Norling (rugby referee), Peter Scudamore (National Hunt jockey), Derek Thompson (*Channel 4* racing).
Commission Home 10%; US 15%; Translation 15%.

John Farquharson (Curtis Brown Group Ltd)

162–8 Regent Street, London W1R 5TB
☎ 01–872 0331
Telex 261536 Fax 01–872 0332

Contact *Vivienne Schuster, Vanessa Holt*

FOUNDED 1919. Now trading as **Curtis Brown Group Ltd** following the merger with Curtis Brown Ltd in January 1989. 'We pride ourselves on being a general agency.' *Handle* commercial and literary fiction, and general non-fiction. *Special interests* bestseller fiction, top crime novels. No academic, no technical, no scripts. Unsolicited mss welcome. Send synopsis plus first 3–4 chapters (5000 words or so), together with c.v. in first instance.
Commission Home 10%; US 20%; Translation 20%. *Overseas associates* John Farquharson, New York.

Film Link Literary Agency

31 Oakdene Drive, Tolworth, Surrey KT5 9NH
☎ 01–330 3182

Contact *Yvonne Heather*

FOUNDED 1979. *Handle* fiction, general non-fiction and TV scripts. No poetry or short stories. No unsolicited mss. Send synopsis, sample pages and introductory letter, together with s.a.e. No reading fee. CLIENTS include Peter May and Michael Elder (writers for *Take the High Road*).
Commission Home 10%; Overseas 15–20%.

Film Rights Ltd

483 South Bank House, Black Prince Road,
London SE1 7SJ
☎ 01–735 7151

Contact *Laurence Fitch*

FOUNDED 1932. Only handle stage/radio/TV/film scripts. Do not consider unsolicited mss or synopses. Preliminary letter giving full details, including c.v. of the writer, essential. No reading fee.
Commission Home 10%; US 15%; Translation 20% 'sometimes'.

Laurence Fitch Ltd

483 South Bank House, Black Prince Road,
London SE1 7SJ
☎ 01–735 7151

Contact *Laurence Fitch, Judy Quinn*

FOUNDED 1954. Scripts only, for all media. Particularly interested in plays for the stage, especially comedies. Ambivalent about unsolicited scripts; writers should send a preliminary letter. Can take up to 3 months to consider mss. CLIENTS include John Chapman, Ray Cooney and Dodie Smith.
Commission Home 10%; US 15%; Translation 20% 'sometimes'.

Jill Foster Ltd

19A Queen's Gate Terrace, London SW7 5PR
☎ 01–581 0084

Contact *Jill Foster, Alison Finch, Ann Foster*

FOUNDED 1976. *Handle* non-fiction and scripts only (mainly TV, drama and comedy). No fiction, short stories or poetry. No unsolicited mss; approach by letter in the first instance. No reading fee. CLIENTS include Paul Hines, Julia Jones, Chris Ralling, Colin Bostock-Smith, Susan Wilkins.
Commission Home 10%; US 15%; Translation 15%.

Fraser & Dunlop Scripts Ltd

See **The Peters Fraser & Dunlop Group**

French's

26 Binney Street, London W1
☎ 01–629 4159

Contact *John French, Janet Welch*

FOUNDED 1973. *Handle* novels and factual material; also scripts for all media. No religious or medical books. No unsolicited mss. 'For unpublished authors we offer a reading service at £30 per mss, inclusive of VAT and postage.' Interested authors should write a letter in the first instance. CLIENTS include James Duke, Barry Heath, Mal Middleton, Shaun Prendergast.
Commission Home 10%.

Jüri Gabriel

35 Camberwell Grove, London SE5 8JA
☎ 01–703 6186

Contact *Jüri Gabriel*

Handle fiction and non-fiction; also scripts for TV/radio/theatre but only have one client playwright to date. No short stories generally unless exceptional circumstances or a collection, and no articles, verse or books for children. Unsolicited mss welcome if accompanied by s.a.e. and letter giving sufficient information about author's writing experience, aims, etc. CLIENTS Nigel Cawthorne; Colonel John Cross; Nigel Foster; Robert Irwin; John Outram; Major Ewen Southby-Tailyour; Dr Robert Youngson.
Commission Home 10%; US 20%; Translation 20%.

Pamela Gillis Management

46 Sheldon Avenue, London N6 4JR
☎ 01–340 7868

Contact *Pamela Gillis*

FOUNDED 1975. TV scripts and radio material. No books. Prefer preliminary letter of introduction. No reading fee.
Commission 10% Home and Abroad.

Eric Glass Ltd

28 Berkeley Square, London W1X 6HD
☎ 01–629 7162
Telex 296759 KALLIN G Fax 01–499 6780

Contact *Eric Glass, Janet Crowley*

FOUNDED 1934. Fiction and non-fiction. TITLES include *Gioconda* Wolf Mankowitz; *The Prime Ministers* ed. William Douglas-Home; *Somerset And All The Maughams* Robin Maugham; *The Unforgiving Minute* Beverley Nichols. No poetry. Handle scripts both for publication and production in all media. Resumés and sample chapters in the first instance (complete mss by request) with return postage. No reading fee. CLIENTS include Philip King, Gleston Trevor/Adam Hall, Alfred Shaughnessy, the estates of Jean Cocteau and Jean-Paul Sartre, Wolf Mankowitz, William Douglas-Home and Warwick Deeping.
Commission Home 10%; US 15%; Translation 20% (minimum rates). *Overseas associates* in USA, Germany, Scandinavia, France, Italy, Spain, Czechoslovakia, Holland, Greece, Poland, Australia, South Africa, Japan.

Goodwin Associates

12 Rabbit Row, Kensington Church Street, London W8 4DX
☎ 01–229 8805

Contact *Ms Phil Kelvin*

FOUNDED 1977. *Handle* scripts for film/TV/theatre/radio only. No prose or poetry. Welcome unsolicited mss with return postage. No reading fee. CLIENTS include Susan Boyd, Jim Hill, Stephen Lowe, Louise Page, Christina Reid, Fay Weldon.
Commission 10% on all sales.

Christine Green (Authors' Agent) Ltd

2 Barbon Close, London WC1N 3JX
☎ 01–831 4956 Fax 01–831 4840

Contact *Christine Green*

FOUNDED 1984. *Handle* fiction (general and literary); general non-fiction. No scripts, poetry

or children's. Unsolicited mss welcome if return postage included. Initial letter and synopsis preferred. No reading fee.
Commission Home 10%; US 15%; Translation 20%.

Elaine Greene Ltd

31 Newington Green, Islington,
London N16 9PU
☎ 01–249 2971

Contact *Elaine Greene, Carol Heaton, Ilsa Yardley*

A small, choosy agency that really likes to involve itself with its authors. Novels and quality non-fiction, journalists' books. No academic, no original scripts for theatre, film or TV. *Special interests* crime writing. No unsolicited mss without preliminary letter. CLIENTS include Colin Forbes, P. D. James, Conor Cruise O'Brien, William Shawcross.
Commission Home 10%; US 15%; Translation 20%.

The Jane Gregory Agency

Riverside Studios, Crisp Road, London W6 9RL
☎ 01–741 3646
Telex 268141 METMAK G Fax 01–846 9039

Contact *Jane Gregory, Felicia Dykstra*

FOUNDED 1982. *Handle* fiction and non-fiction. No plays, poetry, academic or children's. No unsolicited mss; preliminary letter essential. No reading fee. Represent three American companies, including **Simon & Schuster.**
Commission Home 10%; US 20%; Translation 20%.

Gregory & Radice Author's Agents

Riverside Studios, Crisp Road, London W6 9RL
☎ 01–741 3646
Telex 268141 METMAK G Fax 01–846 9039

Contact *Jane Gregory, Lisanne Radice*

FOUNDED 1986. *Handle* crime and thrillers only; a single-minded approach makes them specialists in the field. No scripts. No unsolicited mss. Preliminary letter with synopsis and couple of sample chapters (plus return postage) essential. No reading fee.
Commission Home 10%; US 20%; Translation 20%.

David Grossman Literary Agency Ltd

110–114 Clerkenwell Road, London EC1M 5SA
☎ 01–251 5046
Telex 263404 BK BIZ G

Contact *David Grossman*

FOUNDED 1976. Full-length fiction and general non-fiction. No verse or technical books for students and no original screenplays or teleplays, but sell performance rights in works existing in volume form. *Special interests* suspense and thriller writers, historical novelists, sagas, biographies, political affairs, health, contemporary history, travel, film, anything controversial; good writing of all kinds. Prefer a preliminary letter giving full description of the work. No unsolicited mss. No reading fee.
Commission rates vary for different markets.
Overseas associates throughout Europe, Japan, Brazil and USA.

June Hall Literary Agency

5th Floor, The Chambers, Chelsea Harbour, Lots Road, London SW10 0XF
☎ 01–352 4233 Fax 01–352 7356

Contact *Shân Morley-Jones, Lucinda Culpin*
Consultant *June Hall*
Managing Director *Michael Sissons*

FOUNDED 1979. Fiction and general non-fiction. No scripts. No unsolicited material. Preliminary letter and s.a.e. essential. No reading fee.
Commission on application.

Roger Hancock Ltd

Greener House, 66–8 Haymarket,
London SW1Y 4AW
☎ 01–839 6753 Fax 01–930 8458

Contact *'The company'*

FOUNDED 1961. *Special interest* drama and light entertainment. Scripts only. No books. Unsolicited mss not welcome. Initial phone call required. No reading fee.
Commission 10% throughout.

Xandra Hardie Literary Agency

9 Elsworthy Terrace, London NW3 3DR
☎ 01–722 0178 Fax 01–586 6230

Contact *Xandra Hardie*

FOUNDED 1985. *Handle* literary fiction, thrillers, biographies, political and social affairs, and illustrated books. No scripts, children's or down-market fiction. *Special interests* poetry and art. No unsolicited mss. Approach by letter

in first instance. CLIENTS John Carey; Dr Pauline Cutting; Geoff Dyer; Simon Williams.
Commission Home 20%; US 20%; Translation 20%.

Hatton & Baker Ltd

18 Jermyn Street, London SW1Y 6HN
☎ 01–439 2971 Fax 01–439 7633

Contact *Terence Baker, Richard Hatton*

FOUNDED 1980. *Handle* scripts and screenplays only. No books. No reading fee.
Commission Home 10%; US 15%; Translation 15%. *Overseas associates* worldwide.

Headline Enterprises Ltd

19A Queen's Gate Terrace, London SW7 5PR
☎ 01–584 8568

Contact *Malcolm Hamer, Jill Foster, Alison Finch*

FOUNDED 1971. *Handle* non-fiction only, especially sporting/leisure, show business autobiography, guide books, food and wine. No fiction or poetry. No unsolicited mss; writers should send a letter in the first instance. No reading fee. CLIENTS include Bill Breckon, Chris Dodd, Gareth Edwards, Ray French, David Lemmon, Tony Pawson, Simon Reed, Cliff Temple.
Commission Home 10–15%; US 20%.

A. M. Heath & Co. Ltd

79 St Martin's Lane, London WC2N 4AA
☎ 01–836 4271
Telex 27370 Fax 01–497 2561

Contact *Mark Hamilton, William Hamilton, Michael Thomas, Sara Fisher*

FOUNDED 1919. *Handle* fiction and general non-fiction. No scripts or poetry. Preliminary letter and synopsis essential. No reading fee. CLIENTS include Saul Bellow, Anita Brookner and Jean Plaidy.
Commission Home 10%; US 15%; Translation 20%; Film & TV 15%. *Overseas associates* in USA.

Duncan Heath Associates Ltd

Paramount House, 162–70 Wardour Street, London W1V 3AT
☎ 01–439 1471/2111 Fax 01–439 7274

Contact *Ian Amos*

FOUNDED 1973. *Handle* film/TV/theatre scripts. No books. No unsolicited mss. Preliminary letter essential. No reading fee.
Commission 10% throughout. *Overseas associates* ICM New York and Los Angeles.

David Higham Associates Ltd

5–8 Lower John Street, Golden Square, London W1R 4HA
☎ 01–437 7888
Telex 28910 HIGHAM G Fax 01–437 1072

Contact *Anthony Goff*; scripts *John Rush, Elizabeth Cree*

FOUNDED 1935. *Handle* fiction, general non-fiction; biography, history, current affairs, art, music, etc. Also scripts. Preliminary letter with synopsis essential in first instance. No reading fee. CLIENTS include John Le Carré, James Herbert, Russell Hoban and Alice Walker.
Commission Home 10%; US 15%; Translation 19%.

Valerie Hoskins (in association with Jeremy Conway Ltd)

Eagle House, 109 Jermyn Street, London SW1Y 6HB
☎ 01–839 2121

Contact *Valerie Hoskins*

FOUNDED 1983. Script agent dealing in film, theatre, television and radio. *Special interests* feature films. No unsolicited scripts; preliminary letter of introduction essential. No reading fee. CLIENTS include Peter Berry, Daniel Boyle, Tony Craze, Kit Hesketh-Harvey, Robin Miller, Jeremy Newson, John Peacock, Gillian Richmond.
Commission Home 10%; US 20% (maximum).

Tanja Howarth

19 New Row, London WC2N 4LA
☎ 01–240 5553
Telex 27370 Fax 01–379 0969

Contact *Tanja Howarth*

FOUNDED 1970. Interested in taking on both fiction and non-fiction from British writers. No children's books, plays or poetry, but all other subjects considered providing the treatment is intelligent. Unsolicited mss welcome with return postage. Preliminary letter preferred. No reading fee. Also an established agent for foreign literature, particularly from the German language (*The Perfume* Patrick Süskind; Heinrich Böll, Friedrich Dürrenmatt). Reputation for

smooth efficiency.
Commission Home 10%; Translation 15%.

Michael Imison Playwrights Ltd

28 Almeida Street, Islington, London N1 1TD
☎ 01–354 3174
Telex 934999 TX Link G Fax 01–359 6273

Contact *Michael Imison, Alan Brodie*

FOUNDED 1944. Michael Imison is the brother of Richard Imison, deputy head of BBC radio drama. *Handles* plays, plus books based on scripts, e.g. *Yes Minister*, TV, radio and theatre. Specialise in theatre writing. No fiction or general books. *Special interests* writers motivated primarily by writing for the theatre, translators, particularly from the Russian and Italian languages. Unsolicited mss not welcome. Initial letter (plus s.a.e.) with recommendation from a known theatre professional essential. No reading fee. CLIENTS include David Edgar, Dario Fo, John Godber, Doug Lucie, the Noel Coward estate.
Commission Home 10%; US and Translation 12.5%.
Overseas associates Judy Ferris at Stagewise, Sydney, Australia; Abbe Levin, New York.

International Copyright Bureau Ltd

Suite 8, 26 Charing Cross Road,
London WC2H 0DG
☎ 01–836 5912 Fax 01–379 7731

Contact *Joy Westendarp*

FOUNDED 1905. *Handle* exclusively scripts for TV/theatre/film/radio. No books. Preliminary letter for unsolicited material essential.
Commission Home 10%; US 15%; Translation 19%. *Overseas agents* in New York and most foreign countries.

International Scripts

1 Norland Square, Holland Park,
London W11 4PX
☎ 01–229 0736

Contact *Bob Tanner, Mrs J. Lawson, Liz Moseley*

FOUNDED 1980 by Bob Tanner. *Handle* all types of books, as well as scripts for all media. No poetry. Unsolicited mss welcome, though preliminary letter with synopsis preferred. Works with agents worldwide. CLIENTS include Peter Haining, Robert A. Heinlein, Shaun Hutson, Richard Laymon.
Commission Home 10–15%; US 20%; Translation 20%. *Overseas associates* include **Ralph Vicinanza, Spectrum,** New York.

Jane Judd Literary Agency

6 Thornhill Grove, London N1 1JG
☎ 01–607 0273

Contact *Jane Judd*

FOUNDED 1986. *Handle* general non-fiction and fiction: historical sagas; cookery; humour (*Kenny Everett Loo Book*); pop/rock (*Who Sang What in Rock 'n' Roll*); biography/autobiography; investigative journalism; health; women's interest; fantasy. No scripts, academic, gardening, DIY or popular fiction. 'Looking for good sagas/women's read but not Mills & Boon-type'; also crime and travel writing and literary fiction. Approach with letter, synopsis and sample chapter, plus s.a.e. in first instance. Initial telephone call helpful in the case of non-fiction. CLIENTS Patrick Anthony; Jillie Collings; Heather Hay; Stephen Marley; John Pidgeon; Elliot Philipp; David Winner.
Commission Home 20%; US 20%; Translation 20%.

Juvenilia

Avington, near Winchester,
Hampshire SO21 1DB
☎ 0962 78253 Fax 0962 64649

Contact *Rosemary Bromley*

FOUNDED 1973. *Handle* young/teen fiction, picture books, and non-fiction. Also scripts for TV and radio. No poetry or short stories unless part of a collection or picture book material. No unsolicited mss. Preliminary letter with s.a.e. and full details of work and author in first instance. Phone calls not advised. CLIENTS include Denis Bond, Wendy Etyton, Helen Morgan, Tom Tully, Jennifer Zabel.
Commission Home 10%; US 15%; Translation 20%.

Frances Kelly

111 Clifton Road, Kingston upon Thames,
Surrey KT2 6PL
☎ 01–549 7830

Contact *Frances Kelly*

FOUNDED 1978. *Handle* non-fiction, including illustrated: biography, history, art, self-help, food & wine; also academic non-fiction in all disciplines. No scripts except for existing clients. No unsolicited mss. Prefer letter with brief description of work or synopsis and c.v.

with reply postage.
Commission Home 10%; US 20%; Translation 20%.

Lemon, Unna and Durbridge Ltd

24–32 Pottery Lane, London W11 4LZ
☎ 01–727 1346/229 9216
Telex 27618 Author G Fax 01–727 9037

Directors *Sheila Lemon, Stephen Durbridge, Wendy Gresser, Girsha Reid, Nigel Britten*
Contact *Nigel Britten, Bethan Evans*

Theatrical literary agency, which came out of the merging of Lemon & Durbridge Ltd with **Harvey Unna & Stephen Durbridge Ltd** in 1989. Theatre, TV, film and radio scripts. No books, No unsolicited mss; preliminary letter and outline essential. No reading fee.
Commission Home 10%; US and Translation varies. *Overseas associates* worldwide.

L'Epine Smith & Carney Associates

10 Wyndham Place, London W1H 1AS
☎ 01–724 0739

Contact *Eric L'Epine Smith*

FOUNDED 1957. Fiction – only interested in good material. Welcome unsolicited mss preceded by introductory letter or phone call. Prefer synopses in the first instance.
Commission Home 10%.

Christopher Little

49 Queen Victoria Street, London EC4N 4SA
☎ 01–236 5881
Telex 883968 Fax 01–236 7625

Contact *C. J. Little, A. Barclay, B. Godfrey*

FOUNDED 1979. *Handle* full length fiction, non-fiction, film scripts, TV scripts. *Special interests* crime, thrillers, historical fiction. Unsolicited mss welcome. No reading fee. CLIENTS include Erin Pizzey, A. J. Quinnell, Carolyn Terry and W. Wright (alias David Graham).
Commission Home 20%; US 20%; Translation 20%.

Lloyd-George & Coward

12 Fairfax Place, Dartmouth, Devon TQ6 9AE
☎ 08043 2448

Contact *Bruce Coward*

FOUNDED 1959. *Handle* biography, travel, natural history, general fiction and nautical. No drama scripts, poetry, educational, academic or translations. *Special interests* nautical. No unsolicited mss; send introductory letter with synopsis and s.a.e. No reading fee. CLIENTS include Wallace Breem, Jane Gillespie, Tom Jaine, Jeremy Purseglove.
Commission Home 10%; US 15%. *Overseas associates* Lyle Steele & Co., New York.

London Independent Books Ltd

1A Montague Mews North, London W1H 1AJ
☎ 01–706 0486

Contact *Mrs C. Whitaker*

FOUNDED 1971. A self-styled 'small and idiosyncratic' agency, which handles fiction and non-fiction reflecting the tastes of the proprietors. All subjects considered (except computer books) providing the treatment is strong and saleable. Scripts handled only if by existing clients. *Special interests* boats, travel, travelogues, commercial fiction. No unsolicited mss; letter, synopsis and first two chapters with return postage the best approach. No reading fee. CLIENTS 'none are household names, yet!'
Commission Home 15%; US 20%; Translation 20%.

London Management

235–41 Regent Street, London W1R 7AG
☎ 01–493 1610
Telex 27498 Fax 01–408 0065

Contact *Heather Jeeves, Tony Peake* (general), *Marc Berlin* (TV/film/theatre)

FOUNDED 1959. Part of the biggest show-biz agency in the country. Recent build up on the book side. Sympathetic to new talent. *Handle* full-length fiction and general non-fiction, including illustrated books, craft, health, music, theatre, film, the arts, graphic design, humour/cartoon, military. No science fiction/fantasy, educational, short stories, category romance or children's. *Special interests* South African fiction and non-fiction. Writers should approach by telephone in the first instance, followed by letter with synopsis, sample chapters and s.a.e. No unsolicited mss. No reading fee.
Commission Home 10%; US 19%; Translation 19%. *Overseas associates* **The Lantz Office,** New York, plus full coverage by foreign rights agents.

Andrew Lownie Agency

122 Bedford Court Mansions, Bedford Square, London WC1B 3AH
☎ 01–636 4917 Fax 01–436 1324

Contact *Andrew Lownie, Patricia Reynolds*

FOUNDED 1988. Mainly non-fiction. No scripts, science fiction, poetry, children's. *Special interests* books on intelligence. Prefer approach by letter with synopsis and sample chapters in first instance. CLIENTS Theo Aronson; Joyce Cary estate; Paul James; Judge James Pickles; Tom Pocock. TITLES include the authorised biography of Joan Sutherland, and biographies of Lenin, Nelson and Princess Margaret.
Commission Home 10%; US 20%; Translation 20%.

Maclean Dubois (Writers & Agents)

10 Rutland Square, Edinburgh EH1 2AS
☎ 031–229 6185 Fax 031–228 1319

Contact *Charles Maclean, Piers Schreiber, Patrick Deedes-Vincke* (Paris)

FOUNDED 1977. General fiction and non-fiction, children's, biography, history, photography. No poetry or plays (unless, occasionally, for own authors). *Special interests* literary fiction, Scottish history and topography, food and wine, historical fiction. Unsolicited mss welcome. Reading fee for supply of detailed report on mss offered. Writers should approach the agency by phone or in writing for explanation of terms. CLIENTS include Robin Jenkins, Colin Mackay (literary fiction), Ken Begg (thrillers), David Williams (photos), Helen Mackenzie (children's) Seamus Carney (Scottish history).
Commission Home 10%; US 20%; Translation varies. *Overseas associates* Patrick Deedes-Vincke, 38 bis Rue de Rivoli, 75004 Paris.

Bill McLean Personal Management

23B Deodar Road, Putney, London SW15 2NP
☎ 01–789 8191

Contact *Bill McLean*

FOUNDED 1972. *Handle* scripts only for all media. No books, no unsolicited mss. Phone call or introductory letter essential. No reading fee. CLIENTS Peter Batt, Dwynwen Berry, Jane Galletly, Bill Lyons, John Maynard, Les Miller, Jeffrey Segal, Frank Vickery, Mark Wheatley.
Commission Home 10%.

Andrew Mann Ltd

1 Old Compton Street, London W1V 5PH
☎ 01–734 4751

Contact *Anne Dewe, Tina Betts*

FOUNDED 1975. *Handle* fiction and general non-fiction; film/TV/theatre/radio scripts. No unsolicited mss. Preliminary letter, synopsis and s.a.e. essential. No reading fee. Associate agencies overseas.
Commission Home 10%; US 15%; Translation 20%.

Manuscript Research

5 St Pauls Mews, Shepton Mallet, Somerset BA4 5BN
☎ 0749 5435

Contact *Graham Jenkins*

FOUNDED 1988. *Handle* fiction: thrillers, historical novels, crime, general; biographies; children's. Also scripts for TV/radio. No technical, religious, science fiction, poetry, or short stories unless from established clients. *Special interests* Revision/rewriting scripts for selected clients. Optional criticism service available. Approach by letter with s.a.e. in first instance. CLIENTS include Tom Barrat, Tom Clarkson, Nicholai Kollantoy.
Commission Home 10%; US 20%.

Marjacq Scripts Ltd

32 Cumberland Mansions, Nutford Place, London W1H 5ZB
☎ 01–724 0565 Fax 01–723-3405

Contact *Jacqui Lyons*

FOUNDED 1974. Fiction and non-fiction, plus radio and TV scripts. No children's or religious. Unsolicited mss welcome with s.a.e. but telephone conversation first preferred. No reading fee.
Commission Home 10%; US 10%; Translation 20%.

Marlu Literary Agency

26 Stratford Road, London W8 6QD
☎ 01–937 5161 Telex 268141

Contact *Mary Hall Mayer*

All subjects except children's and poetry. *Special interests* general fiction, non-fiction,

computer and visual books.
Commission Home 10%; US 20%.

Marsh & Sheil Ltd

43 Doughty Street, London WC1N 2LF
☎ 01–405 7473
Telex 94013093 MARS G Fax 01–831 2127

Contact *Paul Marsh, Susanna Nicklin*

FOUNDED 1985. Marsh & Sheil deals in translation rights only, on behalf of selected British and American agents. No unsolicited mss, ideas or synopses. CLIENTS include **Anthony Sheil Associates, Wallace Literary Agency,** Don Congdon Associates and Watkins Loomis.
Commission Translation 10%.

Jenifer Marshall Dunkley

8–26 Hollybush Road, London SW15 3LE
☎ 01–788 5805

Contact *Jenifer Marshall Dunkley*

FOUNDED 1983. *Handle* children's picture books and novels, adult fiction, fantasy and some adult non-fiction. Occasionally scripts for TV/radio/theatre. *Special interests* music, food, wine, literature. No unsolicited mss without phone call first. Prefer preliminary letter with synopsis, s.a.e. and initial fee of £5. CLIENTS include Mark Brooker, Les Brown, Mike Webb, Judith Windeler.
Commission Home 10%; US 15%; Translation 7.5%.

Blanche Marvin

21A St John's Wood High Street,
London NW8 7NG
☎ 01–722 2313

Contact *Blanche Marvin*

FOUNDED 1968. *Handle* general non-fiction, film, radio, TV and play scripts. No poetry. Send c.v. and outline of the work in the first instance. No reading fee.
Commission 12½% throughout.

MBA Literary Agents Ltd

45 Fitzroy Street, London W1P 5HR
☎ 01–387 2076/4785

Contact *Diana Tyler, John Richard Parker, Meg Davis, Ruth Needham*

FOUNDED 1971. *Handle* full-length fiction and non-fiction; particularly interested in science fiction/fantasy. Also scripts for all media a speciality. No reading fee but preliminary letter with outline and s.a.e. essential.
Commission Home 10%; US 20%; Translation 20%; Theatre, TV, Radio 10%; Film 10–15%.

Richard Milne Ltd

28 Makepeace Avenue, London N6 6EJ
☎ 01–340 7007

Contact *R. M. Sharples, K. N. Sharples*

FOUNDED 1956. Specialises in drama and comedy scripts for radio and television, but are not presently in the market for new clients – they are 'fully committed in handling work by authors we already represent'. No unsolicited mss.
Commission Home 10%; US 15%; Translation 25%.

William Morris Agency UK Ltd

31–2 Soho Square, London W1V 5DG
☎ 01–434 2191
Telex 27928 Fax 01–437 4427

Contact *Lavinia Trevor*

FOUNDED 1967. *Handle* fiction and general non-fiction. No scripts, academic, technical, poetry or children's. Welcome unsolicited mss but must be preceded by a preliminary letter with s.a.e.
Commission Home 10%; US 20%; Translation 20%.

Michael Motley Ltd

78 Gloucester Terrace, London W2 3HH
☎ 01–723 2973

Contact *Michael Motley*

FOUNDED 1973. *Handle* all subjects except short mss (e.g. freelance journalism), poetry, and original dramatic material. No scripts. *Special interest* crime novels. Unsolicited mss will be considered but must be preceded by a preliminary letter with s.a.e. No reading fee. CLIENTS include Simon Brett, Doug Nye, K. M. Peyton, Barry Turner.
Commission Home 10%; US 15%; Translation 20%. *Overseas associates* in all publishing centres.

The Maggie Noach Literary Agency

21 Redan Street, London W14 0AB
☎ 01–602 2451

Contact *Maggie Noach*

FOUNDED 1982. Pronounced 'no-ack'. Ex-**A. P.**

Watt. *Handle* a wide range of books, including literary fiction, general non-fiction, and some children's. Film/TV rights handled in association with **Linda Seifert Associates**. No scientific, academic or specialist non-fiction, no romantic fiction, poetry or books for the very young. Recommended for promising young writers but few new clients taken on as it is considered vital to give individual attention to each author's work. Unsolicited mss not welcome. Approach by letter giving a brief description of the book and enclosing a few sample pages. Return postage essential. No reading fee.
Commission Home 10%; US 20%; Translation 20%.

Andrew Nurnberg Associates Ltd

Clerkenwell House, 45–7 Clerkenwell Green, London EC1R 0HT
☎ 01–251 0321
Telex 23353 Fax 01–251 0584

Directors *Andrew Nurnberg, Klaasje Mul, Sarah Nundy*

FOUNDED mid-1970s. *Specialises* in foreign rights, representing leading authors and agents.

Deborah Owen Ltd

78 Narrow Street, Limehouse, London E14 8BP
☎ 01–987 5119/5441 Fax 01–538 4004

Contact *Deborah Owen, Judith Dooling*

FOUNDED 1971. Wife of a well-known politician. Very high-powered. 'Not for old ladies who write knitting books.' *Handle* international fiction and non-fiction (books which can be translated into a number of languages). No scripts, poetry, science fiction, children's books, short stories. No unsolicited mss. Not taking on new authors ('haven't done so for some time'). CLIENTS include Jeffrey Archer, Amos Oz, Ellis Peters, Delia Smith.
Commission Home 10%; US 15%; Translation 15%.

Mark Paterson & Associates

10 Brook Street, Wivenhoe, Colchester, Essex CO7 9DS
☎ 0206 225433
Telex 988805 PATEM G Fax 0206 222990

Contact *Mark Paterson*

FOUNDED 1961. *Specialises* in psychiatric books, psychoanalytical and psychotherapy. No song or play scripts. No articles. No unsolicited mss. Prefer preliminary letter. May charge reading fee. CLIENTS include Hugh Brogan, Vivian Cook, Sir Arthur Evans, Peter Moss, Dorothy Richardson, Hugh Schonfield, D. W. Winnicott. Represents the estate of Sigmund Freud.
Commission 20% throughout (including sub-agent's commission).

John Pawsey

Hollybrae, Hill Brow Road, Liss, Hants GU33 7PS
☎ 0730 893065

Contact *John Pawsey*

FOUNDED 1981. *Handle* non-fiction and fiction; show business (Dudley Moore biography), gardening (*Illustrated Encyclopedia of Trees and Shrubs*), travel, sport (*The Cricketing Cowdreys*), cookery, humour (*How to Survive School*), and leisure. Also thrillers, crime, war, women's and contemporary fiction. Experience in the publishing business has helped to attract some top names. No scripts, poetry, science fiction, academic or educational. *Special interests* sport, political, current affairs, and popular fiction. Preliminary letter with s.a.e. essential. No reading fee.
Commission Home 10%; US 19%; Translation 19%.

Norman Payne TV Scripts (Albemarle Scripts)

109 Ullswater Crescent, London SW15 3RE
☎ 01–546 9747

Contact *Norman Payne*

FOUNDED 1947. Television and radio scripts, but mostly television. Particularly interested in comedy sitcom and sketch material. Prospective writers should write a letter in the first instance. No reading fee.
Commission Home 10%. *Overseas associates* West Germany (Cologne).

Penman Literary Agency

175 Pall Mall, Leigh-on-Sea, Essex SS9 1RE
☎ 0702 74438

Contact *Leonard G. Stubbs*

FOUNDED 1950. *Handle* mainly fiction, and a small amount of non-fiction (biography and autobiography). Occasional scripts. No Westerns. No unsolicited mss. Prefer prelimin-

ary letter with synopsis. No reading fee.
Commission Home 10%; Overseas 15%.

The Peters Fraser & Dunlop Group Ltd

5th Floor, The Chambers, Chelsea Harbour, Lots Road, London SW10 0XF
☎ 01–376 7676 Fax 01–352 7356

Contact *Michael Sissons* (books), *Anthony Jones* (film/TV), *Pat Kavanagh* (books and serials), *Norman North* (TV drama/fiction), *Caroline Dawnay* (books), *Charles Walker* (TV documentary/books), *Araminta Whitley* (books), *Kenneth Ewing & Gordon Dickerson* (theatre), *Tim Corrie* (film), *Richard Wakeley* (film/TV), *Mark Lucas* (books), *Maureen Vincent & Ginette Chambers* (acting), *Shan Morley Jones & Lucinda Culpin* (books/June Hall agency)

FOUNDED April 1988 as a result of the merger of A. D. Peters & Co Ltd and Fraser & Dunlop. **The June Hall Literary Agency** joined the group in November. *Handle* all sorts of books, plus scripts. No third-rate DIY. *Special interests* 'Building careers for writers of talent.' Michael Sissons, Pat Kavanagh (married to Julian Barnes) and Anthony Jones are one of the most high-powered teams in London. Handle the Evelyn Waugh estate. Fraser & Dunlop bring their experience as a show business agency to the group. Also good for radio/TV writing. No unsolicited mss. Prospective clients should write 'a full and honest letter, with a clear account of what he/she has done and wants to do.' No reading fee. CLIENTS include Sally Beauman, Margaret Drabble, Clive James, Robert McCrum, John Mortimer, John Osborne, Douglas Reeman, Ruth Rendell, Anthony Sampson, Gerald Seymour, Tom Stoppard.
Commission Home 10%; US 20%; Translation 20%.

Laurence Pollinger Ltd

18 Maddox Street, London W1R 0EU
☎ 01–629 9761 Fax 01–629 9765

Contact *Gerald J. Pollinger, Margaret Pepper, Romany van Bosch, Juliet Burton* (Negotiating Editor), *Lesley Hadcroft* (children's books)

FOUNDED 1958. A division of Pearn, Pollinger & Higham. *Handle* all types of books except pure science, academic and technological. No plays. Authors include Graham Greene and the literary estates of H. E. Bates, Scott Fitzgerald, D. H. Lawrence and other notables. Good for romantic fiction. Unsolicited mss welcome if preceded by letter (not phone). Charge £5 contribution towards editorial costs.
Commission Home 15%; US 15%; Translation 20%.

Murray Pollinger

4 Garrick Street, London WC2E 9BH
☎ 01–836 6781

Contact *Murray Pollinger, Gina Pollinger*

FOUNDED 1969. Part of the Pollinger dynasty (Murray is the youngest son of Laurence) with a particularly strong name for new writers. Securely based on Roald Dahl and one or two big selling literary novelists. *Handle* all types of general fiction and non-fiction, except poetry, plays and travel. No scripts of any kind. No unsolicited mss; writers should send a letter with synopsis and names of other agents and publishers previously approached. CLIENTS include J. M. Coetzee, Roald Dahl, John Gribbin, Molly Keane, Penelope Lively, Lyall Watson.
Commission Home 10%; Foreign 20%. *Overseas associates* in all major cultural centres.

Shelley Power Literary Agency Ltd

PO Box 149A, Surbiton, Surrey KT6 5JH
48 Kings Road, Long Ditton, Surrey KT6 5JF
☎ 01–398 7723 Fax 01–398 8723

Contact *Shelley Power*

FOUNDED 1976. *Handle* general commercial fiction, quality fiction, business books, self-help, film and entertainment, investigative exposés, writers from South Africa. No scripts, short stories, children's or poetry. Preliminary letter with brief outline of project (plus s.a.e.) essential, and should be sent to PO Box, not Kings Road address. No reading fee. CLIENTS include Kenneth Cameron, Stephen Gray, Peter Lambley, Sutherland Lyall, Lewis Nkosi, Madge Swindells, Roger Wilkes.
Commission Home 10%; US 15–19%; Translation 19%.

PVA Management Ltd

Alpha Tower, Paradise Circus,
Birmingham B1 1TT
☎ 021–643 4011

Contact *Ruth Adcock*

FOUNDED 1978. Mainly non-fiction with some fiction. Scripts. Prefer preliminary letter with synopsis and return postage.
Commission Home and Abroad 15%. *Overseas*

associates Paul Vaughan Associates, Los Angeles.

Radala & Associates

17 Avenue Mansions, Finchley Road,
London NW3 7AXZ
☎ 01–794 4495
Telex 295441 Fax 01–209 1231

Contact *Richard Gollner, Neil Hornick, István Siklôs*

Do not specialise in particular areas of publishing but simply handle anything their clients can produce 'if we think it has prospects'. Radala 'invented' the popular computing book, and handled over 1000 titles in the early 1980s. Also handle theatre, film, TV, radio and the popular arts; writing from Eastern Europe; and psychotherapy. Provide editorial services, mastermind projects of their own, and will often recommend expert independent professional readers if they can't read something themselves.

"We avoid on principle mss entitled 'Battle of Hedgehog River', 'My battle of the Bulge' or anything else with 'My' in the title. Rabidly right-wing military thrillers with titles like 'Red Menace at Dawn' or 'Red Curtains over Greenham' get short shrift. Thinly disguised autobiographical novels entitled 'Page Three Girl' tend to make us gloomy. Anything in which a female victim gladly bares her breast to the whip is liable to end up in the office shredder. Plays written in broad Gaelic vernacular are difficult to push. Our drawerful of decaying Raymond Chandler and John Le Carré pastiches is full to overflowing. Esoteric studies written for a target readership of three fellow-enthusiasts in Surrey do not excite our commercial taste-buds. We don't want to read your closely-typed 300-page true story about how you rescued, nursed, reared and trained an injured budgie. Save your epic 'Sword 'n' Sorcery' trilogy for some more deserving victim. World War Two reminiscences have all been written. Really. Believe me."

Prospective clients should send a shortish letter plus synopsis '(that's a synopsis – not a 30-page abridged version!)' and sample chapter (double-spaced). Especially like letters which show that authors 'already know where to place such simple items as commas, full-stops and hyphens'.

Commission Home 10%; US 15–20%; Translation 20%. *Overseas associates* **Writers House Inc.** (Al Zuckermann), New York, plus agents throughout Europe.

Douglas Rae Management

28 Charing Cross Road, London WC2H 0DB
☎ 01–836 3903

Contact *Douglas Rae*

FOUNDED 1975. Novels, biographies, screenplays, theatre and TV plays. No short stories or poetry. Good reputation for both film and television rights, the main work of the company. Not so happy with books. *Special interests* novels with film and television potential. Unsolicited mss not welcome. Prefer introductory letter, enclosing s.a.e. 'Not taking on new clients at present,' though. No reading fee. CLIENTS include John Briley and Derek Marlowe.

Commission Home 10%; US 15%; Translation 20%.

Margaret Ramsay Ltd

14A Goodwins Court, St Martin's Lane,
London WC2N 4LL
☎ 01–240 0691/836 7403

Contact *Margaret Ramsay, Tom Erhardt* (foreign rights), *Stephanie Tanner* (television)

Established in the 1960s. The grand dame of the agency business Margaret (Peggy) Ramsay has been immortalised in book, play and film as Joe Orton's business brain. During 1988 the following plays on in London or touring have come out of the Margaret Ramsay agency: *Les Liaisons Dangereuses; Shirley Valentine; The Secret Rapture; Henceforward* ... Also handles scripts for TV, radio and film. Writers should approach by letter or phone in the first instance. No reading fee. CLIENTS include Alan Ayckbourn, Christopher Hampton and David Hare.

Commission Home 10%; US 10%; Translation 10%. *Overseas associates* South America, France, Germany, Holland, Israel, Italy, Japan and Scandinavia.

Jim Reynolds Associates

Westbury Mill, Westbury,
Northamptonshire NN13 5JS
☎ 0280 701582 Fax 0280 703640

Contact *Jim Reynolds*

FOUNDED 1988. *Handle* military history; social history; political history; current affairs; investigative journalism; biography; cricket; and quality fiction. No scripts, category fiction, instructional, technical, scientific, business, DIY, children's or poetry. No unsolicited mss. Prefer initial letter describing proposed submission or project, with outline on author's history and

s.a.e. CLIENTS include Martin Adeney, Sir Anthony Farr-Hockley, Dr Alan Gilmour, Graham Leach, John Pertwee, Peter West.
Commission Home 10%; US 19%; Translation 19%. *Overseas associates* Robert Ducas USA; Peter Fritz, Germany; Monical Heyum, Scandinavia; Mary Kling, France; Dennis Linder, Italy; Julio Yanez, Spain; William Miller, Japan.

Rogers, Coleridge & White Ltd

20 Powis Mews, London W11 1JN
☎ 01-221 3717
Telex 25930 DEBROG G Fax 01-221 9084

Contact *Deborah Rogers, Gill Coleridge, Patricia White, Ann Warnford Davis* (foreign rights)

FOUNDED 1967. Recent change of name from Deborah Rogers Ltd. *Handle* fiction and non-fiction, also children's books. No poetry, plays or technical books. Rights representative in UK for several New York agents.
Commission Home 10%; US 15%. *Overseas associates* ICM, New York.

Rostrum Literary Agency Ltd

Suite 477, Royal Exchange, Manchester M2 7DD
☎ 061-456 8035 Fax 061-483 4747

Directors *Eric Falk, Marg Falk*

FOUNDED 1986. *Handle* full-length fiction and non-fiction; biography and autobiography (ghostwriting facilities available); also film, TV, radio and theatre scripts. No poetry or short stories. No unsolicited mss. Preliminary letter with s.a.e. in the first instance. CLIENTS include Christopher Beddows, Joe Cooper, Shirley Goode, Molly Lillis, Robert Redmond, Roderick Wilkinson and Jane Woodrow.
Commission Home 10%; Overseas 19%.

Herta Ryder

c/o Toby Eady Associates Ltd, 7 Gledhow Gardens, London SW5 0BL
☎ 01-948 1010/370 6292

Contact *Herta Ryder*

FOUNDED 1984. *Handle* fiction; non-fiction (except technical/textbooks); children's (particularly for older children); popular music (i.e. 'lives' rather than specialist); military history; German books of quality (London representative of Liepman AG, Zurich). No scripts, poetry, individual short stories or articles. Reliable and conscientious. *Special interests* children's and books from Canada. Unsolicited mss considered but explanatory letter preferred in the first instance. CLIENTS include Judy Blume, Gwyneth Jones (Ann Halam), Jean Morris, Farley Mowat.
Commission Home 10%; US 15%; Translation 20%. *Overseas associates* Harold Ober Associates, New York, plus associates in most other countries.

Tessa Sayle Agency

11 Jubilee Place, London SW3 3TE
☎ 01-823 3883 Fax 01-823 3363

Contact *Tessa Sayle* (books), *Penny Tackaberry* (drama)

FOUNDED 1976 under present ownership; (previously traded as Hope, Leresche & Sayle). *Handle* fiction: literary novels rather than category fiction; non-fiction: current affairs, social issues, biographies, historical; drama (TV, film and theatre): contemporary social issues, or drama with comedy, rather than broad comedy. No children's, textbooks, science fiction, fantasy, horror or musicals. No unsolicited mss. Preliminary letter essential, including a brief biographical note and a synopsis. No reading fee. CLIENTS include (books) Peter Benson, Margaret Forster, Thomas Keneally, Phillip Knightley, David Pallister, William Styron, Mary Wesley; (drama) Shelagh Delaney, Robert David McDonald, Geoff McQueen, Ayshe Raif, Trix Worrell.
Commission Home 10%; US 20%; Translation 20%. *Overseas associates* in USA, Japan and throughout Europe.

Linda Seifert Associates

18 Ladbroke Terrace, London W11 3PG
☎ 01-229 5163/221 0692
Telex Linda London 21879 G Fax 01-221 0637

Contact *Linda Seifert, Elizabeth Dench*

FOUNDED 1972. *Handle* scripts for television and film only. Unsolicited mss will be read, but a letter with sample of work and c.v. (plus s.a.e.) is preferred. CLIENTS include Tony Grisoni *Queen of Hearts,* Michael Radford *White Mischief,* Stephen Volk *Gothic.*
Commission Home 10%. *Overseas associates* The Agency, Triad (both Los Angeles).

James Sharkey Associates Ltd

3rd Floor, 15 Golden Square, London W1R 3AG
☎ 01-434 3801 Telex 295251 JSALON G
Contact *Sebastian Born*

FOUNDED 1983. Actors' and literary agency.

Special interests all dramatic scripts: film/TV/ theatre/radio. Some books. Preliminary letter preferred in the first instance. No reading fee.
Commission 10% across the board.

Vincent Shaw Associates

20 Jays Mews, Kensington Gore,
London SW7 2EP
☎ 01–581 8215 Fax 01–225 1079

Contact *Vincent Shaw, Cherry Palfrey*

FOUNDED 1954. *Handle* TV, radio and theatre scripts only. Unsolicited mss welcome; approach in writing (no phone calls) enclosing s.a.e.
Commission Home 10%; US and Translation by negotiation. *Overseas associates* Herman Chessid, New York.

Anthony Sheil Associates Ltd

43 Doughty Street, London WC1N 2LF
☎ 01–405 9351
Telex 946240 Fax 01–831 2127

Contact *Anthony Sheil, Giles Gordon, Mic Cheetham, Vivien Green, Richard Scott Simon* (books), *Janet Fillingham* (film drama), *Paul Marsh* (Marsh & Sheil foreign).

FOUNDED 1962. *Handle* full-length fiction and non-fiction. Also theatre, film, radio and TV scripts. Unsolicited mss welcome. Preliminary letter and return postage essential. No reading fee. CLIENTS include Peter Ackroyd, Catherine Cookson, John Fowles, Sue Townsend.
Commission Home 10%; US 20%; Translation 20%. *Overseas offices* Anthony Sheil Inc., c/o Sanford J. Greenburger Associates, 55 Fifth Avenue, NY 10003, New York, USA.

Caroline Sheldon Literary Agency

7 Hillgate Place, London W8 7SS
☎ 01–727 9102

Contact *Caroline Sheldon*

FOUNDED 1985. *Handle* adult fiction, and in particular women's, both commercial sagas and literary novels. Also full-length children's fiction (15,000 word minimum). No TV/film scripts unless by clients who also write books. Send letter with all relevant details of ambitions and four chapters of proposed book (large s.a.e.). No reading fee.
Commission Home 10%; US 20%; Translation 20% handled by Jennifer Luithlen, The Rowans, 88 Holmfield Road, Leicester.

Jeffrey Simmons

10 Lowndes Square, London SW1X 9HA
☎ 01–235 8852

Contact *Jeffrey Simmons*

FOUNDED 1978. *Handle* biography and autobiography, cinema and theatre, fiction (both quality and commercial), history, law and crime, politics and world affairs, parapsychology, sports and travel (but not exclusively). No children's books, cookery, crafts and hobbies, gardening. Film scripts handled only if by book-writing clients. *Special interests* personality books of all sorts and fiction from young writers (i.e. under 40) with a future. Writers become clients by personal introduction or by letter, enclosing a synopsis if possible, a brief biography of the author, a note of any previously published books, plus a list of any publishers and agents who have already seen the mss. CLIENTS include Michael Bentine, Fenton Bresler, Doris Collins, Adrienne Corri, Daniel Easterman, John Feltwell, Tim Fitzgeorge-Parker, Greenpeace Books, Fred Lawrence Guiles, Rosie Swale.
Commission Home 10–15%; US 15-20%; Translation 20%.

Richard Scott Simon Ltd

43 Doughty Street, London WC1N 2LF
☎ 01–405 9351

Contact *Richard Simon, Vivien Green*

FOUNDED 1971. *Handle* general non-fiction and fiction, biography, travel, cookery, humour. No scripts, romantic novels, poetry, academic, scientific, educational or children's. Preliminary letter with s.a.e. essential. CLIENTS include Rabbi Lionel Blue, Melvyn Bragg, Helen Forrester, Susan Hill, Tom Sharpe, Carolyn Slaughter, Rose Tremain. Recent titles: *Rich* Melvyn Bragg; *Blood Orange* Sam Llewellyn; *Zest for Life* Barbara Griggs; *The Sadness of Witches* Janice Eliot, *The Double Eagle* Stephen Brook.
Commission Home 10%; US 15%; Translation 20%. *Overseas associates* **Georges Borchardt Inc.** UK representative for **Farrar, Straus and Giroux Inc.**

Carol Smith Literary Agency

25 Hornton Court, Kensington High Street,
London W8 7RT
☏ 01–937 4874

Contact *Carol Smith*

FOUNDED 1976. Ex-**A. P. Watt.** *Handle* general fiction of all sorts and general non-fiction. Scripts for TV/film only rarely. Absolutely no technical; occasionally children's. Reputed to be good on encouraging talented young novelists. Unsolicited mss welcome with return postage. Introductory letter preferred. No reading fee. CLIENTS include Alexander Frater, Sarah Harrison, Katie Stewart, Mike Wilks.
Commission Home 10%; US 15%; Translation 20%.

Solo Syndication & Literary Agency Ltd

49–53 Kensington High Street, London W8 5ED
☏ 01–376 2166
Telex 925235 SOLO G Fax 01–938 3165

Contact *Don Short* (Chairman), *John Appleton* (Senior Executive & Accounts), *Trevor York* (Syndication Manager)

FOUNDED 1978. *Handle* non-fiction. *Special interests* celebrity autobiographies, unauthorised biographies, outback & adventure stories, wildlife, nature & ecology, crime, fashion, beauty & health. Also some fiction but only from established authors only. No unsolicited mss. Preliminary letter essential. CLIENTS include Britt Ekland, Mike Gatting, Sir James Mancham, James Oram, Fred Perry.
Commission Home 15%; US 20%; Translation 20–30%.
Also specialises in worldwide newspaper syndication of photos, features, cartoons. Professional contributors only. CLIENTS include *Daily Mail, Mail on Sunday, YOU Magazine, The Evening Standard,* Guinness Books, *Guiness Book of Records,* News Limited of Australia and others. Also fifty Fleet Street and international freelance journalists. Syndication commission terms: 50/50%.

Elaine Steel

25–7 Oxford Street, London W1R 1RF
☏ 01–437 1090
Telex 8954713 ALFA G Fax 01–434 1726

Contact *Elaine Steel*

FOUNDED 1986. Fiction and non-fiction. Scripts. No technical or academic. Prefer initial phone call or letter. CLIENTS include Les Blair, Karl Francis, Troy Kennedy Martin, G. F. Newman.
Commission Home 10%; US 20%; Translation 20%. *Overseas associates* Susan Burgholz, New York; Geoffrey Sandford, Los Angeles.

Abner Stein

10 Roland Gardens, London SW7 3PH
☏ 01–373 0456/370 7859 Fax 01–370 6316

Contact *Abner Stein*

FOUNDED 1971. *Handle* full-length fiction and non-fiction. General non-fiction only; no scientific, technical, etc. No scripts. Prefer letter and outline in the first instance rather than unsolicited mss.
Commission Home 10%; US 15%; Translation 20%.

Micheline Steinberg

110 Frognal, London NW3 6XU
☏ 01–794 0414

Contact *Micheline Steinberg*

FOUNDED 1988. Specialises in plays for stage, TV, radio and film. Prefer preliminary letter and s.a.e. in the first instance. Dramatic associate for **Laurence Pollinger Limited.**
Commission Home 10%; Abroad 15%.

The Stone Syndicate

9 Mountacre Close, London SE26 6SX
☏ 01–670 4419

Contact *Charles Garvie, Chancery Stone*

FOUNDED 1989. Short fiction only: 'unconventional noir, especially crime passionnel, macabre, horror (not schlock) and fantasy – but no wizards or barbarians. No scripts. No novels, women's fiction, feminism or sexism; no buddy-buddy fiction, slice-of-life vignettes or Catherine Cookson imitations. Nothing that would be suitable for *Woman's Own,* and positively no art.' *Special interests* 'Keep it dark!' No unsolicited mss. Prefer preliminary letter with details of author's history; include s.a.e. and please ensure that drafts are easily legible.
Commission Home 50%; US 50%.

Peter Tauber Press Agency

94 East End Road, London N3 2SX
☏ 01–346 4165

Contact Directors *Peter Tauber, Robert Tauber*

FOUNDED 1950. *Handle* autobiographies and exposé biographies of the famous only, well researched spicy historical romance (over 100,000 words), gripping thrillers incorporating specialised knowledge and literature. Unpublished fiction writers under 50 only. No poetry, short stories, scripts, plays or children's. Preliminary letter with synopsis, c.v. and s.a.e. essential. No reading fee.
Commission Home 20%; US 20%; Translation 20%.

J. M. Thurley

213 Linen Hall, 156–170 Regent Street,
London W1R 5TA
☎ 01–437 9545/6

Contact *Jon Thurley, Mary Alderman*

FOUNDED 1976. *Handle* all types of fiction, non-fiction, coffee table books, etc. Also scripts for TV/radio/theatre. No short stories or children's illustrated books. No unsolicited mss; approach by letter in the first instance. No reading fee.
Commission Home 10%; US 15%; Translation 15%.

Harvey Unna & Stephen Durbridge Ltd

See **Lemon, Unna & Durbridge Ltd**

Vardey & Brunton Associates

Studio 8, 125 Moore Park Road,
London SW6 4PS
☎ 01–384 1248 Fax 01–384 1246

Contact *Carolyn Brunton, Lucinda Vardey*

FOUNDED 1985. All general fiction and non-fiction, including illustrated books. No scripts, children's, science fiction or academic. Approach by letter outlining book in the first instance. CLIENTS include Julia Baird, Ian Taylor, Ben Wicks. Represent US & Canadian publishers and agents including Addison-Wesley, David Godine, Penguin Canada, Madison Press and Key Porter Books.
Commission Home 10%; US 20%; Translation 20%. *Overseas associates* Lucinda Vardey Agency Ltd, Toronto.

Ed Victor Ltd

162 Wardour Street, London W1V 3AT
☎ 01–734 4795 Telex 263361

Contact *Ed Victor, Maggie Phillips, Caroline Daubery*

FOUNDED 1976. *Handle* a broad range, from Iris Murdoch to Irving Wallace, Paula Yates to Stephen Spender. Tend towards the more commercial ends of the fiction and non-fiction spectrums. No scripts, no academic. Preliminary letter essential, setting out very concisely and clearly what the book aims to do. No unsolicited mss. Take on 'very few new writers'. After trying book publishing and literary magazines, Ed Victor, an ebullient American, found his true vocation. Strong opinions, very pushy and works hard for those whose intelligence he respects. Loves nothing more than a good title auction. CLIENTS include Douglas Adams, Jack Higgins, Erica Jong, Iris Murdoch, Erich Segal, Stephen Spender, Irving Wallace.
Commission Home 15%; US 15%; Translation 20%.

S. Walker Literary Agency

96 Church Lane, Goldington, Bedford MK41 0AS
☎ 0234 216229

Contact *Alan Oldfield, Cora-Louise Oldfield, E. K. Walker*

FOUNDED 1939. *Handle* full-length fiction and some non-fiction. No poetry or short topical articles. No unsolicited mss. Preliminary letter enclosing synopsis and return postage essential.
Commission Home 10%; US 20%; Translation 20%. *Overseas associates* Work in conjunction with agencies in most European countries and also negotiate directly with foreign publishers.

Cecily Ware Literary Agents

19C John Spencer Square, Canonbury,
London N1 2LZ
☎ 01–359 3787

Contact *Cecily Ware, Gilly Schuster, Elizabeth Comstock-Smith*

FOUNDED 1972. Primarily a film and television script agency, representing work in all areas: drama, children's, series/serials, adaptations, comedies, etc. Also *handles* children's books, radio and theatre. Very few new clients being taken on. No unsolicited mss or phone calls, and no synopses; approach in writing only. No reading fee.
Commission Home 10%; US 10–20% by arrangement.

Warner Chappell Plays Ltd (formerly English Theatre Guild)

129 Park Street, London W1Y 3FA
☎ 01–629 7600
Telex 268403 Fax 01–499 9718

Contact *Michael Callahan*

Chappell are both agents and publishers of scripts for the theatre. No unsolicited mss; introductory letter essential. No reading fee. CLIENTS include Ray Cooney, Arthur Miller, John Steinbeck.
Commission Home 10%; US 20%. *Overseas representatives* in USA, Canada, Australia, New Zealand, India, South Africa and Zimbabwe.

Watson, Little Ltd

Suite 8, 26 Charing Cross Road,
London WC2H 0DG
☎ 01–836 5880/379 3077 Fax 01–379 7731

Contact *Sheila Watson, Amanda Little*

Very catholic range of subjects. *Specialist interests* military, gardening and business books. No scripts. Would not be interested in an author who wishes to be a purely academic writer. Always write a preliminary ('intelligent') letter rather than send unsolicited synopsis. £10 reading fee.
Commission Home 10%; US 19%; Translation 19%. *Overseas associates* McIntosh & Otis, New York; Mohrbooks, Zurich; La Nouvelle Agence, Paris; Agenzia Letteria Internazionale, Milan; Rombach & Partners, Netherlands; Suzanne Palme, Scandinavia; Carmene Balcells, Spanish & Portuguese (world-wide); Tuttle-Mori, Japan. Works with several dramatic and film/TV agencies.

A. P. Watt

20 John Street, London WC1 2DR
☎ 01–405 6774
Telex 297903 APWATT G Fax 01–831 2154

Contact *Hilary Rubinstein, Caradoc King, Rod Hall* (plays), *Pamela Todd* (children's)

FOUNDED 1875. The oldest established literary agency in the world. *Handle* all full-length typescripts, including children's books, screenplays for film and TV, and plays. No poetry, academic or specialist works. Unsolicited mss and outlines welcome, preceded preferably by introductory letter, plus return postage. No reading fee. CLIENTS include Nadine Gordimer, Michael Holroyd, Lucy Irvine, Garrison Keillor, Alison Lurie, Jan Morris, Frank Muir, Graham Swift, Bill Tidy. Represent, too, the Yeats and Kipling estates.
Commission Home 10%; US 20%; Translation 20%. *Overseas associates* **Ellen Levine Inc.** (USA).

Dinah Wiener Ltd

27 Arlington Road, London NW1 7ER
☎ 01–388 2577 Telex 264550

Contact *Dinah Wiener*

FOUNDED 1985. *Handle* fiction and general non-fiction: auto/biography popular science, cookery. No scripts, children's or poetry. Approach with preliminary letter in first instance, giving full but brief c.v. of past work and future plans. Mss submitted must include s.a.e. and be typed in double-spacing. CLIENTS include Dalene Matthee, Michael Thornton, Danah Zohar.
Commission Home 15%; US 20%; Translation 20%. *Overseas office* in New York.
w

David Wilkinson Associates

Greener House, 66–8 Haymarket,
London SW1Y 4AW
☎ 01–839 6753 Telex 265871 RESRHL 001

Contact *David Wilkinson, Abigail Concannon*

General fiction and non-fiction, and scripts. No unsolicited material. Prefer initial phone call or introductory letter. No reading fee.
Commission varies according to contract.

Copyright and Moral Right

It is good to know that authors have moral rights. Like me you may find this difficult to believe since for most publishers of my acquaintance 'morality' is not a word that trips easily off their tongues. Still, it must be true because the new Copyright Bill fills ten pages in saying so.

Reduced to their essentials, the moral rights that are now ours, all ours, are the right 'to be identified as the author of a work' and the right 'to object to derogatory treatment'. In the way lawyers have of trying to stop us worrying about vague generalisations by making them yet more vague, the first right is now commonly referred to as the right of paternity (should this not be 'maternity'?) and the second as the right to integrity.

I have got so far as to work out that paternity implies identification. If I am father of the book, this fact should be proclaimed loudly and clearly. Otherwise there might be those who assume the worst of the milkman.

But is it not axiomatic that an author should be 'identified in or on each copy or, if that is not appropriate, in some other manner likely to bring his identity to the notice of the person acquiring the copy?' For most of the books on my shelves paternity blazes forth like a bright beacon. Invariably the name of the author appears in bolder type than the title of his work while on the rear of the dust jacket I am given a more than adequate run down on his life and times.

But wait. I have before me what is quite evidently a ghosted biography. The name of a famous showbusiness personality is flashed across the title page while the true author is lost in the acknowledgements, recognised only by those who know how to interpret a line of thanks to A.N. Other 'for helping me to marshal my thoughts into logical order'. So perhaps we can assume that under the Copyright Act, A.N. Other will emerge from the shadows. No, we cannot. Ghosted biographies will remain ghosted because moral rights 'can be waived by written agreement or with the consent of the author'. And A.N. Other needs the work.

The procedure is easier for journalists. They do not have to sign away their moral rights because they do not have any to begin with. Newspaper and magazine publishers successfully lobbied the government to spare them the pain of having to think too carefully about moral responsibilities to their contributors.

It is the same for writers who sell their efforts to 'an encyclopedia, dictionary, yearbook or other collective work of reference' which puts paid to hopes of anyone, apart from the editor, achieving a decent credit in *The Writer's Handbook*.

But if right of paternity is little more than a restatement of the existing position, we can surely expect more from the right of integrity. This is supposed to deter a publisher from changing an author's text to an extent that 'amounts to distortion or mutilation ... or is otherwise prejudicial to the honour or reputation of the author'. If he is unable to resist the urge to amend a text out of recognition, the full force of the law can be brought to bear on the miscreant, assuming, of course, that the writer can afford a lawyer or, indeed, find one who is prepared to take on a case in such a murky area.

Since the Copyright Act has nothing to say about competing moral rights, I suppose I have no redress against an editor who committed me to one of the most horrible abominations of English misusage by changing 'he' to 'he/she' throughout a lengthy text. She explained that as a feminist she too had moral rights. The only difference was that her moral rights were more important than mine. She should go far in publishing.

The Basis of Copyright

Copyright extends to books, articles, plays, films and records. In most books a copyright notice appears on one of the front pages. In its simplest form this is the symbol © followed by the name of the copyright owner and the year of first publication. The assertion of copyright may be emphasised by the phrase 'All rights reserved', and in case there are any lingering doubts the reader may be warned that 'No part of this publication may be reproduced or transmitted in any form or by any means without permission'.

But this is to overstate the case. It is perfectly legitimate for a writer to quote from someone else's work for 'purposes of criticism or review' as long as 'sufficient acknowledgement' is given. What he must not do is to lift 'a substantial part' of a copyright work without permission. Unfortunately, there is little agreement on what constitutes 'a substantial part', since the Copyright Act does not define the term. Legal precedents suggest that the quality of the 'part' and its value to the user must be taken into account as well as its length in determining whether it is 'substantial'. This explains how, in one case, four lines from a thirty-two line poem were held to amount to 'a substantial part'. On the other hand, even a 'substantial' quotation from a copyright work may be acceptable if a reviewer or critic is engaged in 'fair dealing' with his subject. But no-one should be surprised to hear that 'fair dealing' is another of those terms which is open to legal interpretation.

What Does Copyright Cover?

In Britain, copyright protection lasts for fifty years from the end of the year in which the author dies. For a published work of joint authorship, protection runs from the end of the year of the death of the author who dies last. The fifty year rule applies to all written work including letters.

Freelance Journalists

According to the 1988 Copyright Act, freelancers automatically own the copyright of written, commissioned material. An editor acquires only those rights intended by both parties at the time of commissioning. At issue here is not simply the right to have a say on how material is used after its first publication but the more sensitive issue of supplementary fees.

Copyright on Ideas

In radio and television, in particular, writers have the problem of trying to sell ideas for which it is almost impossible to stake an exclusive claim. So much unsolicited material comes the way of the script departments, that duplication of ideas is inevitable.

Frequent complaints of plagiarism have led major production companies to point out the risks whenever they acknowledge an unsolicited synopsis or script. For example, **Thames Television** warns correspondents, 'it is often the case that we are currently considering or have already considered ideas that may be similar to your own'. The standard letter goes on:

> The fact that we are prepared to consider your material implies no obligation on our part to use your work. Equally, it does not mean that you are under any obligation to Thames: you are free to submit your material to any other parties you wish. We cannot undertake to consider your work on any basis of confidentiality. We must be free to discuss your work openly in the course of our consideration ...'

If these conditions are not acceptable, the letter concludes, 'we will not be able to consider your material'.

It is a fair warning though probably of little comfort to those who have suffered the attention of unscrupulous rivals. In a highly competitive, fast-moving business, manuscripts can end up in the wrong hands. If there are worries on this score, a useful precaution is to copy a manuscript, send it to yourself by registered post, then deposit the package and dated receipt at a bank or other safe place. At least then no one can fault your memory on essential detail.

Copyright on Characters

Even when a script is accepted for broadcasting, problems of copyright can still occur. A frequent source of dispute is the lifting of characters from one series to another when there are two or more writers involved. Kenneth Royce had this experience when his detective, George Bulman was transferred from *The XYY Man*, a TV adaptation of four Royce books, to a new series, *Strangers*, and later to yet another series called *Bulman*. By then Kenneth Royce's involvement was limited to 'one begrudging credit on the last episode of every series'.

Disputes of this sort will doubtless continue under the new Copyright Act. 'TV people like to believe that the character becomes their own', writes Kenneth Royce, 'forgetting that without the author's original, there would be no such character'. As a minimum precaution he urges a writer approaching a TV deal 'to resist strongly any attempt to change the names of his characters'. Why make stealing easier than it already is?

Copyright in Titles

If copyright over characters is difficult to establish, it is near impossible with titles. Only when a title is distinctive and clearly identified with the work of a particular author is there any chance of gaining an injunction against its use, or something very close to it, by another writer.

US Copyright

The US Copyright Act of 1909 provided for two separate terms of copyright, a period of twenty-eight years from publication followed by a renewal period of a further twenty-eight years. A new copyright act, which came into force in January 1978, made changes in the duration of copyright protection and set out rules for the transition of existing works.

Copyrights registered before 1950 and renewed before 1978 were automatically extended by the new act until December of the seventy-fifth year of the original date of registration. This meant that all copyrights in their second term were extended for nineteen years. But copyrights registered after 1950 and before December 1977 had to be renewed. The repercussions continue to this day since a work published in 1960 had to be renewed before 31 December 1988 (1960 + 28) in order to obtain protection for the full seventy-five year period.

Works created after the new law came into force are automatically protected for the author's lifetime, and for an additional fifty years after the author's death.

The Economics of Freelancing

The economics of newspaper and magazine publishing have helped to promote the freelancer. It makes sense for editors to keep a news team on the payroll, but no sense at all to take on board occasional contributors who can just as easily work from home. Quite a few of the top freelancers are journalists who previously held full-time jobs. Though income is variable and the demands heavy, none of them would willingly go back to regular employment.

For the newcomer, *The Writer's Handbook* listings of press and periodicals identifies receptive editors and advises on how best to make an approach. But there is no substitute for a careful study of the publication in which you hope to see your byline. It is not simply a matter of getting the subject matter right; there is also the style and length of an article to consider. What will attract one publication will repel another.

The aim of the freelancer who wants to make all or a regular part of his income from writing should be to move quickly from speculative work – where it is up to the editor to accept or reject whatever is sent in – to commissioned articles where the journalist can claim certain rights. Wherever possible, before accepting a commission, extract some sort of agreement in writing. True, a verbal commitment is binding, but if disaster strikes, like a paper folding or the editor changing his job, it is often difficult to prove that the commission was ever made.

The other advantage of a written agreement is that it compels both sides to think carefully about what is involved. What level of expenses is required? Do you want part of the fee up front? (The answer here must always be 'Yes'.) What happens if the material submitted does not fulfil the terms of the commission or is suitable but not published for other reasons? In the first case, the full fee should be paid.

Beware of talking too freely about great ideas for articles before you have a piece of paper acknowledging that you are the writer who will transform them into copy. In the chaos of the typical newspaper or magazine office, ideas are common property.

A freelancer who contributes regularly to a single publication has the right to ask for a contract, renewable say every year or six months. One of the many virtues of a contract is that it offers an element of security in an otherwise highly insecure business. At the very least, it can be waved at the bank manager when asking for an extension of the overdraft.

Both the **National Union of Journalists** and the **Institute of Journalists** have freelance sections which offer constructive advice to members and give welcome backing in disputes where a journalist who speaks for himself is liable to be shouted down. The NUJ has a code of practice for the treatment of freelancers. It decrees that conditions and rates of pay should be established clearly when work is accepted or commissioned, that freelancers should be paid for providing background information and research material, and that work commissioned or accepted should be paid for at a date agreed which should normally be no more than a month after delivery. Material submitted speculatively should be accepted or rejected within two weeks of delivery. If an editor wants more time to decide he should negotiate a holding fee. Other clauses relate to expenses (to be paid on the same basis as for permanent staff), copyright (to remain with the freelancer unless there is a signed agreement to transfer) and the responsibility of staff journalists to watch over the interests of their freelance colleagues.

The rewards of freelancing vary wildly and though where possible we have shown the minimum rates on offer from papers and journals, it must be emphasised that all publications are prepared to pay over the odds for contributors and articles they really want. Not that they will meekly concede special rates. Hard bargaining may be called for, not least with editors of national papers who will not blink at paying their in-house feature writers £30,000 or more a year.

As a general guide there are the comprehensive freelance agreements negotiated by the NUJ with leading publishers. For magazines, the highest band is £270 per thousand words for features and £27 per hundred words for news. This applies to magazines like *Bella*, *Expression*, *Smash Hits* and *Radio Times*. On the lowest band (*Asian Times*, *Everywoman*) rates fall to £90 per thousand words for features and £9 per hundred words for news.

Many journals, including some of the most prestigious, pay below these rates. When it is clear that a publication is run on a shoestring, you may feel justified in giving it support by contributing on derisory terms. But as a principle, writers should not expect, or be expected, to provide a charity service for their readers.

On the national press, news reports start at £16.50 for up to two hundred words and features at £175 per thousand words (£200 for Sundays). The regional and local press is more of a gamble. The NUJ minimum for weekly papers is £1.1 for up to and including 10 lines and 11.1p per line thereafter. The rate for dailies is £1.95 for up to and including 10 lines and 15.1p per line thereafter. But if our research shows anything, it is that in the provinces, all deals are possible. Newspaper editors who plead poverty are seldom to be taken seriously.

Radio and TV

The rates for radio and television start at £28.15 for a three-minute BBC Radio news report, plus £6.36 for each extra minute; £34.69 for a two-minute television news report, plus £8.61 for each extra minute. Radio talks and interviews of up to five minutes are valued at a minimum of £33.90. The corresponding rate for radio features and documentaries starts at £128.80 for up to seven minutes, plus £18.40 per minute thereafter.

Not Quite All is Vanity

Some Thoughts on Self Publishing

There is nothing inherently wrong in paying for the publication of your own book. This apparently obvious point is worth making because the vanity publisher is so often cast as the villain of the writing trade.

In fact, many of the big houses engage in vanity publishing, if not on a regular basis, by charging, or by agreeing to bring out an otherwise unprofitable book on condition that the author or his sponsor guarantees to buy a minimum number of copies (sufficient to cover costs and earn the publisher a reasonable return).

Another common illusion is to assume that vanity publishers only deal with the work of cranks who wouldn't get within a mile of a regular publisher. But it is sheer nonsense to assume, with *The Writers' and Artists' Yearbook*, that 'if a work is worth publishing, sooner or later a publisher will be prepared to publish it at his own expense'. The judgement of the literary establishment is by no means infallible and there are many fine books on the market which have been subsidised by their authors after being rejected by the experts.

To take a random example, it is sobering to reflect that Alice might never have got to Wonderland if Lewis Carroll had not embarked on some DIY publishing. And it is no use arguing, as many do, that what is now regarded as a classic cannot be mentioned in the same breath as vanity publishing. At the time, Carroll's detractors might well have assumed that his money was being wasted to satisfy his pride.

The real problem of vanity publishing is not so much that it caters for those who for one reason or another find themselves outside the magic circle, but that it attracts some sharp business people who put their own profit way ahead of any other considerations such as providing a half decent promotion and marketing service for their clients. Publishing is an expensive business. If an author proposes investing in his own books, he should at least make sure that his money is put to good purpose.

The Society of Authors offers sound advice on what to look out for.

1. Do not take a flattering report on your manuscript at face value. The publisher may simply be motivated by a desire to do business at your expense.
2. Be suspicious of vague promises of quality production. Subsidised books are often tatty books.
3. Regard with suspicion promises to sell television and film rights, serialisation and other money-making options. The chances of getting your money back from subsidiary rights are remote.
4. Be wary of cop-out clauses in the contract which enable the publisher to renege on his initial pitch. For example, if he tells you that he can sell two thousand copies, do not believe him when he says that it makes sense to try the market with a first print-run of five hundred copies. Or rather, do believe him but do not expect him to reprint if the market does not respond.

Always remember that a vanity publisher will want his cut irrespective of sales. For the author who is intent on self-financing, a cheaper route to publication can be via the nearest printer who will be happy to quote for producing any number of copies. The writer must then turn designer, copy editor, publicist and salesman to achieve what a conventional publisher sets out to do. This may be altogether too much for the beginner though professional help is at hand from the **Self Publishing Association** (c/o Malvern Publishing Company, Lloyds Bank Chambers, 18 High Street, Upton-upon-Severn, Worcestershire WR8 0HD. Tel 06846 4666).

For a £25 subscription, an author can submit a manuscript to an editorial panel. If it is thought to be worth publishing, the association will take care of the entire production process, leaving the author responsible only for the cost of cut-price printing. A thousand copies of a 192-page hardback costs about £2350, about a third of the sum charged by a vanity publisher. Any profit goes straight to the author.

A useful guide to self-publishing has been written by Jan Wynne-Tyson (see **Centaur Press**). Appropriately enough, he has published it himself.

National Newspapers

Daily Express

Ludgate House, 245 Blackfriars Road,
London SE1 9UX
☎ 01–928 8000
Telex 21841 Fax 01–633 0244

Owner *United Newspapers plc*
Editor *Nicholas Lloyd*
Circulation 1.63 million

Unsolicited mss generally welcome, though the weekly total is 'too numerous to count'. The general rule of thumb is to approach in writing with an idea; all departments are prepared to look at mss without commitment.
Payment depends on the nature of the article accepted.

News Editor *Michael Parry*

Diary Editor *Ross Benson*
Features Editor *Craig MacKenzie*
Literary Editor *Peter Grosvenor*
Sports Editor *David Emery*
Women's Page *Heather McGlone*

The *Daily Express* magazine is *dx.* **Editor** *Jane Owen.* A weekly colour magazine distributed in the south of England. (See also **Magazines** section.)

Daily Mail

Northcliffe House, 2 Derry Street, Kensington,
London W8 5TT
☎ 01–938 6000 Telex 28301

Owner *Lord Rothermere*
Editor *Sir David English*
Circulation 1.78 million

In-house feature writers and regular columnists provide much of the material. Photo-stories and crusading features often appear; it's essential to hit the right note to be a successful Mail writer, so close scrutiny of the paper is strongly advised. Not a good bet for the unseasoned.

News Editor *Ian Monk*

Diary Editor *Nigel Dempster*
Features Editor *Susan Douglas*
Literary Editor *Gordon McKenzie*
Sports Editor *Peter Lea*
Women's Page (Femail) *Diana Hutchinson*

Daily Mirror

Holborn Circus, London EC1P 1DQ
☎ 01–353 0246
Telex 27286 Fax 01–822 3405

Owner *Robert Maxwell*
Editor *Richard Stott*
Circulation 3.15 million

No freelance opportunities for the inexperienced. Strong writers who understand what the tabloid market demands are, however, always needed.

News Editor *Tom Hendry*

Diary Editor *Garth Gibbs*
Features Editor *Roger Collier*
Literary Editor *George Thaw*
Sports Editor *Keith Fisher*
Women's Page *Christena Appleyard*

Daily Star

Ludgate House, 245 Blackfriars Road,
London SE1 9UX
☎ 01–928 8000
Telex 21841 Fax 01–633 0244

Owner *United Newspapers plc*
Editor *Brian Hitchen*
Circulation 966,533

At one time in competition with *The Sun* for 'most flesh and least hard news' title but returned to more family fare to halt slide in circulation. Freelance opportunities almost non-existent. Few features and both these and news coverage supplied in-house or from regular outsiders.

News Editor *Graham Jones*

Entertainments *Patt Codd*
Features Editor *Mike Parker*

Sports Editor *Phil Rostron*
Women's Page *Carole Malone*

The Daily Telegraph

Peterborough Court, South Quay Plaza, 181 Marsh Wall, Isle of Dogs, London E14 9SR
☎ 01–538 5000
Telex 22874 Fax 01–515 4195

Owner *Daily Telegraph plc*
Editor *Max Hastings*
Circulation 1.1 million

Unsolicited mss not generally welcome – 'all are carefully read and considered, but only about one in a thousand is accepted for publication'. As they receive about 20 weekly, this means about one a year. Contenders should approach the paper in writing making clear their authority for writing on that subject. No fiction.

News Editor *James Allan* Tip-offs or news reports from *bona fide* journalists. Must phone the news desk in first instance. *Words* initial 200. *Payment* minimum £10 (tip).

Arts Editor *Miriam Gross*
Business Editor *Roland Gribben*
Diary Editor *David Twiston-Davies* Diary pieces always interesting, contact *Peterborough* (Diary column).
Features Editor *Veronica Wadley* By commission from established contributors. However, new writers are tried out by arrangement with the features editor. Approach in writing. *Words* 1500.
Payment c. £60–£450 and by arrangement.
Literary Editor *Nicholas Shakespeare*
Sports Editor *David Welch* Occasional opportunities for specialised items.

Colour supplement weekly called Telegraph Weekend Magazine. (See also **Magazines** section.)

Financial Times

1 Southwark Bridge, London SE1 9HL
☎ 01–873 3000
Telex 8954871 Fax 01–407 5700

Owner *Pearson plc*
Editor *Sir Geoffrey Owen*
Circulation 278,577

FOUNDED 1888. Business and finance oriented certainly, but by no means as 'featureless' as some suppose. All feature ideas must be discussed with the department's editor in advance. Not snowed under with unsolicited contributions – they get only about one a week, the lowest of any national newspaper. Approach in writing in the first instance.

News Editor *David Walker*

Arts Editor *J.D.F. Jones*
City/Financial Editor *Martin Dickson*
Features Editor *Peter Martin*
Literary Editor *Anthony Curtis*
Sports Editor *Michael Thompson-Noel*
Women's Page *Lucia van der Post*

The Guardian

119 Farringdon Road, London EC1R 3ER
☎ 01–278 2332
Telex 8811746 Fax 01–837 2114

Owner *The Scot Trust*
Editor *Peter Preston*
Circulation 438,054

Probably the greatest opportunities for freelance writers of all the nationals, if only because it has the greatest number of specialised pages which use freelance work. But mss should be directed at a specific slot.

News Editor *Paul Johnson* No opportunities except in those regions where there is presently no local contact for news stories.

'Computer Guardian' Editor *Jack Schofield* A major part of Thursday's paper, almost all written by freelancers. Expertise essential – but not a trade page, written for 'the interested man in the street', and from the user's point of view. Prefer delivery of mss by disk or electronic mail.
Diary Editor *Andrew Moncur*
Education Editor *John Fairhall* Expert pieces on modern education (covers many pages of Tuesday's paper).
Features Editor *Richard Gott* Receive up to 30 unsolicited mss a day; these are passed on to relevant page editors.
'Grassroots' Editor *John Course* Manchester-based 'forum' page dealing with a wide variety of subjects: 'the only rule of thumb is: nothing to do with London', and ordinarily not by London writers. However, the page is heavily oversubscribed; probably only 1% of contributions are successful.
'Guardian Tomorrow' Editor *Ann Shearer* Social welfare, psychology and theology, both academic and popular. Experts who write well rather than journalists. Forward looking, offbeat. Maximum of twelve pieces weekly.
Media Editor *Georgina Henry* Approximately 4 pieces a week plus diary. Outside contributions are considered. All aspects of modern media, advertising, PR, consumer trends in arts/enter-

tainments. Background insight important. Best approach: note followed by phone call.
Women's Page *Brenda Polan* Since the revamp now has '**Women's Page**' every day. This includes 'Guardian Style', 'First Person', 'Third Person', 'Choices'. Unsolicited mss used if they show an appreciation of the page in question.

The Independent

40 City Road, London EC1Y 2DB
☎ 01–253 1222
Telex 9419611 Fax 01–608 1149

Owner *Newspapers Publishing plc*
Editor *Andreas Whittam Smith*
Circulation 361,000

FOUNDED October 1986, the first new quality national in over 130 years, and the first newspaper to be very precisely targeted and researched before its launch. Aimed at a professional/office working readership, better educated and more affluent than their parents, the label 'the first yuppie newspaper' is not without justification. The content is geared towards those who only have time to dip into a paper at odd times during the day. Particularly strong on its arts/media coverage. The paper has a high proportion of feature material, and theoretically opportunities for freelancers are good. However, unsolicited mss are not welcome; most pieces originate in-house or from known and trusted outsiders. Ideas should be submitted in writing.

News Editor *John Price*

Arts Editor *Thomas Sutcliffe*
Business Editor *Sarah Hogg*
Features Editor *Matthew Symonds*
Literary Editor *Sebastian Faulks*
Sports Editor *Charles Burgess*

Colour supplement Saturday *The Independent Magazine.* **Editor** *Alexander Chancellor.* (See also **Magazines** section.)

The Mail on Sunday

Northcliffe House, 2 Derry Street, Kensington, London W8 5TT
☎ 01–938 6000 Telex 28372

Owner *Lord Rothermere*
Editor *Stewart Steven*
Circulation 1.9 million

Sunday paper with a high proportion of newsy features and articles. Experience and judgement required to break into its band of regular feature writers.

News Editor *Graeme Gourlay*

Diary *Nigel Dempster*
Features Editor *Alan Cochrane*
Literary Editor *Paula Johnson*
Sports Editor *Roger Kelly*
Women's Page *Lesley White*

The Mail on Sunday magazine is *You.* **Editor** *Nicholas Gordon.* Many feature articles are supplied entirely by freelance writers. (See also **Magazines** section.)

Morning Star

74 Luke Street, London EC2A 4PY
☎ 01–739 6166
Telex 916463 Fax 01–739 5463

Editor *Tony Chater*
Circulation 25,000

Not to be confused with the *Daily Star*, the *Morning Star* is our farthest left national daily. Those with a penchant for a Marxist reading of events and ideas can try their luck, though feature space is as competitive here as in the other nationals.

News Editor *Roger Bagley*

Arts/Features Editor *Paul Corry*
Literary Editor *Kay Holmes*
Sports Editor *Tony Braisby*
Women's Page *Kay Holmes*

The News of the World

1 Virginia Street, London E1 9XR
☎ 01–782 4000
Telex 262136 Fax 01–583 9504

Owner *News International – Rupert Murdoch*
Editor *Patsy Chapman*
Circulation 5.36 million

Highest circulation paper. Patsy Chapman has taken over from Wendy Henry, who was the first female national newspaper editor.

News Editor *Robert Warren*

Diary *Paul Connew*
Entertainments *Stuart White*
Features Editor *Paul Connew*
Literary Editor *Roy Stockdill*
Sports Editor *Bill Bateson*
Women's Page *Unity Hall*

The News of the World supplement is *Sunday Magazine.* **Editor** *Colin Jenkins* FOUNDED 1981, this weekly colour supplement magazine welcomes freelance writers' ideas and material. (See also **Magazines** section).

The Observer

Chelsea Bridge House, Queenstown Road,
London SW8 4NN
☏ 01–627 0700
Telex 772532 Fax 01–627 5570

Owner *Lonhro plc*
Editor *Donald Trelford*
Circulation 722,008

FOUNDED 1791. WEEKLY. Occupies the middle ground of Sunday newspaper politics. Unsolicited mss are not generally welcome, 'except from distinguished, established writers'. Receives too many unsolicited offerings. No news, fiction, or 'special pages' opportunities. However, Features concede that 'occasional opportunities' arise.

News Editor *John Shirley*

Arts/Features Editor *Gillian Widdicombe*
Business Editor *Melvyn Marckus*
Diary Editor *Tim Walker*
Literary Editor *Blake Morrison*
Sports Editor *David Hunn*
Women's Page *Anne Barr*
The Observer magazine is *M.* **Editor** *Angela Palmer.* Freelance writers are used extensively, but come from an experienced and comprehensive pool of writers. (See also **Magazines** section.)

The People

Holborn Circus, London EC1P 1DQ
☏ 01–353 0246
Telex 266888 Fax 01–822 3864

Owner *Robert Maxwell*
Editor *Wendy Henry*
Circulation 2.7 million

Slightly up-market version of *The News of the World.* Keen on exposés and big name gossip.

News Editor *David Farr*

Arts Editor *Maurice Krais*
Features Editor *Jill Guyte*
Sports Editor *N. Holtham*
Women's Page *Jill Guyte*

The paper's colour supplement magazine is *People Magazine.* **Editor** *Phil Swift.*

Scotland on Sunday

20 North Bridge, Edinburgh EH1 1YT
☏ 031–225 2468 Fax 031–220 2443

Owner *The Scotsman Ltd*
Editor *Andrew Jaspan*

News Editor *Bill Mackintosh*

Launched late 1988 and already selling 80,000 copies weekly by mid 1989. Also now colour magazine supplement containing features on personalities, etc., launched April 1989. **Editor** *Tim Willis.*

The Sun

1 Virginia Street, London E1 9XP
☏ 01–782 4100/1/2/3/4
Telex 267827 Fax 01–583 9513

Owner *News International – Rupert Murdoch*
Editor *Kelvin Mackenzie*
Circulation 4.2 million

Highest circulation daily newspaper. Right wing populist outlook; very keen on gossip, pop stars, tv soap, scandals and exposés of all kinds. Not much room for feature writers; 'investigative journalism' of a certain hue is always in demand, however. Was top of Press Councils Complaints League in 1987.

News Editor *Tom Petrie*

Features Editor *Stuart Higgins*
Sports Editor *David Balmforth*
Women's Page *Sue Carroll*

Sunday Express

Ludgate House, 245 Blackfriars Road,
London SE1 9UX
☏ 01–928 8000
Telex 21841 Fax 01–633 0244

Owner *United Newspapers plc*
Editor *Robin Esser*
Circulation 2 million

FOUNDED 1918. Unsolicited mss are generally welcome. Prefer to be approached in writing with an idea. One of that rare breed, a newspaper which still uses fiction. *Payment* by arrangement.

News Editor *Henry Macrory* Occasional news features by experienced journalists only. All submissions must be preceded by ideas. *Words* 750.

Diary Editor *Lady Olga Maitland*
Features Editor *Max Davidson* General features *Words* 1000. Profiles of personalities

Words 900. Showbiz features *Words* 1000–1500.
Fiction Editor *Max Davidson* Short stories of around 1800 words.
Literary Editor *Graham Lord*
Women's Page *Daphne Broadhead*

The weekly Sunday Express Magazine **Editor** *Dee Nolan* does not welcome unsolicited mss. (See also **Magazines** section.)

Sunday Mirror

Mirror Group Newspapers, 33 Holborn,
London EC1P 1DQ
☎ 01–353 0246
Telex 27286 Fax 01–822 2160

Owner *Robert Maxwell*
Editor *Eve Pollard*
Circulation 2.9 million

Eve Pollard's husband, Nick Lloyd, is editor of *The Daily Express.*

The Sunday Mirror receives anything up to 90 unsolicited mss weekly. In general terms, these are welcome, though the paper patiently points out it has 'more time for contributors who have taken the trouble to study the market'. Initial contact in writing preferred, unless 'a live news situation'. No fiction.

News Editor *John McShane* The news desk is very much in the market for tip-offs and inside information. Contributors would be expected to work with staff writers on news stories.

Features Editor *Robert Wilson* 'Anyone who has obviously studied the market will be dealt with constructively and courteously.' Cherishes its record as a breeding ground for new talent.
Diary Editor *Robert Wilson*
Literary Editor *Albert Jacobs*
Sports Editor *Anthony Smith*
Women's Page *Katherine Hadley*

Colour supplement *Sunday Mirror Magazine.* **Editor** *Eve Pollard.*

Sunday Sport

Marten House, 39–47 East Road,
London N1 6AH
☎ 01–251 2544
Telex 269277 Fax 01–608 1979

Owner *David Sullivan*
Editor *Drew Robertson*
Circulation 600,000

FOUNDED 1986. Sunday tabloid catering for a particular sector of the male 18–35 readership. As concerned with 'glamour' (for which, read page 3) as with human interest, news, features and sport. Unsolicited mss are welcome; they apparently receive about 90 a week. Approach should be made by phone in the case of news and sports items, by letter for features. No fiction.
Payment is negotiable, agreed in advance and made on publication.

News Editor *Howard Sounes* Offbeat news, human interest, preferably with photographs.

Features Editor *Christine Roderick* Regular items: 'Glamour', Showbiz and television, as well as general interest.
Sports Editor *Bobby Moore* Hardhitting sports stories on major soccer clubs and their personalities, and leading clubs and people in other sports. Strong quotations to back up the news angle essential.

Sunday Telegraph

Peterborough Court, South Quay, 181 Marsh
Wall, London E14 9SR
☎ 01–538 5000 Fax 01–538 5000

Owner *Conrad Black*
Editor *Peregrine Worsthorne*
Circulation 693,431

Right of centre quality Sunday paper (meaning it has the least tendency to bend its ear to the scandals of the hour). Traditionally starchy and correct, it is in the process of trying to pep up its image to attract a younger readership. Editorial resources of *The Daily Telegraph* and *Sunday Telegraph* have been pooled to create a seven-day news-gathering operation. The move aims to inject more of *The Daily Telegraph's* editorial punch behind *The Sunday Telegraph.*

The Sunday Times

1 Pennington Street, London E1 9XY
☎ 01–782 5000 Fax 01–782 5658

Owner *News International – Rupert Murdoch*
Editor *Andrew Neil*
Circulation 1.3 million

FOUNDED 1820. Generally right of centre with a strong crusading, investigative tradition. Unsolicited mss are always welcome, especially on the features pages, which are, by virtue of the sheer size of the newspaper, more extensive than other papers. Approach the relevant editor with an idea in writing. Close scrutiny of the style of each section of the paper is strongly advised before sending mss. No fiction. All fees by negotiation.

News Editor *Michael Williams* Opportunities

are very rare.

Arts Editor *John Whitley*
Business Editor *Roger Eglin*
Atticus (Political Diary) *Michael Jones*
Entertainments Editor *Patrick Stoddart*
Features Editor *Tony Bambridge* Submissions are always welcome, but the paper commissions its own, uses staff writers or works with literary agents, by and large. The features sections where most opportunities exist are 'Screen', 'Look', 'Leisure' and 'Spectrum'.
Literary Editor *Penny Perrick*
Look Editor (includes Women's/Beauty/Fashion) *Kate Carr*

Distributed with The Sunday Times is the weekly colour supplement *The Sunday Times Magazine.* **Editor** *Philip Clarke.* (See also **Magazines** section.)

The Times

1 Pennington Street, London E1 9XN
☎ 01–782 5000
Telex 946240 Fax 01–583 9519

Owner *News International – Rupert Murdoch*
Editor *Charles Wilson*
Circulation 436,298

Generally right (though columns/features can range in tone from diehard to libertarian). *The Times* receives a great many unsolicited offerings. Writers with feature ideas should approach by letter in the first instance. No fiction.

News Editor *John Jinks*

Business Editor *David Brewerton*
Features Editor *Richard Williams*
Home News Editor *John Jinks* Approach by phone.
Literary Editor *Phillip Howard*
Sports Editor *Tom Clarke*
Women's Page *Brigit Callaghan*

Today

Allen House, 70 Vauxhall Bridge Road, London SW1V 2RP
☎ 01–630 1300
Telex 919925 Fax 01–630 6839

Owner *News UK Ltd*
Editor *David Montgomery*
Circulation 548,362

The first of the new technology papers. Originally middle-of-the-road but under Rupert Murdoch, turned sharply to the right. Feature opportunities look to be declining fast.

News Editor *Colin Myler*

Business Editor *Cathy Gunn*
Entertainments Editor *June Walton*
Features Editor *Tessa Hilton*
Sports Editor *David Alexander*
Women's Page *Tessa Hilton*

Wales on Sunday

Thomson House, Havelock Street, Cardiff CF1 1WR
☎ 0222 223333

Owner *Western Mail & Echo Ltd*
Editor *John Humphries*

News Editor *Denis Gane*

Launched March 1989 and described by John Humphries as a 'three-in-one publication': 16-page news magazine; 24-page sports tabloid; 40-page broadsheet newspaper. Expected circulation 60,000.

Regional Newspapers

Regional newspapers are listed in alphabetical order by town or county. Thus the *Daily Record* appears under 'G' for Glasgow.

Aberdeen

Evening Express

PO Box 43, Lang Stracht, Mastrick,
Aberdeen AB9 8AF
☎ 0224 690222 Fax 0224 694613

Owner *Thomson Regional Newspapers*
Editor *Richard J. Williamson*
Circulation 80,764

Unsolicited mss welcome 'but if possible on a controlled basis'. Receive up to four a week.

News Editor *David Smith* Freelance news contributors welcome.

Features Editor *Andrew Knight* Women, fashion, showbiz, health, hobbies, property – anything will be considered on its merits.
Payment £30–40.

The Press & Journal

PO Box 43, Lang Stracht, Mastrick,
Aberdeen AB9 8AF
☎ 0224 690222 Fax 0224 685738

Owner *Thomson Regional Newspapers*
Editor *Harry Roulston*
Circulation 112,862

A well-established regional daily which receives more unsolicited mss a week than the *Sunday Mirror* – about 120 on average. Unsolicited mss are nevertheless welcome; approach should be made in writing. No fiction.

News Editor *Eric Stevenson* Wide variety of hard or offbeat news items, relating to 'the northern half of Scotland'. *Words* 500.
Payment by arrangement.

Features Editor *Norman Harper* Tightly written topical pieces, preferably with a Scottish flavour.
Words 1000.
Payment by arrangement.

Basildon

Evening Echo

Newspaper House, Chester Hall Lane, Basildon,
Essex SS14 3BL
☎ 0268 22792 Fax 0268 532060

Owner *Westminster Press*
Editor *Jim Worsdale*
Circulation 60,723

Rely almost entirely on staff/regular writers' contributions, but will consider material sent on spec. Approach the editor in writing.

Bath

Bath & West Evening Chronicle

33 Westgate Street, Bath, Avon BA1 1EW
☎ 0225 444044 Fax 0225 445969

Owner *Wessex Newspapers*
Editor *David Flintham*
Circulation 27,188

News Editor *Simon Whitby*

Features Editor *David Hamlett*
Women's Page *Tina Currie*

Belfast

Belfast Telegraph

Royal Avenue, Belfast BT1 1EB
☎ 0232 321242 Fax 0232 242287

Owner *Thomson Regional Newspapers*
Editor *Roy Lilley*
Circulation 150,000

News Editor *Norman Jenkinson*

Features Editor *Tom Carson*
Women's Page *Lindy McDowell*

Plus colour supplement 4 times yearly.

The Irish News

Donegall Street, Belfast BT1 2GE
☎ 0232 242614 Fax 0232 231282

Editor *Jim Fitzpatrick*
Circulation 42,439

News Editor *Noel Russell*

Features Editor *John Foster*

News Letter

Donegall Street, Belfast BT1 2GB
☎ 0232 244441 Fax 0232 230715

Owner *Century Newspapers Ltd*
Editor *Sam Butler*
Circulation 44,483

News Editor *Harry Robinson*

Arts Editor *Billy Kennedy*
Features Editor *Harry Robinson*
Women's Page *Niki Hill*

Also 6 issues a year of supplement *Accent* with *Sunday News*. **Editor** *Tony Bradley*.

Birmingham

Daily News

78–9 Francis Road, Edgbaston, Birmingham B16 8SP
☎ 021–454 8800 Fax 021–455 9458

Owner *Reed International*
Editor *Malcolm Ward*
Circulation 300,000

FOUNDED 1984. Britain's first free daily newspaper. Unsolicited mss generally welcome. Approach the editor in writing in the first instance.

News Editor *Claire Wolfe*

Birmingham Evening Mail

28 Colmore Circus, Birmingham B4 6AX
☎ 021–236 3366 Fax 021–233 3958

Owner *The Birmingham Post & Mail Ltd*
Editor *Ian Dowell*
Circulation 287,554

Features Editor *Dan Mason*
Women's Page *Barbara Henderson*

Freelance contributions are welcome, particularly topics of interest to the West Midlands, and Women's Page pieces offering original and lively comment.

Birmingham Post

28 Colmore Circus, Birmingham B4 6AX
☎ 021–236 3366 Fax 021–233 3958

Owner *The Birmingham Post & Mail Ltd*
Editor *Peter Saunders*
Circulation 28,500

One of the leading regional newspapers. Freelance contributions are welcome.

News Editor *Nigel Pipkin*

Features Editor *Jonathan Daumler-Ford*
Women's Page Editor *Barbara Henderson* Particularly welcomes topics of interest to the West Midlands, and Women's Page pieces offering original and lively comment.

Sunday Mercury

28 Colmore Circus, Birmingham B4 6AZ
☎ 021–236 3366 Fax 021–233 3958

Editor *John Bradbury*
Circulation 168,024

News Editor *Bob Haywood*

Features Editor *Peter Whitehouse*

Blackburn

Lancashire Evening Telegraph

New Telegraph House, High Street, Blackburn, Lancashire BB1 1HT
☎ 0254 63588 Fax 0254 680429

Owner *Thomson Regional Newspapers*
Editor *Peter Butterfield*
Circulation 57,627

Both news stories and feature material with an East Lancashire flavour welcome. Approach in writing with an idea in the first instance. No fiction.

News Editor *David Allin*

Features Editor *Neil Preston* Either a local angle or written by a local person.

Blackpool

West Lancashire Evening Gazette

PO Box 20, Preston New Road, Blackpool, Lancashire FY4 4VA
☎ 0253 66136 Fax 0253 694152

Owner *United Newspapers*
Editor *Peter Charlton*
Circulation 52,892

In theory unsolicited mss are welcome. Approach the editor in writing with an idea.

Bolton

Bolton Evening News

Newspaper House, Churchgate, Bolton, Lancashire BL1 1HU
☎ 0204 22345 Fax 0204 385103

Owner *Northern Counties Newspapers*
Editor *Chris Walder*
Circulation 53,490

News Editor *Melvyn Horrocks*

Features Editor *Derrick Grocock*
Women's Page *Angela Kelly*

Bournemouth

Evening Echo

Richmond Hill, Bournemouth BH2 6HH
☎ 0202 24601 Fax 0202 24601

Owner *Southern Newspapers Ltd*
Editor *Pat Fleming*
Circulation 57,076

FOUNDED 1900. Unsolicited mss welcome, but the needs of the paper are specialised and the rejection rate is high. Receive and use a large number of features from established agencies. Ideas in writing, rather than by phone. Prefer to see finished copy, or well thought out suggestions backed up by evidence of writing ability.

News Editor *Ray Horsfield* Few opportunities.

Bradford

Telegraph & Argus

Hall Ings, Bradford BD1 1JR
☎ 0274 729511 Fax 0274 723634

Owner *Bradford & District Newspapers*
Editor *Mike Glover*
Circulation 80,531

Unsolicited mss not welcome. Approach in writing with samples of work. No fiction.

News Editor *Malcolm Hoddy*

Features Editor *Julie Hanson* Local features and general interest. Showbiz pieces. *Words* 600–1000, max. 1500.

Payment NUJ rates for members; negotiable for others.

Brighton

Evening Argus

89 North Road, Brighton BN1 4AU
☎ 0273 606799 Fax 0273 607215

Owner *Southern Publishing (Westminster Press) Ltd*
Editor *Terry Page*
Circulation 94,000

News Editor *Chris Oswick*

Features Editor *Tim Curran*

Bristol

Evening Post

Temple Way, Old Market, Bristol BS99 7HD
☎ 0272 260080 Fax 0272 279568

Owner *Bristol United Press Ltd*
Editor *Brian Jones*
Circulation 110,617

Unsolicited mss welcome; they get around a dozen a week. Approach in writing with ideas.

News Editor *Tim Davey*

Features Editor *Jim Keay*

Western Daily Press

Temple Way, Bristol BS99 7HD
☎ 0272 260080 Fax 0272 279568

Owner *Bristol United Press*
Editor *Ian Beales*
Circulation 72,167

News Editor *Richard Duce*

Features Editor *Derek Whitfield*

Burton upon Trent

Burton Mail

65–8 High Street, Burton upon Trent, Staffs DE14 1LE
☎ 0283 512345

Editor *Brian Vertigen*
Circulation 22,000

News/Features Editor *Andrew Parker*

Cambridge

Cambridge Evening News

51 Newmarket Road, Cambridge CB5 8EJ
☎ 0223 358877 Fax 0223 61720

Owner *Cambridge Newspapers Ltd*
Editor *Robert Satchwell*
Circulation 47,003

News Editor *Chris Elliott*

Features Editor *Rodney Tibbs*

Cardiff

South Wales Echo

Thomson House, Cardiff CF1 1WR
☎ 0222 223333

Owner *Thomson Regional Newspapers*
Editor *Geoffrey Rich*
Circulation 100,704

News Editor *Stuart Minton*

Features Editor *John Scantlebury*
Women's Page *Jenny Longhurst*

Western Mail

Thomson House, Cardiff CF1 1WR
☎ 0222 223333

Owner *Thomson Regional Newspapers*
Editor *John Humphries*
Circulation 76,500

Mss welcome if of a topical nature, and preferably of Welsh interest. No short stories or travel. Approach in writing to the features editor, who receives 5–10 mss daily.

News Editor *Peter Curtis*

Features Editor *Gareth Jenkins* 'Usual subjects already well covered, e.g. motoring, travel, books, gardening. We look for the unusual.' *Words* max. 1000. *Payment* dependent on quality and importance.
Also opportunities on women's page. **Editor** *Sharon Davey*

Carlisle

Evening News & Star

Newspaper House, Dalston Road, Carlisle CA2 5UA
☎ 0228 23488 Fax 0228 23488 ext. 249

Owner *Cumbrian Newspaper Group Ltd*
Editor *J. Vernon Addison*

News Editor *Steve Johnston*

Features Editor *Jane Loughran*

Chatham

Evening Post

395 High Street, Chatham, Kent ME4 4PG
☎ 0634 830600 Fax 0634 829479

Owner *Kent Messenger Group*
Editor *David Jones*
Circulation 29,500

News Editor *Peter Walker*

Features Editor *Deborah Penn*

Cheltenham

Gloucestershire Echo

1 Clarence Parade, Cheltenham, Gloucestershire GL50 3NY
☎ 0242 526261 Fax 0242 578395

Owner *Northcliffe Newspapers*
Editor *Adrian Faber*
Circulation 29,512

News Editor *Alison Graham*

Colchester

Evening Gazette

Oriel House, 43–4 North Hill, Colchester CO1 1TZ
☎ 0206 761212 Fax 0206 715386

Owner *Essex County Newspapers*
Editor *Ken Runicles*
Circulation 31,913

Unsolicited mss not generally used, as 'we rely on regular contributions' and don't receive very many.

News Editor *Dick Lumsden*

Features Editor *Kelvin Brown*

Coventry

Coventry Evening Telegraph

Corporation Street, Coventry CV1 1FP
☎ 0203 633633 Fax 0203 631736

Owner *Coventry Newspapers Ltd*
Editor *Geoffrey Elliott*

Circulation 93,000

Owned by Ralph Ingersoll, American press baron. Unsolicited mss are read, but few are published. Approach in writing with an idea. No fiction. **Features** max. 600 words. *Payment* £25–30. All unsolicited material should be addressed to the editor.

Darlington

The Northern Echo

Priestgate, Darlington, Co. Durham DL1 1NF
☎ 0325 381313 Fax 0325 380539

Owner *North of England Newspapers*
Editor *Allan Prosser*
Circulation 89,890

FOUNDED 1870. DAILY. Freelance pieces welcome if arranged by telephone first.

News Editor *Rachel Campey* Reports involving the North-East or North Yorkshire. Preferably phoned in. *Words* and *payment* by negotiation.

Features Editor *David Bellew* Background pieces to topical news stories relevant to the area. Must be arranged with the features editor before submission of any material. *Words* and *payment* by negotiation. **Fiction** Serialisation of bestsellers only; **Holiday Pages/Supplements** *David Kelly*; **Local industrial reports** *Terry Murdon*; **Sports** *Nick Helliwell.* Also 'Special pages'.
Words and *payment* by arrangement.

Derby

Derby Evening Telegraph

Northcliffe House, Derby DE1 2DW
☎ 0332 291111 Fax 0332 290280

Owner *Northcliffe Newspapers*
Editor *Neil Fowler*

News Editor *Stan Szecowka*

Features Editor *Chris Ward*

Devon

Herald Express

See under *Torquay*

Doncaster

The Doncaster Star

40 Duke Street, Doncaster DN1 3EA
☎ 0302 344001 Fax 0302 329072

Owner *Sheffield Newspapers Ltd*
Editor *Adrian Taylor*

All unsolicited material to the editor.

Dundee

The Courier and Advertiser

7 Bank Street, Dundee DD1 9HU
☎ 0382 23131 Fax 0382 27159

Editor *Iain Stewart*

News Editor *Irene Rowe*

Features Editor *Eddy McLaren*
Women's Page *Sandra Young*

Welcome features on a wide variety of subjects, not only of local/Scottish interest. Two pages devoted to features each weekend, supplied by freelancers and in-house. Also Women's Page/Thursday Pop Page. Only rule of thumb: keep it short. *Words* max. 500. Very occasionally publish fiction.

Evening Telegraph & Post

7 Bank Street, Dundee DD1 9HU
☎ 0382 23131 Fax 0382 27159

Editor *Harold Pirie*
Circulation 48,395

News Editor *Alan Proctor* All material should be addressed to the editor.

East Anglia

East Anglian Daily Times

See under *Ipswich*

Eastern Daily Press

See under *Norwich*

Eastern Evening News

See under *Norwich*

Edinburgh

Evening News

20 North Bridge, Edinburgh EH1 1YT
☎ 031–225 2468 Fax 031–225 7302

Owner *Thomson Regional Newspapers*
Editor *Terry Quinn*
Circulation 123,356

FOUNDED 1873. Unsolicited feature material welcome. Approach by telephone call to appropriate editor.

News Editor *Douglas Middleton* NUJ only.

Features Editor *Bill Clapperton* Features for 'Weekender' magazine supplement of broad general interest/historical interest. Occasionally run 'Platform' pieces (i.e. sounding off, topical or opinion pieces). *Words* 1000.
Payment NUJ/House rates.

The Scotsman

20 North Bridge, Edinburgh EH1 1YT
☎ 031–225 2468 Fax 031–225 3304

Owner *The Scotsman Publications Ltd*
Editor *Magnus Linklater*
Circulation 97,100

Despite its smallish circulation, a national Scottish newspaper of quality. Conservative in outlook, it vies with the *Glasgow Herald* for the top dog position in the Scottish press. Many unsolicited mss come in, and stand a good chance of being read, although a small army of regulars supply much of the feature material not written in-house.

News Editor *James Seaton*

Features Editor *Robert Cowan* The features page carries a great variety of articles. The 6-page *Weekend* section ditto, including book reviews and travel articles.

Exeter

Express & Echo

160 Sidwell Street, Exeter EX4 6SB
☎ 0392 73051 Fax 0392 221566

Owner *Western Times Co. Ltd*
Editor *John Budworth*
Circulation 36,210

News Editor *Dave Murdock*

Features Editor *Dave Murdock*

Glasgow

Daily Record

Anderston Quay, Glasgow G3 8DA
☎ 041–248 7000 Fax 041–242 3145/6

Owner *Mirror Group Newspapers*
Editor *Endell Laird*
Circulation 763,866

Mass market Scottish tabloid.

News Editor *M. B. Speed*

Features Editor *R. Steel*
Women's Page *Fiona Black*

Evening Times

195 Albion Street, Glasgow G1 1QP
☎ 041–552 6255 Fax 041–553 1335

Owner *Lonrho plc*
Editor *George McKechnie*
Circulation 187,091

News Editor *Robbie Wallace*

Features Editor *Russell Kyle*
Women's Page *Rosemary Long*

Glasgow Herald

195 Albion Street, Glasgow G1 1QP
☎ 041–552 6255 Fax 041–552 2288

Owner *Lonrho plc*
Editor *Arnold Kemp*
Circulation 127,636

Lively quality Scottish daily whose readership spreads beyond the city of Glasgow.

Arts Editor *John Fowler*
Business Editor *R. E. Dundas*
Diary *T. Shields*
Features Editor *Raymond Gardner*
Sports *E. Rodger*
Women's Page *Anne Simpson*

Sunday Mail

Anderston Quay, Glasgow G3 8DA
☎ 041–248 7000 Fax 041–242 3145

Owner *Scottish Daily Record*
Editor *Noel Young*
Circulation 866,642

Downmarket Scottish Sunday paper, plus monthly magazine *Sunday Mail Magazine*. **Editor** *Noel Young*.

Sunday Post

144 Port Dundas Road, Glasgow G4 0HZ
☎ 041–332 9933 Fax 041–331 1595

Owner *D. C. Thomson & Co Ltd*
Editor *William Anderson*
Circulation 1,481,640

All material should be sent to the editor. Now also producing monthly magazine *First Sunday*. **Editor** *Maggie Dun*. (See also **Magazines** section.)

Gloucester

The Citizen

St John's Lane, Gloucester GL1 2AY
☎ 0452 424442 Fax 0452 505597

Owner *Northcliffe Newspapers*
Editor *Michael Lowe*
Circulation 40,000

News Editor *R. Gardiner*

Gloucestershire Echo

See under *Cheltenham*

Greenock

Greenock Telegraph

2 Crawfurd Street, Greenock PA15 1LH
☎ 0475 26511 Fax 0475 83734

Owner *Orr, Pollock & Co Ltd*
Editor *Kenneth Thomson*
Circulation 21,799

Unsolicited mss are considered 'if they relate to the newspaper's general interests'. Don't receive too many. Approach by letter. No fiction.

Grimsby

Grimsby Evening Telegraph

80 Cleethorpe Road, Grimsby, South Humberside DN31 3EH
☎ 0472 359232 Fax 0472 359232 ext. 233

Owner *Northcliffe Newspapers*
Editor *Peter Moore*
Circulation 74,000

Combined with sister paper, *Scunthorpe Evening Telegraph*.

In general welcomes unsolicited mss. Receives 'not too many'. Approach in writing. No fiction.

News Editor *J. V. McDonagh* Hard news stories welcome. Approach in haste by telephone. No fiction.

Guernsey

Guernsey Evening Press & Star

Braye Road, Vale, Guernsey Channel Islands
☎ 0481 45866 Fax 0481 49250

Editor *Dave Prigent*
Circulation 16,449

Arts Editor *Peter Witterick*
Features Editor *Peter Witterick*
Women's Page *Julie Mosley*

Halifax

Evening Courier

PO Box 19, Halifax, West Yorkshire HX1 2SF
☎ 0422 65711 Fax 0422 330021

Editor *Edward Riley*
Circulation 37,873

News Editor *Richard Whitaker*

Features Editor *William Marshall*

Hartlepool

Mail (Hartlepool)

Clarence Road, Hartlepool, County Cleveland TS24 8BX
☎ 0429 274441 Fax 0429 869024

Owner *Sunderland & Hartlepool Publishing Ltd*
Editor *Andrew C. Smith*
Circulation 29,365

Huddersfield

Huddersfield Daily Examiner

Ramsden Street, Huddersfield, West Yorkshire HD1 2TD
☎ 0484 537444 Fax 0484 538356

Editor *Ivan M. Lee*
Circulation 44,118

News Editor *P. D. Hinchcliffe*

Features Editor *Malcolm Cruise*

Hull

Hull Daily Mail

PO Box 34, 84 Jameson Street, Hull HU1 3LF
☎ 0482 27111 Fax 0482 27111 ext. 232

Owner *Northcliffe Newspapers*
Editor *Michael Wood*
Circulation 107,113

News Editor *Mark Acheson*

Features Editor *Roy Woodcock*
Women's Page *Jo Davison*

Ipswich

East Anglian Daily Times

30 Lower Brook Street, Ipswich, Suffolk IP4 1AN

☎ 0473 230023 Fax 0473 225296

Owner *East Anglian Daily Times Co Ltd*
Editor *Ken Rice*
Circulation 48,470

FOUNDED 1874. Unsolicited mss generally unwelcome; 3 or 4 received a week, almost none are used. Prefer to be approached in writing in the first instance. No fiction.

News Editor *Andrew Culf* Hard news stories involving East Anglia (Suffolk, Essex particularly) or individuals resident in the area are always of interest. *Words* vary.
Payment NUJ rates.

Features Editor *Cathy Brown* Mostly in-house, but will occasionally buy in when the subject is of strong Suffolk/East Anglian interest. Photo features preferred (extra payment). *Words* 1000. *Payment* £15. Special advertisement features are regularly run. Some opportunities here. *Words* 1000. *Payment* £20.

Evening Star

30 Lower Brook Street, Ipswich, Suffolk 1P4 1AN
☎ 0473 230023 Fax 0473 225296

Owner *East Anglian Daily Times Co Ltd*
Editor *Crawford Gillan*
Circulation 36,664

News Editor *Terry Hunt*

Features Editor *Carol Carver*
Women's Page *Judy Rimmer*

Ireland

The Irish News

See under *Belfast*

Jersey

Jersey Evening Post

Five Oaks, St Saviour, Jersey Channel Islands
☎ 0534 73333 Fax 0534 79681

Editor *M. Rumfitt*
Circulation 24,128

News Editor *Philip Jeune*

Features Editor *P. Stuckey*
Women's Page *Dena Bond*

Kent

Kent Evening Post

See under *Chatham*

Kent Messenger

See under *Maidstone*

Kent & Sussex Courier

See under *Tunbridge Wells*

Kettering

Evening Telegraph

Northfield Avenue, Kettering,
Northants NN16 9JN
☎ 0536 81111 Fax 0536 410101

Owner *EMAP*
Editor *Paul Deal*
Circulation 42,804

News Editor *Dave Lewis*

Features Editor *Mark Adams*
Women's Page *Fiona Fitzgibbon*

Lancashire

Lancashire Evening Post

See under *Preston*

Lancashire Evening Telegraph

See under *Blackburn*

West Lancashire Evening Gazette

See under *Blackpool*

Leamington Spa

Leamington & District Morning News

PO Box 45, Tachbrook Road,
Leamington Spa CV31 3EP
☏ 0926 421122 Fax 0926 313591

Owner *Heart of England Newspaper Group*
Editor *Bruce Harrison*
Circulation 10,950

News Editor *John Wilson*

Leeds

Yorkshire Evening Post

Wellington Street, Leeds,
West Yorkshire LS1 1RF
☏ 0532 432701 Fax 0532 443430

Owner *Yorkshire Post Newspapers Ltd*
Editor *Christopher Bye*
Circulation 149,405

News Editor *Ian Hamilton*

Diary *Derek Naylor*
Features Editor *Howard Corry*
Women's Page *Anne Patch*

Evening sister of the *Yorkshire Post*.

Yorkshire Post

Wellington Street, Leeds,
West Yorkshire LS1 1RF
☏ 0532 432701 Fax 0532 443430

Owner *Yorkshire Post Newspapers Ltd*
Editor *John Edwards*
Circulation 92,998

A serious-minded, quality regional daily with a generally conservative outlook. 3 or 4 unsolicited mss arrive a day; all will be considered. Initial approach in writing preferred. All submissions should be addressed to the editor. No fiction. **Features** open to suggestions in all fields (though ordinarily commissioned from specialist writers).

Leicester

Leicester Mercury

St Georges Street, Leicester LE1 9FQ
☏ 0533 512512

Owner *Northcliffe Newspapers*
Editor *Alex Leys*
Circulation 150,000

News Editor *Hugh Berlyn*

Lincoln

Lincolnshire Echo

Brayford Wharf East, Lincoln LN5 7AT
☏ 0522 25252 Fax 0522 45759

Owner *Northcliffe Newspapers*
Editor *Cliff Smith*
Circulation 34,513

News Editor *Michael Robson*

Liverpool

Daily Post

PO Box 48, Old Hall Street, Liverpool L69 3EB
☏ 051–227 2000 Fax 051–236 4682

Owner *Liverpool Daily Post & Echo Ltd*
Editor *John Griffith*
Circulation 72,000

Unsolicited mss welcome. Receive about six a day. Approach in writing with an idea. No fiction.

News Editor *Nick Garbutt*

Features Editor *Peter Surridge* Local, national/international news, current affairs, profiles – with pictures. *Words* 800–1000. *Payment* £30–50.

Liverpool Echo

PO Box 48, Old Hall Street, Liverpool L69 3EB
☏ 051–227 2000 Fax 051–236 4682

Owner *Liverpool Daily Post & Echo Ltd*
Editor *Chris Oakley*
Circulation 211,213

One of the major regional dailies. Unsolicited mss welcome; they receive on average 20 a week. Prefer to be approached in writing first.

News Editor *Alf Green*

Features Editor *Carolyn Taylor*. *Words* 1000.

London

Evening Standard

Northcliffe House, 2 Derry Street, Kensington, London W8 5EE
☎ 01–938 6000 Fax 01–937 3193

Owner *Lord Rothermere*
Editor *John Leese*
Circulation 460,106

Long-established and staunchly conservative evening paper serving Londoners with news and feature material. Genuine opportunities for general ut particularly London-based features, which abound particularly at the weekend.

News Editor *Philip Evans*

Arts Editor *Michael Owen*
Features Editor *Richard Addis*
Literary Editor *Pat Miller*
Sports Editor *Douglas Jackson*

The *Evening Standard* magazine is *ES*. **Editor** *John Leese*. Monthly magazine issued with the *Evening Standard*. (See also **Magazines** section.)

Maidstone

Kent Messenger

Messenger House, New Hythe Lane, Larkfield, Maidstone, Kent ME20 6SG
☎ 0622 717880 Fax 0622 719637

Owner *Kent Messenger Group*
Editor *John Evans*
Circulation 46,000

Manchester

Manchester Evening News

164 Deansgate, Manchester M60 2RD
☎ 061–832 7200 Fax 061–832 5351

Owner *Manchester Evening News Ltd*
Editor *Michael Unger*
Circulation 320,000

One of the major regional dailies. Unsolicited mss are welcome. Initial approach in writing preferred. No news or fiction opportunities.

Features Editor *Ken Wood* Personality pieces and showbiz profiles particularly welcome. *Words* 1000. *Payment* by negotiation.

Middlesbrough

Evening Gazette

Borough Road, Middlesbrough, Cleveland TS1 3AZ
☎ 0642 245401 Fax 0642 210565

Owner *Thomson Regional Newspapers*
Editor *Peter Darling*
Circulation 77,000

News Editor *Peter Morris*

Features Editor *David Whinyates*
Women's Page *Christine Lane*

Mold

Evening Leader

Mold Business Park, Wrexham Road, Mold, Clwyd CH7 1XY
☎ 0352 700022 Fax 0352 700048

Owner *North Wales Newspapers*
Editor *Reg Herbert*

News Editor *Steven Rogers*

Features Editor *Jeremy Smith*
Women's Page *Gail Cooper*

Newcastle upon Tyne

Evening Chronicle

Thomson House, Groat Market, Newcastle upon Tyne NE1 1ED
☎ 091–232 7500

Owner *Thomson Regional Newspapers*
Editor *Graeme Stanton*
Circulation 148,683

Receive 'an awful lot' of unsolicited material, much of which they can't use. Approach initially in writing.

News Editor *David Trout*

Features Editor *Ian Wilson* Limited opportunities due to full-time feature staff. *Words* max. 1000.
Sports Editor *John Gibson*

The Journal

Thomson House, Groat Market, Newcastle upon Tyne NE1 1ED
☎ 091–232 7500 Fax 091–232 2256

Owner *Thomson Regional Newspapers*
Editor *Christopher Cox*

Circulation 60,000

News Editor *Tom Patterson*

Features Editor *Tony Henderson*
Women's Page *Avril Deane*

Sunday Sun

Thomson House, Groat Market,
Newcastle upon Tyne NE1 1ED
☎ 091–232 7500 Fax 091–232 2256

Owner *Thomson Regional Newspapers*
Editor *Jim Buglass*
Circulation 125,058

News Editor *Alistair Baker* All material should go to the news editor.

Newport

South Wales Argus

Cardiff Road, Maesglas, Newport,
Gwent NP9 1QW
☎ 0633 810000 Fax 0633 810100

Editor *Steve Hoselitz*
Circulation 42,385

News Editor *Peter John*

Features Editor *Lesley Williams*
Women's Page *Josephine Type*

The North of England

The Northern Echo

See under *Darlington*

Northampton

Chronicle and Echo

Upper Mounts, Northampton NN1 3HR
☎ 0604 231122 Fax 0604 233000

Owner *Northampton Mercury Co Ltd*
Editor *Clive Hutchby*
Circulation 40,000

Unsolicited mss are 'not necessarily unwelcome but opportunities to use them are rare'. Some 3 or 4 arrive weekly. Approach in writing with an idea. No fiction.

News Editor *Mrs J. Oldfield*

Features Editor *George Frew*

Northamptonshire Evening Telegraph

See under *Kettering*

Northcliffe Newspapers Group Ltd

Editorial Department, 31–2 John Street,
London WC1N 2QB
☎ 01–242 7070

Editor *Bill Sneyd*

Central editorial office of the regional papers belonging to the group: *The Citizen* (Gloucester); *Daily Mail* (Hull); *Derby Evening Telegraph; Evening Sentinel* (Stoke); *Gloucestershire Echo* (Cheltenham); *Grimsby Evening Telegraph; Herald Express* (Torquay); *Leicester Mercury; Lincolnshire Echo; Scunthorpe Evening Telegraph; South Wales Evening Post.* See separate listings for details.

Norwich

Eastern Daily Press

Prospect House, Rouen Road,
Norwich NR1 1RE
☎ 0603 628311 Fax 0603 612930

Owner *Eastern Counties Newspapers*
Editor *Lawrence Sear*
Circulation 91,331

Unsolicited mss welcome. Approach in writing. News if relevant to Norfolk. Features up to 900 words. Other pieces by commission. Submissions and suggestions to the editor.

Eastern Evening News

Prospect House, Rouen Road,
Norwich NR1 1RE
☎ 0603 628311 Fax 0603 612930

Owner *Eastern Counties Newspapers*
Editor *Peter Ware*
Circulation 51,976

News Editor *Paul Durrant*

Features Editor *Philippa Bowes*

Nottingham

Evening Post Nottingham

Forman Street, Nottingham NG1 4AB
☎ 0602 482000 Fax 0602 484116

Owner *T. Bailey Forman Ltd*
Editor *Barrie Williams*

Circulation 133,161

Unsolicited mss welcome. Send ideas in writing.

Features Editor *Tony Moss* Good local interest only. *Words* max. 800. No fiction.

Nuneaton

Evening Tribune

Watling House, Whitacre Road, Nuneaton, Warwicks CV11 6BJ
☎ 0203 382251 Fax 0203 641055

Owner *Watling Publications Ltd*
Editor *Roger Jeffery*
Circulation 13,710

All material to be addressed to the editor.

Oldham

Evening Chronicle

PO Box 47, Union Street, Oldham, Lancashire OL1 1EQ
☎ 061–633 2121 Fax 061–627 0905

Owner *Hirst Kidd & Rennie Ltd*
Editor *Gordon Maxwell*
Circulation 40,996

'We welcome the good but not the bad'. Receive two or three mss weekly.

News Editor *Jim Williams*

Oswestry

Evening Leader

See under *Mold*

Oxford

Oxford Mail

Osney Mead, Oxford OX2 0EJ
☎ 0865 244988 Fax 0865 790423

Owner *Oxford & County Newspapers*
Editor *Edward Duller*
Circulation 40,646

Unsolicited mss are considered; a great many unsuitable offerings are received. Approach in writing with an idea rather than phoning. No fiction. All fees negotiable.

News Editor *John Chipperfield* Phone first.

Features Editor *Jon Hartridge* Any features of topical or historical significance. *Words* max. 800.

Paisley

Paisley Daily Express

14 New Street, Paisley, Scotland PA1 1XY
☎ 041–887 7911

Owner *Lonrho plc*
Editor *Murray Stevenson*
Circulation 13,000

Unsolicited mss welcome only if of genuine Paisley interest. The paper does not commission work, and will consider submitted material: 'we are more in the business of encouraging amateur writers on local topics than professionals. The budget does not extend to "scale" fees'. *Words* 1000–1500.
Payment maximum £25. All submissions to the editor.

Peterborough

Evening Telegraph Peterborough

Telegraph House, 57 Priestgate, Peterborough PE1 1JW
☎ 0733 555111 Fax 0733 555188

Owner *EMAP*
Editor *David Rowell*
Circulation 33,056

Unsolicited mss not welcome. Approaches should be made in writing.

Plymouth

Evening Herald Plymouth

Leicester Harmsworth House, 65 New George Street, Plymouth, Devon PL1 1RE
☎ 0752 266626 Fax 0752 267580

Owner *Western Morning News Co Ltd*
Editor *Alan Cooper*
Circulation 60,413

News Editor *Peter Hagan*

All material to be addressed to the editor or news editor.

Sunday Independent

Burrington Way, Plymouth PL5 3LN
☎ 0752 777151 Fax 0752 780680

Owner *West of England Newspapers Ltd*
Editor *John Noble*

Portsmouth

The News
The News Centre, Hilsea, Portsmouth PO2 9SX
☎ 0705 664488 Fax 0705 690904

Owner *Portsmouth Printing & Publishing Ltd*
Editor *R. C. C. Poulton*
Circulation 92,506

Unsolicited mss not generally welcome. Approach by letter.

News Editor *Chris Owen*

Features Editor *Keith Ridley* General subjects of SE Hants interest. *Words* max. 600. No fiction.
Sports Editor *Chris Erskine* Sports background features. *Words* max. 600.

Preston

Lancashire Evening Post
Olivers Place, Eastway, Fulwood, Preston, Lancashire PR2 4ZA
☎ 0772 54841 Fax 0772 563288

Owner *United Newspapers plc*
Editor *Steve Kendall*
Circulation 71,364

Generally unsolicited mss are not welcome. Receive anything up to 100 a year. All ideas in writing to the editor.

Reading

Evening Post
PO Box 22, Tessa Road, Reading, Berks RG1 8NS
☎ 0734 575833 Fax 0734 503592

Owner *Thomson Regional Newspapers*
Editor *Trevor Wade*
Circulation 35,047

Unsolicited mss welcome. They get one or two every day, plus mountains of PR material. Finished copy only – no phone calls or written ideas. Fiction very rarely used.

News Editor *Jane Wyatt*

Features Editor *Simon Hedger* Topical subjects, particularly of Thames Valley interest. *Words* 800–1000.

Scarborough

Scarborough Evening News
17–23 Aberdeen Walk, Scarborough, Yorkshire YO11 1BB
☎ 0723 363636

Editor *John Bird*
Circulation 18,585

News Editor *Charles Graves*

Arts Editor *Jeannie Swales*
Women's Page *Elizabeth Johnson*

Scotland

Daily Record
See under *Glasgow*

The Scotsman
See under *Edinburgh*

Sunday Mail
See under *Glasgow*

Sunday Post
See under *Glasgow*

Scunthorpe

Scunthorpe Evening Telegraph
Doncaster Road, Scunthorpe DN15 7RG
☎ 0724 843421 Fax 0724 853495

Owner *Northcliffe Newspapers*
Editor *P. L. Moore*
Circulation 74,000

News Editor *Russell Ward*

All correspondence should go to the news editor.

Sheffield

The Star
York Street, Sheffield S1 1PU
☎ 0742 767676 Fax 0742 753551

Owner *United Newspapers plc*
Editor *Michael Corner*
Circulation 153,606

Unsolicited mss not welcome unless topical and local.

News Editor *Martin Ross* Do accept contributions from freelance news reporters if they relate to the area.

Features Editor *Stuart Machin* Very rarely require outside features, unless on specialised subject.
Payment negotiable.

Shropshire

Shropshire Star

See under *Telford*

South Shields

Shields Gazette and Shipping Telegraph

Chapter Row, South Shields,
Tyne & Wear NE33 1BL
☎ 091–455 4661 Fax 091–456 8270

Owner *Northern Press*
Editor *Kie Miskelly*
Circulation 28,091

Features Editor *Margaret Nicholls*

Women's Page *Janis Blower*

Southampton

Southern Evening Echo

45 Above Bar, Southampton SO9 7BA
☎ 0703 634134 Fax 0703 630428

Owner *Southern Newspapers Ltd*
Editor *Duncan Jeffery*
Circulation 86,000

Unsolicited mss are 'tolerated'. Few are received. Approach in writing with strong ideas; staff supply almost all the material. All correspondence should be addressed to the editor.

Stoke on Trent

Evening Sentinel

Sentinel House, Etruria, Stoke on Trent,
Staffs ST1 5SS
☎ 0782 289800 Fax 0782 280781

Owner *Northcliffe Newspapers*
Editor *Sean Dooley*
Circulation 107,502

News Editor *Michael Wood* All material should be sent to the news editor.

Sunderland

Sunderland Echo

Pennywell Industrial Estate, Pennywell,
Sunderland, Tyne & Wear SR4 9ER
☎ 091–534 3011 Fax 091–534 5975

Owner *Portsmouth & Sunderland Newspapers*
Editor *Andrew Hughes*
Circulation 66,815

News Editor *Ian Holland*

Swansea

South Wales Evening Post

Adelaide Street, Swansea, Glamorgan SA1 1QT
☎ 0792 50841 Fax 0792 55386

Owner *Northcliffe Newspapers*
Editor *Nicholas Carter*
Circulation 66,445

News Editor *Kay Byrne*

Features Editor *George Edwards*
Women's Page *Betty Hughes*

Swindon

Evening Advertiser

100 Victoria Road, Swindon, Wiltshire SN1 3BE
☎ 0793 28144 Fax 0793 23883

Owner *Wiltshire Newspapers*
Editor *John Mayhew*
Circulation 36,410

Unsolicited mss welcome, and many are received. Finished copy much preferred to ideas. 'All need to be strongly related to or relevant to the town of Swindon, Borough of Thamesdown, or the county of Wiltshire, in that order of interest.' Little scope for non-staff work. Fees by the editor's valuation if by non-NUJ members.

News Editor *Alan Johnson*

Features Editor *Pauline Leighton*

Fiction Seldom used. Absolutely no poetry. Special Pages numerous and various.

Thomson Regional Newspapers Ltd
3rd Floor, Pemberton House, East Harding Street, London EC4A 3AS
☎ 01–353 9131

Editor *George Sivell*

London office of the group which owns the following regional daily papers: *Belfast Telegraph; Evening News* (Edinburgh); *Evening Chronicle* (Newcastle); *Evening Express* (Aberdeen); *Evening Gazette* (Middlesbrough); *Evening Post* (Reading); *The Journal* (Newcastle); *Lancashire Evening Telegraph; The Press & Journal* (Aberdeen); *South Wales Echo* (Cardiff); *Sunday Sun* (Newcastle); *Western Mail* (Cardiff). See separate listings for details.

Telford

Shropshire Star
Ketley, Telford, Shropshire TF1 4HU
☎ 0952 242424 Fax 0952 254605

Owner *Shropshire Newspapers Ltd*
Editor *Robert Jones*
Circulation 97,730

Unsolicited mss not welcome. Essential to approach the editor in writing in the first instance with ideas. No news, no fiction.

Features *Mike Bailey* Limited opportunities here; mostly use in-house or syndicated material. *Words* max. 1200.

Torquay

Herald Express
Harmsworth House, Barton Hill Road, Torquay TQ1 1BD
☎ 0803 213213

Owner *Western Times Co. Ltd*
Editor *J. C. Mitchell*
Circulation 30,000

Unsolicited mss generally not welcome. Receive about 2 dozen a year. Approach the editor in writing.

Tunbridge Wells

Kent & Sussex Courier
Longfield Road, Tunbridge Wells, Kent TN2 3HL
☎ 0892 26262

Owner *Courier Printing & Publishing Co. Ltd*
Editor *William Stengel*

Wales

South Wales Argus
See under *Newport*

South Wales Echo
See under *Cardiff*

South Wales Evening Post
See under *Swansea*

Western Mail
See under *Cardiff*

The West of England

Western Daily Press
See under *Bristol*

Weymouth

Dorset Evening Echo
57 St Thomas Street, Weymouth, Dorset DT4 8EQ
☎ 0305 784804

Owner *Southern Newspapers plc*
Editor *Michael Woods*
Circulation 23,459

News Editor *Paul Thomas*

Wolverhampton

Express & Star
Queen Street, Wolverhampton, West Midlands WV1 3BU
☎ 0902 313131 Fax 0902 21467

Owner *Midlands News Association*
Editor *Keith Parker*
Circulation 245,872

News Editor *Derek Tucker*

Arts Editor *Barry Cox*
Features Editor *Barry Cox*
Women's Page *Marion Brennan*

Worcester

Evening News
Berrows House, Worcester WR2 5JX
☏ 0905 748200 Fax 0905 429605

Owner *Berrow's West Midlands Ltd*
Editor *David Griffin*
Circulation 29,256

News Editor *Paul Ricketts*

Arts Editor *David Ford*
Features Editor *Chris Lloyd*
Women's Page *Mary Johns*

York

Yorkshire Evening Press
15 Coney Street, York YO1 1YN
☏ 0904 653051 Fax 0904 611488

Owner *York & County Press*
Editor *Richard Wooldridge*
Circulation 54,019

Unsolicited mss not generally welcome, unless submitted by journalists of proven ability. Receive about six a week. Approach in writing only – 'phone calls always come at the wrong time, and we'd have to see the written work anyway'. No fiction.

News Editor *Bill Hearld* Accredited journalists only.

Features Editor *Malcolm Baylis* Exceptional pieces of local relevance considered. *Words* 1000.
Payment negotiable.

Yorkshire

Yorkshire Evening Post
See under *Leeds*

Yorkshire Post
See under *Leeds*

The Long Arm of the Law of Libel

Writers beware! The cost of libel went up again last year. If resort to the law was part of the retail price index (and some people are as familiar with the courts as with their local supermarket), the rate of inflation would sky rocket.

Most of the recent big pay-outs have hit the pockets of the newspaper proprietors but not just those in the mass circulation league. Two years ago, a former Royal Navy officer, Martin Packard, won £450,000 from the Greek newspaper *Eleftherotypia*, with a circulation of only 50 in Britain. Last March, a jury awarded an envelope company £300,000 against the trade paper *Stationery Trade News*, and in July, a firm of solicitors won £310,000 damages from an Arabic-language magazine.

Journalists and broadcasters may regard these awards with equanimity. Most are covered by their employers who take on the whole cost of any libel action, though there have been a few cases of freelancers being left in the soup. Authors, on the other hand, are in an entirely different class. Rarely do publishers assume full responsibility for libel.

A typical contract includes a warranty clause which entitles the publisher to be indemnified by the author against damages and costs resulting from a libel action. At best, a publisher will offer to share the costs up to a certain level.

For the author, the pain of committing libel does not stop at the chequebook. Anyone who feels himself disparaged can apply to judge in chambers for an *ex parte* injunction banning the book's distribution and sale. This can happen just a few hours before publication.

The most notable recent case involved Norman Tebbit whose biography had to be speedily amended before it went on sale. For a more contentious tome, an injunction can lead to its permanent withdrawal.

The wise and economical course is to check out the hazards before a manuscript goes to print. The litmus test for libel is to ask, 'Would the words complained of tend to lower the plaintiff in the estimation of right-thinking members of society?' Or, more simply, 'Would you like it said about you?'

It may be that the defendant did not intend libel. No matter. All that the plaintiff need show is that the statement would be understood by reasonable people to refer to him. There is a clear warning here for fiction writers not to venture too close to real life. It may seem a neat idea to introduce friends and neighbours into a story – it is so much easier to describe people you know – but if one of them is cast as a villain and recognises himself, albeit in an unlikely role, then a solicitor's letter will surely follow.

Names, too, can be a trap for the unwary. If a novel features a corrupt member of parliament, a financier who fiddles his tax or a vicar with an obsessive interest in choirboys, it is as well to check in the directories that the names given to these characters do not correspond to flesh and blood people. Since one cannot libel the dead, a valuable and safe source of names is *Who Was Who?*

In books it is the biographers of contemporary or near-contemporary figures who tread the narrowest line. To state a known fact about an individual, that he behaved deviously or dishonestly, for example, may raise questions about his friends, associates or family which they feel bound to contest. In such cases the best hope for the writer is the plaintiff's awareness that publicity generated by his action will cause him yet more pain. As Dr Johnson reminds us, 'Few attacks either of ridicule or invective make much noise but with the help of those they provoke.'

Where a libel has been committed unintentionally or 'innocently', it is possible to alleviate the consequences by an 'offer to make amends'. This usually involves a published apology and a settlement of costs. Otherwise, unless it can be established that a statement, however defamatory, is true in substance and fact (a difficult trick to pull off), the defence against libel will probably turn on the assertion that the words complained of are fair comment on a matter of public interest. This is where the wheel turns full circle because writers, who are themselves inclined to rush to law when they feel aggrieved, often hear the 'fair comment' defence from reviewers who have savaged their work. The perimeters of 'fair comment' are wide enough to protect, in essence, the principles of free speech, so that, according to precedent, 'However wrong the opinion expressed may be in point of truth, or however prejudiced the writer, it may still be within the prescribed limit'. In other words, it is one thing to argue that a person's *views* are lunatic but quite another to assert that *he* is a lunatic.

At the very least, the author of a controversial work should insist that his publisher has the manuscript read for libel and he should make sure his contract does not allow for unlimited liability. In 1972 David Irving, whose book *The Destruction of Convoy PQ17* had been the subject of a successful libel action, was in turn sued by his publishers, **Cassell Ltd**, who sought to recover the libel damages and costs they had paid out. The claim was for £100,000. But fortunately for Irving he had taken the advice of **The Society of Authors** and amended his contract. He was liable only for breaches of his warranty that the book was free of libel unknown to the publisher. Irving argued that Cassell knew all the relevant facts before an action was brought. In the end, Cassell did not proceed with the claim.

Bigger and yet bigger awards have led to demands for a reform of the libel laws. Critics point out that libel is the only major category of civil case to be tried by jury. Would it not make sense to rely on a judge to put a value on a tarnished reputation or at least allow him to direct the jury on the appropriate price bracket for a particular libel?

Another sensible proposal is to enable the Court of Appeal to substitute its own finding when it disagrees with a jury's figure for damages. At the moment, all the Court of Appeal can do is to set aside an award, leaving the plaintiff to start all over again – assuming that he has the stomach for a re-run.

Then again, a Scottish Lord Chancellor might be expected to extend the rule applicable in his own country, that a libel plaintiff has to prove a damaged reputation. In England, once the words are shown to be libellous, hefty damages can be obtained even if no real harm has resulted.

But all this is so much idle speculation. The reform of the libel laws has been on the cards for decades but politicians have shown little enthusiasm largely, one suspects, because they see themselves as beneficiaries of any law which inhibits free expression outside Parliament.

The only consolation for the latest generation of writers is to know that their predecessors came through and, in some cases, prospered despite draconian libel laws. Norman Sherry, in his biography of Graham Greene, tells that when the great man was trembling on the publication of his first real success, *Stamboul Train*, a libel action was threatened by J.B. Priestley, who saw himself ridiculed in the book. **Heinemann**, who published both authors, made it clear that if they were to lose one of their authors, it would be Greene who would have to go. But instead 'Greene had to share the cost of the changes

Priestley required and the changes had to be made immediately from a public telephone box, without time for reflection'.

Evidently, the law of libel can make for an exciting life. And whatever the cost, living dangerously is at least good copy for the memoirs.

Magazines

Accountancy

40 Bernard Street, London WC1N 1LD
☏ 01–628 7060 Fax 01–833 2085

Owner *Institute of Chartered Accountants of England and Wales*
Editor *Brian O'Kane*
Circulation 68,000

FOUNDED 1889. MONTHLY. Written ideas welcome. Approach by phone with news items.

Features *Gillian Bird* Accounting/tax/business-related articles of high technical content aimed at professional/managerial readers. Maximum 800–3000 words.
Payment £87 per printed page.

Main features *Gillian Bird* Major feature articles comprising part or all of cover story. Features list available. Material planned and commissioned at least six months in advance. Maximum 800–5000 words.
Payment £87 per printed page or by negotiation.

News *Julia Irvine* News items: investigative reports related to City, EEC, industry, accounting and international accountancy in business context. Maximum 500 words. Commentary: opinionated piece on any similar subject; accounting ideas – technical based; economic trends – up-to-date reviews or predictions. Maximum 1200 words.
Payment by arrangement.

Accountancy Age

32–4 Broadwick Street, London W1A 2HG
☏ 01–439 4242
Telex 23918 VNUG Fax 01–437 7001

Owner *VNU*
Editor *Robert Bruce*
Circulation 77,000

FOUNDED 1969. WEEKLY. Unsolicited mss welcome, and ideas may be suggested in writing or by telephone provided they are clearly thought out.

Features Topics right across the accountancy/business/financial world. Maximum 1500 words.
Payment at NUJ rates.

The Accountant's Magazine

27 Queen Street, Edinburgh EH2 1LA
☏ 031–225 5673
Telex 727530 Fax 031–225 3813

Owner *The Accountant's Publishing Co.*
Editor *Winifred Elliott*
Circulation 13,800

FOUNDED 1897. MONTHLY. New contributors are welcome, but should approach in writing in the first instance.

Features Articles welcome on topics of interest to the accountancy profession; finance, business, management etc. Must be authoritative. Maximum 3000 words (1000–2000 preferred).
Payment by negotiation.

ADviser

Harman Savory Ltd, 1 Winckley Street, Preston PR1 2AA
☏ 0772 201536

Owner *British Dietetic Association*
Editor *Neil Donnelly*
Circulation 3000

FOUNDED 1981. QUARTERLY. Unsolicited manuscripts welcome from dietitians and nutritionists. Make initial approach in writing. All pieces should be appropriate to dietitians. Maximum 1200 words.
Payment £40–50.

African Affairs

Dept. of Politics, University of Bristol, 12 Priory Road, Bristol BS8 1TU
☏ 0272 303200
Telex 445938 Fax 0272 732657

Owner *Royal African Society*
Editor *Richard Hodder-Williams, Peter*

Woodward
Circulation 2250

FOUNDED 1901. QUARTERLY learned journal publishing articles on contemporary developments on the African continent. Unsolicited mss welcome.

Features Should be well researched and written in a style that is immediately accessible to the intelligent lay reader. Maximum 8000 words. *Payment* for non-academics may be up to £40 per 1000 words. No payment for academics.

Amateur Film Maker

33 Gassiot Way, Sutton, Surrey SM1 3AZ
☏ 01–644 0839

Owner *Film Maker Publications*
Editor *Tony Pattison*
Circulation 3000

FOUNDED 1930. BI-MONTHLY of the Institute of Amateur Cinematographers. Reports news and views of the Institute. Unsolicited mss welcome, but all contributions are unpaid.

Amateur Gardening

Westover House, West Quay Road, Poole, Dorset BH15 1JG
☏ 0202 680586 Fax 0202 674335

Owner *IPC Magazines Ltd*
Editor *Graham Clarke*
Circulation 84,935

FOUNDED 1884. WEEKLY. New contributions are welcome provided that they have a professional approach. Of the twenty unsolicited manuscripts received each week, ninety per cent are returned as unsuitable.

Features Topical and practical gardening articles. Maximum 1100 words.

News Gardening news items are compiled and edited in-house. Maximum 200 words. One-off gardening features have to be agreed with the editor before submission. Maximum 1100 words.
Payment at IPC/NUJ rates.

Amateur Photographer

Prospect House, 9–13 Ewell Road, Cheam, Surrey SM1 4QQ
☏ 01-661 4300

Owner *Business Press International*
Editor-in-Chief *George Hughes*
Circulation 90,550

For the competent amateur with a technical interest. Freelancers are used but writers should be aware that there is ordinarily no use for words without pictures.

Amateur Stage

83 George Street, London W1H 5PL
☏ 01–486 1732

Owner *Platform Publications Ltd*
Editor *Charles Vance*

Ambit

17 Priory Gardens, Highgate, London N6 5QY
☏ 01–340 3566

Owner /Editor *Dr Martin Bax*
Circulation 2000

FOUNDED 1959. QUARTERLY literary magazine. Publishes short stories, experimental fiction and poetry, but no features. A large number of unsolicited manuscripts received. But these are welcomed if accompanied by an s.a.e. All approaches should be made in writing, never by phone.

The American

114–15 West Street, Farnham, Surrey GU9 7HL
☏ 0252 713366 Fax 0252 724951

Owner *British American Newspapers Ltd*
Editor *Robert Pickens*
Circulation 15,000

FOUNDED 1976. FORTNIGHTLY community newspaper for US citizens resident in the UK and as such requires a strong American angle in every story. 'We are on the lookout for items on business and commerce, diplomacy, and international relations, defence, and "people" stories'. Maximum '5 minutes read'.
Payment 'modest but negotiable'. First approach in writing with sample of previous work.

Angling Times

Bretton Court, Bretton, Peterborough PE3 8DZ
☏ 0733 266222 Fax 0733 265515

Owner *EMAP Pursuit Publications*
Editor *Neil Pope*
Circulation 126,155

Do not send your fishing stories here: this weekly is more concerned with angling news than feature material, most of which is provided by their large staff. Occasional features from outsiders.

Features Editor *Kevin Willmott*
Payment NUJ rates.

Animal World

Causeway, Horsham, West Sussex RH12 1HG
☎ 0403 64181
Telex 878484 Fax 0403 41048

Owner *RSPCA*
Editor *Elizabeth Winson*
Circulation 60,000

BI-MONTHLY RSPCA magazine. Most technical articles (pet care etc.) are written in-house. Unsolicited mss welcome.

Features and fiction Articles and stories should not contradict RSPCA policy. Illustrative photographs welcome. Maximum 1000 words.
Payment £18 (more for illustrated articles).

Annabel

80 Kingsway East, Dundee, Scotland DD1 9QJ
☎ 0382 44276 Fax 0382 42397

Owner *D. C. Thomson & Co. Ltd*
Editor *Catriona-Mairi MacInnes*
Circulation 162,185

Apart from the domestic content of the magazine, material is mainly supplied by freelance writers (this is typical of a D. C. Thomson publication). Currently trying to change its image, and going for a younger, *Daily Mail*-reading audience. Need general women's interest features, interviews and topical articles. Also fiction, which doesn't have to be about marriage: 'we've also published Fay Weldon'. Maximum 3000 words. A good bet for freelancers; although 'the slush pile' does not generally yield much in the way of ready-made features, it can provide new writers for the future.
Payment fees negotiable.

Features Editor *Catriona-Mairi MacInnes*

The Antique Collector

Eagle House, 50 Marshall Street,
London W1V 1LR
☎ 01–439 5000
Telex 263879 NATMAG G Fax 01–439 5177

Owner *National Magazine Co. Ltd*
Editor *David Coombs*
Circulation 16,500

FOUNDED 1930. MONTHLY. Opportunities for freelance features. It is best to submit ideas in writing. Feature articles have a set format: maximum 2000 words with eight illustrations in colour and/or black and white. Their acceptance depends primarily on how authoritative and informative they are.
Payment by negotiation.

The Antique Dealer and Collectors' Guide

King's Reach Tower, Stamford Street,
London SE1 9LS
☎ 01–261 6894 Telex 915748 MAGDIV G

Owner *IPC Magazines Ltd*
Editor *Philip Bartlam*
Circulation 14,139

FOUNDED 1946. MONTHLY covering all aspects of the antiques and fine art world. Unsolicited mss are welcomed.

Features Maximum 1500 words. Practical but readable articles welcomed on the history, design, authenticity, restoration and market aspects of antiques and fine art.

News *Philip Bartlam* Maximum 150 words. Items welcomed on events, sales, museums, exhibitions, antiques fairs and markets.
Payment £76 per 1000 words.

Apollo

4 Davies Street, London W1Y 1LH
☎ 01–629 4331

Owner *A. Cluff, N. Attallah*
Editor *Anna Somers Cocks*
Circulation *c.* 15,000

MONTHLY. A magazine for art collectors, art historians and dealers. Articles are either art historical or critical, and almost always written by experts in their fields. Unsolicited mss not welcome.

The Architectural Review

9 Queen Anne's Gate, London SW1H 9BY
☎ 01–222 4333
Telex 8953505 Fax 01–222 5196

Owner *The Architectural Press*
Editor *Peter Davey*

MONTHLY. Unsolicited mss welcome, but no news stories – only features.

Arena

The Old Laundry, Ossington Buildings,
London W1M 3HY
☎ 01–935 8232 Fax 01–935 2237

Owner *Wagadon Ltd*

Editor *Nick Logan*

New style and general interest magazine for the young and trendy man about town. Male fashion, intelligent feature articles.

Features Editor *Dylan Jones* Wide range of subject matter: film, television, politics, business, music, media, design, art, architecture, theatre – profiles and articles. Some space allocated to fiction but usually extracted from books, or commissioned from upcoming 'name' writers.
Payment £80–90 per 1000 words.

Art & Craft

Scholastic Publications Ltd, Marlborough House, Holly Walk, Leamington Spa, Warwickshire CV32 4LS
☎ 0926 813910 Fax 0926 883331

Owner *Scholastic Publications Ltd*
Editor *Eileen Lowcock*
Circulation 23,000

FOUNDED 1936. MONTHLY aimed at a specialist market – the needs of primary school teachers and pupils. Ideas and synopses considered for commission.

Features *Eileen Lowcock* Most of our contributors are primary school teachers or art and craft specialists familiar with the needs of our specialised market. Insufficient research from outside contributions is often a problem.

News handled by in-house staff. No opportunities.

Art Monthly

36 Great Russell Street, London WC1B 3PP
☎ 01–580 4168

Owner *Britannia Art Publications*
Editor *Peter Townsend, Jack Wendler*
Circulation 4000

FOUNDED 1976. MONTHLY. News and features of relevance to those interested in modern art. Unsolicited manuscripts, of which approximately two per month are received, are welcome.

Features Alongside exhibition reviews; usually 600–1000 words long and almost invariably commissioned. Articles (up to 3000 words in length) are published on art theory (e.g. modernism, post-modernism), individual artists, art history (of the modern period) and issues affecting the arts (e.g. funding and arts education). Book reviews are usually 600–1000 words long, occasionally more (up to 3000).
Payment in all cases negotiable, and all contributions should be addressed to the editors.

News Brief reports on conferences, public art etc. (250–300 words).

The Artist (Inc. Art & Artists)

Caxton House, 63–5 High Street, Tenterden, Kent TN30 6BD
☎ 05806 3673

Owner *Irene Briers*
Editor *Sally Bulgin*
Circulation 17,000

FOUNDED 1931. MONTHLY.

Features *Sally Bulgin* Art journalists, artists, art tutors and writers with a good knowledge of art materials are invited to write to the editor with ideas for practical, discursive and informative features about art, materials and artists.

Arts Review

69 Faroe Road, London W14 0EL
☎ 01–603 7530

Editor *Graham Hughes*

A vehicle for both London and regional reviews of arts events. Opportunities for reviewers exist, depending on your specialisation and the region you represent. They do have a large number of such people already.
Payment currently £30 per 1000 words but under review. Special rates for special jobs: Arts Review Year Book, published annually in December, carries longer theme articles which are better paid.

Artscribe International

41 North Road, London N7 9DP
☎ 01–609 4565 Telex 24453 OMNIBUG

Editor *Stuart Morgan*
Circulation 12,000

FOUNDED 1975. BI-MONTHLY. Unsolicited mss welcome, but freelance opportunities are limited.

Features *Stuart Morgan* Most pieces are commissioned. Unlikely that freelance pieces will be used unless by established art critics. Length and *payment* varies.

News *Stuart Morgan/Ian Brunskill* Most news stories written by staff but pieces on major events in the art world are considered. Contact editor in first instance.

Reviews *Ian Brunskill* Opportunities are

greatest here: reviews of exhibitions more likely to be used than feature articles. Maximum 600 words.
Payment negotiable.

Artswest

Regional Magazines, Finance House, Barnfield Road, Exeter, Devon EX1 1QR
☎ 0392 216766 Fax 0392 71050

Owner *Town & Country Magazines*
Editor *Mrs Jan Beart-Albrecht*
Circulation 25,500

FOUNDED 1987. MONTHLY. Features articles on the arts in the South West. Unsolicited mss welcome. Maximum 2000–2500 words.
Payment approximately £50. First approach in writing.

Athletics Weekly

Bretton Court, Bretton, Peterborough PE3 8DZ
☎ 0733 261144

Editor *Keith Nelson*
Circulation 26,394

FOUNDED 1945. WEEKLY. Features news and articles on track and field athletics, road running and cross-country. Includes interviews, profiles, historical articles and exclusive news. Length and *payment* of all articles by arrangement. Unsolicited mss welcome.

The Author

84 Drayton Gardens, London SW10 9SB
☎ 01–373 6642

Owner *The Society of Authors*
Editor *Derek Parker*
Manager *Kate Pool*
Circulation 5000

FOUNDED 1890. QUARTERLY journal of **The Society of Authors.** Unsolicited mss not welcome.

Autocar & Motor

38–42 Hampton Road, Teddington, Middlesex TW11 0JE
☎ 01–977 8787
Telex 8952440 HAYMRT G Fax 01–977 0517

Owner *Haymarket Magazines Ltd*
Editor *Bob Murray*

FOUNDED 1895. WEEKLY. All news stories, features, interviews, scoops, ideas, tip-offs and photographs welcome.

Features *Michael Harvey*
News *Jill Stanton*
Payment negotiable from a minimum of £100 per 1000 words.

Baby Magazine

21 Cross Street, Islington, London N1 2BH
☎ 01–359 3575
Telex 263174 MKPG Fax 01–354 3461

Owner *Harrington Kilbridge & Partners*
Editor *Mrs J. Harrington*

QUARTERLY for mothers with children up to school age (0–5 years). Always interested in new writers who should contact *Carole James* for further details.

The Banker

102–108 Clerkenwell Road, London EC1M 5SA
☎ 01–251 9321 Telex 23700 FINBI G

Owner *Financial Times*
Editor *Gavin Shreeve*
Circulation 13,200

FOUNDED 1926. MONTHLY. News and features on banking, finance, and the capital markets worldwide.

Basketball Monthly

'The Hollies', Hoton, Leicestershire LE12 5SF
☎ 0509 880208 Fax 0509 881563

Owner *Celebrity Group*
Editor *Richard Taylor*
Circulation 10,000

FOUNDED 1961. MONTHLY. Official journal of the English Basketball Association. Features technical, specialist, foreign and personality pieces for basketball enthusiasts. Unsolicited mss welcome.

BBC WILDLIFE Magazine

Broadcasting House, Whiteladies Road, Bristol BS8 2LR
☎ 0272 732211 Fax 0272 744114

Owner *BBC Enterprises Ltd* and *Wildlife Publications Ltd*
Editor *Rosamund Kidman Cox*

FOUNDED 1983. MONTHLY. Unsolicited mss not welcome.

Competition The magazine runs an annual competition for professional and amateur writers with a first prize of £1000.

Features Most features commissioned from

amateur writers with expert knowledge on wildlife or conservation subjects. Unsolicited mss are usually rejected. Maximum 2000 words. *Payment* £120–200.

News Most news stories commissioned from known freelancers. Maximum 800 words. *Payment* £40–80.

Bedfordshire Life

Chapel House, Chapel Lane, St Ives, Huntingdon, Cambridgeshire PE17 4DX
☏ 0480 62844

Owner *A. L. Robinson*
Editor *Arnold Hadwin*
Circulation 9500

FOUNDED 1972 as part of *Northamptonshire & Bedfordshire Life* which split into two separate magazines in 1988. MONTHLY magazine featuring articles which are 'geographically relevant'. Maximum 1000–1500 words, plus three or four good quality photographs. Welcome unsolicited mss. First approach in writing.
Payment varies.

Bee World

18 North Road, Cardiff CF1 3DY
☏ 0222 372409 Telex 23152 MONREF G 8390

Owner *International Bee Research Association*
Editor *Mrs P. A. Munn*
Circulation 2000

FOUNDED 1919. QUARTERLY. High-quality factual journal with international readership. Features apicultural science and technology. Unsolicited mss welcome.

Bella

H. Bauer Publishing, Shirley House, 25 Camden Road, London NW1 9LL
☏ 01–284 0909

Owner *Bauer Publishing*
Editor-in-Chief *Jackie Highe*
Circulation 1.3 million

FOUNDED in the UK in October 1987. Latest German import into the women's weekly magazine market. A soft-centred, traditional read.

Senior Features Editor *Sue Reid* Maximum 1200–1300 words.

Senior Fiction Editor *Linda O'Byrne* Maximum 1500-1800 words.
Payment varies.

Best

10th Floor, Portland House, Stag Place, London SW1E 5AU
☏ 01–245 8847

Owner *G & J (UK)*
Editor *Sally Pearce*
Circulation 993,541

FOUNDED 1987. WEEKLY women's magazine; stablemate of *Prima*. Important for would-be contributors to study the magazine to understand the style, which differs from most women's weeklies. Multiple features, news, short stories on all topics of interest to women. First approach in writing with s.a.e.

Features Editor *Liz Murphy* Maximum length 1500 words.

Fiction 'Five-minute Story' maximum 1500 words. *Payment* £100. Short Story maximum 2500 words. *Payment* £150.

Bicycle

Northern & Shell Building, PO Box 381, Millharbour, London E14 9TW
☏ 01–987 5090 Telex 24676

Owner *Northern & Shell plc*
Editor *Ben Orme*
Circulation 16,000

FOUNDED 1981. MONTHLY for cyclists and cycling enthusiasts. Unsolicited mss welcome.

Features Maximum 3000 words.

Fiction Maximum 800 words (plus illustration ideas).

The Big Paper

The Design Council, 28 Haymarket, London SW1Y 4SU
☏ 01–839 8000 Fax 01–925 2130

Owner *The Design Council*
Editor *Ms Morven MacKillop*
Circulation 7,000

FOUNDED 1987. Published three times a year (for each school term). Features design-related topics of interest and use to primary schools and teachers. The magazine gets its name from its centre pages, which fold from A3 to A2 to A1 to create a large worksheet-cum-poster. A theme is chosen for each issue – i.e. size, shape or colour – two-page spread with A1 game or worksheet.

Welcome ideas. Approach in writing in first instance with ideas of subjects covered, pictures and illustrations.

Book Reviews *Ms Morven MacKillop* Book reviews welcome from 'qualified' people only.
Payment £20 per review.

Features *Ms Morven MacKillop* Mostly commissioned or written in-house but unsolicited mss are welcome from writers with an interest in primary education and design.

News *Ms Morven MacKillop* Maximum 100 words.
Payment £100 per 1000 words.

Bike Magazine

2 St John's Place, St John's Square,
London EC1M 4DE
☎ 01–608 1511

Owner *EMAP Nationals Ltd*
Editor *'Mac' McDiarmid*
Circulation 60,000

FOUNDED 1972 MONTHLY. News and features on motorcycling. Do not welcome unsolicited mss. Receive 'too many'. First approach with idea in writing.

Features Maximum 2500 words.

News Maximum 500 words.
Payment £100 per 1000 words.

Birds

The Lodge, Sandy, Bedfordshire SG19 2DL
☎ 0767 80551
Telex 82469 RSPB Fax 0767 292365

Owner *Royal Society for the Protection of Birds*
Editor *R. A. Hume*
Circulation 351,000

QUARTERLY magazine which covers not only wild birds, but wildlife, international and conservation topics as well. No interest in features on pet birds. Usually commission, but mss or ideas welcome. Interested, too, in photographers submitting colour transparencies as photo-features, especially unusual bird behaviour.

Black Beauty & Hair

Hawker Publications, 13 Park House, 140
Battersea Park Road, London SW11 4NB
☎ 01–720 2108

Owner *Hawker Publications*
Editor *Irene Shelley*
Circulation 20,000

QUARTERLY. Unsolicited contributions welcome.

Features Interested in mss from beauty/fashion writers with a knowledge of the Afro Caribbean beauty scene. Emphasis on humorous but authoritative articles that relate to clothes, hair, life, lifestyle, sexual politics, women's interest. Maximum 900 words.
Payment £80 per 1000 words.

Blitz

40–42 Newman Street, London W1P 3PA
☎ 01–436 5211 Fax 01–436 5290

Owner *Cadogan Press Group*
Editor *Simon Tesler*
Circulation 60,000

Magazine covering media-related subjects and current affairs: music, film, fashion, art, politics and style. Aimed at a 'hip' intelligent 18–35 audience. Most articles are commissioned; unsolicited mss unlikely to be accepted.

Blue Jeans & Patches

D. C. Thomson & Co. Ltd, Albert Square,
Dundee DD1 9QJ
☎ 0382 23131 Fax 0382 22214

Owner *D. C. Thomson & Co. Ltd*
Editor *Val Kerr*
Circulation 200,000

FOUNDED 1977. WEEKLY. Unsolicited mss welcome, but about 100 are received each week. All approaches should be made in writing.

Features *Jane Rattray* Features on popular trivia: information on jeans, hair, romance, etc. A lot of light-hearted information and interesting facts. Maximum 1500 words.
Payment £40.

Fiction *Nicky Gilray* Very keen for good-quality short stories – bearing in mind that they are for the teenage-girl market. Maximum 1500 words.
Payment £55.

Pop *Lesley Johnson* Interviews (mainly question and answer type) with chart bands who have a teenage appeal. Gossipy style: nothing too technical. Maximum 1500 words.
Payment £40.

Blueprint

26 Cramer Street, London W1M 3HE
☎ 01–486 7419 Fax 01–486 1451

Owner *Wordsearch Ltd*
Editor *Deyan Sudjic*

Circulation 10,000

FOUNDED 1983. TEN ISSUES YEARLY. Features on design and architecture. Maximum 3000 words. Do not welcome unsolicited mss as 'the odds are against people getting the tone right without talking to us first'. Approach by phone in the first instance.
Payment negotiable.

Boat International

The Courtyard, Queens House, 55-6 Lincoln's Inn Fields, London WC2A 3LJ
☎ 01–831 0884 Fax 01–242 3588

Owner *Sterling Publications*
Editor *Jason Holtom*
Circulation 35,000

FOUNDED 1983. MONTHLY. Welcome unsolicited mss.

Features Maximum 2500 words. *Payment* £100 per 100 words.

News Maximum 300 words. *Payment* £100 per 1000 words. First approach in writing.

Book and Magazine Collecctor

43–5 St Mary's Road, Ealing, London W5 5RQ
☎ 01–579 1082

Owner *Diamond Publishing Group Ltd*
Editor *John Dean*
Circulation 11,900

FOUNDED 1984. MONTHLY. Welcome unsolicited feature items. First approach in writing. Maximum 3000 words.
Payment £30 per 1000 words.

Bookdealer

Suite 34, 26 Charing Cross Road, London WC2H 0DH
☎ 01–240 5890 Fax 01–379 5770

Editor *Barry Shaw*

WEEKLY trade paper which acts almost exclusively as a platform for people wishing to buy or sell rare or out-of-print books. Six-page editorial only; occasional articles and regular book reviews done by regular freelance writers.

Books

43 Museum Street, London WC1A 1LY
☎ 01–404 0304 Fax 01–242 0762

Editor *Matthew Bray*
Circulation 100,000

Formerly known as *Books and Bookmen.* A consumer rather than trade magazine, dealing chiefly with features on authors, reviews of books, and general aspects of the publishing business.
Payment negotiable.

The Bookseller

12 Dyott Street, London WC1A 1DF
☎ 01–836 8911 Fax 01–836 2909

Owner *J. Whitaker & Sons Ltd*
Editor *Louis Baum*

Trade journal of the publishing and book trade. Essential guide to what is being done to whom. Trade news and features, including special features, company news, trends in publishing etc., are ordinarily done in-house or commissioned from experts within the business. Unsolicited mss rarely used. Approach in writing first.

Features Editors *Helen Paddock*

News Editor *Penny Mountain*

Brides and Setting Up Home

Vogue House, Hanover Square, London W1R 0AD
☎ 01–499 9080
Telex 27338 VOLON G Fax 01–493 1345

Owner *Condé Nast Publications*
Editor *Sandra Boler*
Circulation 70,026

BI-MONTHLY. Freelance contributions are considered provided they are relevant. Much of the magazine is produced in-house, but a good feature on cakes, jewellery, music, flowers etc. is always welcome. Prospective contributors should telephone with their idea in first instance. Maximum (features) 1000 words.
Payment £120.

The British Bandsman

The Old House, 64 London End, Beaconsfield, Bucks HP9 2JD
☎ 0494 674411

Owner *Austin Catelinet*
Editor *Peter Wilson*

FOUNDED 1887. WEEKLY. News on brass bands and features on brass instruments and music. Welcome contributions but no payment.

British Birds

Fountains, Park Lane, Blunham,
Bedford MK44 3NJ
☏ 0767 40025

Owner *British Birds Ltd*
Editor *Dr J. T. R. Sharrock*
Circulation 10,000

FOUNDED 1907. MONTHLY ornithological magazine published by non-profit-making company. Unsolicited mss welcome, but from ornithologists only.

Features Well-researched, original material relating to West Palearctic birds. Maximum 6000 words.

News *Mike Everett/Robin Prytherch* News items ranging from conservation to humour. Maximum 200 words.
Payment all contributions are unpaid.

British Medical Journal

BMA House, Tavistock Square,
London WC1H 9JR
☏ 01–387 4499

Owner *British Medical Association*
Editor *Dr Stephen Lock*

No market for freelance writers.

Broadcast

100 Avenue Road, Swiss Cottage,
London NW3 3TP
☏ 01–935 6611 Telex 299973 TIP LNG

Owner *International Thomson*
Editor *Marta Wohrle*
Circulation 9500

FOUNDED 1960. WEEKLY. Opportunities do exist for freelance contributions, but write in the first instance to the relevant editor.

Features *Sue Griffin* Mainly broadcasting issues. Maximum 1500 words.
Payment £113 per 1000 words.

News *Marta Wohrle* News stories on broadcasting. Maximum 400 words.
Payment £115 per 1000 words.

The Brownie

17–19 Buckingham Palace Road,
London SW1W 0PT
☏ 01–834 6242

Owner *Girl Guides Association*
Editor *Lynn Hurdwell*

FOUNDED 1962. FORTNIGHTLY. Aimed at Brownies aged 7–10 years.

Articles Crafts and simple make-it-yourself items using inexpensive or scrap materials.

Features Of general interest. Maximum 350–400 words.
Payment £26 per 1000 words pro rata.

Fiction Brownie content an advantage. No adventures involving children in dangerous situations – day or night – unaccompanied. Maximum 1000 words.
Payment £26 per 1000 words pro rata.

Building

Builder House, 1 Millharbour, London E14 9RA
☏ 01–537 2222 Telex BUILDAG 25212

Owner *The Builder Group plc*
Editor *Graham Rimmer*
Circulation 21,500

FOUNDED 1842. WEEKLY. Features articles on aspects of the modern building industry. Unsolicited mss not welcome, but freelancers with specialist knowledge of the industry are often used.

Features Focus on the modern industry, no building history required. Maximum 1500 words.
Payment by arrangement.

News Maximum 500 words.
Payment by arrangement.

The Burlington Magazine

6 Bloomsbury Square, London WC1A 2LP
☏ 01–430 0481
Telex 291072 Fax 01–242 1205

Owner *The Burlington Magazine Publications Ltd*
Editor *Caroline Elam*

FOUNDED 1903. MONTHLY. Unsolicited contributions are welcome provided they are on the subject of art history and are previously unpublished. All preliminary approaches should be made in writing.

Exhibition Reviews Usually commissioned, but occasionally unsolicited reviews are published if appropriate. Maximum 1000 words.
Payment £75 (maximum).

Main Articles Maximum 4500 words.
Payment £60 (maximum).

Shorter Notices Maximum 2000 words.
Payment £30 (maximum).

Business

234 Kings Road, London SW3 5UA
☎ 01–351 7351
Telex 914549 INTMAG G Fax 01–351 2794

Owner *Condé Nast Publications, Financial Times*
Editor *Stephen Fay*
Circulation 47,000

FOUNDED 1986. MONTHLY. Some opportunities for freelance feature writers, but unsolicited manuscripts are not welcomed. Prospective contributors are best advised to write in the first instance with feature ideas. Maximum 2500 words.
Payment £200 per 1000 words.

Business Traveller

388-96 Oxford Street, London W1N 9HE
☎ 01–629 4688
Telex 8814624 Fax 01–629 6572

Owner *Perry Publications*
Editor *Gillian Upton*
Circulation 40,000

MONTHLY. Receive a steady flow of unsolicited contributions but they are usually 'irrelevant to our market'. Would-be contributors best advised to study the magazine first. First approach in writing.
Payment 'variable'.

Cambridgeshire Life

Chapel House, Chapel Lane, St Ives, Huntingdon, Cambridgeshire PE17 4DX
☎ 0480 62844

Owner *A. L. Robinson*
Editor *Arnold Hadwin*
Circulation 9500

FOUNDED 1965. MONTHLY magazine featuring 'geographically relevant' articles. Maximum 1000-1500 words, plus three or four good quality photographs. Welcome unsolicited mss. First approach in writing.
Payment varies.

Camcorder User

57–9 Rochester Place, London NW1 9JU
☎ 01–485 0011

Owner *W. V. Publications*
Deputy Editor *Ian Campbell*
Circulation 30,000

FOUNDED 1988. MONTHLY. Covers the expanding interest in camcorders with features on creative technique, shooting advice, new equipment, accessory round-ups and interesting applications on location. Unsolicited mss welcome. Maximum 1000 words.
Payment £75 minimum plus illustrations.

Campaign

22 Lancaster Gate, London W2 3LY
☎ 01–402 5266

Owner *Haymarket Publishing*
Editor *Christine Barker*
Circulation 23,008

FOUNDED 1968. WEEKLY. Lively magazine serving the advertising and related industries. Freelance contributors are best advised to write in the first instance.

Features Articles of up to 1500–2000 words.
Payment £100 per 1000 words.

News *Steve Redmond* Relevant news stories of up to 300 words.
Payment £35–£50.
Also 'City', 'Diary', 'News Review' and 'Media' sections.

Camping and Caravanning

11 Lower Grosvenor Place, London SW1W 0EY
☎ 01–828 1012

Owner *Camping and Caravanning Club*
Editor *Peter Frost*
Circulation 88,000

FOUNDED 1901. MONTHLY. Unsolicited, relevant mss are welcomed. Journalists with camping and caravanning knowledge should write if they have ideas for features. Also interested in features on regions of Britain, and outdoor pieces in general.

Features Items and pieces, up to a maximum of 1200 words, are only welcome if illustrated.

Camping & Walking

Link House, Dingwall Avenue, Croydon CR9 2TA
☎ 01–686 2599
Telex 947709 Fax 01–760 0973

Owner *Link House Magazines Ltd*
Editor *Philip Pond*

FOUNDED 1961. MONTHLY. magazine with features on walking and camping for the family. Especially interested in sites reports. Maximum 1500 words. Welcome unsolicited mss.

Canal and Riverboat

Stanley House, 9 West Street, Epsom, Surrey KT18 7RL
☎ 0372741411 Fax 0372744493
Telex 291561 VIASOS G (AEM)

Owner *A. E. Morgan Publications Ltd*
Editor *Norman Alborough*
Circulation 16,000

Unsolicited mss are welcomed and prospective contributors are advised to make initial approach in writing.

Features *Norman Alborough* Maximum 2000 words on all aspects of waterways and narrow boats and motor cruisers, including cruising reports, practical advice etc. Unusual ideas and personal comments are particularly welcome.
Payment around £50.

Fiction Only considered when subject matter is relevant. Maximum 1500 words.
Payment around £35.

News *David Mascord* Items up to 300 words on Inland Waterways System, plus photographs if possible.
Payment £10.

Capital Gay

38 Mount Pleasant, London WC1X 0AP
☎ 01–2783764 Telex 261177

Owner *Stonewall Press Ltd*
Editor *Graham McKerrow*
Circulation 16,733

FOUNDED 1981. WEEKLY newspaper with social and political news and features for London's gay community.

Arts & Entertainments *Pas Paschali* Some freelance work. Maximum 250 words.
Payment 'low'.

Features *Graham McKerrow* Maximum 1500 words.
Payment negotiable.

News *Graham McKerrow* Some freelance work. Maximum 400 words.
Payment negotiable. First approach in writing.

Car

FF Publishing, 97 Earls Court Road, London W8 6QH
☎ 01–370 0333 Fax 01–373 7544

Owner *FF Publishing Ltd*
Editor *Gavin Green*
Circulation 130,000

FOUNDED 1962. MONTHLY. Unsolicited manuscripts of at least 1500 words are welcomed.

Features are usually commissioned from staff and known writers, but other material on new and old cars, special events and travel experiences is considered. Maximum 3000 words.

Fiction Short stories and satire (up to 3000 words) considered.
Payment £150–£200 per 1000 words (negotiable).

News Items (up to 250 words) and photographs are always welcome, especially on new car models.
Payment £50 (negotiable).

Cars and Car Conversions Magazine

Link House, Dingwall Avenue, Croydon, Surrey CR9 2TA
☎ 01–686 2599 Telex 947709 LINKHOG

Owner *Link House Magazines Ltd*
Editor *Nigel Fryatt*
Circulation 80,000

FOUNDED 1965. MONTHLY. Unsolicited mss are welcomed, but preferably after previous contact. Prospective contributors are advised to make initial contact by telephone.

Features *Nigel Fryatt* Welcome technical articles on current motorsport and unusual sport-oriented roadcars.
Payment and length by negotiation.

Cat World

10 Western Road, Shoreham-by-Sea, West Sussex BN4 5WD
☎ 0273 462000

Owner *D. M. & J. H. Colchester*
Editor *Joan Moore*
Circulation 15,000

FOUNDED 1981. MONTHLY. Welcome unsolicited mss. Prefer to be approached in writing.

Features Lively first-hand experience features on every aspect of the cat. Breeding features and veterinary articles by acknowledged experts only. Maximum 1000 words.

Payment £25 per 1000 words.

News Short, concise, factual/humorous items concerning cats. Maximum 100 words.
Payment £5.

Poems Maximum 50 words.
Payment £6.

Catholic Herald

Lamb's Passage, Bunhill Row,
London EC1Y 8TQ
☎ 01–588 3101 Fax 01-256 9728

Editor *Peter Stanford*
Circulation 30,000

Feature material from freelancers is used. Interested not only in straight Catholic issues but also general humanitarian matters, Third World etc. No demand for freelance news writers 'unless they happen to be on the spot'.
Payment by arrangement.

Caves & Caving

342 The Green, Eccleston, Chorley,
Lancs PR7 5TP
☎ 0257 452763

Owner *British Cave Research Association*
Editor *Andy Hall*
Circulation 3000

FOUNDED 1970. QUARTERLY. Covers news on British and foreign caving activities, equipment reports, reviews, letters, expeditions, etc.

Features Expedition reports, new exploration in the UK, history of exploration articles. Maximum 1500–2000 words.

News Regional items from all over the UK. Maximum 1000 words. Welcome unsolicited mss.

Certified Accountant

Westgate House, Spital Street, Dartford,
Kent DA1 2EQ
☎ 0322 79131
Telex 896747 Fax 0322 20628

Editor *Leon Hopkins*
Circulation 32,000

MONTHLY. Specialist, professional readership; unsolicited mss not welcome. About 100 are received each year and prospective contributors are advised to make initial contact in writing. No news or fiction.

Features Professional articles and accountancy analyses. Maximum 3000 words. All features tend to be commissioned.
Payment £150.

Chacom

1 Westgate, Pennylands, Skelmersdale,
Lancs WN8 8LP
☎ 0695 21436

Owner *C. & W. Lancs Chamber of Commerce*
Editor *Mrs Babs Murphy*
Circulation 3000

FOUNDED 1984. MONTHLY for commerce and industry. Unsolicited mss welcome.

Feature Various topical areas of business, exports, Chamber of Commerce business, etc.

News Items on commerce and industry. Maximum 1500 words.
Payment minimal.

Challenge

Revenue Buildings, Chapel Road, Worthing,
West Sussex BN11 1BQ
☎ 0903 214198

Owner *Challenge Literature Fellowship*
Editor *Donald Banks*
Circulation 10,000

FOUNDED 1958. MONTHLY Christian newspaper which welcomes unsolicited mss. Prospective contributors should send for sample copy of writers' guidelines.

Fiction Short children's stories. Maximum 600 words.

News Items up to 500 words (with pictures preferably) 'showing God at work', and human interest photostories. 'Churchy' items not wanted.
Payment negotiable.

Channel TV Times

The TV Centre, St Helier, Jersey, Channel Islands
☎ 0534 68999
Telex 4192265 CTVJYG Fax 0534 59446

Owner *Channel Television Ltd*
Publications Manager *Gordon J. de Ste Croix*
Editor *Stuart C. Guilliard*
Circulation 8800

FOUNDED 1962. WEEKLY. Mainly about the Channel Islands. Unsolicited mss will be considered and are welcomed, but only on subjects of particular relevance to Channel Islanders, local history, lifestyle and island events/entertainments.

Features Maximum 2000 words.
Payment £30 per 1000 words.

Chat

195 Knightsbridge, London SW7 1RE
☏ 01–589 8877 Fax 01–225 2449

Owner *ITP*
Editor *Terry Tavner*
Circulation 515,000

FOUNDED 1985. WEEKLY women's tabloid. No unsolicited contributions; the magazine receives far too many of these. The features editor may be approached by phone with an idea.

Deputy Editor *Helen Gardner* News items usually around 400-500 words.

Features Editor *Maire Fahey* Maximum 700 words.

Cheshire Life

The Old Custom House, 70 Watergate Street, Chester CH1 2LA
☏ 0244 45226 Fax 0244 48430

Owner *Oyston Group*
Editor *Jane Fickling*
Circulation 10,000

FOUNDED 1934. MONTHLY. Features articles on homes, gardens, personalities, business, farming, conservation, heritage, books, fashion, arts, science – anything which has a Cheshire connection somewhere. Welcome unsolicited mss. Maximum 500–1500 words.
Payment £50 minimum.

News 'Not a lot – small diary items only.' First approach in writing. Maximum 150 words.
Payment £15–20.

Chess

Railway Road, Sutton Coldfield, West Midlands B73 6AZ
☏ 021–354 2536/7 Fax 021-355 0655

Owner *Pergamon Press*
Editor *Paul Lamford*
Circulation 12,000

FOUNDED 1935. MONTHLY magazine which reviews the international chess scene in an entertaining and light-hearted style. Unsolicited mss are not welcome. Query letter in the first instance.

Chic

15 Britannia Street, London WC1X 9JP
☏ 01–837 3033

Owner *Channel Media Ltd*
Editor *Kay-Lee Menadó*
Circulation 28,000 (ABC)

FOUNDED 1984. Acquired by Channel Media Ltd and relaunched with new look in March 1988. MONTHLY glossy magazine aimed at a young black readership. Unsolicited mss are welcome, but prospective contributors are advised to write in the first instance with idea.
Payment NUJ rates.

Child Education

Scholastic Publications, Marlborough House, Holly Walk, Leamington Spa, Warwickshire CV32 4LS
☏ 0926 813910

Owner *Scholastic Publications*
Editor *Gill Moore*
Circulation 63,000

FOUNDED 1923. MONTHLY magazine aimed at nursery, pre-school playgroup, infant and first teachers. Articles relating to education for 4–7 year age group written by teachers are welcome. Maximum 2000 words. First approach in writing with synopsis. No unsolicited mss.

Choice

Apex House, Oundle Road, Peterborough PE2 9NP
☏ 0733 555123

Owner *EMAP*
Editor *Annette Brown*
Circulation 87,000

MONTHLY magazine for retirement planning. Aimed at 'better off' people approaching retiring age (i.e. 50–60). Unsolicited mss are not welcome; approach in writing only.

Deputy Editor *Gill Bendall*

Features on items, hobbies and adventure affecting people approaching retirement age considered. Maximum usually 800 words (occasionally 1500 words).
Payment £80–100.

Finance Features on finance/property/legal matters affecting the magazine's readership.

News All items affecting the magazine's readership: pensions, state benefits, caring for elderly

relatives. Maximum 100 words.
Payment up to £25.

Christian Herald

Herald House, Dominion Road, Worthing, West Sussex BN14 8JP
☏ 0903 821082

Owner *Herald House Ltd*
Editor *Colin Reeves*
Circulation 27,000

FOUNDED 1866. WEEKLY. Conservative evangelical Christian magazine aimed at adults with families. Most theological and spiritual articles are commissioned.

Family Focus Short articles on wide range of subjects, some religious, some non-religious. Articles should appeal to whole family, but particularly women. Maximum 200–500 words.
Payment at Herald House rates.

Christian Science, Monitor

Eggington House, 25–8 Buckingham Gate, London SW1E 6LD
☏ 01–630 8666

Owner *Christian Science Publishing Society*
Contact *British Isles Correspondent*

The London office is not an editorial one, and all unsolicited material is passed on to head office in the United States for consideration. WEEKLY in Britain, the *Monitor* has a larger circulation in America, where it is a DAILY paper. Always on the look-out for general interest feature material which appeals to an international audience.

Church News

College Gate House, Bury St Edmunds, Suffolk IP33 1NN
☏ 0284 735530

Owner *Home Words & Canon Cecil Rhodes*
Editor *Canon Cecil Rhodes*
Circulation 95,000

FOUNDED 1946. Small MONTHLY magazine featuring news and information on events, persons, religious subjects and debates. Unsolicited mss welcome. Maximum 600 words for articles.
Payment by agreement.

Church of England Newspaper

Livingstone House, 11 Carteret Street, London SW1H 9DJ
☏ 01–222 3464 Fax 01–222 5414

Owner *Christian Weekly Newspapers Ltd*
Editor *John K. Martin*
Circulation 12,500

FOUNDED 1828. WEEKLY. Almost all material is commissioned, but unsolicited mss are considered.

Features *Polly Hudson* Unless commissioned, preliminary enquiry is essential. Maximum 1200 words.
Payment at NUJ/IOJ rates.

News *Colin Blakely* News items must be sent promptly and must have a church/Christian relevance. Maximum 200-400 words.

Church Times

7 Portugal Street, London WC2A 2HP
☏ 01–405 0844 Fax 01–405 5071

Owner *The Canterbury Press*
Editor *John Whale*
Circulation 44,797

FOUNDED 1863. WEEKLY. Bought by The Canterbury Press mid 1989. Unsolicited mss considered.

Features *John Whale* Articles on religious or social topics. Length 700–1500 words.
Payment £25 per 1000 words minimum.

News *Susan Young* Occasional reports on out-of-London events, but only when commissioned. Length and *Payment* by arrangement.

City Limits

8–15 Aylesbury Street, London EC1R 0LR
☏ 01–250 1299

Owner *London Voice Ltd*
Editor *Ian Pye*
Circulation 24,000

FOUNDED in 1981. WEEKLY independent, cooperatively-owned London publication with news, reviews and features. Recommend first approach by telephone. 'We have a lead period of six weeks so we advise would-be contributors to contact us well in advance.'

Features Maximum 1500–2000 words.
Payment £66 per 1000 words.

Reviews Maximum 250 words.
Payment £16.50 per review.

News Maximum 250 words. Welcome unsolicited material.

Classical Guitar

Olsover House, 43 Sackville Road, Newcastle-upon-Tyne NE6 5TA
☎ 091–276 0448 Fax 091-276 1623

Owner *Ashley Mark Publishing Company*
Editor *Colin Cooper*

FOUNDED 1982. MONTHLY

Concert reviews *Chris Kilvington* Maximum 250 words.
Payment by arrangement.

Features *Colin Cooper* Usually written by staff writers. Maximum 1500 words.
Payment by arrangement.

News *Colin Cooper* Small paragraphs and festival concert reports welcome.
Payment none. First approach in writing.

Classical Music

241 Shaftesbury Avenue, London WC2H 8EH
☎ 01–836 2383
Telex 264675 GILDED G Fax 01–528 7991

Owner *Rhinegold Publishing Ltd*
Editor *Graeme Kay*

FOUNDED 1976. FORTNIGHTLY. A specialist magazine using precisely targeted news and feature articles, so unsolicited manuscripts are not welcome. Prospective contributors may approach in writing with an idea, but should familiarise themselves beforehand with the style and market of the magazine.
Payment from £50 per 1000 words.

Climber and Hillwalker

Floor 7, The Plaza Tower, The Plaza, East Kilbride, Glasgow G74 1LW
☎ 03552 42464

Owner *Holmes McDougall Ltd*
Editor *Cameron McNeish*
Circulation 20,000

FOUNDED 1962. MONTHLY. Unsolicited mss welcome (they receive about ten a day). Finished features only – no ideas.

Features Freelance features (maximum 2000 words) are accepted on climbing, mountaineering and hillwalking in UK and abroad. The standard of writing must be extremely high.
Payment negotiable.

News No freelance opportunities as all items are handled in-house.

Club International

2 Archer Street, London W1V 7HE
☎ 01–734 9191 Telex 22638

Owner *Paul Raymond*
Editor *Stephen Bleach*
Circulation 180,000

FOUNDED 1972. MONTHLY. Features, fiction and short, humorous items 'in the style of *Viz, Private Eye, Punch* etc'.

Features and **Fiction** Maximum 2500 words.
Payment £100 per 1000 words.

Shorts 200–750 words.
Payment negotiable.

Coarse Fishing Today

Bretton Court, Bretton, Peterborough PE3 8DZ
☎ 0733 264666 Fax 0733 265515

Owner *EMAP Pursuit Publications*
Editor *Neil Pope*
Circulation 23,109

FOUNDED 1983. BI-MONTHLY. Unsolicited material on all coarse fishing subjects is very welcome and prospective contributors are advised to make initial contact by telephone. As the magazine is aimed at experienced anglers, submissions should be in-depth studies.

Features Maximum 2500 words. All articles should be illustrated either with black and white photos or colour transparencies.

Fiction Usually one piece per issue and humorous submissions are preferred.
Payment by arrangement.

Company

National Magazine House, 72 Broadwick Street, London W1V 2BP
☎ 01–439 5000

Owner *National Magazine Co. Ltd*
Editor *Gill Hudson*
Circulation 185,932

Glossy women's MONTHLY magazine, founded to appeal to the independent and intelligent young woman. Consider themselves a good market for freelancers: 'we've got more space for them, as we have fewer staff feature writers'. 1500–2000 words. Keen to encourage bright new young talent, but uncommissioned material rarely accepted. Feature outlines preferred plus evidence of writing ability, namely cuttings.

Computer Weekly

Quadrant House, The Quadrant, Sutton,
Surrey SM2 5AS
☏ 01–661 3122

Owner *Reed Business Publishing*
Editor *John Lamb*
Circulation 113,000

FOUNDED 1966. Unsolicited material generally not welcome unless an outline has been discussed and agreed. Unsolicited items (up to 700 words) are welcomed for the 'Platform' section, but there is no fee. No fiction.

Features *Julia Vowler* Always looking for new, good writers with specialised industry knowledge. Maximum 1200 words. Special Show Features for industry events (e.g. previews) up to 1200 words.

News *Angeli Mehta* Maximum 300 words. Some possibilities for regional or foreign news items only.
Payment £120 per 1000 words.

Computing

32–4 Broadwick Street, London W1A 2HG
☏ 01–439 4242 Telex 23918 VNU G

Owner *VNU*
Editor *Sarah Underwood*
Circulation 116,000

WEEKLY. New contributors are welcome, and are advised to write in the first instance with ideas.

Connections

Sea Containers House, 20 Upper Ground,
London SE1 9PF

Editor *Alison Booth*
Circulation over 2 million

TWICE-YEARLY magazine of Sealink Ferries, distributed to those travelling with the company. Carry around 3 articles per issue, mostly connected with places en route. Unsolicited material not generally welcome, nor ideas; happy with their current contributors, and commission when necessary.

Contemporary Review

61 Carey Street, London WC2A 2JG
☏ 0252 713883

Owner *Contemporary Review Co. Ltd*
Editor *Betty Abel*

FOUNDED 1866. MONTHLY. One of the first periodicals to devote considerable space to the arts. Today it remains liberal without any specific political affilations. A wide spectrum of interests includes home affairs and politics, literature and the arts, history, travel and religion. There is also a monthly book section, quarterly fiction and film reviews. Unsolicited mss welcome. Maximum 3000 words. No fiction.

Cosmopolitan

National Magazine House, 72 Broadwick Street,
London W1V 2BP
☏ 01–439 7144

Owner *National Magazine Co. Ltd*
Editor *Linda Kelsey*
Circulation 387,000

Popular mix of articles, emotional advice and strong fiction designed to appeal to the early-twenties modern-minded female. Known to have a policy of not considering unsolicited mss, but does nevertheless sometimes look at those it receives as it is always on the look-out for new writers. 'The thing to do is to ring the features desk with an idea; if they are interested they will ask to see something.'

Features Editor (and long-standing humour writer for the magazine) *Marcelle D'Argy Smith.*

Cotswold Life

West One House, 23 St George's Road,
Cheltenham, Gloucestershire GL50 3DT
☏ 0242 226367/226373

Owner *Beshara Press*
Editor *John Drinkwater*
Circulation *c.* 10,000

FOUNDED 1968. MONTHLY. News and features on life in the Cotswolds. Most news written in-house but welcome contributions for features on interesting places and people; reminiscences of Cotswold life in years gone by; historical features on any aspect of Cotswold life. First approach in writing. Maximum 1500-2000 words for features.
Payment by negotiation after publication.

Country Homes and Interiors

Carlton House, 25 Newman Street,
London W1P 3HA
☏ 01–631 3939

Owner *Carlton Magazines Ltd*
Editor *Vanessa Berridge*

Circulation 97,600

FOUNDED 1986, MONTHLY. The best approach for prospective contributors is with an idea in writing as unsolicited manuscripts are not welcome.

Features *Vanessa Berridge, Julia Watson* There are two main features per month, one a personality interview, the other an examination of a topic of interest to an intelligent, affluent readership (both women and men) aged 25–44. Maximum 1500–2000 words.
Payment negotiable.

Travel *Julia Watson* Articles 1200 words. Also hotel reviews, leisure pursuits, week-ending pieces in England and abroad. Length 750 words.
Payment negotiable.

Country Life

King's Reach Tower, Stamford Street, London SE1 9LS
☎ 01–261 7058 Fax 01–261 5139

Owner *IPC Magazines Ltd*
Editor *Jenny Greene*
Circulation 54,500

Features which relate to the countryside, wildlife, rural events, sports and pursuits, of interest to well-heeled country dwellers welcome. Strong, informed material rather than amateur enthusiasm.
Payment £106 per 1000 words minimum, more if exceptional.

Country Living

National Magazine House, 72 Broadwick Street, London W1V 2BP
☎ 01–439 5294 Fax 01–437 6886

Editor *Deirdre McSharry*
Circulation 162,225

Regards itself as a women's magazine, but has a strong male readership as well. Upmarket, takes living in the country seriously (generally in a soft-focus middle-class way) and tends to be people-oriented. Welcome features on people, conservation, wildlife, houses, gardens, animals, country businesses etc. Suggestions welcome. Pays good fees and very keen to use literate and well researched material; often uses 'name writers'. Articles are mostly commissioned; writers new to the magazine should send a synopsis and examples of published work.
Payment negotiable, but never less than £150 per 1000 words, often more.

Country Sports

59 Kennington Road, London SW1 7PZ
☎ 01–928 4742

Owner *British Field Sports Society*
Editor *Derek Bingham*
Circulation 50,000

FOUNDED 1983. THRICE-YEARLY. No unsolicited mss.

Country Times and Landscape

Evro Publishing Ltd, Thames House, 5–6 Church Street, Twickenham, Middlesex TW1 3NJ
☎ 01–891 6070
Telex 01–895 2440 Fax 01–891 4373

Owner *Haymarket*
Editor *Simon Courtauld*

Formerly *Out of Town* FOUNDED in 1983 and relaunched as *Country Times* May 1988. Merged with *Landscape* in October 1988. MONTHLY. Unsolicited mss not used 'very often' but welcome contributions. First approach in writing.

The Countryman

Sheep Street, Burford OX8 4LH
☎ 099382 2258

Owner *The Countryman Ltd*
Editor *Christopher Hall*
Circulation 78,000

FOUNDED 1927. QUARTERLY. Unsolicited mss with s.a.e. welcome; about 75 received each week. Prospective contributors are advised to make initial approach in writing having read a few issues of the magazine to understand its character.

Creative Camera

Battersea Arts Centre, Old Town Hall Lavender Hill, London SW11 5TF
☎ 01–924 3017

Owner *Registered Charity*
Editor *Peter Turner*
Circulation *c.* 6000

FOUNDED 1968. MONTHLY. Most of the magazine's content is commissioned, but new contributors are welcome and are best advised to approach in writing.

Features Reviews of photographic books and

exhibitions. Maximum 750 words.
Payment £50.

Creative Review
50 Poland Street, London W1V 4AX
☎ 01–439 4222

Editor *Lewis Blackwell*

The trade magazine of advertising and related industries, including film, design and illustration. Expert contributors only. Send in samples of work, whether published or not; feature needs are organised on a commission basis, and writers of talent may be taken up.

The Cricketer International
29 Cavendish Road, Redhill, Surrey RH1 4AH
☎ 0737 772221 Fax 0737 771720

Owner *Ben G. Brocklehurst*
Editorial Director *Christopher Martin-Jenkins*
Executive Editor *Peter Perchard*
Circulation 42,000

FOUNDED 1921. MONTHLY. Unsolicited mss welcome.

Cue World
Cavalier House, 202 Hagley Road, Edgbaston, Birmingham B16 9PQ
☎ 021-455 6230

Owner *Snooker Publications Ltd*
Editor *John Dee*
Circulation 24,000

FOUNDED 1976. MONTHLY for snooker enthusiasts. Unsolicited mss not welcome. All approaches should be made in writing.

The Dalesman
Dalesman Publishing Company Ltd, Clapham, Lancaster LA2 8EB
☎ 04685 225

Owner *Dalesman Publishing Company Ltd*
Editor *David Joy*
Circulation 56,000

FOUNDED 1939. Just celebrated its 50th birthday in 1989, and now the biggest-selling regional publication of its kind in the country. MONTHLY magazine with articles of specific Yorkshire interest. Welcome unsolicited mss and receive approximately ten per day. First approach in writing. Maximum 2000 words.
Payment negotiable.

Dance & Dancers
248 High Street, Croydon, Surrey CR0 1NF
☎ 01–681 7817

Owner *Plusloop Ltd*
Editor *John Percival*

FOUNDED 1950. MONTHLY magazine covering ballet and modern dance throughout the world.

Features *John Percival* 'There is opportunity for writers of good quality with special preference for knowledge of ballet as performer.'

News *Nadine Meisner* Almost all information is written in-house. Preliminary discussion is always advisable.
Payment 'low'.

Dance Theatre Journal
Laban Centre for Movement Dance, Laurie Grove, London SE14 6NH
☎ 01–692 4070

Owner *Laban Centre for Movement & Dance*
Co-Editors *Chris de Marigny, Deirdre McMahon*

FOUNDED 1983. QUARTERLY. Interested in features on every aspect of the contemporary dance scene. Unsolicited mss welcome. Specially interested in articles concerning issues such as the funding policy for dance as well as critical assessments of choreographers' work and latest developments in various schools of contemporary dance. 1000–3000 words.
Payment £20 per 1000 words.

The Dancing Times
Clerkenwell House, 45–7 Clerkenwell Green, London EC1R 0BE
☎ 01–250 3006

Owner *Private company*
Editor *Mary Clarke*

FOUNDED 1910. MONTHLY. Welcome approaches in writing from specialist dance writers and photographers only.

Darts World
2 Park Lane, Croydon, Surrey CR9 1HA
☎ 01–681 2837

Owner *World Magazines Ltd*
Editor *A. J. Wood*
Circulation 24,500

Features Welcome single articles or series on technique and instruction. Maximum 1200 words.

Fiction Short stories with darts theme of no more than 1000 words.

News Maximum 800 words. Tournament reports, general and personality news required.
Payment negotiable.

Decanter

Priory House, 8 Battersea Park Road,
London SW8 4BG
☏ 01–627 8181
Telex 946240 CWEASY Ref 19010760

Editor *David Rowe*
Circulation 30,000

FOUNDED 1975. Glossy wines and spirits magazine. Unsolicited material welcome, but an advance telephone call is appreciated. No fiction.

News and **Features** All items and articles should concern wines, spirits or food and related subjects.

Departures

6 Haymarket, London SW1Y 4BS
☏ 01–930 4411
Telex 8950931 Fax 01–930 4842

Owner *American Express*
Editor *Willie Landels*
Circulation 500,000

FOUNDED 1984. BI-MONTHLY. A literary travel magazine, specialising in high-quality travel writing and glossy colour photography. Prospective contributors are best advised to approach with an idea in writing only.

Features Editor *Margaret Hickey*

Derbyshire County Magazine

Norman House, Heritage Gate, Derby DE1 1NV
☏ 0332 43075 Fax 0332 292125

Owner *Oyston Group of Publications*
Editor *Sue Allen*
Circulation 8000

FOUNDED 1986. MONTHLY. Welcome unsolicited contributions. Prefer initial approach in writing.

News *Ruth Houghton* Diary Section (b&w pix appreciated). Maximum 200 words.
Payment £15.

Features *Sue Allen* County interest: people, places, events, plus photos. Maximum 600 words.
Payment £35–75.
Also news of local events for Social Pages (including photos). Maximum 200 words.
Payment £40.

Derbyshire Life and Countryside

Lodge Land, Derby DE1 3HE
☏ 0332 47087 Fax 0332 290688

Owner *B. C. Wood*
Editor *Vivienne Irish*
Circulation 12,185

FOUNDED 1931. MONTHLY. Unsolicited mss and photos on and of Derbyshire welcome. Best approach in writing with ideas.

Descent

51 Timbers Square, Roath,
South Glamorgan CF2 3SH
☏ 0222 486557

Owner *Ambit Publications*
Editor *Chris Howes*

FOUNDED 1969. BI-MONTHLY for cavers. Submissions welcome from freelance contributors who can write accurately and knowledgeably on any aspect of caves, mines, or underground structures.

Features Maximum 2500 words. General interest articles of under 1000 words always welcome, especially if supported by photographs/illustrations.
Payment on publication according to page area filled.

Design

28 Haymarket, London SW1Y 4SU
☏ 01–839 8000 Fax 01–925 2130

Owner *Design Council*
Editor *Marion Hancock*
Circulation 15,000

FOUNDED 1949. MONTHLY. Unsolicited mss not welcome; approach by phone or in writing.

Book Reviews Various lengths.
Payment approximately £120 per 1000 words.

Features On most design-related areas, particularly product and consumer goods design. Interviews with designers, managers and consult-

ancies. Maximum 1500 words.
Payment £120–140 per 1000 words.

Designing

The Design Council, 28 Haymarket,
London SW1Y 4SU
☎ 01–839 8000 Fax 01–925 2130

Owner *The Design Council*
Editor *Ms Morven MacKillop*
Circulation 7,000

Published three times per year (for each school term). A 32-page paper with news, features, book reviews and special supplements. Design-related subjects on a wide range and on work going on in schools. Welcome unsolicited mss from writers with an interest in education and design. 'We do not receive enough.' First approach in writing with ideas of subjects covered, ideas of pictures and illustrations. Primary and secondary schools and student readership.

Book Reviews *Ms Morven MacKillop* 'Qualified' people can offer to review books.
Payment £20 per review.

Features *Ms Morven MacKillop* Science, engineering, textiles, graphics, cookery, work being done in secondary schools. Maximum 800–1200 words.
Payment £100 per 1000 words.
Also special supplements in designing – eight pages per topic. 'Much of the material is written in-house, but we would like to hear from new authors.' Maximum 8–12 eight-hundred-word pages.
Payment £100 per 1000 words.

News *Ms Morven MacKillop* Short paragraphs on relevant events. Maximum 100–300 words.
Payment £100 per 1000 words.

Devon Life

Regional Magazines, Finance House, Barnfield Road, Exeter, Devon EX1 1QR
☎ 0392 216766 Fax 0392 71050

Owner *Town & Country Magazines*
Editor *Mrs Jan Beart-Albrecht*
Circulation 9,000

FOUNDED 1965. MONTHLY. Features articles on any aspect of life in Devon. Unsolicited mss welcome. Maximum 2000–2500 words.
Payment approximately £50. First approach in writing.

Dimensions

Headway Publications Ltd, Greater London House, Hampstead, London NW1 7QQ
☎ 01–377 4633 Fax 01–383 7486/7570
Telex 922488 Bureau G Ref HWY

Owner *Headway Publications*
Editor *Michael Imeson*
Circulation 300,000

FOUNDED 1989. QUARTERLY National Westminster Bank magazine on money matters and lifestyle. Most articles are commissioned so unsolicited mss are rarely used.

Director

10 Belgrave Square, London SW1X 8PH
☎ 01–235 9122

Editor *George Bickerstaffe*
Circulation 36,000

Published by the Institute of Directors for its members. Wide range of features from design to employment and general interest articles; plus book reviews, technology, health. Use regulars, but unsolicited mss will be considered.
Payment negotiable.

Discover Europe

Huntsman House, Hale Wharf, Ferry Lane,
London N17 9PF
☎ 01–801 3344

Owner *Discovery Press*
Editor *Lyn Thompson*
Circulation 100,000

FOUNDED 1985. BI-MONTHLY. A travel information magazine, covering Europe. Unsolicited mss are not welcome; prefer to discuss material with the writer before it is submitted.

Features on places of interest to the traveller. Maximum 1000 words.

News should be brief.
Payment £80.

Dog and Country

Corry's Farm, Roestock Lane, Colney Heath, St Albans, Herts AL4 0QW
☎ 0727 22614

Owner *Gilbertson & Page Limited*
Editor *Edward Askwith*

QUARTERLY magazine featuring gundog training, veterinary, countryside matters and gardening. Unsolicited mss welcome. Sold by subscription only.

Features Articles, maximum 1200 words, based on actual experience or expert knowledge of household, gun and working dogs, natural history, game, coarse and sea angling, and conservation.
Payment £7.50 per A5 page.
Most articles occupy two pages or more.

Dog World

9 Tufton Street, Ashford, Kent TN23 1QN
☎ 0233 621877 Fax 0233 45669

Owner *Dog World Ltd*
Editor *Simon Parsons*
Circulation 31,489

FOUNDED 1908. WEEKLY magazine for people 'seriously interested in pedigree dogs'. Unsolicited mss welcome provided they are suitable. Best approach in writing first.

News Freelance reports on court cases, local government issues, etc. involving dogs.

Features Well-researched historical items or other items of unusual interest concerning dogs. Maximum 1000 words. Photographs of unusual 'doggy' situations always of interest.
Payment £40 max.

Fiction Seldom.

Dorset Life

Market Street, Crewkerne, Somerset TA18 7JU
☎ 0460 73076

Owner *Smart Print Publications Ltd*
Editor *Jack Rayfield*
Circulation 9,500

FOUNDED 1977. MONTHLY magazine with features on any subject of interest (historical, geographical, arts, crafts) to people living in Dorset. Maximum 1000–1500 words. Welcome unsolicited mss. First approach in writing.
Payment negotiable.

Drama

British Theatre Association, Regent's College, Inner Circle, Regent's Park, London NW1 4NW
☎ 01–935 2571 Fax 01–224 2457

Owner *British Theatre Association*
Editor *Christopher Edwards*
Circulation 7000

FOUNDED 1919. QUARTERLY. theatre review. Unsolicited manuscripts are rarely used, due to a shortage of space, but prospective contributors are advised to approach by phone or in writing (with samples of their work). All enquiries should be directed to the **Assistant Editor** *Sabeha Syed.* Feature articles on current theatrical scene (bearing in mind that *Drama* is a quarterly), interviews and profiles. Maximum *c.*3000 words.
Payment £30–40 per printed page. Also book reviews; maximum *c.*1500 words. *Payment* £15–30.

dx (Daily Express magazine)

121 Fleet Street, London EC4P 4JT
☎ 01–353 8000 Telex 21841

Owner *United Newspapers plc*
Editor *Jane Owen*
Circulation 1.69 million

Stop Press Title withdrawn; replaced by **Forty-Eight Hours**. Features on homes, fashion and beauty, shopping, entertainment, travel, politics, property. Interested in considering ideas from freelance writers. Write with idea in the first instance. Plenty of scope for big pictures. Maximum 1500 words.
Payment negotiable.

Early Days

16 Trinity Churchyard, Guildford, Surrey GU1 3RR
☎ 0483 577533

Owner *Bond Clarkson Russell*
Editor *Fiona Macpherson*
Circulation 400,000

FOUNDED 1984. 'Birth' and 'Weaning' editions dealing with all aspects of the first few months of a baby's life. Unsolicited mss not welcome as all features are commissioned. Readers' letters on relevant issues and experiences are considered for publication. No fees.

Early Times

Brighton Business Centre, 95 Ditchling Road, Brighton BN1 4SB
☎ 0273 675374

Owner *Garth Publications Ltd*
Editor *Robert Dunkley*
Circulation 50,000

WEEKLY quality newspaper aimed at bright, enquiring children. First issue in January 1988 sold out on the day of issue. Originally

conceived for the 8–14 age group but now attracting a wider age range. News and features on national and international issues. Mainly use a pool of freelance writers but welcome items of 300 words maximum.
Payment £100 per 1000 words.

The Economist

25 St James's Street, London SW1A 1HG
☏ 01–839 7000
Telex 24344 Fax 01–839 2968

Owner 50% *Financial Times*, 50% *individual shareholders*
Editor *Rupert Pennant-Rea*
Circulation 349,030

FOUNDED 1843 WEEKLY. Prospective contributors should approach the editor in writing. Unsolicited contributions are not welcomed.

Edinburgh Review

22 George Square, Edinburgh EH8 9LF
☏ 031–667 1011 ext 2412

Owner *Polygon Books*
Editor *Peter Kravitz*
Circulation 1500

FOUNDED 1969. QUARTERLY. Articles and fiction on Scottish and international literary, cultural and philosophical themes. Unsolicited contributions are welcome (1600 received each year) but prospective contributors are strongly advised to study the magazine first. Maximum for fiction should be 6000 words, and translations from little-known world writers are particularly welcome. Feature articles do not have to be tied in to a recent anniversary, and interest will be shown in accessible articles on philosophy and its relationship to literature. In addition each issue now contains an Encyclopaedia Supplement, consisting of approximately twenty pages of short items on matters of cultural and political importance which aims to show knowledge and ideas to be 'the collective property of humankind'. Entries for this supplement may vary from just a few words to a maximum of 1000.

Education

21–7 Lamb's Conduit Street, London WC1N 3NJ
☏ 01–242 2548

Owner *Longman Group*
Editor *George Low*
Circulation 10,000

WEEKLY journal read by educational administrators and professionals; articles which appeal to these groups only. Practical administration, and 'how schools are run', plus comment on the state of administration at the present time. Freelancers tend to be a regular network of writers.
Payment at NUJ rates.

Education + Training

62 Toller Lane, Bradford,
West Yorkshire BD8 9BY
☏ 0274 499821 Fax 0274 547143

Owner *MCB University Press Ltd*
Editor *Derek Bradley*
Circulation *c.* 3000

FOUNDED 1959. BI-MONTHLY. Unsolicited mss are welcomed provided they are practically orientated and not purely academic. No fees are paid for contributions.

8000 Plus

Future Publishing, 4 Queen Street, Bath BA1 1EJ
☏ 0225 446034 Fax 0225 446019

Owner *Chris Anderson*
Editor *Steve Patient*
Circulation 28,365

FOUNDED 1986. MONTHLY. Unsolicited contributions welcome. Receive about 6 or 7 per month but prefer to be approached in writing in first instance.

Features *Steve Patient, Sharon Bradley* 'We will welcome any interesting feature-length articles on writing whether PCW specific or not. Good illustrations required as well.' Maximum 3500 words.
Payment open to negotiation but in the region of £200.

Special Pages *Steve Patient, Sharon Bradley*

'Case in Point' feature monthly – original uses to which people have put their Amstrad PCWs. Good illustrations important. Maximum 1600 words.
Payment approx. £100 but negotiable.

Elle

Rex House, 4–12 Lower Regent Street,
London SW1Y 4PE
☏ 01–930 9050

Owner *Hachette*
Editor *Sally Brampton*
Circulation 250,000

FOUNDED 1985. MONTHLY glossy. Unsolicited contributions, of which twenty are received each week, are only welcome if written specifically for *Elle*. Prospective contributors are best advised to approach the relevant editor in writing.

Features *Jane McCarthy* Maximum 2000 words.

News (Insight) *Carl Hindmarch* Short articles on current/cultural events with emphasis on national and not just London-based readership. Maximum 500 words.
Payment for all pieces £150 per 1000 words.

Embroidery

PO Box 42B, East Molesley, Surrey KT8 9BB
☎ 01–943 1229

Owner *Embroiderers' Guild*
Editor *Valerie Campbell-Harding*
Circulation 12,600

FOUNDED 1933. QUARTERLY. Features articles on embroidery techniques, historical and foreign embroidery, and specific artists' work with illustrations. Also reviews. Unsolicited mss welcome. Maximum 1000 words.
Payment £40–50.

Empire

42 Great Portland Street, London W1N 5AH
☎ 01–436 5430

Owner *East Midlands Allied Press plc*
Editor *Barry McIlheney*

MONTHLY magazine – the modern guide to screen entertainment, launched 1989 at the Cannes Film Festival. Aims to 'cover the world of films in a comprehensive, adult, intelligent and witty package'. Although the majority of Empire will be devoted to films and the people behind them, it will also be looking at the developments and technology behind television and video. Wide selection of in-depth features and stories on all the main releases of the month. Also reviews. Unsolicited mss welcome. Prefer initial approach in writing.

Features *Barry McIlheney* Short features on behind the scenes in films. Maximum 1000 words.
Payment £100.

Encounter

44 Great Windmill Street, London W1V 7PA
☎ 01–434 3063

Owner *Encounter Ltd*
Editors *Melvin J. Laskey, Anthony Hartley, Richard Mayne*
Circulation 20,000

FOUNDED 1953. 10 ISSUES PER YEAR Publishes reportage and articles of a political and philosophical interest together with one short story per issue and a maximum of six poems. Intending contributors are strongly advised to study the magazine in advance. Unsolicited manuscripts generally welcome but thousands are received each year and, due to lack of space, very few accepted. Short stories should be 5000 words maximum.
Payment £10 per 1000 words, and should be sent to the literary editor. *Payment* for poetry varies. S.a.e. is essential if unsuitable work is to be returned.

The Engineer

30 Calderwood Street, London SE18 6QH
☎ 01–855 7777
Telex 896238 MORGAN G Fax 01–316 3040

Owner *Morgan-Grampian*
Editor *John Pullin*
Circulation 40,000

FOUNDED 1956. WEEKLY news magazine for engineers and managers.

Features *Martin Ince* Most outside contributors are specially commissioned, but good ideas are always welcome. Maximum 2000 words.
Payment by arrangement.

News *Peter Eustace* Some scope for specialist regional freelancers and for tip-offs. Maximum 500 words.
Payment by arrangement.

Techscan *Colin MacIlwain* Technology news. Freelance opportunities available as for **News.** Maximum 500 words.
Payment by arrangement.

Engineering

28 Haymarket, London SW1Y 4SU
☎ 01–839 8000 Fax 01–925 2130

Owner *The Design Council*
Editor *Richard Wood*
Circulation 22,000

FOUNDED 1866. MONTHLY. Unsolicited manuscripts not welcome, but prospective contributors may approach by telephone with an idea, which should be followed up with a written synopsis.

Features *Andrew Beevers* Developments in technology, product design, marketing and trade. Maximum 1800 words.
Payment £200.

News *Andrew Beevers* Little opportunity for freelancers here, but 'outstanding new developments in technology' always considered. maximum 350 words.
Payment £40. Applications, also, of advanced plastic composite materials are of great interest – good stories in this area always required. Maximum 1800 words.
Payment £200.

Environment Now

The Old Beet House, Silver Street, Askrigg, Wensleydale, North Yorkshire DL8 3HS
☎ 0969 50659

Owner *Hyde Park Publications*
Editor *Robin Murrell*
Circulation 32,000

FOUNDED 1987. Bought by Hyde Park Publications in 1988. BI-MONTHLY. Features on all aspects of the environment from energy through waste management and pollution, to habitat and species protection, and urban environment, will be considered. Good photographic coverage essential – can be arranged by magazine if required.

News Items done in-house. Welcome unsolicited mss. Prefer to be approached in writing.

ES (Evening Standard magazine)

Northcliffe House, 2 Derry Street, Kensington, London W8 5EE
☎ 01–938 6000 Telex 21909

Owner *Lord Rothermere*

MONTHLY magazine issued with the London *Evening Standard.*

Associate Editor *Maggie Alderson,* to whom all unsolicited mss should be addressed. Potential contributors should study the magazine first for its style and content.
Payment by negotiation.

European Investor

Boundary House, 91–3 Charterhouse Street, London EC1M 6HR
☎ 01–250 0646 Fax 01–250 0637

Owner *Charterhouse Communications Ltd*
Editor *Iain Yule*
Circulation 70,000

FOUNDED 1988. BI-MONTHLY. Features personal finance reporting from major European Financial cities. Welcome unsolicited contributions but prefer approach in writing in first instance.

News and Features Maximum 2000 words.
Payment £100 per 1000 words.

Evergreen

PO Box 52, Cheltenham, Gloucestershire
☎ 0242 577775

Editor *R. Faiers*
Circulation 73,000

FOUNDED 1985. QUARTERLY Features Britain's famous people and infamous characters, its natural beauty, towns and villages, nostalgia, traditions, odd customs, legends, folklore, crafts, etc. Unsolicited contributions welcome but receive a great many. Prefer to be approached in writing in first instance. Maximum 1500 words, minimum 500.
Payment £15 per 1000 words (articles), £4 (poems).

Everywoman

34 Islington Green, London N1 8DU
☎ 01–359 5496

Editor *Barbara Rogers*
Circulation 15,000

Magazine which provides general news and features angled towards women's current affairs interest, health, employment and money, and relationships, rather than being a traditional 'for women' lifestyle consumer glossy. Contributors are strongly advised to study the magazine, and indicate which section submissions are intended for.

Excel Magazine

Lex House, 3–6 Alfred Place, London WC1 7EB
☎ 01–323 3232
Telex 9419132 LEXBSL G Fax 01–631 0035

Owner *Springwood Publishing Ltd*
Editor *Rod Fountain*
Circulation 60,000

FOUNDED 1986. MONTHLY. Magazine with news and features on the business and financial world with special interest in career and management development. Receives 100 unsolicited mss per month. Prefer to see a synopsis or brief outline for features in the first instance.

Features Offbeat, witty, business-related generic stories, or profiles of young men and women in business.

Odds Short quirky items on unusual business matters, success or failure.

Payment by arrangement not less than £100 per 1000 words.

Executive Post

2–4 Fitzwilliam Gate, Sheffield S1 4JH
☎ 0742 704603 Fax 0742 755200/755208

Editor *Alison Bird*
Circulation 130,000

Mailed to jobseekers registered with PER (Professional and Executive Recruitment). Will consider any aspect of executive-level employment or jobhunting as a feature. Limited news opportunities.
Payment negotiable.

Executive Travel

242 Vauxhall Bridge Road, London SW1V 1AU
☎ 01–821 1155
Telex 924015 TRANEW G Fax 01–630 1000

Editor *Mike Toynbee*
Circulation 49,738

FOUNDED 1979. MONTHLY aimed at business travellers. Unsolicited mss welcome.

The Expatriate

25 Brighton Road, South Croydon, Surrey CR2 6EA
☎ 01–681 5545 Telex 295112 NHG G

Owner *Expatriate Publications Ltd*
Editor *Jack Walder*
Circulation *c.* 500

FOUNDED 1977. MONTHLY serving the British expatriate community. Unsolicited mss are welcome.

Features Special features on working in particular countries. Psychological problems for spouses, education difficulties, pensions, investment and taxation features, health matters. Maximum 1200 words.

News Information on special facilities for expatriates, e.g. mail-order presents, financial services, relocation agents, etc. Maximum 1000 words.
Payment negotiable.

Expatxtra!

PO Box 300, Jersey, Channel Islands
☎ 0534 36241

Owner *Expatxtra Ltd*
Editor *Catherine Richmond*
Circulation 15,000

FOUNDED 1982. MONTHLY aimed at working or retired UK expatriates. The magazine is dominated by its laid-back style. It is therefore important to look at a copy before sending mss. No news or fiction.

Features *Vikki Clair* Up to a maximum of 1500 words on travel, fashion, education, etc. Articles on all financial matters are popular, e.g. taxation, investment, banking, life assurance, etc.
Payment £100 per 1000 words.

Expression

20–26 Brunswick Place, London N1 6DJ
☎ 01–490 1444

Editor *Geoffrey Aquilina-Ross*
Circulation 570,000

Upmarket glossy mailed to American Express cardmembers. Features always welcome on travel, food, wine and general consumer matters – anything of genuine interest to the discerning with a disposable income. Some features are produced in-house, others by regular freelancers, but they occasionally find unsolicited articles which hit the right note.
Payment £150 per printed page (generally between 800 and 1000 words).

The Face

The Old Laundry, Ossington Buildings, London W1M 3HY
☎ 01–935 8232 Fax 01–935 2237

Owner *Wagadon Ltd*
Editor *Nick Logan*
Circulation 82,000

FOUNDED 1980. Perhaps the ultimate magazine of the Style Generation, concerned with who's what and what's cool. Profiles, interviews and stories. No fiction. Acquaintance with the 'voice' of *The Face* is essential before sending mss on spec.

Features 3000 words.
Payment £80 per 1000 words.
New contributors should telephone with their ideas and speak to the **Features Editor** *Katherine Flett.* Also **Intro** (diary) pages, with photo-based short pieces (350 words).
Payment as for features.

Diary Editor *Lindsay Baker* No news stories.

Family Circle

King's Reach Tower, Stamford Street,
London SE1 9LS
☎ 01–261 5000
Telex 915748 Fax 01–261 5929

Owner *IPC Magazines Ltd*
Editor *Jill Churchill*
Circulation 625,290

FOUNDED 1964. 13 ISSUES PER YEAR. Most of the magazine's material is produced in-house, and there is very little scope for freelancers. Unsolicited material is never used, although manuscripts are received every week. Prospective contributors are best advised to send written ideas to the relevant editor.

Beauty *Helen Speed*

Cookery *Sara Lewis*

Fashion *Janine Steggles*

Features *Carrie Taylor* Very little outside work commissioned. Maximum 2500–3000 words.

Fiction *Gill Adams* Serial fiction, maximum 6000 words.

Home *Caroline Rodriguez*

News ('Full Circle') *Vivien Donald*
Payment for all contributions not less than £100 per 1000 words.

Farming News

Morgan Grampian House, 30 Calderwood Street,
London SE18 6QH
☎ 01–855 7777 Fax 01–854 6795

Owner *Morgan Grampian Ltd*
Editor *Marcus Oliver*
Circulation *c.* 90,000

Occasionally use freelance writers.

Farmers Weekly

Carew House, Railway Approach, Wallington,
Surrey SM6 0DX
☎ 01–661 4867

Owner *Reed Business Publising*
Editor *Ted Fellows*
Circulation 102,000

Wide-ranging feature material relating to practising farmers' problems and interests, plus news stories. Farm life, practical or general interest, also specific sections on arable, livestock farming, etc. Unsolicited mss considered
Payment negotiable.

Fast Lane

Prospect House, 9–13 Ewell Road, Cheam,
Surrey SM1 4QQ
☎ 01–661 4384
Telex 892084 REEDBP G Fax 01–643 8203

Owner *Prospect Magazines*
Editor *Peter Dron*
Circulation 55,400

FOUNDED 1984. Monthly car magazine. Many unsolicited mss are received but they are rarely used. Prospective contributors are advised to make initial approach in writing.

The Field

6 Sheet Street, Windsor, Berkshire SL4 1BG
☎ 0753 056061

Owner *Mail Newspapers Ltd*
Editor *J. A. Spencer*
Circulation 34,380

FOUNDED 1853. MONTHLY magazine for those serious about the British countryside and its pleasures. Unsolicited mss welcome; preliminary approach should first be made in writing.

Features Exceptional work on any subject concerning the countryside, but tends to be mainly commissioned.
Payment varies according to material.

Fifty Plus

Millbank Publishing, 25 Catherine Street,
London WC2B 5JW
☎ 01–379 3036 Fax 01–240 6840

Owner *Millbank Publishing*
Editor *Alison Davies*
Circulation 20,000

FOUNDED 1982. BI-MONTHLY. Opportunities in news and features only.

Features Well illustrated (colour and black and white, good quality transparencies) items on second careers, crafts and hobbies. Maximum 1500 words.
Payment negotiable.

News Maximum 1500 words.
Payment negotiable. First approach in writing with s.a.e.

Film Monthly

1 Golden Square, London W1R 3AB
☎ 01–437 0626

Owner *Argus Specialist Publications Ltd*
Editor *Ken Ferguson*

Features on the film, video and TV scene. S.a.e. essential for return of unsolicited material.
Payment by arrangement.

Film Review

Spotlight Publications Ltd, Greater London House, Hampstead Road, London NW1 7QZ
☎ 01–387 6611 Telex 299485 MUSIC G

Owner *Spotlight Publications Ltd*
Editor *David Aldridge*
Circulation 37,000

MONTHLY. Profiles, interviews and special reports on films. Welcome unsolicited material for consideration.

Financial Weekly

14 Greville Street, London EC1N 8SB
☎ 01–405 2622 Fax 01–831 2625

Owner *Staff and other investors*
Editor *Tom Lloyd*
Circulation 15,000

FOUNDED 1979. WEEKLY. There are few opportunities for freelancers here, as most of the stories and features are produced in-house. Unsolicited manuscripts not encouraged.

Features *Edward Russell-Walling* The occasional 'perspective' feature, well written, well researched and accompanied by appropriate artwork might be bought. Maximum 1500 words.

News *John Manley* Exclusive news story, supported by evidence and analysis, might be bought very occasionally, Maximum 800 words.
Payment £100 per 1000 words.

First Choice

Home & Law Publishing, Greater London House, Hampstead Road, London NW1 7QQ
☎ 01–388 3171
Telex 269470 Fax 01–387 9518

Owner *Maxwell Pergamon Publishing Corporation plc*
Editor *Helene Hodge*
Circulation 3.5 million

Published TWICE YEARLY. Recipes, humour, items of women's and family interest. Will consider unsolicited mss if they tie in with planned editorial. First approach by phone preferred.

First Down

Spendlove Centre, Enstone Road, Charlbury, Oxon OX7 3PQ
☎ 0608 811266 Fax 0608 811380

Owner *Mediawatch Ltd*
Editor *Alan Lees*
Circulation 45,000

FOUNDED 1986. Unsolicited mss welcome.

Features *Alan Lees* Ideas for commission are welcome.

News *Neil Rowlands* Tip-offs and news items, maximum 300 words, relating to American football in the UK.
Payment by negotiation.

First Sunday

D. C. Thomson & Co. Ltd, Albert Square, Dundee DD1 9QJ
☎ 0382 23131 ext. 4147

Owner *D. C. Thomson & Co. Ltd*
Editor *Maggie Dun*
Circulation 1,400,000

MONTHLY. Unsolicited contributions welcome but prefer to be approached in writing in first instance.

Features A wide variety of features, from human interest to humour, celebrities/royalties.

Fiction Not established as yet, but do consider short stories on any theme.
Payment varies.

Fitness

Deltamere Ltd, 40 Bowling Green Lane, London EC1R 0NE
☎ 01–278 0333 Telex 267247

Editor *Sharon Gethings*
Circulation 75,000

FOUNDED 1983. MONTHLY. Freelance contributions are welcome, but it is advisable to write with ideas in the first instance.

Flairnews

Flair Enterprises, 5 Lothian Court, Midhurst Road, Eastbourne BA22 9HN

BI-MONTHLY journal 'by writers for writers'. Annual subscription £10. Useful source of contact between writers with information, reports, etc. on the publishing world.

Focus

31 Shottsford, Wessex Gardens,
London W2 5LG
☎ 01–229 9298

Owner *British Science Fiction Association*
Editor *Liz Holliday*
Circulation 1100

FOUNDED 1979. TRIENNIAL. The writers' magazine of the BSFA, containing articles of interest to science fiction writers at all stages of their careers. Unsolicited mss and proposals welcome. Maximum usually 4000 words.
Focus also has a workshop section, in which fiction is published and criticised. Promising authors are welcome to submit but only on the understanding that their mss, if accepted, will be 'workshopped'. *Maximum* usually 2500 words.
No Payment.

Folk Roots

PO Box 337, London N4 1TW
☎ 01–340 9651

Owner *Southern Rag Ltd*
Editor *Ian A. Anderson*
Circulation 12,000

FOUNDED 1979. MONTHLY. Unsolicited mss welcome, but a large number are received and an initial phone call is preferred.

Features Folk and roots music, and musicians. Maximum 3000 words.
Payment c. £30 per 1000 words.

Football Monthly

28 Croydon Road, Reigate, Surrey RH2 0PG
☎ 0737 221158 Fax 0737 223047

Owner *Proud Print Ltd*
Editor *Tony Pullein*
Circulation 30,000

FOUNDED 1951. MONTHLY.

Features 'All contributions are considered. Prefer interviews with current players/managers.' Maximum 1600 words.
Payment from £30 depending upon topicality, etc.
Historical items compiled by team of regular contributors.

Forty Eight Hours

See **dx Magazine**

Garden Answers

Bushfield House, Orton Centre,
Peterborough PE2 0UW
☎ 0733 237111
Telex 32157 Fax 0733 231137

Owner *EMAP*
Editor *Ray Edwards*
Circulation 67,565

FOUNDED 1982. MONTHLY. 'It is unlikely that unsolicited manuscripts will be used, as writers rarely consider the style and format of the magazine before writing.' Prospective contributors should approach the editor in writing.

Garden News

Bushfield House, Orton Centre,
Peterborough PE2 0UW
☎ 0733 237111
Telex 32157 Fax 0733 231137

Owner *EMAP*
Editor *Adam Pasco*
Circulation 123,852

FOUNDED 1958. WEEKLY. Britain's biggest selling gardening publication. News, advice on growing flowers, fruit and vegetables, plus colourful features on all aspects of gardening for the committed grower. Contributions of news and features are welcome, especially if accompanied by photos or illustrations. First contact the editor before submitting any material.

Gay Times inc. Gay News

283 Camden High Street, London NW1 7BX
☎ 01–482 2576

Owner *Millivres Ltd*
Editor *John Marshall*

Publish a wide range of feature articles on all aspects of gay life, and general interest likely to appeal to the gay community. Includes arts reviews and news section. Use regular freelance writers and also consider unsolicited contributions. Also publish fiction.

Features Editor *Peter Burton*
Payment negotiable.

Gibbons Stamp Monthly

Stanley Gibbons, 5 Parkside, Ringwood, Hants BH24 3SH
☎ 0425 472363 Telex 41271 Fax 0425 470247

Owner *Stanley Gibbons Ltd*
Editor *Hugh Jefferies*
Circulation 21,000

FOUNDED 1890. MONTHLY. News and features. Welcome unsolicited mss, particularly feature items of a specialised nature. Approach first in writing or by phone.

Features *Hugh Jefferies* Articles of specialised nature or general stamp features. Maximum 2000–2500 words.
Payment £17–25 per 1000 words.

News *Michael Briggs* Any philatelic news item. Maximum 1000 words.
No payment.

Girl

King's Reach Tower, Stamford Street, London SE1 9LS
☎ 01–261 6311

Owner *IPC Magazines Ltd*
Editor *Lesley Robb*
Circulation 134,244

Teen magazine for girls. Feature fashion and beauty magazine for 10–15 year-olds. One photostory per issue.

Girl About Town

141–3 Drury Lane, London WC2B 5TS
☎ 01–836 4433 Fax 01–836 3156

Owner *Girl About Town Magazine Ltd*
Editor *Louisa Saunders*
Circulation 125,000

FOUNDED 1972. WEEKLY free distribution magazine for women. Some news 'but they'd have to beat us to it'. Some features, but standards are 'exacting' and would not commission from unknown writers. No fiction. Unsolicited mss 'have occasionally proved useful'. Receive 5–10 weekly. Maximum for news 200 words. *Payment £25.* Maximum for features 1600 words. *Payment* £100 per 1000 words.

Giroscope

c/o Girobank plc, Bootle, Merseyside G1R 0AA
☎ 051–966 2798
Telex 628021 Fax 051–523 6078

Editor *Ned Halley*
Circulation 1.5 million

BI-MONTHLY. Girobank's magazine for customers. Carries Girobank financial information and general interest features in each issue. Articles are welcome on housing, personal finance, holidays and leisure, and similar consumer-interest topics.

Gloss

Baltic Chambers, 50 Wellington Street, Glasgow G2 6HJ
☎ 041–248 7799/221 2658

Owner *Loraine Chassels*
Editor *Loraine Chassels*
Circulation 50,000

FOUNDED July 1985. MONTHLY Glasgow/Edinburgh glossy. Unsolicited mss welcome; any approach in writing should include a telephone number.

Features *Carlo Tedescht* Maximum 3000 words.
Payment £15–50.

Golden Age

111–17 Victoria Street, Bristol BS1 6AX
☎ 0272 299521

Owner *Tony Davies*
Editorial Director *Richard Davies*
Editor *David Colvin*
Circulation South West edition: 200,000/ National edition: 300,000

FOUNDED 1982. MONTHLY. Unsolicited mss welcome but first approach by brief letter recommended.

Features Informative features on pre-retirement/retirement issues: financial, property, travel, welfare rights, health care, leisure. Maximum 1250 words.
Payment negotiable.

Fiction 'With a mature perspective'.
Payment negotiable.

News Hard news relevant to the retired or those about to retire. Maximum 500 words.
Payment negotiable.

Golf World

Advance House, 37 Millharbour, Isle of Dogs, London E14 9TX
☎ 01–538 1031 Fax 01–538 4106

Owner *New York Times*
Editor *Robert Green*
Circulation 106,457

FOUNDED 1962. MONTHLY. Unsolicited mss not welcome, but prospective contributors should approach in writing with ideas.

Good Food Retailing

3rd Floor, 58 High Street, Sutton, Surrey SM1 1EZ
☎ 01–853 5444

Owner *Robert Farrand*
Editor *Nicola Graimes*
Circulation 11,700

FOUNDED 1980. MONTHLY. Serves the food retailing industry. Unsolicited mss are welcome.

Good Holiday Magazine

1–2 Dawes Court, 93 High Street, Esher, Surrey KT10 9QD
☎ 0372 69799 Fax 0372 66365

Owner *John Hill*
Editor *John Hill*
Circulation 120,000

FOUNDED 1986. QUARTERLY. Unsolicited mss are welcomed. Articles should be biased towards holiday-makers rather than travellers as this is a holiday magazine and in all cases the price of everything from teas and coffees to major purchases should be included along with the relevant rates of exchange. All articles should be illustrated by either high-quality slides or well-printed colour prints. The magazine concentrates mainly on Europe rather than long-haul destinations and the ordinary (ie mass market) rather than the extraordinary. Any queries regarding work/commissioning must be in writing.
Payment approx. £100 per article.

Good Housekeeping

National Magazine House, 72 Broadwick Street, London W1V 2BP
☎ 01–439 5000 Telex 263879

Owner *National Magazine Co. Ltd*
Editor *Noelle Walsh*
Circulation 353,000

FOUNDED 1922. MONTHLY glossy. Freelance contributors are advised to write in the first instance to the appropriate editor. Unsolicited manuscripts are always read, but are not encouraged.

Features *Gillian Fairchild* Most features are specially commissioned, but original ideas are welcome, and should be sent with a short synopsis, plus relevant cuttings showing previous examples of work published.

Fiction *Gillian Fairchild* Most fiction is received from agents or publishers, though unsolicited manuscripts will be read.

News *Anne Woodham* 'Newslines', four pages of short news stories on subjects from food and travel to film stars and money. Maximum 350 words.
Payment £120 per 1000 words.

Good Ski Guide

1–2 Dawes Court, 93 High Street, Esher, Surrey KT10 9QD
☎ 0372 69799 Telex 8951417

Owner *John Hill*
Editor *John Hill*
Circulation 200,000

FOUNDED 1976. QUARTERLY. Unsolicited mss are welcome from writers with a knowledge of skiing and ski resorts. Up to 2000 manuscripts are solicited through the magazine. Prospective contributors should make first contact in writing as ideas and work need to be seen before any discussion can take place.
Payment 'better than NUJ'.
ASSOCIATE TITLES *A-Z Resorts Guide* and *A-Z Fashion and Equipment Guide.*

Gramophone

177-9 Kenton Road, Harrow HA3 0HA
☎ 01–907 4476

Editor *Christopher Pollard*
Circulation 67,127

Classical music magazine, of which 95% is reviews. At any time they are using around 50 regular freelance writers, who provide classical music reviews, and on occasion, features or interviews. Reviewing is the starting place on the magazine, however. Submit samples of work, whether published or not, to the editor.

Granta

Bill Buford, 44A Hobson Street, Cambridge CB1 1NL
☎ 0223 315290

Editor *Bill Buford*

Magazine of literature and politics published in book form in association with **Penguin.** High-brow, diverse, contemporary, it works in a thematic way. Presently QUARTERLY, but may increase to six times yearly in 1990. Do consider unsolicited mss and fiction, and do a lot of

commissioning. Important to read the magazine first to appreciate its very particular fusion of cultural and political interests. No reviews.
Payment depends on length, but not less than £100 per 1000 words.

The Great Outdoors

Ravenseft House, 302–4 St Vincent Street, Glasgow G2 5NL
☏ 041–221 7000

Owner *Holmes McDougall Ltd*
Editor *Peter Evans*
Circulation 27,000

FOUNDED 1978. MONTHLY. Deals with walking, backpacking and countryside topics. Unsolicited mss are welcome.

Features Well-written and illustrated items on relevant topics. Maximum 2000 words.
Payment £70–80.

News Short topical items or photographs. Maximum 300 words.
Payment £10–20.

Greenscene

Parkdale, Dunham Road, Altrincham, Cheshire WA14 4OG
☏ 061–928 0793

Owner *Vegetarian Society UK Ltd*
Editor *Juliet Gellatley*
Circulation 5000

FIRST ISSUE March 1988. Aimed at 13–18 age group. Welcome non-fiction stories with animal welfare, environmental or vegetarian angle. Particularly interested in animal rights issues. Short stories. Unsolicited contributions welcome.
Payment negotiable (small).

Hairflair

20–26 Brunswick Place, London N1 6DJ
☏ 01–490 1444

Owner *Redwood Publishing*
Editor *Sue Rouse*
Circulation 50,000

FOUNDED 1982. MONTHLY featuring original, interesting hair-related ideas written in a young, lively style to appeal to readership aged 16–24 years. Unsolicited mss not welcome, but ideas in writing are considered.

Features Maximum 1000 words.
Payment £75 per 1000 words.

David Hall's Match Fishing Magazine

60 Hillmorton Road, Rugby, Warwickshire CV22 5AF
☏ 0788 535218

Owner *Chrisreel Ltd*
Editor *David Hall*
Circulation 19,000

FOUNDED 1987. BI-MONTHLY. Dealing with all aspects of match fishing. News and features on pollution, fishing matches, events and general fishing topics. Unsolicited mss welcome. Maximum 2000 words.
Payment £40.

Handgunner

Handgunner Ltd, Seychelles House, Brightlingsea, Essex CO7 0NN
☏ 0206 305204

Owner *J. A. Stevenson*
Editor *J. A. Stevenson*
Circulation 28,000

FOUNDED 1980. BI-MONTHLY. Unsolicited mss are welcome, but material should be incisive and in-depth. Make initial contact by telephone.

Features Firearms in economic, political, industrial, police, military and technical fields. Top-quality material can be used. Length is dictated by subject matter.
Payment about £20 per page.

Harpers & Queen

National Magazine House, 72 Broadwick Street, London W1V 2BP
☏ 01–439 5000

Owner *National Magazine Co. Ltd*
Editor *Nicholas Coleridge*
Circulation 100,000

MONTHLY. Up-market glossy that combines the Sloaney and the streetwise. Receive 1000 unsolicited mss a year and publish 4 or 5 of these. Approach in writing (not phone) with ideas.

Features *Meredith Smith* Ideas only in the first instance.

Fiction *Selina Hastings* Fiction welcome. Maximum 6000 words.

News *Nicholas Coleridge* Snippets welcome if

very original.
Payment negotiable.

Health Now

Seymour House, South Street, Godalming, Surrey GU7 1BZ
☎ 0483 426064
Telex 859511 Fax 0483 426005

Editor *Alice Peet*
Circulation 350,000

FOUNDED 1977. BI-MONTHLY. Unsolicited mss welcome only if related to the specialised interests of the magazine. Prospective contributors are advised to make their first approach in writing.

Here's Health

Victory House, 14 Leicester Place, Leicester Square, London WC2H 7NB
☎ 01–437 9011 Telex 01–494 0497

Owner *Argus Press Ltd*
Editor *Sarah Bounds*
Circulation 44,469

FOUNDED 1956. MONTHLY dealing with health, environment, diet and natural therapies. Prospective contributors should telephone the editor in first instance.

Features Maximum 1500 words.
Payment £100 per 1000 words.

Hi-Fi News and Record Review

Link House, Dingwall Avenue, Croydon, Surrey CR9 2TA
☎ 01–686 2599

Owner *Link House Magazines Ltd*
Editor *Steve Harris*
Circulation 39,000

FOUNDED 1956. MONTHLY. Write in the first instance with suggestions based on knowledge of the magazine's style and subject. All articles must be written from an informed technical or enthusiast viewpoint.
Payment rates are negotiable, according to technical content of the item concerned.

High Life

Greater London House, Hampstead Road, London NW1 7QQ
☎ 01–377 4633 Fax 01–383 7570

Owner *Headway Publications*
Editor *William Davis*
Circulation 275,000

MONTHLY glossy. British Airways in flight magazine. Almost all the content is commissioned, so there are few opportunities for freelancers and unsolicited manuscripts are not welcome. Approach with ideas in writing only.

HIM

283 Camden High Street, London NW1 7BX
☎ 01–482 2576

Owner *Millivres Ltd*
Editor *Bryan Derbyshire*

MONTHLY gay magazine. Formerly known as *National Gay*. Carries listings (entertainment, gay pubs and clubs), pin-ups, news and features.

News Editor *David Smith*

Holiday Which?

2 Marylebone Road, London NW1 4DX
☎ 01–486 5544 Fax 01–935 1606

Owner *Consumers' Association*
Editor *Jonathan Sheppard*
Circulation 170,000

QUARTERLY. All research and writing is by permanent staff or by occasional special commission. No real opportunities for freelancers. Unsolicited mss not considered.

Home and Country

39 Eccleston Street, London SW1W 9NT
☎ 01–730 0307

Owner *National Federation of Women's Institutes*
Editor *Penny Kitchen*
Circulation 104,000

FOUNDED 1919. Official MONTHLY journal of the Federation of Women's Institutes, containing articles on a wide range of subjects of interest to women. Strong environmental country slant. Unsolicited mss welcome.
Payment by arrangement.

Home Farm

Broad Leys Publishing Company, Buriton House, Station Road, Newport, Saffron Walden, Essex CB11 3PL
☎ 0799 40922 Fax 0799 41367

Owner *D. & K. Thear*
Editor *Katie Thear*
Circulation 14,000

FOUNDED 1975. BI-MONTHLY journal of the Small

Farmers' Association. Unsolicited mss welcome, and around 30 are received every week. Articles should be detailed and practical, based on first-hand knowledge about aspects of small farming and country living. 'We do not welcome twee urban nostalgia about the countryside.' 'Poetry Corner' publishes verse which 'reflects some aspect of country living today'.

Home & Freezer Digest

Glenthorne House, Hammersmith Grove,
London W6 0LG
☎ 01–846 9922
Telex 919001 Fax 01–741 7762

Owner *British European Associated Publishers*
Acting Editor *Shirley Shelton*
Circulation 180,000

FOUNDED 1974. MONTHLY for freezer owners. Unsolicited mss welcome, but most features are commissioned.

Homebrew Today

Victory House, Leicester Place,
London WC2H 7NB
☎ 01–437 9011 Fax 01–434 0656

Owner *Argus Health Publications*
Editor *Evelyn Barrett*
Circulation 250,000

FOUNDED 1986. QUARTERLY features articles on all aspects of home brewing and the use of homemade wine in cooking, etc. Unsolicited mss welcome.

Homes and Gardens

King's Reach Tower, Stamford Street,
London SE1 9LS
☎ 01–261 5678 Telex 915748 MAGDIV G

Owner *IPC Magazines Ltd/Reed Publishing*
Editor *Amanda Evans*
Circulation 230,000

FOUNDED 1919. MONTHLY. Almost all published articles are specially commissioned. No fiction or poetry. Best to approach in writing with an idea.

Homes Overseas

387 City Road, London EC1V 1NA
☎ 01–278 9232 Fax 01–833 2892

Owner *Cresta Holdings plc*
Editor *Gail Filer*
Editorial consultant *Michael Furnell*
Circulation 17,000

FOUNDED 1965. MONTHLY of interest to those buying or owning property abroad, particularly those areas popular for tourism: south of Spain, Algarve, France, Italy, Cyprus, Malta.

Features Maximum 1000 words.
Payment by arrangement.

News Up-to-date information on new housing developments for holidays or retirement. Maximum 750 words.
Payment £30 or by arrangement.

Horse and Hound

King's Reach Tower, Stamford Street,
London SE1 9LS
☎ 01–261 6315 Telex 915748 MAGDIV G

Owner *IPC Magazines Ltd*
Editor *Michael Clayton*
Circulation 72,000

WEEKLY. The oldest equestrian magazine on the market. Now re-launched with modern make-up, and sharper news and feature sections. Contains regular veterinary advice and instructional articles, as well as authoritative news and comment on fox hunting, international showjumping, horse trials, dressage, driving and cross-country riding. Also weekly racing and point-to-points, breeding reports and articles. The magazine nowadays includes a weekly junior and young rider section. Regular books and art reviews, and humorous articles and cartoons are frequently published. Plenty of opportunities for freelancers. Welcome unsolicited contributions.
Payment NUJ rates.

Horse & Pony

Bretton Court, Bretton, Peterborough PE3 8DZ
☎ 0733 264666 Fax 0733 265515

Owner *EMAP*
Editor *Sarah Haw*
Circulation 50,130

Magazine for young (12–16) owners and addicts of the horse. Features include horse-care articles, pony club news, celebrities in the horse world. Not really interested in freelancers; most feature material is produced in-house by staff writers.

Horse and Rider

104 Ash Road, Sutton, Surrey SM3 9LD
☎ 01–641 4911

Owner *D. J. Murphy (Pubishers) Ltd*

Editor *Janet Evans*
Circulation 30,000

FOUNDED 1949. MONTHLY. Unsolicited mss welcome, and should be addressed to the editor. Adult readership, largely horse-owning. Fiction especially welcome. General interest features welcome. News and instructional features, which make up the bulk of the magazine, are almost all commissioned. Approach in writing with ideas.

House Beautiful

National Magazine House, 72 Broadwick Street, London W1V 2BP
☎ 01–439 5000

Owner *National Magazines Ltd*
Editor *Pat Roberts*

A revival of a Sixties magazine which promises 'all you want from where you live'. Launched March 1989 and directed at the home-making woman rather than the DIY male. 100 pages of easy reading features and facts. Regular features about mortgages and house prices, horoscopes, etc. Contact the editor.

House Buyer

137 George Lane, South Woodford, London E18 1AJ
☎ 01–530 7555

Owner *Brittain Publications*
Editor *Con Crowley*
Circulation 18,000

MONTHLY magazine with features and articles for house buyers, including features on retirement homes, and mortgage information. No unsolicited mss.

House & Garden

Vogue House, Hanover Square, London W1R 0AD
☎ 01–499 9080
Telex 27338 VOLON G Fax 01–493 1345

Owner *Condé Nast Publications Ltd*
Editor *Robert Harling*
Circulation 140,000

Much of the feature material is produced in-house, but the magazine does commission a small number of features from freelancers, particularly in the wine and food sections. Ideas and mss will be considered, especially from photographers.
Payment rates vary according to subject, length, rights, etc., particularly in the food section where recipes are involved.

Ice Hockey World and Skating Review

9 Victoria Road, Mundesley-on-Sea, Norfolk NR11 8JG
☎ 0263 720038

Editor *Phil Drackett*
Circulation 5000

FOUNDED 1935. MONTHLY during the season. Submissions welcome if preceded by letter/phone. All mss to be addressed to the editor.

Features always welcome. Maximum 1000 words.
Payment maximum £25.

Fiction rarely, but interested in occasional good short story, Maximum 1000 words.
Payment by negotiation.

News from local stringers, but occasional vacancies.

I D Magazine

27–9 Macklin Street, London WC2E 5LX
☎ 01–430 0871

Owner *Levelprint*
Editor *John Godfrey*
Circulation *c.* 50,000

Fashion and style magazine for both sexes aged 16–24. Very hip. 'We have opportunities for freelance writers but can't offer fees for non-commissioned work.' Tend to use known writers. A different theme each issue – past themes included the green politics issue, taste, and film – means it is advisable to discuss feature ideas in the first instance.

Ideal Home

King's Reach Tower, Stamford Street, London SE1 9LS
☎ 01–261 6505

Owner *IPC Magazines Ltd*
Editor *Terence Whelan*
Circulation 268,809

FOUNDED 1920. MONTHLY glossy. Unsolicited feature articles are welcome when appropriate to the magazine (one or two are received each week). Prospective contributors wishing to submit ideas should do so in writing to the editor. Home interest features: length of article and *payment* negotiable. Features should be on furnishings and decoration of houses, kitchens or bathrooms; interior design soft furnishings; furniture; home improvements, etc. No fiction.

News Editor *Linda Gray* Suggestions/press releases etc.
Payment negotiable.

The Illustrated London News

91–3 Southwark Street, London SE1 0HX
☏ 01–928 2111 Fax 01–620 1594

Owner *James Sherwood*
Editor-in-Chief *James Bishop*
Circulation 55,034

FOUNDED 1842. Now only SIX ISSUES YEARLY. There are few opportunities for freelancers but all unsolicited manuscripts are read – on average, ten a week. The best approach is with an idea in writing.

In Britain

Thames Tower, Black's Road, London W6 9EL
☏ 01–846 9000 Telex 21231 BTAADM G

Owner *BTA*
Editor *Bryn Frank*
Circulation 100,000

Magazine of the British Tourist Authority, about things to do and places to visit. Unsolicited mss not encouraged.

The Independent Magazine

40 City Road, London EC1Y 2DB
☏ 01–956 1760 Fax 01–962 0016

Owner *Newspaper Publishing*
Editor *Alexander Chancellor*
Circulation 450,000

FOUNDED 1986. WEEKLY colour supplement to *The Independent.* Most articles are commissioned but unsolicited mss do get read. Prefer initial approach in writing. Similar opportunities to those of other newspaper magazines.

News/Features/Fiction *Lucy Tuck, Justine Picardie* Length and payment varies according to contract.

Picture Stores *Colin Jacobson*

Inform

The Newbourne Group, Home & Law Publishing, Greater London House, Hampstead Road, London NW1 7QQ
☏ 01–388 3171
Telex 269470 Fax 01–387 9518

Owner *Robert Maxwell*
Editor *Debbi Scholes*
Circulation 300,000

BI-ANNUAL magazine with articles on health education and general interest items for teenagers. 'Occasionally' welcome unsolicited mss. First approach by phone.

Infusion

16 Trinity Churchyard, Guildford, Surrey GU1 3RR
☏ 0483 577533

Owner *Bond Clarkson Russell*
Editor *Fiona Macpherson*
Circulation 800,000

FOUNDED 1986. THREE ISSUES YEARLY dealing with women's general interest, health, leisure and all subjects related to tea. All editorial features are commissioned. Approach with ideas only.

InterCity

Redwood Publishing, 20–26 Brunswick Place, London N1 6DJ
☏ 01–490 1444
Telex 265871 Ref 81: RED001 Fax 01–490 0494

Owner *Redwood Publishing,* sponsored by British Rail
Editor *Peter Crookston*
Circulation 250,000

FOUNDED 1985. 10 ISSUES PER YEAR. Complimentary business magazine distributed to passengers on InterCity rail routes. Receive two unsolicited mss weekly, but prefer to be approached by phone with idea initially, followed up by a letter with cuttings if the writer's work is unknown to the editor.

Deputy Editor *Beth Richards*

Interior Design

Audit House, Field End Road, Eastcote, Ruislip, Middlesex HA4 9LT
☏ 01–868 4499

Owner *AGB Business Publications Ltd*
Editor *Carl Gardner*
Circulation 10,000

The business magazine of the commercial interior design industry (no domestic interior design interest). Freelance opportunities are limited, as much of the material is produced in-house or by commission, but informed contributions, case studies etc. are always considered. (Also do *Lighting Design* supplement, for which

informed contributions are also welcome.)
Payment £120 per 1000 words.

Interzone

124 Osborne Road, Brighton,
East Sussex BN1 6LU
☏ 0273 504710

Owner *David Pringle*
Editors *David Pringle, Simon Ounsley*
Circulation 10,000

FOUNDED 1982. BI-MONTHLY magazine of science fiction and fantasy fiction. Unsolicited mss are welcome from writers who have a knowledge of the magazine and its contents.

Fiction Science fiction and fantasy stories. Preferred length 2000-6000 words.
Payment £30 per 1000 words.

Features Science fiction and fantasy book reviews, film reviews, interviews with writers and occasional short articles. Length and *payment* by arrangement.

Investors Chronicle

Greystoke Place, Fetter Lane, London EC4A 1ND
☏ 01–405 6969
Telex 883694 IC LDN G Fax 01–405 5276

Owner *Financial Times*
Associate Editor *David Webster*
Circulation 60,000

FOUNDED 1861. WEEKLY. Opportunities for freelance contributors in the survey section only. All approaches should be made in writing. Over thirty surveys are published each year on a wide variety of subjects mainly with a financial, business or investment emphasis. Copies of survey list and synopses of individual surveys are obtainable from the Associate Editor. Maximum 1000 words.
Payment from £100.

Irish Post

Lex House, South Road, Southall,
Middlesex UB1 1SQ
☏ 01–574 2058/3916

Owner *Irish Post Ltd*
Editor *Donal Mooney*
Circulation 78,000

FOUNDED 1970. WEEKLY. News and features relating to the Irish community in Britain. Welcome unsolicited mss. First approach by telephone.

ISMS

26 Hurford Street, Maes y Coed, Pontypridd,
mid Glamorgan, South Wales CF37 1EW
☏ 0443 485292

Owner *Fiifi Annobil*
Editor *Fiifi Annobil*
Circulation 10,000

FOUNDED 1988. MONTHLY. International magazine for the general interest reader with a penchant for intelligent reading. Features extensive reading in the arts: poetry, short stories, fine art, books, jazz, classical music, films, theatre, photography, dance, etc; also societies, memoirs, philosophy, psychology, the environment, medicine and business. Modernistic approach. Avant garde and surreal welcome. Has a general soft spot for illustrated articles. Unsolicited mss and ideas welcome. Best approach by phone first.

Features Maximum 2500 words.
Payment £40.

Fiction Lots of room. Contact the editor.

News relies on freelance material completely.

Jackie

D. C. Thomson, Albert Square, Dundee DD1 9QJ
☏ 0382 23131 Fax 0382 22214

Owner *D. C. Thomson & Co. Ltd*
Editor *Gayle Anderson*
Circulation 250,000

FOUNDED 1964. WEEKLY. Scope for freelance contributors; write in the first instance to the relevant editor.

Features *Tracey Butler* Emotional/fun features dealing with boys, school, friends, parents and growing up. Maximum 1500 words.

Fiction *Ria Legatt* Romantic/humorous text stories and serials. Also photostories. Maximum 1500 words.
Payment for all contributions £45 minimum.

Jazz Journal International

113–17 Farringdon Road, London EC1R 3BT
☏ 01–278 0631

Owner *Jazz Journal Ltd*
Editor-in-Chief *Eddie Cook*
Circulation 11,500

FOUNDED 1948. MONTHLY. A specialised jazz magazine using only expert contributors whose work is known to the editor. Unsolicited mss not welcome, with the exception of news material (for which *no payment* is made).

Jewish Chronicle

25 Furnival Street, London EC4A 1JT
☎ 01–405 9252 Fax 01–405 9040

Owner *Kessler Foundation*
Editor *Geoffrey D. Paul*
Circulation 50,000

Unsolicited mss welcome if 'the specific interests of our readership are borne in mind by writers'. Approach in writing unless it's urgent current news. No fiction. In all cases, maximum 2000 words.
Payment negotiable. This also applies to the *Jewish Chronicle Colour Magazine.*

News Editor (home) *Hyam Corney;* (foreign) *J. Finklestone*

Colour Magazine/Supplements *Gerald Jacobs*

Features Editor *Meir Persoff*

Women's Page *Jan Shure*

Jewish Quarterly

PO Box 1148, London NW5 2AZ
☎ 01–485 4062

Owner *Jewish Literary Trust Ltd*
Editor *Colin Shindler*

FOUNDED 1953. QUARTERLY. Features Jewish literature, politics, music, film, poetry, history, dance, community, autobiography, Hebrew, Yiddish, Israel/Middle East. Unsolicited mss welcome. Prefer letter or phone call in first instance.

The Journalist

NUJ, Acorn House, 314–20 Gray's Inn Road, London WC1X 8DP
☎ 01–278 7916 Telex 892384

Owner *National Union of Journalists*
Editor *Tim Gopsill*
Circulation 35,000

MONTHLY journal of the NUJ. Pieces of interest to journalists or relevant to the industry welcome, though most material is produced in-house and outside contributions are not usually paid for.

Just Seventeen

52–5 Carnaby Street, London W1V 1PF
☎ 01–437 8050

Owner *EMAP Metro*
Editor *Bev Hillier*
Circulation 300,000

FOUNDED 1983. WEEKLY. Top of the mid-teen market. News, articles and fiction of interest to girls aged from about 12–18. Ideas are sought in all areas. Prospective contributors should send ideas to the relevant editorial department, then follow up with phone call.

Beauty *Liz Silvester*

Features *Jeanette Baker*

Fiction *Jacqui Deevoy* No more than 2000 words.

News Editor *Jane Goldman*
Payment £90 per 1000 words.

Kennel Gazette

Kennel Club, 1–5 Clarges Street, Piccadilly, London W1Y 8AB
☎ 01–493 6651

Owner *Kennel Club*
Editor *Charles Colborn*
Circulation 15,000

FOUNDED 1873. MONTHLY concerning dogs and their breeding, Unsolicited mss welcome.

Features Maximum 2500 words.

Fiction Maximum 1500 words.

News Maximum 500 words.
Payment £40 per 1000 words.

Keyboard Player

18 Tileyard Road, off York Way, London N7 9AN
☎ 01–609 5781/2 Fax 01–609 5928

Owner *Mr S. Miller & Mr I. Seymour*
Editor *Steve Miller*
Circulation 14,000

FOUNDED 1979. Unsolicited mss welcome. Prospective contributors should make initial contact in writing to the Editor who is particularly interested in hearing from writers with a technical/playing knowledge of any keyboard instrument.

Knit and Stitch

PO Box 553, Iver, Bucks SL0 0PD
☏ 0753 656395 Fax 0753 656844

Owner *Ingrid Publishing Ltd*
Editor *Sheila Berriff*
Circulation 30,000

FOUNDED 1985. BI-MONTHLY. Mostly patterns, with occasional features. Unsolicited mss not welcome; approach in writing only.

Labour Party News

150 Walworth Road, London SE17 1JT
☏ 01–703 0833

Owner *Labour Party*
Editor *Nigel Williamson*
Circulation 210,000

FOUNDED 1987. BI-MONTHLY. Welcome unsolicited material (with s.a.e.).

Features Contemporary politics.

News Short items, maximum 200-250 words.

Reviews Books and films of a directly political interest only.

The Lady

39–40 Bedford Street, Strand,
London WC2E 9ER
☏ 01–379 4717

Owner *T. G. A. Bowles*
Editor *Joan L. Grahame*
Circulation 63,847

FOUNDED 1885. WEEKLY. Unsolicited manuscripts are welcome; they get about 5000 every year. Nothing is accepted on politics, religion or medicine, or on topics covered by staff writers, i.e. fashion and beauty, household, gardening, finance and shopping.

Features Pieces on British and foreign travel are particularly welcome, and on all other topics except those already mentioned. Maximum 1500 words. All material to the editor.
Payment £42 per 1000 words.
All photographs to support articles should be taken and printed in black and white. *Payment* £12–15 per photo used.

Leisure Management Magazine

40 Bancroft, Hitchin, Hertfordshire SG5 1LA
☏ 0462 31385 Fax 0462 33909

Owner *Dicestar Ltd*
Editor *Liz Terry*
Circulation 17,000

FOUNDED 1981. MONTHLY. Available on subscription. Looking at leisure as a business. Read by policy makers, managers, investors, architects, and all those concerned with the development of leisure, recreation, tourism, entertainment, sports, hotel, heritage and countryside matters. Welcomes unsolicited manuscripts, cartoons, news and ideas.

Lincolnshire Life

Plot No. 40, Burghley Park Close, Poplar Park,
North Hykeham, Lincoln LN6 9UD
☏ 0522 500832

Owner *A. L. Robinson*
Editor *David N. Robinson*
Circulation 8000

FOUNDED 1961. MONTHLY. Features 'geographically relevant' articles on local history, tradition, nature and architecture. 'The magazine is based on unsolicited contributions' and they receive a great deal. First approach in writing with s.a.e.

The Listener

199 Old Marylebone Road, London NW1 5QS
☏ 01–258 3581

Owner *BBC* and *ITV*
Editor *Alan Coren*
Circulation 30,000

WEEKLY. The magazine of broadcasting. International in scope, stylishly literate in approach and presentation, committed not only to all aspects of television and radio, but also to broad coverage of politics, business, design, technology, books, music, sport, arts and entertainment. *The Listener* is happy to discuss and commission work from the best freelance writers and cartoonists. Suggestions and outlines must be submitted in writing only.
Payment by negotiation.

Literary Review

51 Beak Street, London W1R 3LF
☏ 01–437 9392 Fax 01–439 6489

Owner *Namara Group*
Editor *Auberon Waugh*
Circulation 15,000

FOUNDED 1979. MONTHLY. Publishes book reviews (commissioned), features and articles on literary subjects, plus short fiction. Prospective contributors are best advised to contact the editor in writing. Unsolicited manuscripts not

welcome (over 500 a month are currently received).
Payment book reviews: £25 for 800 words; literary features: £25–50 for maximum 1000 words; short stories: £50 for up to 2000 words.

Living Magazine

King's Reach Tower, Stamford Street,
London SE1 9LS
☎ 01–261 5000

Owner *IPC Magazines Ltd*
Editor *Olwen Rice*
Circulation 333,620

Women's and family interest glossy magazine sold at supermarket check-outs and newsagents. Most features are commissioned from outside freelance writers, but **Deputy Editor** *Barbara Baker* is keen to encourage new talent and will look at unsolicited mss. Also welcome preliminary letters with outline ideas in the first instance. Wide-ranging feature needs include family, education, medical issues, 'successful women in small business'-type one-offs, and major issues (divorce, drugs, etc.).
Payment by arrangement.

London Magazine

30 Thurloe Place, London SW7 2HQ
☎ 01–589 0618

Owner *Alan Ross*
Editor *Alan Ross*
Circulation *c.* 4500

FOUNDED 1954. BI-MONTHLY. Art, memoirs, travel, poetry, criticism, theatre, music, cinema, book reviews, photographs. According to *The Times,* ' *London Magazine* is far and away the most readable and level-headed, not to mention best value for money, of the literary magazines.' Receives 150–200 unsolicted mss weekly. Prefers to be approached in writing.

Fiction Maximum 5000 words. Unsolicited mss welcome; s.a.e. essential.
Payment £100 maximum.

London Review of Books

Tavistock House South, Tavistock Square,
London WC1H 9JZ
☎ 01–388 6751

Owner *LRB Ltd*
Editor *Karl Miller, Mary-Kay Wilmers*
Circulation 20,000

FOUNDED 1980. FORTNIGHTLY. Fiction, news, poems and short stories, plus reviews, essays and articles on political, literary, cultural and scientific subjects. Unsolicited contributions welcome (approximately 35 received each week) and it is best to contact the editor in writing. There is one editorial department covering all aspects of the magazine.
Payment £50 per 1000 words for prose; £30 per poem.

Look-in

195 Knightsbridge, London SW7 1RS
☎ 01–589 8877 Telex 27813

Owner *ITV Publications Ltd*
Editor *Colin Shelbourn*
Circulation 204,000

FOUNDED 1971. WEEKLY children's TV magazine featuring ITV programmes and personalities. Unsolicited mss not generally welcome; prospective contributors are advised to make initial approach in writing.

Features TV, pop, sport, general interest, quizzes, etc. – all aimed at children aged 7–12.
Payment by negotiation.

Looking Good

Newspaper House, Derngate,
Northampton NN1 1NN
☎ 0604 24711 Fax 0604 31285

Owner *Thomson Regional Newspapers*
Editor *Bryan Jones*
Circulation 22,000

FOUNDED 1984. MONTHLY fashion, beauty and health magazine. Open to ideas in writing. Contact the editor.

LOOKS

42 Great Portland Street, London W1N 5AH
☎ 01–436 5430
Telex 32157 Fax 01–631 0781

Owner *EMAP*
Editor *Moray Prunty*
Circulation 200,000

MONTHLY magazine for young women aged 15–20, which concentrates on fashion, beauty and hair matters, as well as general interest features, including celebrity news and interviews, fiction, quizzes, etc. Freelance writers are occasionally used in all areas of the magazine. Contact the

editor with ideas.
Payment varies.

Loving

King's Reach Tower, Stamford Street,
London SE1 9LS
☏ 01–261 6376

Owner *IPC Magazines Ltd*
Editor *Lorna Read*
Circulation 70,000

MONTHLY. Any good story with a romantic slant considered. Also historical romance. The 'Something Different' section allows authors to experiment with the genre; even crime or science fiction stories might fit the bill. Acceptable story lengths 1000-5000 words. Would-be authors are advised to read the magazine thoroughly and send s.a.e. for guidelines.

Machine Knitting Monthly

3 Bridge Avenue, Maidenhead,
Berkshire SL6 1RR
☏ 0628 770289

Owner *Anne Smith*
Editor *Anne Smith*
Circulation 55,000

FOUNDED 1986. MONTHLY. Will consider unsolicited mss as long as they are applicable to this specialist publication. 'We have our own regular contributors each month but I'm always willing to look at new ideas from other writers.' First approach in writing.

The Magazine

Fredrica House, 12 Oval Road,
London NW1 7DH
☏ 01–482 2821 Fax 01–485 2758

Owner *Reed International*
Editor *Lisa Freedman*
Circulation 61,703

FOUNDED 1982. MONTHLY. Welcome unsolicited contributions and ideas by phone.

Features General – high glamour, with witty topical London items. Maximum 2000 words.
Payment £200-300.

Fiction Occasional short stories. Maximum 3000 words.
Payment £150.

Interiors – specific topics dealt with monthly.

Magazine Week

Mitre House, 44 Fleet Street (entrance in Mitre Court), London EC4Y 1BS
☏ 01–583 3030

Owner *Bouverie Publishing Co.*
Editor *Tony Loynes*
Circulation 12,000

FOUNDED March 1988. WEEKLY magazine of features and news for everyone who works in the magazine industry.

Features Maximum 1200 words.

News Maximum 400 words. No unsolicited mss. Query phone call in the first instance; generally only use material written by professional journalists.
Payment NUJ rates.

Management Today

22 Lancaster Gate, London W2 3LJ
☏ 01–402 4200

Owner *Management Publications Ltd*
Editor *Lance Knobel*
Circulation 103,000

General business topics and features. A brief synopsis to the editor.
Payment negotiable.

Marketing Week

St Giles House, 50 Poland Street,
London W1V 4AX
☏ 01–439 4222

Owner *Centaur Communications*
Editor *Stuart Smith*
Circulation 41,276

Trade magazine of the marketing industry. Features on all aspects of the business written in a newsy and up-to-the-minute style from expert commentators always welcome. Ideas first to **Features Editor** *Martin Croft.*
Payment negotiable.

Match

Stirling House, Bretton Court, Bretton,
Peterborough PE3 8DJ
☏ 0733 260333 Fax 0733 265515

Owner *EMAP*
Editor *Melvyn Bagnall*
Circulation 107,841

FOUNDED 1979. WEEKLY football magazine aimed at 10–17 year olds. Consult the news editor before making any submission. Contact may be made either by telephone or in writing. Most material is generated in-house by a strong news and features team.

Features/News *Paul Stratton* Good and original material is always welcome. Maximum 600 words. Quality Scottish material will also be considered.
Payment negotiable.

Maternity and Mothercraft

Greater London House, Hampstead Road,
London NW1 7QQ
☎ 01–388 3171

Owner *The Newbourne Group*
Editor *Catherine Fleischmann*
Circulation 100,000

FOUNDED 1965. BI-MONTHLY. Unsolicited mss are not welcome, but any prospective contributor should make initial contact by telephone.

Features There is a features list and there are occasional opportunities for writers with relevent experience. (Being a mother of young children is an added advantage.) Maximum 600–700 words.

Matrix

114 Guildhall Street, Folkestone, Kent CT20 1ES
☎ 0303 52939 (evenings)

Owner *British Science Fiction Association*
Editor *Maureen Porter*
Circulation 1000

FOUNDED 1965. BI-MONTHLY newsletter of the BSFA giving all science fiction-oriented news, gossip, pre-publication details of new SF books, details of SF societies, magazines, media, etc. Initial approach in writing preferred. No fiction. No literary criticism or author interviews.
No Payment.

The Mayfair Times

47 Upper Grosvenor Street, London W1X 9PG
☎ 01–629 3378
Telex 296472 Fundin G Fax 01–629 9303

Owner *Wetherell Publications*
Editor *Peter I. Wright*
Circulation 20,000

FOUNDED 1985. MONTHLY. Features on Mayfair of interest to both residential and commercial readers. Welcome unsolicited mss.

Melody Maker

26th Floor, King's Reach Tower, Stamford Street,
London SE1 9LS
☎ 01–261 5670

Owner *IPC Magazines Ltd*
Editor *Allan Jones*
Circulation 69,313

Freelance contributors are used on this tabloid magazine competitor to *NME* and *Sounds*. Opportunities exist in reviewing and features.

Features Editor *Ted Mico* A large in-house team plus around six regulars produce the feature material. Send in sample reviews, whether published or not, on pop, rock, soul, funk, etc. to **Reviews Editor** *Everett True*.
Payment NUJ rates in all cases.

Mensa Magazine

British Mensa Ltd, Mensa House, St John's
Square, Wolverhampton WV2 4AH
☎ 0902 772771/2/3

Owner *British Mensa Ltd*
Editor *Simon Clark*
Circulation 23,500

MONTHLY. Unsolicited mss welcome. Priority is given to members of the Society, but contributions from non-members are also considered.
No Payment.

Features *Simon Clark* Any general interest topic (e.g. science, travel, education, astrology, etc.) maximum 2500 words. Pieces should be entertaining, informative and concise. Other short articles (500–1200 words) which offer the writer's own opinions on controversial issues are welcome.

Mind Your Own Business

106 Church Road, London SE19 2UB
☎ 01–771 3614 Fax 01–771 4592

Owner *B. Gledhill, M. Brown*
Editor *Bill Gledhill*
Circulation 61,000

FOUNDED 1978. MONTHLY. Unsolicited material with management appeal is welcomed. About 12 articles are received each week, of which one or two may be of interest.

Features *Bill Gledhill* Should appeal to management.

Fiction *Sarah Pritchard* Light-hearted, humorous articles with a moral to the story and management-oriented.

Payment £80–120 per 1000 words approx. Minimum NUJ rates, final fee assessed on quality of finished material.

Mizz

27th Floor, King's Reach Tower, Stamford Street, London SE1 9LS
☎ 01–261 6319

Owner *IPC Magazines Ltd*
Editor *Simon Geller*
Circulation 190,000

FORTNIGHTLY magazine for the 15–19 year-old girl: 'a useful rule of thumb is to write for a 16 year-old'. A wide range of freelance articles welcome, from emotional issues to careers to beauty features. Also fiction – short stories published every issue. Send samples with a letter, or an idea with synopsis in the case of features; the finished mss in the case of fiction, to Simon Geller.

Model Journal

8 Balham Hill, London SW12 9DS
☎ 01–675 4039 Fax 01–675 3542

Editor/Publisher *Marcel C. Mueller*
Circulation 42,000

FOUNDED 1988. MONTHLY. Trade newspaper for models, model agents, photographers, make-up artists, stylists, designers, etc. Covers all aspects of fashion & photographic modelling. Interested in model-related themes. Prospective contributors should approach by phone in first instance.
Payment negotiable.

Modern Machine Knitting

PO Box 175, Kingston upon Thames, Surrey KT2 6HA
☎ 01–546 2444 Fax 01–549 8399

Owner *Modern Knitting Ltd*
Editor *Loraine McCarthy*
Circulation 35,000

FOUNDED 1951. MONTHLY. Anything related to machine knitting and related items. Unsolicited material welcome as is initial approach in writing.

Features Fill 3 pages of magazine including illustrations, diagrams, etc.
Payment £25 per page.

Money & Family Wealth

Stonehart Leisure Magazines, 67–71 Goswell Road, London EC1V 7EN
☎ 01–250 1881 Fax 01–251 5665

Owner *Stonehart Magazines*
Editor *Andrew Etchells*
Circulation 64,244

FOUNDED 1987. MONTHLY. Welcome unsolicited mss, with s.a.e. First approach in writing.
Payment from £100 per 1000 words.

Money Week

Meed House, 21 John Street, London WC1N 2BP
☎ 01–404 5513 Fax 01–405 6639

Owner *EMAP*
Editor *Nick Morgan*
Circulation 31,000

Enthusiastic about freelance writers. As *Money Week* is aimed at the financial services industry, so writers tend to be specialised, or experienced financial journalists. Major part of the magazine is given to features of around 800 words on all aspects of the industry.

News Editor *Sara McConnell*
Payment £150 per 1000 words.

Moneycare

Greater London House, Hampstead Road, London NW1 7QQ
☎ 01–377 4633
Telex 922488 Bureau G Fax 01–383 7486

Owner *Headway Publications*
Editor *Michael Imeson*
Circulation 900,000

The National Westminster Bank Magazine. FOUNDED 1983. QUARTERLY on money management. Most articles are commissioned so unsolicited mss are rarely used.

More!

42 Great Portland Street, London W1N 5AH
☎ 01–436 5430

Owner *EMAP Metro*
Circulation 214,692

First edition April 1988. FORTNIGHTLY women's magazine aimed at the working woman aged 18–30. News and features plus a lot of 'how-to' articles. Fairly short, snappy style. Maximum 1700 words. Will consider unsolicited items but highly recommend that the magazine should be studied for style of writing.

Features Editor *Gillian Carter*
Payment £150 per 1000 words.

The Mortgage Magazine

12 Sutton Row, London W1V 5FH
☏ 01–734 5716

Owner *Brass Tacks Publishing*
Editor *Stephen Quirke*
Circulation 20,000

FOUNDED 1986. MONTHLY magazine covering finance and property. Unsolicited mss welcome. Make initial approach by telephone to discuss idea, and follow up in writing.

Features Ideas concerning finance and building are always welcome. More peripheral subjects such as interior design, legal matters and housing politics will also be considered.
Payment £100 per 1000 words.

Mother

12–18 Paul Street, London EC2A 4JS
☏ 01–247 8233
Telex 8951167 Fax 01–377 9709

Owner *Argus Consumer Publications Ltd*
Editor *Sarah Touquet*
Circulation 73,029

FOUNDED 1936. MONTHLY. New contributors are welcome, but should study the specific style of the magazine in advance. The best approach is in writing with an idea.

Features Bright, lively features on being a mother and on aspects of babies and children. No fiction. Maximum 1500 words.
Payment varies.

News Very little opportunity for freelancers, as the magazine's lead time is 3 months in advance. Maximum 200 words.
Payment varies.

Mother and Baby

12–18 Paul Street, London EC2A 4JS
☏ 01–247 8233
Telex 8951167 Fax 01–377 9709

Owner *Argus Press Ltd*
Editor-in-Chief *Else Powell*
Circulation 121,000

FOUNDED 1956. MONTHLY. No unsolicited mss, except personal 'birth stories' and 'View-point' pieces. Approaches may be made by telephone or in writing.

Motor Boat & Yachting

Quadrant House, The Quadrant, Sutton, Surrey SM2 5AS
☏ 01–661 3298
Telex 892084 REED BP G Fax 01–643 2144

Owner *Reed Business Publishing*
Editor *Tom Willis*
Circulation 37,000

FOUNDED 1904. MONTHLY for those interested in motor cruising.

Features *Tom Willis* Cruising features and practical features especially welcome. Illustrations (mostly colour) as important as the text. Maximum 3000 words.
Payment £75 per 1000 words or by arrangement.

News *Alan Harper* Factual pieces and opinion. Maximum 200 words.
Payment up to £30 per item.

Motor Caravan World

2A Granville Road, Sidcup, Kent
☏ 01–302 6150

Owner *Stone Industrial Publications Ltd*
Editor *Bob Griffiths*

FOUNDED 1975. MONTHLY. Welcome unsolicited mss. Prefer not to receive preliminary enquiries by phone or letter. Features travel sites, etc. for motor caravans and any news relating to motor caravaning: sites, new sites, rallies, interviews, pictures. Also dealer profiles. Length varies according to subject.
Payment **News** £5–£25; **Features** £20–35.

Motor Cycle News

PO Box 11, Huxloe Place, High Street, Kettering NN16 8SS
☏ 0536 81651

Owner *EMAP*
Editor *Malcolm Gough*
Circulation 123,819

Use freelancers, but mostly an established network of contributors. As a WEEKLY, the magazine is news-oriented: particularly keen on motor cycle sport, especially road racing. Feature material is mostly produced in-house. Ideas to deputy editor *Peter Bolt*.

Motorway Express

Newspaper House, 22 Vineyard Road, Wellington, Shropshire TF1 1DJ
☎ 0952 251100

Owner *Promotional Newspapers Ltd*
Editor *Ron Newell Evans*
Circulation 250,000

MONTHLY magazine which welcomes unsolicited manuscripts. Prospective contributors may make initial contact either in writing or by telephone.

Mountain Bike UK

Woodstock House, Luton Road, Faversham, Kent ME13 8HQ
☎ 0795 538903

Owner *Pacificon Ltd*
Editor *Tyn Manley*
Circulation 30,000

FOUNDED May 1988. Unsolicited mss are welcomed if informative articles on mountain biking. Maximum 2500 words. Prospective contributors are advised to make initial approach in writing.
Payment negotiable.

Moxaic

26 Hurford Street, Maes y Coed, Pontypridd, Mid Glamorgan, South Wales CF37 1EW
☎ 0443 485292

Owner *Skillvision Ltd*
Editor *Fiifi Annobil*
Circulation 25,000

FOUNDED 1987. QUARTERLY. Audience: the art world – students, practitioners, collectors, etc. Large format quarterly with the aim of establishing an up-to-date artistic representation of all nations. Prospective contributors should contact the editor. Exhibits works, too, by modern artists; send good slides or prints with detailed resumé, self portraits, and s.a.e.

Ms London

7–9 Rathbone Street, London W1V 1AF
☎ 01–636 6651 Fax 01–872 0806

Owner *Employment Publications*
Editor *Trudy Culross*
Circulation 128,331

FOUNDED 1968. WEEKLY Unsolicited mss welcome but prefer approach in writing with an idea.

Features *Trudy Culross* Ideas welcome; always interested to hear from new writers. Maximum 1500 words.
Payment £100 per 1000 words.

News done in-house but follow-up feature ideas welcome.

Music and Musicians International

8 Primrose Mews, 1A Sharpleshall Street, London NW1 8YL
☎ 01–586 8591 Fax 01–586 1549

Owner *Orpheus Publications*
Editor *Christopher James*
Circulation 7000

FOUNDED 1952. MONTHLY dealing with areas related to the classical music world. Welcome unsolicited mss and ideas in writing.

News Current events in classical music world: developments in relevant technology, appointments, important sponsorship schemes, etc. Maximum 500 words.
Payment £30 per 1000 words.

Features Articles welcome on any classical music related area. Maximum 2000 words.
Payment £30 per 1000 words.

Reviews Concert, record, book reviews. Maximum 500 words.
Payment £30 per 1000 words.

The Musical Times

8 Lower James Street, London W1R 4DN
☎ 01–734 8080 Fax 01–586 8591

Owner *Filmtrax plc*
Editor *Eric Wen*

Serious-minded journal with a scholarly approach to its subject.
Payment negotiable.

My Guy

King's Reach Tower, Stamford Street, London SE1 9LS
☎ 01–261 5000

Owner *IPC Magazines Ltd*
Editor *Lesley Robb*

FOUNDED 1977, WEEKLY teen magazine for girls. No longer 'require freelance contributions'.

My Story

PO Box 94, London W4 2ER
☎ 01–995 0590

Owner *Atlantic Publishing Co.*

Editor *Geoff Kemp*
Circulation 38,000

FOUNDED 1956. MONTHLY. Downbeat romantic story magazine. Fiction only, provided it is in keeping with the usual style publishing. Best to study previous issues before sending anything in. *My Story* receives around 250 mss a week.
Payment £14 per 1000 words.

My Weekly

80 East Kingsway, Dundee DD4 8SL
☏ 0382 44276

Owner *D. C. Thomson & Co. Ltd*
Editor *S. Monks*
Circulation 696,279

A traditional women's WEEKLY which, like others in the D. C. Thomson stable, is currently trying to attract a younger readership, and compete for the young working woman's attention in the marketplace (while not alienating its traditional, loyal readership). Particularly interested in humour and human interest pieces which by their very nature appeal to all age groups: 1000–1500 words; and fiction. Three stories a week range from the emotional to the off beat and unexpected: 2000–4000 words. Also serials. D.C. Thomson has long had a philosophy of consultation and help for writers of promise.
Payment negotiable.

Nature

4 Little Essex Street, London WC2R 3LF
☏ 01–836 6633 Fax 01–370 4204

Owner *Macmillan Magazines Ltd*
Editor *John Maddox*
Circulation 42,500

Covers all fields of science. Very little use for freelance writers or unsolicited mss; approaches specialists when appropriate. No features. Articles and news on science policy only.

Netball

Francis House, Francis Street,
London SW1P 1DE
☏ 01–828 2176

Owner *All England Netball Association Ltd*
Editor *Sylvia Eastley*
Circulation 5000

FOUNDED 1940. QUARTERLY. No freelance or unsolicited mss are accepted.

Network

VNU House, 32–4 Broadwick Street,
London W1A 2HG
☏ 01–439 4242 Fax 01–437 8985

Owner *VNU Business Publications*
Editor *Susan Ablett*
Circulation 22,000

MONTHLY. Unsolicited mss never used. Best approach by writing with written synopses.

Features *Susan Ablett* Case studies of user sites, or pieces on the business/technical issues raised by distributed data processing. Maximum 4000 words.
Payment £110 per 1000 words.

New Democrat

9 Poland Street, London W1V 3DG
☏ 01–434 1059

Owner *Letterhurst Ltd*
Editor *Harry Cowie*
Circulation 8000

FOUNDED 1982, published FIVE TIMES YEARLY. Unsolicited mss welcome. Submissions should be in writing.

Features Profiles, or features on policies and events of interest to Social and Liberal Democrat supporters. Maximum 1500 words.
No *Payment*.

New Home Economics

Forbes Publications Ltd, 120 Bayswater Road,
Queensway, London W2 3JH
☏ 01–229 9322

Owner *Forbes Publications Ltd*
Editor *Dilys Wells*
Circulation 4763

TEN ISSUES YEARLY. Contributors should bear in mind that all readers are fully qualified home economists or students of the subject.

Features Article of up to 1200 words welcome on the topics listed below.

News Items welcomed on food and nutrition, textile studies, childcare and development, health education, money topics and consumer education. Maximum 500 words.
Payment by negotiation.

New Humanist

88 Islington High Street, London N1 8EW
☎ 01–226 7251

Owner *Rationalist Press Association*
Editor *Jim Herrick*
Circulation 3000

FOUNDED 1885. QUARTERLY. Unsolicited mss welcome.

Features Articles with a humanist perspective are welcome in the following fields: religion (critical), humanism, human rights, philosophy, current events, literature, history and science. Usual length 2000–4000 words.
Payment negotiable, but 'minimal'. No fiction.

Book reviews by arrangement with the editor. Usually 750–1000 words.

New Internationalist

42 Hythe Bridge Street, Oxford OX1 2EP
☎ 0865 728181

Owner *New Internationalist Publications Ltd*
Co-editors *Vanessa Baird, Chris Brazier, Pater Stalker*
Circulation 65,000 worldwide

Concerned with world poverty and global issues of peace and politics, with emphasis on the Third World: radical, and broadly leftist in approach, though unaligned. Difficult to use unsolicited material, as they work to a theme each month, and the editor commissions features on that basis. The way in is to send examples of published or unpublished work; writers of interest are taken up.

New Left Review

6 Meard Street, London W1V 3HR
☎ 01–734 8839

Editor *Robin Blackburn*
Circulation 35,000

Magazine of theoretical politics, history and related issues, plus (to a lesser degree) a Marxist reading of the arts and humanities. Material generally provided by academics and expert commentators in the field rather than journalists.
No Payment.

New Musical Express

King's Reach Tower, Stamford Street, London SE1 9LS
☎ 01–261 5000

Owner *IPC Magazines Ltd*
Editor *Alan Lewis*
Circulation 99,000

Britain's best selling musical. WEEKLY. The *NME* does use freelancers, but always for reviews in the first instance. Specialisation in areas of music (or film, which is also covered) is a help.

Review editors: Books *Sean O'Hagan* **Film** *Gavin Mead* **LPs** *Alan Jackson* **Live** *Helen Mead.* Send in examples of work, whether published or specially written samples.

New Socialist

150 Walworth Road, London SE17 1JT
☎ 01–703 0833

Owner *Labour Party*
Editor *Nigel Williamson*
Circulation 16,000

FOUNDED 1981. BI-MONTHLY. Unsolicited mss (with s.a.e.) welcome.

Features Articles on socialist themes. Maximum 2000–3000 words.

News 'Frontline' section – short news items. 500 words.

Reviews *Nigel Williamson* Short reviews of film, theatre, music, television, books, etc. 500 words.

New Statesman and Society

Foundation House, Perseverance Works, 38 Kingsland Road, London E2 8BA
☎ 01–739 3211 Fax 01–739 9307

Owner *Statesman and Nation Publishing Co.*
Editor *Stuart Weir*
Circulation 39,700

WEEKLY magazine of the political left which is the result of a merger in May 1988 of *New Statesman* and *New Society.* Unsolicited contributions welcome. New contributors are best advised to contact the **Deputy Editor** *Philip Dodd.*

Literary Editor *Tony Gould*

Arts & Media Editor *Sally Townsend*

Political Editor *Sarah Benton*

New Woman

King's House, 8–10 Haymarket, London SW1Y
☎ 01–839 8272 Fax 01–925 0721

Owner *Murdoch Magazines (UK) Ltd*
Editor *Frankie McGowan*

MONTHLY. Unsolicited contributions welcome but prefer initial approach in writing.

News *Guy Pierce*

Features *Hilary Smith*

Fiction *Suzanne Askhorn*

Beauty *Liz Earle*

Fashion *Jillie Murphy.*

19 (incorporating Honey)

King's Reach Tower, Stamford Street, London SE1 9LS
☎ 01–261 6360

Owner *IPC Magazine Ltd*
Editor *Maureen Rice*
Circulation 165,000

MONTHLY magazine aimed at the 17–20 year old girl. A little different to the usual teen magazine mix: *19* are now aiming for a 50/50 balance between the fashion/lifestyle aspects and meatier, newsier material on *Young Guardian* lines, e.g. articles on women in prison, and life in East Berlin. Also 'Speak for Yourself', a platform page for ordinary readers rather than professional journalists to speak out on any subject. 40% of the magazine's feature material is commissioned, ordinarily from established freelancers. 'But we're always keen to see original bold vigorous writing from people just starting out ...' Letter with ideas first to the **Deputy Editor** *Ursula Kenny.*

Northamptonshire Life

Chapel House, Chapel Lane, St Ives, Huntingdon, Cambridgeshire PE17 4DX
☎ 0480 62844

Owner *A. L. Robinson*
Editor *Arnold Hadwin*
Circulation 9500

FOUNDED 1972 as *Northamptonshire & Bedfordshire Life,* now two magazines, one for each county. MONTHLY magazine featuring articles which are 'geographically relevant'. Maximum 100–1500 words, plus three or four good quality photographs. Welcome unsolicited mss. First approach in writing.
Payment varies.

Nostalgia

29 Enford Street, London W1H 1DG
☎ 01–706 4256 Fax 01–706 3798

Owner *Nostalgic Enterprises Ltd*
Editor *Sue Malins*
Circulation *c.* 52,000

FOUNDED 1988. BI-MONTHLY. Welcome unsolicited mss; prefer approach with ideas in writing in first instance. **Features** 2000 words.
Payment negotiable.

Number One

28th Floor, King's Reach Tower, Stamford Street, London SE1 9LU
☎ 01–261 5000 Fax 01–261 6034

Owner *IPC Magazines Ltd*
Editor *Colin Irwin*
Circulation 149,000

FOUNDED 1982. WEEKLY. Reviews films, videos, stories and gossip about television. Interviews with leading pop/TV, film personalities.

Features *David Martin* Interviews and 'concept' feature ideas. Must be written in light, humorous style.
Payment negotiable.

Film/TV Pages *Kate Davies* Reviews
Payment negotiable.

Nursing Times

4 Little Essex Street, London WC2R 3LF
☎ 01–379 0970

Owner *Macmillan Magazines Ltd*
Editor *Linda Davidson*

A large proportion of *Nursing Times* feature content is from unsolicited contributions sent on spec., although they also commission articles. Pieces on all aspects of nursing and health care, both practical and theoretical, written in a lively and contemporary way, are welcome.
Payment varies; NUJ rates of £108 per 1000 words for commissioned work.

Observer Magazine

Chelsea Bridge House, Queenstown Road, London SW8 4NN
☎ 01–627 0700 Fax 01–627 5572

Editor *Angela Palmer*

Contact *Victoria Summerley, Sue Matthias*

First colour supplement to be bound with a spine. Freelance writers used extensively, but an experienced and competitive pool of writers; only very strong ideas and demonstrable talent will succeed here.

Office Secretary

Streatfield House, Carterton, Oxford OX8 3XZ
☎ 0993 845484 Fax 0993 845882

Owner *Trade Media Ltd*
Editor *Penny Commerford*
Circulation 150,000

FOUNDED 1986. QUARTERLY. Features articles of interest to female office staff aged 25–50. Unsolicited mss welcome.

Features Chatty but informative pieces on current affairs, health, office-related topics. Maximum 2500 words.
Payment £100 per 1000 words or by negotiation.

On Board Windsurfing Magazine

Andrew House, 2A Granville Road,
Sidcup, Kent DA14 4BN
☎ 01–302 6069

Owner *Stone Industrial Publications Ltd*

FOUNDED 1970. MONTHLY. Official magazine for the UK Boardsailing Association and the Scottish and Irish Associations. On line for mid 1989 was the launch of *Surf Magazine* devoted to surfing only. Freelance opportunities foreseen along the same lines as for *On Board.* Same rates applicable.

Features and **News** Short items about local and regional teams, etc. Maximum 1500–2000 words.
Payment £35 with picture(s).

Opera

1A Mountgrove Road, London N5 2LU
☎ 01–359 1037 Fax 01–354 2700

Owner *Opera Magazine Ltd*
Editor *Rodney Milnes*
Circulation 14,000

FOUNDED 1950. MONTHLY review of the current opera scene. Almost all articles are commissioned and unsolicited mss are not welcome. All approaches should be made in writing.

Opera Now

9-13 Grape Street, London WC2H 8DR
☎ 01–836 7131 Fax 01–836 9982

Owner *Condé Nast Publications*
Editor *Mel Cooper*
Circulation 40,000

LAUNCHED 1989 with a massive pre-launch campaign and exhaustive market research. Initial print run four times larger than that of its 40-year-old rival *Opera.* Aims to take the fear out of talking and seeing opera. Unsolicited mss welcome; prefer approach in writing.

Profiles Maximum 2500 words.

Reviews of CDs, videos, recorded material. Maximum 500 words. No reviews of performances.

Options

King's Reach Tower, Stamford Street,
London SE1 9LS
☎ 01–261 5000

Owner *IPC Magazines Ltd*
Editor *Jo Foley*
Circulation 226,380

Options aims to entertain the modern renaissance woman, worker, mother and wife; more for the woman who has arrived than the *Cosmopolitan* emotional and sexual issues market. Almost all written by freelancers, these tend to be a regular bunch, but new writers are encouraged, and 'commissioned non-commissioned pieces' are requested from new feature writers of promise. The full page 'Talking Point' column is a platform for even the most amateur writer with something to say.

Paperback Inferno

1 The Flaxyard, Woodfall Lane, Little Neston,
South Wirral L64 4BT
☎ 051–336 3355

Owner *British Science Fiction Association*
Editor *Andy Sawyer*
Circulation 1000

FOUNDED 1977. BI-MONTHLY. Publishes reviews of Science Fiction paperbacks and professional SF magazines. Unsolicited material not welcome as all reviews are commissioned.

Parents

Victory House, Leicester Place, London WC2H 7NB
☎ 01–437 9011 Fax 01–434 0656

Owner *Argus Press Ltd*
Editor *Daphne Metland*
Circulation 95,129

FOUNDED 1976. MONTHLY. Very little opportunity for freelancers. Tend to do most writing in-house.

Penthouse

Northern & Shell Building, PO Box 381, Millharbour, London E14 9TW
☎ 01–987 5090 Telex 24676 NORSHL G

Owner *Richard Desmond*
Editor *Linzi Drew*

Managing Editor *Isabel Koprowski*
Circulation *c.*100,000

FOUNDED 1965. 13 ISSUES YEARLY.

Features *Isabel Koprowski* Maximum 3500 words.
Payment negotiable 'but generally pretty good'. Unsolicited mss welcome, 'but most of those we do receive are unsuitable because the authors haven't looked at the magazine'. First approach by phone or in writing with ideas.

News *Sandy Robertson* Limited opportunities for unsolicited material. Must have a fairly long-term appeal.

People Magazine

See National Newspapers Section

People's Friend

80 Kingsway East, Dundee DD4 8SL
☎ 0382 44276

Owner *D. C. Thomson & Co. Ltd*
Editor *Douglas Neilson*
Circulation 566,000

Traditional WEEKLY magazine which caters for a family audience. Mostly fiction; short stories should be suitable for family reading: 'the normal problems of the normal family next door'. Any length from 1000–3000 words. Not much of a market for non-fiction, but short filler articles of 500–2000 words are welcome.
Payment negotiable.

Performance Tuning

538 Ipswich Road, Slough SL1 4EQ
☎ 0753 820161 Fax 0753 22691

Owner *C. W. Editorial Ltd*
Editor *Ian Ward*
Circulation 35,000

Formerly entitled *Sports Car Monthly*. Relaunched as *Performance Tuning* January 1988. Features on tuned or modified cars, both sports and saloon. Maximum 2500 words. No unsolicited mss. First approach in writing.
Payment negotiable.

Personnel Management

1 Hills Place, London W1R 1AG
☎ 01–734 1773 Telex 51714 PRINTN G

Owner *Personnel Publications Ltd*
Editor *Susanne Lawrence*
Circulation 42,000

FOUNDED 1969. MONTHLY specialist magazine for personnel managers. Unsolicited mss welcome, from specialists in the personnel and training fields only.

Features *Susanne Lawrence* Only interested in material written by specialists in their field. Occasional scope for articles by those with experience or knowledge of employment, industrial relations, training, pay areas. Maximum 3000 words.
Payment NUJ rates.

News *David Turner* Sometimes interested in reports of events where staff member was not present. Length varies.
Payment NUJ rates.

Photography

1 Golden Square, London W1R 3AB
☎ 01–437 0626 Fax 01–437 1006

Owner *ASP*
Editor *Tom Ang*
Circulation 26,000

FOUNDED 1986. MONTHLY. Unsolicited contributions welcome. Initial phone call preferred.

News Anything with relevance to photography, including gossip, media, market, foreign.
Payment negotiable.

Features Not necessarily photographic in content. World-class photography plus strong story

– political, topical, travel, historical, 'green', etc.
Payment c. £100 per 1000 words.

Pins and Needles

4 Brandon Road, London N7
☏ 01–609 2177 Fax 01–700 4985

Owner *Quarto Int.*
Editor *Susan Peverill*

FOUNDED 1949. A craft magazine specialising in knitting and sewing. Unsolicited contributions welcome but prefer initial approach in writing. 'Most of our freelancers actually make, knit or sew the items featured – ideas along these lines always welcome.'
Payment £80 per 1000 plus extra for making costs, subject to negotiation.

Plays and Players

248 High Street, Croydon, Surrey CR0 1NF
☏ 01–681 7817

Owner *Plus Publications*
Editor *Natasha Curry*
Circulation 8000

Theatre MONTHLY, which publishes a mixture of reviews, features on aspects of the theatre, festival reports, etc. Rarely use unsolicited material, but writers of talent are taken up. Almost all material is commissioned.
Payment under review, but small.

Plays International

Greenwood Court, Harlescott,
Shrewsbury SY1 3TB

Owner *Plays International Ltd*
Editor *Peter Roberts*

Freelance writers are used, but are a well-established team of regulars, and unsolicited material cannot be considered. The magazine is a mixture of interviews, reviews and a complete play text every month. One-off pieces are only rarely commissioned.

Poetry Review

21 Earls Court Square, London SW5 9DE
☏ 01–373 7861

Owner *The Poetry Society*
Editor *Peter Forbes*
Circulation 4000

FOUNDED 1909. QUARTERLY poetry magazine. Approximately 5000 unsolicited mss received each year (mostly poetry) and these are welcome, but the odds should be taken into account by prospective contributors. Almost all prose is commissioned. A preliminary letter is advisable before submitting reviews or features.

Pony

104 Ash Road, Sutton, Surrey SM3 9LD
☏ 01–641 4911

Owner *Marion O'Sullivan*
Editor *Kate Austin*
Circulation 36,000

FOUNDED 1948. Lively MONTHLY aimed at 10–18 year olds. News, instruction on riding, stable management, veterinary care, interviews. Features welcomed. Not more than 1500 words.
Payment £50 per 1000 words.
News written in-house. Welcome photographs and illustrations (serious/cartoon). Regular short story of not more than 1800 words.
Payment £50 per 1000 words. Prefer to be approached in writing first.

Powerboating International

The Poplars, New Road, Armitage,
Staffordshire WS15 4BJ
☏ 0543 491818
Telex 335622 Fax 0543 490515

Owner *Pat Ainge*
Editor *Pat Ainge*
Circulation 8000

FOUNDED 1983. MONTHLY. This is a specialised powerboat racing magazine whose policy is to welcome outside contributions, especially from overseas. Length and *payment* negotiable. At present only one or two unsolicited contributions are received a month.

Practical Boat Owner

c/o IPC Magazines, Westover House, West Quay Road, Poole, Dorset
☏ 0202 680593

Owner *IPC Magazines Ltd*
Editor *George Taylor*
Circulation 68,547

MONTHLY. For the beginner and the experienced owner. Reports on coastal cruising, pleasure sailing, and marine information. Colour supplement, *Cruising,* in June, August and October.

Practical Computing

Reed Business Publishing Ltd, Quadrant House, The Quadrant, Sutton, Surrey SM2 5AS
☎ 01–661 3633
Telex 892084/REEDBP G Fax 01–661 8943

Owner *Reed Business Publishing*
Editor *Ian Stobie*
Circulation 33,515

FOUNDED 1977. MONTHLY. '... interested in personal computers and the way they are used in large company environments, not at home.' Prospective contributors should ring the editor in the first instance. Prefer not to receive unsolicited mss.
Payment negotiable.

Practical Gardening

Bushfield House, Orton Centre, Peterborough, Cambs PE2 0UW
☎ 0733 237111
Telex 32157 Fax 0733 231137

Owner *EMAP*
Editor *Mike Wyatt*
Circulation 92,519

FOUNDED 1960. MONTHLY. Unsolicited mss welcome, but there are few acceptances out of 150 offered each year. Submit ideas in writing.

Features Occasionally features/photos on gardens (not famous gardens or stately homes) are required provided they are in keeping with the magazine's style. Maximum 1200 words.
Payment from £70 per 1000 words.

Practical Health

King's Reach Tower, Stamford Street, London SE1 9LS
☎ 01–261 5000

Owner *IPC Magazines Ltd*
Editor *Michele Simmons*
Circulation *c.*200,000

QUARTERLY. No unsolicited mss. Query letter in the first instance with samples of style.

Practical Householder

Greater London House, Hampstead Road, London NW1 7QQ
☎ 01–388 3171 Fax 01–387 9518

Owner *Home & Law Magazines Ltd*
Editor *David Bridle*
Circulation 50,000

FOUNDED 1955. MONTHLY. Features on DIY/home improvement subjects. Do not really welcome unsolicited mss. prefer initial approach in writing to the editor.

Practical Motorist

Unit 8, Forest Close, Ebblake Industrial Estate, Verwood, Wimborne, Dorset BH21 6DQ
☎ 0202 823581

Owner *Practical Motorist Ltd* (A member of the Mayfair Publishing Group)
Editor *Denis Rea*
Circulation 40,000

FOUNDED 1934. MONTHLY. Welcome unsolicited mss. All approaches should be made to the editor. Maximum 1500 words.
Payment 'on merit'. 'Ours is a very specialised field and not many can hope to match our established contributors.'

Practical Photography

Bushfield House, Orton Centre, Peterborough, Cambs PE2 0UW
☎ 0733 237111
Telex 32157 Fax 0733 231137

Owner *EMAP*
Editor *Richard Hopkins*
Circulation 105,408

MONTHLY. Unsolicited mss welcome if relevant to the magazine and its readers. Preliminary approach may be made by telephone. Always interested in new ideas.

Features Anything relevant to the readership, but not 'the sort of feature produced by staff writers'. Bear in mind that there is a three-month lead time. Maximum 2000 words.
Payment varies.

News Only 'hot' news applicable to a monthly magazine. Maximum 800 words.
Payment varies.

Prediction

Link House, Dingwall Avenue, Croydon CR9 2TA
☎ 01–686 2599
Telex 947709 LINKHO G Fax 01–760 0973

Owner *Link House Magazines Ltd*
Editor *Jo Logan*
Circulation 35,000

FOUNDED 1936. MONTHLY. The magazine covers astrology and topics with an occult slant and unsolicited material in these areas is welcome. Receive 200–300 mss every year.

Astrology Pieces ranging from 800–2000 words should be practical as well of general interest. Charts and astro data should accompany them, especially if profiles.
Payment £25–75.

Features *Jo Logan* Articles on mysteries of the earth, alternative medicine, psychical/occult experiences and phenomena are considered. Maximum 2000 words.

News *Jon Taylor* News items of interest to readership welcome. Maximum 300 words.
No Payment.

Prima

Portland House, Stag Place, London SW1E 5AU
☏ 01–245 8700

Owner *G & J*
Editor *Sue James*
Circulation 1,000,000

FOUNDED 1986. MONTHLY. Top selling women's magazine. A German import.

Features *Sharon Maxwell Magnus* Features are mostly practical and written by specialists or commissioned from known freelancers. Unsolicited mss not welcome.

Private Eye

6 Carlisle Street, London W1V 5RG
☏ 01–437 4017

Owner *Pressdram*
Editor *Ian Hislop*
Circulation 210,000

FOUNDED 1961. FORTNIGHTLY satirical and investigative magazine. Prospective contributors are best advised to approach the editor in writing. News stories and feature ideas are always welcome, as are cartoons. All jokes written in-house.
Payment in all cases is 'not great', and length of piece varies as appropriate.

Property Mail

The Press Centre, 57 Riverside Estate, Sir Thomas Longley Road, Frindsbury, Rochester, Kent ME2 4DP
☏ 0634 290774

Owner *Property Mail Ltd*
Editor *Fred Nixon*
Circulation 607,000

FOUNDED 1983. WEEKLY. Plans are afoot to expand from eight editions to twelve by the end of 1989. Unsolicited manuscripts are welcome, but prospective contributors are welcome to make a preliminary approach by telephone.

Psychic News

20 Earlham Street, London WC2H 9LW
☏ 01–240 3032/3/4 Fax 01–379 0620

Owner *Psychic Press Ltd*
Editor *Tony Ortzen*

FOUNDED 1932. *Psychic News* is the world's only WEEKLY spiritualist newspaper. It covers such subjects as psychic research, hauntings, ghosts, poltergeists, spiritual healing, survival after death and paranormal gifts. Never use unsolicited mss (although receive enormous amounts).

Punch

Ludgate House, 245 Blackfriars Road, London SE1 9UX
☏ 01–583 9199 Telex LDN 265863

Owner *United Newspapers*
Editor *David Taylor*
Circulation 65,000

FOUNDED 1841. WEEKLY humorous magazine. New image is taking it a long way from dentists' waiting rooms. Unsolicited contributions 'are encouraged', but prospective contributors should note that *Punch* receives 50–60 unsolicited manuscripts per week. Only finished pieces are accepted and these should be around 1200 words, typed and accompanied by an s.a.e.

Q

42 Great Portland Street, London W1N 5AH
☏ 01–436 5430

Owner *EMAP Metro*
Editor *Mark Ellen*
Circulation 98,000

FOUNDED 1986. MONTHLY. Glossy aimed at educated rock music enthusiasts in their thirties. Few opportunities for freelance writers, and unsolicited mss are strongly discouraged. Prospective contributors should approach in writing only.

RA

Friends of the Royal Academy, Royal Academy of Arts, Burlington House, Piccadilly, London W1V 0DS
☏ 01–734 9052/439 7438 Fax 01–434 0837

Owner *Friends of the Royal Academy*

Editor *Nick Tite*
Circulation 55,000

FOUNDED 1983. QUARTERLY magazine with a controlled circulation. Articles relating to or about the Royal Academy, its members and exhibitions. Unsolicited mss considered but no unsolicited material has yet been published. Important to make initial contact in writing. Features should be no longer than 1500 words.
Payment £100.

The Racing Pigeon

19 Doughty Street, London WC1N 2PT
☎ 01-242 0565 Fax 01–831 0056

Owner *The R. P. Publishing Co. Ltd*
Editor *Colin Osman*
Circulation 33,000

FOUNDED 1898. WEEKLY news magazine for racing pigeon enthusiasts. Only specialist writers considered. Maximum 1000 words. Unsolicited mss welcome.

Radio Times

33 Marylebone High Street, London W1M 4AA
☎ 01–580 5577

Owner *BBC Enterprises*
Editor *Nicholas Brett*
Circulation 3,224,038

WEEKLY. Best selling house magazine. Christmas issue tops 11 million. Detailed BBC television and radio listings in this magazine are accompanied by interviews and feature material relevant to the week's output. 95% of this is provided by freelance writers, but, obviously, the topicality of the pieces needed means close consultation with editors. Unlikely to use the unsolicited material they receive, but do take up writers of interest to work on future projects.

Features Editor *Veronica Hitchcock*

The Railway Magazine

Prospect House, 9–13 Ewell Road, Cheam, Surrey SM1 4QQ
☎ 01–661 4480/1/2 Telex 892084

Owner *Reed Business Publishing*
Editor *Peter Kelly*
Circulation 38,000

FOUNDED 1897. MONTHLY. Welcome unsolicited mss for features. Maximum 2000 words.
Payment negotiable.

The Rambler

1–5 Wandsworth Road, London SW8 2XX
☎ 01–582 6878

Owner *Ramblers' Association*
Editor *Linda Hart*
Circulation 65,000

BI-MONTHLY. Unsolicited material welcome.

Features Freelance features are invited on walking in Britain and abroad, the natural world and conservation. Articles should be 1500–2000 words long.
Payment around £75 per 1000 words.

The Reader's Digest

25 Berkeley Square, London W1X 6AB
☎ 01–629 8144

Owner *Reader's Digest Association Ltd*
Editor *Russell Twisk*
Circulation 1.6 million

In theory, a good market for general interest features of around 2500 words. However, 'a tiny proportion' comes from freelance writers, all of which are specially commissioned. Recently has decided to toughen its image with a move into investigative journalism. The Reader's Digest is to sell 10% of its non-voting stock to the public, part of a move to meet tax law changes which require the foundations that own the company to reduce their stake to 50% by the year 2000. Opportunities exist for short humorous contributions to regular features – 'Life's Like That', 'Humour in Uniform'. Fee £150.

Record Collector

43 St Mary's Road, Ealing, London W5 5RQ
☎ 01–579 1082

Owner *Johnny Dean*
Editor *Peter Doggett*

FOUNDED 1979. MONTHLY. Features detailed, well-researched articles on any aspect of record collecting or any collectable artist in the field of popular music (1950s–1980s) with complete discographies where appropriate. Unsolicited mss welcome. Prefer initial phone call in the first instance.
Payment by negotiation.

Record Mirror (RM)

United Magazines, 245 Blackfriars Road,
London SE1 9UX
☎ 01–928 8000

Owner *United Magazines plc*
Editor *Betty Page*
Circulation 52,000

FOUNDED 1954. WEEKLY. Unsolicited manuscripts are not welcome except as examples of a writer's work not intended for publication. Prospective contributors are advised to make initial contact by telephone.

Features *Eleanor Levy* Opportunities for young, new writers with specific feature ideas.

News *Robin Smith* News tips used occasionally.

Review Pages (Lives) *Tim Nicholson* Opportunities for young writers nationwide wanting to review young new bands.
Payment NUJ rates.

Resident Abroad

108 Clerkenwell Road, London EC1M 5SA
☎ 01–251 9321
Telex 23700 FINBI G Fax 01–251 4686

Owner *Financial Times*
Editor *William Essex*
Circulation 17,919

FOUNDED 1979 MONTHLY magazine aimed at British expatriates. Unsolicited mss welcome.

Features of up to 2000 words on finance, employment opportunities and other topics likely to appeal to readership, such as living conditions in 'likely countries'.

Fiction rarely published, but exceptional, relevant stories (no longer than 2000 words) might be considered.
Payment on acceptance £100 per 1000 words.

The RIBA Journal

39 Moreland Street, London EC1V 8BB

Owner *RIBA Magazines Ltd*
Editor *Richard Wilcock*
Circulation 27,500

MONTHLY journal of Royal Institute of British Architects. Now incorporating RIBA Interiors.

Features Specialist articles on architecture/interiors and matters of practice. Maximum 1200 words.
Payment £100 per 1000 words.

Riding

Corner House, Foston, Grantham NG16 2JU
☎ 0400 82032

Owner *Scott Publications Ltd*
Editor *Helen Scott*
Circulation *c.*34,000

Most of the writers on *Riding* are freelancers. It's aimed at a mostly adult, horse-owning audience: the 'serious leisure rider'. Feature opportunities are limited, as regular columnists take up much of the magazine. However, new and authoritative writers always welcome.
Payment negotiable.

Rugby World and Post

Weir Bank, Bray-on-Thames,
Maidenhead SL6 2ED
☎ 0628 770011
Telex 847591 Fax 0628 39519

Owner *Rugby Publishing*
Editor *Nigel Starmer-Smith*
Circulation 30,000

MONTHLY. Features of special rugby interest. Unsolicited contributions welcome but prior approach by phone or in writing preferred.

Running Magazine

67–71 Goswell Road, London EC1V 7EN
☎ 01–250 1881

Owner *Stonehart Magazines Ltd*
Editor *David Calderwood*
Circulation 54,461

Freelancers are used, but are mostly a team of regular contributors. Specialist knowledge is needed to have advice features accepted – 'we would never publish a 'how-to' feature from someone without expert knowledge'. However, they do accept and publish personal accounts from readers – personal experience running stories are welcome.

RYA News

Royal Yachting Association, RYA House,
Romsey Road, Eastleigh, Hampshire SO5 4YA
☎ 0703 629962
Telex 47393 BOATIN G Fax 0703 629924

Owner *Royal Yachting Association*
Editor *Carol Baker*
Circulation 65,000

FOUNDED 1975. QUARTERLY. Unsolicited mss welcome if they concern general cruising matters with a RYA slant. Prospective contributors are advised to make their first approach in writing.

Features Maximum 1500 words.
Payment negotiable but small.

Saga Magazine

The Saga Building, Bouverie Square, Folkestone, Kent CT20 5SL
☎ 0303 47523
Telex 966331 Fax 0303 48622

Owner *Saga Publishing Ltd*
Editor *Paul Bach*
Circulation 650,000

FOUNDED 1984 from *Saga News*. TEN ISSUES PER YEAR. '*Saga Magazine* sets out to celebrate the role of older people in society. It reflects their achievements, promotes their skills, protects their interests, campaigns on their behalf. A warm personal approach, addressing the readership in an upbeat and positive manner.' It has a hard core of celebrated commentators/writers (e.g. Brian Redhead) as regular contributors but there is scope for well-written features. Subjects include achievement, hobbies, finance, food, wine, social comment, motoring, fitness, diet, etc. Maximum 1600 words (preferred length 1000–1200).
Payment 'Very competitive'.

Sailplane and Gliding

281 Queen Edith's Way, Cambridge CB1 4NH
☎ 0223 247725

Owner *British Gliding Association*
Editor *Gillian Bryce-Smith*
Circulation 8000

FOUNDED 1930. BI-MONTHLY for gliding enthusiasts. A specialised magazine with very few opportunities for freelancers.
Payment No fees for contributions.

Sales Direction

2 St John's Place, London EC1M 4DE
☎ 01–253 2427 Fax 01–608 0865

Owner *Sales Direction Magazine Ltd*
Editor *Nick de Cent*
Circulation 25,000

FOUNDED 1986. MONTHLY. Unsolicited mss are welcome as long as they are relevant to sales management/business readership. It is strongly advised that initial contact (either by telephone or in writing) is made with an idea before full submission is made.

Features Lifestyle features up to 1000 words and interesting sports pursuits relevant to business people.

Interviews with top sales directors and business people in the public eye. Prior discussion essential. Between 1500 and 2000 words.

News No longer than 300 words.
Payment £100 per 1000 words.

Sales and Marketing Management

ISE Publications Ltd, Georgian House, 31 Upper George Street, Luton, Bedfordshire LU1 2RD
☎ 0582 456767 Fax 0582 453640

Owner *David Waller*
Editor *Mark Towers*
Circulation 19,843

ELEVEN ISSUES YEARLY. A great many unsolicited mss are received. These are welcome if on topics relevant to sales and marketing management. Prospective contributors are advised to make initial contact in writing and to present other published work where possible.

Features up to 2000 words dealing with sales techniques, training, technology, modern management practice, etc, are welcome. No fiction.
Payment negotiable.

Sanity

22–4 Underwood Street, London N1 7JG
☎ 01–250 4010

Owner *CND Publications Ltd*
Editor *Ben Webb*
Circulation 40,000

FOUNDED 1961. MONTHLY CND magazine. Unsolicited mss are welcomed. About 100 mss come in each month, but most are not suitable for publication.

Features Mostly written by people involved in the peace movement or with specialist political/scientific knowledge. Maximum 3000 words.

News Most news is commissioned on arms race, international and domestic news. Maximum 500 words.
Payment NUJ rates.

Scotland's Runner

62 Kelvingrove Street, Glasgow G3 7SA
☎ 041–332 5738

Owner *Scotrun Publications*
Editor *Alan Campbell*
Circulation 10,000

FOUNDED 1986. MONTHLY with features on athletics, fitness, nutrition and health. Welcome unsolicited mss. First approach in writing.

The Scots Magazine

D. C. Thomson & Co. Ltd, 7–25 Bank Street, Dundee DD1 9HU
☎ 0382 23131
Telex 76380 Fax 0382 27159

Owner *D. C. Thomson & Co. Ltd*
Editor *Maurice Fleming*
Circulation 82,000

FOUNDED 1739. MONTHLY. 'It has to be stressed that this is a magazine produced in Scotland for people who know the country. It's not an "outside" view of Scotland. Besides a core of regular writers, we do consider any good freelance work which comes our way for any category in the magazine. A study of the magazine is advised.'

Features Maximum 4000 words.
Payment 'according to quality and length'.

Fiction 'Must depict Scottish life and character – not sordid or depressing; good plot essential.'
Payment as for features.

News Brief stories of interest.
Payment by arrangement. Photographic features (colour transparencies), and also series are open to freelancers.

Scottish Field

The Plaza Tower, East Kilbride, Glasgow G74 1LW
☎ 03552 46444

Owner *Holmes McDougall Ltd*
Editor *Joe Stirling*
Circulation 20,000

FOUNDED 1903. MONTHLY.

Features *Joe Stirling* Articles of breadth and authority with a Scottish dimension and good visual impact. Maximum 1200 words.
Payment 'above average'.

Fiction *Joe Stirling* One short story monthly by Scottish author or on well-defined Scottish subject. Maximum 1400 words.
Payment 'above average'. Welcome unsolicited mss but writers should study the market.

Scottish Football Today

c/o Forth Sports Marketing Ltd, 3 Marchfield Grove, Edinburgh EH4 5BN
☎ 031–336 2374

Owner *Forth Sports Marketing Ltd*
Editor *Norman Sutherland*
Circulation *c.*20,000

FOUNDED 1985. MONTHLY. Unsolicited mss are welcome. Receive approximately ten per month. First approach in writing.

Screen

29 Old Compton Street, London W1V 5PL
☎ 01–734 5455

Owner *Society for Education in Film & Television*

Editor *Mandy Merck*
Circulation 2,500

QUARTERLY academic journal of film and television studies for a readership ranging from undergraduates to media professionals. There are no specific departments but articles – based on a knowledge of the magazine and its markets – are welcome from freelancers. The best approach is with an idea in writing.

Screen International

6–7 Great Chapel Street, London W1V 4BR
☎ 01–734 9452

Owner *King Publications Ltd*
Editor *Chris Goodwin*

Trade paper of the film, video and television industries. No unsolicited mss, though expert freelance writers are occasionally used in all areas.

Sea Breezes

202 Cotton Exchange Building, Old Hall Street, Liverpool L3 9LA
☎ 051–236 3935

Owner *Jocast Ltd*
Editor *Mr C. H. Milsom*
Circulation 18,500

FOUNDED 1919. MONTHLY. The magazine covers virtually everything relating to ships and seamen of a non-technical nature. Unsolicited mss welcome; they should be thoroughly researched and accompanied by relevant photographs.

Articles about nautical history, shipping company histories, epic voyages, etc. should be up to 4000 words.
Payment £6 per 1000 words.

She Magazine

National Magazine House, 72 Broadwick Street, London W1V 2BP
☎ 01–439 5000 Fax 01–437 6886

Owner *National Magazine Co. Ltd*
Editor *Sally O'Sullivan*
Circulation 204,000

MONTHLY. Women's glossy with less gloss and much more general interest reading than comparable monthlies. Feature material can include social issues, health, spiritual matters, unusual subjects of any kind, as well as traditionally 'female' concerns. Articles should be of around 1200 words. Fiction is used from time to time; again, general rather than 'women's' reading. Regular freelancers used, but open to new talent.
Payment NUJ rates.

Shoot Magazine

King's Reach Tower, Stamford Street, London SE1 9LS
☎ 01–261 6287
Telex 915748 Fax 01–829 7707

Owner *IPC Magazines Ltd*
Managing Editor *Peter Stewart*
Circulation 170,000

FOUNDED 1969. WEEKLY football magazine. Present ideas for news, features or colour photo-features to the editor in writing. No unsolicited mss.

Features Hard-hitting, topical and offbeat. 450–1500 words.

News Items welcome, especially exclusive gossip and transfer speculation. Maximum 150 words.
Payment £36–75.

Shooting and Conservation

Marford Mill, Rossett, Wrexham, Clwyd LL11 0HL
☎ 0244 570881 Fax 0244 571678

Owner *BASC*
Editor *A. German-Lloyd*
Circulation 81,892

QUARTERLY. Unsolicited mss are welcome. In both **Features** and **Fiction** sections, good articles, stories on shooting, conservation and related areas, of up to 2000 words, are always sought.
Payment negotiable.

Shooting News

Unit 21, Plymouth Road Ind. Estate, Tavistock, Devon PL19 9QN
☎ 0822 616460

Owner *V. Gardner*
Editor *C. Binmore*
Circulation 13,050

FOUNDED 1982. WEEKLY. Unsolicited material is welcome, six or seven submissions are received each week, and a list of special editions and subjects covered by the magazine is available on request.

Features Should be on any fieldsport topic and no longer than 1500 words.

News Items considered. No fiction.
Payment Rates available on request.

Shooting Times & Country

10 Sheet Street, Windsor, Berkshire SL4 1BG
☎ 0753 856061 Fax 0753 859652

Owner *Associated Newspapers Holdings plc*
Editor *Jonathan Young*
Circulation 42,000

FOUNDED 1882. WEEKLY. Articles on shooting, fishing and related countryside topics. Unsolicited mss considered. Maximum 950 words.
Payment by negotiation.

The Sign

St Mary's Works, St Mary's Plain, Norwich NR3 3BH
☎ 0603 616563

Owner *Chansitor Publications*
Editor *Rev R. D. Hacking*
Circulation 256,000

FOUNDED 1907. MONTHLY inset for Church of England parish magazines. Unsolicited mss welcome.

News, Features and **Fiction** all considered. Maximum 400 words.
Payment negotiable.

Signature

7–11 St John's Hill, London SW11 1TN
☎ 01–228 3344

Owner *Reed Publishing Services*
Editor *Mary Ratcliffe*

Circulation 200,000

RELAUNCHED 1986. The magazine for Diners Club Cardholders, issued TEN TIMES YEARLY. Unsolicited mss rarely used, but written suggestions welcome.

Features Most of the main features are commissioned from regular writers. Most articles are based on travel or food. Maximum 2000 words.
Payment negotiable.

Special One special section each month on subjects such as health, sport, gardening and fashion. Maximum 1000 words.
Payment negotiable.

Singles Magazine

23 Abingdon Road, London W8 6AH
☎ 01–938 1011 Fax 01–937 3146

Owner *John Patterson*
Editor *Lorraine Furneaux*
Circulation 23,000

FOUNDED 1976. MONTHLY magazine for single people. Unsolicited mss welcome; ideas in writing only.

Features Anything of interest to, or directly concerning, single people. Maximum 2500 words.
Payment from £35–45 per 1000 words.

News All news items required at least six weeks ahead. Maximum 2500 words.
Payment from £35–45 per 1000 words.

Ski Survey

118 Eaton Square, London SW1W 9AF
☎ 01–245 1033 Fax 01–245 1258

Owner *Ski Club of Great Britain*
Editor *Elisabeth Hussey*
Circulation 26,624

FOUNDED 1903. FIVE ISSUES YEARLY. All articles are commissioned.

The Skier

1 Grimsdells Corner, Sycamore Road, Amersham, Bucks HP6 5EL
☎ 0494 728967
Telex 838791 JMC Fax 0494 722626

Owner *Charles Hallifax*
Editor *Charles Hallifax*
Circulation 25,000

MONTHLY from September to January. Unsolicited manuscripts welcome. Approximately 15 are received each season.

Features of 1000–3000 words on any topic involving 'action' such as skiing, climbing, white-water rafting, etc. Articles of about 1000–3000 words, written from personal first hand experience and full of information, are particularly welcome.

News Items of varying length are always welcome.
Payment negotiable.

Skiing UK

15 Woodlands Terrace, Glasgow G3 6DF
☎ 041–332 8247 Fax 041–331 2652

Owner *Skiing UK Ltd*
Editor *Ian McMillan*
Circulation 12,500

FOUNDED 1985. SEVEN ISSUES YEARLY. Unsolicited mss are welcome on all skiing topics. Approach either in writing or by telephone. No fiction.

Features Should be no longer than 1200 words.
Payment per 1000 words.

News Items should be no longer than 300 words.
Payment per 100 words.

Slimmer

Tolland, Lydeard St Lawrence, Taunton, Somerset TA4 3PS
☎ 098423014

Owner *Slimmer Publications Ltd*
Editor *Judith Wills*
Circulation 140,058

FOUNDED 1976. BI-MONTHLY. Freelance contributors should write with synopsis and c.v., or with cuttings of previously published work. Ideas for features are preferred to completed manuscripts.

Features First-person slimming stories and features on nutrition, research, etc. Must be in a chatty style. Maximum 1500 words.
Payment £10 per 100 words.

News Titbits – serious or amusing – on slimming and fitness. Maximum 200 words.
Payment £10 per 100 words on publication.

Slimming

Victory House, 14 Leicester Place,
London WC2H 7QP
☏ 01–437 9011

Owner *Argus Press Ltd*
Editor *Patience Bulkeley*
Circulation 250,000

FOUNDED 1969. BI-MONTHLY. Basically a scientific magazine with most of its material written by staff, so freelance opportunities are very few indeed. There is some scope for first-person experiences of weight control/loss, but only a small number of those received prove suitable. It is best to approach with an idea in writing.
Payment by negotiation.

Smash Hits

52–5 Carnaby Street, London W1V 1PF
☏ 01–437 8050 Fax 01–494 0851

Owner *EMAP Metro*
Circulation 756,540

FOUNDED 1979. FORTNIGHTLY. Top of the mid-teen market. Unsolicited manuscripts are not accepted, but prospective contributors may approach in writing.

Snooker Scene

Cavalier House, 202 Hagley Road, Edgbaston,
Birmingham B16 9PQ
☏ 021–454 2931

Owner *Everton's News Agency*
Editor *Clive Everton*
Circulation 18,000

FOUNDED 1971. MONTHLY. Unsolicited material is not welcome; any approach should be in writing with an idea.

Social and Liberal Democrat News

4 Cowley Street, London SW1P 3NB
☏ 01–222 7999 Fax 01–222 7904

Owner *Social and Liberal Democrats*
Editor *Mike Harskin*

FOUNDED March 1988. WEEKLY. As with the political parties, this is the result of the merger of two publications, *Liberal News* and *The Social Democrat*. Political and social topics of interest to party members and supporters. Unsolicited contributions welcome.

Features Maximum 800 words.

News Maximum 350 words.
Payment All contributions are unpaid.

Somerset & Avon Life

St Lawrence House, Broad Street,
Bristol BS1 2EX
☏ 0272 291069 Fax 0272 225633

Owner *Town & Country Magazines Ltd*
Editor *Heidi Best*
Circulation 9000

FOUNDED 1976. MONTHLY.

Features 'We use a fair percentage of freelance contributors.' Welcome ideas. First approach in writing. Maximum 1300 words.
Payment by arrangement.

News Only small items which will still be newsworthy eight weeks after submission. Maximum 200 words.
Payment by arrangement.

Sounds

Greater London House, Hampstead Road,
London NW1 7QZ
☏ 01–387 6611
Telex 299485 MUSIC G Fax 01–388 5010

Owner *Punch Publications*
Editor *Tony Stewart*
Circulation 58,417

Popular music WEEKLY tabloid. 99% of their material is provided by freelancers. Send trial review in to be considered for work; review writers of talent can go on to writing features.

Reviews Editor *Robbi Millar*

Features Editor *Tony Stewart*
Payment £82.40 per 1000 words.

South Magazine

New Zealand House, 13th Floor, Haymarket,
London SW1Y 4TS
☏ 01–930 8411
Telex 8814201 Fax 01–930 0980 (Group 3)

Publisher *Humayun Gauhar*
Editor *Raana Gauhar*
Circulation 86,000

FOUNDED 1980. MONTHLY magazine of the Third World. Unsolicited mss considered, but it's better to make initial contact in writing so that editors can consider the subject and discuss it with writer. Many articles are received from all over the world.

Arts & Leisure Of interest to the Third World.

Business & Finance *Melvyn Westlake*

Features *Raana Gauhar, Judith Vidal Hall* Any Third World topic is considered, as long as it carries a strong business and financial interest.

Fiction Rarely published.

Science/Technology *Maria Elena Hurtado* Innovations in the field – all pieces must consider the problems of the Third World.
Payment Finance and political features £140 per 1000 words; Arts & Leisure £100 per 1000 words.

Spare Rib

27 Clerkenwell Close, London EC1R 0AT
☎ 01–253 9792

Circulation 25,000

MONTHLY. Leading feminist publication. **Features Editor** *Marcel Farry*

The Spectator

56 Doughty Street, London WC1N 2LL
☎ 01–405 1706
Telex 27124 Fax 01–242 0603

Owner *The Spectator (1828) Ltd*
Editor *Charles Moore*
Circulation 37,000

FOUNDED 1828. WEEKLY political and literary magazine. Taken over April 1988 by the Telegraph Newspaper Group. Maximum length for all contributions is 1500 words, and prospective contributors should write in the first instance to the relevant editor. Unsolicited manuscripts welcomed, but over 20 received every week.

Arts *Jenny Naipaul*

Books *Mark Amory*

Features *Charles Moore, Dominic Lawson*

News *Charles Moore*
Payment in all cases is 'small'.

The Sporting Life

Orbit House, 1 New Fetter Lane,
London EC4A 1AR
☎ 01–822 3291

Owner *Mirror Group Newspapers Ltd*
Editor *Monty Court*
Circulation 95,181

DAILY newspaper of the horse-racing world. Always on the look-out for specialised racing writers – not necessarily established sports writers, but certainly well-informed. No unsolicited mss. Phone or write with an idea in first instance. The talented will be taken up and used again.

Contact *Alastair Down* (Features Editor).

Sporting Life Weekender

Orbit House, 1 New Fetter Lane,
London EC4A 1AR
☎ 01–822 2089 Fax 01–583 3885

Owner *Odhams Newspapers Ltd*
Editor *Neil Cook*
Circulation 40,000

FOUNDED 1983. WEEKLY. Prospective contributors should write with ideas in first instance as no articles are published before discussion.
Payment NUJ rates.

Squash Player International

Stanley House, 9 West Street, Epsom,
Surrey KT18 7RL
☎ 03727 41411
Telex 291 561 via SOS G (AEM) Fax 03727 44493

Owner *A. E. Morgan Publications Ltd*
Editor *I. R. McKenzie*
Circulation 10,000

MONTHLY. Mss welcome; sample material and synopsis preferred.

Features Instructive club and commercial news.

News Tournament reports.

Squash World

Chiltern House, 184 High Street, Berkhamsted,
Hertfordshire HP4 3AP
☎ 04428 74947 Fax 04428 63152

Owner *Dennis Fairey Publishing Ltd*
Editor *Larry Halpin*
Circulation 10,000

FOUNDED 1986. MONTHLY. Unsolicited mss welcome; approach by telephone with ideas. Resident experts generally cover topics of health, diet, fitness and coaching, but material of 1200–1500 words from other experts would be considered.

Features *Larry Halpin* Phone with ideas for articles of 1200–1500 words.

News *Larry Halpin* Stories of a maximum of 500 words on tournaments, new clubs, sponsorship,

etc., always welcome.
Payment by negotiation.

The Stage and Television Today

47 Bermondsey Street, London SE1 3XT
☎ 01–403 1818

Owner *Carson and Comerford Ltd*
Editor *Peter Hepple*
Circulation 43,422

FOUNDED 1880. WEEKLY. Unsolicited manuscripts are not welcome; prospective contributors should write with ideas in the first instance.

Features Occasional feature suggestions are considered. Preference is given to material with a business or financial orientation rather than personal pieces or interviews. Maximum 1200 words.
Payment £100 per 1000 words.

News News stories from outside London are always welcome. Maximum 300 words.
Payment minimum £10.

The Strad

4th Floor, Centro House, Mandela Street, London NW1
☎ 01–388 9995

Owner *Orpheus Publications*
Editor *Eric Wen*
Circulation 10,000

FOUNDED 1889. MONTHLY for classical string musicians and enthusiasts. Unsolicited mss welcome.

Features Profiles of string players and musical instruments. Maximum 3000 words.
Payment £150.

Sunday

PO Box 7, 2nd Floor, 214 Gray's Inn Road, London WC1X 8EZ
☎ 01–782 7000
Telex 297918 KRM G Fax 01–782 7373

Owner *News Group Newspapers Ltd*
Editor *Colin Jenkins*
Circulation 5,200,000

FOUNDED 1981. WEEKLY colour supplement magazine published with *The News of the World*. Freelance writers' ideas and material are always welcome. Showbiz interviews and strong human-interest features make up most of the content, but there are no strict rules about what is 'interesting'.

Features *Pete Picton*
Length and *payment* subject to negotiation.

Sunday Express Magazine

Ludgate House, 245 Blackfriars Road, London SE1 9UX
☎ 01–928 8000 Fax 01–928 7262

Owner *United Newspapers plc*
Editor *Dee Nolan*
Circulation 2,206,494

WEEKLY. Unsolicited mss are not welcome or considered, as features on all topics are commissioned from freelance writers. Any ideas, however, should be offered in writing.

Sunday Mirror Magazine

Colour supplement to Sunday Mirror. See **National Newspapers Section**.

The Sunday Times Magazine

214 Gray's Inn Road, London WC1X 8EZ
☎ 01–782 7000

Owner *News International*
Editor *Philip Clarke*
Circulation 1,300,000

FOUNDED 1962. WEEKLY colour supplement distributed with *The Sunday Times*. Almost all features are specially commissioned. Prospective contributors should write in the first instance with ideas. No unsolicited mss are accepted.

Supercar Classics

FF Publishing, 97 Earls Court Road, London W8 6QH
☎ 01–370 0333 Fax 01–244 8692

Owner *FF Publishing Ltd*
Editor *Mark Gillies*
Circulation 40,000

FOUNDED 1983. MONTHLY. Unsolicited mss of at least 1000 words are welcome: make initial contact either by phone or in writing.

Features are usually commissioned from staff and known writers, but other reports of classic older cars, no longer in production, would be welcome. Maximum 3000 words. Short stories about motoring experiences are considered.
Payment £100–200 per 1000 words (negotiable).

Survival Weaponry & Techniques

Castle House, 97 High Street, Colchester, Essex CO1 1TH
☎ 0206 562244

Owner *Aceville Publications Ltd*
Editor *Greg Payne*

MONTHLY publication on outdoor survival techniques. The only unsolicited material welcomed are specialist articles from experienced survival writers. Articles are paid for on publication.
Payment £14 per 1000 words.

Swimming Times

Harold Fern House, Derby Square, Loughborough LE11 0AL
☎ 0509 234433

Owner *Amateur Swimming Association*
Editor *K. T. Glendenning*
Circulation 16,092

FOUNDED 1923. MONTHLY about competitive swimming and associated subjects. Unsolicited mss welcome.

Features Technical articles on swimming, water polo, diving or synchronised swimming. Length and *payment* negotiable.

Symbiosis

43 James Street, Scarborough, North Yorkshire YO12 7PH
☎ 0723 367870

Owner *Eric & Sue Twose*
Editor *Eric Twose*
Circulation 'growing'

FOUNDED 1988. BI-MONTHLY. Independent non-profit-making national magazine devoted to positive environmental, humanist and spiritual alternatives. Features green & nuclear issues; animal welfare; food & health; political & social oppression/human rights; alternative energy, medicine and lifestyles; meditation & mysticism; music related to things environmental; humanist & spiritual; social issues. Unsolicited contributions very welcome.
No payment.

The Tablet

48 Great Peter Street, London SW1P 2HB
☎ 01–222 7462

Owner *The Tablet Publishing Co Ltd*
Editor *John Wilkins*
Circulation 14,402

FOUNDED 1840. WEEKLY. Quality magazine featuring articles of interest to Roman Catholic laity and clergy. On average, five unsolicited manuscripts are received daily, but these are only accepted when relevant. The usual article length is 1500 words.
Payment is approximately £50 upwards. All approaches should be made in writing.

Taste

Greencoat House, Francis Street, London SW1P 1DG
☎ 01–834 1717 Fax 01–828 0270

Owner *Focus Magazines Ltd*
Editor *Paul Dymond*

A small staff means articles are mostly by freelance writers, and usually commissioned. Always on the look-out for 'new regulars' though. Food, travel, cookery, wine/drink, good living, and general interest features with a foodie angle. Glossy and upmarket. New writers should approach the editor with ideas and samples of written work, whether published or not.

The Tatler

Vogue House, Hanover Square, London W1R 0ED
☎ 01–499 9080

Owner *Condé Nast Publications Ltd*
Editor *Emma Soames*
Circulation 49,124

Upmarket glossy from the *Vogue* stable. New writers should send in copies of either published work or unpublished material; writers of promise will be taken up. The magazine works largely on a commission basis: they are unlikely to publish unsolicited features, but will ask writers to work to specific projects.

Features Editor *Rebecca Fraser*

Associate Editor *David Jenkins*

Telegraph Weekend Magazine

Peterborough Court, Southquay, 181 Marsh Wall, London E14 9SR
☎ 01–538 5000

Editor *Nigel Horne*
Circulation 700,000

WEEKLY magazine supplement to the *Sunday Telegraph.* Well-written articles on subjects of national interest with a human angle. Must have very good picture potential. Interested contrib-

utors should write in first instance.
Payment negotiable.

Television Week

21 John Street, London WC1N 2BP
☎ 01–404 5513

Owner *EMAP Maclaren*
Managing Editor *Peter Lloyd*
Circulation 15,000

FOUNDED 1988. WEEKLY. No unsolicited mss. Approach in writing in first instance.

Features *John Marshall* UK and international stories on all aspects of TV production and distribution. Contact by phone to discuss ideas. Maximum 2000 words.
Payment £120 per 1000 words.

Tennis World

Chiltern House, 184 High Street,
Berkhamsted, Herts HP4 3AP
☎ 04427 74947/8 Fax 04427 3055

Owner *Dennis Fairey Publishing Ltd*
Editor *Alastair McIver*
Circulation 15,500

FOUNDED 1969. MONTHLY. Unsolicited mss welcome.

Features Any ideas on tennis features or tennis personalities are welcome. Maximum 1000 words.
Payment £75–100.

The Tennis Times

Ludgate House, 160 Tower Bridge Road,
London SE1
☎ 01–407 9111

Editor *Ryk Richardson*

All matters relating to tennis and the tennis world. Unsolicited contributions welcome. Prefer approach in writing though.

News Send factual details – may generate an article.

Features player profiles, product news and events by prior arrangement with the editor.

Fiction occasionally 'if amusing'.

Texas Homecare Magazine

Home & Law Publishing, Greater London House,
Hampstead Road, London NW1 7QQ
☎ 01–388 3171
Telex 269470 Fax 01–387 9518

Owner *Robert Maxwell*
Editor *Debbi Scholes*
Circulation 3.5 million

THRICE YEARLY with features on DIY and gardening. Will consider unsolicited mss if they 'fit the planned editorial'. First approach by phone.

This England

PO Box 52, Cheltenham, Glos GL50 1YQ
☎ 0242 577775

Owner *This England Ltd*
Editor *Roy Faiers*
Circulation 180,000

Published FOUR TIMES YEARLY, and with a strong overseas readership. Celebration of England and all things English: famous people, natural beauty, towns and villages, history, traditions, customs and legends, crafts, etc. Generally a rural basis, with the 'Forgetmenots' section publishing readers' recollections and nostalgia. Receive up to 100 unsolicited pieces a week. 250–2000 word articles will be considered.
Payment negotiable.

This Lincolnshire

Plot No. 40, Burghley Park Close, Poplar Park,
North Hykeham, Lincoln LN6 9UD
☎ 0522 500792

Owner *A. L. Robinson*
Editor *Arnold Hadwin*

FOUNDED 1987. BI-MONTHLY. Features articles on local activities and social issues. Welcome unsolicited mss. First approach in writing.
Payment varies.

Time

Time & Life Building, New Bond Street,
London W1Y 0AA
☎ 01–499 4080 Telex 22557

Owner *Time Inc.*
Editor *William Mader* (London Bureau Chief)
Circulation 509,000,000 (worldwide)

FOUNDED 1923. WEEKLY current affairs and news magazine. There are no opportunities for freelancers on *Time* as almost all the magazine's content is written by staff members from the various bureaux around the world. Unsolicited manuscripts are not read.

Time Out

Tower House, Southampton Street,
London WC2E 7HD
☎ 01–836 4411 Fax 01–836 7118

Owner *Tony Elliott*
Editor *Simon Garfield*
Circulation 90,000

FOUNDED 1968. WEEKLY magazine of news and entertainment in London.

Features *John Morrish* 'Usually written by staff writers or commissioned, but it's always worth submitting an idea if particularly apt to the magazine.' Maximum 2500 words.

Fiction *Simon Garfield* and *John Morrish* Creative writing competitions at Christmas. Maximum 2500 words.

News *Andy Bell* Despite having a permanent team of staff news writers, always willing to accept contributions from new journalists, 'should their material be relevant to the issue'. Maximum Sidelines 250 words; Features 1000 words. Other sections occasionally take on freelance writers. Submit pieces to section heads (see masthead of current issue).

The Times Educational Supplement

Priory House, St John's Lane, London EC1M 4BX
☎ 01–253 3000 Telex 24460 TTSUPP

Owner *News International*
Editor *Stuart MacLure CBE*
Circulation 109,000

FOUNDED 1910. WEEKLY. New contributors are welcome, and should phone with ideas for news or features, write for reviews.

Arts and Books *Heather Neill* Unsolicited reviews are not accepted. Anyone wanting to review should write, sending examples of their work and full details of their academic and professional background to either the literary editor or the media and resources editor. Maximum 1200 words.

Features *Bob Doe* 'Platform': a weekly slot for a well-informed, and cogently-argued viewpoint, maximum 1500 words; 'Second Opinion': a shorter comment on an issue of the day by somebody well placed to write on the subject, maximum 570 words; 'Features': longer articles on contemporary practical subjects of general interest to the *TES* reader, maximum 1000–1500 words; longer or multi-part features are rarely accepted.
Payment varies.
'Extra' *Joyce Arnold* Subjects covered include: science, travel, music, modern languages, home economics, school visits, primary education, history, geography, mathematics, health, life skills, environmental education, CDT, special needs. Articles should relate to current educational practice. Age range covered is primary to sixth form. Maximum 1000–1300 words.
Payment £65 per 1000 words.

Media/Resources Editor *Gillie Macdonald*

The Times Educational Supplement Scotland

37 George Street, Edinburgh EH2 2HN
☎ 031–220 1100 Fax 031–220 1616

Owner *Times Newspapers Ltd*
Editor *Willis Pickard*
Circulation 6500

FOUNDED 1965. WEEKLY. Unsolicited mss welcome, but many more are received than can be used.

Features Articles on education in Scotland. Maximum 1500 words.
Payment NUJ rates for NUJ members.

News News items on education in Scotland. Maximum 600 words.

The Times Higher Education Supplement

Priory House, St John's Lane, London EC1M 4BX
☎ 01–253 3000
Telex 24460 Fax 01–608 1599

Owner *Times Newspapers Ltd*
Editor *Peter Scott*
Circulation 15,367

FOUNDED 1971. WEEKLY. Unsolicited mss are welcome but most articles and *all* book reviews are commissioned. 'In most cases it is better to write, but in the case of news stories it is all right to phone.'
Payment NUJ rates.

Books *Brian Morton*

Features *Peter Aspden* Most articles are commissioned from academics in higher education.

News *David Jobbins* Very occasionally freelance opportunities.

Science *Jon Turney*

Science Books *Robbie Vickers*

The Times Literary Supplement

Priory House, St John's Lane, London EC1M 4BX
☎ 01–253 3000
Telex 24460 TTSUPP Fax 01–608 1599

Owner *News International*
Editor *Jeremy Treglown*
Circulation 30,000

FOUNDED 1902. WEEKLY review of literature. Contributors should approach in writing and be familiar with the general level of writing in the *TLS*.

Literary Discoveries *Alan Hollinghurst*

Poems *Alan Jenkins*

Short Stories *Holly Eley*

News *Isabel Fonseca* News stories and general articles concerned with literature, publishing and new intellectual developments anywhere in the world. Length by agreement.
Payment NUJ rates.

Titbits

Northcliffe House, London EC4Y 0JA
☎ 01–583 0350 Fax 01–583 2133

Owner *Mail Newspapers plc*
Editor *Brian Lee*
Circulation 120,000

FOUNDED 1881. MONTHLY. There are opportunities for freelance contributors with features on show business, television, pop music, medical topics, women's interests, animals and pets, royalty, and the supernatural. Unsolicited manuscripts are welcome, but many are received every day so write with ideas in first instance. Articles with pictures (or picture references) stand the best chance.

Features Maximum 1500 words.
Payment £80–120. No news stories or fiction required.

Today's Guide

17–19 Buckingham Palace Road,
London SW1W 0PT
☎ 01–834 6242 Fax 01–828 8317

Owner *Girl Guides Association*
Editor *Diana Wallace*
Circulation 25,000

FOUNDED 1962. MONTHLY aimed at Girl Guides aged 10–14 years. Unsolicited mss welcome.

Features and Fiction General interest with a Guiding background. Maximum 750–1000 words.
Payment £26 per 1000 words pro rata.

Today's Runner

Bretton Court, Bretton, Peterborough PE3 8DZ
☎ 0733 264666 Fax 0733 265515

Owner *EMAP Pursuit Publishing*
Editor *Paul Richardson*
Circulation 40,000

FOUNDED 1985. MONTHLY. Instructional articles on running and fitness, plus running-related activities and health.

Features Specialist knowledge an advantage. Opportunities are wide, but approach with idea in first instance.

News 'Lots of opportunities, especially if backed by photographs.'

Townswoman

ECN Special Publications, 69 Thorpe Road,
Norwich NR1 1TB
☎ 0603 619421 Fax 0603 615973

Owner *National Union of Townswomen's Guilds*
Editor *Moira Eagling*
Circulation 39,631

FOUNDED 1933. ELEVEN ISSUES YEARLY (no issue in August). No unsolicited mss; few opportunities as in-house editorial staff are strong.

Tracks

52 Charlbert Street, London NW8 7BU
☎ 01–722 0167 Fax 01–483 2534

Owner *Trevor Wells*
Editor *Phil McNeill*
Circulation 500,000

FOUNDED 1985. MONTHLY aimed at compact disc, singles and album buyers, mainly of chart music but also country, retro and film soundtracks. The magazine also covers films, video and books. Unsolicited manuscripts are not welcome: telephone with idea in the first instance and follow up with brief synopsis in writing.

Features Should be tied in with monthly albums/singles releases. Also major film/video releases, books and compact discs. There is also a new band section focusing predominantly on signed bands. Freelance suggestions welcome in this area, particularly exclusive access to big-name artists. Maximum 2000 words.
Payment £84 per 1000 words.

News Some opportunity for freelance contributions. Inside information, not available from usual PR sources, is welcome. Maximum 200 words.
Payment £84 per 1000 words (£10 minimum).

Reviews As for features. Maximum 350 words.
Payment £84 per 1000 words (£10 minimum).

Traditional Homes (incorporating Period Homes)

Schweppes House, Grosvenor Road, St Albans, Herts AL1 3TN
☎ 0727 59166 Fax 0727 64218

Owner *Burleigh Magazines Ltd*
Circulation 33,500

FOUNDED 1984. Merged with Period Homes in 1988. MONTHLY magazine covering conservation, restoration, architecture, antiques and interior design. Unsolicited mss are welcome.
Payment £100 per 1000 words.

Traditional Interior Decoration

Burleigh Magazines Ltd, Schweppes House, Grosvenor Road, St Albans, Herts AL1 3TN
☎ 0727 59166

Owner *Benn Consumer Publications*
Editor *Jo Newson*
Circulation 40,000

FOUNDED 1986. BI-MONTHLY. Unsolicited mss welcome. They receive around six per issue.

Features Up to 2500 words considered on houses with impressive interiors; design and designers; historic interiors and furnishing; fabrics and wallpaper; crafts.

News Under 'Carousel' section, short write-ups of maximum 500 words are welcome on conservation, interiors, events, exhibitions in art and antiques world. Other sections include 'Bazaar' which covers new products and companies including crafts and design, and 'Under the Hammer' which covers auctions. Maximum 2500 words.
Payment varies.

Trailfinder Magazine

42–8 Earls Court Road, London W8 6EJ
☎ 01–938 3366
Telex 919670 Fax 01–937 9294

Owner *Trailfinders Ltd*
Editors *David Thompson, Linda Zeff*
Circulation 175,000

FOUNDED 1970. THREE ISSUES YEARLY (March, July & December). Unsolicited mss are welcome and prospective contributors should make initial contact in writing. No fiction.

Features *Linda Zeff* Lightweight, anecdotal travel features, specialising in Asia, Australasia, Far East, North and South America and Africa are welcome. Maximum 1000 words.
Payment £50 (plus £15 for accompanying colour transparency; £10 B & W).

Traveller

45 Brompton Road, London SW3 1DE
☎ 01–581 4130
Telex 297155 WEXAS G Fax 01–589 8418

Owner *Dr I. M. Wilson, Wexas*
Editor *Caroline Sanders*
Circulation 33,000

FOUNDED 1970. THREE ISSUES YEARLY. Unsolicited mss welcome, but a preliminary letter is preferred.

Features Five colour features per issue – authors should supply pictures. Contributors' guidelines available with s.a.e., but all articles should be off-beat, independent, and travel-based. Maximum 2000 words.
Payment £50 per 1000 words.

Tribune

308 Gray's Inn Road, London WC1X 8DY
☎ 01–278 0911

Owner *Tribune Publications Ltd*
Editor *Phil Kelly*
Circulation 10,000

'We have plenty of opportunities for freelancers. Miniscule fees may possibly be available for commissioned work only.' Contact the editor in first instance. Opportunities in features – current affairs with the emphasis on left politics; reviewing, and newswriting. Either send mss in on spec., or ring to discuss an idea.

Features Editor *Paul Anderson*

Trout Fisherman

Bretton Court, Bretton, Peterborough PE3 8DZ
☎ 0733 264666 Fax 0733 265515

Owner *EMAP Pursuit Publishing*
Editor *Chris Dawn*
Circulation 36,000

FOUNDED 1977. MONTHLY instructive magazine on trout fishing. Most of the articles are commissioned, but unsolicited mss and quality colour transparencies welcome.

Features *Steve Windsor* Maximum 1500 words. *Payment* varies.

True Romances

12–18 Paul Street, London EC2A 4JS
☎ 01–247 8233
Telex 8951167 Fax 01–377 9709

Owner *Argus Press Ltd*
Managing Editor *Veronica Dunn*
Circulation 74,187

FOUNDED 1934. MONTHLY. Romantic fiction aimed at the teen/16–19 year-olds market. Occasionally use unsolicited mss. Subjects: teenage/young love, written in first-person. More off-beat than others in this market. 'Lovemaking takes place only within long-term faithful relationships.' Sad stories, stories with a twist welcome. 1000–6000 words.
Payment negotiable on acceptance.

News/Features all written in-house.

True Story

12–18 Paul Street, London EC2A 4JS
☎ 01–247 8233 Fax 01–377 9709

Owner *Argus Press Ltd*
Editor *Veronica Dunn*

MONTHLY Unsolicited contributions welcome but receive 80–100 weekly. Nevertheless prefer to be approached with complete mss rather than with outline ideas.

News and **Features** written in-house.

Fiction Welcome mss from 'bright, new writers'. Maximum 6000 words, minimum 1000.
Payment varies.

The Truth

1 Leighton Road, London NW5 2QD
☎ 01–485 9290

Owner *Stranger than Fiction Ltd*
Editor *Stephen Caplin*

FOUNDED 1987. MONTHLY magazine rivalling *Private Eye*. News, features and fiction. Most material supplied by staff writers but welcome contributions if 'very funny'. Features which would support good visual ideas particularly welcome. Maximum 2000 words. First approach in writing but allow at least a month for a reply as they are 'snowed under' with unsolicited material.

TV Times

247 Tottenham Court Road, London W1P 0AU
☎ 01–323 3222
Telex 24643 Fax 01–580 3986

Owner *Reed International*
Editor *Richard Barber*
Circulation 3,003,017

FOUNDED 1968. WEEKLY magazine of listings and features serving the viewers of Independent Television. Almost no freelance contributions used, except where the writer is known and trusted by the magazine. No unsolicited contributions. Reed International bought ITP, the publisher of TV Times for £113 million, and a further £2 million a quarter for up to three and a half years as long as the exclusive television listings survive.

20/20

Tower House, Southampton Street,
London WC2E 7HD
☎ 01–836 4411 Fax 01–836 7118

Owner *Tony Elliot*
Editor *Don Atyeo*
Circulation 60,000 (estimate)

LAUNCHED 1989. MONTHLY national spin-off from Time Out, London's best selling guide. Provides features and information on the coming month's arts and entertainment. It also covers stories relevant to a young (18–40), intelligent, educated, arts & entertainment oriented readership. Welcomes unsolicited mss and ideas in writing.

Features *Pete Silverton* Plenty of opportunities. Maximum 6000 words.
Payment £140 per 1000 words.

The Universe

33–39 Bowling Green Lane, London EC1R 0AB
☎ 01–278 7321 Fax 01–278 7320

Owner *Universe Publications Ltd*
Editor *Tom Murphy*
Circulation 160,902

Occasional use of new writers, though a substantial network of regular contributors exists. Interested in a very wide range of material, all subjects which might bear on

Christian life, from politics to occasional fiction. *Payment* negotiable.

Vector

23 Oakfield Road, Croydon, Surrey CR0 2UD
☎ 01–688 6081

Owner *British Science Fiction Association*
Editor *David V. Barrett*
Circulation 1300

FOUNDED 1957. BI-MONTHLY. The critical journal of the BSFA, containing articles mainly about science fiction and its writers. Unsolicited mss welcome, especially if authoritative and well-written, but most contributors are either professional science fiction authors or BSFA members. No fiction.

Book Reviews *Paul Kincaid* Most are submitted by BSFA members. Should be no longer than 500 words.

Features Articles up to 4000 words are welcome. Interviews with SF authors, editors, publishers etc. are welcome. Maximum length 4000 words.
No *Payment.*

The Vegan

33–5 George Street, Oxford OX1 2AY
☎ 0865 722166

Owner *Vegan Society*
Editor *Barry Kew*
Circulation 7000

FOUNDED 1944. QUARTERLY. Features articles on the ethical, health, ecological and other aspects of veganism. Unsolicited mss welcome. Maximum 1500 words.
Payment negotiable.

Veteran Car

Acorns, Oak Lane, Easterton, Devizes, Wiltshire SN10 4PD
☎ 0380 812649

Owner *The Veteran Car Club of Great Britain*
Editor *Malcolm Jeal*
Circulation 2000

FOUNDED 1938. BI-MONTHLY magazine which exists primarily for the benefit of members of The Veteran Car Club of Great Britain, although it is available on subscription to non-members. It is concerned with all aspects of the old vehicle hobby – events, restoration, history, current world news, legislation, etc., relating to pre-1919 motor cars. Some contributions are from professional writers, but 'no budget for paid contributions'. Approach in writing in the first instance.

Video Today

1 Golden Square, London W1R 3AB
☎ 01–437 0626 Fax 01–437 1006

Owner *Argus Specialist Publications*
Editor *Chris Adam-Smith*
Circulation 30,000

FOUNDED 1981. MONTHLY. Main interest lies in film-related interviews and features. Approach with ideas in writing. No unsolicited mss.
Payment on publication by agreement.

Video Trade Weekly

20 Bowling Green Lane, London EC1
☎ 01–250 3077 Fax 01–608 0304

Owner *United Trade Press*
Editor *Julie Lefebve*
Circulation 10,000

FOUNDED 1981. WEEKLY. Welcome unsolicited mss and ideas in writing.

News *Jo Jeffery* Freelance stories on video-related topics.

Features *Peter Dean* Approach the editor with ideas. Photos appreciated.

Video World Magazine

The Northern & Shell Building, PO Box 381, Millharbour, London E14 9TW
☎ 01–987 5090
Telex 24676 (NORSHL G) Fax 01–987 2160

Owner *Richard Desmond*
Editor *Jonathan Richards*
Circulation 32,000

FOUNDED 1984. MONTHLY. Features on anything relevant to film and video. Welcome unsolicited contributions.

Vogue

Vogue House, Hanover Square, London W1R 0AD
☎ 01–499 9080
Telex 27338 VOLON G Fax 01–493 1345

Owner *Condé Nast Publications Ltd*
Editor *Liz Tilberis*
Circulation 177,187

Features are upmarket general interest rather than 'women's', with a good proportion of highbrow art and literary articles, as well as travel features, gardens, food, home interest, reviews. Typically of Condé Nast magazines, tend to use known writers and commission what's needed, rather than using unsolicited mss. Contacts are useful. No fiction.

Features Editor *Alex Schulman*

The Voice

370 Coldharbour Lane, London SW9 8PL
☎ 01–737 7377 Fax 01–274 8994

Owner *Vee Tee Ay Media Resources*
Editor *Steve Pope*
Circulation 45,000

FOUNDED 1982. WEEKLY newspaper, particularly aimed at the Black British community. Unsolicited contributions welcome. Best approach in writing though. Few opportunities except in **Features**. Maximum 1000 words.
Payment £75 per 1000 words.

Voyager

7–11 St John's Hill, London SW11 1TE
☎ 01–228 3344

Owner *Reed Publishing Services*
Editor *Roger St Pierre*

FOUNDED 1986. MONTHLY. No opportunities for freelance work at the moment.

Waterways World

Kottingham House, Dale Street, Burton-on-Trent, Staffs DE14 3TD
☎ 0283 42721 Telex 342260 Zilec G

Owner *Waterway Productions Ltd*
Editor *Hugh Potter*
Circulation 20,593

FOUNDED 1972. MONTHLY magazine for inland waterway enthusiasts. Unsolicited mss welcome, provided the writer has a good knowledge of the subject. No fiction.

Features *Hugh Potter* Articles (preferably illustrated) are published on all aspects of inland waterways in Britain and abroad including recreational and commercial boating on rivers and canals.

News *Euan Corrie* Maximum 500 words.
Payment £25 per 1000 words.

Wedding and Home

Greater London House, Hampstead Road, London NW1 7QQ
☎ 01–388 3171 Fax 01–387 9518

Owner *Home and Law Publishing Ltd*
Editor *Maggi Taylor*
Circulation 50,000

BI-MONTHLY for women planning their wedding, honeymoon and first home. Most features are written in-house or commissioned from known freelancers. Unsolicited mss are not welcome, but approaches may be made in writing.

Weekend

Temple House, Tudor Street, London EC4
☎ 01–353 6000

Owner *Mail Newspapers plc*
Editor *Grant Lockhart*
Circulation 280,000

FOUNDED 1953. WEEKLY. Freelance contributions are welcome and should be sent to the features editor.

Features *Guy Simpson* Preferred subjects are showbiz features, especially British and American 'soaps', royalty, fashion and beauty, general interest and true-life dramas. Maximum 800 words.
Payment £100 per 800 words.

Weekly News

Albert Square, Dundee DD1 9QJ
☎ 0382 23131

Owner *D. C. Thomson & Co. Ltd*
Editor *W. Kelly*
Circulation 670,502

Newsy, family-oriented magazine designed to appeal to the busy housewife. 'We get a lot of unsolicited stuff and there is great loss of life among them.' Usually commission, but writers of promise will be taken up. Series include showbiz, royals and television. No fiction.
Payment negotiable.

Weight Watchers Magazine

141–3 Drury Lane, London WC2B 5TS
☎ 01–836 4433 Fax 01–836 3156/2610

Owner *GAT Publishing*
Editor *Harriet Cross*
Circulation 107,000

BI-MONTHLY. For slimmers and the health-conscious. Unsolicited mss not normally accepted, but approaches may be made in writing.

Features are usually commissioned by editor or features editor – length and *payment* vary depending on subject.

What Camera

Prospect House, 9–13 Ewell Road,
Cheam, Surrey SM1 4QQ
☏ 01–661 4300 Fax 01–642 6562

Owner *Reed Business Publishing*
Editor *Keith Wilson*
Circulation *c.* 75,000

FOUNDED 1988. MONTHLY. Few opportunities except in the Supplement section, and many more openings for copy which is accompanied by good photography.

What Car?

38–42 Hampton Road, Teddington,
Middlesex TW11 0JE
☏ 01–977 8787 Fax 01–977 9792

Owner *Haymarket Publishing Ltd*
Editor *Sam Brown*
Circulation 136,019

Reports on cars, and consumer-based articles to do with motoring generally. Freelancers are used for both, but testing is only offered to the few, and general articles on aspects of driving must be by writers known and trusted by the magazine, as conclusions arrived at can be controversial, and need to be scrupulously researched. Not interested in receiving unsolicited mss.
Payment NUJ rates.

What Diet & Lifestyle

AIM Publications Ltd, Silver House,
31–5 Beak Street, London W1R 3LD
☏ 01–437 0796 Fax 01-437 8787

Owner *D. C. Thomson & Co. Ltd*
Editor *Helen Williams*
Circulation 45,000

FOUNDED 1983. BI-MONTHLY. Unsolicited mss not welcome as all news and feature articles are written by in-house or regular commissioned freelance writers.

What Hi-Fi

Haymarket Magazines Ltd, 10–12 The Causeway,
Teddington, Middlesex TW11 0HE
☏ 01–943 5533 Fax 01–943 1057

Owner *Haymarket Magazines Ltd*
Editor *Simon Davies*
Circulation 65,018

FOUNDED 1976. MONTHLY. Features on hi-fi, music, retailing and new technology. No unsolicited contributions. Prior consultation with the editor essential.

Features *Simon Davies* General or more specific on hi-fi, music, retailing and new technology pertinent to the consumer electronics market. Length 2500–3000 words.
Payment £65 per page.

Reviews Specific product reviews. Generally from an established pool of reviewers; 'only exceptionally will a review from an unknown source be accepted'.

What Investment

Ground Floor, Boundary House,
91–3 Charterhouse Street, London EC1M 6HR
☏ 01–250 0646 Fax 01–250 0637

Owner *Charterhouse Communications*
Editor *Peter Fuller*
Circulation 25,530

FOUNDED 1983. MONTHLY. Features articles on a variety of savings and investment matters. Unsolicited mss not welcome. All approaches should be made in writing.

Features Maximum 2000 words (usually less).
Payment NUJ rates.

What Mortgage

Boundary House, 91–3 Charterhouse Street,
London EC1M 6HR
☏ 01–250 0646 Fax 01–250 0637

Owner *Charterhouse Communications*
Editor *Valerie Bayes*
Circulation 20,000

FOUNDED 1983. MONTHLY magazine on property purchase, choice and finance. Unsolicited mss welcome; prospective contributors may make initial contact either by telephone or in writing.

Features Up to 1500 words on related topics are considered. Particularly welcome are new

angles, new ideas or specialities.
Payment £100 per 1000 words.

What Restaurant & Theatre

Ajmal House, Hayes Road, Southall,
Middlesex UB2 5NG
☎ 01–843 2160

Owner *Finis Coronat Opus Ltd*
Editor *Helen Sniadek*

FOUNDED 1988. MONTHLY.

News handled in-house. No opportunities.

Features *Helen Sniadek* All aspects of London and the south-east restaurant scene of interest to consumers. Also theatre reviews and interviews. Maximum 1500 words.
Payment negotiable.
Reviews *Helen Sniadek* Brief reviews of restaurants and theatre shows – West End and fringe. Maximum 300 words.
Payment negotiable.

What Satellite

57–9 Rochester Place, London NW1 9JU
☎ 01–485 0011

Owner *W. V. Publications*
Editor *Alan Smith*

FOUNDED 1989. MONTHLY. Equipment guide to consumer satellite TV receivers. Comprehensive coverage of all types available, dish system tests, satellite channel listings, installation advice and programming features. Unsolicited mss welcome. Maximum 1000 words.
Payment £75 minimum plus illustrations.

What Video

57–9 Rochester Place, London NW1 9JU
☎ 01–485 0011

Owner *W. V. Publications*
Editor *Colin Goode*
Circulation 40,000

FOUNDED 1980. MONTHLY. Features on video equipment and user features on video – TVs, VCRs, camcorders, accessories. Welcome unsolicited mss. Particularly interested in application features – 'outside broadcast' video movies, novel trips with video. Maximum 1000 words.
Payment £75 minimum plus illustrations.

What's New in Building

Morgan-Grampian House, 30 Calderwood Street,
London SE18 6QH
☎ 01–855 7777 Telex 896238

Owner *Morgan-Grampian Ltd*
Editor *Derrick Jolley*
Circulation 35,500

MONTHLY. Specialist magazine covering new products for building; unsolicited manuscripts are not generally welcome. The only freelance work is rewriting press-release material. This is offered on a monthly basis of 25–50 items of about 150 words each.
Payment £5 per item.

What's New in Farming

Morgan-Grampian House, 30 Calderwood Street,
London SE18 6QH
☎ 01–855 7777 ext. 3420 Telex 896238

Owner *United Newspapers*
Editor *Jonathan Theobald*
Circulation 75,000

FOUNDED 1977. MONTHLY. The magazine is primarily a guide to new agricultural products, with little feature space. Most copy is written in-house, and unsolicited mss are not welcome.

Features *Claire Cronin/Jonathan Theobald* Articles on relevant agricultural topics. Maximum 2000 words.
Payment negotiable.

What's New in Interiors

Morgan-Grampian House, 30 Calderwood Street,
Woolwich, London SE18 6QH
☎ 01–885 7777
Telex 896238 Morgan G Fax 01–855 2342

Owner *Morgan-Grampian Ltd*
Editor *Anthea Bain*
Circulation 13,519

FOUNDED 1981. TEN ISSUES YEARLY, plus specialist supplements (5 in 1989). Aimed at interior designers, architects and specifiers. Unsolicited manuscripts welcome if they are exclusive, well-researched and aimed at readership. Make initial contact in writing or by telephone.

Features Good, technical journalists who know the contract interiors market are always sought. Maximum 1500 words. Opportunity for writers of interiors application stories and specialised

profiles.
Payment £110 per 1000 words.

What's On in London

182 Pentonville Road, London N1 9LB
☎ 01–278 4393 Fax 01–837 5838

Owner *E. G. Shaw*
Editor *David Parkes-Bristow*
Circulation 38,000

FOUNDED 1932. WEEKLY guide and information magazine. Features and reviews. Like to receive well thought out and well presented mss. Articles should have London/Home Counties connection, although during the summer they can be of much wider tourist/historic interest, especially relating to unusual traditions and events. Prefer first approach to editor by telephone.
Payment by arrangement.

Cinema *Michael Darvell*

Pop Music *Jon Homer*

Classical Music *Marshall Julius*

Theatre *Lydia Conway*

Wine

Thames House, 5–6 Church Street, Twickenham, Middlesex TW1 3NJ
☎ 01–891 6070 Fax 01–891 4373

Owner *The Evro Publishing Co.*
Editor *Margaret Rand*
Circulation 40,000

FOUNDED 1983. MONTHLY. Unsolicited mss not welcome.

News and **Features** Wine, food and travel stories. Prospective contributors should approach in writing.

Wisden Cricket Monthly

6 Beech Lane, Guildford, Surrey GU2 5ES
☎ 0483 32573

Owner *Wisden Cricket Magazines Ltd*
Editor *David Frith*
Circulation *c.*42,000

FOUNDED 1979. MONTHLY. Very few uncommissioned articles are used, but would-be contributors are 'not discouraged'. Approach in writing.
Payment rates vary.

Woman

King's Reach Tower, Stamford Street, London SE1 9LS
☎ 01–261 5944
Telex 915748 Fax 01–261 5997

Owner *IPC Magazines Ltd*
Editor *David Durman*
Circulation 1.5 million

Recently celebrated its 50th anniversary in 1988.

Features Editor *Mary Frances* Maximum 1500 words.

Books Editor *Catherine Evans* Unsolicited mss not accepted.

Woman and Home

King's Reach Tower, Stamford Street, London SE1 9LS
☎ 01–261 5423 Telex 915748 MAGDIV G

Owner *IPC Magazines Ltd*
Editor *Sue Dobson*
Circulation 600,000

FOUNDED 1926. MONTHLY. Unsolicited contributions, of which 200 are received each month, are not welcome; prospective contributors are advised to write with ideas, plus photocopies of other published work or details of magazines to which they have contributed. Most freelance work is specially commissioned.

Features *Lyn Brookes*

Fiction *Kati Nichol* Short stories are usually submitted by agents, serials are always submitted by agents or publishers.

Other Departments Fashion, knitting, beauty, home, cookery and travel, all covered by staff writers and specially commissioned freelancers. No poetry is published. S.a.e essential for return of mss.
Payment *c.*£90 per 1000 words.

Woman's Journal

King's Reach Tower, Stamford Street, London SE1 9LS
☎ 01–261 6220
Telex 915748 MAGDIV G Fax 01–261 6023

Owner *IPC Magazines Ltd*
Editor *Laurie Purden* MBE

MONTHLY. Unsolicited non-fiction mss welcome.

Features *Jane Dowdeswell* Maximum 3000 words. Major features are generally commissioned but new ideas on all subjects

welcome.
Payment negotiable.

Fiction *Christie Hickman* Maximum 4000 words. Unsolicited material is not accepted; stories are mainly bought from agents and publishers direct.

Design and Homes *Jane Graining* **Fashion** *Alex Parnell* **Food** *Katie Stewart* **Health and Beauty** *Susan Irvine.*

Woman's Own

King's Reach Tower, Stamford Street,
London SE1 9LS
☎ 01–261 5474 Telex 915748 MAGDIV

Owner *IPC Magazines Ltd*
Editor *Bridget Rowe*
Circulation 967,852

WEEKLY. Prospective contributors should contact the features editor in writing in the first instance before making a submission.

Features *Sarah Crompton*

Fiction *Susan Oudot* Unsolicited fiction mss are not accepted, but there is an annual short story competition, for which the first prize in 1988 was £5000. Maximum for fiction 3500 words.

Woman's Realm

King's Reach Tower, Stamford Street,
London SE1 9LS
☎ 01–261 5708

Owner *IPC Magazines Ltd*
Editor *Ann Wallace*
Circulation 608,034

FOUNDED 1958. WEEKLY. Scope here for freelancers who should write in the first instance to the appropriate editor.

Features *Christine Evans* Interested in one-page human interest pieces or emotional features. 1200–2000 words. *Payment* at NUJ rates. Best vehicle for new freelancers is the half-page humorous slot, described as 'wry looks at family life', *c.*700 words. *Payment* £100.

Fiction *Sally Bowden* One short story and a serial instalment used every week. Aimed at an intelligent, family-minded woman aged 23 upwards. Very wide range; not much romance. A high standard of writing is essential. Serials are usually bought from agents or publishers but ideas for serials (with sample chapter) welcome. 1000–4000 words.
Payment £150 and upwards.

Woman's Story

12–18 Paul Street, London EC2A 4JS
☎ 01–247 8233
Telex 8951167 Fax 01–377 9709

Owner *Argus Consumer Publications*
Managing Editor *Veronica Dunn*
Circulation 57,754

MONTHLY sister magazine to *True Story* and *True Romances.*

Fiction Welcome; finished mss, not ideas, should be addressed to the editor. No serials. Receive 80–100 mss weekly. Subjects: romantic, domestic crises, marriage and job problems. Aimed at an older (25+), slightly more sophisticated market than its sister magazines. No explicit sex. Written in first-or third-person, possibly from a man's viewpoint. Twists of plot, uncertain or sad endings are frequent features. 1500–5000 words.
Payment on acceptance.

Woman's Weekly

King's Reach Tower, Stamford Street,
London SE1 9LS
☎ 01–261 6131

Owner *IPC Magazines Ltd*
Editor *Judith Hall*
Circulation 1.8 million

Mass market women's WEEKLY.

Features Editor *Eileen McCarroll* Focus on strong human interest stories, film and television personalities, as well as more traditional, homemaking subjects. Regularly use freelancers, but at this level tend to be experienced magazine journalists.

Fiction Editor *Gaynor Davies* Short stories 1500–5000 words; serials of 20,000–50,000 words. Guidelines for fiction writers - 'a strong romantic emotional sensual theme ... with a conflict not resolved until the end' (serials); short stories are more varied. Receive around 500 unsolicited stories a month.

Woman's World

25 Newman Street, London W1P 3HA
☎ 01–631 3939

Owner *IPC Magazines Ltd*
Editor *Kerry MacKenzie*
Circulation 207,150

FOUNDED 1977. MONTHLY. Freelance contributions are welcome, but it is best to write with ideas and samples of published work in the first instance. Approximately 150 unsolicited mss are received every week.

Workbox

40 Silver Street, Wiveliscombe,
Somerset TA4 2NY
☏ 0984 24033

Owner *Audrey Babington*
Editor *Audrey Babington*
Circulation 35,000

FOUNDED 1984. BI-ANNUAL. The magazine caters for the enthusiast and professional in all branches of needlecrafts.

Features covers a very wide range of needlecrafts but no 'how-to-make' items.

News Any items welcome, especially about new products, processes, etc., and events. S.a.e. essential.
Payment by arrangement.

The World of Interiors

234 King's Road, London SW3 5UA
☏ 01–351 5177 Fax 01–351 2794

Owner *Condé Nast*
Editor *Min Hogg*
Circulation 69,000

FOUNDED 1981. MONTHLY. Best approach by phone with an idea rather than by letter or on spec.

Features *Leslie Geddes-Brown* Approx. 75% of feature material is commissioned. Subjects tend to be found by us, but we are delighted to receive suggestions of houses unpublished elsewhere, and would love to find new writers. Always happy to look at sample writing, articles, etc.

World of Knitting

1–2 East Market Street, Newport, Gwent NP9 2AY
☏ 0633 58216

Owner *Sandra Williams*
Editor *Sandra Williams*
Circulation 29,114

FOUNDED 1983. Unsolicited mss welcome on knitting and related crafts. Prospective contributors are advised to make initial contact in writing, outlining proposal, and accompanied by illustration where appropriate. No fiction.

Features Up to 1000 words on yarns, knitwear fashions as well as 'how-to-make' pieces. Special features, e.g. picture knitting, Fair Isle patterns, etc., are particularly sought after.

News Reports up to 1000 words on knitting-related subjects.
Payment around £50 per 1000 words.

World Soccer

King's Reach Tower, Stamford Street,
London SE1 9LS
☏ 01–261 5636 Fax 01–261 5638

Owner *Websters Publications/IPC Magazines Ltd*
Editor *Keir Radnedge*

FOUNDED 1960. MONTHLY. Unsolicited material welcome but approach by phone or in writing would be preferable. News and features on world soccer.

Writers' Monthly

The Writer Ltd, 18–20 High Road,
London N22 6DN
☏ 01–888 1242

Owner *The Writer Ltd*
Contributing Editor *Joanne Mallabar*
Circulation 9,000

FOUNDED 1984. MONTHLY magazine (incorporating *The Writer*) aimed at freelance writers, both beginners and professionals. News and features of interest to writers.

Features Maximum 2000 words. 'Always on the look-out for new writers'.

News compiled in-house; very little scope for outside contributors.

Monthly short story competition open to subscribers, plus two major annual ones. The winning story is published in future editions of the magazine, subject to available space. Query letter with synopsis in the first instance. 'The main reason for material being rejected is usually because writers have not studied the magazine. Articles should be informative, practical and concise.'

Yachting Monthly

Room 2209, King's Reach Tower, Stamford Street,
London SE1 9LS
☏ 01–261 6040
Telex 915748 MAGDIV G Fax 01–261 6704

Owner *IPC Magazines Ltd*
Editor *Andrew Bray*
Circulation 48,360

FOUNDED 1906. MONTHLY magazine for yachting enthusiasts. Unsolicited mss are welcome, but between 50 and 80 are received each month. Prospective contributors should make initial contact in writing.

Features *Howard Cheedle* A wide range of features concerned with maritime subjects and cruising under sail; well-researched and innovative material always welcome, especially if accompanied by colour transparencies. Maximum 3000 words.
Payment maximum £76 per 1000 words.

News *Andrew Bray* News items up to a maximum of 500 words are received from a series of correspondents 'Around the Coast'.
Payment £5.03 per 100 words.

You and Your Barclaycard

Advertising Department, Barclaycard,
Northampton NN1 1SG
☎ 0604 252296 Fax 0604 253153

Owner *Barclaycard*
Editor *D. M. Shine*
Circulation 4–5 million

FOUNDED 1983. BI-MONTHLY. Practical product-oriented features, e.g. lighting, furniture, fashion, etc. Do not welcome unsolicited mss but will consider suggestions for future topics. Approach in writing in the first instance.

You Magazine (Mail on Sunday)

Northcliffe House, 2 Derry Street,
London W8 5EE
☎ 01–938 6000

Editor *Nicholas Gordon*

Lively, substantial colour supplement whose many feature articles are supplied entirely by freelance writers. These tend to be established magazine journalists: 'as far as we know there hasn't yet been a single case of an unsolicited feature ending in publication'. In such a competitive market there is a glut of talent anyway. On the other hand, always hoping to find new writers who understand their needs. Articles, whether general interest or issue based, are always people orientated, and interview based. This is the only general guideline in writing for the magazine; otherwise, it's a strong idea that counts. Send these to the **Commissioning Editor** *John Koski*.

Young Mother

PO Box 20, Owen Road, Diss, Norfolk IP22 3HH

Owner *Bounty Family Publications Ltd*
Editor *Alison Mackonodrie*
Circulation 67,500

FOUNDED 1986. BI-MONTHLY. Features information and articles of interest to families with young children aged 0–5 years. Unsolicited mss with s.a.e. welcome. Ideas in writing are preferred.

Features Maximum 1500 words.
Payment by negotiation.

Your Horse

Bretton Court, Bretton, Peterborough,
Cambs PE3 8DZ
☎ 0733 264666 Fax 0733 265515

Owner *EMAP Pursuit Publishing*
Editor & Publisher *Lesley Eccles*
Circulation 39,765

A magazine for all ages which deals with practical horsecare: the skills and problems involved in keeping or riding horses. They get a lot of unsolicited offerings from knowledgeable readers, some of which are used. But it's best to send ideas to the editor in the first instance.
Payment by negotiation.

Your Money

361A Upper Richmond Road West,
London SW14 8QN
☎ 01–392 1378 Fax 01–878 0341

Owner *Fredericks Place Holdings plc*
Editor *Jeanne Griffiths*
Circulation 40,000

FOUNDED 1987. BI-MONTHLY. News and features on the financial world. No unsolicited mss. Willing to discuss ideas. Contact either by phone or in writing.

Yours Newspaper

Apex House, Oundle Road,
Peterborough PE2 9NP
☎ 0733 555123 Fax 0733 312025

Owner *Choice Publications*
Editor *Neil Patrick*
Circulation 118,256

FOUNDED 1973. MONTHLY. Readership is in the age group of 55 plus and unsolicited mss are welcome.

Features Maximum 1000 words, and genuinely appealing to readership, would be considered.

Fiction One piece of fiction each month. Average *payment* for short story £70. Very rare that unsolicited submissions are accepted.

News Short newsy items (300–500 words) of interest to readership are welcome. *Payment* negotiable.

Words and Pictures

Writing for Sound and Screen

Historians of the British film industry look back with misty eyes to the great days of Ealing, a studio which, over twenty years, turned out some forty quality movies. Not all classics by any means but quintessentially home-grown productions which bear intermittent revival.

But another way of judging the Ealing achievement is to ask why it was that an accumulation of so much talent – the brightest and best producers, writers, directors and actors in British film making, so it was said – could not manage *more* in twenty years. What were so many clever chaps doing all that time, for heaven's sake?

Today, the same might be asked of British television and by the same process of inquiry. Yes, of course, there are wonderful programmes to be seen; even the occasional humdinger which clears the pubs before closing time. But on the most generous estimates, the total achievement cannot justify the welter of self congratulation which issues forth from the BBC and ITV and which seems to be taken seriously by all those who *still* refer to British television as the best in the world.

The BBC alone has an income of well over a thousand million pounds. How do they spend all that money? Not on writers, that's for sure. In fact, most of it seems to go on regurgitating old favourites.

Nostalgia is in fashion. Remember the great days when *Z Cars, Panorama* and *The Forsythe Saga* were gripping the nation? Colin McCabe devoted his South Bank Show lecture to the creative Sixties but then missed his point by showing programme extracts of such mind-numbing awfulness that it was impossible to understand what all the fuss was about.

Some vintage programmes are good enough to repeat – and repeat – and repeat, but how long the BBC can hope to pull audiences for yet another re-run of *Fawlty Towers* (aged 12), *The Good Life* (coming up for 15) and *Some Mothers Do 'Ave 'Em* (a doddery 16) is open to dispute. Probably for a long time given the feeble effort going into producing new programmes.

A **Writers' Guild** survey published in late 1988 showed a steady decline in the amount of original work appearing on our screens. In a sample week of 254 hours of programmes, the BBC showed only three and half hours of new drama with nearly ten and a half hours of repeats and non-original drama. The rest of the input consisted of game shows, imported programmes, news and current affairs, sport and variety.

The figures for ITV were much better with thirteen and a half hours of new material and three and a half hours of repeats but over a longer period the trend towards more repeats was unmistakable.

Last March, Michael Checkland, BBC Director General, acknowledged mounting criticism of the number of repeats with the announcement of a £7 million boost for drama and entertainment of which £5 million is to be allocated to independent production companies.

Here, if anywhere, are the mould breakers of television. Given their first impetus by the creation of Channel 4, the independents have thrived on government instructions to the

BBC and ITV to take 25 per cent of their programmes from outsiders by 1990.

The showcase for the independents is 'Film on Four', a commissioning slot for the best original drama on television, and source of quality, low-budget movies for the British cinema. That such films as *Wish You Were Here, My Beautiful Launderette, A Room With a View* and *Mona Lisa* reached the screen at all is thanks entirely to financial backing from Channel 4 (often short of 100 per cent, but enough to start the ball rolling) and the readiness of the independent producers to take risks.

Still it would be more encouraging if senior producers within the BBC and ITV showed an interest in new ideas and new talent.

Reporting in *The Guardian* on the last year's television jamboree at the Edinburgh Festival, Carl Sarler launched a blazing attack on the diehards of corny broadcasting:

> 'Not one word was spoken of music, musical comedy, revues, sketch shows, documentary comedy or comedy drama. And when one senior executive said the reason for the lack of new departures was a dearth of writing talent and that only 20 writers in the country can be used, none disagreed.
>
> 'That is, of course, palpable nonsense. The truth is that these people are scared to death of anything new, and especially of the work required by themselves to develop it. James Moir, for the BBC, claimed pride in their recent comedy record. Maybe with justification – but given his personal record of cavalier refusal to acknowledge, let alone read, new scripts, we can only assume he intends to run *Yes, Prime Minister* until Paul Eddington is as old as Churchill.'

The terrible irony, of course, is that while this mutual admiration society was in session, the Edinburgh Festival was showing off enough writing talent to keep the networks busy until the next conference of mutual backslappers.

The dearth of imagination shows most obviously in television comedy. While extravagant rewards are promised to those who can come up with a winning formula, there is little agreement on what is likely to make people laugh. Maybe the answer is to be found in the advice and information leaflets put out by the BBC:

> 'The laughs should arise naturally and logically from the interactions of character and plot, not from a string of gags and funny lines fired off into the blue. Where so many beginners go wrong is that they provide no situation: the characters are not at grips with each other over some matter that is important to them, in which something crucial is at stake. Famous comedy series like *Dad's Army, The Good Life, Porridge* and *Sorry* were very different, but they all had one thing in common: fundamentally they were about the serious matter of sheer survival in the teeth of perilous circumstances. This is what made them funny. Do not be seduced into following in the steps of somebody like, say, Roy Clarke since it needs great experience and tremendous skill to pull off something like *The Last of the Summer Wine*.'

The cynic might respond that what makes *The Last of the Summer Wine* exceptional is that it was one of the last original ideas to reach the comedy screen. Today, the secret of success seems to be to stick to the old ideas, preferably for actors who are already made famous by earlier situation comedies.

According to Dennis Main Wilson, famed producer of *The Goons, Hancock's Half Hour* and *Till Death Us Do Part*, the trouble with the way comedy is done now is that it is management-led instead of talent-led. 'It used to be management's job to support, now they dictate. More and more producers are just given formats to occupy.'

To illustrate his point, Main Wilson tells the story of a midday meeting in the BBC bar with a man called Sullivan.

> 'He was a day-crew scene-shifter, I knew him well. He bought me an unusually large drink and shoved some papers into my hand. 'Read that,' he said. I went away and read it, and when I came back I said, 'I'll buy it.'
>
> 'I don't think a modern producer could even say that; he'd have to refer it round and round the departments and it might never get bought. Well, it was the first episode of *Citizen Smith*. And John Sullivan went on to write *Dear John*, and *Only Fools and Horses*. Now when he comes into that bar, he buys all his mates drinks.'

That comedy is expensive to produce (£70,000 to £100,000 an hour) deters budget controllers from taking chances. For the same reason they are liable to chop series which are not immediately popular.

The prospects of success are improved enormously if the writer is in an alliance with an agent who specialises in TV (see **Agents** listing). But agents who stay in business are very choosy about their clients. Not one of them will move a step on behalf of a dubious or untried talent.

The way forward for comedy writers could be eased considerably if there were more opportunities to try out ideas and to test viewer reaction. This valuable function used to be performed by *Comedy Playhouse*, a weekly slot for pilot episodes, which the BBC unaccountably axed some years ago. First timers should campaign for its revival. And every writer must wish for an end to the tyranny of the thirty-minute rule. That situation comedy is in such a poor way is surely not entirely unrelated to the problem of having to squeeze every story line into a half hour. At the moment, the schedules are as rigid as a school timetable and every bit as stultifying.

It is much the same for drama though the BBC in Birmingham deserves credit for commissioning eight writers new to television for the 'Debut on Two' slot. A three-month search for scripts including workshops in six cities attracted 3500 entries. Whether or not the project will be repeated is presently unclear but these competitive schemes are attractive to sponsors (the 'Debut on Two' had support from Barclays) and are likely to crop up elsewhere on the BBC or on other channels.

On a wider front it would be churlish to ignore the satellite networks. But it is still hazardous to predict what benefits, if any, they will bring to writers. It is argued that even if all the new channels survive (by no means a certainty), they will make little difference to programme makers here because satellite and cable output will consist predominantly of American imports.

This must be taken as the accountant's option – buying in programmes is at least two-thirds cheaper than origination. But viewers may not be ready to cooperate. Audience research suggests that indigenously produced programmes of high quality are far more popular than the drop-offs from the Hollywood conveyor belt.

A deluge of inferior product, from home or overseas, will have an adverse effect on advertising revenue which in turn will force the programme makers to mend their ways. This is what happened when the BBC and ITV began to share the screen in the mid 1950s. Viewers were thrown a lot of rubbish early on but over a period standards did improve. Does anyone argue that television today on four channels is not infinitely better than the television of thirty years ago when it was dominated by a single public service channel?

Maybe the satellites will take advantage of the new EEC-backed fund which is to allocate £1.5 million a year to European writers of television and film scripts. The aim is to reverse the domination of American productions. How the money is to be distributed still has to be decided but in traditional Common Market style a start has been made by advertising for an administrator. At £20,000 a year he is likely to make more out of the project than any of his clients.

For the newcomer, an increasingly popular way in to television script writing is via training and promotional videos, directly commissioned by industry. Budgets are tight and there is little opportunity for imaginitive writing (business clients are notoriously conservative). But new writers are welcome and a few corporate videos can do wonders for a beginner's reputation.

The problems for writers involved in corporate television is the absence of any guidelines on payment. No doubt **The Writers' Guild** and other professional associations will soon have something to say about this. Meanwhile, the writer must fend for himself. Since he is working to a tight brief, usually with material supplied by the client, he is expected to surrender copyright. There is therefore no question of repeat fees or royalties. But if the production company is honest and the client is sensible enough to want a professional writer, the rewards can be up to the level of network television and far beyond that of radio.

A guess at a standard rate would be £2000 plus for an hour-long programme. Some writers prefer to value their time on a daily rate and this too is generally acceptable.

If a writer and production company have not previously worked together it is as well to ask for an advance on payment to show goodwill. Some production companies with respectable client lists are nonetheless run on a shoestring. They are not above telling their accounts departments that when it comes to payments, writers are last in the pecking order.

The next step from corporate television might be into drama documentaries (though here the writer who is his own director has the best chance of success) or light entertainment.

Another favoured point of entry is copywriting for TV commercials. Working within a 30-second time slot is not at all a bad training for visual storytelling.

Radio Drama

Whatever happens to television, BBC radio is likely to remain the biggest single market for writers. In addition to special reports, story readings and talks, Radios 3 and 4 transmit some five hundred new plays every year – fifty times more than the National Theatre and the Royal Shakespeare Company put together. This output amounts to an annual 96 hours on Radio 3 (1.5 per cent of the total) and 852 hours on Radio 4 (11 per cent). In addition, the BBC World Service puts out one hundred and thirty plays a year, mostly adaptations of stage and television productions, interspersed with an increasing number of original plays. No other country does so many radio plays. The main slots on Radio 4 are:

The Monday Play (repeated Saturday afternoons) 75 or 90 minutes or sometimes longer. Opportunities for original writing on complex themes. Also a showcase for classic stage plays and occasional dramatisation of novels.

Saturday Night Theatre (repeated Monday afternoons) 75 or 90 minutes.
Family entertainment with a strong narrative line.

The Afternoon Play (Wednesday and Thursday) 45 to 55 minutes.
A balanced diet of original entertainment and demanding plays.

Thirty Minute Play (Tuesday afternoon)
Drama equivalent of the short story.

At least seventy new writers achieve production each year. But competition is stiff. Richard Imison, chief script editor and deputy head of radio drama, receives up to 10,000 scripts a year, of which only 5 per cent make the grade.

The consolation is that all submissions are paid the compliment of serious and often valuably constructive criticism. There are four full-time and eight part-time readers who study all scripts that are remotely viable. Each week a shortlist is drawn up and discussed at a Thursday morning editorial meeting. Decisions are made then about who gets commissioned and what goes into what slot.

The BBC is enormously helpful in advising writers how to structure and present their work. Various publications are available from any of seven production centres (see BBC TV listings) and occasional seminars for aspiring playwrights are run by the Script Unit.

Last year the BBC launched a Young Playwrights Festival with two weeks of radio drama placings set aside for writers aged between 15 and 30. It is too early to predict the future of the project but there is strong support for making it an annual event.

For every newcomer the critical pointer to success is an understanding of the potential and limitations of sound. Even established writers fall into the error of including too many characters (confusing the listener particularly if they talk over each other) or of failing to ring the changes in pace and location. The longer the sequence the more difficult it is to sustain interest.

Probably the best advice to newcomers is encompassed in the list of questions script readers must consider before recommending a play.

- Is it basically a good story?
- If it is, are the characters and dialogue equally good?
- If they are, will it make good *radio*?
- If it will, to which spot is it best suited?
- If the script is viable on all the counts listed above, is it the right length? If not, can it be cut or expanded without artistic loss? If so, where? Even if the script is still viable, how might it be improved? Is the beginning sufficiently compelling? Is the cast too big? Does it maintain dramatic tension? Is everything that should be conveyed sufficiently well planted in the *dialogue*?
- If it's a good story, well told in radio terms, are there any special problems? (e.g. controversial themes liable to misunderstanding by the audience; foreign settings calling for difficult or expensive casting; technical backgrounds likely to attract expert criticism; etc.)
- If the play passes on all these counts, it's obviously a strong possibility for broadcast. How could the author make it *better*?

To start on the right side of the script reader is to follow certain basic rules of presentation – rules which apply with equal force to any form of script writing.

- Use a typewriter or word processor. Handwritten scripts are hardly ever considered.
- Type on one side of the paper only. (A4 size preferably.)
- Make sure all the pages are firmly fastened and numbered consecutively.
- Use plenty of spacing.
- Put your name and address on the title page.
- Give names of characters in full throughout the script and clearly separate them from speech.
- Clearly distinguish technical information such as location changes and sound effects from speech.

- Attach a synopsis of the play to the completed script together with a full cast list and notes on the main characters.

With at least a thousand submissions under consideration at any one time, nobody should expect a quick response. A two or three months wait is common even for a straight rejection. A further wait suggests that the writer has become part of the BBC's internal politics. Somebody for some reason is nervous of saying 'yes' but reluctant to say 'no'. Early in his career when Alan Bennett sent a play to the BBC (television in this case) they took so long to think about it that when an acceptance did come through the play had been on in the West End for six months.

Radio Features and Comedy

Beyond drama, to talks and features, there is another crowd of writers jostling for attention. But they have more of a problem in identifying the best person to contact with a proposal. Most of the production centres have features editors and in London the heads of department or their minions will pass on an idea to whatever producer they think might be interested.

However, long-established programmes like *Woman's Hour* or *You and Yours* have their own pecking order of contributors. The editors do not seem to spend much time assessing material from unknown outsiders. Much depends on sheer good fortune – catching the right producer with the right idea at the right time. It also helps to boast expert knowledge. The views of everyman are little appreciated except on *Any Answers*.

Comedy programmes like *Week Ending* and *The News Headlines* are in the market for short sketches. Success here can be an entrée to the world of comedy series where, for once, there is a dearth of good material. But if demand is high so is the failure rate. Perhaps the broadcasters are their own worst enemies in calling for more and yet more situation comedies – a patch of humour which has been so heavily cultivated as to be close to exhaustion. Iconoclastic humour in the tradition of *The Goons* is now a rarity though when it is tried, as in the marvellous *Radio Active* series, the BBC achieves its declared objective of reaching a younger audience.

Morning Story is a great radio institution which relies exclusively on outside contributors. With a quarter-hour slot, anything of more than two and a half thousand words is overwritten. A strong plot stands a better chance with the editor than impressive writing. Steer clear of controversial topics.

Specialist journalists who are not career broadcasters can often find themselves a comfortable niche within the BBC, in sports, say, or current affairs where they are not so much reporters as professional interviewers. The call for expertise also attracts certain voluble academics.

Educational broadcasting is thick with specialists but is ever hungry for more. Despite having to stick with a narrow curriculum and to work on pathetic budgets, programmes for schools and colleges are a good training ground for writers and presenters.

So too is local radio, though if anything, funds are tighter than in education. The recent cuts imposed by the BBC – up to ten per cent over the next five years – will leave many local stations floundering. Independent radio is in not much better shape with many stations running at a loss or barely breaking even. Still, they do attract enthusiastic and hard-working staff who are open to ideas and willing to take chances.

Basic Pay

Radio, Television and Film

The Writers' Guild, The Society of Authors and **The National Union of Journalists** have led the way in negotiating minimum fees for writers of radio and television scripts. Full details of their agreement with the broadcasting authorities can be obtained from these bodies (see **Professional Associations** Section) but the following is a guideline to the offers that writers might expect from the BBC and ITV.

Radio

- A beginner in radio drama should receive at least £957 for a 60-minute script. For an established writer – one who has three or more plays to his credit – the minimum rate goes up to £1455.
- Fees for dramatisations range from 65 to 85 per cent of the full drama rate depending on the degree of original material and dialogue.
- An attendance payment of £24.25 per production is paid to established writers.
- For talks, the level of fees starts at £9.15 per minute for script only and £12.45 per minute for script and read.
- Features and documentaries begin at £16.50 per minute with a minimum fee of £115.50.
- Higher fees are limited to writer's experience and to 'the particular circumstances of the engagement'.
- Fees for short stories start at a beginner's rate of £82 for 15 minutes rising to £107.50 for writers who have contributed six or more stories.
- Repeat fees are nearly always part of an agreement but terms vary according to the type of production.
- Basic rates for news reporting are covered by an NUJ agreement with the BBC and the Association of Independent Radio Contractors.
- For the BBC, news reports start at £25.10 for up to two minutes, plus £5.65 for each extra minute on network radio. Local radio is £12.85 for up to two minutes, plus £4.62 for each extra minute.
- In the commercial sector, news reports make £13.50 for the first two minutes and £4.50 a minute thereafter.
- There are special day rates and separately negotiated fees for specialist reporting, such as sports coverage.

Television

For a sixty-minute teleplay, the BBC will pay an established writer at least £4950; a beginner £3145. The corresponding figures for ITV are £5824 for the established writer; £4139 for a writer new to television, but with a solid reputation in books, film, radio or theatre; and £3967 for other writers.

- The day rates for attendance at read-throughs and rehearsals is £45 for the BBC and £44 for ITV.
- The NUJ agreement on news reporting guarantees BBC rate to freelancers of £30.94 for up to two minutes and £7.68 for each extra minute. The ITV rate is tied to a minimum of £32.61.

Feature Films

An agreement between **The Writers' Guild, The British Film and Television Producers' Association** and **The Independent Programme Producers' Association** allows for a minimum writer's fee of £20,000 on a high-budget feature film (in excess of £1½ million) and £12,000 on a lower-budget movie. Writers can also expect additional TV fees to cover transmission at home and abroad.

The contrast with Hollywood rates is instructive. There, the writer gets a development deal: money to write a first draft and a set of revisions. The Minimum Basic Agreement is set at $35,000 for that task, with three times that if the picture is made. Established writers will get six-figure sums as up front guarantees. Screenwriters can earn more than £1 million, depending on their track record and their agent's bravado.

For television, the gap between what British and American writers can expect to earn is as wide as the Atlantic. In the States, the Writers' Guild minima are $6800 for an idea, $10,017 for a script and $1000 a day for revisions. For the first repeats of their shows, writers get half as much again, while for foreign sales, the return is 35 per cent.

And last year, they went on strike for more!

National and Regional Television

The BBC

BBC Television

Television Centre, London W12 7RJ
☏ 01–743 8000

Managing Editor News/Current Affairs *Chris Cramer*
Editor, Current Affairs *Tony Hall*
Head of Drama *Peter Goodchild*
Features & Documentaries *Colin Cameron*
Light Entertainment *James Moir*
Comedy *Gareth Gwenlan*
Music & Arts *Leslie Megahey*
Religious Programmes *John Whale*
Children's Programmes *Anna Home*
Series & Serials *Peter Cregeen*
Community Programmes *Tony Laryea*

BBC Breakfast Time

Wood Lane, London W12 8QT
☏ 01–576 7506

Editor *Bob Wheaton*
Contact *Forward Planning*

BBC TV Documentary Features

Kensington House, Richmond Way, London W14 0AX
☏ 01–743 1272

Managing Editor Documentary Features *Hugh Purcell*

BBC TV Leeds (North East)

Broadcasting Centre, Woodhouse Lane, Leeds LS2 9PX
☏ 0532 441188

Since the reorganisation of the BBC television regions in 1987, Leeds is now the head of the North East region. Though presently its major production is the nightly news magazine programme *Look North*, there are plans to expand the repertoire. No drama department.

Features Editor *Mark Roland*

News Editor *John Lingham*

BBC TV Midlands

Broadcasting Centre, Pebble Mill Road, Birmingham B5 7QQ
☏ 021–414 8888

Home of the Pebble Mill Studio.

Head of Drama *Michael Wearing* OUTPUT *Run For the Lifeboat; Lovebirds; Air Base; Rainbow.*

News & Current Affairs *Richard Thompson*

Also makers of one-offs like *Cool It* with Phil Cool; *Ebony*, the black magazine series: *Top Gear* and *Farming*. *Farming's* **Editor** *Mike Fitzgerald* will seriously consider unsolicited material if well researched.

BBC TV North East (Newcastle upon Tyne)

Broadcasting House, 54 New Bridge Street, Newcastle upon Tyne NE99 2NE
☏ 091–232 1313

Although Leeds is now the headquarters of the North East region, Newcastle continues to make its own programmes.

Features Editor *John Mappleback* Features, documentaries and drama come under this department. Very little drama is made, but there is a strong feature-making unit, particularly for programmes of direct local relevance. They make forty 30-minute programmes a year, some of which are nationally broadcast.

News and Current Affairs *John Bird*

BBC TV North West

New Broadcasting House, Oxford Road, Manchester M60 1SJ
☏ 061-236 8444

Network production in Manchester breaks down into 4 departments: features, children's, sports and entertainments.

Features (General Programmes) *Brass Tacks John Drury.*
Open Air Editor Sue Woodward

Children's Editor *Edward Pugh* No childrens' drama – light entertainment for kids, like *It's Wicked* and *The Saturday Picture Show.*

Entertainments in a fragmented state at the moment. OUTPUT *No Limits*

Executive Producer, Independent Productions *Peter Ridsdale Scott* Deals with proposals from independent producers (which the BBC is increasingly using), though not direct from writers alone.

BBC TV Northern Ireland

Broadcasting House, 25-7 Ormeau Avenue,
Belfast BT2 8HQ
☎ 0232 244400

News & Current Affairs (Acting) *Keith Baker*
Drama *Robert Cooper*
General Programmes *Ian Kennedy* OUTPUT *A Taste of Ireland* (food series)
Religious Programmes *Rev. James Skelly*
Series: *Spotlight* **Editor** *Andy Colman*
Sport *Jim Neilly*

BBC TV (Norwich) East

St Catherine's Close, All Saints Green,
Norwich NR1 3ND
☎ 0603 619331

The second centre (after Elstree) of the BBC TV South and East region. They occasionally make network programmes; Norwich is more than a regional opt-out station simply making its own local news programmes. Very locally oriented scripts should be sent to their small features unit.

Features *Robert Bufton*

BBC TV Nottingham (BBC Midlands)

York House, Mansfield Road, Nottingham
☎ 0602 472395

An opt-out station from BBC TV Midlands Birmingham office, and served by the programmes made in Birmingham. Nottingham makes local news only.

BBC TV Plymouth (South West)

Broadcasting House, Seymour Road,
Plymouth PL3 5BD
☎ 0752 229201

Programmes for the South West region are made in the regional network centre in Bristol. Plymouth makes one 'opt-out' programme for its own region a week. Direct mss to the Bristol office.

BBC Scotland (Aberdeen)

Beechgrove Terrace, Aberdeen AB9 2ZT
☎ 0224 625233 Telex 739622

No real market. BBC Aberdeen make features, but these are nearly always commissioned.

BBC Scotland (Dundee)

12–13 Dock Street, Dundee DD1 4BT
☎ 0382 25025

News only.

BBC Scotland (Edinburgh)

Broadcasting House, 5 Queen Street,
Edinburgh EH2 1JF
☎ 031–225 3131

All programmes made in Glasgow.

BBC TV Scotland (Glasgow)

Broadcasting House, Queen Margaret Drive,
Glasgow G12 8DG
☎ 041–330 2345

Head of Drama *Bill Bryden* 'A strong commitment to drama production.' Previous productions in the *Play on One* slot: *Down Where the Buffalo Go; The Dumroamin' Rising; The Dark Room.* Also, the award winning serial *Tutti Frutti.*

Head of Features *David Martin* encompasses the old Light Entertainment department, plus documentaries.

Special Projects *Desmond Wilcox: The Visit.* No children's programmes except those made in the Gaelic department.

Head of Gaelic *Ken McQuarrie.*

BBC South and East

BBC Elstree Centre, Clarendon Road,
Borehamwood, Herts WD6 1JF
☎ 01–953 6100

Home of the history and archaeology unit,

Global Report and the general programmes unit which makes leisure and one-off programmes. No drama production.

History & Archaeology *Bruce Norman* *Timewatch* and *The Great Journeys* series.

Global Report *Barry Dixon* Documentary programmes on, for example, Third World issues. Usually devised and made in-house.

General Programmes *Peter Massey* OUTPUT *Mastermind, Masterteam,* chess and bridge programmes, and *Lifeline.*

BBC TV South West

Broadcasting House, Whiteladies Road, Clifton, Bristol BS8 2LR
☎ 0272 732211

Bristol no longer has a drama department, but does have a strong features department, and houses the BBC's much praised natural history unit.

Features *Daniel Wolf* OUTPUT has included *Antiques Roadshow, Scott Free, Whicker's World, Probation, Under Sail, Mountain Men* and *The Healing Arts.*

Natural History *Andrew Neal* Programmes have included *Kingdom of the Ice Bear, The Living Planet, The Living Isles* and *Wildlife on One.* Specialist writers only.

BBC TV Southampton (South West)

South Western House, Canute Road, Southampton SO9 1PF
☎ 0703 226201

Programmes for the South West region are made in Bristol, to whom all mss and programme ideas should be sent. Southampton makes one weekly local opt-out programme only.

BBC Wales (Cardiff)

Broadcasting House, Llantrisant Road, Llandaff, Cardiff CF5 2YQ
☎ 0222 564888

News & Current Affairs *Gwilym Owen*

General Programmes *Huw Brian Williams*

Children's Programmes *Dyfed Glynn Jones* BBC Wales also make programmes for S4C in Welsh.

BBC Wales (Bangor)

Broadcasting House, Meirion Road, Bangor LL57 2BY
☎ 0248 362214

News only.

Independent Television

Anglia Television

Anglia House, Norwich NR1 3JG
☎ 0603 615151
Telex 97424 Fax 0603 631032

The Company's subsidiary, Anglia Films, produces drama series and films for the ITV network. Current productions include the Malcolm Bradbury story *Anything More Would Be Greedy, Goldeneye* and *The Chief.* Other networked programmes include the *Survival* wildlife documentaries, *Go Fishing, Knightmare* (computer game), *Anything Goes* (leisure & travel), *About Anglia* (news), *Anglia Reports* (current affairs), *Cross Question* (political), *Farming Diary*, Folio (arts).

Managing Director, Anglia Films *Graeme McDonald*

Controller News Programmes *Jim Wilson*

Political Editor *Malcolm Allsop*

Border Television

Television Centre, Durranhill, Carlisle, Cumbria CA1 3NT
☎ 0228 25101 Telex 64122

Contact *Paul Corley* (Programme Controller)

News Editor *Lis Howell*

Documentaries *Paul Corley* Most scripts are provided in-house but are occasionally commissioned. Writers should not submit written work apart from notes before their ideas have been fully discussed. In last couple of years, Border has greatly increased its programme production, including children's television – features and documentaries rather than drama. Also contributes programmes to Channel 4: *The Drove, Sheer Genius, The Writing on the Wall, The Hills Are Alive.*

Central Independent Television

East Midlands Television Centre, Lenton Lane, Nottingham NG7 2NA
☎ 0602 863322 Telex 377696

Contact *Christopher Walker* (Head of Scripts)

'Although some television companies ask to see a synopsis first, the Script Unit always prefers to read scripts from new writers. However, it is rare for a finished script to be purchased – writers are normally assessed for possible future commissions.' A few single plays are made by the company, but the bulk of the Drama output takes the form of series and serials. The Light Entertainment department makes situation comedy series, and other shows which need sketches and one liners. Young People's Programmes include single plays for the *Dramarama* slot, serials and light entertainment. The Script Unit welcomes scripts and tries to read everything which comes in. 'However, this process does take time, so writers should not expect an instant response.'

Channel 4

60 Charlotte Street, London W1P 2AX
☎ 01–631 4444

Launched in November 1982, Channel 4 broadcasts 135 hours of programmes a week, all of them made by independent producers or other independent television companies. *Brookside* is one such programme and was rumoured to become Britain's first four-nightly soap in 1989. Also in 1989 came rumours of Channel 4 being forced into competition with ITV companies, which would put Channel 4's remit under considerable strain. Channel 4 does not make any of its great diversity of programmes, except for the weekly *Right to Reply, Comment, Book Choice,* and the role of its commissioning editors is to sift through proposals for programmes and see interesting projects through to broadcast.

Director of Programmes *Liz Forgan*
Controller of Factual Programmes *John Willis*
Controller of Arts & Entertainment *Mike Bolland*
Head of Fiction *David Rose*
Education *Gwynn Pritchard*
Drama Series *Peter Ansorge*
Young People *Stephen Garrett*
Multi Cultural *Farrukh Dhondy*
Documentaries *Peter Moore*
Current Affairs *David Lloyd*

Channel Television

The Television Centre, St Helier,
Jersey, Channel Isles
☎ 0534 73999

Chairman *John Riley*

News, current affairs and documentaries provide the bulk of programmes. Make programmes for the network. Ideas are assessed but only commissioned after sale is made to the network.

Director of Programmes *Michael Lucas* OUTPUT Regular weekday magazine programme *Channel Report*; monthly religious magazine programme *Link Up*; series for Channel 4 on islands throughout Great Britain, *Great British Isles.*

Grampian Television

Queen's Cross, Aberdeen AB9 2XJ
☎ 0224 646464

Grampian Television serves an area stretching from Fife to Shetland.

Documentaries *Edward Brocklebank* OUTPUT *The Blood Is Strong* – a trilogy of hour long programmes for Channel 4 on the Gaelic Scots and their fortunes at home and abroad.

News & Current Affairs *Alistair Gracie*

Other areas of production, light entertainment, schools, children's and religious programmes, come under **Head of Production** *George Mitchell.* These tend to be for regional broadcast only. Light entertainment is usually of the chat show/quiz show sort, and children's programmes are both light entertainment and educational.

Granada Television

Granada TV Centre, Manchester M60 9EA
☎ 061–832 7211

Director of Programmes *Steve Morrison*

Drama *Sally Head* Drama series, film production. OUTPUT *Small World; Game, Set and Match* (13-part film); *After the War; The Return of Sherlock Holmes; The Magic Toyshop.* Opportunities for freelance writers have decreased of late but will consider mss from professional writers. All mss to Head of Scripts.

Features *Andrew McLaughlin*

Light Entertainment *David Liddiment* OUTPUT *The Krypton Factor; Busman's Holiday.* Unlikely to be opportunities for the freelance writer.

Arts *David Boulton*

News & Current Affairs *Ray Fitzwalter*

Sport *Paul Doherty*

HTV Wales

TV Centre, Cardiff CF5 6XJ
☏ 0222 590590

Productions sought with an authentic Welsh dimension.

News *Bob Symonds*
Features *Cenwyn Edwards*
Drama/Fiction *Graham Jones*
Light Entertainment *Peter Elias Jones*

Documentaries *Cenwyn Edwards* OUTPUT: Drama *Wall of Tyranny; Ballroom; Better Days.* Documentaries *To Ride a Wild Horse; The Pity of War.* Light Entertainment *Tom Jones, Born To Be Me.* Health series *Stress.*

HTV West

Television Centre, Bath Road, Bristol BS4 3HG
☏ 0272 778366

Head of News & Current Affairs *Steve Matthews*

There are no heads of departments as such (unlike its sister company HTV Wales).

Director of Programmes *Derek Clark*

Strong local programme making in all departments has included feature programmes like *Along the Cotswold Way* and *The Royal Forest of Dean.*

London Weekend Television

South Bank Television Centre, Kent House, Upper Ground, London SE1 9LT
☏ 01–261 3434 Telex 91823

Controller of Entertainment *Marcus Plantin*
Controller of Drama and Arts *Nick Elliott*
Head of Arts *Melvyn Bragg*
Controller of Features & Current Affairs *Jane Hewland*

Makers of weekend entertainment programmes like *You Bet, Surprise Surprise, Me and My Girl, Hot Metal.* Drama series such as *London's Burning*; also *The South Bank Show* and *Aspel & Company.* Provides a large proportion of the network's drama and light entertainment, and is a major supplier to Channel 4.

Scottish Television

Cowcaddens, Glasgow G2 3PR
☏ 041–332 9999

Controller of News, Sport & Current Affairs *David Scott*
Controller of Features *Alistair Moffat*
Controller of Drama *Robert Love*
Controller of Entertainment *Sandy Ross*

'Encouragingly, an increasing number of STV programmes are networked, and seen nationally. The detective series *Taggart*; the popular series *Take the High Road*; network series *Bookie*; *The Campbells* (a co-production with Canadian television) and a series of children's plays which are part of the *Dramarama* series.

Sianel Pedwar Cymru (Welsh 4th Channel)

Clos Sophia, Cardiff CF1 9XY
☏ 0222 343421 Telex 497146 Pedwar G

Deputy Programme Controller *Deryk Williams*

S4C commissions some four and a half hours of programmes from independent producers each week, to be produced in Welsh. Demand exists for drama scripts, comedy and documentary programmes.

Thames Television

Thames Television House, 306 Euston Road, London NW1 3BB
☏ 01–387 9494

Head of Factual Programmes *Roger Bolton*
Controller Drama *Lloyd Shirley*
Controller Features *Catherine Freeman*
Head of Comedy *James Gilbert*
Head of Variety *John Fisher*
Controller of Light Entertainment *John Howard Davies*
Head of News and Current Affairs *Barrie Sales*

Perhaps the strongest of drama production departments: *Minder, London Embassy, The Fear, Rumpole of the Bailey, The Bill, Hannay.* Light Entertainment: *The Benny Hill Show, The Des O'Connor Show, Give Us a Clue, After Henry, All at No 20, Home James, Strike It Lucky.* Documentaries and features: *Unknown Chaplin, A Source of Innocent Merriment, The Mikado, Take 6 Cooks, Mavis on 4, Catherine.* Children's programmes: *Rainbow, Sooty, Splash, Creepie Crawlies, The Gemini Factor.*

TSW – Television South West

Derry's Cross, Plymouth PL1 2SP
☏ 0752 663322 Telex 45566

Head of News *Richard Myers*
Head of Documentaries *Frank Wintle*
Features/Drama/Light Entertainment *Paul*

Stewart Laing

Network OUTPUT has included the adult educational series *Food: Fad or Fact?, Three Score Years and Then?*, and a five-part series on architectural oddities and follies entitled *Bats in the Belfry*. Other documentaries: *Surcouf – Diving to Disaster; A Head of Time* and *Affairs of the Hart*, an hour-long documentary on stag hunting. TV's only canine quiz show called *That's My Dog*. For Channel 4 a drama entitled *Someday Man*. Young people's programmes: *Look and See*, and *Gus Honeybun's Magic Birthdays*.

TVS Television

Television Centre, Northam,
Southampton SO9 5HZ
☎ 0703 634211
Telex 477217 Fax 0703 221598

Contact *Graham Benson*, (Controller of Drama), *Corinne Cartier* (Script & Development Executive)

Controller Entertainment *Gill Stribling-Wright*
Head of Features *John Miller*
Children's Programmes *Nigel Pickard*
Head of Religious Programmes *Andrew Bau*
Local Documentaries *Anthony Howard*
Youth Programming *John Dale*
Head of News & Sport *David Morris Jones*

Full range of regional and network ITV programmes from drama to documentary, children's programmes and light entertainment. OUTPUT: *A Guilty Thing Surprised* and *Shake Hands Forever* both by Ruth Rendell; *Gentlemen and Players* (drama series for ITV); *Mandela* (Channel 4 film); *That's Love* (situation comedy); *Tahiti Witness* and *Inside the Bank of England* (networked documentaries); *Mr Majeika* (children's series); *Americas Cup* (sailing series for Channel 4); *Frocks on the Box* (networked fashion series). Keen to encourage new writing as far as possible. Only look at unsolicited mss passed through literary agents, independent production companies, etc.

Tyne Tees Television Limited

The Television Centre, City Road,
Newcastle upon Tyne NE1 2AL
☎ 091–261 0181 Telex 53279

Director of Programmes *Geraint Davies*
Controller of Entertainment Programmes *Trish Kinane*
Factual Programmes *Jim Manson*
News and Sport *Dave Picken*
Religious Programmes *Paul Black*

Programme OUTPUT has included *Northern Life* (news magazine); *Extra Time* (sport); *Commercial Break* (business); *Crosswits* (quiz); *Kellyvision* (children's); *Morning Worship* (religious).

Ulster Television

Havelock House, Ormeau Road,
Belfast BT7 1EB
☎ 0232 328122 Telex 74654

News & Current Affairs *Gary Gillespie*
Sports Editor *Colm McWilliams*

General programme planning comes under the office of **Assistant Controllers** *Michael Beattie* and *Andrew Crockart*. Michael Beattie is particularly responsible for current affairs; Andrew Crockart for documentary features. Drama, light entertainment, children's and religious programme ideas can be addressed to either. Credits include *Shadow in a Landscape*, a dramatised documentary on the life and work of Irish impressionist painter Roderic O'Connor; *After the Gold*, a profile of the Belfast-born pianist, Barry Douglas; *Celtic Church in Ireland*; the networked series *Sing Out*; a series of book programmes, *The Write Stuff; No Poor Parish*, a series of documentaries.

Yorkshire Television

Television Centre, Leeds LS3 1JS
☎ 0532 438283 Telex 557232

Editor *Richard Gregory*
Controller of Drama *Keith Richardson*

Drama series, film productions, studio plays and long-running series like *Emmerdale Farm*. Always looking for strong writing in these areas, and make great use of agents to find it. Around 20 unsolicited mss received weekly. Unknowns should submit at least the first act, ideally the first episode if submitting a series, and synopsis.

Documentaries *Grant McKee* Opportunities are rare here, as scripts are usually provided by producers. However, adaptations of published work put to the department as a documentary subject are considered. OUTPUT has included *First Tuesday*.

Light Entertainment *Vernon Lawrence* Comedy series like *Home to Roost* and *Singles*. Opportunities for writers of series/episodes in theory, but in reality there is a well-established circle of professionals in this area which it is difficult to infiltrate. Best approach is through a good agent.

Regional Features *David Lowen* Documentaries and special features. No scripts, ideas only. Previous OUTPUT has included *Calendar Commentary, Calendar Lunchtime Live, You and E.Y.E., Enterprize '88.*

National Radio

BBC Radio (News and current affairs)

Broadcasting House, London W1A 1AA
☎ 01–580 4468

Editor News and Current Affairs Radio *Jenny Abramsky*

RADIO 4 EDITORS **Kaleidoscope** *Richard Bannerman* **Today** *Phil Harding* **The World at One/The World This Weekend** *Martin Cox* **PM** *Roger Mosey* **Woman's Hour** *Clare Selerie-Grey* **The World Tonight** *Margaret Budy* **Motoring Unit** *Irene Mallis* **Week Ending** *Contact the producer* **You and Yours** *Ken Vass.*
RADIO 3 **Contact** *Ann Winder* at Room 8053, Broadcasting House. Features, Arts and Education department welcomes either finished mss or written ideas for 20- or 40-minute talks and documentaries for broadcast on the BBC's 'classical music station'.
RADIO 2 There are no general opportunities for original work, but welcomes and uses contributions from outside writers to existing series. These change with the seasons, but presently include **The News Huddlines** *Dirk Maggs* (Producer).

BBC Radio (fiction and drama opportunities)

Broadcasting House, London W1A 1AA
☎ 01–580 4468

Contact *Duncan Minshull* (Short stories on Radio, incl. Morning Story), *Enyd Williams* (Afternoon play, 30 minutes of Series & Serials) *Ned Chaillet* (Saturday Night Theatre, R3 Studio 3, Stage Classics) *Caroline Rafael* (30 minute Play, Monday Play).

Contributions to 'Morning Story' should be sent to *Duncan Minshull*, 'Morning Story', Room 6114, at the above address. The evening drama slots on Radio 4 are: 'Classical Serial' (for obvious reasons not a good bet for new writing); 'Thirty Minutes of Series and Serials' (open to new plays); 'Saturday Night Theatre' (open to new writing of either 75 or 90 minutes length). Scripts should be sent to *Enyd Williams* at Room 6087, although it should be noted that currently they are fully scheduled for the next two years and any incoming mss have to have 'stunning potential', 'Fear on Four' (open to new plays) scripts to *Richard Imison* (**Deputy Head Radio Drama**). Probably the best bet for new plays on Radio 4 is 'Afternoon Play'. Its producers are too numerous to list here; scripts should be sent to **Senior Script Editor** *Penny Gold.*

BBC External Services

Central Talks and Features Department, Bush House, Strand, London WC2B 4PH
☎ 01–240 3456

Contact *Mary Raine*

Provide scripts in English for translation and broadcast by the 35 foreign language services that make up the BBC External Services. Cover the following areas: (a) analysis of international current affairs; (b) cultural, social and economic affairs in Britain; (c) science, technology and export promotion. Contributors should bear in mind that the target audience cannot be taken to have a ready familiarity with life in this country or with British institutions. Translation skills are not necessary, as this is done exclusively by their own professionals.

BBC Northern Ireland

Broadcasting House, 25–7 Ormeau Avenue, Belfast BT2 8HQ
☎ 0232 244400

Contact *Robin Harris* (Head of Radio)

Also see **Radio Foyle** in **Local Radio** section.

BBC Radio Scotland

Queen Margaret Drive, Glasgow G12 8DG
☎ 041–339 8844
5 Queen Street, Edinburgh EH2 1JF
☎ 031–225 3131

Editor News & Current Affairs *Jack Regan*

(G) **Fiction/Drama Producer** *Stewart Conn* (E) **Comedy** *Colin Gilbert* (G) **Talks and Features** *Mike Shaw* (E)

Produces a full range of news and current affairs programmes, comedy; documentaries; drama; short stories; talks and features. The emphasis is on speech-based programmes (rather than music, etc.) and programmes reflecting Scottish culture.
Scottish BBC Radio has two aspects: a national radio service contributed to by programme-making in Glasgow, Edinburgh, Aberdeen and Dundee; and the local community stations, which take the national programmes and splice this with local material. These stations are **BBC Aberdeen, BBC Highland**, nan Gaideheal, Orkney, Shetland, **BBC Solway** and **Tweed**.

BBC Radio Scotland (Dundee)

66 The Nethergate, Dundee
☏ 0382 202481

Small office producing news coverage only. No openings.

BBC Wales

Broadcasting House, Llantrisant Road, Llandaff, Cardiff CF5 2YQ
☏ 0222 564888

Contact *Meirion Edwards* (Head of Radio)

As with **BBC Radio Scotland**, there are two aspects to the working of the Welsh network. There are three centres of programme-making, in Cardiff, Bangor and Swansea, for the national Welsh BBC network, but in addition two community stations which provide local material for local audiences. See **Radio Clwyd** and **Radio Gwent** in the **Local Radio** section.

BBC Wales (Bangor)

Broadcasting House, Meirion Road,
Bangor LL57 2BY
☏ 0248 370880

Contact *Elwyn Jones* (Senior Producer)

BBC Radio Wales (Swansea)

32 Alexandra Road, Swansea SA1 5DT
☏ 0792 654986

Contact *Sulwyn Thomas* (Station Manager)

Independent Radio News

Communications House, Gough Square,
London EC4P 4LP
☏ 01–353 1010

News Editor *John Perkins*

IRN supplies national and international news coverage to all independent local radio stations throughout Britain.

Local Radio

BBC Local Radio

BBC Radio Aberdeen

Beechgrove Terrace, Aberdeen AB9 2ZT
☎ 0224 625233 Telex 739622

Editor *Greg Russell*

No real market. Only involved in features (don't make any drama) and these are virtually all commissioned. News, local only.

BBC Radio Bedfordshire

PO Box 476, Hastings Street, Luton, Bedfordshire LU1 5BA
☎ 0582 459111 Telex 825979 RADBED G

Station Manager *Mike Gibbons*
Contact *Ann Jones* (Programme Organiser)

No news opportunities, and few in drama and light entertainment. Locally written contributions about Bedfordshire, north and west Hertfordshire and north Buckinghamshire are encouraged. Particularly interested in historical topics (five minutes maximum). Also encourage freelance contributions from the community across a wide range of radio output, including interview and feature material.
The station very occasionally broadcasts drama – its first professional play was aired recently. Stringent local criteria are applied in selection.

BBC Radio Cambridgeshire

104 Hills Road, Cambridge CB2 1LD
☎ 0223 315970
Peterborough Studio: Broadway Court, Broadway, Peterborough PE1 1RP
☎ 0733 312832

Contact *Margaret Hyde* (Station Manager), *Rowland Myers* (Programme Organiser)

Each autumn the station runs a short story competition with £500 worth of prize money in adult and children's sections. The winning stories are broadcast. Short stories are also regularly featured in the weekday 1–4 pm programme presented by Bill Dod.

BBC Radio Cleveland

Broadcasting House, PO Box 1548, Middlesbrough, Cleveland TS1 5DG
☎ 0642 225211

Contact *Mick Wormald* (Programme Organiser)

Material used is almost exclusively local to Cleveland, County Durham and North Yorkshire, or written by local writers.

BBC Radio Clwyd

The Old School House, Glanrafon Road, Mold CH7 1PA
☎ 0352 59111

Contact *Tony Todd* (Senior Producer)

BBC Radio Cornwall

Phoenix Wharf, Truro, Cornwall TR1 1UA
☎ 0872 75421

Contact *Andy Joynson* (Programme Organiser)

Opportunities exist for Cornish poetry and literature on the Sunday afternoon arts programme, *Seen and Heard*, produced by Tim Hubbard.

BBC Radio Cumbria

Hilltop Heights, London Road, Carlisle CA1 2NA
☎ 0228 31661

Contact *Kath Worrell* (Programme Organiser)

Not very many opportunities for writers, apart from *Write Now*, a weekly half-hour regional local writing programme, shared with Radios Merseyside (see entry), Manchester and Lanca-

shire.
Contact *Caroline Adams* on 051–708 5500.

BBC Radio Derby

PO Box 269, Derby DE1 3HL
☏ 0332 361111

Contact *Bryan Harris* (Station Manager)

BBC Radio Devon

PO Box 100, Exeter EX4 4DB
☏ 0392 215651 Telex 42440

Manager *Roy Corlett*
Contact *John Lilley*

Special projects mounted annually have included a short story competition (1985), also a playwriting competition (1986), Armada Playwriting competition (1988), and a playwriting competition for 1989 in conjunction with the Theatre Royal (Plymouth) applause club and the local *Evening Herald* newspaper.

BBC Essex

198 New London Road, Chelmsford CM2 9XB
☏ 0245 262393

Station Manager *Richard Lucas*
Contact *Keith Roberts* (Programme Organiser)

No regular outlets for writers but do mount special projects from time to time, and these are well publicised on the air.

BBC Radio Foyle

PO Box 927, Londonderry BT48 7NE
☏ 0504 262244/5/6

Contact *Joe Mahon*

Radio Foyle broadcasts both its own programmes and those made for Belfast – for national transmission. Occasionally programmes made by Radio Foyle will be taken up by the national network.

BBC Radio Furness

Hartington Street, Barrow-in-Furness, Cumbria LA14 5FH
☏ 0229 36767

Contact *Keith Daniels* (Senior Producer)

A **Radio Cumbria** community sub-station.

BBC Radio Gwent

Powys House, Cwmbran, Gwent NP44 1YF
☏ 0633 372727

Contact *Adrian Hearn* (Senior Producer)

BBC Radio Highland

Broadcasting House, 7 Culduthel Road, Inverness IV2 4AD
☏ 0463 221711

Contact *Allan Campbell* (Station Manager)

BBC Radio Humberside

63 Jameson Street, Hull, North Humberside HU1 3NU
☏ 0482 23232 Telex 597031

Programme Organiser *Geoff Hibbert*
Contact *Margaret Garbett*

Broadcast a daily short story each afternoon at 2.35 pm. 75% of material is provided by local writers.

BBC Radio Kent

Sun Pier, Chatham, Kent ME4 4EZ
☏ 0634 830505 Telex 965011

Contact *Jim Latham* (Manager)

Opportunities exist for writers on the afternoon magazine programme, plus the specialist arts programme *Scene and Heard*. Features need to be of strong local interest, as do drama/fiction, for which there are few openings. Occasional commissions are made for local interest documentaries and other one-off programmes.

BBC Radio Lancashire

King Street, Blackburn BB2 2EA
☏ 0254 62411

Manager *Michael Chapman*
Contact *Programme Organiser*

Not very many opportunities for writers, apart from *Write Now*, a weekly half-hour regional local writing programme, shared with Radios Merseyside (see entry), Manchester & Cumbria.
Contact *Caroline Adams* on 051–708 5500.

BBC Radio Leeds

Broadcasting House, Woodhouse Lane, Leeds LS2 9PN
☏ 0532 442131

Contact *Abha Sood Adams* (Producer, Features Unit)

A monthly workshop on the *Afternoon Show* in which resident poet, Martyn Wiley, sets 'homework' for listeners, and then, in a series of features a month later, reads out the poems, and comments.

BBC Radio Leicester

Epic House, Charles Street, Leicester LE1 3SH
☎ 0533 27113

Station Manager *Jeremy Robinson*

BBC Radio Lincolnshire

PO Box 219, Newport, Lincoln LN1 3XY
☎ 0522 40011 Telex 56186

Manager *David Wilkinson*
Contact *Alan Stennett*

Unsolicited material only considered if locally relevant. Maximum 1000 words; straight narrative preferred, ideally with a topical content.

BBC Radio London

See **Greater London Radio**

BBC Radio Manchester

New Broadcasting House, PO Box 90, Oxford Road, Manchester M60 1SJ
☎ 061–228 3434

Contact *Martin Henfield* (Editor, Local Programmes)

Very few opportunities, apart from *Write Now*, a weekly half-hour regional local writing programme, shared with Radios Merseyside (see entry), Lancashire & Cumbria.
Contact *Caroline Adams* on 051–708 5500.

BBC Radio Merseyside

55 Paradise Street, Liverpool L1 3BP
☎ 051–708 5500

Contact *Caroline Adams*
News Editor *Liam Fogarty*

No opportunities in news. Very rarely in light entertainment, drama or fiction. However, there is *Write Now,* a new weekly half-hour regional writing programme, shared with Radios Lancashire, Manchester & Cumbria, which features work by local talent from the North West only. Short stories (maximum 1200 words), poetry and features on writing. Broadcast Friday evening at 7.30.

BBC Radio Newcastle

Broadcasting Centre, PO Box
Newcastle upon Tyne NE99 1RN
☎ 091–232 4141

Manager *Tony Fish*

Opportunities for freelance writers are extremely rare.

BBC Radio Norfolk

Norfolk Tower, Surrey Street, Norwich NR1 3PA
☎ 0603 617411 Telex 975515

Contact *Keith Salmon* (Station Manager)

Features/Documentaries *Keith Salmon* Good local material welcome, but must relate directly to Norfolk and north Suffolk.

BBC Radio Northampton

PO Box 1107, Abington Street,
Northampton NN1 2BE
☎ 0604 239100

Contact *Nigel Dyson*

Literary outlets limited but they do occur occasionally, e.g. short story competitions/poetry week, and are trailed accordingly.

BBC Radio Nottingham

York House, Mansfield Road,
Nottingham NG1 3JB
☎ 0602 415161

Contact *Nick Brunger* (Programme Organiser)

BBC Radio Oxford

269 Banbury Road, Oxford OX2 7DW
☎ 0865 311444 Fax 0865 311915

Contact *Stewart Woodcock* (Programme Organiser)

Limited opportunities: short stories are used from time to time.

BBC Radio Sheffield

60 Westbourne Road, Sheffield S10 2QU
☎ 0742 686185

Contact *Frank Mansfield* (Programme Organiser)

'Radio Sheffield is keen to develop local writing

talent through the radio station. We broadcast short stories from local writers on merit.' Plays are broadcast 'very occasionally'. Poetry workshops held twice a week. Also involved with **Sheffield City Libraries** in a scheme called 'Write Back', and hope to broadcast material coming out of this in the near future.

BBC Radio Shropshire

PO Box 397, Shrewsbury, Shropshire SY1 3TT
☎ 0743 248484 Telex 35187

Station Manager *Lawrie Bloomfield*

Few opportunities, if any, at the moment: owing to recent cuts, the station can no longer accommodate the poetry/prose outlet for local creative talent.

BBC Radio Solent

South Western House, Canute Road, Southampton SO9 4PJ
☎ 0703 631311 Telex 47420

Station Manager *Steve Panton*

Occasional short story competitions.

BBC Radio Solway

Loves Walk, Dumfries DG1 1NZ
☎ 0387 68008
Telex 776671 Fax 0387 52568

Editor *Colin Caley*

BBC Radio Sussex

Marlborough Place, Brighton, Sussex BN1 1TU
☎ 0273 680231

Contact *Greg Ainger* (Programme Organiser)

Weekly short story slot featuring creative local talent. Have in the past mounted a short story competition and hope to do so again in the near future.

BBC Radio Tweed

Municipal Buildings, High Street, Selkirk TD7 4BU
☎ 0750 21884 Fax 0750 22400

Contact *Colin Wight* (Senior Producer)

BBC Radio WM

PO Box 206, Birmingham B5 7SD
☎ 021–414 8484

Contact *Tony Inchley* (Editor)

Interested in short stories, plays, documentaries, preferably but not necessarily local interest.

BBC Radio York

20 Bootham Row, York YO3 7BR
☎ 0904 641351 Fax 0904 610937

Station Manager *Barry Stockdale*
Programme Organiser *Chris Choi*

'A limited outlet for short stories and features provided they are either set locally or have some other local relevance.'

Beacon Radio

PO Box 303, 267 Tettenhall Road, Wolverhampton WV6 0DQ
☎ 0902 757211
Telex 336919 Fax 0902 745456/755163

Contact *Pete Wagstaff* (Programme Controller)

Greater London Radio

PO Box 4LG, 35A Marylebone High Street, London W1A 4LG
☎ 01–486 7611

Contact *Tony Freeman*

Formerly known as **BBC Radio London.**

Independent Local Radio

BRMB

PO Box 555, Radio House, Aston Road North, Birmingham B6 4BX
☎ 021–359 4481 Telex 339707

Programme Controller *Mike Owen*
Light Entertainment *Robin Valk*
Contact *Mike Owen*

Occasionally use drama; hold an annual short story competition; have some demand for comedy material; and there are opportunities for writers in the various feature series the station puts out.
News *Brian Sheppard*

Brunel Radio

PO Box 2020, Swindon SN4 7EX
PO Box 2020, Watershed, Canon's Road, Bristol BS9 7EN
☎ 0793 848600/0272 258600
Telex 44450 (Swindon) Fax 0793 853929

Contact *Mike Henfield* (Network Controller)

A radio station specifically aimed at a more

mature audience. Some opportunities for short stories, regular short story and poetry competitions.

Capital Radio

PO Box 958, Euston Tower, London NW1 3DR
☎ 01–388 1288

Contact *Nicholas Wheeler*

Britain's largest commercial radio station. Recently acquired a package of minority stakes in thirteen independent local radio stations. Also has a 60% holding in Monte Carlo-based Riviera Radio. Nicholas Wheeler covers current affairs, features, news and talks. Opportunities exist on the daily (weekdays) 7 pm programme *The Way It Is*, and on the 7.30–midnight *Mike Dicken Show*. Also opportunities for comedy writing.

Chiltern Radio

Chiltern Road, Dunstable,
Bedfordshire LU6 1HQ
☎ 0582 666001 Telex 825175

Radio Scripts Contact *Paul Robinson*
News Editor *Andy Diprose*

Part of the Chiltern Network. See also **Northants Radio**. Opportunities existing for radio drama only, and these are rare. However, if a script is of exceptional local interest, Chiltern Radio will consider it.

CNFM

PO Box 1000, Vision Park, Chivers Way, Histon,
Cambridge CB4 4WW
☎ 0223 235255 Fax 0223 235161

Contact *Andy Gillies* (Station Manager)

Sister station of **Hereward Radio.** Not usually any openings as all material is compiled and presented by in-house staff.

County Sound

The Friary, Guildford, Surrey GU1 4YX
☎ 0483 505566 Fax 0483 33126

Contact *Paul Owens* (Deputy Programme Controller)

Devonair Radio

35–7 St David's Hill, Exeter EX4 4DA
☎ 0392 430703
Telex 42496 Fax 0392 411893

Now owned by **Capital Radio**. No opportunities for freelance writers.

Downtown Radio (DTR)

Newtownards, Co. Down,
Northern Ireland BT23 4ES
☎ 0247 815555 Telex 747570

Programme Head *John Rosborough*

Downtown Radio ran a highly successful short story competition in 1988, attracting over 400 stories. The competition has become an annual event and writers will be asked to submit material during the winter and early spring. For further information, write to Derek Ray at the station.

Essex Radio

Radio House, Cliftown Road, Southend on Sea,
Essex SS1 1SX
☎ 0702 333711
Telex 995480 Fax 0702 345224
Radio House, 53 Duke Street, Chelmsford,
CM1 1SX
☎ 0245 251141

Editor *Bob Smith*
Contact *Keith Rogers* (Programme Controller)

No real opportunities for writers' work as such, but will often interview local authors of published books.

Fox FM

Brush House, Pony Road, Cowley,
Oxfordshire OX4 2XR
☎ 0865 748787

Contact *Tom Hunter* (Managing Director)

Awarded the local independent radio franchise for the Oxford and Banbury area in 1988, and planned to be on the air by the middle of September 1989. Backed by an impressive list of shareholders including the Blackwell Group of Companies. Welcome suggestions and unsolicited contributions.

GEM-AM

Nottingham NG1 7AP
Derby DE1 3AA/Leicester LE1 7RW
☎ 0602 581731
Telex 37463 Fax 0602 585087

Contact *Chris Hughes* (Programme Controller)

Part of the Radio Trent Group. Runs the same

short story series/competition as **Trent FM** (see entry).

GWR Radio

PO Box 2000, Swindon SN4 7EX
PO Box 2000, Watershed, Cannon's Road, Bristol BS9 7EN
☎ 0793 853222/0272 279900
Telex 44450 (Swindon)

Contact *Mark Seaman* (Network Controller)

Very few opportunities. Almost all material originates in-house.

Hereward Radio

PO Box 225, Queensgate Centre, Peterborough PE1 1XJ
☎ 0733 46225
Telex 32738 Fax 0733 42714

Contact *Adrian Crookes* (Head of Programmes)

Not usually any openings offered to writers as all material is compiled and presented by in-house staff.

Invicta FM

15 Station Road East, Canterbury, Kent CT1 2RB
☎ 0227 67661 Telex 965360

Contact *Roger Day* (Programme Controller)

LBC

Communications House, Gough Square, London EC4P 4LP
☎ 01–353 1010

Contact *Peter Thornton* (Programme Controller)

Leicester Sound

Granville House, Granville Road, Leicester LE1 7RW
☎ 0533 551616 Telex 341953

Contact *Chris Hughes* (Programme Controller)

Annual short story competition at the end of each year.

Marcher Sound

The Studios, Mold Road, Gwersyllt, Wrexham LL11 4AF
☎ 0978 752202 Telex 63140

Contact *Paul Mewies* (Programme Controller)

Mercia Sound

Hertford Place, Coventry, West Midlands CV1 3TT
☎ 0203 633933 Telex 31413

News Editor *Colin Palmer*
Contact *Stuart Linnell* (Managing Director/Programme Controller)

Metro Radio

Newcastle upon Tyne NE99 1BB
☎ 091–488 3131 Telex 537428

Contact *Steve Martin* (Features Editor)

Very few opportunities for writers.

Moray Firth Radio

PO Box 271, Scourgurie Place, Inverness IV3 6SF
☎ 0463 224433 Telex 75643

Contact *Brian Anderson* (Programme Controlller)

Northants Radio

71B Abington Street, Northampton NN1 2HW
☎ 0604 29811 Fax 0604 250666

Contact *Paul Robinson* (Programme Controller)

Part of the Chiltern Network. See also **Chiltern Radio**.

NorthSound

45 King's Gate, Aberdeen AB2 6BL
☎ 0224 632234 Telex 739883

Contact *Peter Strachan* (Senior Producer)

Ocean Sound Ltd

Whittle Avenue, Segensworth West, Fareham, Hants PO15 5PA
☎ 04895 89911 Telex 47474

News *Peter Solomons*
Contact *Michael Betton* (Programme Controller)

For economic reasons, Ocean Sound rarely considers commissioning an external writer to produce drama/short stories for the station. All submissions are, however, considered, but only those with a special local connection are likely to be taken further. Ocean Sound runs a very popular children's short story competition. Most of the entrants (and in the past the winners) are beginners.

Orwell FM 97.1

Electric House, Lloyds Avenue, Ipswich, Suffolk IP1 3HZ
☎ 0473 216971
Telex 98548 Fax 0473 230350

Contact *Daragh Croxson* (Head of News)

Features Editor/Group Programme Controller *Sally Gordon* Few openings here; 'even fewer' in drama and light entertainment.

Pennine Radio

PO Box 235, Pennine House, Forster Square, Bradford BD1 5NP
☎ 0274 731521

Contact *Colin Slade* (Programme Controller), *Martin Lee* (Presentation Controller)

Piccadilly Radio/Key 103

127–31 The Piazza, Piccadilly Plaza, Manchester M1 4AW
☎ 061–236 9913 Telex 667203

Contact *Michael Briscoe* (Programme Controller)

Documentaries Submit draft plans for discussion. **Drama** Of a 'pop' nature, especially short comedies or soaps. No light entertainment. **Features** Of local interest only. **News** Qualified journalists only.

Plymouth Sound

Earl's Acre, Alma Road, Plymouth PL3 4HX
☎ 0752 227272 Fax 0752 670730

Contact *Louise Churchill* (Head of Programmes)

Radio Aire

PO Box 362, Leeds LS3 1LR
☎ 0532 452299 Fax 0532 421830

Contact *Christa Ackroyd* (Programme Controller)

Radio Broadland

St Georges Plain, 47–9 Colegate, Norwich NR3 1DB
☎ 0603 630621 Telex 975186

Contact *Mike Stewart* (Programme Controller), *Dick Hutchinson* (Features Producer)

Radio City (Sound of Merseyside)

PO Box 194, Liverpool L69 1LD
☎ 051–227 5100 Telex 628277

Contact *Brian Harvey*

Opportunities for writers are very few and far between.

Radio Clyde

Clydebank Business Park, Clydebank G81 2RX
☎ 041–941 1111
Telex 779537 Fax 041–952 0080

Contact *Hamish Wilson* (Head of Drama), *Alex Dickson* (Programme Controller)

Radio Clyde and the IBA, together with the **Society of Authors** and **The Writers' Guild**, launched a major new commissioning scheme for radio drama in 1989. The aim is to create a regular strand of specially-produced plays for independent radio stations. Members of the Society or Guild will be asked to submit outlines for previously unsubmitted work towards a one-hour production for radio – preference for contemporary themes, and no special emphasis on Scottish works. Accepted outlines will lead to full-length script commissions for production at Radio Clyde's drama department under Hamish Wilson's supervision. Few opportunities outside of this, as programmes usually originate in-house or by commission. All documentary material is made in-house. Good local news items always considered.

Radio Forth

Forth House, Forth Street, Edinburgh EH1 3LF
☎ 031–556 9255 Telex 727374

Contact *Tom Steele* (Programmes Director)

Features *Alec Shuttleworth* Opportunities in the two-minute feature series *The Story of ...* **Light Entertainment** *Tom Steele* Sixty-second *Radio Cartoons*. **News** *David Johnston* News stories welcome from freelancers.

Radio Hallam

PO Box 194, Hartshead, Sheffield S1 1GP
☎ 0742 766766
Telex 547338 Fax 0742 738909

Contact *Dean Pepall* (Presentation Co-ordinator)

Radio Luxembourg (London) Ltd

38 Hertford Street, London W1Y 8BA
☎ 01–493 5961 Telex 263912

Contact *Rodney Collins* (Editor)

Some freelance opportunities in news only.

Radio Mercury

Broadfield House, Brighton Road, Crawley, West Sussex RH11 9TT
☎ 0293 519161 Telex 87503

Programme Controller *J. Wellington*

No fiction or features opportunities. The newsroom occasionally take freelance news stories, though most of these come from established contacts.

Radio Stoke

Cheapside, Hanley, Stoke on Trent ST1 1JJ
☎ 0782 208080 Telex 36104

Programme Organiser *Mervyn Gamage*
Contact *Arthur Wood*

The station has long had a policy of encouraging material suitable for a Radio Stoke audience, whether this be short or longer essays, short stories, original research and writing on local history, or other subjects of local interest. The station is particularly keen on receiving these from locally-based authors. Very occasionally use scripts of great local relevance. (All scripts lacking local links are rejected.)

Radio Tay

PO Box 123, Dundee DD1 9UF
☎ 0382 200800 Telex 76412

Contact *Sandy Wilkie* (Station Manager/Director)

See also sister station **Radio Forth**.

Radio 210

PO Box 210, Reading RG3 5RZ
☎ 0734 413131 Telex 848503

Contact *Phil Coope* (Programme Controller)

Radio Wyvern

PO Box 22, 5–6 Barbourne Terrace, Worcester WR1 3JS
☎ 0905 612212 Telex 335292

Contact *Norman Bilton* (Managing Director)

One of the smallest of the regional radio stations; has little money for contributors. Very occasionally, a local writer may be commissioned to produce something of interest to the Wyvern audience.

Red Dragon Radio

Radio House, West Canal Wharf, Cardiff CF1 5XJ
☎ 0222 384041

Contact *Peter Milburn* (Programme Controller)

See also **Red Rose Radio** based in Preston.

Red Rose Radio

PO Box 301, St Paul's Square, Preston, Lancashire PR1 1YE
☎ 0772 556301 Telex 677610

Contact *Dave Lincoln* (Head of Programmes)

See also sister station **Red Dragon Radio**.

Saxon FM 96.4

Long Brackland, Bury St Edmunds, Suffolk IP33 1JY
☎ 0284 701511 Telex 98548

Contact *Sally Gordon* (Programme Controller)

Severn Sound

PO Box 388, 67 Southgate Street, Gloucester GL1 2DQ
☎ 0452 423791 Telex 0437271

Contact *Eddie Vickers* (Programme Controller), *Steve Ellis*

Signal Radio

Stoke Road, Stoke on Trent ST4 2SR
☎ 0782 417111
Telex 367444 Fax 0782 744110

Contact *John Evington* (Programme Controller)

Sound FM

Granville House, Granville Road, Leicester LE1 7RW
☎ 0533 551616 Fax 0533 550869

Contact *Chris Hughes* (Programme Controller)

Part of the Radio Trent Group. Runs the same short story series/competition as **Trent FM** (see entry).

Southern Sound Radio

PO Box 2000, Brighton, Sussex BN41 2SS
☏ 0273 430111 Fax 0273 430098

Programme Controller *Jeremy Scott*

Swansea Sound

Victoria Road, Gowerton, Swansea SA4 3AB
☏ 0792 893751 Telex 48594

Contact *David Thomas* (Programme Controller)

Features, Drama and Fiction, Light Entertainment *David Thomas*
News *Hugh Turnbull*

TFM Radio

74 Dovecot Street, Stockton on Tees TS18 1HB
☏ 0642 615111
Telex 587232 Fax 0642 674402

Programme Controller *Brian Lister*
Features *Heather Raw*

Limited opportunities but always willing to consider new ideas.

Trent FM

29–31 Castlegate, Nottingham NG1 7AP
☏ 0602 581731
Telex 37463 RADTRENT Fax 0602 585087
Derby station: Market Place, Derby DE1 3AA
☏ 0332 292945 Fax 0332 292229

Contact Nottingham & Derby *Chris Hughes* (Programme Controller)

Few opportunities, although a short story series/competition is run annually. **Documentaries** 'perhaps if locally orientated and discussed upfront'. **Features** *John Shaw* Rarely used. **Light Entertainment** Christmas material only.

Two Counties Radio

5 Southcote Road, Bournemouth BH1 3LR
☏ 0202 294881
Telex 418362 Fax 0202 299314

Programme Administrator *Rosemary Mundy*
Programme Controller *Stan Horobin*

Viking FM

Commercial Road, Hull HU1 2SG
☏ 0482 25141
Telex 597572 Fax 0482 25141 ext. 226

Contact *Alma Cooper* (News Editor)
Features *Steve King*

West Sound

Radio House, 54 Holmston Road, Ayr KA7 3BE
☏ 0292 283662 Telex 776235

Contact *John McCauley* (Programme Controller)

Weekly arts programme, Thursdays at 6 pm, which covers all aspects of the arts, including writing.

Film TV and Video Production Companies

Abbey Video Ltd
Five Lamps Studio, West Avenue,
Derby DE1 3HR
☏ 0332 40693

Contact *Richard Faulkner*

Makers of corporate video for a variety of industrial clients.

Acme Arts Ltd
12 Vauxhall Grove, London SW8 1SY
☏ 01–735 9099

Contact *Jim Field*

Horticultural and educational films for television and video. Plans for children's video, too, towards the end of 1989.

A.C.T. Films Ltd
111 Wardour Street, London W1A 4AY
☏ 01–437 8506 Fax 01–437 8268

Contact *Richard Gates*

Low budget features, television documentary. Unsolicited mss welcome. 'We are pleased to read anything and are prepared to try and help writers revise scripts to make them acceptable.'

Action Time
Wrendel House, 2 Whitworth Street West,
Manchester M1 5WX
☏ 061–236 8999 Fax 061–236 8845

Contact *Steven Leahy*

Moved from London to Manchester in 1988. Makers of television programmes: 'format shows' like *Game For a Laugh, Odd One Out* and *The Krypton Factor*, both for the UK and America. Recent work includes *Busman's Holiday* and *Connections.*

Adam Video Productions
21 Dungarvan Avenue, Roehampton,
London SW15 5QU
☏ 01–876 3333

Contact *John McAdam*

Audio – video corporate identity, staff training and safety at work. *Specialises* in marketing support and corporate identity productions to industry, commerce and education. *Special areas* optical/opthalmic. No unsolicited mss but welcome any new creative work: 'any collection of works that will sell the product or message'.

After Image Ltd
32 Acre Lane, London SW2 5SG
☏ 01–737 7300 Fax 01–326 1850

Contact *Jane Thorburn*

Makers of television, with a particular interest in the arts and unusual people and events. OUTPUT *Alter Image*, the alternative arts magazine, with no presenter; *Pookiesnackenburger* (musical series); *Map of Dreams* (arts video, dance and effects). After Image concentrate on the visual aspects of television; interested to read new writing, and to work with author towards new pieces, specifically for television.

Aisling Films Ltd
17–21 Bruce Street, Belfast BT2 7JD
☏ 0232 327434 Fax 0232 327820

Contact *Bill Miskelly*

Film and television drama and documentary. No unsolicited mss. Interested in all new work, but 'don't have the time to comment on unsolicited scripts'. OUTPUT *The End of the World Man* (children's feature film); *The Schooner* (TV drama).

The Britt Allcroft Group Limited

61 Devonshire Road, Southampton SO1 2GR
☎ 0703 331661
Telex 47408 BALAHA G Fax 0703 332206

Contact *Britt Allcroft, Angus Wright*

Specialists in children's and family television. Properties: *Thomas the Tank Engine & Friends; Here Comes Mumfie; Shining Time Station.*

Allied Stars

55 Park Lane, London W1
☎ 01–493 1050

Contact *Luke Randolph*

Feature films. OUTPUT *Chariots of Fire; Breaking Glass; F/X Murder by Illusion.* Only feature films and TV series considered.

Amber Films

5–9 side (rear), Newcastle upon Tyne NE1 3JE
☎ 091–232 2000

Contact *Kitty Fitzgerald*

Television programmes, cinema and animation. OUTPUT, with a drama/scripted content, has included *Keeping Time, Byker, Seacoal, T. Dan Smith, Shields Stories.* Plus many documentaries.

Antelope Films Ltd

3 Fitzroy Square, London W1P 5AH
☎ 01–387 4454
Telex 266205 AFLG Fax 01–388 9935

Contact *Clive Syddall* (Chief Executive)

Producers of drama and television documentaries. Welcome unsolicited mss. OUTPUT has included *The Triple Crown: The Paradox of the Papacy, The Spirit of the Alcazar: 50 years in a Spanish City, Vidal in Venice, Heart of the Dragon* (12-part series on China for Channel 4), *Portrait of the Soviet Union* (7-part series for Turner Broadcasting); *Testament* (7-part series for Channel 4); *Global Rivals* (3-part series for PBS). Currently in production *Pasternak* (2 drama documentaries for LWT); *The Margot Fonteyn Story* (90-minute special for Channel 4)' *International Terror* (3-part series for Channel 4); *Midas Touch* (6-part series for BBC). In development: several drama and international documentary series.

Antonine Productions/Black Cat Studios

830 Springfield Road, Glasgow G31 4HG
☎ 041–554 4667

Contact *Paddy Higson*

Films for television, feature films. Production slate 1989/90 full.

Aspect Corporate Communications

36 Percy Street, London W1P 9FG
☎ 01–636 5303

Contact *Sally Davidson*

Drama, documentary and corporate television.

Aspen Spafax Television

Aspen House, 1 Gayford Road,
London W12 9BY
☎ 01–743 8618 Fax 01–740 9333

Contact *Mike Raggett, Amanda Thompson*

Commercials and corporate film and video production for corporate communications, company and product promotion. OUTPUT has included training films for accountants Peat, Marwick, McLintock; promotional videos for the Leeds Building Society, Tie Rack, ICI, Glaxo and British Gas.

Astramead Ltd

38 Gloucester Mews, London W2 3HE
☎ 01–723 4678

Contact *Mark Shivas*

Television programmes, cinema and drama on film and video. OUTPUT has included the television series *Telford's Change* and *Late Starter* for BBC; *The Price* for Channel 4; *Can You Hear Me at the Back?* and *Kipling*, presented on West End stage, the latter shown also on Channel 4.

Athos Film Productions Ltd

65 High Street, Hampton Hill,
Middlesex TW12 1NH
☎ 01–783 0533 Fax 01–783 1757

Contact *Peter Bucknall* (Director)

Films and videos. No unsolicited mss. Interested in seeing CVs.

Aurora Sound and Vision

5 Hellesdon Hall Industrial Park, Hellesdon Park Road, Norwich NR6 5DR
☎ 0603 789509 Fax 0603 402844

Contact *Steve Bloomfield*

Video marketing and training programmes; radio drama and radio commercials. Only undertake commissioned work (except for radio drama) and only interested in seeing unsolicited mss as examples of work.

Robert Austen Communications Ltd

The Chequers, 2 Church Street, High Wycombe, Bucks HP11 2DE
☎ 0494 443777 Fax 0494 464353
Telex 265871 MONREF G TCC/097

Contact *Bob Austen, Charlene Hamlin*

Film and video – commercials, corporate, documentary, dramatised documentary.

AVC Group

Walters Farm Road, Tonbridge, Kent TN9 1QT
☎ 0732 365107 Fax 0732 362600

Contact *Brian Adams*

A specialist business communication company who work as consultants for corporate clients in the field of conferences, corporate and financial communications, PR events and award ceremonies, safety, sales and marketing, and training.

Michael Barratt Ltd

5–7 Forlease Road, Maidenhead, Berks SL6 1RP
☎ 0628 770800 Fax 0628 770144

Contact *Michael Barratt*

Corporate and educational video, also television programmes. Wide range of publishing work, too, including company newspapers, brochures and training manuals.

Peter Batty Productions

Claremont House, Renfrew Road, Kingston, Surrey KT2 7NT
☎ 01–942 6304
Telex 261507 MONREF 2685 Fax 01–336 1661

Contact *Peter Batty*

Television programmes and commercials. Primarily broadcast documentaries. Recent OUTPUT has included *The Divided Union* (5-part series on the American Civil War) and *Fonteyn and Nureyev: The Perfect Partnership* (a one-off for Channel 4).

Beat Ltd

See **Wall to Wall Television/The Media Show Ltd**

Behr Cinematography

22 Redington Road, London NW3 7RG
☎ 01–794 2535

Contact *Arnold Behr, Betty Burghes*

Documentary, educational, corporate film and video on subjects ranging from care of the terminally ill, through sport for the handicapped, to custom building of motor cars. No unsolicited mss.

Bentorm Ltd

26B Thorney Crescent, London SW11 3TR
☎ 01–585 1592

Contact *David Deutsch*

Television and cinema producers, particularly in drama and arts fields. OUTPUT has included *Shakespeare Lives* and *Reflections*, both for Channel 4, and the feature film *The Chain* (script by Jack Rosenthal). More recently, 3 adaptations of Somerset Maugham's short stories for Anglia TV.

Paul Berriff Productions Ltd

The Chestnuts, Woodfield Lane, Hessle, North Humberside HU13 0EW
☎ 0482 641158

Contact *Paul Berriff*

Television, documentary features. OUTPUT has included *Lakeland Rock* for Channel 4, *Lifeboat* series for BBC1, *Fire* for BBC's 40 Minutes, *Animal Squad* for BBC1 and *Dianne's Children* for BBC2. More recent achievements include *Rescue* – a 13-part documentary for ITV in 1989.

Bevanfield Films

22 Soho Square, London W1V 5FJ
☎ 01–287 0628

Contact *Mary Swindale*

Television programmes, cinema and animation.

Martin Bird Productions

Saucelands, Coolham, Horsham,
West Sussex RH13 8QG
☎ 0403 87620 Fax 0403 87647

Contact *Alastair Martin-Bird*

Makers of film and video, specialising predominantly in programmes covering equestrianism and the countryside. Do not welcome unsolicited mss but always looking for new writers who are fully acquainted with the subject.

Black Cat Studios

See **Antonine Productions**

Blackrod

Threeways House, 40–4 Clipstone Street,
London W1P 7EA
☎ 01–637 9376
Telex 269859 Fax 01–580 9143

Contact *Penny Hayes*

Corporate television – drama and documentary. One of the biggest corporate video makers, and they have won a fistful of awards for excellence in the field.

Matt Boney Associates

'Woodside', Holdfast Lane, Grayswood,
Haslemere, Surrey GU27 2EU
☎ 0428 56178

Contact *Matt Boney*

Video, television – commercials, documentaries, sport and travel. No unsolicited mss.

British Lion Screen Entertainment Ltd

Pinewood Studios, Iver, Bucks SL0 0NH
☎ 0753 651700 Telex 847505

Contact *Peter R.E. Snell* (Chief Executive)

Film production. OUTPUT *Turtle Diary; Lady Jane; A Prayer for the Dying.* No unsolicited mss.

Broadcast Communications plc

14 King Street, Covent Garden,
London WC2E 8HN
☎ 01–240 6941

Contact *Michael Braham, Susan Lowery*

Factual/current affairs/business programmes and corporate video. OUTPUT: Television – *The Business Programme, Business Daily;* Corporate – training, customer care, safety at work, and financial matters such as pensions. 'All material has a tendency towards the financial sector, where most of our clients come from'. No unsolicited mss.

Broadside Ltd

74 Moss Lane, Pinner, Middlesex HA5 3AU
☎ 01–866 5271

Contact *Angela Spindler-Brown*

An all woman independent production company. OUTPUT has included a current affairs series for Channel 4; *Thinking about conflict, Female Focus* and *Five Women Photographers*, also for Channel 4.

Broadwick Productions

78 Romilly Road, London N4 2QX
☎ 01–226 7157 Fax 01–354 5875

Contact *Sarah Wickham, Simon Lethbridge*

Wide range of corporate productions including documentary, educational, financial, point-of-sale programme-making, production of pop promos and training. Unsolicited mss welcome. 'Always attempt to use at least two new writers each year for corporate production. Opportunity varies according to quantity and quality of incoming work.'

Brook Productions

103–9 Wardour Street, London W1V 3TD
☎ 01–439 9871

Contact *Anne Lapping*

Makers of arts, current affairs, documentary and music television. OUTPUT has included *A Week in Politics* for Channel 4, *Shape of the World, Voices, The Writing on the Wall* and *David Low.*

Burbank Film & Video Ltd

Ebury Rooms, Bury Lane, Rickmansworth, Herts
WD3 1DT
☎ 0923 771222 Fax 0923 896059

Contact *Rae Evans*

Film and video documentaries. Commercial, industrial, medical and scientific films, video programmes and children's television; programmes for industry, commerce and television. Will consider unsolicited mss, but 'as our output is so specialised, we feel it may be a wasted effort by writers'. Mostly use staff writers.

Burrill Productions

19 Cranbury Road, London SW6 2NS
☏ 01–736 8673

Contact *Timothy Burrill*

Feature film production company. OUTPUT *Alpha Beta* for BBC; *Tess* Roman Polanski; *Pirates of Penzance; Supergirl; The Fourth Protocol.* No unsolicited mss. Policy of encouragement for new screenwriters.

Arthur Butten Animation

11 South Road, Saffron Walden,
Essex CB11 3DG

Contact *Arthur Butten*

Animated films, commercials and documentary inserts. *Specialises* in animation. OUTPUT has included feature films: *Animal Farm, Yellow Submarine, The Snowman*; also many commercials for clients like *Daily Telegraph* 'Hitchhikers' Guide to the Universe'.

Camden Productions

20 Jeffreys Street, London NW1 9PR
☏ 01–482 0527

Contact *Theresa FitzGerald, Philip Kemp*

Camden Productions consists of two writers and develops their work exclusively. No unsolicited mss.

Caravel Film Techniques Limited

The Great Barn Studios, Cippenham Lane,
Slough, Berks SL1 5AU
☏ 0753 821218

Contact *Nick See*

Film, video, television – documentary and commercials. No unsolicited mss. 'We keep a file on writers' details and always welcome any new information'.

Pearl Catlin Associates

16A Carlisle Mansions, Carlisle Place,
London SW1P 1HX
☏ 01–834 1660 Fax 01–828 5898

Contact *Pearl Catlin, Philip Bond, Douglas Neill*

Commercials, promotional, corporate – film and video. No unsolicited mss but interested in creative ideas.

Celador Productions Limited

39 Long Acre, London WC2E 9JT
☏ 01–240 8101
Telex 264593 COMCEL G Fax 01–836 1117

Contact *Bob Louis*

Television: primarily entertainment programming for all broadcast channels, including factual entertainment, game shows, variety, plus selected documentary and drama output including *Delorean* and *Don't Cry for Me Sergeant Major.*

Chameleon Television Ltd

The Magistretti Building, 1 Harcourt Place, West Street, Leeds LS1 4RB
☏ 0532 438536

Contact *Chris Lister*

Television – including documentaries for Channel 4, ITV and BBC; PR videos for corporate clients.

Chapel Studios

Quebec Street, Langley Park, Durham DH7 9XA
☏ 091–373 0449 Fax 091–373 0449

Contact *Ian Farnworth, Stefan Gemski*

Corporate video makers: bio-technology; civil, mechanical, electrical and chemical engineering; automotive and defence industry; financial; motorsport; power generation; health and safety. No unsolicited mss. All scriptwriting done inhouse.

Chatsworth Television Ltd

97–9 Dean Street, London W1V 5RA
☏ 01–734 4302/434 1731
Telex 28604 Fax 01–437 3301

Contact *Malcolm Heyworth*

Drama and light entertainment television producers, with 16 years of experience.

Cheerleader Productions

The Trocadero, 19 Rupert Street,
London W1V 7FS
☏ 01–287 3333

Contact *Charles Balchin*

Sports programme makers. Have produced American football, sumo wrestling, power-spirit racing, tennis and golf programmes for Channel 4. Also corporate video makers.

CHG Communications

108 Clarendon Road, London W11 2HR
☎ 01–727 4269 Fax 01–727 3918

Contact *Jeremy Hamp, Charlotte Cain*

Television drama; corporate film and video. OUTPUT has included a 3-part drama for Ford Motors on customer care (with 'lip sync' into twelve languages); technical service training video programmes, and a one-hour television play. Commissioned work only. No unsolicited mss, although always keen to meet scriptwriters.

Chromavision Ltd

200 York Road, London SW11 3SA
☎ 01–223 9312

Contact *Jeremy Jacobs, Adam Woods*

Makers of video – documentary; commercials; corporate; training; point-of-sale. OUTPUT includes TV and cinema commercials. Unsolicited mss welcome but have a regular team of writers specialising in various subjects.

Chrysalis TV Group Ltd

Threeways House, 40–44 Clipstone Street, London W1P 7EA
☎ 01–436 8891 Fax 01–436 3523

Contact *Shelley Miller, Nick Hicks-Beach*

Programmes for all British broadcast channels, with particular expertise in the documentary field and magazine programmes. Recent OUTPUT has included *See For Yourself* (BBC); several editions of *Equinox* (Channel 4); *Des Res* (pilot sitcom for LWT); and a weekly community magazine programme *Action* for TVS. Currently developing a five-day-a-week soap opera with the BBC and an action drama series with ABC Distribution in USA. Welcome unsolicited mss, time permitting, and are always interested in new script/programme proposals.

Cinexsa Film Productions Limited

209 Manygate Lane, Shepperton, Middlesex TW17 9ER
☎ 0932 225950 Fax 01–436 6327

Contact *Jimmy Wright*

Film, video and TV – documentary and commercials. No unsolicited mss but 'new writing is welcomed'.

City Photographic and Video Services

1–4 Caer Street, Swansea SA1 3PP
☎ 0792 467688/650742

Contact *R.H. Kneath*

Film, video and TV – commercials and documentary. Welcome unsolicited mss. 'Willing to look into any ideas.'

Cleveland Productions

5 Rainbow Court, Oxhey, Herts WD1 4RP
☎ 0923 54000

Contact *Michael Gosling*

Film and video – documentary and commercials.

Colchester Film and Video

Workshop, 21 St Peter's Street, Colchester CO1 1EW
☎ 0206 560255

Contact *Paul Pelowski*

Promotion and documentary work for the voluntary and arts sectors.

Colstar Communications Entertainment Ltd

1 Wardour Mews, D'Arblay Street, London W1V 3FF
☎ 01–437 5725 Fax 01–439 8305

Contact *Stephen Goddard*

International distributors of broadcast programming for all media: documentaries, short films, drama programme specials and series. Library includes films and series on art, the sciences, history, sport and nature. TITLES include *The National Gallery – A Private View; Kenneth Clark's Romantic Classic Art; The Wandering Company; The Life and Times of Lord Mountbatten; The Monkey's Paw; The Man Who Loves Giants; The Most Dangerous Animal.*

Compass Film Productions Ltd

Third Floor, 18–19 Warwick Street, London W1R 5RB
☎ 01–439 6456

Contact *Simon Heaven*

Specialists since 1974 in documentary, educational and promotional programmes for television and corporate clients. Recent OUTPUT has included *Another Way of Life* (on mental handicap); *Music of the Outsiders*, and *Concerning Cancer* for Channel 4.

Component Television Productions Ltd

1 Newman Passage, London W1P 3PF
☎ 01–631 4400

Contact *Gaby Bedford*

Corporate videos, documentary, drama, retail videos, TV. Welcome unsolicited mss, 'of documentary style only'. 'Most of our work is commissioned but we are open to ideas, particularly for Channel 4 programming.'

Consolidated Productions Ltd

5 Jubilee Place, London SW3 3TD
☎ 01–376 5151 Fax 01–225 2890

Contact *Annette Kiely*

Worldwide television. OUTPUT has included *Deceptions*, mini-series co-produced with Columbia and BBC; *Gathering of Old Men*, 2-hour feature film; *Where Do I Come From?*, animated cartoon; *Nightmare Years*, 8-hour mini-series about Second World War; *Campion* for BBC.

Cosmos Productions

42–4 Hanway Street, London W1P 9DE
☎ 01–631 3041

Contact *Ronis Varlaam*

Television makers. OUTPUT has included *Enthusiasts* (six half-hour documentaries), plus *Well You Didn't Expect Us To Sit Around Doing Nothing Did You?* (on unemployment) – both for Channel 4.

David Cox Associates

Portman House, Portland Road, Jesmond, Newcastle upon Tyne NE2 1AQ
☎ 091–261 6881

Contact *Peter Brown*

Film and video production company with many commercial clients.

Creative Film Makers Ltd

Pottery Lane House, 34A Pottery Lane, London W11 4LZ
☎ 01–229 5131 Fax 01–229 4999

Contact *Michael Seligman, Julian Roberts*

Corporate and sports documentaries; commercials; TV programmes. OUTPUT has included *Golden Greats of Golf* and various corporate or sports programmes for clients like Nestlé, Benson & Hedges, Wimpey, Bouygues. Always open to suggestions but have hardly ever received unsolicited material of any value. Keen, though, to encourage new writers.

The Crew

186 Monkmoor Road, Shrewsbury, Shropshire SY2 5BH
☎ 0743 3684 Fax 0743 4009

Contact *Simon Rea*

Film and video makers – in-house communications; training; sales; corporate. Welcome unsolicited mss.

Cromdale Films Limited

12 St Paul's Road, London N1 2QN
☎ 01–226 0178

Contact *Ian Lloyd*

Film video and TV – drama and documentary. OUTPUT *The Face of Darkness* (feature film); *Drift to Dawn* (rock music drama); *The Overdue Treatment* (documentary).

Crystalvision Productions Ltd

Communications House, Blue Riband Estate, Roman Way, Croydon CR9 3RA
☎ 01–681 7171
Telex 881 4079 Fax 01–681 2340

Contact *Fraser Ashford* (Executive Producer)

Film, video, TV and cable/satellite programming – children's, documentary, drama, music, sports. OUTPUT *Shady Tales* (13-part drama co-production for Thames TV); *The History of Cricket; The Other China; World Invitation Club Basketball Championships; Nicky & the Newsgang* (children's). Welcome unsolicited material which should have treatment/outline page. 'Each project is studied on merit; if the story/idea is good we would work with new writers.'

CTR Productions

31 Lismore Crescent, Broadfield, Crawley, West Sussex RH11 9DA
☎ 0293 548475

Contact *Ian Cunningham, Roseanne Coils*

Video and television – documentary, music, children's, religion. Specialise in promotional work/documentaries for churches, schools, education authorities and voluntary organisations. Particularly interested currently in children's work. OUTPUT has included *Sex Matters* for Channel 4 and *Christians and Trade Unions.*

Cwmni'r Castell Cyf

1 Coed Pella Road, Colwyn Bay, Clwyd LL29 7AT
☎ 0492 533148

Contact *Elwyn Vaughan Williams*

Television programmes. OUTPUT has included *The Scouts Holiday*, a mute comedy film and *Galw Gari*, light entertainment – both for S4C; various other light entertainment programmes with comedy sketches.

Dareks Production House

58 Wickham Road, Beckenham, Kent BR3 2RQ
☎ 01–658 2012

Contact *David Crossman*

Independent producers of broadcast television – factual and fictional programmes for ITV and Channel 4. OUTPUT *The Cannon & Ball Show; Metal Mickey; The Pocket Money Programme.* Unsolicited mss welcome: 'we are looking for original minds, and have an interest in tragic situations in modern contexts.' No longer interested in situation comedy scripts; short film stories welcome.

Dateline Productions Ltd

79 Dean Street, London W1V 5HA
☎ 01–437 4510/1834

Contact *Miranda Watts*

Film and video – documentary and corporate. Welcome unsolicited mss. 'We are always interested in widening our list of possible writers.'

DBA Television

21 Ormeau Avenue, Belfast BT2 8HD
☎ 0232 231197 Telex 747001

Contact *David Barker*

Long-established makers of documentary. Recent OUTPUT has included *Power in the Blood* for Arena BBC2; *Learning to Lose* and *Dust on the Bible* for Channel 4. New series *Nothing to Fear* with writer Damian Gorman for Channel 4.

DBI Communication

21 Congreve Close, Warwick CV34 5RQ
☎ 0926 497695/58901 (edit studio)

Contact *David B. Impey*

Video – corporate, promotion, safety, training and sales. Do not welcome unsolicited mss as most programmes are 'customised'. OUTPUT has included *Play Safe* with Keith Chegwin (about the dangers of children entering quarries), shown in schools nationwide.

Deptford Beach Productions Ltd

79 Wardour Street, London W1V 3TH
☎ 01–734 8508

Contact *Tony Kirkhope*

FOUNDED 1985 to make independent productions for Channel 4. OUTPUT includes documentary about Jean-Luc Godard, directed and written by him.

Destination Productions

Chandos House, 74 Chandos Avenue, Whetstone, London N20 9DZ
☎ 01–445 3178

Contact *Barry Weitz*

Makers of TV documentary and commercials, plus corporate video. Recent OUTPUT has included a drama documentary on housing; various commercials for the Entertainment Corporation; and training films for clients like British Telecom. Welcome unsolicited mss and happy to collaborate with new writers.

Dibgate Productions Ltd

Studio 4, Parkstead Lodge, 31 Upper Park Road, London NW3 2UL
☎ 01–722 5634

Contact *Nicholas Parsons*

Make documentary and travel films for television and, increasingly in recent years, shorts for cinema audiences. OUTPUT has included *A Fair Way to Play, Mad Dogs and Cricketers, Relatively Greek, Viva Menorca* and *Terribly British.*

Diverse Productions Ltd

6 Gorleston Street, London W14 8XS
☎ 01–688 6336 Fax 01–603 2148

Contact *Frank Dynes, Graham Walker*

Corporate video, and television – current affairs, satellite business news, and educational programme; all produced in-house. Recent OUTPUT has included *9-II-5, Open at One*, and *Not On Sunday*.

Drake A-V Video Ltd

89 St Fagans Road, Fairwater, Cardiff CF5 3AE
☎ 0222 560333 Fax 0222 554909
Telex 497618 TYPES G DRAKED

Contact *Ian Lewis*

Corporate A-V film and video – mostly documentary and promotional. No unsolicited mss. Query letter and brief synopsis in the first instance.

East Anglian Film-Makers

22 Colegate, Norwich NR3 1BQ
☎ 0603 622313

Contact *Alistair Reid*

Film and video – drama, documentary, non-broadcast, community, promos and corporate. OUTPUT tends to be arts- or community-based; also education, local government/authorities, etc. Welcome unsolicited mss and encourage new writing.

Edinburgh Film & Video Productions

Nine Mile Burn, by Penicuik,
Midlothian EH26 9LT
☎ 0968 72131

Contact *R. Crichton*

Film, TV drama and documentary. OUTPUT has included *Silent Mouse; The Curious Case of Santa Claus; The Stamp of Greatness.* Welcome new writing.

The Elstree (Production) Co Ltd

Goldcrest Elstree Studios, Shenley Road,
Borehamwood, Herts WD6 1JG
☎ 01–953 1600 Telex 922436 E FILMS G

Produces feature films and television drama/situation comedy. OUTPUT includes *Prospects* for Euston Films/Channel 4; *Rude Health* for Channel 4 and *Great Expectations* for Disney Channel. No unsolicited scripts at present.

Emitel

65 Beak Street, Soho, London W1R 3LF
☎ 01–439 9882

Contact *Malcolm Craddock*

Corporate video, training and educational films, sponsored films.

Enigma Productions Ltd

11–15 Queen's Gate Place Mews,
London SW7 5BG
☎ 01–581 0238 Fax 01–225 2230

Contact *David Puttnam*

Underwent a major relaunch in 1988 following David Puttnam's resignation from Columbia Pictures Hollywood. Backed by Warner Brothers, NatWest, Fujisankei Communications and British Satellite Broadcasting, and 'could provide the model for a new beginning for British cinema' (David Puttnam). 'We shall use British crews but with writers, actors and directors from around the world.' Projects in development include *Memphis Belle* (true story of an American B-17 bomber crew in Second World War); *Opera Europa* (comedy about a multinational opera company); *The October Circle* (Soviet political thriller).

Enlightenment AV & Video

The Studio, Warrens Lane, Botesdale, Diss,
Norfolk IP22 1BW
☎ 0379 898434 Fax 0379 898987

Contact *Adrian Tayler*

Video productions for training and industrial marketing. All scripts currently produced in-house, or commissioned by a client for a specific project, but will consider unsolicited mss if appropriate to their market, e.g. technical subjects such as insurance, animal health or computers.

Epic Communications

22 Brighton Square, Brighton, Sussex BN1 1HD
☎ 0273 728686/821567

Contact *Alan Holden* (Production Director), *Tracy Garrett* (Production Manager)

Film and video – corporate training, medical, interactive video production.

Equal Time

Heath Lodge, Heathside, London NW3 1BL
☎ 01–431 1927

Contact *Martin Mimms*

Documentaries on music, the arts and current affairs. Few opportunities as use mostly broadcast material in collaboration with BBC, ITV, etc. 'But if you've had a chat with the BBC or ITV and they like what you do, we'd be willing to see it.'

Eurofilm Productions Ltd

47 Ossington Street, London W2 4LY
☎ 01–243 1613

Contact *Andrzej Swoboda*

OUTPUT has included *Modern Polish Composers* for Channel 4 and *King Size*, a short science fiction comedy feature.

Euston Films

365 Euston Road, London NW1 3AR
☎ 01–387 0911 Fax 01–388 2122

Contact *Joanna Willett*

Feature films; television series and serials. OUTPUT has included *Bellman and True, Consuming Passions* and *The Fear*.

Fairwater Films

389 Newport Road, Cardiff CF2 1RP
☎ 0222 460302
Telex 497492 CHACOM G Fax 0222 489785

Contact *Naomi Jones*

Makers of animated films. OUTPUT has included a cartoon series for S4C, *Hanner Dwsin, The Shoe People* (Tram). Recent productions include *Satellite City*, and various ads, etc.

Fidelity Films Ltd

34–6 Oak End Way, Gerrards Cross, Bucks SL9 8BR
☎ 0753 884646
Telex 846723 AUDVIS G Fax 0753 887163

Contacts *John Fewlass, Graham Harris*

Corporate, training, sales and exhibition videos. Welcome unsolicited mss; 'always willing to try new scriptwriters'.

Filmessence Limited

302 Clive Court, London W9 1SF
☎ 01–289 5850

Contact *Don Morrison*

Film and video – drama, documentary and commercials. Unsolicited mss welcome.

Filmfair Ltd

Jacobs Well Mews, London W1H 5PD
☎ 01–935 1596 Fax 01–935 0229

Contact *Lewis Rudd*

FOUNDED 1966. Makers of children's and educational television, cable and video. OUTPUT *The Wombles; Paddington Bear; Portland Bill; The Perishers; The Blunders; Bangers and Mash.* 'If unsolicited mss come in, they are read.'

First Choice

See **Humphrey Barclay Productions**

Fitting Images Ltd

Alfred House, 127A Outlands Drive, Weybridge, Surrey KT13 9LB
☎ 0932 840056 Fax 0932 858075

Contact *Sue Fleetwood* (Managing Director)

Film, and video: point-of-sale; health and safety; corporate; induction; team building; customer relations; keyboard skills; security. Unsolicited mss welcome.

Five Lamps Production Company

Five Lamps Studio, West Avenue, Derby DE1 3HR
☎ 0332 383322 Fax 0332 291268

Contact *Mollie Kirkland, David Regan*

Part of the Five Lamps Group; formerly traded as Concept for Communications Ltd. Industrial video, conferences and audio visual. Total in-house facilities, including writing. No unsolicited mss.

Flamingo Pictures

47 Lonsdale Square, London N1 1EW
☎ 01–607 9958

Contact *Christine Oestreicher*

Television programmes and cinema films.

Mostly cinema and of that, mostly fiction. OUTPUT has included *Every Picture Tells a Story* for Channel 4, *Loser Takes All*, Graham Green, for cinema release in 1989 and *Dibs*, in development.

FM Television Limited

92 Water Lane, Wilmslow, Cheshire SK9 5BB
☏ 0625 533580
Telex 667028 WILSEC G   Fax 0625 531992

Contact *Hilary Pinnock*

Sports programmes for international broadcasters; corporate videos for industry. OUTPUT *Budweiser Grand Prix* series for powerboats, world dragster car racing. No unsolicited mss.

Forever Films

7A–9 Earlham Street, London WC2H 9LL
☏ 01–836 5105

Contact *Clare Downs*

Describe their intended audience as 'specialised to crossover feature film audience'. OUTPUT *The Dress* (short romantic fantasy, BAFTA award winner); *High Season* (serious comedy feature); *Buster's Bedroom* (absurdist drama). No unsolicited mss. Very interested in writing which has energy and wit, with a serious undertone.

Formula Communications

3 Avebury Court, Mark Road, Maryland's Avenue, Hemel Hempstead, Hertfordshire HP2 7TA
☏ 0442 63885/61358

Contact *Colleen Bending, Steve Arnold*

Video – commercials, corporate, training; AV multi-image production, conferences, presentations.

Mark Forstater Productions Ltd

8A Trebeck Street, London W1V 7RL
☏ 01–408 0733   Fax 01–499 8772
Telex 8954665 VBSTLX G Ref MFP

Contact *Nicola Lund*

Active in the selection, development and production of material for film, television and theatre. OUTPUT *Monty Python and the Holy Grail; The Odd Job; The Grass is Singing; Xtro; Forbidden; The Fantasist.* Unsolicited mss considered, but prefer writers to send synopses in the first instance.

Fowler and Wowrek Film Co. Ltd

2nd Floor, 12 D'Arblay Street,
London W1V 3FP
☏ 01–734 5877

Contact *Yanina Wowrek*

Commercials, pop videos and corporate. OUTPUT has included a 'Style Council' pop video; *Water Safety* (C.0.1); and *Hypothermia in Elderly* (C.0.1). Welcome unsolicited mss.

Freeway Films

31 Albany Street, Edinburgh EH1 3QN
☏ 031–557 0882   Fax 031–558 3137

Contact *John McGrath, Susie Brown*

Film outlet fo John McGrath's work. OUTPUT has included *Blood Red Roses* and *There is a Happy Land* for Channel 4. *The Dressmaker,* from the novel by Beryl Bainbridge, scripted by John McGrath, for *Film on 4* International and British Screen. Recent projects: *Border Warfare*, a 3-part series on Anglo-Scots relations, and *The Long Roads*, a feature film.

Frontroom Productions Ltd

79 Wardour Street, London W1
☏ 01–734 4603

Contact *Angela Topping*

Television and cinema, both shorts and full-length features. OUTPUT has included *Acceptable Levels, Ursula Glenys, Intimate Strangers* and *The Love Child.*

Gateway Audio Visual and Video

472 Green Lanes, London N13 5XF
☏ 01–882 0177

Contact *Graham L. Smart*

Producers of video and film for sponsors. Work has included marketing, training and corporate programmes for various clients; also TV commercials. No unsolicited mss but 'always on the look-out for new scriptwriters'.

John Gau Productions

Burston House, 1 Burston Road, Putney,
London SW15
☏ 01–788 8811   Fax 01–789 0903

Contact *Susan Gau*

Documentaries and series for television, plus corporate video. OUTPUT has included *Assignment Adventure, Moneyspinner* and *Sputniks, Bleeps and Mr Perry* for Channel 4, the *Korea* series for BBC1, and *Reaching for the Skies* for BBC2.

Gibb Rose Organisation Ltd

Pinewood Studios, Iver, Bucks SL0 0NH
☏ 0753 651700
Telex 847505 PINEW G Fax 0753 656935

Contact *Sydney Rose* (Managing Director), *Keith Belcher* (Creative Director)

Film, video and TV. Corporate and sales videos through to independent productions for ITV (music, film, documentary) to full feature film. Unsolicited mss not welcome unless at full screenplay level. 'We will examine ideas and scripts after initial discussion with the author.'

Adrian Gilpin Television

Kilchurn House, South Street, Rotherfield, East Sussex TN6 3LU
☏ 0892 853267

Contact *Adrian Gilpin*

Originally theatre production company; currently expanding and concentrating on TV/film production. Looking mainly for TV comedy scripts at the moment.

Bob Godfrey Films

199 King's Cross Road, London WC1X 9DB
☏ 01–278 5711 Fax 01–278 6809

Contact *Mike Hayes*

Animated films, children's TV series, adult political work, plus shorts for cinema and television. Do not have time to read mss – have been inundated with them in the past and not been able to sift through them even. Best approach by phone or letter in first instance. Cannot sponsor writers in any way ... 'only do films for people who'll pay us!'

Goldcrest Films and Television Ltd

36–44 Brewer Street, London W1R 3HP
☏ 01–437 8696/953 1600
Telex 267458 Goldcr Fax 01–437 4448

Once stood for all that was best in the British film industry. 1987, bought by Masterman, a company jointly owned by the producer-entrepreneur Brent Walker and the Merchant Newy Offices Pension Fund. Modest productions promised. Developing material for feature films but only scripts through agents with directors attached.

Grasshopper Productions Ltd

50 Peel Street, London W8 7PD
☏ 01–229 1181

Contact *Joy Whitby*

Children's Programmes and adult drama. FOUNDED 1970 by Joy Whitby, who has no use for outside writing as this is her own area of expertise. No unsolicited mss.

Greenpark Productions Ltd

St Wilfrids, 101 Honor Oak Park, London SE23 3LB
☏ 01–699 7234 Telex 25247 GPK

Contact *David Morphet*

Makers of short, documentary, specialised and business-sponsored films; video and television (general). Welcome unsolicited mss.

Greenpoint Films

5A Noel Street, London W1V 3RB
☏ 01–437 6492

Contact *Ann Scott, Patrick Cassavetti*

A small company whose members act as individual producers and directors. Check before sending unsolicited material.

Colin Gregg Films Ltd

Floor 2, 1–6 Falconberg Court, London W1V 5SG
☏ 01–439 0257

Contact *Colin Gregg*

Feature films for Channel 4 and BBC2. OUTPUT *Remembrance; To The Lighthouse; Lamb; Hard Travelling; We Think The World of You.* Unsolicited mss are welcome. Original scripts are preferred to adapted material.

Griffin Productions

Balfour House, 46–54 Great Titchfield Street, London W1P 7AE
☏ 01–636 5066 Fax 01–436 3232

Contact *Adam Clapham*

Documentary and drama television. OUTPUT has

included *Painting With Light* for BBC; *Odyssey* for Channel 4 and *Betrayal* (mini series) for ITV.

Nick Hague Productions Ltd

Film House, 142 Wardour Street,
London W1V 3AU
☎ 01–637 4904/01–734 1600
Telex 24865 SVCLTD G   Fax 01–437 1854

Contact *Nick Hague, Michael Algar, Rosalind Allen*

Film, video and TV – commercials, corporate, drama, documentary. No unsolicited mss.

David Hall Productions

30–38 Dock Street, Leeds LS10 1JF
☎ 0532 422586

Contact *David Hall*

Makers of television drama and documentaries, film, corporate video. Welcomes unsolicited mss. Encourages and supports new writing but 'unfortunately I do not have the financial resources to provide development funding for speculative projects'. OUTPUT *Maggie's Children* and *All of You Out There* (both documentaries for Channel 4); *Silver Shadows* (feature film in development), and various regional documentaries for Yorkshire Television.

Hamilton Perry

Merged with ICM International in 1988 to form **HPICM International** (see entry).

Handmade Films

26 Cadogan Square, London SW1X 0JP
☎ 01–581 1265
Telex 8951338 EURODO   Fax 01–584 7338

OUTPUT has included *Mona Lisa; The Missionary; Time Bandits; Withnail and I; The Lonely Passion of Judith Hearne* and, more recently, *The Raggedy Rawney; Checking Out, How To Get Ahead in Advertising.* Company policy is not to accept unsolicited mss direct from writers, though they do consider submissions from literary agents, publishers and producers.

John Hemson

The Bakehouse, Media Resource Centre,
Bedford Road, Aspley Guise, Milton
Keynes MK17 8DH
☎ 0908 583062

Contact *John Hemson*

Film and television – training, sales, documentary. Wishes to encourage new writing. Unsolicited mss welcome.

Philip Hinden

33 Albert Street, London NW1 7LU
☎ 01–380 0375

Contact *V. Marsh*

Producer of quiz panel game shows for TV and theatre. No unsolicited material welcome but always interested in new ideas/writing.

Hines Television Ltd

Britannic Building, Hargreaves Street, Burnley,
Lancs BB11 1DU
☎ 0282 52521   Fax 0282 30297

Contact *David E. Hines, Peter Hunt, Lawrence Windley*

Television – broadcast and corporate. Moving towards more drama this year.

Holmes Associates

10–16 Rathbone Street, London W1P 1AH
☎ 01–637 8251   Fax 01–637 9024

Contact *Andrew Holmes*

Prolific originators, producers and packagers of children's, comedy, documentary, drama and music television. OUTPUT has included *Piece of Cake* (drama mini-series for LWT); documentaries – *Arts Weekly* and *Well Being* for Channel 4; children's – *Chish 'n' Fips* for Central and *Video & Chips* for HTV; music – *Four Up Two Down* for Channel 4.

HPICM International

53 Frith Street, London W1V 5TE
☎ 01–434 0929

Contact *John Wyatt*

Formerly ICM but merged with Hamilton Perry in 1988. Prominent makers of corporate video for major commercial and industrial clients.

Humphrey Barclay Productions

7 Garrick Street, London WC2E 9AR
☎ 01–240 1128   Fax 01–497 9242

Contact *Al Mitchell, Tony Humphreys*

TV – situation comedy and drama. Recently set up a subsidiary company **First Choice**, run by producer/writer Moira Williams. Both HBP and First Choice have a joint administrative base with

Barclay, ex-LWT, as director of both. HBP will continue to concentrate on fully commissioned projects, while First Choice plans to acquire and develop scripts through a development fund, financed by the parent company. OUTPUT (HBP) *Relative Strangers* (Channel 4); *Hot Metal* (LWT); *Thompson* (BBC); *Surgical Spirit* (Granada); *Behaving Badly* (Channel 4); *Desmonds* (Channel 4). Projects in development (First Choice) include *Mary and Richard* (feature film); *The Excursion to the Source* (TV adaptation of Elizabeth Taylor's novel).

ICE International Video Films Ltd

31 King Street West, Manchester M3 2PN
☎ 061–834 3992

Contact *David Kent-Watson*

TV and video – film and drama. OUTPUT has included *Into the Darkness; Assassinator; Kill.* Welcome unsolicited mss; always looking for new writers.

ICP – Innovative and Creative Productions

Studio Centre, Ackhurst Road, Chorley, Lancs PR7 1ND
☎ 02572 66411/4 Fax 02572 68490

Contact *Michael Mulvihill*

Multi-media production for a great variety of clients.

The Ideas Factory

1st Floor, Kingston Mill, Chestergate, Stockport SK3 0AG
☎ 061–474 7786

Contact *Martin Duffy*

Film, video and TV. OUTPUT has included *Don't Just Sit There* for Channel 4; *Telethon '88* for Granada, and various corporate productions. Special interests: adventure, travel, activities, and disability.

Illuminations

16 Newman Passage, London W1P 3PE
☎ 01–580 7877 Telex 23152 Monref G

Contact *Linda Zuck*

Primarily a documentary production company, making cultural programmes for a Channel 4 audience. OUTPUT has included *State of the Art* (6-part documentary series); *Ghosts in the Machine* (6-part video compilation series); plus other documentaries about art and television. No unsolicited mss.

Image Productions

4F Newton Court, Wavertree Technology Park, Liverpool L13 1EJ
☎ 051–259 5551 Fax 051–259 5551

Contact *Paul Grice*

Corporate video production aimed principally at training and sales promotion.

Imagicians

8 Newburgh Street, London W1V 1LH
☎ 01–439 2244
Telex 299200 MOLI G Fax 01–734 6813

Contact *Alan Scales*

Diverse productions, from television documentary features to in-flight videos and corporate production. OUTPUT has included *The Great Palace – the Story of Parliament; Mary Wesley – Not That Sort of Girl*, (documentary on the writer) for BBC; *Roller Hockey* sports series for Channel 4; various corporate videos for clients like ICI, IBM and British Telecom.

Inca Video & Film Productions

Park House Studios, PO Box 111,, London SE26 5DB
☎ 01–778 7318

Contact *Peter Ashton*

Video and film – travel, commercials, promotional and sales. No unsolicited mss.

Independent Business Television Ltd

PO Box 4BE, 22–5 Portman Close, London W1A 4BE
☎ 01–487 4474 Fax 01–997 8738

Contact *Sue Tramontini, Patrick Veale*

Film and video – drama and documentary. Recent OUTPUT includes mostly corporate productions for the public sector, multinationals, etc. No unsolicited mss.

Independent Film Production Associates

87 Dean Street, London W1V 5AA
☎ 01–734 3847
Telex 265871 Ref MMU441 Fax 01–734 0776

Contact *Aileen McCracken*

Makers of documentary and entertainment television, plus corporate video. Unsolicited mss are 'sometimes welcome ... if it's good we go with it.'

Independent Producers Ltd

65 Shelton Street, London WC2H 9HE
☎ 01–240 3742 Fax 01–240 8267

Contact *Jan Martin*

Corporate – extending from drama to point-of-sale and documentary.

Infovision Ltd

63 White Lion Street, London N1 9PP
☎ 01–837 0012

Contact *John Mayhew* (Managing Director)

Corporate video makers in the areas of training, marketing, and internal communications. Household-name clients.

In-House Corporate Video

The Boundary House, Old Warwick Road, Lapworth, Warwickshire B94 6LU
☎ 056433958

Contact *John Pluck* (Senior Producer)

Corporate films and videos for training, marketing and public relations. No unsolicited mss, but interested in hearing from writers with corporate experience, with a sample of writing in this area.

Insight Productions Ltd

Gidleigh Studio, Gidleigh, Chagford, Newton Abbot, Devon TQ13 8HP

Contact *Brian Skilton*

TV and film – drama, documentary and light entertainment. OUTPUT has included *Taming the Flood, Streets Ahead* and *Dartmoor The Threatened Wilderness,* all series for Channel 4; *Playing Away* (feature film – 'Film on 4'). No unsolicited mss. 'We welcome new ideas or scripts for films for cinema or TV but prefer to discuss the subject before accepting a script to read or comment upon.'

Interesting Television Ltd

The Boundary House, Old Warwick Road, Lapworth, Warwickshire B94 6LU
☎ 056433958 Fax 056433619

Contact *John Pluck* (Senior Producer)

Produce broadcast television documentaries and feature series on film and video for ITV and BBC TV. Will be increasingly looking towards cable, satellite and home video to broaden output. Welcome ideas for television documentaries. Send a treatment in the first instance, particularly if the subject is 'outside our area of current interest'. OUTPUT has included television programmes on heritage and antiques, and industry. Projects on heritage and sports for the home video front.

Peter Isaac Ltd

94 High Street, Bildeston, Suffolk IP7 7EB
☎ 0449 741248

Contact *Peter Isaac*

Film, video and TV – documentary and commercials. Special interest in medical and animal husbandry. Open to new writing but no unsolicited mss. OUTPUT has included *Cats* (RSPCA Corporate); *Understanding Chemotherapy; Early Detection of Breast Cancer; Understanding Cystic Fibrosis.*

Isolde Films Ltd

4 Kensingon Park Gardens, London W11 3HB
☎ 01–727 3541
Telex 267409 Isolde G Fax 01–727 3632

Contact *Maureen Murray*

Film and television – drama and documentary. OUTPUT has included *Mozart in Japan* (TV film); *Maria Callas* (TV film); *Testimony* (film); *In From The Cold* (portrait of Richard Burton); *Dvorak In Love?* No unsolicited mss.

Brian Jenkinson Film & Television Productions Ltd

32 Heaton Road, Newcastle upon Tyne NE6 1SD
☎ 091–276 1970 Fax 091–265 3026

Contact *Brian Jenkinson*

Commercials, news and drama.

Paul Joyce Productions

5 Townley Road, Dulwich, London SE22
☎ 01–693 6006

Contact *Paul Joyce*

Development and production of arts, adventure, current affairs, documentary, drama and music, television and cinema. OUTPUT has included *Nothing as it Seems* (the films of Nicolas Roeg), *The Man Who Left His Soul on Film, Summer Lightning* for 'Film on 4', *Out of the Blue and Into the Black* (about Dennis Hopper) and *Tickets for the Titanic: Everyone a Winner*, with Jonathan Pryce and Anna Carteret.

Michael Kann Associates Ltd

4 Beak Street Studios, 65–9 Beak Street, London W1R 3LF
☎ 01–439 9882 Fax 01–734 8574

Contact *Michael Kann, Julian Harvey, Kate Davidson*

Corporate films, including documentary and drama. CLIENTS include Ford Motor Co., British Council, Ladbroke Holidays and Hotels. No unsolicited mss but always looking for fresh, new writing.

Kay Communications Ltd

Gauntley Court Studios, Gauntley Court, Nottingham NG7 5HD
☎ 0602 781333 Fax 0602 783734

Contact *John Alexander*

Makers of industrial video programmes and training programmes. Scripts written in-house. No unsolicited mss.

Knaves Acre Productions

The Crest, Hoe Lane, Abinger Hammer, Dorking, Surrey RH5 6RL
☎ 0306 731007

Contact *Bryan Izzard*

Makers of broadcast television principally for Channel 4 and ITV. Unusual biographies of unusual composers, comedy (particularly sitcom), popular video drama. Recent OUTPUT has included *A Ladies Knight* (MOR music show featuring Sir Geraint Evans) and *Spread A Little Happiness* (profile of Vivian Ellis), both for HTV; *Stars on a Dark Night* – music special for Channel 4 in 1989. Unsolicited mss welcome.

Landseer Film and Television Productions

100 St Martin's Lane, London WC2N 4AZ
☎ 01–240 3161 Fax 01–240 8975

Arts, adventure, children's, current affairs, documentary, drama and music television. Principally arts documentaries (and videos of performances), but also television drama. OUTPUT has included *Mr Pye* with Derek Jacobi and *A Penny for Your Dreams*, a co-production with BBC Wales and S4C.

Lawson Productions Ltd

2 Clarendon Close, London W2 2NS
☎ 01–706 3111 Fax 01–706 3035

Contact *Sarah Lawson*

Film & TV – drama and comedy. OUTPUT has included *That's Love* (UK and US); *Home to Roost* (US version); *The Dawning* with Anthony Hopkins. No unsolicited mss unless via agents. Always welcome new talent.

Limehouse Productions

The Trocadero, 19 Rupert Street, London W1V 7FS
☎ 01–287 3333

Contact *Iain Bruce, Richard Key*

Dramatic adaptations made for television and video (mostly video). OUTPUT has included *But What if it's Raining; Rocket to the Moon; To Have and To Hold.* 'Not besieged' by unsolicited scripts, which are welcome direct from writers.

Lodestar Productions Ltd

15 Eyot Gardens, London W6 9TN
☎ 01–748 8517

Contact *Peter Coulson*

Film and TV – drama and documentary. Documentaries include *Odyssey* (Channel 4); *Nature* (BBC) and *Natural World* (BBC); drama developments include *Unflinching* (NFDF); *Anna's Story* (Channel 4 – 'Film on Four'). Projects tend to have 'a world about us nature'; a wilderness/exploring bias. Do commission from new writers but tend to come by way of recommendation.

London Film Productions Ltd

44A Floral Street, London WC2E 9DA
☎ 01–379 3366
Telex 896805 Fax 01–240 7065

Contact *Rosie Bunting*

Makers of a wide range of international television and film. OUTPUT has included *The Scarlet Pimpernel; Kim; Country Girls; Poldark; I Claudius.* No unsolicited material considered.

Loose Alliance

80 Appley Lane North, Appley Bridge, Wigan WN6 9AQ
☎ 02575 4825

Contact *Alan Marsden, Janice Davinson*

Film, video and TV – drama, documentary, commercials. Camera services, including steadicam on 130 episodes of *Brookside*. Unsolicited mss very welcome. Particularly interested in work from Northern writers, keen to foster low-budget broadcast drama.

LTV Productions

53 Kirkgate, Shipley, Bradford BD8 3LU
☎ 0274 585289 Fax 0274 531698

Contact *Simon Allison*

Video – drama and documentary; company training and sales promotion. No unsolicited mss.

Magda Films Ltd

12 Winchester Place, London N6 5HJ
☎ 01–341 7966

Contact *Lorne Magory*

Film, video and TV – corporate, documentary, children's drama. Encourage and welcome new writers/unsolicited mss.

Magic Hour Films Ltd

143 Chatsworth Road, London NW2 5QT
☎ 01–459 3074

Contact *B. M. Ford, L. de Villiers*

Makers of television and films for a serious adult audience. Documentaries, drama series, serials, shorts. OUTPUT has included *Life in Oasis, Alice!* and *Comparison – The World Through Working Women's Eyes.* Projects in development include a documentary on Third World Debt and a current affairs series on money, as well as a new drama series. Unsolicited mss welcome, provided an s.a.e is included for their return. 'We read all unsolicited manuscripts and try to encourage new writing.'

Malone Gill Productions Ltd

16 Newman Passage, London W1P 3PE
☎ 01–580 6594
Telex 8951182 Fax 01–255 1473

Contact *Georgina Denison*

Mainly documentary, but also some drama productions. OUTPUT has included *Paul Gauguin: The Savage Dream; Vintage: A History of Wine* (by Hugh Johnson); *No Man Hath Seen God; Matisse in Nice; Space Craft; Pride of Place: Building the American Dream; Treasure Houses of Britain.* Prefer an outline proposal with letter in the first instance. 'Always interested in seeing new writing of quality.'

Marking Inc Productions

5 Mercer Street, Covent Garden, London WC2H 9QP
☎ 01–240 2345

Contact *Stacy Marking*

Film and TV – drama and documentary. OUTPUT *Guide to Genius* series for Channel 4. Query letter in the first instance.

Martak Ltd

Prospect Place, Mill Lane, Alton, Hampshire GU34 2SX
☎ 0420 88011 Fax 0420 82497

Contact *Bruce Vigar, Chris Wade*

Film and video documentary; corporate training, sales, promotion and education. Welcome unsolicited mss and willing to work with new writers.

The Media Show Ltd

See **Wall to Wall Television/The Media Show Ltd**

Medialab Ltd

Chelsea Wharf, 15 Lots Road, London SW10 0QH
☎ 01–351 5814 Fax 01–351 7898

Contact *John Gaydon* (Chairman)

FOUNDED 1982. Film and video production. Pop promos, TV documentaries, video label and a feature film with Godley & Creme. Interested in ideas for pop promos, investigative journalistic documentaries and feature films.

Medical & Scientific Productions

PO Box 493, Cookham, Maidenhead, Berks SL6 9TD
☎ 06285 31148
Telex 849462 Fax 0628 810029

Contact *Peter Fogarty*

Corporate – medical programmes for health care

professionals. Welcome health care ideas. No unsolicited mss.

Meditel Productions Ltd

Bedford Chambers, The Piazza, Covent Garden, London WC2 8HA
☎ 01–836 9216/9364
Telex 262284 Ref 3348
Fax 01–831 9489/405 1656

Contact *John Shenton, Jad Adams*

Intelligent documentaries, afternoon programmes factually-based with an element of fun; evening programmes with hard story lines (no fun required). OUTPUT has included *Food – Fad or Fact?* (a series taking a scientific look at attitudes to food); *AIDS – The Unheard Voices* (questioning the evidence that HIV causes AIDS); many documentaries on health care and the drug industry. No unsolicited mss; writers should submit programme ideas on factual subjects including drama/documentary ideas with strong story lines. Either previous experience is essential, or new writers will work closely with a producer appointed by the company.

Bill Melendez Productions Ltd

32–4 Great Marlborough Street, London W1V 1HA
☎ 01–439 4411/734 0691 Fax 01–439 6808

Contact *Steven Melendez, Graeme Spurway*

Animated films aimed mainly at a family audience, produced largely for the American market, and prime-time network broadcasting. Also develops and produces feature films (six so far). OUTPUT has included *Peanuts* (half-hour TV specials); *The Lion, The Witch and The Wardrobe; Babar the Elephant* (TV specials); IT Dick Deadeye or Duty Done, a rock musical based on Gilbert & Sullivan operettas. Generally produces own projects or work in collaboration with other producers/TV companies; 'however, three of the above walked in through the door'. Always interested in seeing new scripts and ideas.

Merchant Ivory Productions

46 Lexington Street, London W1P 3LH
☎ 01–437 1200

Contact *Ismail Merchant, Paul Bradley*

The darlings of the art houses: makers of quality, literate cinema for an international market. OUTPUT has included *Shakespeare Wallah, Heat and Dust, The Bostonians, Quartet, Room With A View, Maurice,* and *Slaves of New York.* Latterly going strong with E.M. Forster.

The Mersey Television Company Ltd

18 Rodney Street, Liverpool L1 2TQ
☎ 051–708 7846

Contact *Andrew Corrie*

Makers of television programmes – drama and fiction serials for popular consumption only. OUTPUT includes *Brookside* and *What Now?* for Channel 4.

Metcalf & Mills Ltd

101 Charing Cross Road, London WC2H 0DT
☎ 01–287 0814 Fax 01–434 1539

Contact *Charlotte Metcalf*

Commercials, concert films, documentary, pop promos, television. Welcome unsolicited mss. 'Being such a small, young company, we are open to anything'. OUTPUT includes *Vivat Regina*, a documentary for Channel 4; *Anthrax Live; Julian Cope Live; Aswad Live*; also TV commercials for *Atlantic Soul Classics, Tango in the Night, Bryan Ferry's Greatest Hits, The Hits Album*, and many more.

Metropolis Pictures Ltd

147 Crouch Hill, London N8 9QH
☎ 01–340 4649

Contact *Nick Dubrule*

A small independent film production company producing commissioned works for television. Its track record has been in quality documentaries/drama documentaries, though there are plans to produce low-budget fictional projects in the future. OUTPUT includes *Before Hindsight* (documentary feature on 1930s newsreels); *10 Years in An Open Necked Shirt*, featuring John Cooper Clarke; *The Rupert Bear Story*, directed by Terry Jones; *My Mama Done Told Me (A Torch Song)*, a TV special on the theme of obsessive love, featuring Lynn Seymour, for Channel 4. Very interested in working with new writers; but are presently too small a company to cope with unsolicited mss.

Midnight Films Ltd

26 Soho Square, London W1V 5FJ
☎ 01–434 0011
Telex 268157 OJKG Fax 01–434 9625

Contact *Michael Hamlyn*

FOUNDED 1976. Became active in 1981 when Julien Temple and Michael Hamlyn formed a partnership to produce *The Secret Policeman's Other Ball*. Developed *Absolute Beginners* until Julien Temple left to set up his own company. OUTPUT includes *White City* (1985), a music feature starring Pete Townshend; *U2 Rattle and Hum*, a full-length feature film – part concert film/part cinema verité documentary, directed by Phil Joanou; numerous pop promos for major international artists. Feature projects in development.

John Mills Video Productions

11 Hope Street, Liverpool L1 9BJ
☏ 051–709 9822 Fax 051–709 6585

Contact *Andrew Mills*

Corporate and training videos. No unsolicited mss.

Mirus Productions

9 Carnaby Street, London W1V 1PG
☏ 01–439 7113

Contact *Mike Wallington*

Documentary, music and arts television. OUTPUT includes many programmes for Channel 4, most recently *This Joint is Jumping* and *Colonial Madness* (1987), *One Love* and *Art Tatum* (1988), *Family Saga* (1989).

MJW Productions

13 Carlisle Road, London NW6 6TL
☏ 01–968 6542

Contact *Margaret Williams*

Makers of television programmes, cinema, corporate and educational video. OUTPUT has included a series for the Design Council and a Channel 13 film (New York) about composer Steve Reich. More recent productions include *Bodystyles* and *Different Trains* (Channel 4); *Noël A Paris* (Antenne 2 France).

MNV

7 Althorp Road, Wandsworth Common, London SW17 7ED
☏ 01–767 7501

Contact *Michael Norman*

Video – corporate, training, communications. Video publishing – special interest. Also conference television. OUTPUT includes special interest videos for Reader's Digest Home Video Library, and much big-screen TV work for conferences. No unsolicited mss but interested in new writers.

Mosaic Film & Video Productions

68 Clarence Road, Teddington, Middlesex TW11 0BW
☏ 01–977 5554

Contact *Adrian Antrum*

Film and video: TV and corporate documentaries. Areas of interest: social, spiritual/religious, metaphysical, paranormal, environmental. No unsolicited mss. All new writing is commissioned or self generated.

Moving Direction

Ground Floor, 97 Strawberry Vale, Twickenham, Middlesex TW15 4SJ
☏ 01–891 2604

Contact *Shaun Gale* (Director/Producer)

Makers of documentary and fictional productions on video and film. Welcome unsolicited mss. Open to new ideas and prefer writing in screenplay form. OUTPUT has included *Truckers Delight*, a documentary about truck racing; *Dick Head*, a gangster spoof for children's television; *'Presenting' in an Ideal World*, a corporate production for Panasonic UK.

Multiple Image Productions Ltd

168 Ferme Park Road, London N8 9SE
☏ 01–348 8635

Contact *Tim Langford*

TV drama and documentary. Corporate and educational training and promotional films. Welcome unsolicited mss. Interested in exploring co-production possibilities and nurturing new talent. OUTPUT has included *We're Not Mad ... We're Angry; Looking Back; Right to be Understood.*

New Decade Film & Video

61–3 Beak Street, London W1R 3LF
☏ 01–437 4284

Contact *Stanley Marks*

Film, video, TV documentary; corporate video. Produce mainly advertising, public relations, training and recruiting programmes.

Normandy Film Productions

49 Observatory Road, East Sheen,
London SW14 7QB
☎ 01–878 2646

Contact *David Turnbull*

Broadcast film/TV. Drama-documentaries, and arts. Welcome unsolicited mss. 'Wish to encourage new writing.' OUTPUT *The Song & The Story* (Prix Jeunesse, Munich 1982, BAFTA nominated); *The Meisel Mystery* (arts/documentary about the search for, reconstruction, and performance of the lost score for Eisenstein's *Oktober*).

Ocean Pictures Ltd

25 Melody Road, London SW18 2QW
☎ 01–870 5345

Contact *Roger Brown, Lucinda Sturgis*

Particularly interested in docu-drama and drama for film and TV.

Original Image

12–18 Grosvenor Gardens, London SW1H 0DH
☎ 01–824 8257
Telex 8956658 TPSG Fax 01–730 4293

Contact *Michael O'Toole, John Link*

Film/video – documentaries, drama, training, corporate. OUTPUT *Daley Thompson's Bodyshop* (Channel 4); in-flight entertainment; aircraft safety video demonstrations; financial and legal training. Welcome unsolicited mss. Wish to encourage new writing.

Orion Picture Corporation

31–2 Soho Square, London W1V 3FF

London office of an American giant.

Oxford Film & Video Makers

The Stables, North Place, Headington,
Oxford 0X3 9HY
☎ 0865 60074

Contact *Anne Marie Sweeney*

Makers of film and video for community, educational, trade union audiences. OUTPUT *Aids: Myth and Reality; Road or Reservation.* Unsolicited mss not welcome; 'we have enough work on already'. Though all their productions involve new writing, most of it is done in-house on a low budget.

Pace Productions Ltd

12 The Green, Newport Pagnell,
Bucks MK16 0JW
☎ 0908 618767 Fax 0908 617641

Contact *Chris Pettit, Aileen Spankie*

Film/video – drama, documentary, corporate and commercials.

Pacesetter Enterprises Ltd

1 Wardour Mews, D'Arblay Street,
London W1V 3FF
☎ 01–437 5725 Fax 01–439 8305

Production, co-production of international broadcast programming. A wholly-owned subsidiary of Colstar Communications and Entertainment Ltd. Credits include *The Wandering Company, In Search of Wildlife*. In development: *Brabant Antartica – A Survey, In Search of Wildlife*, second and third series. Currently looking for new co-production properties – in drama, documentary, the arts, sciences and nature.

Palace Productions

16–17 Wardour Mews, London W1V 3FF
☎ 01–734 7060

Contact *Stephen Wooley, Nik Powell*

OUTPUT includes *Company of Wolves; Absolute Beginners; Mona Lisa*; co-produced *Letter to Brezhnev; Chinese Boxes; The Courier, Siesta.* Unsolicited mss not welcome. As a small company, they aim to encourage new writing but can only do so 'on a limited basis'. Formed a TV arm, Palace TV, early 1989, headed by Martin Auty.

Parallax Pictures Ltd

7 Denmark Street, London WC2H 8LS
☎ 01–836 1478

Contact *Sally Hibbin*

Documentaries and commercials; projects for Channel 4.

Paramount Pictures (UK) Ltd

UAP House, 45 Beadon Road, London W6 0EG
☎ 01–741 9041 Fax 01–748 8990

'It is Paramount's policy not to accept unsolicited scripts'.

Peak Viewing Film and Video Productions Ltd

130 Canalot Production Studios, 222 Kensal Road, London W10 5BN
☎ 01–969 7139

Contact *Wendy Smith*

Film and video non-broadcast programmes for commercial business and voluntary organisations. Contributions to broadcast documentaries. Interested in feature film ideas and screenplays.

Pelicula Films

7 Queen Margaret Road, Glasgow G20 6DP
☎ 041–945 3333

Contact *Mike Alexander*

Television producers. Makers of drama documentaries for Channel 4, including *Gramsci, Down Home* and *Scapa Flow – 1919*.

Picture Base International

13–14 Golden Square, London W1R 3AG
☎ 01–287 5800 Fax 01–287 3779

Contact *Caroline Dring*

Television drama and films, and hoping to move into low-budget films in the future. OUTPUT *Little Match Girl* (HTV); *Child of Love* ('Film on Four' for SC4 and Channel 4); *Passion and Paradise* (HTV; ABC, USA; CTV, Canada).

Picture Palace Productions Ltd

1 Beak Street Studios, 65–9 Beak Street, London W1R 3LF
☎ 01–439 9882

Contact *Malcolm Craddock*

Television and cinema film and drama. OUTPUT *Tandoori Nights* series; *Ping Pong* (for 'Film on 4 International'); *Four Minutes* for Channel 4; *Eurocops, Hunting The Squirrel; Firing The Bullets.*

Picture Partnership Productions Ltd

73 Newman Street, London W1R 3LS
☎ 01–637 8056

Contact *Brian Eastman*

FOUNDED 1978. Picture Partnership makes feature films and popular entertainment television, with the emphasis on comedy. OUTPUT has included *Blott on the Landscape* and *Words of Love* (BBC); *Whoops Apocalypse* (ITC); *Porterhouse Blue* (Channel 4); *Agatha Christie's Poirot* and *Forever Green* (LWT). Unsolicited mss welcome if relevant to their particular field. In general terms encourage new writing.

Phil Pilley Productions

Lee International Studios, Studios Road, Shepperton, Middlesex TW17 0QD
☎ 0932 562611 Fax 0932 568989

Contact *Phil Pilley, Julie Bailey*

Film and video for TV. Mainly sports, including documentaries for the BBC and ITV. Unsolicited ideas and synopses welcome.

Polygram Movies

30 Berkeley Square, London W1X 5DB
☎ 01–493 8800

Contact *Michael Kuhn*

Music-related visual programming, suspense/thriller movies with psychological depth and integrated commercial musical score.

Portman Entertainment

Pinewood Studios, Iver Heath, Buckinghamshire SL0 0NH
☎ 0753 630366

Contact *Victor Glynn*

Feature films and mini-series for television. OUTPUT *Praying Mantis; Letters to an Unknown Lover; Tusitala; A Woman of Substance; Hold the Dream* (Bradford-Portman co-production). They receive a great many unsolicited scripts, all of them so far unsuitable for production. Letters with treatments/outlines are read in hope: send these before submitting a finished script.

Poseidon Productions Ltd

113–17 Wardour Street, London W1V 3TD
☎ 01–734 4441/5140
Telex 22347 POSFILM Fax 01–437 0638

Contact *Frixos Constantine*

Television and film makers/distributors, for educated art-loving film audience. Specialise in supplying film facilities and co-productions in Soviet Union. Own office in Moscow.

Pretty Clever Pictures Ltd

Post 59, Shepperton Studios, Studios Road, Shepperton, Middlesex TW17 0QD
☏ 0932 562611 Fax 0932 568989

Contact *Geraldine Morgan*

Formerly Peter Claridge Pictures Ltd. Film and video – commercials, corporate communication, promos, special projects and titles. Welcome unsolicited mss.

Primetime Television Limited

Seymour Mews House, Seymour Mews, Wigmore Street, London W1H 9PE
☏ 01–935 9000
Telex 22872 TV Film G Fax 01–487 3975

Contact *Deirdre Simms*

Family drama, including children's, natural history and adult drama series (political, thrillers). OUTPUT has included *Gunfighters, Waltz Through the Hills, Fortunes of War* (BBC); *Durrell in Russia* and *Ourselves and Other Animals* (Channel 4); *Return to Treasure Island* (HTV) and *Seal Morning* (Central). Welcome unsolicited mss. Wish to extend range of material and original writing.

The Production Pool Ltd

52 Tottenham Street, London W1P 9PG
☏ 01–323 0691 Fax 01–436 6287

Contact *Ann Wingate*

Film and television drama. 'Always interested to read new scripts'. OUTPUT *Making Waves*, short film for British screen and Channel 4. Three drama projects in development.

Quad Production Co.

Studio One, 2 Downshire Hill, Hampstead, London NW3 1NR
☏ 01–435 6953 Fax 01–433 1048

Contact *Andy Dean, Graham Grimshaw*

Conferences, events and video production mainly for corporate clients. Specialises in programmes with an element of entertainment, especially comedy. Welcome unsolicited mss.

Quanta Ltd

12 Wicks Drive, Chippenham, Wiltshire SN15 3ES
☏ 0249 660599

Contact *Nicholas Jones*

FOUNDED 1982. Documentary makers, with science programming a speciality. Also interactive corporate video. OUTPUT *Horizon* (BBC2); *Equinox* (Channel 4). A relatively young company, Quanta currently write all their own material in-house. No unsolicited mss.

Ragdoll Productions

34 Harborne Road, Edgbaston, Birmingham B15 3AA
☏ 021–454 5453/4344

Contact *Anne Wood*

Makers of children's television programmes. OUTPUT has included *Pob's Programme* and *Pob's Playtime* for Channel 4 and *Playbox* for Central Television.

Alvin Rakoff Productions Ltd

1 The Orchard, Chiswick, London W4 1JZ
☏ 01–994 1269

Contact *Alvin Rakoff*

TV and film. OUTPUT *Paradise Postponed* (TV mini-series); *A Voyage Round my Father; The First Olympics – 1986; Dirty Tricks* (film). Welcome unsolicited mss.

Red Rooster Films

11–13 Macklin Street, London WC2B 5NH
☏ 01–405 8147
Telex 291829 TLX G Fax 01–831 0679

Contact *Linda James, Christian Routh*

An independent film and television production company, whose productions range from drama series and feature films to documentaries, all destined for international distribution. Previously specialised in quality drama for children. OUTPUT *Joni Jones* (5-part drama series about a 1940s Welsh childhood); *The Flea and the Giants* (3-part documentary series on the technological revolution); *Coming Up Roses* (feature film for S4C); *Just Ask for Diamond* (comedy feature film for **Twentieth Century Fox** and King's Road Entertainment). Although unsolicited mss are not encouraged, treatments or outlines are welcome, and are much more likely to receive a prompt response.

Renaissance Vision

Unit 16, Drayton Industrial Estate, Taverham Road, Drayton, Norwich NR8 6RL
☏ 0603 260280 Fax 0603 260585

Contact *B. Gardner*

Video – full range of corporate work (training, sales, promotional, etc.).

Riverfront Pictures Ltd

Dock Cottages, Peartree Lane, Glamis Road, Wapping, London E1 9SR
☏ 01–481 2939 Fax 01–480 5520

Contact *Jeff Perks, Tony Freeth* (Joint Producers/Directors)

Arts, comedy, documentary, drama, music, and young people's programmes. Production of broadcast programmes, specialising in cultural subjects, with an emphasis on music programmes. OUTPUT *Our Lives; A Wee Bit Cheeky; Everyone a Special Kind of Artist; Breaking Through; The New Eastenders; Cola Cowboys; Raag Rung; Chorus Theatre of Manipur*, all for Channel 4, and *Night Moves* for the BBC.

Cecil Rowe Productions

2nd Floor, 12–13 Poland Street, London W1V 3DE
☏ 01–734 6525 Fax 01–437 0985

Contact *Cecil Rowe*

Mainly corporate programming; also developing broadcast proposals, chiefly documentary. OUTPUT in the business sector includes recruiting, sales and marketing, public relations and employee communication programmes; broadcast OUTPUT tends to be in arts, social commentary, dance, children's programming. Unsolicited mss welcome. 'Keen to nurture fresh talent, explore new approaches and ideas.'

Roymark Ltd

36 Soho Square, London W1V 5DG
☏ 01–437 9121 Fax 01–734 9785

Contact *Andrew G. B. Kerr*

Film, video and TV – drama and documentary. OUTPUT has included programmes for government, public and private companies.

Schonfeld Productions International/SPI 80 Ltd

BCM-Summer, London WC1N 3XX
☏ 01–435 1007

Contact *Victor Schonfeld*

Drama, arts, natural history, current affairs, documentary films for television and cinema. OUTPUT has included *Shattered Dreams, The Animals Film, Courage Along the Divide* and *And I Don't Have to Do the Dishes*.

Scope Picture Productions Ltd

123 Blythswood Street, Glasgow G2 4EN
☏ 041–248 3123 Fax 041–248 3423

Contact *Alison Bye, Bill Gordon*

Corporate film and video; broadcast documentaries and sport; TV commercials. OUTPUT has included *Waste Without Wasteland; Locate in Scotland; Scottish Eye*; also Scottish football coverage weekly. Unsolicited mss, realistic scripts and ideas welcome.

The Shooting Picture Co. Ltd

44 Lexington Street, London W1R 3LH
☏ 01–734 9566 Fax 01–734 9303

Contact *Jillo Waddington*

Film and video – commercials. CLIENTS include British Gas, Coca-Cola, Adams Childrenswear, NatWest Bank. Welcome unsolicited mss.

Siren Film & Video Co-op

Customs House, St Hilda's, Middlesbrough, Cleveland TS2 1EA
☏ 0642 221298

Contact *Peter Woodhouse*

Local distribution to community groups, etc., plus work for Channel 4.

Siriol Productions

3 Mount Stuart Square, Butetown, Cardiff CF1 6RW
☏ 0222 488400 Fax 0222 481552

Contact *Robin Lyons*

Animated films aimed at a family audience. OUTPUT TV specials: *A Winter Story; Space Baby;* serials: *Super Ted; Wil Cwac Cwac;* also *The Easter Egg; The Princess and The Goblin; Gerald of Wales*. Ideas and scripts for animated programmes are welcome (though no unsolicited mss has so far been produced). Shorts and full-length films. Presently most of the writing is done by Robin Lyons, but new blood will be needed in the future.

Skippon Video Associates

43 Drury Lane, London WC2B 5RT
☏ 01–240 8777 Fax 01–240 8779

Have their own team of scriptwriters and do not welcome unsolicited material from outside.

Spectacle Films Ltd

16 Chelmsford Road, London E11 1BS
☎ 01–539 2306

Contact *Roger Ashton-Griffiths*

Film/video – corporate. OUTPUT ranging from corporate communications to training. Clients include Tesco Stores, Peugeot. All aspects of business television covered.

Spectel Productions Limited

744–6 Warwick Road, Tyseley,
Birmingham B11 2HG
☎ 021–708 0931

Contact *David Webster*

Film and video – documentary, corporate and video publishing.

Tom Steel Productions

56 Sutherland Square, London SE17 3EL
☎ 01–701 6695

Contact *Tom Steel*

Documentary television. The company write and develop their own material (though not necessarily always). OUTPUT has included *Touch and Go – the Battle for Crete* and *Scotland's Story* (24 half-hour episodes for Channel 4).

Strawberry Productions Ltd

36 Priory Avenue, London W4 1TY
☎ 01–994 4494

Contact *John Black*

Film, video and TV – drama and documentary; corporate and video publishing. Welcome unsolicited mss.

Swanlind TV

The Production Centre, Stafford Road,
Fordhouses, Wolverhampton
☎ 0902 7848848/789212 Fax 0902 788840
Telex 338490 Swanlind Chacom G

Contact *Tom Coyne*

Film, video and TV – commercials, corporate and drama. OUTPUT *Hidden Attractions* (1987 award-winning drama); *It's No Big Deal* (1988 award-winning drama); *Great Western Experience* (TV and video release about the Great Western Railway). 'Looking for new writers in corporate field.' Synopses of broadcast ideas welcome.

Teletape Video Ltd

8 Nuffield Road, Cambridge CB4 1TF
☎ 0223 315014 Fax 0223 321686

Contact *Bernard Mulhern* (Head of Production)

Video and TV – documentary and commercials. Mostly corporate and training programmes for a wide range of companies. All work is commissioned; do not welcome unsolicited mss but always interested in new writers working in their field.

The Television Co-operative

100 Fawnbrake Avenue, London SE24 0BZ
☎ 01–738 7789

Contact *John Underwood*

A television production company specialising in the media, arts and politics. OUTPUT has included programmes for Channel 4, the National Trust and the British Council.

Teliesyn

3 Mount Stuart Square, The Docks,
Cardiff CF1 6EE
☎ 0222 480911 Fax 0222 481552

Contact *Mary Simmonds, Richard Staniforth*

Film and video – broadcast TV drama, documentary music and sport. Will consider unsolicited mss only if accompanied by synopsis. Encourage new writing wherever possible, often with a script editor on hand. Involved in the Celtic Film Festival and Cyfle (Welsh Language Film Training course). OUTPUT *Will Six* (1920s period drama); *Paris–Dakar Motor Rally; Dihirod Dyfed* (West Wales murder drama series); *In Two Minds* (feature film); *Cracking Up* (documentary series for Channel 4).

Third Eye Productions Ltd

Unit 210, Canalot Studios, 222 Kensal Road,
London W10 5BN
☎ 01–960 5652 Fax 01–960 8790

Contact *Marsha Fitzpatrick*

Makers of television and film documentary programmes for the BBC and Channel 4. Recent OUTPUT includes *Master Class; Yani's Monkeys;*

The Perfect Pickle Programme; The Encircled Sea.

Treasure City Photographic

1–4 Caer Street, Swansea SA1 3PP
☎ 0792 650742

Contact *Royston Kneath*

Video production (and photography). OUTPUT has included film and video animation and short demos. Welcome unsolicited mss and always willing to help new writing where possible.

Triangle Two Ltd

33 Rathbone Place, London W1P 1AD
☎ 01–637 0667 Fax 01–436 4410

Contact *Vincent Joyce*

Film and video for non-broadcast use: museums, exhibitions, companies. OUTPUT has included *Operation Overlord* for the D-Day Museum and *Time Machine* for the Geological Museum; also marketing multi-image production for King's Cross Development and special performance film for British Aerospace, Farnborough. No unsolicited mss. Prefer to meet writers direct, not via agencies. Writers must be experienced in writing for screen and should be involved in visualisation.

Tridec Television Ltd

2 Dinsdale Road, Croft Industrial Estate, Bromborough, Merseyside L62 3PY
☎ 051–334 7939 Fax 051–647 4839

Contact *Belinda Talbot Smith*

Video makers – corporate identity; training programmes; company profiles and sales promotion. Welcome unsolicited mss and interested in new writers.

Tripod Films Limited

111A Wardour Street, London W1V 3TD
☎ 01–439 0729 Fax 01–437 0304
Telex 8950051 (ONE ONE G) Ref 13643001

Contact *Evan Morgans*

Film and video – TV documentary, corporate, commercials. No unsolicited mss. Most scripts commissioned or written in-house.

Turners Film & Video Productions

7 Pink Lane, Newcastle upon Tyne NE1 5HT
☎ 091–232 1809 Fax 091–232 9823

Contact *John Grant* (Production Director)

Film and video; dramatised documentaries. OUTPUT has included *Glass is Like That!* (film – won the Royal Television Society Award 1988 and was nominated for the IVCA Production Awards in 1989); *Bloody Saturday* (film/ dramatised – with equal success). Welcome unsolicited mss. Policy on new writing: 'To seek out and encourage!'

Twentieth Century Fox Productions Ltd

Twentieth Century House, 31–2 Soho Square, London W1V 6AP
☎ 01–437 7766 Fax 01–437 1625

Contact *Company Secretary*

London office of the American giant.

Ty Gwyn Films Ltd

Y Ty Gwyn, Llanllyfni, Caernarfon, Gwynnedd LL54 6DG
☎ 0286 881235

Contact *Gareth Wynn Jones*

Situation comedy, contemporary gritty Welsh subjects, spy thrillers (spies are the current vogue). Bilingual productions. New writing welcome, in English as well as Welsh. Their primary role is to provide output for the Welsh fourth channel, S4C.

Tyburn Productions Ltd

Pinewood Studios, Iver Heath, Bucks SL0 0NH
☎ 0753 651700 Fax 0753 656844

Contact *Gillian Garrow* (Director of Research & Development)

Television producers, specialising in popular drama. OUTPUT has included TV movies *The Masks of Death, Murder Elite, Courier, The Abbots Cry* and *Peter Cushing: A One-Way Ticket to Hollywood.*

UBA (Developments) plc (United British Artists)

Monro House, 40–42 King Street, London WC2E 8JS
☎ 01–240 9891 Fax 01–379 5748

Contact *Christina Robert* (Creative Affairs

Executive)

Quality feature films and television for an international market. OUTPUT *The Lonely Passion of Judith Hearne; Taffin; Castaway; Turtle Diary.* In development: *Batavia; Rebel Magic; One Last Glimpse; Duke and Duchess of Beverly Hills; Carolina Madness; Windprints; Tale Told by an Idiot; Happy Feet; Kerry Babies; My Old Sweetheart* and *Rosa*, as well as several television projects, including a biopic of Paul Robeson. Prepared to commission new writing whether adapted from another medium or based on a short outline/treatment. Concerned with the quality of the script (*Turtle Diary* was written by Harold Pinter) and breadth of appeal. Do not welcome 'exploitation material'.

Umbrella Films

31 Percy Street, London W1P 9FG
☎ 01–631 0625
Telex 296538 Fax 01–436 9442

Contact *Stacy Bell*

OUTPUT British feature films: *Nineteen Eighty Four; Another Time Another Place; Loose Connections; Hotel du Paradis; Nanou; White Mischief.* No scripts, treatments only.

VATV

17–19 Foley Street, London W1P 7LB
☎ 01–636 9421 Fax 01–436 7426

Contact *Jane Lighting*

An independent television production and international distribution company, specialising in factual programming for television. OUTPUT includes programming for Channel 4, BBC and PBS (USA). The company also produces for the corporate and educational market, and for the home video sell-thru market. A Channel 4 distributor representing 30 other companies for international sales.

Verronmead Ltd

30 Swinton Street, London WC1X 9NX
☎ 01–278 5523 Fax 01–609 3290

Contact *Maureen Harter, David Wood*

Children's programmes, documentaries, drama and women's programmes, many for Channel 4. Recent OUTPUT *Back Home* with TVS. Unsolicited mss and new writing welcome.

Video at Work

10 King Street Lane, Winnersh, Berkshire RG11 5AS
☎ 0734 790500 Fax 0734 793494

Contact *Gerry Clarke*

Corporate video production: sales and training. OUTPUT has included staff training videos for British Airways and Midland Bank. Unsolicited mss welcome.

Videotel Productions/Living Tape Productions

Ramillies House, 1–2 Ramillies Street, London W1V 1DF
☎ 01–439 6301 Telex 298596

Contact *Nick Freethy*

Film video, TV, mainly but not exclusively, of a broadly educational nature. Welcome unsolicited mss in the education and training field only. 'We would like to support new writers who can put up with the ego-bashing they are likely to get from industrial and commercial sponsors.' OUTPUT *Catering with Care* and *Tourism: The Welcome Business* (Open College and Channel 4); *Dead Ahead – AIDS advice for Seafarers* (Royal Navy); *Working with Care* (NHS and Trusthouse Forte); *Oceans of Wealth* (Channel 4).

Vidox Video Productions Ltd

Milton House, Roper Close, Canterbury, Kent CT2 7EP
☎ 0227 763888 Fax 0227 450744

Contact *Robin Ochs*

Makers of corporate and training videos and TV commercials. Welcome unsolicited mss.

Virgin Vision

328 Kensal Road, London NW10 5XJ
☎ 01–968 8888 Telex 892890

Contact *Mike Watts (Managing Director), Anne Barson* (Acquisitions Manager)

Worldwide distributor of feature films and video on all media. Video programming – comedy, education, children's, music and feature film. 1989 slate includes *The Tall Guy, Mystic Pizza, The Rachel Papers, How to Get Ahead in Advertising.*

The Visual Connection (TVC) Ltd

1 Rostrevor Mews, London SW6 5AZ
☎ 01–731 6300 Fax 01–736 9462

Contact *Hugh Price*

Corporate film and video; conference and audiovisual production. Unsolicited mss welcome.

Wall to Wall Television/The Media Show

The Elephant House, 35 Hawley Crescent, London NW1 8NP
☎ 01–485 7424 Fax 01–267 5292

Contact *Andy Lipman*

Documentary series/features. OUTPUT includes *The Sixties* for RSO; *Open the Box* and *The Media Show* for Channel 4. Material is produced in-house, or by commission direct to writers. Rarely use agents. Happy to consider new documentary ideas: write in the first instance with outline. Intended expansion of The Media Show Ltd means 'there should be more opportunities for writers here'.

The Walnut Production Partnership

Crown House, Armley Road, Leeds LS12 2EJ
☎ 0532 456913 Fax 0532 456913

Contact *Geoff Penn*

Corporate videos mainly, plus some film. Welcome script examples from corporate productions to broaden pool of available writers. Also welcome unsolicited mss for independent production with a Northern regional slant.

Watershed Television

53 Queen Square, Bristol BS1 4LH
☎ 0272 276864 Fax 0272 252093

Contact *Liz Keynes, Jenny Jillich, Dene Bristol*

Film and video – corporate; training; commercials. No unsolicited mss; 'we need to see samples of writers' work to consider them for corporates. We encourage new writing but we aren't a training organisation. We need good writers who know what they're doing.'

White City Films

79 Sutton Court Road, Chiswick, London W4 3EQ
☎ 01–994 6795/4856
Telex 265871 Ref 84WCR001 Fax 01–995 9379

Contact *Aubrey Singer*

Films. No unsolicited mss. OUTPUT has included *The Restoration of the Sistine Chapel* (NTV); *The Witness of the Long March* (Channel 4); and more recently, *Return to Saigon; Return to Peking; Joseph Needham, FRS SBA.*

Working Title Films Ltd

10 Livonia Street, London W1V 3PH
☎ 01–493 2424 Fax 01–437 9964

Contact *Tim Bevan, Sarah Radclyffe, Alison Jackson*

Feature films and television programmes, drama and documentary subjects. OUTPUT includes *My Beautiful Laundrette, Caravaggio, A World Apart, Paperhouse, For Queen and Country, The Tall Guy, Diamond Skulls.*

Worldwide Television News

31–6 Foley Street, London W1P 7LB
☎ 01–323 3255 Fax 01–580 1437

Contact *Gerry O'Reilly*

Video and TV documentary and news. OUTPUT has included *Earthfile* (weekly documentary on environment); *Roving Report* (weekly documentary on current affairs), plus many one-off specials. Unsolicited material welcome.

Wright Brothers

22 Woodstock Street, London W1R 1HF
☎ 01–439 8623 Telex 262187 ACTION G

Contact *Alan Wright*

Television documentary and drama. OUTPUT has included *Beyond Belief* (Channel 4); *Route 66* (Central); *Land* (BBC); *Headstart* (UTV). Welcome unsolicited mss provided 'the writers are prepared to be patient'. Keen to encourage new writing for British television.

WSTV Productions Ltd

Magic Eye Studios, 20 Lydden Road, London SW18 4LR
☎ 01–874 0062

Contact *Bill Stewart, Rex Berry, Sian Coombes*

Corporate video, commercials, TV programmes. No unsolicited mss.

Wyke Farmer Productions

Norwich House, Saville Street, Hull HU1 3EG
☎ 0482 226298 Fax 0482 226245

Contact *Jon Levy, Robert Lucas*

Mainly corporate but includes TV documentary and commercials. Welcome unsolicited mss.

Wyvern Television Ltd

18 Landsdown Road, Swindon,
Wiltshire SN1 3N3
☎ 0793 615615

Contact *Fred Shively, Les Jenkinson*

Film and TV – drama and documentary; corporate TV; public relations and training. Welcome unsolicited mss.

Greg Younger Associates

Baron's Croft, Hare Lane, Blindley Heath,
Surrey RH7 6JA
☎ 0342 832515 Fax 0342 833768

Contact *Greg Younger*

Film, video, TV – drama; documentary; commercials. Welcome unsolicited mss.

Yo-Yo Films

108 Grove Park, London SE5 8LE
☎ 01–733 1806

Contact *Philip Bartlett, Laurens Postma*

Film, video and television – drama, documentary and commercials. Welcome unsolicited mss.

Zenith Productions Ltd

15 Saint George Street, London W1R 9DE
☎ 01–499 8006 Fax 01–895 9572

Contact *Archie Tait* (Head of Development)

Feature films and television. Formerly the film production arm of Central TV, now owned by Carlton, leading independent communications company. First independent company to be commissioned by the BBC to produce a ten-part drama series *The Paradise Club*, starring Leslie Grantham. Also the first UK company to adopt the US-style team of writers to produce scripts for series. OUTPUT Films: *Personal Services; Prick Up Your Ears; Wish You Were Here; The Dead; For Queen and Country; Soursweet; Paris by Night; Patty Hearst; The Wolves of Willoughby Chase.* Television: *Fields of Fire I–III; Inspector Morse I–IV; Escape from Sobibor; A Dangerous Life; Shadow of the Cobra; Paradise Club; Startrap.* Unsolicited mss are acceptable.

Zooid Pictures

52 Crouch Hill, London N4 4AA
☎ 01–272 9115

Contact *Richard Philpott, Jasmine Nicholas*

Zooid combine their experimental, multi-media interests with commercial viability. OUTPUT includes *Road Movie* and *Spirit of Albion*, both for Channel 4. Writing has been entirely in-house so far, but if mss which understand their work are submitted they will always be considered.

The Zoom Production Co. Ltd

102 Dean Street, London W1V 5RA
☎ 01–434 3895 Fax 01–734 2751

Contact *Tom Coates*

Film and video – documentary; drama; promotional; training; educational and medical. OUTPUT has included *Wildlife Conservation in the Middle East; Alcoholism in the Workplace; Design is ...* for schools. Unsolicited mss welcome 'if there is a likelihood of attracting sponsorship or financial backing'. Always willing to meet new talent, time permitting.

Theatre Producers

Aba Daba

30 Upper Park Road, London NW3 2UT
☏ 01–722 5395

Plays and satirical pantomimes performed at venues like the Water Rats and the Canal Café in London. The company write all their material themselves. They would be happy to consider some of the great piles of unsolicited mss they receive, were it not for the fact that there is absolutely no money available for outsiders.

Actors Touring Company

Alford House, Aveline Street, London SE11 5DQ
☏ 01–735 8311

Contact *Ceri Sherlock* (Artistic Director)

ATC are well known for producing lively new versions of classic works. They take plays by Shakespeare, Molière, Isben and others, and work with writers in adapting them for ATC use. Unsolicited mss with classic/epic features or intentions are welcome. Intend to work more with writers in the future.

Albemarle of London

74 Mortimer Street, London W1N 7DF
☏ 01–631 0135

Pantomimes only, and Albemarle write their own scripts.

Aldersgate Productions

12 Palace Street, London SW1E 5JF
☏ 01–828 6591

Contact *Ronald Mann* (Secretary)

Produce plays of a broadly Christian nature for the West End and for the main theatre touring circuit. Productions have included *Ride, Ride,* a musical about John Wesley; *Sentenced to Life,* a play about euthanasia; *Song of the Lion,* a one man show about C.S. Lewis. Also co-producers of *The Lion, The Witch and The Wardrobe,* and other Narnia plays.

Almeida Theatre

Almeida Street, Islington, London N1 1TA
☏ 01–226 7432

Contact *Marc Doudey* (Programme co-ordinator)

FOUNDED 1980. The Almeida now has an outstanding reputation in the field of contemporary arts in Britain and throughout the world. It presents a mixture of theatre, dance, mime and music, and one of its main annual events is its internationally acclaimed contemporary music festival. Productions have included *The Saxon Shore* David Rudkin, and *The Tourist Guide* Botho Stauss. Do not welcome unsolicited mss; 'our producing programme is very limited and linked to individual directors and producers'.

Alternative Theatre Company Limited (trading as the Bush Theatre)

Bush Theatre, Shepherds Bush Green, London W12 8QD
☏ 01–602 3703

Contact *David Hunter*

FOUNDED 1972. Produce about six new plays a year (principally British, some foreign) and invite in up to three visiting companies also producing new work – 'we are a writer's theatre'. Scripts are read by a team of associates and then discussed with the management, a process which takes between two and three months. The theatre offers commissions, recommissions to ensure further drafts on promising plays and a guarantee against royalties so writers are not financially penalised even though the plays are produced in a small house. New plays at the Bush have included: *The Tax Exile* Jonathan Gems; *Amabel, Unsuitable for Adults* Terry Johnson; *Duet for One* Tom Kempinski; *Commitments* Dusty Hughes; *The Miss Firecracker Contest, Crimes of the Heart* Beth Henley; *Hard*

Feelings, Progress Doug Lucie; *Writer's Cramp, Candy Kisses* John Byrne; *When I Was a Girl, I Used to Scream and Shout* ... Sharman Macdonald; *Kiss of the Spiderwoman, Mystery of the Rose Bouquet* Manuel Puig; *More Light* Snoo Wilson; *Raping the Gold* Lucy Gannon; *Handful of Stars* Billy Roche; *The Fatherland* Murray Watts.

Yvonne Arnaud Theatre

Millbrook, Guildford, Surrey GU1 3UX
☎ 0483 64571

Contact *Val May* (Director)

New work always considered. Credits include *Sweet William* Bernard Slade; *Groucho* Arthur Marx & Robert Fisher; *It Runs in the Family* Ray Cooney; *Married Love* Peter Luke; *The Secret of Sherlock Holmes* Jeremy Paul; *Over my Dead Body* Michael Sutton & Anthony Fingleton.

Artattack Stage Ltd

Kilchurn House, South Street, Rotherfield, East Sussex TN6 3LU
☎ 0892 853267

Contact *Adrian Gilpin*

FOUNDED 1987. Theatre production company in the process of expanding into TV and film production and seem to be concentrating on new areas now, looking mainly at TV comedy scripts.

Arts Management

Redroofs, Littlewick Green, Maidenhead, Berks.
☎ 0628 822982

Contact *June Rose* (Artistic Director)

Only interested in full-scale children's musicals based on classic titles, and potted versions of Shakespeare for schools. Mss are welcome if they meet these exact requirements. Recent productions have included *Charlie and the Chocolate Factory; The Lion, The Witch and The Wardrobe* (musical); and *Once Upon a Time.*

Belgrade Theatre, Coventry

Belgrade Square, Coventry CV1 1GS
☎ 0203 256431

Contact *Robert Hamlin* (Director)

The Belgrade Theatre regularly presents new work in both main house and studio. Productions in the main house have included the world première of Julian Garner's *Guardian Angels* in autumn 1987; Rob Bettinson's *Bare Necessities* in June 1988; and Paul Kember's *Asylum* in October 1988. Most of the productions in the studio theatre are dedicated to new writing, either first or second productions. 1988 Studio productions included the première of Richard Osborne's *Our Ellen*, the second production of Richard Langridge's *The Act*, and the newly revised *In Touch* by Debbie Horsfield. Most new plays are commissioned.

Birmingham Repertory Theatre

Broad Street, Birmingham B1 2EP
☎ 021–236 6771

Contact *John Adams* (Artistic Director)

In the main theatre, plays are chosen because they fully exploit the epic size of the stage (with its 60-foot proscenium) and auditorium (900 seats in a single curved rake). This applies to new plays as much as to established ones. In the studio theatre, it is unlikely that Birmingham Rep will be able to afford to do many productions of its own, old or new, for the foreseeable future.

Borderline Theatre Company

Darlington New Church, North Harbour Street, Ayr KA8 8AA
☎ 0292 281010

Contact *Morag Fullarton* (Artistic Director)

FOUNDED 1974. A touring company taking shows to main house theatres in city centres and small venues in outlying districts, plus the Edinburgh Festival, Mayfest and, occasionally, London. Mainly new and contemporary work, plus revivals: *Trumpets and Raspberries* Dario Fo; *A Night in the Ukraine* Voxburgh & Laxarus; *Four in a Million* Les Blair; *Shanghied* Liz Lochhead; plus pantomime and children's plays. Synopsis with cast size preferred in the first instance. Borderline try to include one new work every season. 'We are looking for writing which is stimulating, relevant and, above all, entertaining, which will lend itself to dynamic physical presentation.'

Bristol Express Theatre Company

20 Mocatta House, Brady Street, Whitechapel, London E1 5DL
☎ 01–247 4156/7965

Contact *Richard Osborne* (Assistant Director)

Bristol Express, a non-funded professional middle-scale national touring company, has a continuing commitment to the discovery, development and encouragement of new writers and new writing, principally through a research and development programme – consisting of public and private staged and rehearsed readings, skill workshop productions and full productions – called *The Play's The Thing!* 'We look for plays that are socially/emotionally/theatrically/politically significant, analytical and challenging. The company is concerned to produce work which attempts to mix genres (and create new ones!), is eloquent and honest, while remaining accessible and entertaining ... It's unusual for a play sent to (or commissioned by) the company to be accepted on its receipt.' Past productions have included *Child's Play* Jonathan Wolfman; *Winter Darkness* Allan Cubitt; *Prophets in the Black Sky* John Matshikiza; *Lunatic & Lover* Michael Meyer.

Bristol Old Vic Company

Theatre Royal, King Street, Bristol BS1 4ED
☎ 0272 277466

Contact *Paul Unwin* (Artistic Director)

A producing theatre with a script reading committee which meets regularly to consider all new work submitted. New work is produced – both in the main house and the New Vic Studio – and 'we are constantly looking for dynamic, innovative and exciting texts'.

Bush Theatre

See **Alternative Theatre Company**

Cambridge Theatre Company

8 Market Passage, Cambridge CB2 3PE
☎ 0223 357134

Contact *James Williams* (Administrator)

Cambridge Theatre Company have no script facilities, and rarely produce new work. They admit that unsolicited mss are seldom read, though letters and synopses are welcome.

Channel Theatre Trust Ltd

Granville Theatre, Victoria Parade, Ramsgate, Kent CT11 8DG
☎ 0843 588280

Contact *Philip Dart*

Based at the Granville Theatre, the company divides its productions between a commercial season there and Arts Council tours to smaller venues, art centres, etc. It also has an attached Theatre-in-Education and Community Theatre Company. Productions have included Anthony Minghella's *Made in Bangkok*; *The Normal Heart*, the play about AIDS; a new version of *The Canterbury Tales; What the Butler Saw*. Interested in new writing, particularly Theatre-in-Education and small-scale work of quality, but financial restraints often make full-scale production of new work unlikely.

Jean Charles Productions

4A Jointon Road, Folkestone, Kent CT20 2RF
☎ 0303 52413

Contact *Jean Charles*

Jean Charles produces variety, panto and summer shows much of which is scripted elsewhere. However, she is always on the lookout for good new comedy material – sketches and jokes particularly. Write a letter first.

The Chichester Festival Theatre

Festival Theatre Productions Co. Ltd, Oaklands Park, Chichester, Sussex
☎ 0243 784437

Contact *Robin Phillips* (Artistic Director)

1989 sees the opening here of the Minerva Studio theatre. It is this that promises most to new writers. Under the art direction of Sam Mendes, the studio will be looking for new work to promote. Main theatre productions for 1989 included Thomas Hardy's *The Dynasts*.

Churchill Theatre

High Street, Bromley, Kent BR1 1HA
☎ 01–464 7131

Contact *Nick Salmon*

The Churchill produces a broad variety of popular plays, both new and revivals. Recent productions have included *Blithe Spirit* Noël Coward; *Stiff Options* Andrew McCullock & John Flanigan; *Little Women*, new adaptation by Angela Huth; *Time & The Conways* J.B. Priestley; *King's Rhapsody* Ivor Novello; and *Oklahoma*. Most productions go on to either tour or into the West End. New scripts welcome.

City Theatre Productions

11A Friern Mount Drive, London N20 9DP
☎ 01–445 7961

Contact *Jon Rumney*

The company is currently dormant, but if a good script came along, would awake to produce it.

Enjoyed great success at the Edinburgh Festival in the past, with international plays and new work. 'We're after topical interest, humour, a very small cast and strong actors' parts ...'

Alan Clements Productions

Mill House, St Ives Cross, Sutton St James, Spalding, South Lincs
☏ 094 585466

Contact *Alan Clements*

Small-scale operation, producing pantomimes and only one or two plays a year. Of these, very little is new – *Sweeny Todd* being a recent exception. There is generally little hope for new writers here.

Ron Coburn International

Vaudevilla, Elliot Road, Dundee DD2 1SY
☏ 0382 69025

Contact *Ron Coburn*

Ron Coburn writes and produces internationally touring musical variety shows like *A Breath of Scotland* and *The Waggle o' the Kilt*. Venues range from Carnegie Hall to Mablethorpe and Skegness. As the material needs to travel to North America and is usually of a topical nature, it's not feasible to use outside writers.

Michael Codron Ltd

Aldwych Theatre Offices, Aldwych, London WC2B 4DF
☏ 01–240 8291 Fax 01–240 8467

Contact *Joe Scott Parkinson* (General Manager)

Michael Codron Ltd manage the Aldwych and Adelphi theatres, and own the Vaudeville Theatre in London's West End. The plays they produce don't necessarily go into these theatres, but always tend to be big-time West End fare like *Woman in Mind* with Julia Mackenzie. The company had a busy year 1988/89 with productions of *Hapgood, Uncle Vanya, The Sneeze, Re: Joyce* and *Henceforward*. There is no particular rule of thumb on subject matter or treatment, the acid test being 'whether something appeals to Michael'. Straight plays rather than musicals. Generally enthusiastic about new work and resolve to read everything which is submitted.

The Coliseum, Oldham

Fairbottom Street, Oldham OL1 3SW
☏ 061–624 1731

Contact *Paul Kerryson* (Artistic Director)

Considered a good bet for new playwrights, the Coliseum is besieged by more scripts than it can read. However, they do put on new work: 'We like to do new writing that's popular and relevant to our audience ... it's got to be popular.' Do not welcome unsolicited scripts. First approach with letter and synopsis. Previous productions include *A Night on the Tiles* Frank Vickery; *Girlfriends* Howard Goodall; *Stage Fright* Peter Fieldson; *The Steamie* Tony Roper; *Clowns on a School Outing* Ken Campbell. Often plays come by way of contacts or commissions, but good unsolicited scripts still stand a chance. Just don't expect a swift decision.

Communicado Theatre Company

Royal Lyceum Theatre, Grindlay Street, Edinburgh EH3 9AX
☏ 031–229 7404/228 5465 Fax 031–228 3955

Contact *Gerard Mulgrew* (Artistic Director)

FOUNDED 1982. Touring company which 'aims to entertain the widest range of audience'. Want to encourage new writing, especially Scottish. Recent productions include *Blood Wedding*, new translation by David Johnston; *A Bicycle to the Moon* John Harvey; *A Wee Home from Home* Gerald Mulgrew; *Mary Queen of Scots Got Her Head Chopped Off* Liz Lochhead; *Tales of the Arabian Nights* Gerard Mulgrew.

Compass Theatre Ltd

13 Shorts Gardens, London WC2H 9AT
☏ 01–379 7501

Contact *Edward Kemp* (Assistant Director)

Sir Anthony Quayle founded this company in 1984 to produce revivals and large-cast classics; it has a particular interest in touring. Productions have included *The Government Inspector; King Lear, Dandy Dick; The Tempest; St Joan; The Clandestine Marriage*. New scripts are welcome, especially those of a large-scale or epic nature – two such plays have recently been commissioned – though the company is chiefly funded to stage classic work. Exploring ways of pursuing a commitment to new writing through studio productions, readings and workshops attached to major touring productions.

Condor Productions

15 Catherine Street, London WC2B 5JC
☏ 01–240 1444

Contact *Robert Cogo-Fawcett* (Managing Director)

FOUNDED 1987. Produce both new plays and classics. No musicals. Welcome unsolicited mss.

Mervyn Conn Organisation

MC House, 14 Orange Street,
London WC2H 7ED
☏ 01–930 7502

The *Annie* tour is the first theatre Mervyn Conn have produced (ordinarily they produce one-offs like the Silk Cut Country & Western Festival). No facilities for reading mss, and no interest in new work.

Contact Theatre Company

Oxford Road, Manchester M15 6JA
☏ 061–274 3434

Contact *Anthony Clark* (Artistic Director)

FOUNDED 1966. Play predominantly to a young audience (15–35) with a particular interest in new work, especially from the north-west. Up to 5 plays a year are commissioned. Recent OUTPUT has included *Homeland* Ken Blakeson; *Stig of the Dump* adapted by Richard Williams from Clive King's novel; *McAlpine's Fusilier* Kevin Fegan.

Crucible Theatre

55 Norfolk Street, Sheffield S1 1DA
☏ 0742 760621

Contact *Director's secretary*

Under the artistic direction of Clare Venables, the Crucible has developed a strong policy on new writing and tries to do one new main house show a year, with plenty of others appearing in the Studio. All premières over recent years have resulted from commissions to established writers or to new writers of promise. Unsolicited scripts are seen by a reader and a small number may go on to a rehearsed reading/workshop. Finished scripts are always preferred to synopses or ideas. Full devising and commissioning TIE company working in Sheffield and South Yorkshire schools, usually 'concept' based, to reflect school's needs and curriculum, eg racism, sexuality. New plays have included *A Passion in 6 Days* Howard Barker; *Here We Go* Andy de la Tour; *Who Killed Hilda Murrell?* Chris Martin. The TIE Company's commission *Plague of Innocence* by Noel Greig won the Young People's Theatre category in the BTA drama review awards of 1988. Recent translation/adaptation commissions for the main house include Tinch Minter & Anthony Vivis' *The Park* by Botho Strauss (1988), and Stephen Lowe's *William Tell* by Schiller (1989).

Cumberland Theatre Company

Kildrum, Cumberland G67 2BN
☏ 0236 737235

Contact *Robert Robson*

FOUNDED 1979. Popular community entertainment. Productions have included children's shows, new plays, Scottish material, educational and community plays as well as popular theatre. Commission new plays but prefer not to see unsolicited mss unless they really fit the audience.

Charles Dickens Theatre Company

Meadowsweet, Wash Lane, Witnesham, Ipswich, Suffolk IP6 9EW
☏ 047385 672

Contact *Charles Peter Mugleston*

A new company which will consider plays of all kinds. New writing considered; s.a.e. in all cases.

Dramatis Personae Ltd

122 Kennington Road, London SE11 6RE
☏ 01–735 0831

Contact *Nathan Silver*

Run by Nathan Silver and Maria Aitken, the company turns its hand to a variety of production projects (and is currently co-producing with the BBC on arts documentary subjects). Interested to be advised about new plays, which most often come by way of contacts in the business, but can occasionally be taken up from unknowns who send scripts on spec. Good plays are put into provincial rep and brought to London if successful. Letters and synopses preferred in the first instance.

Durham Theatre Company

The Arts Centre, Vane Terrace, Darlington, County Durham DL3 7AX
☏ 0325 469861

Contact *Laurence Sach*

FOUNDED 1977. Audience defined by the range of community venues that the theatre visits throughout County Durham and the north-east. Produce an annual pantomime, a play for junior schools, a popular autumn show and a community production in Durham Cathedral which has included *The Mysteries* and *Godspell*. Prefer to receive brief synopsis and c.v. rather than complete mss. Will always consider new writing if appropriate to the programme demands.

Each World Productions

1 King's House, 396 King's Road,
London SW10 0LL
☎ 01–352 1852

Contact *David Adams, Mandie Joel*

FOUNDED 1984. A minority audience for high-quality drama and drama documentary. Recent OUTPUT *Calming the Waters* – arts documentary filmed in Iraq and Pakistan for Channel 4; world premiere of *Tales From a Long Room* and *Uncle Mort's North Country* by Peter Tinniswood, starring Willie Rushton at Lyric Hammersmith Studio. Do not welcome unsolicited mss but interested in good original scripts. Would prefer a letter from a writer in first instance detailing author's work and project for consideration.

E & B Productions Ltd

Suite 3, Waldorf Chambers, 11 Aldwych,
London WC2B 4DA
☎ 01–836 2795 Fax 01–379 4892

Contact *Paul Elliott, Brian Hewitt-Jones*

Theoretically, at least, interested in seeing new scripts, although the schedule for 1988 was very much taken up with touring shows like *One for the Pot and Pride & Prejudice*, plus 20 pantomimes for the winter. Previous productions include *Run for Your Wife, Double Double, Crown Matrimonial, Gaslight and Crystal Clear, The Secret Life of Cartoons* by Clive Barker. 1989 ventures include *Pirates of Penzance*, a stage adaptation of Catherine Cookson's *The 15 Streets* and *The Buddy Holly Story*.

Field Day Theatre Company

Foyle Arts Centre, Old Foyle College, Lawrence Hill, Derry BT48 7NJ
☎ 0504 360196

Contact *Maureen Loughran* (Administrator)

A touring company which usually commissions its plays from Irish writers. Past productions have included *Pentecost* Stewart Parker. No scripts or ideas as all work is commissioned.

Vanessa Ford Productions Ltd

62 Uverdale Road, London SW10 0SS
☎ 01–352 1948/351 9293

Contact *Vanessa Ford*

Recent work has included *The Magician's Nephew; Winnie the Pooh; The Lion, The Witch and The Wardrobe;* touring and West End. Also classical seasons touring and in London. Often do their own writing and adaptation in-house but also keen to see new plays of all kinds, whether finished scripts, ideas or synopses.

Clare Fox & Brian Kirk Ltd

Suite 17, 26 Charing Cross Road,
London WC2H 0DG
☎ 01–379 4985/4676 Fax 01–379 5898

Contact *Clare Fox*

Producers and general managers from the commercial West End. Past involvement include *Bent* Martin Sherman; *Mr & Mrs Nobody; Breaking the Code, Pack of Lies, Best of Friends* Hugh Whitemore; *Of Mice and Men* John Steinbeck; *The Amen Corner* James Baldwin. Unsolicited mss are welcome, 'but they take a long time to process'. Very interested in new writing.

Robert Fox Limited

6 Beauchamp Place, London SW3 1NG
☎ 01–584 6855/6
Telex 936221 Fax 01–225 1638

Contact *Robert Fox*

In 1987, co-producers of *Chess* in London's West End, Peter Shaffer's *Lettice and Lovage*, and Ronald Harwood's *J. J. Farr*. 1989 co-producer of *Anything Goes*. Scripts, while usually by established playwrights, are always read. Bear in mind, however, that the company is usually concerned with work suitable for West End production.

Freeshooter Productions Ltd

10 Clorane Gardens, London NW3 7PR
☎ 01–794 0414 Fax 01–435 3783

Contact *Andrew Empson* (General Manager)

Past productions have included *The Petition* Wyndhams Theatre; *Siegfried Sassoon* Apollo Theatre; *Kipling* Mermaid Theatre; *St Mark's*

Gospel on tour; *March of the Falsettos* Manchester and the Albery Theatre, London, and *Godspell* on national tour. Also, touring *Shakespeare Cole & Co.* Unsolicited scripts welcome.

Mark Furness Ltd

10 Garrick Street, London WC2E 9BH
☏ 01–836 7373

Contact *Mark Furness*

Recent productions: West End – *'Allo 'Allo; Peter Pan; Dangerous Obsession.* On tour and overseas – *Mating Game; Bedful of Foreigners; The Real Thing*; and new plays *Mixed Feelings* Donald Churchill, *Holiday Swap* Chapman & Pertwee, *The Blue Angel* Andrew Sinclair. Unsolicited scripts at all times welcome. Comedies, dramas and thrillers, also musicals. Often commissions new works.

Gallery Productions Ltd

Number 5, Denmark Street, London WC2
☏ 01–836 8801

Contact *Robert Kennedy, Lee Dean*

A touring company founded in 1985, with almost twenty productions in 1988, and increasingly interested in new work. Past productions include *Blyth Spirit, Widow's Weeds* Anthony Shaffer; *Rough Crossing* Tom Stoppard; *The Haunting* Shirley Jackson. No 'avant-garde' work; prefer contemporary subjects traditionally written. Synopses in the first instance; scripts by invitation.

Gay Sweatshop

PO Box 820, London NW1 8LW
☏ 01–722 1491

Contact *The Administrator*

FOUNDED 1970. Alternative audience, those particularly interested in lesbian and gay theatre and sexual politics. OUTPUT Script-based plays: *Raising the Wreck* Sue Frumin; *Compromised Immunity* Andy Kirby; *This Island's Mine* Philip Osment. Also festivals of new work presented as staged rehearsed readings: *Gay Sweatshop x 10; GS x 12.* Committed to encouraging new work by lesbian, black and disabled playwrights. Work submitted must include representation of those sections of the community which are under represented in mainstream theatre. Welcome unsolicited mss.

Glasgow Citizens Theatre

Gorbals, Glasgow G5 9DS
☏ 041–429 5561

Contact *Giles Havergal*

Citizens Theatre has no formal policy on new writing; although interested in seeing new work, in practice they haven't produced any in the last couple of years. Productions tend to be classic revivals, or else adaptations/translations done by the resident dramatist Robert David MacDonald.

Globe Players Theatre Company

36 St James's Avenue, Hampton Hill, Middlesex TW12 1HN
☏ 01–979 5497

Touring, mostly schools in London and the Home Counties. An established repertoire of plays for younger children and classics for secondary schools. Submissions unlikely to be of use.

Derek Glynne (London) Pty Ltd

25 Haymarket, London SW1Y 4EN
☏ 01–930 1981
Telex 919150 Fax 01–935 6638

Contact *Mrs Denise Parkhurst*

Derek Glynne (who also trades at the same address as The London Company International Plays Ltd) is a producer in partnership with American and Australian producers. There are two aspects of the company's work – taking international companies like the **Royal Shakespeare Company** abroad and producing plays largely for Australian and American audiences. Most of these originate abroad, so in general there is little hope for playwrights here. However, they have recently commissioned a new play, and unsolicited mss/ideas of promise are passed on for consideration. In addition, they are often consulted or asked to co-produce.

Graeae Theatre Company

No. 9, 25 Bayham Street, London NW1

Contact *Jakki Mellor-Ellis*

The only theatre company of disabled actors in England. Productions range from TIE to community shows. OUTPUT *Every Picture Tells a Story; Our House.* Welcome unsolicited mss. Currently performing new writing only, based mainly around disability issues and themes. In the process of setting up workshops for disabled writers.

Great Eastern Stage

Steinkirk Block, Dunkirk Road, Lincoln LN1 3UJ
☎ 0522 534924

Contact *Michael Fry* (Artistic Director)

Small-scale regional (plus national) touring company. Primarily classically-based, but presents one or two new plays each year.

Greenwich Theatre

Crooms Hill, London SE10 8ES
☎ 01–858 4447

Contact *Sue Dunderdale* (Artistic Director)

Strong policy here under Sue Dunderdale's direction to encourage new writing and community involvement. 1989/90 sees the introduction of weekly play readings on Sunday nights, as well as an increased commitment to commissioning new work. Try to include at least one or two new writers each season. 'We want to see exciting new writing which is accessible to our mixed audience.' Positively encourage people to send in scripts, will read them and will respond – less keen on initial approach with ideas. 'like to see a good play.'

Raymond Gubbay Ltd

176A High Street, Barnet, Hertfordshire
☎ 01–441 8940

Although Raymond Gubbay does from time to time act as a theatrical producer, these are mostly one-offs and rarely straight plays. Concentrating on music and active as an exhibition promoter, notably at the Barbican with the City of London Antiques and City of London Fine Arts fairs. Recently became part of EMAP Exhibitions Ltd, a subsidiary of the EMAP Publishing Group.

Half Moon Theatre

213 Mile End Road, London E1 4AA
☎ 01–791 1141

Contact *John Turner* (Artistic Director)

The Half Moon produce six shows a year and are very interested in new writing, but 'we're not a writers' theatre for the sake of it, and aren't prepared to produce new work unless it's of a high standard'. A third to a half of their output meets these exacting requirements. Occasionally commissions to complete further drafts of promising work will be offered. Productions have included *Poppy* Peter Nichols; *Regeneration* Jonathan Moore; *Moll Flanders* Clare Luckham; *Sink the Belgrano* Steven Berkoff; *Elizabeth* Dario Fo (first English translation); and the first English production of the Jamaican pantomime *Trash* by Barbara Gloudon.

Hampstead Theatre

Swiss Cottage Centre, London NW3 3EX
☎ 01–722 9224

Contact *Mathew Lloyd*

A new writing theatre that mainly produces new plays. Scripts are initially assessed by a team of script-readers, and their responses are shared with the management in monthly script meetings. The Literary Manager and/or Artistic Director then read and consider many submissions in more detail, and therefore it may take two to three months to reach a decision. Recent productions include *Observe the Sons of Ulster Marching Towards the Somme* Frank McGuinness; *Ask for the Moon* Shirley Gee; *Curtains* Stephen Bill; *Separation* Tom Kempinski; *Valued Friends* Stephen Jeffreys.

Hazemead Ltd

1st Floor, 235–41 Regent Street,
London W1R 5DD
☎ 01–629 4817

Contact *Anne Chudleigh*

Producers of summer seasons and pantomimes all over the country. Interested in plays, sitcoms and sketches. New writers and scripts come to them principally through recommendation, but unsolicited mss and letters are always welcome.

Philip Hinden

33 Albert Street, London NW1 7LU
☎ 01–380 0375

Contact *V. Marsh*

Producer of quiz panel game shows for TV and theatre. No unsolicited material welcome but always interested in new ideas/writing.

Hiss & Boo Ltd

The Strand Theatre, Aldwych,
London WC2B 5LD
☎ 01–379 5LD Fax 01–240 2056

Contact *Ian Liston*

Productions have included *Double Act, An Ideal Husband, Fertility Dance, Mr Men's Magical Island, Mr Men and the Space Pirates, Nunsense, Corpse!, Groucho: A Life in Revue, See How They Run.* Keen to see and read as much new work as possible, provided a synopsis and introductory letter is offered in the first instance. Unsolicited mss not welcome.

Horseshoe Theatre Company Ltd

The Shrubbery, Cliddesden Road, Basingstoke, Hampshire RG21 3ER
☏ 0256 55844

Contact *Ian Mullins* (Artistic Director)

Productions in the Main House for the 1988/1989 season included *Noises Off* Michael Frayn; *The Cherry Orchard* Anton Chekhov; *Fantastic Mr Fox* Roald Dahl (new adaptation Ian Mullins); *The Reluctant Debutante* William Douglas Home; *Spider's Web* Agatha Christie; *Breaking The Code* Hugh Whitemore; *Pride and Prejudice* Jane Austen (adaptation David Horlock); *From Where I'm Standing* (John Ringham (new play – two nights). In the same season at Central Studio, *Hamlet* William Shakespeare; *Consent* Kevin Eylot, commissioned play developed by students at Queen Mary's College, Basingstoke through workshops with writer and director. A new play for the Main House has been commissioned for 1989/1990 season.

Hull Truck Theatre Company

Spring Street, Hull HU2 8RW
☏ 0482 224800

Contact *Barry Nettleton* (Administrator)

John Godber, the Artistic Director of this high-profile northern company since 1984, has very much dominated the scene with his own successful plays. However, a change of direction is in the offing. Although the company will be doing at least one of John's plays a year, there is a new emphasis on outside writers. (Already this has produced plays like Phil Woods' *The Dock* and Jane Thornton's *Cut and Dried*.) Most of the new plays have been commissioned, and the company admits it doesn't always get around to reading unsolicited mss. Synopses and letters are preferred. Bear in mind the artistic policy of Hull Truck, which is 'accessibility and popularity'. In general they are not interested in musicals, or in plays with many more than 5 characters.

Richard Jackson

59 Knightsbridge, London SW1
☏ 01–235 3671

Independent-minded producer who does 'strong plays which appeal to me'. Besieged by mss and tends to go out for what he wants (particularly European material). Works mainly in smaller-scale London fringe theatres where he can take risks the West End can no longer afford. Credits include bringing *Quentin Crisp* to a theatre audience, *Madame de Sade; The Square; The Bitter Tears of Petra Von Kant; Appearances; Flashpoint.* More recently *Latin* Stephen Fry; *Swimming Pools at War* Yves Navarre; *Matthew, Mark, Luke and Charlie* Robert Gillespie; *Pasolini* Michael Azama; *I Ought to Be in Pictures* Neil Simon; *Starting in the Middle* Sally-Jane Heit's one-woman show (1987). Regularly tours world-wide with Susannah York in *The Human Voice.*

Pola Jones Associates Ltd

5 Dean Street, London W1V 5RN
☏ 01–439 1165 Fax 01–437 3994

Contact *Andre Ptaszynski, Andrew Fell*

FOUNDED 1982. Productions have included *Arturo Ui* with Griff Rhys Jones; *The Nerd* with Rowan Atkinson; *Progress* Doug Lucie and *The Gambler* with Mel Smith. Welcome unsolicited mss. Comedy preferred.

Stephen Joseph Theatre

Valley Bridge Parade, Scarborough YO11 2PL
☏ 0723 370540

Contact *Alan Ayckbourn* (Artistic Director)

A small theatre-in-the-round seating 307 people and additional studio theatre seating 75–90, with positive policy on new work. For obvious reasons, Alan Ayckbourn's work is featured heavily in the repertoire, but plays from other sources are encouraged. Recent productions include *Woman in Black*, adaptation by Stephen Mallatratt; *The Ballroom* Peter King; *The Parasol* Frank Dunai. Up to 80% première productions in each season.

Bill Kenwright Productions

55–9 Shaftesbury Avenue, London W1V 7AA
☏ 01–439 4466 Fax 01–437 8370

Contact *Bill Kenwright*

Both revivals and new shows for West End and touring theatres. New work tends to be by established playwrights: *Artist Descending A Staircase* Tom Stoppard; *The Business of Murder* Richard Harris; *A Fighting Chance* Norman Crisp; *Up On The Roof* Jane Prowse & Simon Moore. For children, *James and the Giant Peach* Herbert Chappell (adapted from Roald Dahl). 'We have no particular system established for the reading of unsolicited mss': send a letter with synopsis and a few sample pages in the first instance.

King's Head Theatre Club

115 Upper Street, London N1 1QN
☏ 01–226 8561

Contact *Amy Beamish* (Casting and Production)

New scripts are welcome and are farmed out to consultants for reading and evaluation. An unpretentious little café theatre, the King's Head nevertheless produces some strong work, notably in 1987 *Diary of a Somebody* by John Lahr, about the life and death of Joe Orton. Other productions have included *Artist Descending A Staircase* Tom Stoppard; *Heyday* Herbert Appleman; *The Secret Garden* adapted by Diana Morgan; *This Savage Parade* Anthony Shaffer; *The Fling* Asher; and Noel Coward's *Easy Virtue*, which transferred to the West End.

David Kirk Productions

12 Panmuir Road, London SW20 0PZ
☏ 01–947 0130

Contact *David Kirk*

Commercially managed, bringing post-London revivals and some new plays to provincial and suburban theatres. Productions usually have two or three TV names in them, but David Kirk is very interested in scripts strong enough not to need these. Not interested in verse plays, rock musicals or 'scripts more suited to the fringe'. No unsolicited mss without preliminary letter and return postage. Productions have included the post-London tours of Alan Ayckbourn's *Taking Steps;* Peter Terson's *Strippers;* Bob Larbey's *A Month of Sundays;* John Lahr's *Diary of a Somebody.* New plays have included *Local Murder* Peter Whalley; *Mr Fothergill's Murder* Peter O'Donnell; *Agenda for Murder* Denis Cleary & Joseph Boyer.

Knightsbridge Theatrical Productions

15 Fetter Lane, London EC4A 1JJ
☏ 01–583 8687

Contact *Mrs S. Gray*

Straight plays suitable for production in the West End only. No musicals. Occasionally plays are taken on tour. New writing is welcome; unsolicited mss will always be considered.

Leeds Playhouse

Calverley Street, Leeds LS2 3AJ
☏ 0532 442141

Contact *John Harrison* (Artistic Director)

'Always on the look-out for new plays, but good ones are hard to find.' Of 10 or 11 plays a season, at least one is likely to be a première. Recently *Torpedoes in the Jacuzzi* Phil Young, which came out of improvisation, and Barry Hillman's *The Amazing Dancing Bear.* Have recently commissioned a play from Leeds-based writer, Kay Mellor. Also do 'regional premières', i.e. plays new to Leeds, though not new as such. Gave the British première of *Colours* by Jean Binnie, a Leeds-based writer, in October 1988.

Leicester Haymarket Theatre

Belgrave Gate, Leicester LE1 3YQ
☏ 0533 530021 Fax 0533 513310

Contact *Peter Lichtenfels*

In 1987, Theatre Director, Peter Lichtenfels brought from his old job at the **Traverse Theatre** in Edinburgh a desire to put on more work in Leicester, both in the studio and main house. Hopes to achieve at least 6 new plays a year. Recent OUTPUT has included *M. Butterfly* David Hwang; *Kirti Sona and Ba* Gyoti Patel: *Fat Pig* a musical by Henry Kreiger & Mark Bramble. Scripts preferred to outline or ideas.

Library Theatre Company

St Peter's Square, Manchester M2 5PD
and Forum Theatre, Leningrad Square, Manchester M22 5RT
☏ 061–236 9422 ext. 295

Contact *Christopher Honer*

Produces contemporary and new work, as well as occasional classics; musicals, broad-appeal plays and popular classics at the Forum Theatre. No unsolicited mss. Send outline of the nature of the script first. Encourage new writing through the commissioning of new plays, and through a programme of staged readings to help writers' development.

Liverpool Playhouse

Williamson Square, Liverpool L1 1EL
☏ 051–709 8478 Fax 051–236 2882

Contact *Kate Rowland* (Associate Director)

Regional theatre very active in promoting new writing, with an impressive record on first plays. Recent productions: *Be Bop Alula* Biu Morrison; *Journeymen Jack* Phil Wood; *Fears and Miseries of the Third Term* by twelve acclaimed writers, such as Catherine Hayes and Frank McGuinness; *A Brusque Affair* Shaun Duggan. Finished scripts preferred to synopses and ideas. Committed to developing new work in both its auditoria. Young Writers Award to be held for a third year.

Logan Theatres Ltd

Tigh-na-Mara, 152 East Clyde Street, Helensburgh G84 7AX
☏ 0436 71503

Contact *Jimmy Logan*

Productions vary, but mostly star Jimmy Logan. Laughter and comedy appealing to a genuine family audience. Past productions include *Run for Your Wife, A Bedful of Foreigners, Not Now Darling* and *Lauder.* Prepared to consider new writing if it is funny and doesn't rely on extraneous four-letter words for laughs.

London Bubble Theatre Company

3–5 Elephant Lane, London SE16 4JD
☏ 01–237 4434

Contact *Peter Rowe*

Plays to a mixed audience of theatregoers and non-theatregoers, wide ranging in terms of age, culture and class. Welcome unsolicited mss but 'our reading service is extremely limited and there can be a considerable wait before we can give a response'. Produce at least one new show a year which is invariably commissioned. Recent OUTPUT *Blood Brothers* Willy Russell; *Can't Pay, Won't Pay* Dario Fo; *Peacemaker; The Caucasian Chalk Circle* Brecht; *A Midsummer Night's Dream.*

The Lyric Theatre, Hammersmith

King Street, London W6 0QL
☏ 01–741 0824

Contact *Peter James* (Director)

Theatre with a long tradition of putting on new work, and always keen to receive scripts, which are read by a permanent team of three. Currently the main house is concentrating on modern European drama, rather than new plays by British playwrights, but the studio is always on the look-out for good new scripts. Productions have included *State of Affairs* Graham Swannell (trans. Duchess); *Mumbo Jumbo* Robin Glendinning (Mobil Prizewinner); *Atonement* Barry Collins; *Asylum* Paul Kember; *Madhouse in Goa* Martin Sherman. Finished scripts only – they take at least 6 weeks to process, but a report is made on every manuscript received.

Cameron Mackintosh

1 Bedford Square, London WC1B 3RA

Producer of *Cats, Les Misérables, Phantom of the Opera, Little Shop of Horrors, Follies* and *Miss Saigon.* Cameron Mackintosh is one of the most important producers in London's West End. Unsolicited scripts are read and considered (there is no literary manager, however) but chances of success are slim. This is because they only produce musicals, and never more than one a year – which is likely to come by way of contacts. Will not, however, be producing any musicals for the stage until 1993 at the earliest, as he is now tied up in producing *Les Misérables.*

The Made in Wales Stage Company

Mount Stuart House, Mount Stuart Square, Cardiff CF1 6DQ
☏ 0222 484017

Contact *Gilly Adams*

Varied audience. Works with Welsh and Wales based actors to create new and exciting plays. Have premiered and toured 17 new plays and toured throughout Wales since the company's formation five years ago. Productions have included *A Blow to Bute Street*, a new play about the changing face of Cardiff's docklands; *On the Black Hill* and *Chane Way*, adap. from Bruce Chatwin's novel *Rural Emsemble Piece.* Also provide workshops, courses and seminars.

Marianne Macnaughten

c/o 8 Redwoods, Alton Road, London SW15 4NL
☏ 0265 731215

Contact *Marianne Macnaughten*

One of the army of freelance directors who also act as producers. Consulted by other producers so often able to pass on good ideas. Interested in new writing but with limited time to acknowledge and read scripts.

Marcellus Productions Ltd

11 Chelverton Road, London SW15 1RN
☏ 01–788 5663

Contact *Jimmy Thompson*

Jimmy Thompson acts more as a director than producer, but is always on the look-out for new plays. Recent productions have included *Don't Misunderstand Me* (Patrick Cargill); *The Quiz Kid* (which was written by the Thompsons); *Wind in the Willows* (Vaudeville Theatre); *My Giddy Aunt* (tour with Mollie Sugden) and *Touch and Go* with Ruth Madoc. Regularly produce a revue for the West End, *The Englishman Amused.* Not really in the market for avant-garde or social plays, but will consider thrillers, revue, farce and romantic comedy.

Lee Menzies Limited

20 Rupert Street, London W1V 7FN
☏ 01–437 0127 Fax 01–439 0297

Contact *Lee Menzies*

Merseyside Everyman Theatre Company

5–9 Hope Street, Liverpool L1 9BH
☏ 051–708 0338 Fax 051–709 0398

Contact *John Doyle* (Artistic Director)

FOUNDED 1964. Of five shows a year, two to three are usually new plays. The theatre tend to produce new versions of old classics, idiosyncratic Shakespeares, Willy Russell, Brecht, rock-and-roll panto – a very catholic repertoire. The common ingredient is an upfront bold style; productions are designed to appeal to non-traditional audiences. 'But no working-class angst plays please. If you spend all day in a tower block, you don't want to go out and see a play about it.' Recent productions have included *Quasimodo, The Winter's Tale, No Holds Baird, Slaughterhouse 5.* 'In theory we welcome unsolicited mss, but in practice we find we don't have the staff to do a proper reading job on them.'

Midland Arts Centre

Cannon Hill Park, Birmingham B12 9QH
☏ 021–440 4221

Contact *Robert Petty*

Home of Cannon Hill Puppet Theatre, Central Junior Television Workshop, City of Birmingham Touring Opera, Birmingham Film and TV Festival, etc., and base for Readers and Writers, an annual festival held in the last two weeks of November.

Barry J. Mishon Associates

159 Great Portland Street, London W1N 5FD
☏ 01–637 7548

Contact *Barry Mishon*

Not in the market for straight plays by either new or established writers. Devise and produce one-offs, events such as *The Night of 100 Stars,* and concerts such as *Mack & Mabel* and *La Cage aux Folles.*

Monstrous Regiment Ltd

123 Tottenham Court Road, London W1P 9HN
☏ 01–387 4790

Contact *The Directors*

FOUNDED 1976. Committed particularly to inventive and innovative ways of looking at scripts, and interested in women's experiences. Policy of encouraging new writing whenever possible and will read unsolicited mss if they can handle them. Productions include *The Colony Marivaux* (trans. Byg Hanna); *Waving* Carol Bunyan; *Island Life* Jenny McLeod, the latter both new plays.

Kenneth More Theatre

Oakfield Road, Ilford, Essex IG1 1BT
☏ 01–553 4464

Contact *Vivyan Ellacott*

Productions range from rock musicals to grand opera, gay theatre to Shakespeare, for an audience of both local senior citizens and young, upwardly mobile East-Enders. Unsolicited mss are not welcome, as there aren't the resources to cope with them; studio plays around 30 minutes long are welcome, however, as there is a great demand for these.

Norman Murray & Anne Chudleigh Ltd

1st floor, 235–41 Regent Street, London W1
☏ 01–629 4871

Contact *Anne Chudleigh*

Present pantomimes, but in general act more as agents than producers, handling light entertainment performers as well as comedy writers. 'We are always looking for new ideas in respect of comedy material, situation comedy and plays.'

Newgate Theatre Company

13 Dafford Street, Larkhall, Bath, Avon BA1 6SW
☎ 0225 318335

Contact *Jo Anderson*

'We need more than a script; we need a concept.' Newgate might be termed 'theatre packagers'; formed as a loose ensemble of actors and directors, they write their own material and respond to specific projects (often on a commission basis) for festivals, the BBC and theatres such as the **Bush, Half Moon** and **Theatre Royal Stratford East.** Credits include London production and tour of *Solstice* Jo Anderson, co-produced by **Bristol Express** in 1988; tour by **Orchard Theatre** company of *Hitler's Whistle* in 1989. New concepts always welcome. At the same address: *Air Play* – designed to 'bridge the ever increasing divide that lies between the lonely writer and the man at the top production desk'. Consists of an experienced major radio drama director, mainstream actors and access to a well-equipped stereo recording facility. Cassettes of plays are made for writers. Cover stage plays, musicals and, in the case of screen and teleplays, incorporate an exposition of visuals. Author's copyright is protected and the all-in cost depends largely on number of lead characters. Details and quotation form by return (no obligation).

Newpalm Productions

26 Cavendish Avenue, Finchley,
London N3 3QN
☎ 01–349 0802

Contact *Phil Compton*

Don't often produce new plays: *As Is* by William M. Hoffman, which came from Broadway to the **Half Moon Theatre** in August 1986 was an exception to this. National tours of *Noises Off, Seven Brides for Seven Brothers* and *Rebecca* at regional repertory theatres are examples of their more usual shows. However, unsolicted mss, whether plays or musicals are welcome; scripts are always preferable to synopses.

North Bank Productions

103B Victoria Road, London NW6 6TD
☎ 01–328 8563 Fax 01–328 8414

Contact *Chris Hayes, Jon Bromwich*

An established production company interested in both revivals and new plays, mostly on tour. New writing often comes to them through writers they know and have used in the past, like Colin Bennet, who wrote *Hancock's Finest Hour* for them. Other productions have included *Educating Rita* Willy Russell; *Funny Peculiar* Mike Stott; *To Kill a Mocking Bird* Christopher Sergel; the People Show No 92. *Whistlestop*. Future productions include *Jane Eyre* Lionel Hamilton; *The Long and the Short and the Tall* Willis Hall.

Northcott Theatre

Stocker Road, Exeter, Devon EX4 4QB
☎ 0392 56182

Contact *George Roman*

A self-producing regional theatre keen to present new writing of quality. However, much of the material which comes in is uninspiring and the Theatre often finds it has to seek out new work. Commissions and contacts are generally the order of the day. 1988/89 productions have included *Bunter* John Judd; *Sherlock Holmes* – the musical, by Leslie Bricusse; *Ancestors & Diamonds* Michael Picardie.

Northumberland Theatre Company

The Playhouse, Bondgate Without, Alnwick,
Northumberland NE66 1PQ
☎ 0665 602586

Contact *Rowan Paterson*

FOUNDED 1978. Predominantly rural, playing to village halls and community centres throughout the Northumberland and Scottish borders. Productions range from established classics to new work and popular comedies, but must be appropriate to our audience. Welcome unsolicited mss but must be suitable for production tours. Encourage new writing and do commission when possible.

Norwich Puppet Theatre

St James, Whitefriars, Norwich,
Norfolk NR3 1TN
☎ 0603 615564

Contact *Pat Holtom*

Mostly a young audience (aged 4–16), although on occasions shows are put on for an adult audience interested in puppetry. Christmas and summer season shows, plus school tours. Unsolicited mss welcome if relevant.

Nottingham Playhouse

Nottingham Theatre Trust, Wellington Circus,
Nottingham NG1 5AF
☎ 0602 474361

Contact *Les Smith* (Director of Writing)

They expect to do around two new plays a season, though no quota exists. Plays must, however, have popular appeal – they have to fill a 700-seat main house. No formal studio space exists though a studio space seating up to 120 has recently opened in the Albert Hall next door, and they have occasional use of this space for rehearsed readings and full productions. Opened with *Island Life* Jenny McLeod (co-production with **Monstrous Regiment**). 1989 plans include *Nottingham First* – three premières by writers new to the stage. Les Smith gets around 300 scripts a year and tries to criticise constructively all of these, though only 5% or so show genuine promise. Past productions include *Y'Shunta Joined,* Barry Heath; *Queer Folk,* Rosie Logan. Unsolicited mss welcome.

Nuffield Theatre

University Road, Southampton SO9 5NH
☎ 0703 617871
Fax 0703 61778 (must be marked 'Nuffield Theatre')

Contact *Patrick Sandford* (Artistic Director)

Well known as a good bet for new playwrights, the Nuffield gets an awful lot of scripts. They tend to do a couple of new plays every season, often by established playwrights, though not as a matter of policy. Recent productions have included *Swallows and Amazons* Denise Deegan & Arthur Ransome; *Fertility Dance* Philip Harland & Carol Thompson. In April 1988 premièred *The Little Heroine* Nell Dunn's first play since *Steaming.* They are open-minded about subject and style, and produce musicals as well as straight plays. Scripts preferred to synopses in the case of writers new to theatre. All will, eventually, be read 'but please be patient. We do not have a large team of paid readers. We read everything ourselves.'

Open Air Theatre

Regent's Park, London NW1 4NP
☎ 01–935 5884

Contact *Ian Talbot* (Artistic Director)

Shakespeare and revivals only, except for summer lunchtime children's theatre which is usually specially commissioned.

Orange Tree Theatre

45 Kew Road, Richmond, Surrey TW9 2NQ
☎ 01–940 3633

Contact *Sam Walters* (Artistic Director)

One of those just-out-of-London fringe theatre venues good for new writing, both full productions and rehearsed readings. New plays have included *Four Attempted Acts* (winner of the Giles Cooper Award), *A Variety of Death Defying Acts, Definitely the Bahamas* and *Dealing with Clair* – all by Martin Crimp; *Revisiting the Alchemist* Charles Jennings; *Brotherhood* Don Taylor; *A Smile on the End of the Line* (trans. Peter Meyer) and *Situation Vacant* (trans. John Burgess) by Michael Vinaver. Prospective playwrights should bear in mind, however, that unsolicited mss are read in one great blitz every spring. Those submitting scripts in the early autumn could be in for a long wait.

Orchard Theatre

108 Newport Road, Barnstaple,
Devon EX32 9BA
☎ 0271 71475

Contact *Bill Buffery* (Artistic Director)

FOUNDED 1969. Plays appealing to a wide age range, which tour some 60 or 70 cities, towns and villages throughout Devon, Cornwall, Dorset, Somerset, Avon and Gloucestershire. Programme includes classics, new adaptations, outstanding modern work, musicals and newly commissioned plays on West Country themes: *The Cuckoo* and *The Lie of the Land* Jane Beeson; *Sedgemoor* and *The Death of Arthur* John Fletcher. 'A large proportion of our work is concerned with the history, literary traditions and present-day life of the region. Unsolicited mss are read, but are usually unsuccessful simply because the theatre is committed to several commissioned new plays at any one time.'

Oxford Stage Company

Beaumont Street, Oxford OX1 2LW
☎ 0865 723238

Contact *John Retallack* (Artistic Director)

A middle-scale touring company. Productions have included *Travesties, Hamlet, Dr Faustus,* new works like *Airbase,* and adaptations like

Tristram Shandy. Unsolicited mss welcome. Produce at least one new play or new adaptation a year.

Paines Plough – The Writers Company

121–2 Tottenham Court Road,
London W1P 9HN
☎ 01–380 1188

Contact *Robin Hooper* (Literary Manager)

Produce new writing. Recent plays have included *Berlin Days* and *Hollywood Nights* Nigel Gearing; *The Way to go Home* Rona Munro; *Germinal* William Gaminara; *Abolition* Gabriel Gbadamosi. They receive around five unsolicited scripts a week and reports are made on all plays received. Writers' workshops held in London. Accompany productions on tour.

Palace Theatre, Watford

Clarendon Road, Watford WD1 1JZ
☎ 0923 35455

Contact *Lou Stein* (Artistic Director)

Important point of policy is the active commissioning of new plays. Recently these have included Stein's own adaptation of *The Adventures of Pinocchio*, Adrian Mitchell's *Woman Overboard, The Patchwork Girl of Oz*, and Louise Page's new play, *Diplomatic Wives*.

Pentameters

Three Horseshoes, 28 Heath Street,
London NW3
☎ 01–435 6757

Contact *Leonie Scott-Matthews*

Occasional plays and poetry readings. Very interested in new plays ('we've been a new writing theatre since 1968') but no resources to deal with an influx of scripts, so send letters and synopses first. Broad-minded in terms of subject matter and style: 'It's not just Soho Poly working-class angst ... we've even put on farce, which isn't supposed to work in fringe venues, but it does.'

James Perry Productions Ltd

1F Morpeth Terrace, Westminster,
London SW1P 1EW
☎ 01–828 2203

Contact *Jimmy Perry*

FOUNDED 1956. James Perry Productions is a small company which exists solely to handle the work of Jimmy Perry, creator of, among others, *It Ain't Half Hot Mum* and *Hi De Hi*.

Plantagenet Productions

Westridge Open Centre, Highclere,
near Newbury, Berks RG15 9PJ
☎ 0635 253322

Contact *Dorothy Rose Gribble*

Recorded library of the spoken word (classical, no unsolicited mss). Short list of drawing-room recitals based at Westridge Open Centre, a showcase for visiting recitals, mainly of music. Venue for small seminars, healing studies and holidays.

Players' Theatre

Villiers Street, Strand, London WC2N 6NG
☎ 01–839 1134

Contact *Reg Wooley, Geoffrey Brown*

Present Victorian music hall entertainment, researched largely from sources like the British Library. No market for playwrights here.

Playfare Productions

1 Hogarth Terrace, London W4
☎ 01–995 0065

Produce plays for children, both classics and fairy tales, for ages 4–14, which are written by a regular team, who know Playfare's needs. No interest in new scripts from other sources.

Polka Children's Theatre

240 The Broadway, London SW19 1SB
☎ 01–542 4258

This Wimbledon theatre is interested in receiving scripts suitable for children of all ages, but principally 3–5, 5–7 and 8–11. 'Our overall writing policy is to present excellent theatre for children which is both educational and entertaining'. Main house productions include original plays connected to school project work; Christmas plays; summer musical-plays; adaptations of classic stories, novels and folk tales; and puppet plays. Plays that need a cast of no more than five to seven people particularly welcome.

Q20 Theatre Company

Ivy Lea, Fyfe Lane, Baildon, Shipley,
West Yorkshire BD17 6DP
☎ 0274 591417/581316

Contact *John Lambert*

Produce shows mainly for school and community venues. Particularly interested in plays for children. Q20 write a lot of their own material, and haven't the resources to pay professional contributors. Write initially with ideas.

Quill Theatre Productions

247 Norwood Road, London SE24 9AG
☎ 01–674 1050

Contact *Ann Parnell McGarry* (Artistic Director)

Quill exist to produce new work and suffer enormous gaps in their production schedule when, as is often the case, decent new work can't be found. Writing can be set in any period, as long as it offers fresh insights, and relationships are strongly and authentically represented. 'Originality of approach is the most important thing.' In the market for serious work, fast witty comedies, musicals and children's plays. Finished scripts are preferred to synopses, unless someone wants to try out 'a truly brilliant idea which we can develop together. We have no preconceptions on size of cast.'

Really Useful Theatre Company

Palace Theatre, Shaftesbury Avenue,
London W1V 8AY
☎ 01–734 0762

Contact *Bridget Hayward* (Director)

Commercial/West End theatre producers whose output has included *Cats, Phantom of the Opera, Starlight Express, Daisy Pulls It Off, Lend Me a Tenor, Arturo Ui.* Have a positive policy towards new writing and will read unsolicited mss.

Michael Redington

10 Maunsel Street, London SW1P 2QL
☎ 01-834 5119

Contact *Michael Redington*

Recent West End productions have included *Breaking the Code* and *The Best of Friends* Hugh Whitemore; *Mr & Mrs Nobody* Keith Waterhouse *Mrs Klein* Nicholas Wright. Interested in new work but unsolicited mss not welcome; new plays generally come to him by way of contacts in the business: 'I am only interested in new work.'

Royal Court Theatre (English Stage Company Ltd)

Sloane Square, London SW1W 8AS
☎ 01–730 5174

Contact *Kate Harwood* (Literary Manager) *Mel Kenyon* (Artistic Assistant)

The English Stage Company was founded by George Devine in 1956 to put on new plays. John Osborne, John Arden and Arnold Wesker, Edward Bond and Caryl Churchill, Howard Barker and Michael Hastings are among the writers this theatre has discovered. Other writers (Christopher Hampton, David Hare) have worked in the literary department. The aim of the Royal Court is to develop and perform the best in new writing for the theatre, encouraging writers from all sections of society to address the problems and possibilities of our times.

Royal Court Young Writer's Festival

Royal Court Young People's Theatre,
309 Portobello Road, London W10 5TD
☎ 01–960 4641

Open to young people up to the age of 25 who live in the regions targeted by each particular festival. Focuses on the process of playwriting: writers and directors from the Royal Court visit 3 regions with 5 centres in each region, leading a workshop on playwriting. A second visit extends this process to the point at which young people attending are invited to submit work for the Festival. Intensive work on the final draft of plays precedes production at the Royal Court Theatre Upstairs, before going on a tour of participating regions.

Royal Exchange Theatre Company

St Ann's Square, Manchester M2 7DH
☎ 061–833 9333 Fax 061–832 0881

Contact *Allan Pollock* (Literary Manager)

FOUNDED 1976. The Royal Exchange has developed a New Writing Policy, which they find is attracting a younger audience to the theatre. They produce English and foreign classics, modern classics, adaptations, as well as new musicals and plays by young dramatists like Jeff Noon, Iain Heggie, Michael Wall and Dolores Walsh. The Royal Exchange receives up to 500 scripts a year, which are read by Michael Fox with a team of readers. Only a tiny percentage is suitable, but opportunities also exist for rehearsed readings, workshops and consultation on new work of promise. Currently there is one writer-in-residence, and a number of plays are commissioned each year. Also, annual award – see the **Mobil Playwriting Competition** under **Prizes.**

The Royal National Theatre

South Bank, London SE1 9PX
☎ 01–928 2033 Telex 297306

Contact *Nicholas Wright*

Unsolicited mss are read, but the majority of The National's new plays come about as a result of a direct commission or from existing contacts with playwrights. There is no quota for new work, though so far more than a third of plays presented have been the work of living playwrights. Writers new to the theatre would need to be of exceptional talent to be successful with a script here, though the NT Studio acts as a bridge between the theatre and a limited number of playwrights, through readings, workshops and discussion. In some cases a new play is presented for a shorter-than-usual run in the Cottesloe Theatre. NT Platforms, 45-minute plays with the minimum of decor, are a further outlet for original work.

Royal Shakespeare Company

Barbican Centre, London EC2Y 8DS
☎ 01–628 3351 Fax 01–628 6247

Contact *Colin Chambers* (Literary Manager)

The literary department at the RSC, headed by Colin Chambers, receives around 500 unsolicited mss a year of which 98 per cent are totally unsuitable. But the RSC is interested in new work and roughly a third of the company's total output is new work. This, however, is generally commissioned and unsolicited offerings from unknowns are rarely successful. Bear in mind that they are *not* interested in straightforwardly biographical plays (they get an awful lot of Lives of Elizabeth I) or singlemindedly topical writing and have no use for reworkings of Shakespeare. They don't generally welcome musicals and particularly not rewritings of *Kiss Me Kate* or *Les Misérables* (these have arrived by the sackful of late). There is, they find, a tendency among playwrights to assume that because the RSC have done a play once, they're in the market for more of the same. Usually the reverse is true, and it's wise to check whether a subject has been covered previously before submitting mss. The RSC doesn't generally hold rehearsed readings and workshops – their 'Early Stages' series (held in early 1987) is unlikely to become a regular event. Does, however, organise festivals in which new work is often a prominent feature.

Stanley Sher Enterprises Ltd

28 Oakhampton Court, Park Avenue, Roundhay, Leeds LS8 2JK
☎ 0532 731348

Contact *Stanley Sher*

FOUNDED 1962. Produce plays for a family audience: pantomime and popular theatre, plus children's productions. Unsolicited mss welcome.

Soho Poly Theatre

16 Ridinghouse Street, London W1P 7PB
☎ 01–580 6982

Contact *Tony Craze* (Art Director)

A new writing theatre, which presented its first revival for some years in 1987. The system for dealing with unsolicited mss is as follows: scripts go out to a team of readers; those they find interesting are passed on to Tony Craze, who invites writers of promise to his Writers' Workshops. An expansion of the workshop programme is under way. In addition, there is an annual three-week-long workshop called Blueprints, especially for young writers and held in the spring. This is designed to help young and inexperienced writers to develop their ideas in the professional environment. Those interested (aged between 16–25) should send a one-page proposal for a play and a few details about themselves. The Soho Poly produces around six shows a year. Output has included *Releevo* David Spencer (winner of the Verity Bargate Award 1986); *The Last Waltz* Gillian Richmond.

SRO Productions Ltd

c/o Independent Theatrical Productions Ltd, Monro House, 40-2 King Street, London WC2E 8JS
☎ 01–240 9891 Fax 01–379 5748

Contact *A. Stirling*

Produce theatre aimed at Everyman: past productions include *Once a Catholic, Candida, A Nightingale Sang, The Streets of London, Born in the Gardens, Beecham, Are You Now Or Have You Ever Been? Wildfire, Steel Magnolias* 'Delighted to read new or experienced authors; particularly the former, who must write the play as they wish to express themselves, not in the way which they think will be the most acceptable to budget-conscious producers – we can always tailor the cloth later!'

Barrie Stacey Productions/Santa Fe Productions Ltd

Flat 8, 132 Charing Cross Road, London WC2H 0LA
☎ 01–836 6220/4128

Contact *Barrie Stacey*

Now setting up tours of various subjects, some Barrie Stacey's, some other writers. Always interested in two- or three-handers for production. Also film synopses.

Stoll Moss Theatres Ltd

Cranbourn Mansions, Cranbourn Street, London WC2H 7AG
☎ 01–437 2274
Telex 296882 Fax 01–434 1217

Contact *Louis Benjamin*

One of the most influential theatrical empires, with twelve theatres, including the Globe, Lyric, Apollo and Queens in Shaftesbury Avenue. These tend to be the theatres which host straight plays, Her Majesty's and the Palladium tend to be musical venues. Recent plays have included *Lettice & Lovage* and *Beyond Reasonable Doubt*. Louis Benjamin comments that after some years as theatre managers, in which other producers brought their own shows into Stoll Moss theatres, the group is now about to move into a new phase. This will mean a return to production, and a policy, still in the planning stage, of considering all kinds of subjects and treatments: 'The size of our operation means we are likely to have a slot for anything which interests us.' The policy will be to read everything, and to reply thoughtfully 'rather than sending a bland rejection note'. Well-constructed synopses and letters are more likely to be considered than finished mss: 'we are looking into the possibility of commissioning plays where we consider the talent merits it.' Although letters/scripts should be addressed to Louis Benjamin, they are passed on to one of his staff for consideration.

Swan Theatre

The Moors, Worcester WR1 3EF
☎ 0905 726969 Fax 0905 723738

Contact *Pat Trueman* (Artistic Director)

Tries to produce one new play each season in the main house and looking towards developing more new work with the re-opening of the Studio Theatre in autumn 1989. Recent productions include *A Child in the Forest*, adapted by David Goodland from the autobiography of Winifred Foley. Also, local writers' workshops continue to be run by the director.

Swansea Little Theatre Ltd

Dylan Thomas Theatre, Maritime Quarter, 7 Gloucester Place, Swansea SA1 1TY
☎ 0792 473238

Contact *Mrs F. Davies* (Secretary)

Produce Anglo-Welsh plays. Regular production of Dylan Thomas' *Under Milkwood*. Repertoire ranges from Shakespeare to family comedies. Include one new play each season as a matter of policy. A panel of reader/producers considers new scripts.

Bob Swash Ltd

44 Lonsdale Square, London N1 1EW
☎ 01–607 8291

Contact *Bob Swash*

OUTPUT has included *One for the Road* and *Shirley Valentine*, both by Willy Russell; *Evita* on tour. New plays not currently welcome as Mr Swash is on sabbatical.

Tabard Theatre

2 Bath Road, Chiswick, London W4 1LW
☎ 01–995 6035

Contact *Sam Dowling*

FOUNDED by Sam Dowling and run as a cooperative. Plays to a wide audience from Hounslow and Greater London area. Since its opening in 1985 have done around 40 new plays. Produce new writing only and aim to encourage it as much as possible. Welcome unsolicited mss. Some workshops during the year – contact the theatre for details.

Talbot Hay Productions Ltd

2A Roebuck Road, Rochester, Kent ME1 1UD
☎ 0634 812584

Contact *Philip Talbot, Pamela Hay*

West End and touring shows. Recent productions include *The Fifteen Streets* Catherine Cookson. Unsolicited mss welcome, 'typed and bound please!'

7:84 Theatre Company, Scotland

302 Buchanan Street, Glasgow G2 3LB
☎ 031–331 2219

Contact *John Haswell* (Associate Artistic Director)

Interested in scripts 'that show an awareness of reality in the 1980s, with particular reference to working-class life in Scotland, and the varied culture that this implies.' Past productions have included Alex Norton's *The Incredible Brechin Beetle Bug* Mat McGinn; *The Albannach* adapted by John McGrath; Alex Norton's *No Mean City* based on the book by A. McArthur & H. Kingsley Long; *The Sash* Hector MacMillan; *Long Story Short* (various writers).

H.M. Tennent Ltd

Globe Theatre, Shaftesbury Avenue, London W1V 7HD
☎ 01–437 3647

Contact *Peter Wilson* (Chief Executive)

Recent productions include Jean Anouilh's *Number One* and Bob Larbey's *A Month of Sundays* (1986 SWET Award for Best Comedy). Interested in reading new works.

Theatr Clwyd

County Civic Centre, Mold, Clwyd CH7 1YA
☎ 0352 56331 Fax 0352 58323

Contact *Toby Robertson* (Artistic Director)

Lively theatre company with a policy of genuine encouragement as far as new writing is concerned. All scripts are passed on to an in-house reader – scripts are preferred to synopses and ideas. Open-minded on subjects – musicals and children's are considered. New work has included *Barnaby and the Old Boys* Keith Baxter; *Self Portrait* Sheila Yeger.

Theatre of Comedy Company

219 Shaftesbury Avenue, London WC2H 8EL
☎ 01–379 3345

Contact *Nica Burns* (Co-producer)

FOUNDED 1983 to produce new work, and regard themselves as a good bet for new plays. Interested in strong comedy in the widest sense – Chekov comes under the definition.

Theatre Foundry

Theatre Foundry Ltd, The Multi-Purpose Centre, Victoria Road, Darlaston, West Midlands
☎ 021–526 6947

Contact *The Artistic Director*

FOUNDED 1982. Small-scale touring company which performs the 'Black Country' boroughs of Walsall Dudley and Sandwell, with emphasis on working-class audiences and neighbourhood groups. 'Our policy is to encourage and advance new writing whenever possible – especially on material about the Black Country.' Welcome unsolicited mss. Large-scale community plays are also part of the company's work pattern. Recent productions include *Red Devils* Debbie Horsfield; *Crossing the Line* Stephen Bill; *Humpshire* and *Junction 10* Les Smith; *One in a Million* David Holman; *Woza Albert* Mtwa, Ngema & Simon; *Ruff Moey* David Calcutt.

Theatre Royal Stratford East

Gerry Raffles Square, London E15 1BN
☎ 01–534 7374

Contact *Jeff Teare* (Associate Director)

Lively East London theatre catering for a very mixed audience, both local and London-wide. A good bet for new work – unsolicited mss are welcome 'and we read them – eventually!' Produce new plays, musicals, classics, youth theatre, plus local community plays/events. Special interest in Asian work.

Theatre Workshop Edinburgh

34 Hamilton Place, Edinburgh EH3 5AX
☎ 031–225 7942

Contact *Adrian Harris* (Artistic Director)

Plays to a young, broad-based audience and much of the work is targeted towards particular groups or communities. OUTPUT has included *Birds of Passage* – a community performance project written by local writers and Jenny Frazer & Steve Brown's *Macburger* – youth theatre production. Welcome unsolicited mss. Enclose s.a.e. Scripts are read by the Director and one other staff member and take about 8–10 weeks to be processed for response. Commission a significant amount of new writing for a wide range of contexts, from large cast community plays to small-scale professional tours. Favour writers based in Scotland, producing material relevant to a contemporary Scottish audience.

Playwright's workshop, plus other courses and classes.

W & J Theatrical Enterprises Ltd

51A Oakwood Road, London NW11 6RJ
☏ 01–458 1608

Contact *W. D. Roberton*

Represent actors and comedians as theatrical agents, also direct farces, and write and direct pantomimes.

Tigerwise Theatrical Management

71 St Georges Square, London SW1V 3QN
☏ 01–828 3349

Contact *Anthony Smee*

Perhaps best known as concert and dance promoters (they handle the touring drumming groups Kodo, Samul Nori, and The Netherlands Dance Theatre). However, also act as producers and have handled a variety of material, including opera, revues, drama, comedy, and one-man shows. No unsolicited mss; letters and synopses in the first instance.

Traverse Theatre

112 West Bow, Grassmarket,
Edinburgh EH1 2HH
☏ 031–226 2633

Contact *Jane Ellis*

The Traverse is the most well-known theatre in Scotland for new writing; indeed it has a policy of putting on nothing but new work by new writers. They also have a strong international programme of work in translation and visiting companies. Recent productions include *Man to Man* and *The Conquest of The South Pole* Manfred Karge; *Dead Dad Dog* John McKay; *Prickly Heat* Simon Donald. Jane Ellis heads a reading panel who read and comment upon every script received. Unsolicited mss welcome.

Andrew Treagus Associates Ltd

18–19 Warwick Street, London W1V 5RB
☏ 01–734 4274
Telex 263899 Fax 01–434 4478

Contact *Andrew Treagus*

Produce shows for a London and provincial audience 'used mainly to commercial fare', from large-scale musicals to small-scale straight plays. Unsolicited mss are welcome. Policy of encouraging new writing with possible play readings, or fringe productions of their work.

Trends Management

54 Lisson Street, London NW1 6ST
☏ 01–723 8001

Theatre production is just one facet of their work (Trends also act as an agency and have an extensive wardrobe department for the designing, making and hiring of costumes). Productions are on the light entertainment side – particularly revues and pantomime. Provide most material for these themselves; shows like *Sweet Charity* and *Palm Beach Revue.* No unsolicited mss.

Tricycle Theatre

269 Kilburn High Road, London NW6 7JR
☏ 01–372 6611

Contact *Nicolas Kent*

FOUNDED 1980. Destroyed by fire in 1987. Re-opening at the end of 1989 with *All or Nothing at all.* Audiences culturally very mixed, both ethnically and in class. Encourage new writing from ethnic minorities. Look for a strong narrative drive with popular appeal. Not 'studio' plays. Run workshops for writers. Most recent production is *Pentecost* by Stewart Parker at the Lyric, Hammersmith.

Triumph Theatre Productions

Suite 4, Waldorf Chambers, 11 Aldwych, London WC2B 4DA
☏ 01–836 0187

Contact *Duncan Weldon, Peter Wilkins*

A major producer of West End and touring shows, mostly revivals but with a regular output of new work. Recent productions have included co-producing *Kiss Me Kate* at the Old Vic; *Caught in the Act; You Never Can Tell; The Deep Blue Sea;* and *A Touch of the Poet;* but also new work like *Melon* Simon Gray; *A Piece of My Mind* Peter Nichols. New work tends to be by established playwrights, but the company are always on the look-out for talented newcomers. They receive a great many unsolicited mss 'and we read them all'. Letters and synopses preferred in the first instance.

Tron Theatre Co.

63 Trongate, Glasgow G1 5H8
☎ 041–552 3748

Contact *Michael Boyd*

FOUNDED 1981. Plays to a very broad cross section of Glasgow and beyond. OUTPUT *Terrestrial Extras* Marcella Evansti; *Muir* and *Losing Alec* Peter Arnott; *Gamblers* Gogol (trans. Chris Hannan); *The Funeral* Hector McMittan. Interested in premieres of ambitious plays by experienced Scottish writers and new Irish work. Unsolicited mss welcome.

Tyne Theatre Company

Tyne Theatre and Opera House, Westgate Road, Newcastle upon Tyne NE1 4AG
☎ 091–232 3366

Contact *Andrew McKinnon* (Artistic Director and Chief Executive)

The Tyne Theatre Company is a newly formed production company based in the Tyne Theatre, a large Victorian lyric theatre in the heart of the city. New writing strategies are still in the process of formulation, but scripts will be read. As there is no literary manager, the reading of scripts is likely to be a fairly lengthy process. The company plans to involve itself in the production of new work, including co-productions with other local companies. Writers' workshops are likely to be arranged and these will be announced separately.

Umbrella Theatre

46A Compton Avenue, Brighton, East Sussex BN1 3PS
☎ 0273 775354

Contact *David Lavender*

Theatre for 'a discerning, intelligent, and adventurous' audience. Particularly interested in new writing from abroad and welcome translations as well as scripts in their original language. Past productions include *Komiker Kaberett* based on the work of Karl Valentin (Germany); *Cabaret Camique* based on the writings of French humourist Pierre Henri Cami; *The World of Cafe ´Waiters* and *Boum! Voila!*, two shows based on original writings for early French cabaret. Unsolicited mss welcome.

Charles Vance

83 George Street, London W1H 5PL
☎ 01–486 1732

Contact *Charles Vance*

In the market for small-scale touring productions and summer season plays, although they haven't done much lately, as Charles Vance has been busy editing *Amateur Stage* and refurbishing the Grand Opera House, York. Recent productions include Vance's own adaptation of *Wuthering Heights*. Do not commission plays, and don't often do new work, though writing of promise stands a good chance of being passed on to someone who does. Occasional try-outs for new work in the Sidmouth repertory theatre.

Viva Theatre Productions Ltd

42–6 St Lukes Mews, London W11 1DG
☎ 01–221 5101 Fax 01–221 3374

Contact *Tracy Bennett*

FOUNDED 1985. General West End theatre audience with bias towards the younger sector. OUTPUT *Pal Joey; Yakety Yak; Metamorphosis; Decadence*. Welcome unsolicited mss. Strongly in favour of new work and try to concentrate on it.

John Wallbank Associates Ltd

St Martin's Theatre, West Street, London WC2N 3NH
☎ 01–379 5665

Contact *John Wallbank*

Plays and musicals suitable for West End production and occasionally touring. New writing is welcome.

Michael Ward Theatre Productions

Radnors, 39 Thames Street, Windsor, Berkshire SL4 1PR
☎ 0753 863982

Contact *Michael Ward*

FOUNDED 1984. Standard touring market audience. Concentrating at the moment on reopening the historic Theatre Royal Margate and will be producing in-house productions that could then either be toured or go direct to London. Unsolicited mss welcome but expect to wait a long time. Encourage new writing though and keep in touch with fringe and try-outs as much as possible.

The Warehouse Theatre Croydon

Dingwall Road, Croydon CR0 2NF
☎ 01–681 1257

Contact *Rachel Braverman* (Script Manager)

South London's new writing theatre, seating 120; producing six new plays a year and also co-producing with companies who share the commitment to new work. The Warehouse continually builds upon a tradition of discovering and nurturing new writers, with activities including a monthly Writers' Workshop and the annual South London Playwriting Festival held in the autumn. Recent productions include *Pommies* by David Allen, *The Astronomer's Garden* by Kevin Hood, and *Dinner* by Mark Bunyan (winner of the 1988 Festival). Receive between 2 and 5 unsolicited scripts a day. The theatre is committed at least 9 months in advance.

Watermill Theatre

Bagnor, Newbury, Berks RG16 8AE
☎ 0635 45834

Contact *Jill Fraser*

The Watermill tries to put on one new piece of work each year. 1988 production *My Wife Whatsername* by Christopher Lillicrap & Jonathan Izard. Also produce regular new Christmas shows for young children aged 5–12 and their families. In 1988, *King Rollo's Stolen Christmas* a musical adventure story by Euan Smith and Peter Murray. Plans for 1989 include a new musical by George Stiles & Anthony Drewe entitled *Just So* and *I Wish, I Wish* by Terence Brady & Charlotte Bingham.

Westminster Productions Ltd

Westminster Theatre, Palace Street,
London SW1E 5JB
☎ 01–828 9361

Contact *Howard Bird* (Administrator)

FOUNDED 1961. Encourages new writing 'which explores fundamental spiritual and moral values in a contemporary and relevant context'. Have produced 29 West End productions/co-productions, five feature films and three video dramas, plus school productions. Plays range from children's/family shows like *The Lion, The Witch and The Wardrobe* to classics like *An Inspector Calls*, plus good new plays. An outline or synopsis in the first instance is essential.

Whirligig Theatre

14 Belvedere Drive, Wimbledon,
London SW19 7BY
☎ 01–947 1732

Contact *David Wood*

Produce one play a year, which tends to be a musical play for children, for primary school audiences and weekend family groups, in major theatres. All new mss should exploit the theatrical nature of children's tastes. Previous productions have included: *The See-Saw Tree, The Selfish Shellfish, The Gingerbread Man; The Old Man of Lochnagar*. David Wood gave a writing course in conjunction with the **British Theatre Association** in 1987.

Michael White

13 Duke Street, St James's, London SW1Y 6DB
☎ 01–839 3971 Fax 01–839 3836

Contact *Michael White*

Contributions are passed by Michael White to a script reader for consideration. Recent productions by this high-output company have included *White Mischief* and *Metropolis*.

Winged Horse Touring Productions

6 The Old Schoolhouse, 1 Dean Path,
Edinburgh EH4 3BG
☎ 031–226 3520

Contact *John Carnegie* (Artistic Director)

FOUNDED 1979. Touring company which plays to a wide variety of diverse audiences in urban and rural venues throughout Scotland and northern England. New plays are the core of their output and are by Scottish-based writers (both established and new) and narrative-based. No unsolicited mss. Receive 'piles' of scripts but tend to seek out authors to commission. However, will consider synopsis with sample dialogue. Recent productions include *Blood and Ice* Liz Lochhead; *Bozzy* Frederic Mohr; *Changed Days* Alan Spence.

Women's Theatre Group

5 Leonard Street, London EC2A 4AQ
☎ 01–251 0202

Contact *The Administrator*

FOUNDED 1974. Tours nationally to a wide range of

venues, including studio theatres, arts centres, universities, colleges, community venues. Audiences vary accordingly – predominantly women though. OUTPUT *Pax* Deborah Levy; *Time Pieces* (company compiled) dir. Lou Wakefield; *Picture Palace* Winsome Pinnock; *Lear's Daughters* from an original idea by Elaine Feinstein. No unsolicited mss. Apply for writing policy details in first instance. Commission 2 new plays a year by women and 50% of commissions are to black writers.

York Theatre Royal

St Leonard's Place, York YO1 2HD
☏ 0904 651862

Contact *Derek Nicholls* (Artistic Director)

Recent productions have included *Charley's Aunt; The American Clock; Pride and Prejudice; Taking Steps; Groping for Words; As You Like It; The Country Wife; The Island of Doctor Moreau; Peter Pan.*

US Publishers

Abingdon Press

201 Eighth Avenue S, Box 801,
Nashville TN 37202
☎ 0101 615 749 6403

Contact *Michael E. Lawrence* (Trade Books), *Davis Perkins* (Reference/Academic Books), *Etta Wilson* (Children's Books)

Publishes fiction (children's only); non-fiction: religious (lay and professional); children's religious books; and academic texts. Average 100 titles a year. Approach in writing with synopsis and samples only.

Harry N. Abrams Inc.

100 Fifth Avenue, New York NY 10011
☎ 0101 212 206 7715
Telex 23–4772 Cable ABRAMBOOK

Publisher/Editor-in-chief *Paul Gottlieb*

Subsidiary of Times Mirror Co. *Publishes* illustrated books: art, design, nature, outdoor recreation; no fiction. Average 90 titles a year. Submit completed mss (no dot matrix) and sample illustrations.

Addison-Wesley Publishing Co. Inc.

General Books Division, Jacob Way,
Reading MA 01867
☎ 0101 617 944 3700
Telex 94–9416 Cable ADIWES

Publisher *David Miller*

Publishes biography, business/economics, health, 'how-to', politics, psychology and science, also finance, health, education and parenting 'by people well known and respected in their field.' No fiction. Average 75 titles a year. Approach in writing or phone call in first instance, then submit synopsis and one sample chapter.

University of Alabama Press

Box 870380, Tuscaloosa AL 35487

Director *Malcolm MacDonald*

Publishes academic books only. 40 titles a year.

Amacom

135 West 50th Street, New York NY 10020
☎ 0101 212 586 8100

Contact *Weldon P. Rackley*

Publishing division of American Management Associations. *Publishes* business and management.

University of Arizona Press

1230 N. Park Avenue, 102, Tucson AZ 85719
☎ 0101 602 621 1441

Director *Stephen Cox*
Editor-in-chief *Gregory McNamee*

FOUNDED 1959. Academic non-fiction only, particularly with a regional-cultural link. Average 40 titles a year.

Atlantic Monthly Press

19 Union Square West, New York NY 10003
☎ 0101 212 645 4462

Editorial Director *Gary Fisketjon*

Publishes general fiction and non-fiction, poetry. Average 60 titles a year. Approach in writing, submitting sample chapter (especially fiction).

Baen Books

3rd Floor, 260 Fifth Avenue, New York NY 10001
☎ 0101 212 532 4111

Chairman/Publisher/Managing Director/ Editor-in-Chief *James Baen*

Publishes science fiction and fantasy only. Welcome unsolicited mss provided they are

accompanied by s.a.e. or International Reply Coupons. Likewise, welcome synopses and covering letter but not just ideas.
Royalties paid twice yearly.

Ballantine/DelRey/Fawcett Books

201 E. 50th Street, New York NY 10022
☏ 0101 212 751 2600

Division of **Random House Inc.** *Publishes* general fiction and non-fiction, science fiction. (Mss not less than 50,000 words.) Average 750 titles a year.

Bantam Books Inc.

666 Fifth Avenue, New York NY 10103
☏ 0101 212 765 6500 Cable BANTAMBOOK NY

President/Publisher *Linda Grey*

Vice-President/Publisher (adult fiction and non-fiction) *Steve Rubin*

A division of the Bantam Doubleday Dell Publishing Group Inc. *Publishes* general fiction and children's books. Category books: mysteries, westerns, romance, war books, science fiction. No poetry or general non-fiction. No queries or unsolicited mss.

IMPRINTS
Spectra (science fiction), **New Age, Bantam New Fiction** (original fiction in trade paperback).

Beacon Press

25 Beacon Street, Boston MA 02108
☏ 0101 617 742 2110 Cable BEAPRESS

Director *Wendy J. Strothman*

Publishes general non-fiction. Average 50 titles a year. Approach in writing or submit synopsis and sample chapters with International Reply Coupons to editorial department.

Beaufort Books Inc.

9 E. 40th Street, New York NY 10016
☏ 0101 212 685 8588

Publishes fiction – mystery, thriller, contemporary and literary novels, including translations from French (no science fiction or first novels). General non-fiction. Average 30–40 titles a year. Write or submit complete mss.

Berkley Publishing Group

200 Madison Avenue, New York NY 10016
☏ 0101 212 951 8848

Editor-in-Chief *Ed Breslin*

Publishes general fiction, including young adult; non-fiction: 'how to', inspirational, family life, philosophy and nutrition. Average 900 titles a year. Submit synopsis and first three chapters (for Ace Science Fiction only). No unsolicited mss.

IMPRINTS
Berkley, Berkley Trade Paperbacks, Jove, Charter, Second Chance at Love, Pacer, Ace Science Fiction.

University of California Press

2120 Berkeley Way, Berkeley CA 94720

Director *James H. Clark*

Publishes academic non-fiction. Also fiction and poetry in translation. Average 225 titles a year. Preliminary letter with outline preferred.

Carolrhoda Books Inc.

241 First Avenue North, Minneapolis MN 55401
☏ 0101 612 332 3345

Publishes children's: nature, biographies, history, beginning readers, world cultures, photo essays.

Carroll & Graf Publishers Inc.

260 Fifth Avenue, New York NY 10001
☏ 0101 212 889 8772 Tek 0101 212 545 7909

Chairman *Herman Graf*
Managing Director *Kent Carroll*

FOUNDED 1983. *Publishes* 'all except for romance – particularly classic mystery and science fiction reprints'. 10 titles in 1988 (and 70 reprints). Welcome unsolicited mss provided they are accompanied by return postage, but prefer query with synopsis in first instance. Any approach in writing with ideas or outlines must be accompanied by s.a.e.
Royalties paid twice yearly.

University of Chicago Press

5801 South Ellis Avenue, Chicago IL 60637
☏ 0101 312 702 7700

Publishes academic non-fiction only.

Contemporary Books

180 North Michigan Avenue, Chicago IL 60601
☎ 0101 312 782 9181

Editorial Director *Nancy Crossman*

Publishes general non-fiction, professional and school test preparation, adult education and sports.

Crown Publishers Inc.

225 Park Avenue South, New York NY 10003
☎ 0101 212 254 1600

Publishes non-fiction only: Americana, animals, art, biography, children's, cookery, health, history, hobbies, 'how-to', humour, music, nature, philosophy, photography, politics, psychology, recreation, reference, science, self-help and sport. Average 250 titles a year. Preliminary letter essential.

IMPRINTS
Clarkson Potter, Orion Books, Harmony and **Julian Press.**

Dell Publishing Co. Inc.

1 Dag Hammarskjold Plaza, New York NY 10017

A division of Bantam Doubleday Dell Publishing Group, Inc.

Publishes (Make sure query is directed to right department.) Fiction: **Delacorte** top-notch commercial fiction; **Dell** mass market paperbacks – sagas, romance, adventure, suspense, horror and war; **Delta** original fiction, non-fiction; **Delacorte** popular non-fiction; **Dell Trade** non-fiction guides; **Yearling** and **Laurel Leaf** children and young adults. Average 500 titles a year. Unsolicited mss: do not send mss, sample chapters or art work; do not register, certify or insure your letter; send only a four-page synopsis with covering letter stating previous work published or relevant experience.

IMPRINTS
Dell, Delacorte Press, Delta Books, Dell Trade Paperbacks, Laurel, Delacorte Press, Yearling and **Laurel Leaf.**

Dorchester Publishing Co. Inc

Suite 1008, 276 Fifth Avenue,
New York NY 10001
☎ 0101 212 725 8811 Fax 0101 212 532 1054

President/Publisher *Gerard Brisman*

Publishes historial romance, horror, adventure, westerns. 140 titles in 1988.

IMPRINTS
Leisure Books *Aurdrey LaFehr* (Submissions Editor) TITLES *Night Flame* Catherine Hart; *Pagoda* R. Karl Largent; western series; men's adventure series. No unsolicited mss. Send first three chapters and a synopsis (plus s.a.e.) for historical romance and horror books. Best approach in other categories is with an idea in writing.

Doubleday

245 Park Avenue, New York NY 10167
☎ 0101 212 765 6500

A division of Bantam Doubleday Dell Group, Inc. *Publishes* fiction for mystery/suspense, science fiction and romance. Send complete mss (60,000–80,000 words) to Crime Club Editor, Science Fiction Editor or Starlight Romance Editor as appropriate.

Farrar, Straus & Giroux Inc.

19 Union Square West, New York NY 10003
☎ 0101 212 741 6900

Children's Editors *Stephen Roxburgh, Margaret Ferguson*

Publishes fiction, picture books and novels for children and young adults. Limited number of non-fiction titles. Approximately 100 titles each year. Submit synopsis and sample chapters (artwork/photographs as part of package).

David R. Godine

Horticultural Hall, 300 Massachusetts Avenue,
Boston MA 02115
☎ 0101 617 536 0761 Fax 0101 617 421 0934

Publishes fiction and non-fiction. Non-fiction: photography, art, history, natural history, children's, poetry, typography and graphic art. 40–50 titles a year.

Harcourt Brace Jovanovich

Children's Division, 1250 Sixth Avenue,
San Diego CA 92101
☎ 0101 619 699 6810

Publishes fiction and non-fiction. Non-fiction: educational, textbooks, biography, travel, children's, science travel, current affairs, history. Also poetry. No unsolicited mss except for children's.

Harlequin Books (New York)

6th Floor, 300 East 42nd Street,
New York NY 10017
☎ 0101 212 682 6080 Fax 0101 212 682 4539

FOUNDED 1949, Harlequin Books is the world's largest publisher of romantic fiction. Head office: Harlequin Books Enterprises Ltd in Toronto. Now has offices in six continents, publishing in over 100 countries in 19 languages. In its early years published a wide variety of books from westerns to cookbooks to classics but have concentrated on romance fiction since 1964. Acquired **Mills & Boon** in 1971. *Publishes* romantic fiction, action & adventure, mystery, science fiction. About 1240 titles in 1988. Welcome unsolicited mss, synopses and ideas for books.

IMPRINTS
Harlequin (Superromance, Romance) *Horst Bausch* TITLES *Working it Out; The Diamond Trap.* **Silhouette** (Desire, Special Edition) *Karen Solem* TITLES *Lady of the Island; Navy Wife.* **Gold Eagle** (Mack Bolan, Able Team) *Randall Toye* TITLES *Border Sweep; Cold Steel.* **Worldwide Library** (Mystery, science fiction) *Randall Toye* TITLES *Paint her Face Dead; Caliban Landing.*
Royalties paid twice yearly. *Overseas subsidiaries* worldwide; joint ventures in France, Germany & Italy.

Harper & Row Publishers Inc.

10 East 53rd Street, New York NY 10022
☎ 0101 212 207 7000

Chief Executive *George Craig*

Jointly owned by Collins and News International. *Publishes* general fiction and non-fiction. Average 500 titles a year.
Vice President/Publisher (paperbacks) *Eddie Bell* **Vice President/Publisher** (adult trade) *William Shinker.*

Harvard University Press

79 Garden Street, Cambridge MA 02138
☎ 0101 617 495 2600 Telex 92–1484

Editor-in-chief *Maud Wilcox*

Publishes scholarly non-fiction only. Average 120 titles a year. Free book catalogue and mss guidelines.

D.C. Heath & Co.

125 Spring Street, Lexington MA 02173
☎ 0101 617 862 6650

Editor-in-chief (Lexington books) *Robert Bovenschule*

Publishes textbooks, professional, scholarly, and software. Textbooks at college level in all subjects. Average 300 titles a year. Preliminary letter essential.

Hippocrene Books Inc.

171 Madison Avenue, New York NY 10016
☎ 0101 212 685 4371

Publishes general non-fiction, and reference books, particularly strong on maps and travel guides. No fiction.

Holiday House Inc.

18 E. 53rd Street, New York NY 10022
☎ 0101 212 688 0085

Vice President/Editor-in-Chief
Margery Cuyler

Publishes children's general fiction and non-fiction (pre-school to secondary school). Average 35–40 titles a year. Submit synopsis and three sample chapters or complete mss without artwork.

Houghton Mifflin Co.

2 Park Street, Boston MA 02108
☎ 0101 617 725 5000
Telex 94–0959 Cables HOUGHTON

Director *Joseph Kanon*

Publishes general fiction including poetry; general non-fiction including 'how to' and self-help. Average 110 titles a year. Approach in writing in the first instance.

University of Illinois Press

54 E. Gregory, Champaign IL 61820
☎ 0101 217 333 0950

Editorial Director *Richard L. Wentworth*

Publishes fiction and non-fiction. Fiction: ethnic, experimental, mainstream, short story collections only, no novels. Non-fiction: scholarly and general – particularly in the humanities and Americana. Average 100 titles a year. Letter first.

Indiana University Press

10th & Morton Streets, Bloomington IN 47405
☏ 0101 812 337 4203

Director *John Gallman*

Publishes scholarly non-fiction. Especially interested in non-fiction works in specific subject areas, of which there is a long list. Query in writing in first instance.

Alfred A. Knopf Inc.

201 E. 50th Street, New York NY 10022
☏ 0101 212 751 2600

Senior Editor *Ashbel Green*
Children's Book Editor *Frances Foster*

Publishes fiction (of literary merit); non-fiction: including scholarly. 200+ titles a year. Submit complete mss (fiction 30,000–150,000 words). Write in first instance for non-fiction (mss should be 40,000–150,000 words).

Lerner Publications Co.

241 First Avenue North, Minneapolis MN 55401
☏ 0101 612 332 3344

Publishes books for children and young adults. Geography, social issues, biographies, history, economics, ethnic studies, science, nature, activities, hi-lo, sports, some fiction.

Little, Brown & Co. Inc.

34 Beacon Street, Boston MA 02108
☏ 0101 617 227 0730 Telex 94–0928

Publishes contemporary popular fiction as well as literary fiction; limited poetry list usually by recognised poets. Non-fiction: 'how-to', distinctive cookbooks, biographies, history, science and sports. Average 100+ titles a year. Mss accepted only from published authors. Write or submit synopsis and sample chapters for both fiction and non-fiction – including artwork in the non-fiction package.

Longman Inc.

95 Church Street, White Plains NY 10601
☏ 0101 914 993 5000

Publishes primary, secondary, tertiary and professional textbooks. No trade, art or children's books. Average 200 titles a year.

Lorevan Publishing Inc./Critic's Choice Paperbacks

31 East 28th Street, New York NY 10016
☏ 0101 212 685 1550

Chairman/Managing Director *Stanley L. Reisner*

FOUNDED 1984. *Publishes* mass market paperbacks: suspense and horror, thriller, historical romance, mysteries, westerns, celebrity biographies, adventure. About 65 titles a year. No unsolicited mss but welcome synopses and ideas for books.
Royalties paid twice yearly.

Louisiana State University Press

Baton Rouge LA 70893
☏ 0101 504 388 6294

Director *L. E. Phillabaum*

Publishes fiction: 2 novels, 2 short story collections and 6 volumes of poetry a year. Non-fiction includes: Southern history, American history, French history, Southern literary criticism, American literary criticism, political philosophy, and some Latin American studies. Average 60 titles a year. Send International Reply Coupons for mss guidelines.

Lyle Stuart Inc.

120 Enterprise Avenue, Secaucus NJ 07094
☏ 0101 201 866 0490/212 736 1141

Publisher *Steven Schragis*

Publishes fiction and non-fiction: biography, gay and lesbian, 'how-to' books, illustrated and self-help. Average 100 titles a year. Unsolicited mss not considered – write in first instance. Strong, even controversial ideas welcome.

McGraw-Hill Book Co.

College Division, 1221 Avenue of the Americas, New York NY 10020
☏ 0101 212 512 2000

Editors-in-Chief (Social Science & Humanities) *Philip A. Butcher*; (Science, Mathematics & Nursing) *David Beleio*; (Business, Economics & Data Processing) *Kaye Pace*; (Engineering & Computer Science) *Eric Munson*

Publishes non-fiction: college textbooks (social, business and physical sciences, and engineering).

Macmillan Publishing Company

Children's Book Department, 866 Third Avenue, New York NY 10022
☎ 0101 212 702 2000

Publishes children's fiction and non-fiction. Average 65 titles a year.

Merrill Publishing Co.

1300 Alum Creek Drive, Columbus OH 43216
☎ 0101 614 890 1111

Parent company Bell & Howell. Education Division *publishes* texts, workbooks and software in science, language, arts, mathematics and social studies for school level. College Division publishes higher level books and materials in humanities, business, mathematics, science and technology. Average 400 titles a year. Send synopsis and three sample chapters.

University of Missouri Press

200 Lewis Hall, Columbia MO 65211
☎ 0101 314 882 7641

Director *Beverly Jarrett*

Fiction and academic non-fiction. Fiction, drama and poetry only considered in February and March of odd-numbered years through Breakthrough Contest. Letter essential. Average 40 titles a year.

MIT Press

55 Hayward Street, Cambridge MA 02142
☎ 0101 617 253 1693

Acquisitions Co-ordinator *Madeline Brown*

Publishes non-fiction: technologically sophisticated books including computer science and artificial intelligence, economics, architecture, cognitive science, linguistics and philosophy. Average 100 titles a year. Submit synopsis, academic resumé and sample chapters.

William Morrow and Co.

105 Madison Avenue, New York NY 10016
☎ 0101 212 889 3050

Publisher *James Landis*

Publishes fiction, including poetry. General non-fiction. Approach only in writing. No unsolicited mss or proposals, which should only be submitted through a literary agent (50,000–100,000 words).

IMPRINTS

Arbor House, Greenwillow Books *Susan Hirschman;* **Lothrop, Lee and Shepard** *Dorothy Briley;* **Morrow Junior** *David Reuther;* **Quill** (trade paperbacks) *Douglas Stumpf & Andrew Ambraziejus.*

University of New Mexico Press

Journalism 220, Albuquerque NM 87131
☎ 0101 505 277 2346

Director *Elizabeth C. Hadas*

Publishes scholarly and regional non-fiction only. No fiction. Average 60 titles a year.

University of North Carolina Press

Box 2288, Chapel Hill NC 27514
☎ 0101 919 966 3561

Editor-in-Chief *Iris Tillman Hill*

Publishes scholarly and regional trade books. No fiction. Particularly interested in American history and Southern studies. Average 60 titles a year.

W.W. Norton & Company

500 Fifth Avenue, New York NY 10110
☎ 0101 212 354 5500 Telex 12–7634

Managing Editor *Liz Malcolm*

Publishes quality fiction and non-fiction. No occult, paranormal, religious, cookbooks, arts and crafts, genre fiction (formula romances, science fiction or westerns), children's books or young adult. Average 213 titles a year. Submit synopsis and two or three sample chapters.

Ohio University Press

Scott Quad, Ohio University, Athens OH 45701
☎ 0101 614 593 1155

Director *Duane Schneider*

Publishes general scholarly non-fiction with emphasis on nineteenth-century literature and culture, and African studies. Average 25–30 titles a year. Approach in writing in first instance.

University of Oklahoma Press

1005 Asp Avenue, Norman OK 73019
☎ 0101 405 325 5111

Editor-in-Chief *John Drayton*

Publishes non-fiction only: American Indian studies, Western American history, classical studies, literary theory and criticism, women's studies. Average 70 titles a year.

Open Court Publishing Co.

Box 599, Peru IL 61354
☎ 0101 815 223 2520

Editorial Director *David Ramsay Steele* (General Books)

Publishes non-fiction: scholarly books, mainly philosophy, psychology, religion, economics and science; also German and French non-fiction translations. Average 30 titles a year. Write or submit synopsis and two or three sample chapters as part of package.

Pantheon Books

201 E. 50th Street, New York NY 10022
☎ 0101 212 751 2600

Contact *Adult Editorial Department* (27th Floor), *Children's Department* (6th Floor)

Publishes fiction: less than five novels a year; some foreign fiction in translation. Non-fiction: political and social subjects, emphasis on Asia, medicine, 'how-to' books. Some children's books. Average 90 titles a year. Write in first instance concerning non-fiction, no mss accepted. No fiction queries accepted at all.

Pelican Publishing Company

1101 Monroe Street, Box 189, Gretna LA 70053
☎ 0101 504 368 1175

Associate Editor *Dean M. Shapiro*

Publishes fiction: very limited requirement (including children's books); non-fiction: general non-fiction (especially cookbooks, travel, art, architecture, and inspirational). Average 30–40 titles a year. Write and submit mss and photocopied samples of artwork (non-fiction); submit synopsis and sample chapters (fiction), but query preferred in the first instance. No multiple submissions. Include International Reply Coupons with all enquiries.

Persea Books Inc.

60 Madison Avenue, New York NY 10010
☎ 0101 212 779 7668

Editorial *Karen Braziller*

Publishes biography, contemporary affairs, literature and criticism, poetry, fiction, belles lettres, and women's studies.

Plenum Publishing

233 Spring Street, New York NY 10013
☎ 0101 212 620 8000

Senior Editor (Trade books) *Linda Greenspan Regan*

Publishes quality non-fiction for the intelligent layman and the professional: sciences, social sciences and humanities.

Pocket Books

1230 Avenue of the Americas,
New York NY 10020
☎ 0101 212 698 7000

Publishes fiction: adult, mystery, science fiction, romance, westerns; non-fiction: history, biography, reference and general books.

IMPRINTS
Washington Square Press – high quality mass market. No unsolicited mss; write in the first instance.

Prentice Hall Inc. Business and Professional Books Division

Gulf & Western, Sylvan Avenue,
Eaglewood Cliffs NJ 07632
☎ 0101 212 592 2000

Publishes 'how to', reference, self-help, and technical non-fiction, on business, economics, sport, law, accountancy, computing and education. Average 150 titles a year. Particularly interested in high level books which will sell well by direct mail marketing.

Princeton University Press

41 William Street, Princeton NJ 08540
☎ 0101 609 452 4900

Editor-in-Chief *Sanford G. Thatcher*

Publishes art history, literary criticism, history, philosophy, religion, political science, economics, anthropology, sociology and science. Also poetry, which is judged solely in competition (mss to *Robert Brown*). Average 150 titles a year.

Putnam Publishing Group

200 Madison Avenue, New York NY 10016
☎ 0101 212 576 8900

Editorial *Gene Brissie, Bernette Ford, Patty Gauch, Neil Nyren*

Publishes general fiction and non-fiction, including children's books. Particularly strong on history, literature, economics, political science, natural science. Major fiction publisher.

Rand McNally & Co.

PO Box 7600, Chicago IL 60680
☎ 0101 312 673 9100

Editor *Jon Leverenz*

Publishes world atlases and maps; road atlases of North America and Europe; city and state maps of the United States and Canada; marketing guides and banking directories; educational wall maps; atlases and globes.

Random House Inc.

201 E. 50th Street, New York NY 10022
☎ 0101 212 751 2600 Fax 0101 212 872 8244

Chairman *Robert Bernstein*
Publisher (Adult books) *Joni Evans*
Editorial Head *Jason Epstein*

FOUNDED 1925. *Publishes* fiction, biography/autobiography, current affairs, history, economics, politics, health, gardening, business, sports, military history, humour, cookbooks. About 100 titles a year. Send synopsis and sample chapters. *Royalties* paid twice yearly.

The Rosen Publishing Group, Inc.

29 East 21st Street, New York NY 10010
☎ 0101 212 777 3017

Publishes non-fiction books for a young adult audience, on careers, personal and guidance subjects; also art, theatre, music and health. Average 45 titles a year. Write with outline and sample chapters.

IMPRINT
Pelion Press Classical music and opera.

St Martin's Press Inc.

175 Fifth Avenue, New York NY 10010
☎ 0101 212 674 5151

FOUNDED 1952. *Publishes* over 1200 new titles a year. General fiction and non-fiction, particularly adult fiction and non-fiction, history, self-help, political science, biography, scholarly, popular reference. Noted for its fiction and mystery programmes. Will consider unsolicited mss but recommend enquiry letter in the first instance.

Schocken Books Inc.

201 East 50th Street, New York NY 10022
☎ 0101 212 751 2600

Publishes serious non-fiction (including reprints), Jewish studies, women's studies, history, and social science, psychology, education.

Scholastic Inc.

730 Broadway, New York NY 10003
☎ 0101 212 505 3000

Editor *Ann Reit*

Publishes teen fiction for girls: romance and historical romance – 40,000–45,000 words. Average 36 titles a year. Sending International Reply Coupons for guidelines essential before submitting mss.

Charles Scribner's Sons

Children's books department, 866 Third Avenue, New York NY 10022
☎ 0101 212 702 7885

Editorial Director *Clare Costello* (Children's books)

Publishes fiction and non-fiction. Fiction: adventure, fantasy, historical, humour, mystery, science fiction and suspense. Send synopsis and sample. Non-fiction: animals, art, biography, health, humour, nature, science and sports. Write in first instance. Average 25 titles a year.

Simon & Schuster

Trade Books Division, 1230 Avenue of the Americas, New York NY 10020
☎ 0101 212 698 7000

Fiction and non-fiction through agents only. No textbooks, specialised, poetry or plays. Unsolicited mss returned unread.

Stanford University Press

Stanford CA 94305–2235
☎ 0101 415 723 9434

Editor *William W. Carver*

Publishes non-fiction only. Scholarly works in all areas of the humanities, social sciences and natural sciences, plus more general interest, middle-brow academic books. Average 65 titles a year. Write in first instance.

Sterling Publishing

387 Park Avenue South, New York NY 10016
☎ 0101 212 532 7160

Contact *Sheila Anne Barry*

Publishes non-fiction only: 'alternative life-style', games/puzzles, 'how-to' books, health, home medical, business, cookery, hobbies, children's humour, occult, pets, recreation, self-help, sports, collecting, wines, woodworking, and reference. Average 80 titles a year. Write in first instance enclosing sample chapter list, synopsis and two sample chapters.

Taplinger Publishing Co.

132 W. 22nd Street, New York NY 10011
☎ 0101 212 741 0801

Editor *Roy Thomas*

Fiction and non-fiction hardbacks. No children's. Fiction: serious and contemporary. Non-fiction: art, calligraphy and belles lettres. Write in first instance. Average 25 titles a year.

IMPRINT
Crescendo music books.

Temple University Press

Broad and Oxford Streets,
Philadelphia PA 19122
☎ 0101 215 787 8787

Editor-in-Chief *Michael Ames*

Publishes scholarly non-fiction only. American history, sociology, women's studies, health care, philosophy, public policy, labour studies, urban studies, photography, and black studies. Average 60 titles a year. Authors generally academics. Write in first instance.

Time-Life Books Inc.

777 Duke Street, Alexandria VA 22314
☎ 0101 703 838 7000

Editor *George Constable*

Publishes non-fiction general interest books only; usually heavily illustrated and originating in-house. No unsolicited mss. Average 45 titles a year.

Times Books Inc.

201 East 50th Street, New York NY 10022
☎ 0101 212 872 8110

Editorial Director *Jonathan B. Segal*

Publishes non-fiction only: business, economics, science and medical, biography, history, women's issues, cookery, current affairs, language and sports. Unsolicited mss not considered. Letter essential. Average 45 titles a year.

Universe Books

381 Park Avenue South, New York NY 10016
☎ 0101 212 685 7400

Editorial Director *Louis Barron*

Publishes non-fiction only: art, architecture and design. Also some illustrated on ballet, crafts, countries, music, nature, and social sciences. Averages 45 titles a year. Synopsis with two to three sample chapters.

Van Nostrand Reinhold Co. Inc.

115 5th Avenue, New York NY 10003
☎ 0101 212 254 3232

Publishes technical and scientific, business, medical, architecture, design, aeronautical, marine, energy, photography, reference, encyclopaedias and handbooks. Distributed in Europe, Middle East and Africa by **Chapman and Hall** (see under **UK Publishers**).

Vanguard Press Inc.

424 Madison Avenue, New York NY 10017
☎ 0101 212 753 3906

Editor-in-Chief *Bernice Woll*

Publishes fiction and non-fiction. Fiction: adventure, experimental, humour, mystery, and literary. Non-fiction: all general and popular areas. No coffee table books, reference or technical. Average 20 titles a year.

Viking Books

40 West 23rd Street, New York NY 10001
☎ 0101 212 337 5200

Senior Editor *Nan Graham*

Publishes hardcover and paperbound books: art, classical literature, fiction, history, politics, biography/autobiography. All unsolicited mss returned unopened. Proposals through agents only.

Walker & Co

720 Fifth Avenue, New York NY 10019
☎ 0101 212 265 3632

Contact *Submissions Editor*

Publishes fiction and non-fiction. Fiction: adventure, mystery, regency romance, spy/thriller, westerns. Non-fiction: Americana, art, biography, business, histories, 'how-to' books, children's, science, history, media, psychiatric, music, nature, sports, parenting, psychology, recreation, reference, popular science, self-help. Average 150 titles a year.

Warner Publishing Co.

666 5th Avenue, New York NY 10103
☎ 0101 212 484 2900

Editor-in-chief *Mel Parker*

Publishes fiction and non-fiction, both hardcover and mass market paperbacks.

University of Wisconsin Press

114 North Murray Street, Madison WI 53715
☎ 0101 608 262 4928

Acquisitions Editor *Barbara Hanrahan*

Publishes academic non-fiction only, and only interested in complete mss.

Yale University Press

302 Temple Street, New Haven CT 06520
☎ 0101 203 432 0960

Publishes academic books.

US Agents

International Reply Coupons

Most agents ask correspondents to pay for any return postage. This can be done by International Reply Coupons, which for a letter costs 55 pence, but when mss are involved check with the Post Office.

Carol Abel Literary Agency

160 West 87th Street, New York NY 10024
☏ 0101 212 724 1168

FOUNDED 1978. *Specialises* in contemporary women's fiction, biographies, thrillers, health and medical, history, and self-help. No science fiction. No scripts. Will consider unsolicited mss but prefer proposal and sample chapters. No reading fee. CLIENTS include Freda Bright, Alexander Kane and Kathy Ketcham.
Commission Home 15%; Dramatic 15%; Foreign 20%. *UK associates* **David Grossman Literary Agency.**

Dominick Abel Literary Agency Inc.

Suite 12C, 498 West End Avenue, New York NY 10024
☏ 0101 212 877 0710

Contact *Dominick Abel* (President)

FOUNDED 1975. Non-fiction and novels. No scripts. Prefers to work with established/ published writers. No unsolicited mss. First approach with query letter and International Reply Coupons. No reading fee.
Commission Home 10%; Dramatic 15%; Foreign 20%. *UK associates* **David Grossman Literary Agency.**

Edward J. Acton Inc.

928 Broadway, New York NY 10010
☏ 0101 212 473 1700

Contact *Jane Dystel*

FOUNDED 1975. *Specialises* in politics, celebrities, sports and historical romances. Non-fiction and novels. No reading fee. CLIENTS include Jason Miller, Tip O'Neill, Jennifer Wilde. *Commission* Home 15%; Dramatic 15%; Foreign 19%.

James Allen Literary Agent (in association with **Virginia Kidd Literary Agents**)

Box 278, Milford PA 18337

Contact *James Allen*

FOUNDED 1974. Prefers to work with established/ published authors. *Specialises* in mysteries, occult, horror, science fiction, historical romance, fantasy, young adult novels and mainstream novels. No juveniles or westerns. No unsolicited mss. No reading fee for outlines. CLIENTS include the estates of Elsie Lee and E. E. "Doc" Smith, also Lisa W. Cantrell, Louise Moeri and David Poyer.
Commission Home 10%; Dramatic 20%; Foreign 20%.

Marcia Amsterdam Agency

Suite 9A, 41 West 82nd Street, New York NY 10024
☏ 0101 212 873 4945

Contact *Marcia Amsterdam*

FOUNDED 1969. *Specialises* in mainstream fiction, horror, suspense, humour, young adult, TV and film scripts. No poetry, 8–10 age group, 'how to' books. No unsolicited mss. First approach by letter only and International Reply Coupons. No reading fee for outlines and synopses. CLIENTS include Kristopher Franklin, Christopher Hinz, Ruby Jean Jensen, William Lovejoy, Joyce Sweeney.
Commission Home 15%; Dramatic 10%; Foreign 15%.

Julian Bach Literary Agency Inc.

747 Third Avenue, New York NY 10017
☏ 0101 212 753 2605

Contact *Julian Bach, Ann Rittenberg*

FOUNDED 1959. *Handle* non-fiction and fiction. TITLES *The Prince of Tides* Pat Conroy; *Hong Kong* Jan Morris; *The Store* Michael Pearson; *The*

Power Game Hedrick Smith. Not interested in juvenile, young adult, science fiction, fantasy, futuristic, poetry, or photography. No scripts. Do not welcome unsolicited mss. For non-fiction – prefer initial approach in writing, detailing idea and relative experience/background; for fiction – a brief synopsis (ie. one typed A4!), sample pages, relative experience, publishing history, etc. Send photocopies which preferably do not need returning. CLIENTS Pat Conroy, Nancy Thayer, Norman Cousins, Jan Morris.
Commission Home 15%; Dramatic 15%; Foreign 20%.

The Balkin Agency

850 West 176th Street, New York NY 10033
☎ 0101 212 781 4198

Contact *Richard Balkin*

FOUNDED 1973. *Specialises* in adult non-fiction only. No reading fee for outlines and synopses.
Commission Home 15%; Foreign 20%.

Virginia Barber Literary Agency Inc.

353 West 21st Street, New York NY 10011
☎ 0101 212 255 6515 Fax 0101 212 255 6515

Contact *Virginia Barber, Mary Evans*

FOUNDED 1974. Non-fiction and novels. No reading fee for outlines and synopses.
Commission Home 15%; Dramatic 15%; Foreign 20%.

Lois Berman

The Little Theatre Building, 240 West 44th Street, New York NY 10036
☎ 0101 212 575 5114

Contact *Lois Berman*

FOUNDED 1972. Dramatic writing only (and only by recommendation).

The Blake Group Literary Agency

Suite 600, One Turtle Creek Village, Dallas TX 75219
☎ 0101 214 520 8562

Contact *Lee B. Halff*

FOUNDED 1979. Prefers to work with established/published authors. Magazine fiction, non-fiction books, novels, textbooks, juvenile books, film, radio, TV and stage scripts, poetry. No reading fee.
Commission Home 10%; Dramatic 15%; Foreign 20%.

The Book Peddlers

18326 Minnetonka Boulevard, Deephaven MN 55391
☎ 0101 612 475 3527

Contact *Vicki Lansky*

FOUNDED 1984. Small agency taking on few new clients. Non-fiction and some syndicated material. No scripts and no novels at the moment. Prefer approach by query letter with International Reply Coupons. No reading fee but once a client's material is accepted a charge of $5 per publisher submission is made. If the mss sells this fee is taken out of the advance; if not the client is billed.
Commission Home 15%; Foreign 20%.

Georges Borchardt Inc.

136 East 57th Street, New York NY 10022
☎ 0101 212 753 5785

FOUNDED 1967. Prefers to work with established/published authors. *Specialises* in fiction, biography and general non-fiction of unusual interest. Does not read mss.
Commission Home 10%; Dramatic 10%; Foreign 20%. *Overseas associate* **Richard Scott Simon Ltd**, London.

Brandt & Brandt Literary Agents Inc.

1501 Broadway, New York NY 10036
☎ 0101 212 840 5760

FOUNDED 1914. Non-fiction books and novels. No poetry or children's books. No unsolicited mss. First approach by letter 'describing background and ambitions'. No reading fee.
Commission Home 10%; Dramatic 10%; Foreign 20%. *UK associates* **A. M. Heath & Co. Ltd.**

Pema Browne Ltd

185 East 85th Street, New York NY 10028
☎ 0101 212 369 1925

Contact *Perry J. Browne*

FOUNDED 1966. *Specialises* in men's adventure, thrillers, mainstream historical, regencies and contemporary romances, young adult, children's, reference, 'how to' and other types of non-fiction. No reading fee. Query letter first with s.a.e. Do not review mss sent to publishers or previously handled by another agent. Mss submitted must include return postage and packaging (no cheques or cash please). *Commission* Home 15%; Dramatic 10%; Foreign 10%.

Connie Clausen Associates

Suite 16H, 250 East 87th Street,
New York NY 10128
☎ 0101 212 427 6135

Contact *Connie Clausen, Susan Lipson*

FOUNDED 1976. Prefers to work with established/published authors. *Specialises* in trade non-fiction of all kinds and some fiction. Does not read unsolicited mss. CLIENTS include Quentin Crisp, Robert Haas.
Commission Home 15%; Dramatic 15%; Foreign 20%. *UK associates* **David Grossman Literary Agency.**

Hy Cohen Literary Agency

111 West 57th Street, New York NY 10019
☎ 0101 212 757 5237

Contact *Hy Cohen* (President)

FOUNDED 1975. Novels and non-fiction. No scripts. Welcome unsolicited mss but prefer synopsis and 100 pages. International Reply Coupons essential. No reading fee. CLIENTS include Robert Ferguson, Elaine Long, Tom Lorenz.
Commission Home 10%; Dramatic 10%; Foreign 10%. *UK associates* Albert Stein.

Ruth Cohen Inc.

Box 7626, Menlo Park CA 94025
☎ 0101 415 854 2054

Contact *Ruth Cohen* (President)

FOUNDED 1982. Prefers to work with established/published authors. *Specialises* in high-quality juvenile, young adult and genre books: historical romance, mystery and western. No reading fee for outlines and synopses; International Reply Coupons essential.
Commission Home 15%; Dramatic 15%; Foreign 20%.

Columbia Literary Associates, Inc.

7902 Nottingham Way, Ellicott City MD 21043
☎ 0101 301 465 1595

Contact *Linda Hayes, Kathryn Jensen*

FOUNDED 1980. *Specialises* in mass market, mainstream adult fiction and non-fiction, contemporary romance (category and single title), suspense, intrigue, cookbooks, general popular non-fiction and book series. No reading fee. Return postage required.
Commission Home 12–15%; Dramatic 20%; Foreign 20%.

Connor Literary Agency

640 West 153rd Street, New York NY 10031
☎ 0101 212 491 5233

Contact *Marlene Connor*

FOUNDED 1985. Specialises in commercial fiction and non-fiction, including thrillers, horror, current affairs, self-help, cookbooks, New Age and 'how to'. Special interest in black writers. No reading fee for outlines.
Commission Home 15%; Foreign 25%.

Richard Curtis Associates, Inc.

Suite 1, 164 East 64th Street, New York NY 10021
☎ 0101 212 371 9481

Contact *Richard Curtis* (President), *Elizabeth Waxse* (Vice President), *Roberta Cohen, Rick Henshaw* (Associates)

FOUNDED 1969. Prefers to work with established/published authors. *Specialises* in commercial fiction of all genres, mainstream fiction and non-fiction. CLIENTS include Greg Benford, Matthew Braun, Janet Dailey.
Commission Home 10–15%; Dramatic 15%; Foreign 20%.

Joan Daves

21 West 26th Street, New York NY 10010-1083
☎ 0101 212 685 9573/9577
Fax 0101 212 685 1781

Contact *Joan Daves, Jennifer Lyons*

FOUNDED 1952. Tradebooks: fiction, non-fiction, juveniles. No science fiction, romance, textbooks. No scripts. No unsolicited mss. Query letter in the first instance. 'A detailed synopsis seems valuable only for non-fiction work. Material submitted should specify the author's background, publishing credits, and similar pertinent information.' No reading fee. CLIENTS include Frederick Franck, the estate of Martin Luther King Jr, Nancy Larrick, Elizabeth Marshall Thomas.
Commission Home 10%; Dramatic 10–25%; Foreign 20%.

Educational Design Services Inc.
Box 253, Wantagh NY 11793
☎ 0101 718 539 4107/516 221 0995

Contact *Bertram Linder* (President)

FOUNDED 1979. *Specialises* in educational material and textbooks. Materials for sale to school markets.
Commission Home 15%; Foreign 25%.

Peter Elek Associates
Box 223, Canal Sreet, Station,
New York NY 10013
☎ 0101 212 431 9368 Fax 0101 212 966 5768

Contact *Liza Lagunoff*

FOUNDED 1979. Prefers to work with established/published authors. *Specialises* in illustrated non-fiction, current affairs, self-help, contemporary biography/autobiography, food, popular culture (all for adults); pre-school and juvenile illustrated fiction, non-fiction; contemporary adventure for adults. No reading fee for outlines. CLIENTS include Nara Atlas, Marc Bloom, Patrick Brogan, Leah Komaiko.
Commission Home 15%; Dramatic 20%; Foreign 20%. *UK Representative* Carolyn Brunton, Vardey/Brunton Associates, London.

Ann Elmo Agency Inc.
60 East 42nd Street, New York NY 10165
☎ 0101 212 661 2880/1/2/3

Contact *Lettie Lee, Mari Cronin, Ann Elmo*

FOUNDED 1940s. Literary and romantic fiction, mysteries, and mainstream; non-fiction in all subjects including biography and self-help. Juvenile (8–12-year-olds) and young adult. Query letter with outline of project in the first instance. No reading fee.
Commission Home 15–20%. *UK associates* **John Johnson Ltd.**

John Farquharson Ltd
Suite 1007, 250 West 57th Street,
New York NY 10107
☎ 0101 212 245 1993

Contact *Deborah Schneider*

FOUNDED 1919 (London), 1980 (New York). Prefers to work with established/published authors. *Specialises* in trade fiction and non-fiction, mysteries. No poetry, short stories or screenplays. No reading fee for outlines. CLIENTS include Carolyn Chute, Wade Davis, Oliver Sacks, Madison Smartt Bell.
Commission Home 10%; Dramatic 10%; Foreign 20%. *Overseas associates* **John Farquharson (Curtis Brown Group Ltd).**

Florence Feiler Literary Agency
1524 Sunset Plaza Drive, Los Angeles CA 90069
☎ 0101 213 652 6920/659 0945

Contact *Florence Feiler*

FOUNDED 1967. *Specialises* in fiction, non-fiction, 'how to', text books, translations, TV and film scripts, tapes. No short stories or pornography. No unsolicited mss. First approach by letter. No reading fee. CLIENTS include literary estates of Isak Dinesen (*Out of Africa* and *Babette's Feast*) and Bess Streeter Aldrich.
Commission Home 10%; Foreign 20%.

Frieda Fishbein Ltd
2556 Hubbard Street, Brooklyn NY 11235
☎ 0101 212 247 4398

Contact *Janice Fishbein* (President)

FOUNDED 1925. Eager to work with new/unpublished writers. *Specialises* in historical romance, historical adventure, male adventure, mysteries, thrillers and family sagas. Also, 'non-reporting' 'how to' ... and non-fiction. Books on the environment, nursing and medicine, plays & screenplays. No poetry, magazine articles or short stories. First approach with query letter. No reading fee for outlines. Reading fees of $60 for first 50,000 words, $1 per 1,000 thereafter. $75 for TV script, screenplay or play. CLIENTS include Thomas Harris, Jeanne Mackin, Thomas Millstead, Alicen White.
Commission Home 10%; Dramatic 10%; Foreign 20%.

Robert A. Freedman Dramatic Agency Inc.
Suite 2310, 1501 Broadway, New York NY 10036
☎ 0101 212 840 5760

Contact *Robert A. Freedman* (President)

FOUNDED 1928 (as Brandt & Brandt Dramatic Department Inc.), under present name since 1984. Prefers to work with established/published authors. *Specialises* in plays and film and TV scripts. Does not read unsolicited mss.
Commission Dramatic 10%.

Samuel French Inc.

45 West 25th Street, New York NY 10010
☎ 0101 212 206 8990

Contact *Lawrence Harbison*

FOUNDED 1830. *Specialises* in plays. No reading fee. International Reply Coupon required. Published playwrights include Neil Simon, Don Nigro, Tina Howe, August Wilson, Jack Sharkey.
Commission 90% book royalties; 10% professional production royalties; 20% amateur production royalties.

Jay Garon-Brooke Associates Inc.

415 Central Park West, 17th Floor,
New York NY 10025
☎ 0101 212 866 3654

Contact *Jay Garon* (President), *Jean Free* (Vice President)

FOUNDED 1951. Fiction and non-fiction, historical & romantic historicals, suspense thrillers, political intrigue, horror & occult, self-help. No category romance, westerns or mysteries. Occasionally handles top-quality scripts. No unsolicited mss. First approach by query letter. No reading fee. CLIENTS include Virginia Coffman, Elizabeth Gage, James Leo Herlihy, Burt Hirschfeld, Patricia Matthews, Jeffrey Sacket, Daoma Winston.
Commission Home 15%; Dramatic 10 – 15%; Foreign 30%. *UK associates* **Abner Stein.**

Max Gartenberg, Literary Agent

15 West 44th Street, New York NY 10036
☎ 0101 212 860 8451

Contact *Max Gartenberg*

FOUNDED 1954. Prefers to work with established/published authors. *Specialises* in non-fiction and fiction trade books. No reading fee for outlines. CLIENTS include William Ashworth, Edwin P. Hoyt, Robert Minton, David Roberts.
Commission Home 10%; Dramatic 10%; Foreign 15%.

Goodman Associates Literary Agents

500 West End Avenue, New York NY 10024

Contact *Arnold* or *Elise Goodman*

FOUNDED 1976. *Specialises* in general adult trade fiction and non-fiction. No fantasy, science fiction, stories, articles or computer books. No reading fee for outlines.
Commission Home 15%; Dramatic 15%; Foreign 20%.

Irene Goodman Literary Agency

521 Fifth Avenue, 17th Floor,
New York NY 10017
☎ 0101 212 688 4286

Contact *Irene Goodman*

FOUNDED 1978. *Specialises* in women's fiction (mass market, category and historical romance), popular non-fiction, reference and westerns. No reading fee for initial query/approach. CLIENTS include Barbara Boswell, John Cooney, Linda Lael Miller.
Commission Home 15%; Dramatic 15%; Foreign 20%.

Sanford J. Greenburger Associates

55 Fifth Avenue, New York NY 10003
☎ 0101 212 206 5600

Contact *Heide Lange, David Black, Diane Cleaver, Nick Ellison, Faith Hamlin, Beth Vesel*

Fiction and non-fiction. No scripts. No unsolicited mss. First approach with query letter and synopsis. No reading fee.

Harold R. Greene Inc.

8455 Beverly Boulevard, Suite 309,
Los Angeles CA 90048
☎ 0101 213 852 4959

Contact *Harold Greene*

FOUNDED 1985. Novels adaptable to films or TV films and film scripts. No unsolicited mss. Best approach 'through a mutual acquaintance'. No reading fee. CLIENTS include George La Fountaine, Richard Henrick, Crawford Kilian.
Commission Home 10%; Dramatic 10%; Foreign 10%.

John Hawkins & Associates Inc.

71 West 23rd Street, Suite 1600,
New York NY 10010
☎ 0101 212 807 7040 Fax 0101 212 807 9555

Contact *John H. Hawkins, William Reiss, Sharon Friedman*

FOUNDED 1893. General trade fiction and non-fiction. No scripts. Prefer query letter in the first instance; submit one-page biography, one to three-page outline and up to 50 sample pages. No reading fee.

Commission Home 10%; Dramatic 10%; Foreign 20%. *UK associate* **Murray Pollinger.**

Heacock Literary Agency Inc.

1523 Sixth Street, Suite 14,
Santa Monica CA 90401
☎ 0101 213 393 6227/213 451 8523/4

Contact *James B. Heacock* (President), *Rosalie G. Heacock* (Vice President)

FOUNDED 1978. Works with a small number of new/unpublished authors. *Specialises* in non-fiction on a wide variety of subjects – diet, health, nutrition, exercise, beauty, women's studies, popular psychology, crafts, business expertise, pregnancy, parenting, alternative health concepts. Celebrity biographies. Novels (by authors who have been previously published by major houses). Film/TV scripts (only for full-time professionals and members of the Writer's Guild). Do not consider unsolicited mss. Queries with International Reply Coupons only. No reading fee. CLIENTS include Dr Joseph Bark, Dr Arnold Fox & Barry Fox, Don & Audrey Wood.
Commission Home 15% on first $50,000 each year & 10% thereafter; Foreign 15% if sold direct, 25% if agent used.

Frederick Hill Associates

2237 Union Street, San Francisco CA 94123
☎ 0101 415 921 2910

Contact *Fred Hill, Bonnie Nadell*

FOUNDED 1979. General fiction and non-fiction. No scripts. First approach with query letter detailing past publishing history, if any. International Reply Coupons required. CLIENTS include Eric Hansen, Katherine Neville, Randy Shilts.
Commission Home 15%; Dramatic 15%; Foreign 20%. *UK associates* Dasha Shenkman Associates.

Hintz & Fitzgerald Inc.

Suite 211, 207 East Buffalo Street,
Milwaukee WI 53202
☎ 0101 414 273 0300

Contact *Sandy Hintz*

FOUNDED 1978. *Specialises* in most adult fiction – mysteries, westerns, science fiction, fantasy, 'how to's, biographies, general non-fiction. No reading fee for outlines. Query first. CLIENTS include Sharyn McCrumb, Nick O'Donohoe.
Commission Home 15%.

International Publisher Associates Inc.

746 West Shore, Sparta NJ 07871
☎ 0101 201 729 9321

Contact *Joe DeRogatis* (Executive Vice President)

FOUNDED 1982. Eager to work with new/unpublished writers. *Specialises* in all types of non-fiction. No reading fee for outlines but include s.a.e.
Commission Home 15%; Foreign 20%.

Sharon Jarvis and Co. Inc.

260 Willard Avenue, Staten Island NY 10314
☎ 0101 718 273 1066

Contact *Sharon Jarvis* (President)

FOUNDED 1985. (Previously known as Jarvis, Braff Ltd). Prefers to work with established/published authors. Does not read unsolicited mss. CLIENTS include Eric Helm, Roger Jewett, Melanie Rawn, Kevin Randle.
Commission Home 15%; Foreign 25%.

JET Literary Associates Inc.

124 East 84th Street, New York NY 10028
☎ 0101 212 879 2578

Contact *J. Trupin* (President)

FOUNDED 1976. Prefers to work with established/published authors. *Specialises* in non-fiction. Will handle novels. Does not read unsolicited mss. CLIENTS include Robert Campbell, David Feldman, Charles Willeford.
Commission Home 15%; Dramatic 15%; Foreign 25%.

Alex Kamaroff Associates

200 Park Avenue, Suite 303 East,
New York NY 10166
☎ 0101 212 557 5557

Contact *Alex Kamaroff, Paul Katz*

FOUNDED 1985. Men's fiction, science fiction, thriller, mystery, category & historical romance, *Star Trek*. No poetry, short stories, 'how to'. No scripts. Will consider unsolicited mss but prefer first three chapters and outline with International Reply Coupons. No reading fee for sample chapters. CLIENTS include Irene Kress, Diana Morgan, Louis Rukeyser.

Commission Home 10%; Dramatic 10%; Foreign 20%.

Kidde, Hoyt and Picard Literary Agency

333 East 51st Street, New York NY 10022
☎ 0101 212 755 9461

Contact *Katherine Kidde* (Chief Associate), *Amy Edminster* (Associate)

FOUNDED 1981. *Specialises* in mainstream and literary fiction, romantic fiction (historical and contemporary), mainstream non-fiction. No reading fee. Query first. CLIENTS include R.M. Humphreys, Helene Lehr, Frank Sherry.
Commission Home 10%; Dramatic 10%; Foreign 10%.

Daniel P. King

5125 North Cumberland Boulevard,
Whitefish Bay WI 53217
☎ 0101 414 964 2903
Telex 724389 Fax 0101 414 964 6860

Contact *Daniel P. King* (President)

FOUNDED 1974. Mainstream fiction, crime and mystery, science fiction. *Specialises* in mystery and non-fiction books on crime and espionage. Scripts handled by representative office in Beverly Hills, California. No unsolicited mss. Send synopsis or sample chapter first but would prefer to see a concise letter (1–2 pages) describing the book. No reading fee unless an author wants a critique on his material. CLIENTS include John Bonnet, John Dunning, Cyril Joyce.
Commission Home 10%; Dramatic 10%; Foreign 20%.

Harvey Klinger Inc.

301 West 53rd Street, New York NY 10019
☎ 0101 212 581 7068

Contact *Harvey Klinger* (President)

FOUNDED 1977. *Specialises* in mainstream fiction (not category romance or mysteries, etc.), non-fiction in the medical, social sciences, autobiography/biography areas. No reading fee for outlines. CLIENTS include C. Terry Cline Jr., Jane Powell, Barbara Wood.
Commission Home 15%; Dramatic 15%; Foreign 25%.

Paul Kohner Inc.

9169 Sunset Blvd, Los Angeles CA 90069
☎ 0101 213 550 1060

Contact *Gary Salt*

FOUNDED 1938. *Handle* a broad range of books for subsidiary rights sales to film and TV. Do not usually handle novel mss directly for placement with publishers as film and TV scripts are the major portion of the business. *Specialise* in true crime, biography and history. Generally prefer non-fiction to fiction in the TV markets but will handle 'whatever we feel has strong potential'. No short stories, poetry, science fiction, gothics. Unsolicited material will always be returned unread. Approach via a third-party reference or query letter with professional resumé. No reading fee. CLIENTS include Evan Hunter, Tony Huston, John Katzenbach, Charles Marowitz, Alan Sharp, Donald Westlake.
Commission Home 10%; Publishing 15%; Dramatic 10%. *UK associates* John Redway & Associates.

Barbara S. Kouts, Literary Agent

788 Ninth Avenue, New York NY 10019
☎ 0101 212 265 6003

FOUNDED 1980. Fiction, non-fiction, children's books. No romances, science fiction, scripts. No unsolicited mss. Query letter in the first instance. No reading fee. CLIENTS include Hal Gieseking, Nancy Mairs, Robert San Souci.
Commission Home 10%; Foreign 20%. *UK associates* **Murray Pollinger.**

The Lantz Office

888 Seventh Avenue, New York NY 10106
☎ 0101 212 586 0200

Contact *Robert Lantz, Joy Harris*

Handles adult non-fiction and fiction. No science fiction. No unsolicited mss. Query letter in the first instance. No reading fee. Film/TV scripts handled by the Los Angeles office at 9255 Sunset Boulevard, Suite 505, Los Angeles, CA 90069.
Commission Home 10%; Dramatic 10%; Foreign 20%. *UK associates* **Abner Stein, London Management.**

Michael Larsen/Elizabeth Pomada Literary Agents

1029 Jones Street, San Francisco CA 94109
☎ 0101 415 673 0939

Contact *Mike Larsen, Elizabeth Pomada*

FOUNDED 1972. Eager to work with new/unpublished writers. Literary fiction, commercial fiction, popular psychology, finance. No scripts. No children's, poetry, westerns. No unsolicited mss. Send first 30 pages and synopsis with International Reply Coupons. No reading fee. CLIENTS include Ruth Coe Chambers, Jay Conrad, Marty Klein, Yvonne Lenard, June Lune Shiplett.
Commission Home 15%; Dramatic 15%; Foreign 20%.

The Lee Allan Agency

P.O. Box 18617, Milwaukee WI 53218
☏ 0101 414 357 7708

Contact *Andrea Knickerbocker, Lee Matthias*

FOUNDED 1983. *Specialises* in mystery, techno-thrillers, war, suspense/thriller, horror, western, science fiction, and fantasy. Commercial fiction, including young adult and mainstream. Some non-fiction, including self-help, cookbooks, humour, true crime, and occult. *Handle* feature film screenplays properly formatted to the Writer's Guild of America guidelines; no TV/stage plays/radio or joke routines. No autobiographies (except for celebrities), scholarly works, articles, short pieces, technical, and 'how to' books. No unsolicited mss. Approach by letter, with International Reply Coupons, giving length/word count. Novels – min. 50,000 words; scripts – min. 90 pages, max. 140 pages. No reading fee. CLIENTS include John Deakins, Franklin Allen Leib, David North, Gary Raisor and John Randall.
Commission Home 10%; Dramatic 10%; Foreign 20%.

Adele Leone Agency Inc.

26 Nantucket Place, Scarsdale NY 10583
☏ 0101 914 961 2965

Contact *Adele Leone, Ralph Leone, Richard James Monaco, Shawna McCarthy*

FOUNDED 1979. Prefers to work with established/published authors. *Specialises* in historical, gothic, regency and contemporary romance, science fiction and fantasy, westerns, horror, men's adventure, thrillers, mystery, biography and general women's and mainstream fiction. Non-fiction: health, nutrition, science, New Age. No scripts. No books on photography, travel. No young adult and children's books; no poetry. Welcome unsolicited mss. Send three chapters and outline in the first instance. International Reply Coupons required. No reading fee. CLIENTS include Simon Hawke, David Pear, Skipp & Spector, Janelle Taylor.
Commission Home 15%; Dramatic 15%; Foreign 10%. *UK associates* **MBA Agency.**

Ellen Levine, Literary Agency Inc.

Suite 1205, 432 Park Avenue South,
New York NY 10016
☏ 0101 212 899 0620

Contact *Diana Finch*

FOUNDED 1980. *Handles* all types of books. No scripts. No unsolicited mss. First approach by letter and proposal, synopsis or sample chapter. Send International Reply Coupons for reply and return of material submitted. No telephone calls. No reading fee.
Commission Home 10%; Dramatic 10%; Foreign 20%. *UK associates* **A.P. Watt.**

Wendy Lipkind Agency

Suite 3E, 165 East 66th Street,
New York NY 10021
☏ 0101 212 628 9653

Contact *Wendy Lipkind* (President)

FOUNDED 1977. *Specialises* in non-fiction (social history, adventure, biography, science, sports, history) and fiction. No reading fee for outlines.
Commission Home 10–15%; Dramatic 10–15%; Foreign 20%.

Lowenstein Associates Inc.

Suite 601, 121 West 25th Street,
New York NY 10001
☏ 0101 212 206 1630

Contact *Barbara Lowenstein* (President)

FOUNDED 1976. *Specialises* in non-fiction (especially science, medical for the general public), and pop psychology, women's and general fiction. No reading fee for outlines. Must query first.
Commission Home 15%; Dramatic 15%; Foreign 20%.

McIntosh & Otis Inc.

310 Madison Avenue, New York NY 10017
☏ 0101 212 687 7400

Contact *Julie Fallowfield* (Adult books), *Dorothy Markinko* (Juvenile)

FOUNDED 1928. Adult and juvenile general trade books, fiction and non-fiction. No cookbooks and textbooks. No scripts. No unsolicited mss. Approach first with a letter indicating nature of the work the writer wishes to submit plus details

of writer's background. No reading fee. CLIENTS include Mary Higgins Clark, Shirley Hazzard, Victoria Holt, Harper Lee.
Commission Home 15%; Dramatic 15%; Foreign 20%. *UK associates* **A.M. Heath & Co. Ltd, Jane Conway-Gordon.**

Denise Marcil Literary Agency Inc.

316 West 82nd Street, 5F, New York NY 10024
☎ 0101 212 580 1071

Contact *Denise Marcil* (President)

FOUNDED 1977. *Specialises* in non-fiction (money, business, health, childcare, parenting, self-help and 'how to's) and commercial fiction, especially women's fiction, mysteries, psychological suspense and horror. Query letters only, with s.a.e. CLIENTS include Elaine Raco Chase, Fayrene Preston, Madge Swindells.
Commission Home 15%; Dramatic 15%; Foreign 20%.

Betty Marks

Suite 9F, 176 East 77th Street,
New York NY 10021
☎ 0101 212 535 8388

Contact *Betty Marks*

FOUNDED 1969. Prefers to work with established/published authors. *Specialises* in journalists' non-fiction. Novels. No reading fee for outlines.
Commission Home 15%; Foreign 20%.

Claudia Menza Literary Agency

237 West 11th Street, New York NY 10014
☎ 0101 212 889 6850

Contact *Claudia Menza* (President)

FOUNDED 1983. *Specialises* in unique fiction and non-fiction dealing with serious subjects (i.e. political and medical issues). No reading fee. No unsolicited mss; queries and synopses only.
Commission Home 15%; Dramatic 15%; Foreign 20%.

The Peter Miller Agency Inc.

Office: 220 West 19th Street, Suite 501,
New York NY 10011
Package address: PO Box 760, Old Chelsea Station, New York NY 10011
☎ 0101 212 929 1222 Fax 0101 212 206 0238

Contact *Peter Miller* (President), *Jonathan Blank* (Director of Development), *Harrilyn Mills* (Associate), *Dan Broch* (Associate)

FOUNDED 1976. Commercial fiction and non-fiction. *Specialises* in true crime and Hollywood biographies. All books with film and television potential. No poetry, pornography, non-commercial academic. No unsolicited mss. Approach by letter with one-page synopsis. Reading fee for unpublished authors. Fee recoupable out of first monies earned. CLIENTS include Vincent T. Bugliosi, Christopher Cook Gilmore, Brigette Roux-Lough, Clifford Schorer, Ted Sennett, Lindsay Wagner.
Commission Home 15%; Dramatic 10–15%; Foreign 20–25%.

Robert P. Mills

c/o Richard Curtis Associates, 164 East 64th Street, New York NY 10021
☎ 0101 212 371 9481

Contact *Richard Curtis*

Multimedia Product Development Inc.

410 South Michigan Avenue, Suite 724,
Chicago IL 60605
☎ 0101 312 922 3063 Fax 0101 312 922 1905

Contact *Jane Jordan Browne*

FOUNDED 1971. Biography, history, current affairs, mainstream novels, genre novels, science, psychology, social science, 'how to'. No autobiography (except celebrities), no poetry. No scripts. No unsolicited mss. Query letter with International Reply Coupons only. No reading fee. CLIENTS include James Kahn, Helen Hooven Santmyer, Donald A. Stanwood, Jean Westin, J. Patrick Wright.
Commission Home 15%; Dramatic 15%; Foreign 15–20%. *UK associates* **A.M. Heath & Co. Ltd.**

B.K. Nelson Literary Agency

Suite 1308A, 303 Fifth Avenue,
New York NY 10016
☎ 0101 212 889 0637/889 8567

Contact *Bonita K. Nelson* (President)

FOUNDED 1978. *Specialises* in business books. Handles New Age, 'how to', computer state of the art and computer science; software/game programmes – high tech and college level. Some historical romance/contemporary novels. No unsolicited mss. First approach with letter. Reading fee. CLIENTS include Msgr Eugene Kevane, Louis Nevaer, Thomas Phelan, Charles Romine.

Commission Home 15%; Dramatic 15%; Foreign 20%.

New England Publishing Associates Inc.

Box 5, Chester CT 06412
☎ 0101 718 788 6641/203 345 4976

Contact *Elizabeth Frost Knappman* (President)

FOUNDED 1983. Mainly non-fiction with some fiction. *Specialises* in current affairs, history, science, women's studies, psychology, biography, true crime. No text books, children's, collections/anthologies. No scripts. Will consider unsolicited mss but prefer query letter or phone call. No reading fee. CLIENTS include William Packard, Tom Renner, Carl Rollyson.
Commission Home 15%. *UK associates* Scott-Ferris Agency. *Representation* throughout Europe and Japan.

The Betsy Nolan Literary Agency

50 West 29th Street, Suite 9 West,
New York NY 10001
☎ 0101 212 799 0700

Contact *Betsy Nolan* (President), *Carla Glasser, Donald Lehr*

FOUNDED 1980. Non-fiction books and novels. No reading fee for outlines.
Commission Home 15%; Foreign 20%.

The Otte Company

9 Goden Street, Belmont MA 02178
☎ 0101 617 484 8505

Contact *Jane H. Otte*

FOUNDED 1973. *Specialises* in adult trade books. Non-fiction books and novels. No scripts. No unsolicited mss. Approach by letter. No reading fee for outlines. CLIENTS include Nathan Aldyne, Philip Craig, Cameron Foote, Michael McDowell, Robert Shaw.
Commission Home 15%; Dramatic 7 ½%; Foreign 20%. *UK associates* **Aitken & Stone Ltd.**

The Ray Peekner Literary Agency Inc.

Box 3308, Bethlehem PA 18017
☎ 0101 215 974 9158

Contact *Barbara Puechner*

FOUNDED 1973. Prefers to work with established/published authors. *Specialises* in mysteries, westerns, mainstream suspense, fantasy. No romance, no scripts, no unsolicited mss. Send a query letter, but most new clients are referred by existing clients. No reading fee. CLIENTS include Bill Crider, Loren D. Estleman, Tracy Hickman, Rob Kantner, Thomas Sullivan, Margaret Weis and G. Clifton Wisler.
Commission Home 10%; Dramatic 10%; Foreign 20%. *UK associates* **Laurence Pollinger Limited.**

Aaron M. Priest Literary Agency

Suite 3902, 122 East 42nd Street,
New York NY 10168
☎ 0101 212 818 0344

Contact *Aaron Priest, Molly Freidrich*

Non-fiction books and novels. No reading fee for outlines. International Reply Coupon required. CLIENTS include Erma Bombeck, Philip Caputo, Elizabeth Forsythe Hailey.
Commission Home 15%.

Susan Ann Protter Literary Agent

Suite 1408, 110 West 40th Street,
New York NY 10018
☎ 0101 212 840 0480

Contact *Susan Protter*

FOUNDED 1971. Fiction, fantasy, mysteries, thrillers, science fiction. Non-fiction: history, auto/biography, science, health. No romantic fiction, poetry, religious, children's, sports manuals. No scripts. First approach with letter and International Reply Coupons. No reading fee. CLIENTS include Terry Bisson, James Colbert, David Hartwell, Robert Edwin Herzstein, Rudy Rucker, Samuel Shem and Michael Weaver.
Commission Home 15%; Dramatic 15%; Foreign 25%. *UK associates* **Abner Stein.**

Raines & Raines

71 Park Avenue, New York NY 10016
☎ 0101 212 684 5160

Contact *Theron Raines, Joan Raines*

FOUNDED 1961. No unsolicited mss.
Commission Home 15%; Foreign 20%.

Helen Rees Literary Agency

308 Commonwealth Avenue, Boston MA 02116
☎ 0101 617 262 2401

Contact *Catherine Mahar*

FOUNDED 1982. *Specialises* in books on health and business. Biography, autobiography, his-

tory. No scholarly, academic, technical books. No scripts. No unsolicited mss. Prefer query letter with International Reply Coupons. No reading fee. CLIENTS include Joan Borysenko, Donna Carpenter, Senator Barry Goldwater, Sandra Mackey.
Commission Home 15%; Foreign 20%.

Rosenstone/Wender

3 East 48th Street, 4th Floor, New York NY 10017
☎ 0101 212 832 8330

Contact *Phyllis Wender, Susan Perlman*

FOUNDED 1981. Fiction, non-fiction, children's and young adult books. Scripts for film, TV and theatre, but not radio. Do not welcome unsolicited mss. Prefer letter outlining the project, the writer's credits, etc. No reading fee. CLIENTS include Mary Kay Blakely, Julia Frey, Simon Gray, David Kendall, Jeffrey Lawe, Loring Mandell, Hugh Whitemore.
Commission Home 10%; Dramatic 10%; Foreign 20%. *UK associates* **A.P. Watt Ltd.**

Jack Scagnetti Literary Agency

Suite 210, 5330 Lankershim Blvd, North Hollywood CA 91601
☎ 0101 818 762 3871

Contact *Jack Scagnetti*

FOUNDED 1974. Prefers to work with established/ published authors. Non-fiction books, novels, film and TV scripts. No reading fee for outlines.
Commission Home 10%; Dramatic 10%; Foreign 15%.

Schaffner Agency Inc.

264 Fifth Avenue, New York NY 10001
☎ 0101 212 689 6888

Contact *Timothy Schaffner, Patrick Delahunt*

FOUNDED 1948. *Specialises* in literary fiction, science fiction, fantasy, biographies, travel, and general non-fiction. Query letter in first instance. No reading fee for outlines. International Reply Coupon required. CLIENTS include Maxine Hong Kingston, Lucius Shepard.
Commission Home 15%; Dramatic 15%; Foreign 20%. *UK associates* **A.M. Heath & Co. Ltd.**

The Susan Schulman Literary Agency Inc.

454 West 44th Street, New York NY 10036
☎ 0101 212 713 1633

Contact *Susan Schulman* (President)

FOUNDED 1978. Prefers to work with established/ published authors. Because of the success of *Women Who Love Too Much, Wife in Law* and *Overparenting*, leans towards titles in the field of psychology and sociology, trends, family issues and women's issues. CLIENTS include Jim Arnosky, Robin Norwood, David Saperstein.
Commission Home 10%; Dramatic 10%, (foreign) 20%; Foreign 20%. *UK associates* **Serafina Clarke.**

Shapiro-Lichtman Talent Agency

8827 Beverly Blvd, Los Angeles CA 90048
☎ 0101 213 859 8877

FOUNDED 1969. Prefers to work with established/ published authors. Film and TV scripts. Does not read unsolicited mss.
Commission Home 10%; Dramatic 10%; Foreign 20%.

Bobbe Siegel, Literary Agency

41 West 83rd Street, New York NY 10024
☎ 0101 212 877 4985

Contact *Bobbe Siegel*

FOUNDED 1975. Prefers to work with established/ published authors. *Specialises* in literary fiction, detective, suspense, historical, science fiction, biography, 'how to', women's subjects, fitness, health, beauty, sports, pop psychology. No scripts. No cookbooks, crafts, juveniles. First approach with letter with International Reply Coupons for response. No reading fee. Will only give a critique if the writer is taken on for representation. CLIENTS include Marlin Bree, Nina Herrmann Donnelley, Margaret Mitchell Dukore, Lew Dykes, Primo Levi.
Commission Home 15%; Dramatic 20%; Foreign 20%. (Foreign/Dramatic split 50/50 with sub-agent). *UK associates* **John Pawsey.**

The Evelyn Singer Literary Agency Inc.

P.O. Box 594, White Plains NY 10602
☎ 0101 914 949 1147/212 799 5203

Contact *Evelyn Singer*

FOUNDED 1951. Prefers to work with established/ published authors. Fiction and non-fiction; adult and juvenile. Adult: health, medicine, 'how to', diet, biography, celebrity, conservation, political; serious novels, suspense, mystery. Juvenile: educational non-fiction for all ages; fiction for the middle and teen levels. No picture books unless the author is or has an experienced book

illustrator. No formula romance, poetry, sex books, occult, textbooks, or specialised material unsuitable for trade market. No scripts. No unsolicited mss. First approach with letter giving writing background, credits, publications, including date of publication and publisher. S.a.e or International Reply Coupons essential. No phone calls. No reading fee. CLIENTS include William Beechcroft, Mary Elting, Franklin Folsom, Michael Folsom, William F. Hallstead.
Commission Home 15%; Dramatic 20%; Foreign 25%. *UK associates* **Laurence Pollinger Limited.**

Singer Media Corporation

3164 Tyler Avenue, Anaheim CA 92801
☎ 0101 714 527 5650

Contact *Donna Hollingshead*

FOUNDED 1944. Contemporary romances, non-fiction, biographies. *Specialises* in psychological self-help. No scripts or personal adventure novels. No unsolicited mss. Letter first. Reading fee for unpublished authors of US$200.00 for a complete critique and suggestions. Fee deducted from advance if publisher found. Worldwide newspaper syndicate. CLIENTS include Dr Frank S. Caprio, Dr Muriel Oberleder, W.E.D. Ross.
Commission Home 15%; Foreign 20%.

Michael Snell Literary Agency

Bridge and Castle Road, Truro MA 02666
☎ 0101 508 349 3781

Contact *Michael Snell* (President), *Patti Smith* (Fiction Editor)

FOUNDED 1980. Eager to work with new/unpublished writers. *Specialises* in business, computer and science books (from professional/reference to popular trade 'how to'); 'how to' and self-help (on all topics, from diet and exercise to sex, psychology and personal finance); mystery and suspense fiction. Will consider unsolicited mss but prefer outline and sample chapter with International Reply Coupons. No reading fee for outlines.
Commission Home 15%; Dramatic 15%; Foreign 15%.

Elyse Sommer Inc.

110-34 73rd Road, P.O. Box 1133,
Forest Hills NY 11375
☎ 0101 718 263 2668

Contact *Elyse Sommer*

FOUNDED 1950. Prefers to work with established/published authors; also well-credentialled people on non-fiction reference books. Specialise non-fiction books, some novels – mysteries and page turners. Good novels for juveniles. No reading fee but s.a.e. must accompany letters and/or manuscripts (no coupons, please). Some book packaging.
Commission Home 15%; Dramatic 20%; Foreign 20%.

Philip G. Spitzer Literary Agency

788 Ninth Avenue, New York NY 10019
☎ 0101 212 265 6003

Contact *Philip Spitzer*

FOUNDED 1969. Prefers to work with established/published authors. *Specialises* in general non-fiction (politics, current events, sports, biography) and fiction, including mystery and suspense. No reading fee for outlines. CLIENTS include Thomas Allen, James Lee Burke, Andre Dubus, Robert Mayer, Norman Polmar, Sam Toperoff.
Commission Home 10%; Dramatic 10%; Foreign 20%. *UK associates* **Murray Pollinger.**

Ellen Lively Steele and Associates

Drawer 447, Organ NM 88052
☎ 0101 505 382 5449 Fax 0101 505 382 9821

FOUNDED 1980. *Specialises* in metaphysical and the occult. Writers must be referred. Novels, film and TV scripts. Does not read unsolicited mss.
Commission Home 10%; Foreign 5%.

Sterling Lord Literistic Inc.

1 Madison Avenue, New York NY 10010
☎ 0101 212 696 2800

Specialises in adult fiction and non-fiction in all genres. No reading fee for outlines.
Commission Home 10%; Dramatic 10%; Foreign 20%.

Gloria Stern Agency (New York)

1230 Park Avenue, New York NY 10128
☎ 0101 212 289 7698

Contact *Gloria Stern*

FOUNDED 1976. 80% non-fiction; 20% serious mainstream fiction. Biography; philosophy/history. *Specialises* in education, women's issues, biographies, serious fiction. No scripts, 'how to' books, poetry, short stories, first fiction of a previously unpublished author. First approach

by letter stating content of book, including one chapter, list of competing books, qualifications as author and International Reply Coupons. No reading fee. CLIENTS include Dian Dincin Buchman, Phillip Hallie, Dr Lester Morrison, Gerald Phillips, Sheila Tobias.
Commission Home 10–15%; Dramatic 10%; Foreign UK 15% shared; Translation 20% shared. *UK associates* **A.M. Heath & Co. Ltd.**

Gloria Stern Agency (Hollywood)

12535 Chandler Blvd, 3 North
Hollywood CA 91607
☎ 0101 818 508 6296

Contact *Gloria Stern*

FOUNDED 1984. Mainstream fiction, fantasy, film scripts. *Specialises* in books on relationships. No books containing gratuitous violence. Approach with a letter and synopsis. Recommendation when applicable. Reading fee charged by the hour.
Commission Home 10–15%; Dramatic 10–15%; Foreign 18%.

H.N. Swanson Inc.

8523 Sunset Blvd, Los Angeles CA 90069
☎ 0101 213 652 5385 Fax 0101 213 652 3690

Contact *B. F. Kamsler*

FOUNDED 1934. Fiction: thrillers, adventure, non-fiction, plays – radio, audio cassettes, television. No scientific, medical, sexploitation. No unsolicited mss. Send a letter with International Reply Coupon in the first instance. No reading fee. CLIENTS include Arthur Hailey, Joseph Hayes, Elmore Leonard.
Commission Home 10%; Dramatic 10%; Foreign 20%. *UK associates* various.

Patricia Teal Literary Agency

2036 Vista Del Rosa, Fullerton CA 92631
☎ 0101 714 738 8333

Contact *Patricia Teal*

FOUNDED 1978. *Specialises* in romance (contemporary and historical). Category fiction: mysteries, men's adventure, horror, occult. Non-fiction: self-help and 'how to' books. No religious/inspirational, autobiography, cookbooks, travel. No scripts. No unsolicited mss. First approach with letter. No reading fee. CLIENTS include D.R. Meredith, Laura Taylor, M. Wills.
Commission Home 10–15%; Dramatic 20%; Foreign 20%. *UK associates* Inpra, **Shelley Power.**

A Total Acting Experience

Suite 100, 14621 Titus, Panorama City CA 91402
☎ 0101 818 901 1044

Contact *Dan A. Bellacicco*

FOUNDED 1984. Will accept new and established writers. *Specialises* in romance, science fiction, mysteries, humour, 'how to' and self-help, juvenile books, film, TV and radio scripts and stage plays. No reading fee. Submit first ten pages only with s.a.e. Fresh original ideas welcomed – but most of all loyalty.
Commission Home 10%; Dramatic 10%; Foreign 10%.

Susan P. Urstadt Inc.

Suite 708, 271 Madison Avenue,
New York NY 10016
☎ 0101 212 808 9810

Contact *Susan P. Urstadt* (President), *Helen F. Pratt* (Associate)

FOUNDED 1975. *Specialises* in literary and commercial fiction, decorative arts and antiques, architecture, gardening, cookery, biography, performing arts, sports, current affairs, lifestyle and current living trends. No unsolicited mss or queries at the moment. CLIENTS include Sven Birkerts, Mick Hales, Allen Lacy, Thomas Powers, Katherine Whiteside.
Commission Home 15%; Dramatic 15%; Foreign 20%.

Ralph M. Vicinanza Ltd

Suite 1205, 432 Park Avenue,
New York NY 10016
☎ 0101 212 725 5133

Contact *Christopher Lotts*

FOUNDED 1978. *Specialises* in history, fantasy and thrillers. No unsolicited mss. CLIENTS include David Brin, John Crowley, Robert Silverberg, Jack Vance.
Commission Home 10%; Foreign 20%.

Carlson Wade

49 Bokee Court, Room K-4, Brooklyn NY 11223
☎ 0101 718 743 6983

Contact *Carlson Wade*

FOUNDED 1949. All types of fiction and non-fiction. No poetry or textbooks. No scripts. Will consider

unsolicited mss but prefer letter of description with International Reply Coupons. Reading fee of $50 for books, $10 for short script.
Commission Home 10%; Dramatic 10%; Foreign 10%.

Austin Wahl Agency Ltd

Suite 342, Monadnock Building, 53 West Jackson Boulevard, Chicago IL 60604
☎ 0101 312 922 3331

FOUNDED 1935. Professional writers only. No reading fee.
Commission Home 15%; Dramatic 10%; Foreign 20%.

Wallace Literary Agency Inc.

177 East 70th Street, New York NY 10021
☎ 0101 212 570 9090

FOUNDED 1988. No unsolicited mss.
Commission Home 10%; Dramatic 10%; Foreign 20%. *UK associates* **A.M. Heath & Co. Ltd,** London.

John A. Ware Literary Agency

392 Central Park West, New York NY 10025
☎ 0101 212 866 4733

Contact *John Ware*

FOUNDED 1978. *Specialises* in biography, investigative journalism, history, health and psychology (academic credentials required). No category fiction (except mysteries and thrillers). Current issues and affairs, sports, oral history, Americana and folklore. Does not read unsolicited mss. No reading fee. CLIENTS include Dr Stephene Ambrose, Jennifer Johnston, Frank Satterthwaite.
Commission Home 10%; Dramatic 10%; Foreign 20%.

Wieser & Wieser Inc.

118 East 25th Street, New York NY 10010
☎ 0101 212 260 0860 Fax 0101 212 505 7186

Contact *Olga B. Wieser, George J. Wieser, Anastasia M. Ashman, Laurence Gershel*

FOUNDED 1976. Prefers to work with established/published authors. *Specialises* in literary and mainstream fiction, serious and popular historical fiction, mass market regencies, general non-fiction: business, finance, aviation, sports, photography, Americana, cookbooks, travel and popular medicine. TV and film scripts. No poetry, children's, science fiction, religious. No unsolicited mss. First approach by letter with International Reply Coupons. No reading fee for outlines. CLIENTS include Dale Brown, Douglas C. Jones, John Nance, Joan Wolf, the editors of Associated Press.
Commission Home 15%; Dramatic 15%; Foreign 20%.

Williams/Wesley/Winant

180 East 79th Street, New York NY 10021
☎ 0101 212 RE-4-0988

Contact *Jean Valentine Winant* (plays), *William A. Winant III* (other submissions)

FOUNDED 1976. *Specialise* in novels, short stories dealing with fantasy, mystery or mythology. Plays for the theatre (any length, any subject). Detective novels (Chandler genre). Welcome unsolicited playscripts, but for other mss a letter in the first instance is required. No reading fee.
Commission Home 10%; Dramatic 10%; Foreign 15%.

Ruth Wreschner, Authors' Representative

10 West 74th Street, New York NY 10023
☎ 0101 212 877 2605

Contact *Ruth Wreschner*

FOUNDED 1981. Prefers to work with established/published authors, but 'will consider very good first novels, both mainstream and genre, particularly British mystery writers'. *Specialises* in popular medicine, health, 'how to' books and fiction. No screenplays or dramatic plays. First approach with query letter and International Reply Coupons. For fiction, a synopsis and first 100 pages; for non-fiction, an outline and two sample chapters. No reading fee. CLIENTS include Cynthia Janus, Samuel Janus, Lucy Freeman, Nathaniel Lehrman, Richard Parrish, David Rudnitsky.

Writers House Inc.

21 West 26th Street, New York NY 10010
☎ 0101 212 685 2400

Contact *Albert Zuckerman* (President), *Amy Berkower* (Executive Vice President), *Merrilee Heifetz* (Vice President), *Susan Cohen* (Vice President), *Megan Howard* (new clients)

FOUNDED 1974. Avant-garde original fiction, thrillers, science fiction, fantasy, contemporary fiction, self-help, children's and young adult books. No poetry, short story collections. No scripts. For consideration of unsolicited mss,

send letter of enquiry, plus synopsis. No reading fee. CLIENTS include Ken Follett, Stephen Hawking.
Commission Home 15%; Dramatic 15%; Foreign 20%. *UK associates* **Blake Friedmann Literary Agency Ltd.**

Writer's Productions

Box 630, Westport CT 06881
☏ 0101 203 227 8199

Contact *David L. Meth*

FOUNDED 1981. Eager to work with new/unpublished writers. Literary, quality fiction & non-fiction. Has a special interest in Asia and Asian Americans, especially Japan and Korea. Interested in important non-fiction on subjects that will have some influence on society. Send a sample of thirty pages, s.a.e. and International Reply Coupons. No reading fee. CLIENTS include Joseph Czarnecki, Ahn Junghyo, Matsumoto Seicho, Jim Truck.
Commission Home 15%; Dramatic 20%; Foreign 20%.

Susan Zeckendorf Associates

Suite 11B, 171 West 57th Street,
New York NY 10019
☏ 0101 212 245 2928

Contact *Susan Zeckendorf* (President)

FOUNDED 1979. Work with new/unpublished writers. *Specialises* in literary fiction; international espionage; mysteries; non-fiction: illustrated, and science. No category romance, science fiction, scripts. No unsolicited mss. Send query letter describing mss. No reading fee. CLIENTS include Doris Jean Austin, Robert Fowler, Diane Lynch Fraser, Una-Mary Parker, Jerry Patterson.
Commission Home 15%; Dramatic 15%; Foreign 20%. *UK associates* **Abner Stein.**

American Press and Journals

The Associated Press
12 Norwich Street, London EC4A 1BT
☎ 01–353 1515

Chief of Bureau *Myron L. Belkind*

Baltimore Sun
14 Gough Square, London EC4A 3DE
☎ 01–353 3531

Chief of Bureau *Gilbert Lewthwaite*

Boston Globe
42 Jubilee Place, London SW3 3TQ
☎ 01–351 3692

Contact *Gordon McKibben*

Business Week
34 Dover Street, London W1X 4BR
☎ 01–493 1451

Bureau Manager *Richard Melcher*

The Christian Science Monitor
Eggington House, 25–8 Buckingham Gate,
London SW1E 6LD
☎ 01–630 8666

Contact *Julian Baum*

Forbes Magazine
PO Box 280, 50A Pall Mall, London SW1
☎ 01–839 7251

Contact *John Marcom*

Fortune Magazine
Time & Life Building, New Bond Street,
London W1Y 0AA
☎ 01–499 4080

Contact *Richard Kirkland*

International Herald Tribune
63 Long Acre, London WC2
☎ 01–836 4802

Contact *Warren Getler*

Journal of Commerce
Bailey House, Old Seacoal Lane,
London EC4M 7LR
☎ 01–489 1932

Contact *Janet Porter*

Life Magazine
Time & Life Building, New Bond Street,
London W1Y 0AA
☎ 01–499 4080

Contact *Liz Nickson*

Los Angeles Times
150 Brompton Road, London SW3 1HX
☎ 01–823 7315

Bureau Chief *Dan Fisher*

Miami Herald
19 Clareville Grove, London SW7 5AU
☎ 01–370 5532

Contact *Peter Slevin*

New York City Tribune
35 Broxash Road, London SW11 6AD
☎ 01–223 8503

Contact *Mark Palmer*

The New York Times
London International Press Centre, 76 Shoe Lane,
London EC4A 3JB
☎ 01–353 8181

Contact *Craig Whitney*

Newsweek
25 Upper Brook Street, London W1Y 1DP
☎ 01–629 8361

Contact *Gerald C. Lubenow*

People Magazine
Time & Life Building, New Bond Street,
London W1Y 0AA
☎ 01–499 4080

Contact *Jerene Jones*

Philadelphia Inquirer
14 Rodborough Road, London NW11 8RY
☎ 01–455 2725

Contact *Michael Leary*

Pittsburgh Post-Gazette
7 Vicarage Gate, Flat 11, London W8 4HH
☎ 01–937 7120

Contact *Fernand Auberjonois*

San Francisco Examiner
53 Devonshire Road, London W5
☎ 01–567 9444

Contact *Dan Ehrlich*

Sports Illustrated
Time & Life Building, New Bond Street,
London W1Y 0AA
☎ 01–499 4080

Contact *Lavinia Scott Elliot*

Time Magazine
Time & Life Building, New Bond Street,
London W1Y 0AA
☎ 01–499 4080

Bureau Chief *B. William Mader*

The Toledo Blade
c/o Reuters Ltd, 85 Fleet Street,
London EC4Y 1EE
☎ 01–735 6905

Chief of Bureau *Fernand Auberjonois*

US News and World Report
72 New Bond Street, London W1Y 0RD
☎ 01–493 4643

Contact *Robin Knight*

Wall Street Journal
London International Press Centre, 76 Shoe Lane,
London EC4A 3JB
☎ 01–353 0671

London Bureau Chief *Kathryn Christensen*

Washington Post
25 Upper Brook Street, London W1Y 2AB
☎ 01–629 8958

Contact *Karen De Young*

Washington Times
21 Chalcot Crescent, London NW1 8YE
☎ 01–722 4553

Bureau Chief *James Morrison*

Professional Associations

ABSA (Association for Business Sponsorship of the Arts)

2 Chester Street, London SW1X 7BB
☎ 01–235 9781

A national independent organisation which was established by the business community, concerned with both the concept and practical details of business sponsorship of the arts, and to represent sponsors' interest. Though ABSA has not yet been involved in the commercial sponsorship of a 'purely literary work', other aspects of writing come up, and writers interested in getting involved in some way should send for *Sponsorship Manual* (£5 including p&p).

The Arts Club

40 Dover Street, London W1X 3RB
☎ 01–499 8581

Membership Secretary *Mrs Ridgway*
Subscription assessed individually (Town £300 maximum; Country £145 maximum)

FOUNDED 1863. Some connection with the arts necessary for membership, which is only available by application with two sponsors.

The Association of Authors' Agents

20 John Street, London WC1N 2DR
☎ 01–405 6774

Secretary *Linda Shaughnessy*
Membership £50 p.a.

FOUNDED 1974. Membership voluntary. The AAA maintains a code of practice, provides a forum for discussion, and represents its members in issues affecting the profession.

Association of Independent Producers (AIP)

17 Great Pulteney Street, London W1R 3DG
☎ 01–434 0181 Fax 01–437 0086

Contact *Tracy Rowe*
Subscription £97.75 p.a.

FOUNDED 1976. Membership open (there are many writer members). Benefits include: an information service, a regular magazine, information packs on various aspects of production, and a free copy of the *Independent Production Handbook*. Offers information about production, how to get in touch with producers etc. The general aims of the association are to encourage film and television production and to broaden the base of finance and exhibition.

Association of Little Presses

89A Petherton Road, London N5 2QT
☎ 01–226 2657

Subscription £7.50 p.a.

FOUNDED 1966. Membership offered to individuals who run small presses; associate membership is available to other interested people or groups. Over 80% of all new poetry in Britain is published by little presses and magazines. ALP publishes a magazine, *Poetry and Little Press Information* (PALPI); information booklets such as *Getting Your Poetry Published* (over 34,000 copies sold since 1973) and the annual *Catalogue of Little Press Books in Print*, plus a regular newsletter. A full list of Little Presses (some of which, like **Bloodaxe Books**, are now sufficiently established and successful to be considered in the mainstream of the business) is available from ALP, or from the Oriel Bookshop, price £1.80 inc. p&p (see **Welsh Arts Council**).

Authors' Club

40 Dover Street, London W1X 3RB
☎ 01–373 5244

Subscription £300 p.a. (Town); £56-76 (Country and young members under 35)

FOUNDED 1891 by Sir Walter Besant. For men and women writers and those with literary interests.

Authors' Licensing and Collecting Society

7 Ridgmount Street, London WC1E 7AE
☎ 01–255 2034

President *Lord Willis*
Secretary General *Janet Hurrell*
Subscription £5 plus VAT (Free to members of **The Society of Authors** and the **Writers' Guild**)

A non-profit making society collecting and distributing payment to writers in areas where they are unable to administer the rights themselves, such as reprography, certain lending rights, private and off-air recording and simultaneous cabling. Open to both writers and their heirs.

BAFTA (British Academy of Film and Television Arts)

195 Piccadilly, London W1V 9LG
☎ 01–734 0022 Fax 01–734 1792

Director *A. J. Bryne*
Ordinary Subscription £75 p.a.

FOUNDED 1947. Membership limited to 'those who have contributed creatively to the industry' over a period of minimum 3 years. Facilities for screening, discussions; encourage research and experimentation; lobby parliament, and make annual awards.

BAPLA (British Association of Picture Libraries and Agencies)

13 Woodberry Crescent, London N10 1PJ
☎ 01–883 2531 Fax 01–883 9215

Administrator *Sal Shuel*

An association of nearly 200 picture libraries and agencies who handle between them more than 100 million images, 'black and white, colour, very old, very new, pretty, terrifying, scientific, absurd, aardvarks, and Zulus and practically everything in between'. The *Directory* (obtainable from the above address) is a guide to members and subject index. Offers advice on costs, etc.

BASCA (British Academy of Songwriters, Composers and Authors)

34 Hanway Street, London W1P 9DE
☎ 01–240 2823

Contact *Bernard Brown*
Subscription from £11.50 p.a.

FOUNDED 1947. The Academy offers advice and support for both established and aspiring songwriters. Issues standard contracts between publishers and writers. Benefits of membership include the quarterly magazine, assessment of beginners' work, and solicitor's advice.

Booksellers Association

154 Buckingham Palace Road,
London SW1W 9TZ
☎ 01–730 8214

FOUNDED 1895 to promote and protect the interest of 3400 bookselling businesses, including independent, chain and multiple. Provides a forum for booksellers and represents their interests on a national and international level. Also, administers the **Whitbread Prize** (see **Prizes** section), and publishes the annual *Directory of Book Publishers and Wholesalers* with detailed information on both.

Book Trust (formerly the National Book League)

Book House, 45 East Hill, London SW18 2QZ
☎ 01–870 9055

Chief Executive *Keith McWilliams*
Subscription £25 p.a.

FOUNDED 1925. Benefits to members include the Book Information Service (which also provides a free service to the public) and access to the Children's Book Foundation. The Foundation acts as a source of advice and information on all aspects of children's literature, with a comprehensive collection of every book published in the last 24 months. Book Trust runs Children's Book Week. Other aspects of its work include organising touring exhibitions, the administering of 14 literary prizes, including the **Booker** (see *Awards, Competitions and Prizes*), and the carrying out of surveys which are then published. *Book Trust* publications include books about books, writers, prizes and education; a free list with order form is available from Book House. Also publishes a quarterly magazine called *Booknews* which is free to members.

British Amateur Press Association

78 Tennyson Road, Stratford, London E15 4DR

Subscription £4.50 p.a.

A non-profit making, non-sectarian society founded in 1890 to 'promote the fellowship of writers, artists, editors, printers, publishers and other craftsmen/women. To encourage them to edit, print and publish, as a hobby, magazines, books and other literary works' by letterpress and other processes. Not an outlet for writing, except between other members in their private publications, but a fraternity providing contacts between amateur writers, journalists, artists, etc.

British American Arts Association

49 Wellington Street, London WC2E 7BN
☎ 01–379 7755

Director *Jennifer Williams*

Organisation addressing the problems of trans-atlantic cultural exchange. Offers advice and counselling in all arts disciplines, runs a conference programme, and takes on special projects. Emphasis is on the non-profit sector. BAAA is not a grant-giving organisation.

British Copyright Council

Copyright House, 29–33 Berners Street, London W1P 4AA

Contact *Geoffrey Adams* (Secretary)

Works for the international acceptance of copyright and acts as a lobby/watchdog organisation on legal and professional matters, on behalf of the trade. An umbrella organisation, which does not deal with individual enquiries.

The British Council

10 Spring Gardens, London SW1A 2BN
☎ 01–930 8466
Telex 8952201 BRICON G Fax 01–839 6347

Contact *Press and Information Section* (01–389 4878) or *Literature Department* (01–389 4069)

The British Council promotes Britain abroad. It provides access to British ideas, talents, expertise and experience in education and training, books and periodicals, the English language, the arts, sciences and technology. It is an independent, non-political organisation represented in more than 80 countries, where it runs 138 offices, 116 libraries and 50 English language schools.

British Film Institute

21 Stephen Street, London W1P 1PL
☎ 01–255 1444 Telex 27624 BFI LDNG

Membership £26.50 (includes monthly Film Bulletin)/£15.75;
Associateship £10.25 (plus concessions)

FOUNDED 1933. Committed to the development of the art and appreciation of film and television. Runs the National Film Theatre and the National Film Archive in London, and funds film theatres in the regions, as well as supporting the making of new films, video and television largely through the **Regional Arts Associations**, but also through direct grants.

British Guild of Travel Writers

90 Corringway, London W5 3HA
☎ 01–998 2223

Chairman *Carol Wright*
Honorary Secretary *Gillian Thomas*
Subscription £30 p.a.

The professional association of travel writers, broadcasters, photographers and editors which aims to serve its membership's interest professionally, and also act as a forum for debate and discussion. Meet monthly. The guild is represented on the BTA, and its members (*c.*135) must earn the majority of their income from travel reporting.

British Science Fiction Association

33 Thornville Road, Hartlepool, Cleveland TS26 8EW

Membership Secretary *Jo Raine*
Subscription £10 p.a.

For both writers and readers of science fiction and fantasy. Publishes *Matrix* (news), *Focus* (fiction), *Vector* (criticism), *Paperback Inferno* (paperback and magazine reviews). Also offers creative writing groups, a magazine chain and an information service.

British Screen Finance

37–39 Oxford Street, London W1R 1RE
☎ 01–434 0291
Telex 888694 BRISCR G Fax 01–434 9933

Contact *Adrian Hodges, Simon Relph*

A private company aided by government grant, taking over from the NFFC in 1986. Backed by consortium including Rank, Channel 4 and Cannon. Divided into two functions: National Film Development Fund for script development (contact *Adrian Hodges*), and production investment (contact *Simon Relph*). Develop around 18 projects per year, and have invested in 35 British films in the last three years.

British Theatre Association

The Darwin Infill Building, Regents College,
Inner Circle, Regents Park, London NW1 4NW
☎ 01–935 2571 Fax 01–224 2457

Director *Sally Meades*
Subscription from £15 p.a.

FOUNDED 1919. Though the British Theatre Association is a membership organisation, the Play Library, the most comprehensive in the world, is open to all. Benefits of membership include the reference and lending sections of the library, a unique theatre information service, and training courses. Publishes *Drama* magazine (see entry).

British Theatre Institute
(incorporating Drama and Theatre Education Council)

c/o NCA, Francis House, Francis Street,
London SW1

The British Theatre Institute was founded in 1971. In 1976 it called a conference of educational bodies which led to the formation of DATEC, the *Drama and Theatre Education Council*. The two joined forces in 1982. Because of this merger the BTI places particular emphasis on education and training. It also acts as a resource office and consultant on all aspects of theatre and drama education. Subscriber members include both individuals and organisations.

Campaign for Press and Broadcasting Freedom

9 Poland Street, London W1V 3DG
☎ 01–437 2795

Subscription £7 p.a. (plus concessions)

Broadly based pressure group, working for more accountable and accessible media in Britain. Advises on right of reply and takes up the issue of the portrayal of minorities (incorporating CARM, the *Campaign Against Racism in the Media*). Members receive *Free Press* (bi-monthly), discounts on publications, and news of campaign progress.

Crime Writers' Association

PO Box 172, Tring, Hertfordshire HP23 5LP
☎ 044 282 8496

Secretary *Anthea Fraser*
Membership £20 (Town); £17 (Country)

Full membership is limited to professional crime-writers, but publishers, literary agents, booksellers, etc., who specialise in crime are eligible for Associate membership. Meetings are held monthly in Soho, with informative talks frequently given by police, Scenes of Crime officers, lawyers, etc. A weekend conference is held annually in different parts of the country. Monthly newsheet, *Red Herrings*. Presents annual awards (Gold Daggers) for year's best crime fiction and non-fiction (see Prizes). Also a separate award, the CWA-Cartier Diamond Dagger presented to an author, rather than a book, for outstanding contribution to the genre. Previous winners include Eric Ambler, P. D. James, and John Le Carré.

The Critics' Circle

c/o The Stage & Television Today, 47
Bermondsey Street, London SE1 3XT
☎ 01–403 1818

President *Rodney Milnes*
Honorary General Secretary *Peter Hepple*
Subscription £8 p.a.

Membership by invitation only. Aims to uphold and promote the art of criticism (and the commercial rates of pay thereof) and preserve the interests of its members, who are professionals involved in criticism of film, drama, music and ballet.

Sean Dorman Manuscript Society

Union Place, Fowey, Cornwall PL23 1BY

Subscription £3.50 p.a. (£1.50 after six months trial period)

FOUNDED 1957. The Society trains its members in all branches of writing by cooperative methods, so avoiding the expense of writing schools. Typescripts are circulated in postal criticism folios, read, and returned with a wide range of opinions. There is also a folio magazine, *Ideas & Markets*, where writing problems and outlets are discussed, and another, *Poetry*, solely for the work of poets and discussion thereon.

Educational Television Association

The King's Manor, Exhibition Square,
York YO1 2EP
☎ 0904 433929

An umbrella organisation for individuals and organisations using television for education and training. Annual awards scheme, and annual conferences. School membership now available.

The English Association

The Vicarage, Priory Gardens, Bedford Park, London W4 1TT
☏ 01-995 4236

Secretary *Ruth Fairbanks-Joseph*

FOUNDED 1906 to promote understanding and appreciation of the English language and its literature. Activities include sponsoring a number of publications and organising lectures and conferences for teachers, plus annual sixth-form conferences. Publications include *English, Year's Work in English Studies* and *Essays and Studies*.

Federation of Broadcasting Unions

c/o BETA, 181–5 Wardour Street, London W1V 4LA
☏ 01–439 7585

Chairman *John Morton* (MU)
Secretary *Paddy Leech* (BETA)

Unions affiliated to the FBU are BETA, EETPU, Equity, Musicians Union, **NUJ** and the **Writers' Guild**.

Federation of Film Unions

111 Wardour Street, London W1V 4AY
☏ 01–437 8506

Contact *Alan Sapper* (Secretary)

Represents unions involved in film production, including the **Writers' Guild**.

Film & Video Press Group

c/o IVCA, 102 Great Russell Street, London WC1E 3LN

Contact *Adam Cook*

A professional association for editors, journalists, and freelance writers in the audio-visual media.

The Gaelic Books Council (An Comann Leabhraichean)

Department of Celtic, University of Glasgow, Glasgow G12 8QQ
☏ 041–339 8855 ext. 5190

Chairman *Professor Derick S. Thomson*

Executive and Editorial Officer *Ian MacDonald*

FOUNDED 1968. Encourages and promotes Gaelic publishing by offering publication grants, commissioning authors, organising competitions, advising readers and providing practical help for writers.

Independent Film, Video & Photography Association

79 Wardour Street, London W1V 3PH
☏ 01–439 0460

Subscription £12 p.a.

FOUNDED 1974. Practical help and advice on script development and funding, for its writer members.

Independent Publishers' Guild

147–9 Gloucester Terrace, London W2 6DX
☏ 01–723 7328

Subscription £30/35 p.a.

FOUNDED 1926. Membership open to independent publishers, packagers and suppliers, i.e. professionals in allied fields. 320 members in the year 1988/89. Regular meetings, conferences, seminars, a bulletin, and a small publishers' group.

Independent Theatre Council

Unit 129, West Block, Westminster Business Square, Durham Street, London SE11 5JA
☏ 01–820 1712

Contact *Philip Bernays*

The management association and representative body for small and middle scale theatres (up to around 250 seats) and touring theatre companies. They negotiate contracts and have standard agreements with Equity on behalf of all professionals working in the theatre. Currently they are negotiating with the **Theatre Writers' Union** and **Writers' Guild** for a contractual agreement covering rights and fee structure for playwrights writing for the fringe theatres.

Institute of Journalists

2 Dock Offices, Surrey Quays, Lower Road, London SE16 2XL
☏ 01–252 1187

Joint General Secretaries *Bill Tadd, Christopher Underwood*
Subscription £45–£135 (by assessment)

FOUNDED 1884. An independent trade union and professional association for writers, broadcasters and journalists in all media. Affiliation available to part time or occasional practitioners. Services include an employment register, a freelance division, and legal advice.

IPPA

50–51 Berwick Street, London W1V 4RD
☎ 01–439 7034 Fax 01–494 2700

Director *Paul Styles*
Deputy Director *John Woodward*
Subscription £350 + VAT (Corporate); £100 + VAT (Individual)

The Independent Programme Producers Association (IPPA) is the trade association for British independent broadcast television producers. FOUNDED 1981 by producers making programmes for the newly-established Channel 4. Now represents more than 600 production companies based throughout the UK and Northern Ireland, advising its members on all matters relating to independent production for television. Services include the publication of an international directory and a regular journal, a seminar programme on current business issues, a business advice service, a specialist industrial relations unit, legal documentation and back-up, and a European producers' network.
IPPA led the campaign for 25% of all new British TV programmes to be made by independent producers, building upon IPPA's original submission to Parliament. In the wake of the Government's commitment to the 25% figure, IPPA has negotiated with the BBC and ITV to establish a code of practice and trading guidelines similar to those previously agreed by the Association with Channel 4. IPPA continues to liaise with all UK broadcasters to influence decisions that may affect independent producers and maintains an active lobby to ensure that the needs of the UK independent sector are properly heard and understood by government in Britain and Europe.

The Library Association

7 Ridgmount Street, London WC1E 7AE
☎ 01–636 7543 Fax 01–436 7218

Chief Executive *George Cunningham*

The professional body for libraries and information specialists, with 25,000 members. The library (reference only, except to members) has a good range of books relevant both to library and publishing matters; both it and the bookshop are open to all.

London Screenwriters' Workshop

37 Victoria Road, Watford,
Hertfordshire WD2 5AY
☎ 0923 31342

Contact *Lawrence Gray*

FOUNDED 1983. A means of contact, discussion and practical help for film and television writers. Meetings, monthly seminars, script workshops. Also acts as a pressure group.

National Union of Journalists (NUJ)

Acorn House, 314 Gray's Inn Road,
London WC1X 8DP
☎ 01–278 7916
Telex 892384 Fax 01–837 8143

General Secretary *Harry Conroy*
Subscription £104 p.a. (freelance)

Trade union. Responsible for wages and conditions agreements which apply throughout the industry. Advice and representation for its members, as well as administering disputes, unemployment and other benefits. Publishes *Freelance Directory* and *Fees Guide*, and *The Journalist*.

New Playwrights Trust

Whitechapel Library, 77 Whitechapel High Street,
London E1 7QX
☎ 01–377 5429

Contact *Susan Croft*
Subscription rates (telephone for details) very reasonable, with group rates also available.

Membership open to would-be playwrights, actors and directors. Organises projects and joint projects including rehearsed readings, workshops and discussions. They run a script reading service, bulletin and library service. Also Link Service between writers and theatre companies. Monthly newsletter. Recent projects include Wordplay '88 and *The Play's the Thing!* – a development programme organised by the **Bristol Express Theatre Company** (see entry under Theatre Producers for more details).

The Newspaper Society

Bloomsbury House, Bloomsbury Square,
74–7 Great Russell Street, London WC1B 3DA
☎ 01–636 7014 Fax 01–631 5119

President *Fred Johnston* (May 1989/90)

Director *Dugal Nisbet-Smith*

Organisation for the provincial/London sub-

urban morning, evening, and weekly newspapers.
At the same address: Guild of British Newspaper Editors, **President** *Don Mildenhall*; Newspaper Conference, a newspaper society organisation concerned primarily with newsgathering facilities in London for the regional press; and the Young Newspapermen's Association for young newspaper executives, **Honorary Secretary** *Paul Mee.*

Office of Arts and Libraries

Horse Guards Road, London SW1P 3AL
☎ 01–270 5866

Among its more routine responsibilities, the OAL funds the British Library, and is responsible for the new library project at St Pancras. It is also responsible for funding to the Arts Council and the Regional Arts Associations.

PEN

7 Dilke Street, London SW3 4JE
☎ 01–352 6303

General Secretary *Josephine Pullein-Thompson* MBE
Subscription £20 (Town Membership); £16 (members living over 50 miles from London, and overseas)

English PEN is part of International PEN, a worldwide association of writers which fights for freedom of expression and speaks out for writers who are imprisoned or harassed for having criticised their governments or for publishing other unpopular views. FOUNDED in London in 1921, International PEN now consists of 87 centres in 63 countries. PEN originally stood for poets, essayists and novelists, but membership is now open to all poets, playwrights, essayists, editors and novelists. A programme of talks and discussion is supplemented by the publication of a twice-yearly broadsheet.

The Penman Club

175 Pall Mall, Leigh on Sea, Essex SS9 1RE
☎ 0702 74438

Subscription £8.25 in the first year; £5.25 thereafter

FOUNDED 1950. International writers' society, offering criticism of members' work, general advice and use of writers' library.

Performing Right Society

29–33 Berners Street, London W1P 4AA
☎ 01–580 5544
Telex 892678 PRSLON Fax 01–631 4138

Collects and distributes royalties arising from performances and broadcasts of its members' copyright music.

The Personal Managers' Association Ltd

1 Summer Road, East Molesey, Surrey KT8 9LX
☎ 01–398 9796

President *Peter Dunlop*
Secretary *Angela Adler*
Subscription £200 p.a.

An association of artists' and dramatists' agents (membership not open to individuals). Monthly meetings, for exchange of information, discussion, and acts as a lobby when necessary. Applicants screened. Maintains a code of conduct. A high proportion of Play Agents are members of the PMA.

Players and Playwrights

St John's Church Hall, Hyde Park Crescent, London W2

Subscription £4 p.a.

FOUNDED 1948. A society for newcomers to play and television writing. Weekly meetings in central London. Run-throughs of members' work are staged, and a discussion follows.

Playwrights Co-operative

117 Waterloo Road, London SE1
☎ 01–633 9811

Contact *The Administrator*

FOUNDED 1981. Has evolved a process of script development – a sequence of readings, discussions and workshops. Also story conferences, rehearsed readings, critical and professional advice, workshops held in London venues, and help in getting the final script produced. Since its inception, an average of 34% of the scripts which have been through the Co-Op have ended in production. Only the talented are accepted for membership; the rest can become 'Playwrights Co-Op Subscribers'.

Playwrights' Workshop

22 Brown Street, Altrincham,
Cheshire WA14 2EU
☎ 061–928 3095

Honorary Secretary *Robert Coupland*
Subscription £2 p.a.

FOUNDED 1949. The Society meets monthly in Manchester, and aims to support playwrights of all kinds interested in furthering their work. Guest speakers on all aspects of the theatre. Annual one-act play competition. Past members include Michael Dines and Harry Kershaw.

The Poetry Society

21 Earl's Court Square, London SW5 9DE
☎ 01–373 7861

President *Dannie Abse*
Chairman *Alan Brownjohn*
Director *Paul Ralph*
Membership £15 (London); £12 (rest of Britain & Ireland); £10 (student, senior citizens, UB40)

FOUNDED 1909 to promote poetry and is now a major arts organisation with a thriving membership. It is Britain's only major organisation dealing exclusively with poetry. Offers a wide range of services and activities including: a poetry bookshop; mail-order service supplying most contemporary poetry publications; regular poetry readings and events with leading poets. Publishes *Poetry Review* quarterly; organises the Poets in Schools scheme, sponsored by W.H. Smith; provides a critical service with professional and detailed advice for aspiring poets; publishes a quarterly information bulletin giving details of new presses, writers' groups and competitions; organises poetry events and workshops for teachers and young people; arranges adult educational courses in association with the University of London; administers competitions such as the **Dylan Thomas Award, Alice Hunt Bartlett Award, National Poetry Competition** (see entries for more details). Membership gives reduced admission charges to Poetry Society events and readings.

Publishers Association

19 Bedford Square, London WC1B 3HJ
☎ 01–580 6321-5/580 7761/323 1548
Telex 267160 PUBASS G Fax 01–636 5375

Chief Executive *Clive Bradley*

The national UK trade association (see also **The Scottish Publishers Association**) with over 500 member companies in the industry. Very much a trade body representing the industry to Government and Commissions, and providing services to publishers. Writers with queries are referred on to **The Society of Authors** or **Writers' Guild**. Publishes the *Directory of Publishing*, in association with Cassell. Also home of the Book Marketing Council, whose task it is to promote books and boost their sale, by running promotions and undertaking market research, etc.

The Romantic Novelists' Association

20 First Avenue, Amersham,
Buckinghamshire HP7 9BJ
☎ 0494 727202

Secretary *Dorothy Entwistle*
Subscription £10 p.a.

Membership is open to published writers of romantic novels or of two or more full-length serials, and also to publishers, literary agents, booksellers and librarians. Meetings are held in London and speakers are often arranged. *RNA News* is published quarterly and issued free to members. Annual award **Romantic Novelists' Association/Netta Muskett Award** (see entry for more details).

The Royal Literary Fund

144 Temple Chambers, Temple Avenue,
London EC4Y 0DT
☎ 01–353 7150

Contact *Mrs Fiona M. Clark* (Secretary)

FOUNDED 1790, the fund makes grants available to authors and their dependents in financial need on a stringently discretionary basis. (See **Bursaries** section.)

Royal Society of Literature

1 Hyde Park Gardens, London W2 2LT
☎ 01–723 5104

President *Lord Jenkins of Hillhead*
Subscription £20 p.a.

FOUNDED 1823. Membership (limited to 300) by application to the secretary with 2 sponsors. Fellowships are conferred by the Society on the proposal of two fellows. Benefits of membership include lectures and poetry readings in the Society's rooms. Recent lecturers have included Melvyn Bragg, Helen Gardner, Francis King and Dilys Powell. Presents the **Royal Society of**

Literature Award, and the **Winifred Holtby Memorial Award** (see **Prizes** section).

Royal Television Society

Tavistock House East, Tavistock Square, London WC1H 9HR
☎ 01-387 1970/1332

Subscription £35; overseas (surface mail) £42; (airmail) £65

FOUNDED 1927. Covers all disciplines involved in the television industry. Provides a forum for debate and conferences on technical, social, and cultural aspects of the medium. Presents Journalism and Programme Awards and runs a wide range of training courses.

Science Fiction Foundation

North East London Polytechnic, Longbridge Road, Dagenham, Essex RM8 2AS
☎ 01-590 7722 ext. 2177

Contact *Joyce Day*

A national academic body for the furtherance of science fiction studies. Publishes *Foundation* three times a year, a magazine containing academic articles about science fiction, and reviews of new fiction.

Scottish Poetry Library Association

Tweeddale Court, 14 High Street, Edinburgh EH1 1TE
☎ 031-557 2876

Director *Tessa Ransford*
Membership £7.50 p.a.

A comprehensive collection of work by Scottish poets in Gaelic, Scots and English, plus the work of international poets. Books, tapes, and magazines. Borrowing is free to all. A postal lending service is also offered, for which there is a small fee. Mobile library which can visit schools and other centres by arrangement. Members receive a newsletter and support the library, whose work includes exhibitions, bibliographies, information and promotion in the field of poetry. **Librarian** *Dr Tom Hubbard.*

The Scottish Publishers Association

25A South West Thistle Street Lane, Edinburgh EH2 1EW
☎ 031-225 5795

Director *Lorraine Fannin*
Publicist *Alison Harley*

The Association represents over 50 Scottish publishers, from multinationals to very small presses, in a number of capacities, but primarily in the cooperative promotion and marketing of their books. The SPA also acts as an information and advice centre for both the trade and general public. It publishes seasonal catalogues, membership lists, a detailed directory of members, and provides its membership with a regular newsletter. The SPA represents its members at international bookfairs, provides opportunities for publishers' training, and carries out market research.

Scottish Society of Playwrights

Tron Theatre, 38 Parnie Street, Glasgow G1 5HB
☎ 041-553 1425

Secretary *Donneil Kennedy*
Membership fee £20

FOUNDED 1973 by a group of playwrights, the society acts as a pressure group for playwrights and negotiates contracts with managements. Full membership is open to anyone who has had a play professionally produced on stage, television or radio.

The Society of Authors

84 Drayton Gardens, London SW10 9SB
☎ 01-373 6642

General Secretary *Mark Le Fanu*
Subscription £45/50 p.a.

FOUNDED 1884. The Society of Authors is an independent trade union with some 4300 members. The Society advises on negotiations with publishers, broadcasting organisations, theatre managers and film companies; takes up complaints and pursues legal action for breach of contract, copyright infringement, etc. Along with the **Writers Guild**, the Society has played a major role in advancing the Minimum Terms Agreement for authors. Among the Society's publications are *The Author* (a quarterly journal) and *Quick Guides* to various aspects of writing. Other services include a pension fund and a group medical insurance scheme. Authors under 35, who are not yet earning a significant income from their writing, may apply for membership at a lower subscription of £32.

The Society of Civil Service Authors

8 Bawtree Close, Sutton, Surrey SM2 5LQ
☎ 01-661 9169

Hon. Secretary *Mrs Joan Hykin*
Subscription £8.50 p.a.

FOUNDED 1935. Aims to encourage authorship by present and past members of the Civil Service and to provide opportunities for social and cultural relationships between civil servants who are authors or who aspire to be authors. Annual competitions, open to members only, are held for short stories, poetry, sonnets, travel articles, humour etc. Members receive *The Civil Service Author* quarterly.

The Society of Indexers

16 Green Road, Birchington, Kent CT7 9JZ
☎ 0843 41115

Contact *Mrs H. C. Troughton* ALA (Secretary)
Subscription £15 p.a.

FOUNDED 1957. Publishes *The Indexer* (bi-annual, April and October); *Micro-Indexer* (bi-annual), dealing with computer indexing, and a quarterly newsletter. Issues an annual list of members, and *(IA) Indexers Available*, listing members and their subject expertise. Also, runs an open-learning course 'Training in Indexing'. Recommends rates of pay – currently £7.50 per hour.

Society of Women Writers and Journalists

2 St Lawrence Close, Edgware,
Middlesex HA8 6RB

Honorary Secretary *Olive McDonald*
Subscription £15 (Town); £12 (Country); £9 (Overseas)

Lectures at monthly lunchtime meetings. Also offers advice to members, seminars, etc. Publishes *The Woman Journalist* issued three times a year.

South Bank Board: Literature Office

Artistic Projects Department, Royal Festival Hall, South Bank, London SE1 8XX
☎ 01–921 0906 Fax 01–928 0063

Literature Officer *Maura Dooley*

Maura Dooley's, aims were to 'create a strong presence for literature on the South Bank'. Her brief covered all aspects of writing, and a venue within the Royal Festival Hall, called The Voice Box, has now been established to house a variety of literature events. Plans include the appointment of a writer in residence. In December 1988, the National Poetry Library moved to the South Bank. The library is open 7 days a week (11am-8pm). **Librarian** *Mary Enright* (tel 01–921 0943).

Television History Centre

42 Queen Square, London WC1N 3AJ
☎ 01–405 6627

Contact *Sharon Goulds, Marilyn Wheatcroft*

Home of the television history workshop, the history centre 'provides a range of resources, materials, information and assistance to help people record their own history'.

Theatre Writers' Union

The Actors' Centre, 4 Chenies Street,
London WC1E 7EP
☎ 01–631 3619

Contact *Membership Secretary*
Membership £55 p.a., if annual income from playwriting is more than £10,000; £33, if more than £2000; £22 if less than £2000; £11 for unwaged. (Reduced rate for anyone joining part way through the year.)

Represents all writers working for the theatre, negotiates for terms and conditions, encourages new writing and presses for further funding. Anybody who has written a play is eligible to join. Activities include forums on new writing; rehearsed readings of new plays; meetings with theatre managements and regional arts associations; surveys; workshops; working parties. Services also include professional advice, support in disputes and assistance with problems. The quarterly General Meetings are the Union's decision-making body. All officers and committees must work within the policies decided at GMs. Branches in Birmingham, London, Manchester, Nottingham, and Wales.

The Translators' Association

84 Drayton Gardens, London SW10 9SB
☎ 01–373 6642

Contact *Kate Pool*

FOUNDED 1958 as a subsidiary group within the **The Society of Authors** to deal exclusively with the special problems of literary translators into the English language. Members are entitled to all the benefits and services of the parent Society without extra charge. The Association offers free legal and general advice and assistance on all matters relating to translators' work, including the vetting of contracts, and information on developments relating to translation including information about improvements in fees. Membership is normally confined to translators who have had their work published in volume or serial form or produced in this country for stage, television or radio. Translators of technical work for industrial firms or Government Departments are in certain cases admitted to membership if their work, though not on general sale, is published by the organisation commissioning the work.

Institute of Translation and Interpreting

318A Finchley Road, London NW3 5HT
☏ 01–794 9931

Membership is open to those who satisfy stringent admission criteria, and can provide evidence of adequate professional translation or interpreting experience. Also offer affiliation and student membership. Benefits include listing in an index which specifies the skills and languages of each member.

Welsh Books Council (Cyngor Llyfrau Cymraeg)

Castell Brychan, Aberystwyth, Dyfed SY23 2JB
☏ 0970 624151 Fax 0970 625385

Contact *Gwerfyl Pierce Jones*

FOUNDED 1961 to stimulate interest in Welsh literature and to support authors. The Council distributes the government grant for Welsh-language publications, promotes and fosters all aspects of both Welsh and Welsh interest book production. Its four departments, Editorial, Design, Publicity and Marketing, and Wholesale Distribution Centre offer central services to publishers in Wales, and writers in Welsh and English are welcome to approach the Editorial Department for advice on how to get their manuscripts published. *Book News From Wales/ Llais Llyfrau*, quarterly, includes book lists, reviews, and articles on various aspects of Welsh writing and publishing.

Writers' Circles

A nationwide network of writers' circles (hundreds of them, too many to list here) exists, designed to provide an informal atmosphere of mutual help and constructive criticism for writers of all grades. Your Regional Arts Association (see Contents for listings) can usually provide a comprehensive list of those in your area.

The Writers' Guild of Great Britain

430 Edgware Road, London W2 1EH
☏ 01–723 8074

General Secretary *Walter J. Jeffrey*
Annual subscription 1% of that part of the author's income earned in the areas in which the Guild operates, with a minimum of £50 and a maximum of £530.

FOUNDED 1959, The Writers' Guild is the writers' trade union, affiliated to the TUC, representing writers in film, radio, television, theatre and publishing. The Guild advises on all aspects of writers' agreements and leads the way in campaigns for minimum terms for writers working in all areas represented by The Guild. In 1979 The Guild, together with the **Theatre Writers' Union**, negotiated the first ever industrial agreement for theatre writers. Along with the **Society of Authors**, it has played a major role in advancing the Minimum Terms Agreement for authors. Membership is by a points system. One major piece of work (a full-length book, an hour-long television or radio play, a feature film, etc.) entitles the author to full membership; lesser work helps to accumulate enough points for full membership, while temporary membership may be enjoyed in the meantime. Temporary members can pay a minimum subscription of £30 in their first year.

Yr Academi Gymreig (Welsh Academy)

3rd Floor, Mount Stuart House, Mount Stuart Square, Cardiff CF1 6DQ
☏ 0222 492064/492025

Contact *Kevin Thomas* (Administrator, English Language Section)

FOUNDED 1959 to encourage writing in Welsh. Membership by election. Publishes *Taliesin*, books on Welsh literature and an English/Welsh dictionary. English language section for Welsh writers in English, and those who write on Welsh themes. Both sections organise readings, conferences and general literary events, including the annual Cardiff Literature Festival. Membership open to all.

Regional Arts Associations

Arts Councils

The Arts Council of Great Britain

105 Piccadilly, London W1V 0AU
☎ 01–629 9495

Chairman *Mr Peter Palumbo*
Secretary General *Luke Rittner*

The 1989/90 grant dispensed by the Arts Council stands at *c*.£150 million. From this fund the Arts Council supports arts organisations, artists, performers, and others: grants can also be made for particular productions, exhibitions and projects. Grants available to individuals are detailed in the free Arts Council folder *Awards & Schemes 1989/90.* The total amount set aside for literature 1989/90 is £720,000, an increase of over 14 per cent.

Drama director *Ian Brown* New writing is supported through *Theatre Writing Allocations* (contact the Drama department for more details). **Literature director** *Alastair Niven* Under its director, the Literature Department has defined education, ethnic minority groups, the touring of literature and translation among its top priorities. P. D. James has been appointed as Chairperson to the Literature Advisory Panel. This year the Arts Council will be giving four grants of £5000 each to individual writers – at least one for short story writers; two for biographical projects. Applicants must have at least one published book. Details available from the Literature Department from June 1989.

Arts Council Northern Ireland

181A Stranmillis Road, Belfast BT9 5DU
☎ 0232 381591

Literature Director *Michael Longley*
Drama Director *Dennis Smith*

Scottish Arts Council

19 Charlotte Square, Edinburgh EH2 4DF
☎ 031–226 6051

Literature Director *Walter Cairns*

The Council's work for Scottish-based professional writers, who have a track record of publication includes, Bursaries considered twice yearly; Travel and Research Grants considered three times yearly; Writing Fellowships, posts usually advertised; International Writing Fellowship organised reciprocally with the Canada Council; Writers in Schools and in Public – a list of writers willing to participate in the schemes is published. Also publishes lists of Scottish writers' groups, awards and literary agents.

Welsh Arts Council

Museum Place, Cardiff CF1 3NX
☎ 0222 394711

Literature Director *Meic Stephens*

Funds literary magazines and bookproduction, Writers on Tour and Bursary Schemes, competitions, the **Welsh Academy (Yr Academi Gymreig)** and the Welsh Books Council, children's literature, annual prizes and readings at the Council's bookshop, Oriel.

Drama Director *Michael Baker*
Of particular interest to writers is the new WAC Drama Committee Theatre Writing policy and programmes for 1990/91, which aim to develop theatrical experience among Wales-based writers through a variety of schemes – in particular, funding writers on year-long attachments.

Regional Arts Associations

Council of Regional Arts Associations

Litton Lodge, 13A Clifton Road, Winchester, Hampshire SO22 5BP

☎ 0962 51063

Literature Secretary *Geoff Swallow* (at **Lincolnshire & Humberside Arts**, see entry for address and telephone number)

CoRAA is a service organisation for the corporate needs of the 13 regional arts associations of England (Scotland and Wales have their own Arts Councils, and are not regionally split in this way). 'Increasingly the RAAs are becoming development agencies for the arts in the regions, and policies develop not only in response to regional demand, but also to develop new initiatives in areas of perceived need, and these – aside from the broad objectives of all RAAs – will vary from region to region.' As well as offering advice and practical help in the form of direct funding, the associations often also initiate arts events, such as touring theatre. Associate membership is offered to individuals; rates vary regionally.

DIRECT GRANTS FOR WRITERS
While most of the RAAs designate part of their budget for allocation direct to writers, this is often a minor proportion, which new or aspiring playwrights stand little chance of receiving. Money is more readily available for the professional, though because of the emphasis on community access to the arts in many of the associations, this is often allocated to writers' appearances in schools etc., rather than to support the writer at the typewriter. It is generally accepted, too, that funding is more accessible to novelists than to playwrights. Direct grants are made to writers of fiction because, usually, there is confidence that the work will be published. The grant or bursary is regarded as an investment of sorts. But for playwrights publication is rarely the end result. Funding is more likely to go into the creation of workshops and performance, to bring along a play and help shape it for public consumption: 'The present structure is as much about performance skills as writing skills', one drama officer remarked, 'though just how the RAAs should be directing these funds has become one of the burning questions of the year.'

Buckinghamshire Arts Association

55 High Street, Aylesbury,
Buckinghamshire HP20 1SA
☎ 0296 434704

Arts Officer *Pat Swell*

FOUNDED 1983, BAA is part of the Regional Arts Association network. It exists to encourage and develop the arts in the county and has an active literature policy. The Association can offer help and advice to writers, writing groups, small presses, etc., and operates a 'Book the Writer' scheme offering subsidy for writers' visits and workshops with their public.

East Midlands Arts

Mountfields House, Forest Road, Loughborough,
Leicestershire LE11 3HU
☎ 0509 218292 Telex 265871

Literature Officer *Debbie Hicks*
Drama Officer *Helen Flack*

Covers Leicestershire, Nottinghamshire, Derbyshire (excluding the High Peak District) and Northamptonshire. A comprehensive information service for writers includes an extensive *Writers' Information Pack*, with details of groups and societies in the region, publishers and publishing information, a list of regional magazines which offer a market for work, advice on approaching the media, on unions, courses and grants. Also available is a directory of writers, primarily to aid people using the Writers' Visits Scheme, and in establishing Writers' Attachments. Writers' bursaries (six a year) are granted for work on a specific project – all forms of writing are eligible except for local history and biography. Writing for the theatre can come under the aegis of both Literature and Drama. A list of writers' groups is available, plus *Foreword*, the literature newsletter, and the free magazine *Steppin' Out*.

Eastern Arts

Cherry Hinton Hall, Cambridge CB1 4DW
☎ 0223 215355

Literature Officer *Richard Ings*
Director of Performing Arts *Richard Hogger*

Covers Bedfordshire, Cambridgeshire, Essex, Hertfordshire, Norfolk and Suffolk. Policy emphasises access for all in as wide an area as possible. As a self-styled arts development agency, great stress is placed upon the support of individuals, particularly in the interests of literature in the community. On the drama side, greater emphasis is placed on the creation of a structure to support the playwright – by means of adequate workshops and performance opportunities, rather than direct grants, though a small fund exists for the commissioning of work. Closely involved with the **Royal Court Young People's Theatre Writing Festival**. The Visiting Writers' Scheme subsidises visits by professional writers to schools and other organisations (and includes many household names). Can also supply lists of literary groups, societies and workshops in the area, plus details of residential creative writing courses.

Greater London Arts

9 White Lion Steet, London N1 9PD
☎ 01–837 8808

Literature Officer *Laurence Baylis*
Drama Officer *Sue Timothy*

Awards and bursaries to individual writers are not currently offered by GLA, though this is under review. Applications are encouraged for projects which support the availability and awareness of contemporary literature, such as book and magazine distribution and representation, promotion and marketing schemes, and book fairs. Grants are also available for readings, performances and workshops involving creative writing of all kinds, as well as one-off publications and film projects. 'Writers in Schools' subsidises the cost of bringing writers into contact with students of all ages.

Lincolnshire and Humberside Arts

St Hugh's, Newport, Lincoln LN1 1RX
☎ 0522 533555

Literature, Film and Media Officer
Geoff Swallow

Covers Lincolnshire and Humberside, developing working partnerships with regional agencies, such as local authorities, library and education services, the broadcast media and the private sector, as well as national arts funding agencies and the book trade. LHA supports the following areas of work: writers' residencies and short-term attachments; writers' commissions; a programme of field worker/animateur posts in strategic centres; the development of writers' workshops through the Writers in Public Scheme; a programme of residential weekends for writers. Supports literature in performance through grants to promoters; a regular programme planning forum; and is developing a regional touring network. It has encouraged the live presentation of contemporary literature by British and foreign writers in major arts venues in the region as well as by independent promoters. LHA also supports independent publishers based in its region, and will consider publication grants to those based elsewhere for first publications by writers from Lincolnshire and Humberside.

Merseyside Arts

Graphic House, Duke Street, Liverpool L1 4JR
☎ 051–709 0671 Fax 051–708 9034

Contact ADO (Drama & Literature) *Theresa Griffin*

Merseyside Arts covers Merseyside, part of Cheshire and part of West Lancashire. The aim of the Association is to encourage the development of opportunities for all people of the region to have access to a wide range of literature and opportunities for writing. Through its touring and education policies, Merseyside Arts encourages venues to promote literature and, in partnership with others, seeks to introduce professional writers to workshops, libraries, educational establishments and the wider community in order to stimulate local literature activity. Through its literature policy, Merseyside Arts has established a publications budget for local writers and is seeking to establish a Merseyside Publishing Company in conjunction with the local authorities of the region. Merseyside Arts provides general advice and support for writers and makes a top priority the work for and by members of the Black, Asian and Chinese communities of the region, young people, women and disabled people.

North West Arts

4th Floor, 12 Harter Street, Manchester M1 6HY
☎ 061–228 3062

Literature Officer (vacant)
Drama Officer *Ivor Davies*

Covers Cheshire, Greater Manchester, Lancashire (except West Lancs), and the High Peak District of Derbyshire. Gives financial assistance to a great variety of projects and schemes, including Lancaster Literature Festival and creative writing courses. A Readers' Service is offered to any writer living in the region who submits original unpublished material at a time when funds are available. Writers should send their work with s.a.e. and postcard with name etc., for filing purposes. The Writers in the Community Scheme subsidises writers' fees and travel expenses, when addressing societies and schools, etc. This scheme is currently under review and is expected to be replaced by a new scheme, operational from late 1989. NWA's Literature Department produces a quarterly magazine, *The Word is Out*.

Northern Arts

9–10 Osborne Terrace, Jesmond,
Newcastle upon Tyne NE2 1NZ
☏ 091–281 6334 Fax 091–281 8430

Literature Officer *Jenny Attala*
Drama Officer *Sheila Harborth*

Covers Cleveland, Cumbria, Durham, Northumberland, and Tyne and Wear, and was the first regional arts association in the country to be set up by local authorities. It supports both organisations and writers and aims to stimulate public interest in artistic events. Offers awards for published writers to release them from work or other commitments for short periods of time to enable them to concentrate on specific literary projects. A separate scheme operates for playwrights by the Northern Playwrights Society. Northern Arts make drama awards to producers only. Also fund writers' residencies, magazines and publishing.

South East Arts

10 Mount Ephraim, Tunbridge Wells,
Kent TN4 8AS
☏ 0892 515210

Literature Officer *Charmian Stowell*
Drama Officer *Robert Henry*

Covers Kent, Surrey and East Sussex (excluding the London boroughs). The Literature panel 'aims to create a high public profile for contemporary writing; and to encourage aspiring writers to develop their skills'. Priorities include Writers' Residencies; the Writers in Performance, Writers in Education, and Writers in the Community schemes. Also the continued support of literature festivals in the region. South East Arts offers a reader service under which a writer can, for a small fee, submit work to professional readers for critical comment.

South West Arts

Bradninch Place, Gandy Street, Exeter EX4 3LS
☏ 0392 218188

Literature Officer *Ingrid Squirrell*
Drama Officer *Moira Sutton*

Covers Avon, Cornwall, Devon, much of Dorset, Gloucestershire and Somerset. 'The central theme running through the Association's constitution is development ... increasing, improving, encouraging, advancing and co-ordinating.' The literature policy aims to promote a healthy environment for writers of all kinds and to encourage a high standard of new writing. The programme includes residential courses, residencies, and writers in education. There is also direct investment in small presses, publishers and community groups. Literary festivals, societies and arts centres are encouraged. 'Although South West Arts cannot act as a literary agency or offer subsidy for work in progress, we do on occasion sponsor special awards, such as the **TSB Peninsula Prize**' (see entry). Also available from SWA is a new service called Second Opinion, which is a free manuscript reading service.

Southern Arts Association

19 Southgate Street, Winchester,
Hampshire SO23 9DQ
☏ 0962 55099

Literature Officer *Jane Spiers*
Marketing and Information Officer (to be appointed)
Drama Officer *Fiona Ellis*

The literature panel decides on funding for fiction and poetry readings, festivals, magazines, bursaries, a literature prize, publications, residencies and attachments. A third of the budget in 1989/90 will be spent on the Writers in Education Scheme.

West Midlands Arts

82 Granville Street, Birmingham B1 2LH
☏ 021–631 3121

Literature/Projects Officer *David Hart*

Covers the West Midlands, Hereford and Worcester, Shropshire, Staffordshire and Warwickshire district. 'Our policy is to cooperate with local authorities and other bodies to support new writing and storytelling in relation to readers, aspiring writers, and as part of educational, community and other groundwork.' The Writers and Storytellers in the Community Scheme pays half the fee for visits, longer attachments and commissions. The latter, like publication grants, are offered through publishers or other local organisations. A reading service offers professional advice on, say, 12 poems or 3 sample chapters, and costs £5. Together with the City Council, WMA supports the major national literature festival, the Birmingham Readers and Writers, held in November. Also publishes *People to People* magazine, 20,000 copies free across the region 3 times a year, and welcomes contributions.

Yorkshire Arts

Glyde House, Bradford BD5 0BQ
☏ 0274 723051

Literature Officer *Jennifer Barraclough*
Drama Officer *Shea Connolly*

'Libraries, publishing houses and the education service all make major contributions to the support of literature. Recognising the resources these agencies command, Yorkshire Arts actively seeks ways of acting in partnership with them, whilst at the same time retaining its particular responsibility for the living writer and the promotion of activities currently outside the scope of these agencies.' Funding goes to the Arvon Foundation at Lumb Bank; the Yorkshire Art Circus for community publishing; the Live Writing Scheme, which subsidises projects involving professional writers and students at all levels; and awards to independent publishers. Also offer support for literature in performance, e.g. the Ilkley Literature Festival, and live poetry events.

Bursaries, Fellowships and Grants

Aosdàna Scheme

The Arts Council (An Chomhairle Ealaíon), 70 Merrion Square, Dublin 2, Eire
☎ 0001 611840

Contact *Literature Officer*

Aosdàna is an affiliation of creative artists engaged in literature, music and the visual arts, and consists of not more than 150 artists who have gained a reputation for achievement and distinction. Membership is by competitive sponsored selection. Members are eligible to receive an annuity for a five-year term to assist them in pursuing their art full time.
Award IR£5500 (annuity)

Arts Council of Great Britain Writers' Bursaries

Arts Council of Great Britain, 105 Piccadilly, London W1V 0AU
☎ 01–629 9495

Three awards to writers of outstanding literary achievement needing financial assistance for the research or writing of their next book. Open to British and non-British subjects resident in England. The precise category of writers' eligibility is re-defined each year. Amount varies according to need.

Arvon Foundation Bursaries

Kilnhurst, Kilnhurst Road, Todmorden, Lancashire OL14 6AX
☎ 070681 6582

Contact *The Administrator*

Has recently received a full award from the Arts Council under its incentive funding scheme and is using the money to establish bursaries. No more details available by the time we go to press.

The Authors' Contingency Fund

The Society of Authors, 84 Drayton Gardens, London SW10 9SB
☎ 01–373 6642

This fund makes modest grants to authors who find themselves in sudden financial difficulties.

The Authors' Foundation

The Society of Authors, 84 Drayton Gardens, London SW10 9SB
☎ 01–373 6642

Annual grants to writers whose publishers's advance is insufficient to cover the costs of research involved. At present, preference is given to non-fiction. Application by letter to The Authors' Foundation giving details, in confidence, of the advance and royalties, together with the reasons for needing additional funding. 1988 grants included: Neil Berry (£2500); Alan Judd (£2500). Total of £12,000 available.

The K. Blundell Trust

The Society of Authors, 84 Drayton Gardens, London SW10 9SB
☎ 01–373 6642

Annual grants to writers whose publishers' advance is insufficient to cover the costs of research. Author must be under 40, has to submit copy of his/her previous book and the work must 'contribute to the greater understanding of existing social and economic organisation'. Application by letter. Final entry date 30 June. 1988 grants included: Anne Karpf (£3000); Nam Rodger (£3000). Total of £15,000 available.

Bursaries in Literature

The Arts Council (An Chomhairle Ealaíon), 70 Merrion Square, Dublin 2, Eire
☎ 0001 611840

Contact *Literature Officer*

Annual competition awarded to creative writers

(fiction, poetry, drama) to enable concentration on, or completion of, specific projects. Final entry date 15 April.
Award £1500–£6000

Fulbridge-Chandler Arts Fellowship Award (in detective and spy fiction)

The Fulbridge Commission, 6 Porter Street, London W1M 2HR
☎ 01–486 7697

Contact *Sarah Newman*

Annual award for three years (89/90, 90/91, 91/92) for detective and spy fiction writing to a British writer to study and research in the United States. Offered by the US–UK Educational Commission in association with the Raymond Chandler Estate to commemorate the centenary of Raymond Chandler. Candidates must be under 35 years of age and will need to demonstrate that a period of work or study in the US can be expected to contribute significantly to his or her future work and to an enhancement of Anglo-American cultural understanding.
Award air travel and grant (£10,000 in 89/90)

The Economist/Richard Casement Internship

The Economist, 25 St James's Street, London SW1A 1HG

Contact *Business Affairs Editor* (re Casement Internship)

For a journalist under 24 to spend three months in the summer writing for *The Economist* about science and technology. Applicants should write a letter of introduction along with an article of approximately 600 words suitable for inclusion in the Science and Technology Section. 1989 entry date 28 February.

European Cultural Foundation

Jan van Goyenkade 5, 1075 HN Amsterdam, Netherlands

Contact *Michael Cullis CVO*, British Director, County End, Bushey Heath, Hertfordshire WD12 1NY
☎ 01–950 1057

Grants programme supporting projects involving at least three and preferably more European countries. Endeavours to increase the awareness of the European dimension of our societies. Concerned primarily with basic values, culture, education, environment, international relations or the problems of European society in general. Given for one year as part of sum required for completion of the project. Details from General Secretariat in Amsterdam.

E. C. Gregory Trust Fund

The Society of Authors, 84 Drayton Gardens, London SW10 9SB
☎ 01–373 6642

Annual competitive awards of varying amounts are made each year for the encouragement of young poets under the age of 30 who can show that they are likely to benefit from an opportunity to give more time to writing. Open only to British-born subjects resident in the UK. Final entry date: 31 October. Presentation date June. 1988 awards included: Michael Symmons Roberts (£7000); Gwyneth Lewis (£6000); Adrian Blackledge (£5000); Simon Armitage (£4000); Robert Crawford (£3000). Total of £25,000 available.

The Guardian Research Fellowship

Nuffield College, Oxford OX1 1NF

Contact *Warden's Secretary*

Annually endowed by the Scott Trust, owner of *The Guardian*, to give someone working in the media the chance to put their experience into a new perspective, publish the outcome and give a *Guardian* lecture. Applications welcomed from journalists and management members, in newspapers, periodicals or broadcasting. Research or study proposals should be directly related to experience of working in the media. Accommodation and meals in college will be provided, and a 'modest supplementary stipend' might be arranged to ensure the Fellow does not lose from the stay. Advertised annually in December.

Francis Head Awards

The Society of Authors, 84 Drayton Gardens, London SW10 9SB
☎ 01–373 6642

Designed to provide grants to established British authors over the age of 35 who need financial help during a period of illness or disablement.

Macaulay Fellowship

The Arts Council (An Chomhairle Ealaíon), 70 Merrion Square, Dublin 2, Eire
☎ 0001 611840

Contact *Literature Officer*

To further the liberal education of a young

creative artist. Candidates for this triennial award must be under 30 on 30 June, or 35 in exceptional circumstances.
Award £3500

The John Masefield Memorial Trust

The Society of Authors, 84 Drayton Gardens, London SW10 9SB
☎ 01–373 6642

This trust makes occasional grants to professional poets (or their immediate dependents) who are faced with sudden financial problems.

Airey Neave Trust National & International Law & Human Freedom Fellowship

Airey Neave Trust, 40 Bernard Street, London WC1N 1LG

Contact *Hannah Scott*

Initiated 1989. Annual (this is the intention) research fellowships for up to 3 years – towards a book or paper – for serious research connected with national and international law, and human freedom. Attached to a particular university – those involved at time of going to press include the universities of: London, Cambridge and Oxford, plus Queen's College, Belfast. Interested applicants should come forward with ideas at the beginning of the year, preferably before March.

Northern Arts Literary Fellowship

Northern Arts, 10 Osborne Terrace, Jesmond, Newcastle upon Tyne NE2 1NZ
☎ 091–281 6334

Contact *Literature Officer*

A competitive fellowship, tenable at, and co-sponsored by the Universities of Durham and Newcastle upon Tyne for a period of two academic years.
Award £10,000 p.a.

Northern Arts Writers Awards

Northern Arts, 10 Osborne Terrace, Jesmond, Newcastle upon Tyne NE2 1NZ
☎ 091–281 6334

Contact *Literature Officer*

Awards are offered to established authors resident in the Northern Arts area on basis of literary merit and financial need. Application spring/summer. Also available, one-month residencies at Tyrone Guthrie Centre, Eire.
Award variable

Oppenheim John Downes Memorial Trust

36 Whitefriars Street, London EC4Y 8BH

Grants to writers and artists of all descriptions who are over the age of 30 and unable to pursue their vocation by reason of their poverty. Applicants must be British by birth and of British parents and grandparents. Awards made annually in December. Final application date 1 November.
Grant variable, but usually between £50 and £1500.

The Margaret Rhondda Award

The Society of Authors, 84 Drayton Gardens, London SW10 9SB
☎ 01–373 6642

Competitive award given to a woman writer as a grant-in-aid towards the expenses of a research project in journalism. Triennial, next awarded 1990. Final entry date 31 December. Presentation date June. Total amount available £500.

The Royal Literary Fund

144 Temple Chambers, Temple Avenue, London EC4Y 0DT
☎ 01–353 7150

Contact *Mrs Fiona Clark*

The Fund helps published authors and their families when in financial need. For further details, write for application form. (See also **Professional Associations** section.)

The Scottish Arts Council Bursaries and Awards

(See entry under **Regional Arts Associations/Arts Councils**.)

Southern Arts Literature Bursaries

19 Southgate Street, Winchester, Hampshire SO23 9DQ
☎ 0962 55099

Contact *Literature Officer*

Discretionary annual bursaries may be awarded for periods of up to one year to authors of published poetry or fiction resident in the Southern Arts Region. Bursaries may be awarded to: (a) writers of literary merit whose work might be expected to benefit from a period of full time writing; and (b) publishers wishing to publish work by local writers, and to small presses based in the region.

Laurence Stern Fellowship

Graduate Centre for Journalism, City University, 223 St John Street, London EC1V 0HB

Contact *Robert Jones*

Awarded to a young journalist experienced enough to work on national stories. It gives them the chance to work on the national desk of the *Washington Post*. Benjamin Bradlee, the *Post*'s executive editor selects from a shortlist drawn up in March.

Thames Television Theatre Writers' Scheme

Teddington Lock, Middlesex TW11 9NT
☎ 01–977 3252

Bursaries awarded to playwrights. Must be sponsored by a theatre who then submit the play for consideration by a panel. Not necessarily awarded annually – depends on quality of work submitted. 1988 winners included: Roselia John Baptiste (Liverpool Playhouse); Don Hale (Paine's Plough); Martin Crimp (Orange Tree); Anne Marie di Mambro (Traverse, Edinburgh); Billy Roche (Bush Theatre); Kevin Hood (Warehouse, Croydon); Allan Cubitt (Guildhall School of Music & Drama). Each award allows the playwright a twelve-month attachment.

Tom-Gallon Trust

The Society of Authors, 84 Drayton Gardens, London SW10 9SB
☎ 01–373 6642

A biennial award is made from this Trust Fund to fiction writers of limited means who have had at least one short story accepted. Authors wishing to enter should send a list of their already published fiction, giving the name of the publisher or periodical in each case and the approximate date of publication; one published short story; a brief statement of their financial position; an undertaking that they intend to devote a substantial amount of time to the writing of fiction as soon as they are financially able to do so; and an s.a.e. for the return of work submitted. Final entry date 20 September 1990. Presentation date June.
Award £500

Travelling Scholarships

The Society of Authors, 84 Drayton Gardens, London SW10 9SB
☎ 01–373 6642

Annual, non-competitive awards for the benefit of British authors to enable them to travel abroad. 1988 winners included: A.L. Barker, Eva Figes, Allan Massie, David Rudkin (£1100 each). Total amount available £4500

UEA Writing Fellowship

University of East Anglia, University Plain, Norwich NR4 7JT
☎ 0603 56161

Contact *Administrative Secretary*

Awarded to a writer of established reputation in any field for the period of the Summer term. The duties of the Fellowship are discussed at an interview. It is assumed that one activity will be the pursuit of the Fellow's own writing. In addition the Fellow will be expected to (a) offer an undergraduate creative writing course in the School of English and American Studies during the Summer term, and to read and grade work received; (b) offer fifteen less formal sessions of 1 hour or more made up of readings, workshops, tutorials, and/or visits to seminars; (c) arrange, with help from UEA and Eastern Arts, additional visits and readings by other writers from outside the University. It is hoped that (b) and (c) above will involve students from the University as a whole; and in some cases participants from the city and the region. Applications for the Fellowship should be lodged with the Administrative Secretary by 1 December each year.
Award £2500

West Midlands Arts Creative Writing Attachment

82 Granville Street, Birmingham B1 2LH
☎ 021–631 3121

Contact *David Hart*

Part of the new Community Links Scheme across all art forms. The Creative Writing Attachment provides a grant for an arts, community, educational or other organisation in the West Midlands Region to establish a creative writing attachment.

Prizes

Joe Ackerley Prize

English Centre of International PEN, 7 Dilke Street, London SW3 4JE
☎ 01–352 6303

Commemorating the novelist/autobiographer, J. R. Ackerley, this prize is awarded for a literary autobiography, written in English and published in the year preceding the award.
1987 winner: Anthony Burgess *Little Wilson and Big God.* 1988 winner: John Healy *The Glass Arena.*
Prize £500

Alexander Prize

Royal Historical Society, University College London, Gower Street, London WC1E 6BT
☎ 01–387 7532

Contact *Literary Director*

Awarded for an historical essay of not more than 8000 words. Competitors may choose their own subject for their essay, but must submit their choice for approval to the Literary Director of the Royal Historical Society.
Prize Medal plus £100

An Duais don bhFilíocht i nGaelige

(Prize for Poetry in Irish)

The Arts Council (An Chomhairle Ealaíon), 70 Merrion Square, Dublin 2, Eire
☎ 0001 611840

Contact *Literature Officer*

Awarded for the best book of poetry in the Irish language published in the preceding three years. Triennial – most recent award 1989.
Prize £1000

Hans Christian Andersen Awards

Book Trust, Book House, 45 East Hill, London SW18 2QZ
☎ 01–870 9055

Contact *IBBY British Section*

The only international prizes for children's literature. Two prizes are awarded to the author and illustrator whose work has made a lasting contribution to children's literature. Biennial – in the even-numbered years.
Award Gold medals

Eileen Anderson/Central Television Drama Award

Central Television, Central House, Broad Street, Birmingham B1 2JP
☎ 021–643 9898

Contact *John Palmer, Diana Harris*

An annual award, initiated in 1987 with money left by the late Dr Eileen Anderson, and now contributed to by Central, to encourage new theatre writing in the Midlands. A stage play or adaptation which has been commissioned or premièred at a venue in the Central region is eligible.
1988 winner: Timberlake Wertenbaker *The Love of The Nightingale* (commissioned by the Royal Shakespeare Company's The Other Place in Stratford).
Prize: £500 plus a unique trophy designed each year by a local College of Education. A plaque is awarded to the theatre which commissioned the work.

Angel Literary Prize

The Angel Hotel, Angel Hill, Bury St Edmonds, Suffolk IP33 1LT
☎ 0284 753926

Contact *Caroline Gough*

This award is intended to stimulate interest in, and support for, writers in East Anglia. Two prizes are given, one for a work of fiction and one for a work of non-fiction. Books must have been published between October and September and written by authors living and working in East Anglia. Entries must be submitted by 31 August.
1988 winners: Ficton: Barbara Vine *The House of Stairs* (Viking); Non-fiction: Ethne Clarke *The Art*

of the Kitchen Garden (Joseph).
Prize Fiction £1000; Non-fiction £500

Arvon Foundation International Poetry Competition

Kilnhurst, Kilnhurst Road, Todmorden, Lancs OL14 6AX
☎ 070–681 6582

Contact *The Administrator*

FOUNDED 1980. Biennial competition (odd years) is for poems written in English and not previously broadcast or published. There are no restrictions on the number of lines, themes, age of entrants or nationality. No limit to the number of entries. Entry fee: £3 per poem.
1987 winner: Selima Hill *The Notebook*.
Prize £5000 (First Prize)

Authors' Club First Novel Award

The Authors' Club, 40 Dover Street, London W1X 3RB
☎ 01–373 5244

INSTITUTED 1954. This award is made for the most promising work published in Britain and is presented at a dinner held at the Authors' Club. Entries for the award are accepted from publishers and must be full-length – short stores are not eligible.
Award £200 plus Silver-mounted Quill

Verity Bargate Award

The Soho Poly Theatre Club, 16 Ridinghouse Street, London W1P 7PD
☎ 01–580 6982

Contact *Annette Clancy* (The Administrator)

To commemorate the late Verity Bargate, founder and director of the **Soho Poly Theatre Club**, this award is presented annually for a new and unperformed play, suitable for performance at the Soho Poly. Send s.a.e. for details; if submitting scripts, enclose one s.a.e. script-size and one standard-size. The Soho Poly also runs an annual young writers course to encourage young playwrights.
Previous winners: David Spencer, Melissa Murray, Mick Maloney.
Award £1000 plus publication by **Methuen** and possible production at the Soho Poly Theatre.

Alice Hunt Bartlett Award

The Poetry Society, 21 Earl's Court Square, London SW5 9DE
☎ 01–373 7861

This award is given to the living poet the Society most wishes to honour and encourage. Special consideration is given to newly emerging poets, as merit warrants. The author must submit a volume of poetry containing no fewer than 20 poems or 400 lines. In the case of translations, the original poet must also be alive and the prize is shared equally between poet and translator.
1988 winner: Sujata Bhatt *Brunizem*.
Award £500

H. E. Bates Short Story Competition

Leisure & Recreation Department, Northampton Borough Council, Guildhall, Northampton
☎ 0604 34734

Contact *Malcolm Johnston*

Named after the late H. E. Bates, one of the masters of the short story form, this competition is for short stories of 2000 words maximum. Any writer resident in Great Britain is eligible, and there are categories for children under 11 and under 16.
Prize £100 (First Prize)

The BBC Wildlife Magazine Awards for Nature Writing

Broadcasting House, Whiteladies Road, Bristol BS8 2LR
☎ 0272 732211

Contact *Rosamund Kidman Cox* (Editor of *BBC Wildlife Magazine*)

Annual competition for professional and amateur writers. Entries should be a single essay either on personal observations of, or thoughts about, nature – general or specific – or about reflections on human relationships with nature. Entry forms from Rosamund Kidman Cox.
Prizes £1000 for best essay by a professional or amateur writer; £400 for best essay by an amateur writer (only if a professional writer wins the top award); £200 for best essay by a young writer aged between 13 and 17; £100 for best essay by a young writer aged 12 or under.

Samuel Beckett Award

Faber & Faber, 3 Queen Square, London WC1N 3AU
☎ 01–278 6881

Contact *Frank Pike*

Jointly sponsored by Channel 4, the Royal Court Theatre and Faber & Faber, this award aims to give support and encouragement to new playwrights at a crucial stage of their careers. Two prizes are given, one for a first play for the stage and another for a first play for television, both to have been professionally performed or transmitted during the calendar year. There is also the possibility of publication by Faber.
Prize £1500 (each category)

David Berry Prize

Royal Historical Society, University College London, Gower Street, London WC1E 6BT
☎ 01–387 7532

Awarded for an unpublished essay on Scottish history within the reigns of James I to James VI, not exceeding 10,000 words. Candidates may select any subject from the relevant period, providing it has been submitted to and approved by the Council of the Royal Historical Society. Triennial – next award 1991.
Prize £100

Best Book of the Sea Award

1 Chesham Street, London SW1X 8NF
☎ 01–235 2884

Contact *Col. Richard Preston*

INSTITUTED 1970 and sponsored by King George's Fund for Sailors, this award is given annually for a work of non-fiction which contributes most to the knowledge and/or enjoyment of those who love the sea. A second award may be given at the discretion of the judges for a work of outstanding merit. To be eligible books must be first published in the UK in the year of the award. Closing date December.
Award £1000

Bimco-Lloyd's List Maritime Book Prize

Lloyd's of London Press Ltd, Sheepen Place, Colchester, Essex CO3 3LP
☎ 0206 772277

Contact *Mrs Patricia Morris*

For the best unpublished manuscript on operational, commercial, technical, financial or legal aspects of any sector of maritime industries and services.
Biennial – next award 1991. Closing date 1 December 1990.
Prize 15,000 Swiss Francs (*c.*£5000)

James Tait Black Memorial Prizes

University of Edinburgh, David Hume Tower, George Square, Edinburgh EH8 9JX
☎ 031–667 1011 ext. 6259

Contact *Department of English Literature*

These prizes, one for biography and one for fiction, were instituted in 1918 in memory of a partner of the publishing firm of **A. & C. Black Ltd**, and since 1979 they have been supported by the Scottish Arts Council. Each prize is awarded for a book published in Britain in the previous twelve months. Previous winners include: Biography: Ruth Dudley Edwards *Victor Gollancz: A Biography*; Victoria Glendinning *Edith Sitwell*; Fiction Jenny Joseph *Persephone*; George Mackay Brown *The Golden Bird*.
Prize £1000 (each)

Boardman Tasker Memorial Award

56 St Michael's Avenue, Bramhall, Stockport, Cheshire SK7 2PL
☎ 061–439 4624

INSTITUTED 1983, this award is given for a work of fiction, non-fiction or poetry, whose central theme is concerned with the mountain environment and which can therefore be said to make an outstanding contribution to mountain literature. Authors of any nationality are eligible, but the book must have been published or distributed in the UK for the first time between 1 November 1989 and 31 October 1990. Entry by publishers only.
1988 winner: Joe Simpson *Touching the Void*.
Prize £1000 (may vary at Trustees' discretion)

Booker Prize for Fiction

Book Trust, Book House, 45 East Hill, London SW18 2QZ
☎ 01–870 9055

The leading British literary prize. It was set up in 1968 by Booker McConnell Ltd, with the intention of rewarding merit, raising the stature of the author in the eyes of the public and increasing the sale of the books. The announcement of the winner has been televised live since 1981, and all books on the shortlist experience a substantial increase in sales. Eligible novels must be written in English by a citizen of Britain, the Commonwealth, the Republic of Ireland, Pakistan or South Africa, and must be published in the UK for the first time between 1 October and 30

September of the year of the prize. Entries are submitted only by UK publishers who may each submit not more than four novels within the appropriate scheduled publication dates. The judges may also ask for certain other eligible novels to be submitted to them. This has led to some controversy during recent years with publishers accused of 'holding back' obvious favourites in order to increase the chances of the prize going to one of their listed authors. Annual award.
Previous winners include: Peter Carey *Oscar and Lucinda* (1988); Penelope Lively (1987), Kingsley Amis (1986), Salman Rushdie (1981).
Prize £20,000

BP Arts Journalism Awards

Arts Council, 105 Piccadilly, London W1V 0AU
☎ 01–629 9495
Council of Regional Arts Associations, Litton Lodge, 13A Clifton Road, Winchester, Hampshire SO22 5BP
☎ 0962 51063

Contact *Arts Council Press Office, or* CoRAA

First presented in 1986 to recognise the contribution made by journalists throughout the UK towards understanding and appreciation of the arts. Sponsored by British Petroleum plc. Four main categories: (a) Best news story or feature article about the arts or heritage in a newspaper or periodical. Reviews excluded. (b) Best radio programme on the arts or heritage. (c) Best television programme on the arts or heritage. (d) A picture or series of pictures published in a newspaper or periodical which best illustrates an event in the arts or heritage.
Prize £1000 1st prize; £250 for runner-up in each category.

Bridport Arts Centre Creative Writing Competition

Arts Centre, South Street, Bridport, Dorset
☎ 0308 27183

Contact *The Administrator*

A competition for poetry and short story writing. Unpublished work only, written in English.
Prizes £1000, £500 & £250 in each category, plus runners-up prizes.

Katharine Briggs Folklore Award

The Folklore Society, c/o University College London, Gower Street, London WC1E 6BT

Contact *Katharine Briggs Convener*

An annual award in November for a book receiving its first British publication in the previous calendar year which has made the most distinguished non-fiction contribution to folklore studies. The term folklore studies is interpreted broadly to include all aspects of traditional and popular culture, narrative, belief, custom and folk arts.
Prize £50 plus engraved goblet.

Bristol Old Vic & HTV West Playwriting Award

Playwriting Award, PO Box 60, Bristol BS99 7NS
☎ 0272 778366

INITIATED 1987, this award is open to any author, amateur or professional, over the age of 18 and resident in the British Isles. Along with the cash prize there is a trophy and the possibility of production on the stage or television.
Award £2000

British Film Institute Book Award

21 Stephen Street, London W1P 1PL
☎ 01–255 1444

Contact *Wayne Drew*

For a book on film or television which is both innovative and accessible with a lively approach to the media. Annual.
Previous winners include: Michael Powell *A Life in Movies*; Leonard J. Leff *Hitchcock and Selznick*.
Award £1000

British Science Fiction Association Award

c/o 33 Thornville Road, Hartlepool, Cleveland TS26 8EW

Contact *The Award Administrator*

Annual awards are given in four categories: Best Novel, Best Short Fiction, Best Media Presentation, Best Artist, for work first published or presented in Britain during the preceding year.
Award Trophy

The British Topography Book Prize

Provincial Booksellers Fairs Association, PO Box 66, Cambridge CB1 3PD
☎ 0223 240921

Contact *Mrs Gina Dolan* (Secretary)

Awarded to the best book on topography published in the UK between June and May. 1987

winner: *Wetland: Life in the Somerset Levels.*
Award £1000

James Cameron Award

City University Graduate Centre for Journalism, Northampton Square, London EC1
☏ 01–253 4399

Contact *The Administrator*

Annual award for journalism. Awarded to a reporter of any nationality, working for the British media, whose work is judged (by a panel of journalists) to have contributed most during the year to the continuance of the Cameron tradition. Administered by the City University Graduate Centre for Journalism. 1988 winner: Michael Buerk, BBC foreign correspondent.

Cartier Diamond Dagger Award

See **Crime Writers' Association Fiction Award**

Catullus Award

The Yeats Club, PO Box 271, Oxford OX2 6DU

FOUNDED 1986 to encourage translators of poetry. Twice yearly open competition for poetry in translation from an ancient language. Send s.a.e. for entry form. Complete original text must accompany translation.
Prize An original sculpture.

Cheltenham Prize

Cheltenham Festival of Literature, c/o Town Hall, Cheltenham, Glos GL50 1QA
☏ 0242 521621

The Cheltenham Prize is awarded annually and is given to the author of a work of literature, who is deemed in the opinion of an independent judge to have made an outstanding contribution to the previous year's literature, but which has not yet received the critical attention it deserves.
Prize £500

Children's Book Award

The Federation of Children's Book Groups, 30 Senneleys Park Road, Northfield, Birmingham B31 1AL
☏ 021–427 4860

Contact *Jenny Blanch*

FOUNDED 1980. Awarded annually by the Federation for best book of fiction suitable for children up to 14 years. It is unique because it is judged by the children themselves.

Previous winner: Korky Paul & Valerie Thomas *Winnie The Witch* (1987).
Award Certificate

The Children's Book Circle Eleanor Farjeon Award

c/o Philippa Milnes-Smith, Penguin Books Ltd, 27 Wright's Lane, London W8 5TZ
☏ 01–938 2200

This award, named in memory of the much loved children's writer, is for distinguished services to children's books either in this country or overseas, and may be given to a librarian, teacher, publisher, bookseller, author, artist, reviewer, television producer, etc. at the discretion of the Children's Book Circle.
1988 winner: National Library for the Handicapped Child.
Award £500

Cholmondeley Awards

The Society of Authors, 84 Drayton Gardens, London SW10 9SB
☏ 01–373 6642

In 1965, the Dowager Marchioness of Cholmondeley established these annual non-competitive awards, for which submissions are not required, for the benefit and encouragement of poets of any age, sex or nationality. Presentation date June.
1988 winners: John Heath-Stubbs, Sean O'Brien, John Whitworth.
Award £6000 (in total, usually divided)

Arthur C. Clarke Award for Science Fiction

Science Fiction Foundation, North East Polytechnic, Longbridge Road, Dagenham, Essex RM8 2AS
☏ 01–590 7722 ext. 2177

Contact *Joyce Day*

ESTABLISHED 1986. The Arthur C. Clarke Award is given yearly to the best Science Fiction novel first published in the UK in the previous calendar year. Both hardcover and paperback books qualify. Made possible by a generous donation from Arthur C. Clarke, this Award is selected by a rotating panel of six judges nominated by the British Science Fiction Association, the International Science Policy Foundation and the Science Fiction Foundation.
Past winners: Margaret Atwood *The Handmaid's Tale* (1987); George Turner *The Sea and Summer* (1988); Rachel Pollock *Unquenchable Fire*

(1989).
Award £1000 for the best science fiction novel published in the UK.

Collins Biennial Religious Book Award

William Collins Sons & Co. Ltd, 8 Grafton Street, London W1X 3LA
☎ 01–493 7070

Contact *Lesley Walmsley*

A biennial award given for a book which has made the most distinguished contribution to the relevance of Christianity in the modern world, written by a living citizen of the Commonwealth, the Republic of Ireland or South Africa.
1987 winner: Gerard W. Hughes *God of Surprises*.
Award £2000

Commonwealth Writers Prize

The Chairman, SPACLALS, University of Wollongong, Wollongong, New South Wales, Australia 2500
☎ (042) 270555
Telex 29022 Fax (042) 270477

Contact *Dr W. McGaw*

ESTABLISHED 1987. Eligible books must be in English, written by a Commonwealth citizen. Novels, plays or collection of one-act plays, and short stories.
1988 winner: Festus Iyayi *Heroes*.
Prizes 1st £10,000; runners-up £500 – eight prizes given at regional level for best entry and best first published in each of the four regions.

The Constable Trophy

Constable Publishers Ltd, 10 Orange Street, London WC2H 7EG
☎ 01–930 0801

Contact Book Trust, Book House, 45 East Hill, London SW18 2QZ

Biennial competition supported by the five northern-based regional arts associations for fiction writers living in the North of England for a previously unpublished novel. The winning entry may be considered for publication by Constable, as may two runners-up.
1988 winner: Paul Sayer.
Prize 1st £1000 plus Trophy and £1000 on acceptance by Constable in advance of royalties.

Thomas Cook Travel Book Awards

Book Trust, Book House, 45 East Hill, London SW18 2QZ
☎ 01–870 9055

The annual awards are given to encourage the art of travel writing in three categories: (a) best travel book, (b) best guide book published in the current year, (c) best illustrated guide book.
1989 winner: Paul Theroux *Riding the Iron Rooster*; Pat & John Underwood *Madeira*; Dr Richard Fisher *The Marco Polo Expedition*.
Previous winners have included: Patrick Leigh Fermor, Patrick Marnham, Geoffrey Moorhouse, Tim Severin, Jonathan Raban.
Awards (a) £7500, (b) 2500, (c) £1000

The Duff Cooper Memorial Prize

24 Blomfield Road, London W9 1AD
☎ 01–286 5050

Contact *The Viscount Norwich*

An annual award for a literary work in the field of biography, history, politics or poetry, published during the previous 24 months. Financed by the interest from a Trust Fund commemorating Duff Cooper, first Viscount Norwich (1890–1954), the prize has two permanent judges, the present Lord Norwich, and the Warden of New College, Oxford, as well as three others who change every five years.
Prize c.£250

Giles Cooper Radio Play Award

BBC Broadcasting House, London W1A 1AA
☎ 01–580 4468

Contact *Richard Imison*

In memory of the great pioneer of radio drama Giles Cooper. Awarded to the best BBC radio play. Aims to encourage established radio drama as well as discovering new talent. Co-sponsored by Methuen London Ltd who will select winners for publication.
Previous winners: Peter Tinniswood *The Village Fête*; Wally K. Daly *Mary's*; Frank Dunne *Dreams of Dublin Bay*; Anna Fox *Nobby's Day*; Nigel D. Moffat *Lifetime* and Richard Nelson *Languages Spoken Here*.

Rose Mary Crawshay Prize

The British Academy, 20–21 Cornwall Terrace, London NW1 4QP
☎ 01–487 5966

Contact *Rosemary Lambeth*

FOUNDED 1888 by Rose Mary Crawshay, this prize is given for a historical or critical work by a woman of any nationality on English literature, with particular preference for a work on Keats, Byron or Shelley. The work must have been published in the preceding 3 years.
Prize normally 2 prizes of £300 each.

John Creasey Memorial Award

Crime Writers' Association, PO Box 172, Tring, Herts HP23 5LP

Contact *The Secretary*

FOUNDED 1973 following the death of crime writer, John Creasey, who founded the **Crime Writers' Association.** This award is given annually for the best crime novel by a previously unpublished author.
Previous winners: Janet Neel *Death's Bright Angel* (1988); Denis Kilcommons *The Dark Apostle* (1987).
Award Cheque (sum varies), plus magnifying glass.

Crime Writers' Association Fiction Award

Crime Writers' Association, PO Box 172, Tring, Herts HP23 5LP

Contact *The Secretary*

Gold Dagger and Silver Dagger Awards for the best crime fiction published during the year. Also Cartier Diamond Dagger awarded annually for a lifetime's achievement in the world of crime fiction.
1988 winners: Gold Dagger: Michael Dibdin *Ratking*; Silver Dagger: Sara Paretsky *Toxic Shock*; Cartier Diamond Dagger: Dick Francis (1989); John Le Carré (1988).
Award Gold- or silver-plated dagger, plus cheque in each case (sum varies).

Crime Writers' Association Non-Fiction Award

Crime Writers' Association, PO Box 172, Tring, Herts HP23 5LP

Contact *The Secretary*

Non-fiction Gold Dagger – an annual award for the best non-fiction crime book published during the year.
1988 winner: Bernard Wasserstein *The Secret Lives of Trebitsch Lincoln*.
Award Cheque (sum varies), plus gold-plated dagger.

Crime Writers' Association Punch Prize

PO Box 172, Tring, Hertfordshire HP23 5LP

Contact *The Secretary*

Sponsored by *Punch* Magazine for the funniest crime novel of the year.
Previous winner: Nancy Livingston *Death in a Distant Land*.
Award cheque

Daily Telegraph Young Science Writer Awards

British Association, Fortress House, 23 Savile Row, London W1X 1AB
☎ 01–494 3326 **Contact**

Julie Dallison

The aim of the competition is to bolster BASA's (British Association for the Advancement of Science) crusade to make the public more aware of the importance of science. Award to a young science journalist for 'putting poetry into science' – for an article giving a fresh view of an existing scientific field. Copy needs to be bright, lively, and suitable for publication in the newspaper – easy for the layman to read, and enjoy.

Isaac Deutscher Memorial Prize

c/o Gerhard Wilkie, 75 St Gabriels Road, Gabriels Road, London NW2 4DU
☎ 01 450 0469

An annual award in recognition of and as encouragement to outstanding research in the Marxist tradition of Isaac Deutscher. Made to the author of an essay or full scale work published or in manuscript. Entries should be submitted by 1 May each year. Recent winner: Professor Teodor Shanin, *Russia 1905–1907: Revolution as a Moment of Truth*.
Award £100

The George Devine Award

23 Ainger Road, London NW3

Contact *Christine Smith*

Annual award administered by the **Royal Court Theatre** to find and support a promising new playwright. Send two copies of the script to Christine Smith by the end of March. Information

leaflet available.
1987 winner: Nick Ward *Apart from George*.
Prize £2000

Denis Devlin Award

The Arts Council (An Chomhairle Ealaíon), 70 Merrion Square, Dublin 2, Eire
☎ 0001 611840

Contact *Literature Officer*

Triennial award for the best book of poetry in English by an Irish poet, published in the preceding three years.
Award £1000 (most recent award – 1989)

Dillons Commonwealth Poetry Prize

Commonwealth Institute, Kensington High Street, London W8 6NQ
☎ 01–603 4535 ext. 255

Contact *Ronald Warwick*

An annual prize, sponsored by Dillons the Bookstore, for a published book of poetry by an author from a Commonwealth country including the UK. Non-English entries in officially recognised languages are accepted with a translation.
1987 winner: Philip Salom *Sky Poems*.
Prize £5000 plus four regional awards of £1000.

DuQuesne Award

The Yeats Club, PO Box 271, Oxford OX2 6DU

FOUNDED 1986 to encourage translators of poetry. Twice yearly open competition for poetry in translation from a *modern* language. Send s.a.e. for entry form. Complete original text must accompany translation.
Prize An original sculpture

Mary Elgin Award

Hodder & Stoughton Ltd, 47 Bedford Square, London WC1B 3DP
☎ 01–636 9851

To encourage gifted new writers of traditional fiction on the **Hodder & Stoughton** publishing list. No restrictions of age, sex or nationality apply, and writers need not be first novelists. Work to have been published or submitted to Hodder & Stoughton during the previous 12 months. Annual.
Award £50

Michael Elliott Prize for the North West

See **The Mobil Playwriting Competition**

European Prize for Translation of Poetry

European Poetry Library, Blijde Inkomststraat 9, B-3000 Leuven, Belgium

Triennial prize offered by the European Commission in Brussels for translations of poetry, written by living poets from other Community countries. Both poems and translations must be in one of the nine official Community languages and the translations must have been published in book form in the previous four years. Next prize 1990. Submit five copies of the translation before the end of 1989, marking envelope: 'European Prize for Translation of Poetry'.
Prize £6000

Christopher Ewart-Biggs Memorial Prize

33A Brondesbury Road, London NW6

Biennial award to any writer, historian, novelist, playwright or journalist whose work is considered by the judges to promote and encourage 'peace and understanding in Ireland, or the strengthening of links between the peoples of Ireland and Britain, or closer cooperation between the partners of the European Community.' Works must have been published in the two year period preceding the prize, and must have been written in either English or French.
1988 joint winners: Mary Holland (The Observer) and David McKittrick (The Independent).
1987 winner: Frank McGuinness *Observe the Sons of Ulster Marching Towards the Somme*.
Prize £4000

Geoffrey Faber Memorial Prize

Faber & Faber Ltd, 3 Queen Square, London WC1N 3AU
☎ 01–278 6881

ESTABLISHED 1963 as a memorial to the founder and first chairman of **Faber & Faber**, this prize is awarded in alternate years for the volume of verse and the volume of prose fiction judged to be of greatest literary merit published in the UK in the preceding two years. Authors must be under 40 at the time of publication and citizens of the UK, Commonwealth, Republic of Ireland or South Africa.

1988 winner: Michael Hofmann *Acrimony*.
Prize £1000

Prudence Farmer Award

New Statesman and Society, Foundation House, Perseverance Works, 38 Kingsland Road, London E2 5BA
☎ 01-739 3211

Contact *Maria Seed*

For the best poem to have been published in the *New Statesman and Society* during the previous year (July–July).
Award £100

Fawcett Society Book Prize

46 Harleyford Road, London SE11 5AY
☎ 01-587 1287

Contact *Beth McHattie*

An annual award to the author of a book (alternately fiction and non-fiction) which has made a substantial contribution to the understanding of women's position in society today. All works submitted for the prize are placed in the **Fawcett Library** at City of London Polytechnic.
1988 winner: Beatrix Campbell *The Iron Ladies: Why Do Women Vote Tory?*
Prize £500

The Kathleen Fidler Award

c/o The Book Trust, 15A Lynedoch Street, Glasgow G3 6EF
☎ 041-332 0391

For an unpublished novel for children aged 8–12, to encourage authors new to writing for this age group. The work must be the author's first attempt to write for this age range.
1988 winner: Charles Morgan *Flight of the Solar Ducks*.
Award £1000 plus publication by **Blackie**.

Sir Banister Fletcher Award

The Authors' Club, 40 Dover Street, London W1X 3RB
☎ 01-373 5244

This award is financed by the income from a Trust left by the late Sir Banister Fletcher, who was President of the Authors' Club for many years. It is presented annually for the best book on architecture or the fine arts published in the preceding year. Submissions: Fletcher Award Committee, RIBA, 66 Portland Place, London W1N 4AD.
Previous winner: Sir Michael Levey *Giambattista Tiepolo: His Life and Art*.
Award £200

The John Florio Prize

The Translators' Association, 84 Drayton Gardens, London SW10 9SB
☎ 01-373 6642

Contact *Kate Pool*

ESTABLISHED 1963 under the auspices of the Italian Institute and the British–Italian Society, this prize is awarded biennially for the best translation into English of a twentieth-century Italian work of literary merit and general interest, published by a British publisher in the two years preceding the prize.
Previous winner: J. G. Nichols.
Prize £900

Glaxo Prize for Medical Writing

The Society of Authors, 84 Drayton Gardens, London SW10 9SB
☎ 01-373 6642

Awarded for a medical textbook written and published in the United Kingdom in the year preceding the award. Final date 30 June. Annual.
1988 winner: P. M. Dean *Molecular Foundations of Drug Receptor Interaction*.
Prizes 1st £1250; 2nd £500

Glenfiddich Awards

W. Grant & Sons Ltd, Independence House, 84 Lower Mortlake Road, Richmond, Surrey TW9 2HS

A series of awards to writers and broadcasters who have contributed most to the civilised appreciation of food and drink through articles, books, illustration and photography published in the UK. Also covers TV and radio programmes, as well as a Special Award for outstanding work or event.
1989 Winners: Food Book of the Year: *English Seafood Cookery* Richard Stein; Drink Book of the Year: *The Wines of Spain and Portugal* Charles Metcalfe & Kathryn McWhirter; Restaurant Writer of the Year & Glenfiddich Trophy: Jeremy Round for articles in *The Independent*; Special Award: Hilly Janes *The Independent* Food Page; Television Programme of the Year: *4 What It's Worth*; Radio Programme of the Year: *Radio 2 Food & Drink*.
Award Overall winner £2000 plus The Glenfiddich Trophy; category winners £500

each, plus case of Glenfiddich Pure Malt Whisky and an engraved commemorative quiach.

GPA Book Award

GPA House, Shannon, County Clare, Eire

Contact *Gerry Dukes*

Awarded for the first time last year to celebrate and identify the best in contemporary Irish writing. Books in the categories of fiction, poetry and general (autobiography, biography, history, essays, belles lettres and criticism) will be considered. Authors must be born in Ireland, or resident there for three years.
Prize IR£50,000

Greenwich Festival Poetry Competition

151 Powis Street, London SE18 6JL
☎ 01–317 8687

Contact *Keith Rusby*

A biennial award on even years for an unpublished poem in English of up to 50 lines by anyone over the age of sixteen.
Prize £1000 total prize money

The Guardian Children's Fiction Award

24 Weymouth Street, London W1N 3FA
☎ 01–580 3479

Contact *Stephanie Nettell*

Annual award for an outstanding work of fiction for children by a British or Commonwealth author, first published in the UK in the preceding year, excluding picture books and previous winners.
1989 winner: Geraldine McCaughrean *A Pack of Lies*. Previous winners include: Ruth Thomas, Ann Schlee, Joan Aiken, James Aldridge.
Award £500

The Guardian Fiction Prize

The Guardian, 119 Farringdon Road, London EC1R 3ER
☎ 01–278 2332

Contact *Literary Editor*

ESTABLISHED 1965. An annual award for a novel published by a British or Commonwealth writer, this is chosen by the Literary Editor in conjunction with *The Guardian*'s regular reviewers of fiction.
1988 winner: Lucy Ellmann *Sweet Desserts*. Previous winners include: Isabel Colegate, Peter Benson.
Prize £1000

The Hawthornden Prize

Hawthornden Castle, Lasswade, Midlothian E818 1EG
☎ 031–440 2180

An annual award for a work of imaginative literature by a British subject under the age of 41 published during the previous year.
Previous winners: Robert Shaw, V. S. Naipaul.
Prize £2000

The Royal Society of Literature Award under W. H. Heinemann Bequest

Royal Society of Literature, 1 Hyde Park Gardens, London W2 2LT
☎ 01–723 5104

Works of any kind of literature may be submitted by their publishers for consideration under this award, but only living authors are considered. Genuine contributions to literature originally written in English are sought, but preference will be given to publications which are unlikely to command large sales: poetry, biography, criticism, etc.
1987 winner: Michael Ignatieff *The Russian Album* (£4000).
Award Amount varies.

Ritz Paris Hemingway Award

75 Rockefellar Plaza, Suite 1809, New York NY 10019

Contact *The Executive Director*

Nominations not accepted from publishers, nor may applications for entry be made. Previous winners: Marquerite Duras *The Lover*; Peter Taylor *A Summons to Memphis*. The richest literary prize for a single award to date.
Award $50,000

Historical Novel Prize in Memory of Georgette Heyer

The Bodley Head, 31 Bedford Square, London WC1B 3SG
☎ 01–255 2393
Transworld Publishers Ltd, Century House, 61–3 Uxbridge Rd, London W5 5SA.
☎ 01–579 2652

Contact *Jill Black* (Bodley Head)

FOUNDED 1977 in memory of the celebrated historical novelist, this is an annual prize for an outstanding previously unpublished historical novel.
Prize £5000

David Higham Prize for Fiction

Book Trust, Book House, 45 East Hill,
London SW18 2QZ
☎ 01–870 9055

An annual award for a first novel or book of short stories published in the UK in the year of the award by an author who is a citizen of Britain, the Commonwealth, the Republic of Ireland, Pakistan or South Africa.
1988 winner: Carol Birch *Life in the Palace*.
Award £1000

Winifred Holtby Memorial Prize

Royal Society of Literature, 1 Hyde Park Gardens,
London W2 2LT
☎ 01–723 5104

An annual award for the best regional work of fiction (or, in some cases non-fiction or poetry) written in English by a living citizen of the UK, Republic of Ireland or the Commonwealth, published in the year of the prize.
1986 winner: Maggie Hemingway *The Bridge*.
Prize £750

Nelson Hurst & Marsh Biography Award

The Authors' Club, 40 Dover Street,
London W1X 3RB
☎ 01–373 5244

A biennial award (odd years) for the most significant biography published over a two year period by a British publisher.
1987 winner: Roland Huntford.
Award £2000 & silver trophy presented at a dinner.

The Jerusalem Prize

Embassy of Israel, 2 Palace Green,
London W8 4QB
☎ 01–937 8050

The Jersualem Prize is awarded to an author whose work expresses the idea of 'the freedom of the individual in society'. Last year it went to the Argentinian writer Ernesto Sabato in recognition of his work expressing the struggle of the individual to preserve his freedom and uniqueness against dictatorial regimes. Ernesto Sabato is the fourteenth recipient of the prize. He follows John M. Coetzee, Milan Kundera, V. S. Naipaul, Graham Greene, Sir Isaiah Berlin, Octavio Paz, Simone de Beauvoir, Eugene Ionesco, Jorge Luis Borges, Ignazio Silone, Andre Schwarz-Bart, Max Frisch and Bertrand Russell.

Mary Vaughan Jones Award

Welsh National Centre for Children's Literature,
c/o Welsh Books Council, Castell Brychan,
Aberystwyth, Dyfed SY23 2JB
☎ 0970 624151

Contact *The Administrator*

For distinguished services to the field of children's literature in Wales over a considerable period of time. This triennial award will next be presented in 1991.
Award £600 plus silver trophy.

The Sir Peter Kent Conservation Book Prize

Book Trust, Book House, 45 East Hill,
London SW18 2QZ
☎ 01–870 9055

ESTABLISHED by BP Exploration Limited. A book on creative conservation of the environment. Entries from publishers in the UK.
1989 winner: Jeremy Purseglove *Taming the Flood*.
Prize £1500

The Martin Luther King Memorial Prize

National Westminster Bank Ltd, 7 Fore Street,
Chard, Somerset TA20 1PJ

Contact *John Brunner*

An annual award for a literary work (including poetry, plays and TV or film scripts) reflecting the ideals to which Dr King dedicated his life, published or performed in the UK during previous calendar year. No enquiries answered without s.a.e.
Prize £100

Kraszna-Krausz Award: Best Book on Photography

Kraszna-Krausz Foundation, 3 King's Grove,
Maidenhead, Berkshire
☎ 0734 789456

Contact *Alan J. Davis*

For the book making the most original and lasting contribution to the art and practice of camera media. Details subject to annual announcement.
Prize £5000

Lakeland Book of the Year

Cumbria Tourist Board, Ashleigh, Holly Road, Windermere LA23 2AQ
☏ 096 62 4444

Contact *Award Secretary*

Now been running since 1984 with a great deal of success. An annual award, funded by Cumbrian author Hunter Davies, for the best book or booklet on any aspect of Cumbria and the English Lake District published in the previous calendar year. Entry date mid-February 1990.
1988 winner: Molly Lefebure *The Bondage of Love: A Biography of Mrs Samuel Taylor Coleridge.*
Award £100

The Library Association Besterman Medal

7 Ridgmount Street, London WC1E 7AE
☏ 01–636 7543

Awarded annually for an outstanding bibliography or guide to the literature first published in the UK during the preceding year. Recommendations for the award are invited from members of The Library Association. Among criteria taken into consideration in making the award are: authority of the work and quality of articles or entries; accessibility and arrangement of the information; scope and coverage; quality of indexing; adequacy of references; accuracy of information; physical presentation; and the originality of the work.
1987 winner: Philip H. Bolton *Dickens Dramatized.*
Award medal

The Library Association Carnegie Medal

The Library Association, 7 Ridgmount Street, London WC1E 7AE
☏ 01–636 7543 Fax 01–436 7218

First awarded in 1936. Presented for an outstanding book for children written in English and first published in the UK during the preceding year. This award is not necessarily restricted to books of an imaginative nature.
1988 winner: Susan Price *The Ghost Drum.*
Award Medal

The Library Association Kate Greenaway Medal

The Library Association, 7 Ridgmount Street, London WC1E 7AE
☏ 01–636 7543 Fax 01–436 7218

First awarded in 1955. Offered annually by the **Library Association** for the most distinguished work in the illustration of children's books first published in the UK during the preceding year.
1988 winner: Adrienne Kennaway *Crafty Chameleon.*
Award Medal

The Library Association McColvin Medal

7 Ridgmount Street, London WC1E 7AE
☏ 01–636 7543

Annual award for an outstanding reference book first published in the UK during the preceding year. Books eligible for consideration include: encyclopedias, general and special; dictionaries, general and special; biographical dictionaries; annuals, yearbooks and directories; handbooks and compendia of data; atlases. Recommendations invited from members of The Library Association.
1987 winner: Geoffrey Campbell-Platt *Fermented Foods of the World: A Dictionary and Guide.*
Award medal

The Library Association Wheatley Medal

7 Ridgmount Street, London WC1E 7AE
☏ 01–636 7543

Annual award for an outstanding index first published in the UK during the preceding three years. Whole work must have originated in the UK and recommendations for the award are invited from members of the Library Association, the Society of Indexers, Publishers and others.
1987 winner: Neil R. Fisk *Index to a Short History of Wilson's School*, 3rd edition.
Award medal

London Tourist Board Guide Book of the Year Award

London Tourist Board, 26 Grosvenor Gardens, London SW1W 0DU
☎ 01–730 3450

Contact *Public Relations Manager*

An annual award for new or substantially revised guidebooks mainly on London and published between 1 June and 31 May. Two categories: (a) general guide, and (b) specialist.
Award Gift and certificate

LWT Plays on Stage

LWT Plays on Stage, South Bank Television Centre, London SE1 9LT
☎ 01–261 3196

Contact *Michael Halifax, Marion Milne*

A live drama competition with a total prize money in 1988 of £44,000 to be divided into 1st, 2nd and 3rd prizes, to help stage three plays judged to be outstanding by a panel of 'distinguished judges'. The competition is open to producers, producing theatres and repertory companies, rather than playwrights direct.
1988 winners: Temba Theatre Company *Glory!* by Felix Cross; The Operating Theatre Company *The Harlot's Curse* by Rodney Archer & Powell Jones; Northumberland Theatre Company *Wor Jackie* by Mike Kirkup & Keith Armstrong, with music by Rick Taylor & Frank Gibbon.
Prizes: 1st £17,000; 2nd £15,000; 3rd £12,000

Sir William Lyons Award

The Guild of Motoring Writers, 2 Pembroke Villas, The Green, Richmond, Surrey TW9 1QF
☎ 01–940 6974

Contact *Jean Peters*

An annual competitive award to encourage young people in automotive journalism and foster interests in motoring and motor industry. Entrance by two essays and interview with Awards Committee. Applicants must be British aged 17–23, and resident in UK. Final entry date 1 October. Presentation date December.
Award £500

Roger Machell Prize

The Society of Authors, 84 Drayton Gardens, London SW10 9SB
☎ 01–373 6642

An annual award for a non-fiction book on any of the performing arts, written in English, the work of one author and first published in the UK. This prize is sponsored by **Hamish Hamilton**. Final entry date 30 November. Presentation April.
1988 winner: Peter Conrad *A Song of Love and Death: The Meaning of Opera*. 1987 winner: Kurt Ganzl *The British Musical Theatre*.
Prize £2000

The Macmillan Prize for a Children's Picture Book

4 Little Essex Street, London WC2R 3LF
☎ 01–836 6633

Contact *Publicity Manager* (Macmillan Children's Books)

'Established in order to stimulate new work from young illustrators in art schools and to help them start their professional lives.' Fiction or non-fiction. Macmillan Children's Books have the option to publish any of the prize winners.
Prizes 1st £500; 2nd £300; 3rd £100.

Macmillan Silver Pen Award

The English Centre of International PEN, 7 Dilke Street, London SW3 4JE
☎ 01–352 6303

An annual award, from nomination by PEN Executive Committee, for an outstanding novel written in English by a British author and published in the UK in the year preceding the prize.
1988 winner: A. L. Barker *The Gooseboy*; 1987 winner: Lewis Nkosi *Mating Birds*.
Prize £500 plus Silver Pen

The Mail on Sunday Novel Competition

Mail on Sunday, Temple House, Temple Avenue, London EC4Y 0JA
☎ 01–353 6000

Annual award, now in its sixth year. Judges look for a character who springs to life in the story.
1988 winners: Bronya Ralley, Kate Smith, Elizabeth Baxter.
Award 1st £400 book tokens; 2nd £300 tokens; 3rd £200 tokens; runners-up £150 tokens.

Arthur Markham Memorial Prize

University of Sheffield, Western Bank, Sheffield S10 2TN
☎ 0742 768555

Contact *Registrar & Secretary*

There are six categories for work specially

written for this annual prize: short story, essay, group of poems, prose account, one-act play, first chapter of a novel on a given subject announced annually. Candidates must be manual workers at a coal mine or have been injured when so employed.
Prize £200

Emil Kurt Maschler Award

Book Trust, Book House, 45 East Hill,
London SW18 2QZ
☎ 01–870 9055

For 'a work of imagination in the children's field in which text and illustration are of excellence and so presented that each enhances, yet balances the other'. Books published in the current year in the UK by a British author and/or artist, or by someone resident for ten years are eligible.
1988 winner: Anthony Browne *Alice's Adventures in Wonderland.*
Award £1000

Somerset Maugham Trust Fund

The Society of Authors, 84 Drayton Gardens,
London SW10 9SB
☎ 01–373 6642

The annual competitive awards arising from this Fund are designed to encourage young writers to travel and to acquaint themselves with the manners and customs of other countries. Candidates must be under 35 and submit a published literary work in volume form in English. They must be British subjects by birth. Final entry date 31 December. Presentation in June.
1988 winners: Jimmy Burns, Carol Ann Duffy, Matthew Kneale.
Award £4000 each

Enid McLeod Literary Prize

Franco–British Society, Room 636, Linen Hall,
162–8 Regent Street, London W1R 5TB

An annual award for a full length work of literature which contributes most to Franco–British understanding. It must be written in English by a citizen of the UK, Commonwealth, the Republic of Ireland, Pakistan or South Africa, and first published in the UK.
Previous winner: Piers Paul Read *The Free Frenchman.*
Prize £100

McVitie's Prize for Scottish Writer of the Year

Michael Kelly Associates, Scottish Legal
Building, 95 Bothwell Street, Glasgow G2 7HY
☎ 041–204 2580

Contact *Alan Clark*

ESTABLISHED 1987. Sponsored by United Biscuits. Imaginative works in English, Scots, or Gaelic, including TV and film scripts. Eligible to writers born or now working in Scotland.
1988 prize shared by Bernard MacLaverty *The Great Profundo* & Edwin Mickleburgh *Beyond the Frozen Sea.*
Prize £5000

MIND Book of the Year – The Allen Lane Award

MIND, 22 Harley Street, London W1N 2ED
☎ 01–637 0741

INAUGURATED 1981, this annual award in memory of Sir Allen Lane, is given to the author of the book, fiction or non-fiction, which furthers public understanding of mental illess, published in the current year.
1988 winner: J. Bernlef *Out of Mind*, trans. from the Dutch by Adrienne Dixon.
Award £1000

Mitchell Prize for the History of Art

21st Floor, 595 Madison Avenue,
New York NY 10022

Contact *Everett Fahy*

There are two annual prizes, one to the author of an outstanding original contribution in English to art history assessed in terms of scholarly, critical and literary merit, and the second to the most promising first book fulfilling the same criteria. Books should have been published in the 18 months preceding presentation date in USA (1 August 1990).
Previous winners: Lee Johnson *The Paintings of Eugene Delacroix*; Cecilia Powell *Turner in the South.*
Prizes 1st $10,000; 2nd $3000

The Mobil Playwriting Competition for the Royal Exchange Theatre Company

Royal Exchange Theatre, St Ann's Square,
Manchester M2 7DH

Contact *The Mobile Playwriting Competition*

Awarded to an original full length play in

English. Entries should be submitted with a pseudonym and with a sealed envelope containing actual identity.
1988 winners: Michael Wall *Amongst the Barbarians*; Rod Williams *No Remission*; Keith Wood *Assuming the Role*; Michele Celeste *Hanging the President*.
Prizes 1st £10,000 with performance by **Royal Exchange Theatre Company** and publication by **Nick Hern Books**; joint 2nd £4000 each. International Prize £3000 for the best play by a foreign writer.
Also runs the **Michael Elliott Prize for the North West** for the best play with a North West setting by a North West writer.
Prize £3000

Scott Moncrieff Prize

The Translators' Association, 84 Drayton Gardens, London SW10 9SB
☎ 01–373 6642

An annual award for the best translation published by a British publisher during the previous year of French twentieth-century work of literary merit and general interest.
Previous winners: Robyn Marsack *Le Poisson-Scorpion* by Nicolas Bouvier;Barbara Wright *Grabinoulor* by Pierre Albert-Birot.
Prize £1500

The Mother Goose Award

Books for Children, Park House, Dollar Street, Cirencester, Glos GL7 2AN
☎ 0285 657081

Contact *Sally Grindley*

For the most exciting newcomer to British children's book illustration.
1988 winner: Emma Chichester Clark *Listen to This* compiled by Laura Cecil (Bodley Head).
Prize £1000 plus a bronze goose egg.

Shiva Naipaul Memorial Prize

The Spectator, 56 Doughty Street, London WC1N 2LL
☎ 01–405 1706

Contact *Julia Mount*

An annual competition for the writer best able to describe a visit to a foreign place or people; for the most acute and profound observation of cultures and/or scenes evidently alien to the writer. Submissions must be unpublished and no more than 4000 words.
Recent winners: William T. Vollmann and Sousa Jamba.
Prize £1000 plus publication in *The Spectator*.

National Poetry Competition

The Poetry Society, 21 Earl's Court Square, London SW5 9DE
☎ 01–373 7861

This is now the major annual poetry competition in Britain. The prizes are each awarded for an unpublished poem of less than 40 lines by anyone over the age of 16 who lives, works or studies in the UK or Republic of Ireland. There is an entry fee of £2 per poem, and a maximum entry of ten poems per writer. Further details and entry form available on receipt of an s.a.e.
Previous winners include Andrew Motion and Ian Duhig.
Prizes 1st £2000, plus publication in a special anthology produced by **The Poetry Society**; 2nd £1000, 3rd £500; plus smaller prizes.

NCR Book Award for Non-Fiction

NCR Book Award, 206 Marylebone Road, London NW1 6LY
☎ 01–725 8244

Contact *The Administrator*

ESTABLISHED 1987 (first award made in 1988), the NCR Book Award for Non-fiction is for a book written in English by a living writer from Britain, the Commonwealth or Republic of Ireland, and first published in the UK. Still the UK's most valuable book prize with a total of £29,500. Publishers only may submit titles, limited to three per imprint. The award will cover all areas of non-fiction except academic, guide books and practical listings (such as cookery books). Titles must be published in the 12 months between 1 April and 31 March. A shortlist of four books will be announced in mid-April and the winning book in mid-May. The aim of the award is to stimulate interest in non-fiction writing, reading and publishing in the UK.
1988 winners: 1st David Thomson *Nairn in Darkness and Light*; runners-up Claire Tomalin *Katherine Mansfield: A Secret Life*; Max Hastings *The Korean War*; Kathleen Tynan *The Life of Kenneth Tynan*; Michael Ignatieff *The Russian Album*; Nirad C. Chaudhuri *Thy Hand, Great Anarch!*
Prizes 1st £25,000; three runners-up on shortlist £1000.

Nobel Prize

c/o The Swedish Embassy, 11 Montagu Place,
London W1
☏ 01–724 2101

Contact *Cultural Attaché*

Allocated yearly to outstanding achievement in science, peace-making and literature. Founded by Alfred Nobel, a chemist who proved his creative ability by inventing dynamite. British winners of the literature prize, first granted in 1901, include Rudyard Kipling, John Galsworthy and Winston Churchill.
Recent winners: Wole Soyinka (Nigeria) 1986; Joseph Brodski (USA) 1987 and Naguib Mahfouz (Egypt) 1988.
The current value of the prize is around $415,000 and this increases by 15% each year.

Observer National Children's Poetry Competition

Observer Magazine, Chelsea Bridge House,
Queenstown Road, London SW8 4NN
☏ 01–627 0700 ext. 3472

Contact *Janet Briggs*

An annual award which takes place in the spring. Young people aged up to 18 may enter poems on any theme. Details are announced in the *Observer* Magazine and are also sent out to schools around the country. In 1989 the panel of judges was led by Poet Laureate Ted Hughes.
Prizes (total) £4000 (including a £1000 school prize).

The Odd Fellows (Manchester Unity)/Friendly Society's Social Concern Book Awards

Book Trust, Book House, 45 East Hill,
London SW18 2QZ
☏ 01–870 9055

An annual award for a book or pamphlet of not less than 10,000 words within a specified area of social concern (varies each year). Entries must have been published in the current year in English and been written by citizens of the Commonwealth, Republic of Ireland, Pakistan or South Africa.
1989 winner: Tessa Lorant Warburg *A Voice at Twilight.*
Award £2000

Outposts Poetry Competition

PO Box 120, Sutton, Surrey SM2 5WG

Contact *Roland John*

Annual competition for an unpublished poem of not more than 40 lines.
Prize c.£1000

Catherine Pakenham Award

Evening Standard, Northcliffe House, 2 Derry Street, London W8 5EE
☏ 01–938 6000

Contact *Managing Editor*

FOUNDED 1970, this is an annual award in memory of Lady Catherine Pakenham, and given for a published or unpublished article (of up to 2500 words) or radio or TV script (but not a short story) by women aged between 18 and 30 involved in or intending to take up a career in journalism.
1987 winner: Amanda Craig.
Previous winners include: Jaci Stephen (*Standard*); Sharon Maxwell (*Cosmopolitan*).
Award £500

Parents Magazine Best Book for Babies Award

Book Trust, Book House, 45 East Hill,
London SW18 2QZ
☏ 01–870 9055

An annual award for the best book for the under-fours (babies and toddlers) published in Britain in the year ending 31 May.
1988 winner: Sarah Pooley *Day of Rhymes.*
Award £1000

The Portico Prize

The Portico Library, 57 Mosley Street,
Manchester M2 3HY
☏ 061–236 6785

Contact *Mrs Janet Allan*

Administered by the Portico Library in Manchester. Awarded for a work of fiction or non-fiction set wholly or mainly in the North West/ Cumbria.
Joint 1988 winners: John Stalker *Stalker*; Margaret Simey *Democracy Rediscovered: A Study of Police Accountability.*
Prize £1500

Pulitzer Prizes

The Pulitzer Prize Board, 702 Journalism, Columbia University, New York NY 10027

Contact *The Secretary*

Awards for journalism, letters, drama and music in US newspapers, and in literature, drama and music by Americans. Deadline February 1 (journalism); March 14 (music & drama); November 11 (letters). 1988 winners (Fiction) Toni Morrison *Beloved*; (Non-fiction) Richard Rhodes *The Making of the Atomic Bomb.*

Radio Times Drama Awards

BBC Publications, PO Box 1AX, 33 Marylebone High Street, London W1 1AX
☎ 01–580 5577

Contact *The Administrator*

Biennial award (even years) for an original work for either radio or television not previously performed in public. Each entry to be supported by a sponsor experienced in production. Details of awards are announced in *Radio Times* in January.
Award £7500 in each category.

Radio Times Radio Comedy Awards

BBC Publications, PO Box 1AX, 33 Marylebone High Street, London W1 1AX
☎ 01–580 5577

Contact *The Administrator*

Biennial award (odd years) for an original 30-minute script capable of being developed into a series. Details of awards announced in *Radio Times* in January.
Awards total £5000

John Llewellyn Rhys Memorial Prize

Book Trust, Book House, 45 East Hill, London SW18 2QZ
☎ 01–870 9055

An annual award for a memorable work of any kind by a writer who is under the age of 35 at the time of publication. Books must have been published in the UK in the year of the award, and the author must be a citizen of Britain or the Commonwealth writing in English.
1988 winner: Mathew Yorke *The March Fence.*
Prize £500

Romantic Novelists' Association Major Award

Dove House Farm, Potter Heigham, Norfolk NR29 5LJ
☎ 0692 670727

Contact *Olga Sinclair*

Annual award now sponsored by Boots the Chemist for the best romantic novel of the year, open to non-members as well as members of the **Romantic Novelists' Association**. Novels must be published between 16 December of previous year and 15 December of the year of entry.
1989 winner: Sarah Woodhouse *The Peacock's Feather.*
1988 winner: Audrey Howard *The Juniper Bush.*
Award £5000

Romantic Novelists' Association/ Netta Muskett Award

20 First Avenue, Amersham, Bucks HP7 9BJ
☎ 0494 727202

Contact *Mrs Dorothy Entwistle*

The award is for unpublished writers in the field of the romantic novel who must join the **Romantic Novelists' Association** as Probationary Members. Mss entered for this award must be specifically written for it.

Royal Society of Literature Awards

see under **Heinemann Bequest** and **Winifred Holtby**.

Runciman Award

Book Trust, Book House, 45 East Hill, London SW18 2QZ
☎ 01–870 9055

INSTITUTED 1985, an annual award by the Anglo-Hellenic League and sponsored by the Onassis Foundation, for a literary work wholly or mainly about Greece. The book may be fiction, poetry, drama or non-fiction and to be eligible must be published in its first English edition in the UK.
Award £1000

Ian St James Awards

c/o Collins Publishers, 8 Grafton Street, London W1X 3LA
☎ 01–493 7070

INITIATED 1989. Presented to 12 previously unpublished authors for short stories of between 5–10,000 words. Administered by Collins who

describe it as 'an opportunity for talented and as yet unpublished writers to achieve recognition'. Ian St James is a thriller writer – it is he who is funding the awards and he hopes to attract both literary and commercial stories. It should be noted here though that Rule 6 states: 'Copyright in the 12 award winning manuscripts will become the property of the Ian St James Trust upon payment of the appropriate prize money to the winning authors.' Winning entries will be published in a paperback anthology by Collins/ Fontana in the spring. Closing date end May.
Award (total amount) £28,000

Schlegel-Tieck Prize

The Translators' Association, 84 Drayton Gardens, London SW10 9SB
☎ 01–373 6642

Contact *Kate Pool*

An annual award for the best translation of a German twentieth-century work of literary merit and interest published by a British publisher during the preceding year.
1988 winners: 1st Ralph Manheim *The Rat* by Günter Grass; 2nd Michael Hoffman *The Double-Bass* by Patrick Suskind.
Prize £2000

Scottish Arts Council Book Awards

Scottish Arts Council, 19 Charlotte Square, Edinburgh EH2 4DF
☎ 031–226 6051

Contact *Literature Department*

A number of awards are given biennially to authors of published books in recognition of high standards in new writing as well as work of established writers. Authors should be Scottish, resident in Scotland or writing books of Scottish interest.
Previous winners include: G. F. Dutton *Squaring the Waves*; James Kelman *Greyhound for Breakfast*; Andro Linklater *Compton Mackenzie: A Life*; Brian McCabe *One Atom to Another*.
Award £750 each

SCSE Book Prizes

School of Education, University of Durham, Leazes Road, Durham DH1 1TA
☎ 091–374 2000

Contact *Dr Batho*

Annual awards given by the Standing Conference on Studies in Education for the best book on education published during the preceding year – by nomination from members of the Standing Conference and publishers.
Prizes £1000 and £500

Signal Poetry for Children Award

Thimble Press, Lockwood, Station Road, South Woodchester, Stroud GL5 5EQ
☎ 0453 873716/2208

Contact *Nancy Chambers*

This award is given annually for particular excellence in one of the following areas: single poetry collections published for children; poetry anthologies published for children; the body of work of a contemporary poet; critical or educational activity promoting poetry for children. All books for children published in Britain are eligible regardless of the original country of publication. Unpublished work is not eligible.
1988: John Mole *Boo to a Goose*, illustrated by Mary Norman.
Award £100

André Simon Memorial Fund Book Awards

61 Church Street, Isleworth, Middlesex TW7 6BE
☎ 01–560 6662

Contact *Tessa Hayward*

Two awards are given annually for the best book on drink and the best on food.
Award £1500; £100 to shortlisted books.

Smarties Prize for Children's Books

Book Trust, Book House, 45 East Hill, London SW18 2QZ
☎ 01–870 9055

ESTABLISHED 1985 to encourage high standards and stimulate interest in books for children, this prize is given for a children's book written in English by a citizen of the UK or an author resident in the UK, and published in the UK in the year ending 31 October. There are three age-group categories: under 5; 6–8 and 9–11. An overall winner from these categories is chosen for the Grand Prix.
1988 Grand Prix winners: Martin Waddell *Can't You Sleep Little Bear?* ill. by Barbara Firth; Susan Hill *Can It Be True?* ill. by Angela Barrett; Theresa Whistler *Rushavenn Time*.
Prizes £8000 (Grand Prix); £1000 (other categories).

W. H. Smith Literary Award

W. H. Smith, 7 Holbein Place,
London SW1W 8NR
☎ 01–730 1200 ext. 5458

Contact *Public Relations*

Annual prize awarded to a UK, Republic of Ireland or Commonwealth citizen for the most oustanding contribution to English literature, published in English in UK in the preceding year.
1989 winner: Dr Christopher Hill *A Turbulent, Seditious and Factious People.*
Previous winners include: Robert Hughes, Doris Lessing, David Hughes, Philip Larkin, Elizabeth Jennings.
Prize £10,000

W. H. Smith Young Writers' Competition

W. H. Smith, 7 Holbein Place,
London SW1W 8NR
☎ 01–730 1200 ext. 5458

Contact *Public Relations*

Annual awards for poems or prose by anyone in the UK under the age of 17. There are three age groups. Sixty-three individual prize-winners have their work included in a paperback every year.
Prize £4000 (Total amount)

Southern Arts Literature Prize

Southern Arts, 19 Southgate Street, Winchester,
Hants SO23 9DQ
☎ 0962 55099

Contact *Literature Officer*

This prize is awarded annually to an author living in the Southern Arts Region who has made the most notable contribution to literature during the year in published fiction, poetry or collection of short stories, or non-fiction.
1988 winner: David Constantine *Madder.*
Prize £1000

The Spectator Young Writer Awards

The Spectator, 56 Doughty Street,
London WC1 2LL
☎ 01–405 1706

An annual competition for aspiring journalists – must be under 25 on 31 Jan. Submissions should be less than 2000 words on a subject of your choice, and suitable for publication in *The Spectator*. Use of a pen name will invalidate the entry. Entry form obtained from above address.
Prizes generous, but vary from year to year depending on sponsors.
The winning article will be published in *The Spectator* and the writer will be commissioned to compose another piece for publication.

Stand Magazine Short Story Competition

Stand Magazine, 179 Wingrove Road,e
Newcastl upon Tyne NE4 9DA
☎ 091–273 3280

Contact *The Administrator*

Biennial award (odd years) for a short story written in English and not published, broadcast or under consideration elsewhere.
Prize £2250 total prize money.

The Winifred Mary Stanford Prize

Hodder & Stoughton, 47 Bedford Square,
London WC1B 3DP
☎ 01–636 9851

This biennial award (even years) is open to any book published in the UK in English which has been in some way inspired by the Christian faith, and written by a man or woman who is under 50 years of age at the time of publication. Literary merit is a prime factor in consideration for the award, but the subject may be from a wide range including poetry, fiction, biography, autobiography, biblical exposition, religious experience and witness. Submission is invited, from publishers only, of books published in the two years prior to the award which is presented at Easter.
Prize £1000

Sunday Express Book of the Year Award

INITIATED 1988. An award for a work of fiction published in the current year. Books are nominated by a panel of judges which invites entries from publishers.
1989 winner: David Lodge *Nice Work*; 1988 winner: Brian Moore *The Colour of Blood.*
Prize £20,000

The Sunday Times Award for Small Publishers

c/o Book Trust, Book House, 45 East Hill,
London SW18 2QZ
☎ 01–870 9055

Contact *Sarah Morgan*

Open to any publisher producing between five

and forty titles a year, which must primarily be original titles, not reprints. Takes place at the beginning of the year when entrants are invited to submit their catalogues for the last twelve months, together with two representative titles. INITIATED in 1988, the first winner was **Fourth Estate**, against strong competition from over 100 entrants.
1989 winner: **Serpent's Tail** – who were presented with £1000 at the *Sunday Times* Literary Banquet in April.

The Sunday Times Special Award for Excellence in Writing

The Sunday Times, 1 Pennington Street, London E1 9XN
☎ 01–782 7000

Contact *Penny Perrick*

INITIATED 1987. Annual award to fiction and non-fiction writers who have not received sufficient recognition. The panel consists of *Sunday Times* journalists, publishers and other figures from the book world.
Previous winners: Anthony Burgess and Seamus Heaney.
Award – whatever the recipient would like – 1988 winner Seamus Heaney asked for a photocopier to be installed in his County Wexford home!

E. Reginald Taylor Essay Competition

Journal of the British Archaeological Association, Institute of Archaeology, 36 Beaumont Street, Oxford OX1 2PG

Contact *Honorary Editor*

An annual prize, in memory of the late E. Reginald Taylor FSA, for the best unpublished essay, not exceeding 7500 words, on a subject of archaeological, art history or antiquarian interest within the period from the Roman era to AD 1830. The essay should show *original* research on its chosen subject, and the author will be invited to read the essay before the Association. In addition, the essay may be published in the Journal of the Association if approved by the Editorial Committee.
Prize £100

Dylan Thomas Award

The Poetry Society, 21 Earl's Court Square, London SW5 9DE
☎ 01–373 7861

An annual award given in alternate years for poetry and short stories, established in 1983 to commemorate Dylan Thomas and encourage the two forms in which he made his outstanding contribution to literature. This is open to all published writers in the UK (all entrants must have had poetry or short stories published within two years of submission). Entries must include published work, but unpublished work may also be included.
1988 winner: John Murray *Master of Ceremonies.*
Prize £1000

Time-Life Silver PEN Award (for non-fiction)

English Centre of International PEN, 7 Dilke Street, London SW3 4JE
☎ 01–352 6303

An annual award, the winner being nominated by the PEN Executive Committee, for an outstanding work of non-fiction written in English and published in England in the year preceding the prize.
1988 winner: John Miller *Friends and Romans: On the Run in Wartime Italy.*
Prize £500 plus silver pen.

Times Educational Supplement Information Book Awards

Times Educational Supplement, Priory House, St John's Lane, London EC1M 4BX
☎ 01–253 3000

Contact *Literary Editor*

There are two annual awards made for Best Information Books, one for the age range 10–16, and another for children up to the age of 9. Books must have been published in Britain or the Commonwealth in the year preceding the award.
1988 winner of the Senior Information Book Award: *Martin Luther King* from the series *People who have helped the World.*
Award £500 (each category)
Also, a third award for Best School Textbook, with age and subject range variable from year to year.
Award £500

Times Literary Supplement/ Cheltenham Literature Festival Poetry Competition

Poetry Competition, Town Hall, Cheltenham, Gloucestershire GL50 1QA
☎ 0242 521621

Annual competition for an unpublished poem of fifty lines in English. Organised as part of the Cheltenham Literature Festival. Fifty shortlisted poems published anonymously in the Times Literary Supplement for a readers' ballot. Details and entry forms from the above address (s.a.e. required). Previous winners include John Fuller, Seamus Heaney, Derek Mahon, Edwin Morgan, Richard Murphy, Sylvia Plath, Craig Raine.
Prizes Readers' choices £500, £250, £100; Judges' choices £500, £250, £100

The Tir Na N-Og Award

Welsh National Centre for Children's Literature, c/o Welsh Books Council, Castell Brychan, Aberystwyth, Dyfed SY23 2JB
☎ 0970 624151

An annual award given to the best original book published for children in the year prior to the announcement. There are two categories: The Best Welsh book and The Best English book with an authentic Welsh background.
Award £500 (each category)

Marten Toonder Award

The Arts Council (An Chomhairle Ealaíon), 70 Merrion Square, Dublin 2, Eire
☎ 0001 611840

Contact *Literature Officer*

A triennial award for creative writers.
Award £3000 (most recent award 1989)

The Betty Trask Awards

The Society of Authors, 84 Drayton Gardens, London SW10 9SB
☎ 01–373 6642

These annual awards are for authors who are under 35 and Commonwealth citizens, awarded on the strength of a first novel (published or unpublished) of a traditional or romantic (rather than experimental) nature. The awards must be used for a period or periods of foreign travel. Final entry date 31 January. Presentation June. 1988 winners: Alex Martin, Candia McWilliam (£6500 each); Georgina Andrewes, James Friel, Glenn Patterson, Susan Webster (£2000 each).
Award £21,000 total prize money.

TSB Peninsula Prize

South West Arts, Bradninch Place, Gandy Street, Exeter EX4 3LS
☎ 0392 218188

Contact *Literature Officer*

An annual award for unpublished works of literature submitted by anyone who is resident in or who can demonstrate strong links with the region served by South West Arts and TSB South West region, i.e. Avon, Berkshire, Cornwall, Devon Dorset, Gloucestershire, Hampshire, Isle of Wight, Oxfordshire, Somerset, West Sussex and Wiltshire.
1988 winner: Steve May *Keeping Faith*.
Prize £1500 plus £1000 advance on royalties, plus additional prizes to value of £1000.

Unicorn Theatre, Young Playwright's Competition

Unicorn Theatre for Children, Arts Theatre, Great Newport Street, London WC2H 7JB
☎ 01–379 3280

Contact *Dorothy Wooder*

Annual awards to young playwrights aged 4–12 years old for plays on a theme decided by the theatre. Entries by the end of December. Three age groups: 4–6; 7–9; 10–12. The plays are judged by a committee of writers and the winners take part in workshops on the plays with members of the Unicorn Theatre Club before performances on stage the following spring.

T. E. Utley Award

The Secretary, T. E. Utley Memorial Fund, 60 St Mary's Mansions, St Mary's Terrace, London W2 1SX

Contact *The Secretary*

Open to writers under 35 years of age for a work of originality in political thought of any colour. Closing date late April. Applicants should contact the Secretary in the first instance for details of presentation.
Award £5000

Ver Poets Open Competition

Haycroft, 61–3 Chiswell Green Lane, St Albans, Herts AL2 3AG
☎ 0727 67005

Contact *May Badman*

An annual competition for unpublished poems of no more than 30 lines written in English. Final entry date end April. Entry fee £1.50 per poem. An anthology of winning/selected poems as well as the adjudicators' report is normally available from mid June.

Prizes £1000 total (£500, £300 and two prizes of £100).

Verbatim Essay Competition

Verbatim, PO Box 199, Aylesbury,
Bucks HP20 1TQ
☎ 0296 27314

Contact *Hazel Hall*

Awarded for original popular articles on any aspect of language, in English, and not more than 1500 words.
Prizes 1st $1000; 2nd $500 and four prizes of $250.

Wandsworth Writers London Competition

Town Hall, Wandsworth High Street,
London SW18 2PU
☎ 01–871 6364

Contact *Assistant Director of Leisure and Amenity Services* (Libraries, Museums & Arts)

An annual competition, open to all writers of 16 and over who live, work or study in the Greater London Area. There are three categories, all for previously unpublished work, in poetry, plays and the short story.
Prize £775 (the total for each class; it's divided between the top three in each category.)

The David Watt Memorial Prize

RTZ Ltd, 6 St James's Square, London SW1Y 4LD

INITIATED 1987 to commemorate the life and work of David Watt. Annual award, open to writers currently engaged in writing for newspapers and journals, in the English language, on international and political affairs. The winners are judged as having made 'outstanding contributions towards the clarification of international and political issues and the promotion of a greater understanding of such issues'.
Prize £2000

Welsh Arts Council Prizes

Welsh Arts Council, Museum Place,
Cardiff CF1 3NX
☎ 0222 394711

Contact *Tony Bianchi*

Annual, non-competitive prizes presented for works of exceptional merit by Welsh authors (by birth or residence) published in Welsh or English during the previous calendar year. There are five prizes for each language in the following categories: poetry, fiction, non-fiction, literary criticism and young writer.
Prize £1000 (each)

Whitbread Book of the Year/ Whitbread Literary Awards

The Booksellers Association of Great Britain & Ireland, 154 Buckingham Palace Road,
London SW1W 9TZ
☎ 01–730 8214

Contact *Andrea Livingstone*

Publishers are invited to submit books for this annual competition designed at writers who have been resident in Great Britain or the Republic of Ireland for five years or more. The awards are made in two stages. Firstly nominations are selected in five categories: novel, first novel, biography, children's novel and poetry. One of these is then voted by the panel of judges as Whitbread Book of the Year.
1988 winners: A.N. Wilson *Tolstoy* (Biography); Peter Porter *The Automatic Oracle* (Poetry); Judy Allen *Awaiting Developments* (Children's); Paul Sayer *The Comforts of Madness* (First Novel and Book of the Year); Salman Rushdie *The Satanic Verses* (Novel).
Awards £20,000 (Book of the Year); £1500 (all nominees).

Whitfield Prize

Royal Historical Society, University College
London, Gower Street, London WC1E 6BT
☎ 01–387 7532

Contact *Literary Director*

An annual award for the best work on English or Welsh history by an author under 40, published in the UK in the preceding calendar year.
Prize £1000

John Whiting Award

Arts Council of Great Britain, 105 Piccadilly,
London W1V 0AU
☎ 01–629 9495

Contact *The Drama Director*

FOUNDED 1965. Annual award to commemorate the life and work of the playwright John Whiting (*The Devils, A Penny for a Song*). Any writer who has received during the previous two calendar years an award through the Arts Council's Theatre Writing Schemes or who has had a première production by a theatre company in receipt of annual subsidy is eligible to apply.

1989 winner: Ian Heggie *American Bagpipes*.
Prize £4000

Mary Wilkins Memorial Poetry Competition

Birmingham & Midland Institute, 9 Margaret Street, Birmingham B3 3BS
☎ 021–236 3591

Contact *Mr Hunt* (The Administrator)

An annual competition for an unpublished poem not exceeding 40 lines, written in English by an author over the age of 15 and living, working or studying in the UK. The poem should not have been entered for any other poetry competition.
Prize £200 (total of four prizes)

H. H. Wingate Prize

Book Trust, Book House, 45 East Hill, London SW18 2QZ
☎ 01–870 9055

An annual award of two prizes (one for fiction, one for non-fiction) for the books which best stimulate an interest in and awareness of themes of Jewish interest. Books must have been published in the UK in the year of the award and be written in English by an author resident in Britain, Commonwealth, Israel, Pakistan, Republic of Ireland or South Africa.
1988 winners: Amos Oz *Black Box* (fiction); Anton Gill *The Journey Back from Hell* (Non-fiction).
Prize £2000 (each category)

Wolfson History Awards

Wolfson Foundation, 251–6 Tottenham Court Road, London W1A 1BZ

Contact *The Director, Wolfson Foundation*

FOUNDED 1972. Two awards totalling £15,000 made annually to authors of published historical works of oustanding scholarship and literary quality. No 1988 winner.
1987 winners: Professor R. R. Davies *Conquest, Co-existence and Change – Wales 1063–1415*; Dr John Pemble *The Mediterranean Passion*.

Yeats Club Awards

The Yeats Club, PO Box 271, Oxford OX2 6DU

FOUNDED 1986. Twice yearly competition for original poetry in English. Send s.a.e. for entry form.
Prize Grand prize £250; 1st prize £100; 2nd prize £50; other awards at the discretion of the judges.

Yorkshire Post Art and Music Awards

Yorkshire Post, PO Box 168, Wellington Street, Leeds LS1 1RF
☎ 0532 432701 ext. 512

Contact *Glenys Miles*

Two annual awards made to authors whose work has contributed most to the understanding and appreciation of art and music. Books should have been published in the preceding year in the UK.
Previous winners: Winton Dean & John Merrill Knapp *Handel's Operas*; James King *Interior Landscapes: A Life of Paul Nash*.
Award £800 each – one for art, one for music.

Yorkshire Post Best First Work Awards

Yorkshire Post, PO Box 168, Wellington Street, Leeds LS1 1RF
☎ 0532 432701 ext. 512

Contact *Glenys Miles*

An annual award for a work by a new author published during the preceding year.
Prize £800

Yorkshire Post Book of the Year Award

Yorkshire Post, PO Box 168, Wellington Street, Leeds LS1 1RF
☎ 0532 432701 ext. 512

Contact *Glenys Miles*

An annual award for the book (either fiction or non-fiction) which, in the opinion of the judges, is the best work published in the preceding year.
1988 winner: William Trevor *The Silence in the Garden*.
Prize £1000

Library Services

Bank of England Reference Library

Threadneedle Street, London EC2R 8AH
☎ 01–601 4715 Telex 885001

Open 9.30 am to 5.00 pm Monday to Friday

Access for research workers by prior arrangement only, when material is not readily available elsewhere.

50,000 volumes of books and periodicals. 3000 periodicals taken. UK and overseas coverage of banking, finance and economics. *Special collections* Central bank reports; UK 17th–19th century economic tracts; Government reports in the field of banking.

BBC Data Enquiry Service

Room 7, 1 Portland Place, London W1A 1AA
☎ 01–927 5998 Fax 01–637 0398

Open 9.00 am to 8.00 pm Monday to Friday

Access Telephone or written enquiries only.

The Enquiry Service is a fee-based information broker. It was set up in 1981 to draw on the extensive information resources of the BBC and works solely for clients from outside the Corporation. The resources include press cuttings and reference libraries whose main strengths are arts and entertainment; biographical information; industrial information; political affairs; political, economic, social events; and world affairs.

British Architectural Library

Royal Institute of British Architects, 66 Portland Place, London W1N 4AD
☎ 01–580 5533 Fax 01–255 1541

Open Monday to Saturday from 10.00 am, closing Monday 5.00 pm, Tuesday, Wednesday, Thursday 8.00 pm, Friday 7.00 pm, Saturday 1.30 pm

Access Open to the general public. 90% of the library is reference and only RIBA members are allowed to borrow from the small reference section.

Collection of drawings, manuscripts, photographs and 400 indexed periodicals. All aspects of architecture, current and historical. Material both technical and aesthetic, covering related fields including: interior design, landscape architecture, topography, the construction industry and applied arts. Brochure available; queries by telephone, letter or in person.

British Film Institute

21 Stephen Street, London W1P 1PL
☎ 01–225 1444 Fax 01–436 7950

Open 10.30 am to 5.00 pm Monday, Tuesday, Thursday, Friday; 1.30 pm to 8.00 pm Wednesday

Open access for reference to BFI members

A vast library of books, pamphlets, newspaper clippings, scripts and other memorabilia relating to the cinema and all its aspects (including video and television).

The British Library Business Information Service

25 Southampton Buildings, Chancery Lane, London WC2A 1AW
☎ 01–323 7979 (Priced Enquiry Service), 01–323 7454 (Free) Fax 01–323 7453
Telex 266959 BT Gold (81) BLI404

Priced Enquiry Service open 10.00 am to 5.00 pm Monday to Friday

Free Service open 9.30 am to 5.00 pm Monday to Friday

Library open 9.30 am to 9.00 pm Monday to Friday; 10.00 am to 1.00 pm Saturday

Open access

A resource facility for those engaged in all aspects of business, an invaluable reference source for specialist journalists.

The British Library India Office Library and Records

197 Blackfriars Road, London SE1 8NG
☎ 01-928 9531 Fax 01-928 9531 ext. 279

Open 9.30 am to 6.00 pm Monday to Friday; 9.30 am to 1.00 pm Saturday

Open access for reference purposes. Long term use and loans to members only.

Contains an extensive stock of printed books, prints, drawings, photographs and manuscripts related to Indological and modern South Asian studies. Large collection of manuscripts in Arabic, Persian, Sanskrit and Tibetan languages. The Records comprise the archives of the East India Company, Board of Control, India Office and Burma Office (1600–1948). *Guide to the India Office Library* by S.C. Sutton is available to researchers.

The British Library Information Sciences Service (successor to The Library Association Library)

7 Ridgmount Street, London WC1E 7AE
☎ 01-323 7688

Open 9.00 am to 6.00 pm Monday, Wednesday, Friday; 9.00 am to 8.00 pm Tuesday and Thursday (9.00 am to 6.00 pm from mid July–September Monday to Friday)

Open access for reference (loans to members of the Association or by British Library form)

Provides British and foreign reference material on librarianship, information science and related subjects. *Special collections* Historical library annual reports and theses on librarianship. Strong on books and all stages of their production.

The British Library Manuscripts Department

Great Russell Street, London WC1B 3DG
☎ 01-323 7508 Fax 01-323 7039

Open 10.00 am to 4.45 pm Monday to Saturday (closed Public Holidays and second week of November)

Access to reading facilities by Reader's Pass

A useful publication, *The British Library: Guide to the catalogues and indexes of the Department of Manuscripts* by M.A.E. Nickson is available (£1.95) to guide the researcher through this vast collection of manuscripts dating from Ancient Greece to the present day. Approximately 85,000 volumes are housed here.

The British Library Map Library

Great Russell Street, London WC1B 3DG
☎ 01-323 7700

Open 9.30 am to 4.30 pm Monday to Saturday

Access by British Library Reader's Pass or Map Library Pass. Application in person, with proof of identity.

A collection of 1.5 million charts, globes and maps, with particular reference to the history of British cartography. Maps for all parts of the world at wide range of scales and dates. *Special collections* King George III Maritime Collection and Topographical Collection, and the Crace Collection of maps and plans of London. Also satellite pictures of all areas of the world.

The British Library Music Library

Great Russell Street, London WC1B 3DG
☎ 01-323 7527

Open 9.30 am to 4.45 pm Monday, Friday, Saturday; 9.30 am to 6.45 pm Tuesday, Wednesday, Thursday

Access by British Library Reader's Pass

Special collections the Royal Music Library (containing almost all Handel's surviving autographed scores) and the Paul Hirsch Music Library. Also a large collection (about one and a quarter million items) of printed music, British and foreign.

The British Library National Sound Archive

29 Exhibition Road, London SW7 2AS
☎ 01-589 6603

Open 10.00 am to 5.00 pm Monday to Friday (Thursday till 9.00 pm)

Open access

Listening service (by appointment) 10.00 am to 5.00 pm Monday to Friday (Thursday till 9.00 pm)

Northern Listening Service at British Library Document Supply Centre, Boston Spa, West Yorkshire. **Open** 9.15 am to 4.30 pm Monday to Friday, ☎ 0937 843434

An archive of over half a million discs and over 45,000 hours of tape recordings including all types of music, oral history, drama, wildlife, selected BBC broadcasts and BBC Sound Archive material.

The British Library Newspaper Library

Colindale Avenue, London NW9 5HE
☏ 01–323 7353

Open 10.00 am to 4.45 pm Monday to Saturday. Last newspaper issue 4.15 pm.

Access by British Library Reader's Pass or Newspaper Library Reader's Pass (available from and valid only for Colindale Avenue). Readers are advised to check availability of newspapers in advance as the Library is very popular.

English provincial, Scottish, Irish, Commonwealth and foreign newspapers from *c.*1700 are housed here. London newspapers from 1801 and most large weekly periodicals are also in stock. (London newspapers pre-dating this are housed in Great Russell Street.)

The British Library Official Publications and Social Sciences Service

Great Russell Street, London WC1B 3DG
☏ 01–323 7536/4207

Open 9.30 am to 4.45 pm Monday, Friday and Saturday; 9.30 am to 8.45 pm Tuesday, Wednesday and Thursday

Access by British Library Reader's Pass

Provides access to current and historical official publications from all countries, plus publications of intergovernmental bodies. Also House of Commons Sessional Papers from 1715; UK legislation; current UK electoral registers and up-to-date reference books on the social sciences with special emphasis on law.

The British Library Oriental and Printed Books Department

14 Store Street, London WC1E 7DG
☏ 01–323 7642/7658

Open 9.30 am to 5.00 pm Monday to Friday; 9.30 am to 1.00 pm Saturday (closed Sundays, Public Holidays and the last complete week of October)

Access to Oriental Reading Room by special pass

A comprehensive collection of printed volumes and manuscripts in the languages or related to the cultures of North Africa, the Near and Middle East and all of Asia.

The British Library Reading Room

Great Russell Street, London WC1B 3DG
☏ 01–636 1544 (Switchboard) 01–323 7678 (Admissions) 01–323 7676 (Bibliographical; holdings enquiries)

Open 9.00 am to 5.00 pm Monday, Friday and Saturday; 9.00 am to 9.00 pm Tuesday, Wednesday, Thursday (closed Sundays, Public Holidays and last week October)

Access by reader's pass

Large and comprehensive stock of books and periodicals relating to the humanities and social sciences for reference and research which cannot easily be done elsewhere. Also exhibitions on literary and historical figures and a permanent exhibition on the history of printing and binding. Telephone enquiries welcome. Leaflet *Applying for a reader's pass* available for guidance.

The British Library Science Reference and Information Service

25 Southampton Buildings, Chancery Lane, London WC2A 1AW
☏ 01–323 7494 Fax 01–323 7930

Open 9.30 am to 9.00 pm Monday to Friday; 10.00 am to 1.00 pm Saturday

Open access

The national library for modern science and technology providing an invaluable resource facility for technical journalists. Telephone enquiries welcome.

British Museum (Natural History) Library

Cromwell Road, London SW7 5BD
☏ 01–938 9191 Fax 01–938 9290

Open 10.00 am to 4.30 pm Monday to Friday

Access by reader's ticket which is issued to *bona fide* researchers on production of identification. The use of the library is free of charge.

The library is in five sections: general; botany; zoology; entomology; palaeontology/mineralogy. The sub-department of ornithology is at Zoological Museum, Akeman Street, Tring, Herts HP23 6AP (tel 0442 834181).
Resources available include books, journals, maps, manuscripts, drawings and photographs

covering all aspects of natural history, including palaeontology and mineralogy, from the 14th century to the present day. Also a historical collection on the Museum itself.

The British Psychological Society

c/o Psychology Library, University of London, Senate House, Mallet Street, London WC1E 7HU
☏ 01-636 4514

Open 9.30 am to 9.30 pm Monday to Thursday; 9.30 am to 6.30 pm Friday; 9.30 am to 5.30 pm Saturday

Access by day ticket available for reference purposes by arrangement

Contains the British Psychological Society collection of periodicals – over 140 titles and books on the subject, some of which are provided by London University. Largely for academic research. General queries referred to Swiss Cottage Public Library which has a very good psychology collection.

British Theatre Association/British Theatre Play Library

After its Arts Council grant was withdrawn, the library closed. It has since been saved by the Robert Holmes a-Court Foundation, and will be rehoused in Cranbourn Mansions, Cranbourn Street, London W1. No dates or other details available at present.

Catholic Central Library

47 Francis Street, London SW1P 1QR
☏ 01-834 6128

Open 10.00 am to 5.00 pm Monday to Friday; 10.00 am to 1.30 pm Saturday

Open access for reference purposes. Non-members must sign in. Members, who pay a subscription, may borrow books.

Contains books, many not readily available elsewhere, on theology, scripture, history of churches of all denominations, and religion worldwide. Also 140 periodicals.

Central Music Library

160 Buckingham Palace Road,
London SW1W 9UD
☏ 01-798 2192

Open 9.30 am to 7.00 pm Monday to Friday; 9.30 am to 5.00 pm Saturday

Open access

Extensive coverage of all aspects of music, including books, periodicals and printed scores.

Centre for Children's Books, Children's Reference Library

Book Trust, Book House, 45 East Hill,
London SW18 2QZ
☏ 01-870 9055

Open 9.00 am to 5.00 pm Monday to Friday

Open access for reference only

A comprehensive collection of children's literature and related books and periodicals. Aims to have all children's titles published within the last two years. An information service covers all aspects of children's literature, including profiles of authors and illustrators. Houses the Linder Collection of books and drawings by Beatrix Potter.

The City Business Library

Gillett House, 55 Basinghall Street,
London EC2V 5BX
☏ 01-638 8215/8216

Open 9.30 am to 5.00 pm Monday to Friday

Open access for reference purposes

Books, pamphlets, periodicals and newspapers of current business interest.

Commonwealth Institute

Kensington High Street, London W8 6NQ
☏ 01-603 4535

Educational Resource Centre open 10.00 am to 5.00 pm Monday to Saturday

Open access for reference purposes

Special collection Books and periodicals on Commonwealth countries.

Information Centre open 10.00 am to 5.00 pm Monday to Saturday

Open access for reference purposes

Large collection of directories and reference books on the Commonwealth. Information on political, social and economic affairs, art, cultural organisations and bibliography.

Commonwealth Secretariat Library

10 Carlton House Terrace, Pall Mall,
London SW1Y 5AH
☏ 01-839 3411 ext. 5013

Open 9.15 am to 5.15 pm Monday to Friday

Access open for reference by arrangement

Extensive reference source concerned with economy, development, trade, production and industry of Commonwealth countries; also sub-library specialising in human resources including women, development and education.

English Folk Dance and Song Society

Vaughan Williams Memorial Library, Cecil Sharp House, 2 Regent's Park Road, London NW1 7AY
☏ 01–485 2206

Open 9.30 am to 5.30 pm Monday to Friday

Access open for reference purposes to the general public on payment of a daily fee. Members may borrow books and use the library free of charge.

A multi-media collection: books, periodicals, manuscripts, tapes, records, films, videos. Mostly British folk culture and how this has developed around the world. Some foreign language material, and some books in English about foreign cultures. Also, the history of the English Folk Dance and Song Society.

Equal Opportunities Commission

Library, Overseas House, Quay Street, Manchester M3 3HN
☏ 061–833 9244 Fax 061–833 9244 ext. 350

Open 9.00 am to 5.00 pm Monday to Friday

Open access for reference purposes. Loans available.

Non-sexist children's books, languages and Equal Opportunities Commission publications. Also an information service with periodicals and press cuttings.

European Communities Commission Information Office

Abbey Buildings, 8 Storey's Gate, Westminster, London SW1 3AT
☏ 01–222 8122

Open 2.00 pm to 5.30 pm Monday to Friday

Open access for reference

Reference works on the European Community, plus copies of all EEC publications.

Farming Information Centre

National Farmers' Union, Agriculture House, Knightsbridge, London SW1X 7NJ
☏ 01–235 5077 Fax 01–235 3526

Open 10.00 am to 4.30 pm Monday to Friday

Open access for reference purposes but telephone first

The politics of agriculture rather than technical aspects. History, statistics since 1870, economics, union affairs. Also a picture library: farmland, machines.

Fawcett Library

City of London Polytechnic, Old Castle Street, London E1 7NT
☏ 01–283 1030

Open during term time 11.00 am to 8.30 pm Monday; 10.00 am to 5.00 pm Wednesday, Thursday, Friday (10.00 am to 5.00 pm Monday to Friday during vacations) **Closed** Tuesdays

Open access to non-Polytechnic members on payment either of annual membership fee: £10 (students/unwaged £5); or one-day fee: £2 (students/unwaged £1)

The leading library for feminist studies and research into all other aspects of women's history with emphasis on social sciences and the humanities. Contains extensive stocks of books, pamphlets, photographs and archive materials. Limited loans to members or via **British Library**. (The **Mary Evans Picture Library** (see entry, Picture Libraries) now acts as agent for the Fawcett Library's pictorial material.)

Fine Arts Library

Central Reference Library, St Martin's Lane, London WC2H 7HP
☏ 01–798 2038

Open 10.00 am to 7.00 pm Monday to Friday; 10.00 am to 5.00 pm Saturday

Access closed

Older books and periodicals earlier than 1970 are in storage and at least three days' notice is required before they can be obtained. An excellent reference source for fine arts and crafts related subjects. Also houses the Preston Blake Collection of works by and about William Blake.

Foreign and Commonwealth Office Library

Cornwall House, Stamford Street,
London SE1 9NS
☏ 01–211 0117

Open 9.30 am to 5.30 pm Monday to Friday

Open access for reference purposes

An extensive stock of books, pamphlets and other reference material on all aspects of socio-economic and political subjects relating to countries covered by the Foreign and Commonwealth Office. Particularly strong on official Commonwealth publications and legislation.

The French Institute (Institut Français du Royaume-Uni)

17 Queensbury Place, London SW7 2DT
☏ 01–589 6211

Open 11.00 am to 8.00 pm Monday; 11.00 am to 6.00 pm Tuesday to Friday; 10.00 am to 1.00 pm Saturday

Open access to reading room; loans to members only

Annual membership £9; students and OAPs £6

A collection of over 70,000 volumes mainly centred on cultural interests with special emphasis on the French language.

Greater London History Library

40 Northampton Road, London EC1R 0HB
☏ 01–633 7132/6759

Open 9.30 am to 4.45 pm Tuesdays to Fridays

Open access for reference purposes

Covers all aspects of the life and development of London, specialising in the history and organisation of local government in general, and London in particular. Books on London history and topography, covering many subjects. Also London directories dating back to 1677, and other source material including acts of parliament, Hansard, reports, statistical returns, atlases, yearbooks and many complete sets of newspapers and magazines. (See also **Photo Libraries**).

HERTIS

Hatfield Polytechnic Library, College Lane,
Hatfield, Herts AL10 9AD
☏ 07072 79678 Fax 07072 79670

Open 8.45 am to 9.30 pm Monday to Thursday; 8.45 am to 7.00 pm Friday; 10.00 am to 1.00 pm Saturday; 2.00 pm to 7.00 pm Sunday. During vacation period open 9.00 am to 5.00 pm Monday to Friday. (These times are for the Hatfield Library only.)

Access to reference material open to public at all HERTIS libraries

The HERTIS group is a college library network served by Hatfield Polytechnic and twelve other colleges of further education which combine to provide a resource facility on engineering, computing, humanities (with particular reference to South East Asia), education, social and business studies as well as building, agriculture, horticulture and art and design.

Holborn Library

32–8 Theobalds Road, London WC1X 8PA
☏ 01–405 2705

Open 9.30 am to 8.00 pm Monday, Thursday; 9.30 am to 6.00 pm Tuesday; 9.30 am to 5.00 pm Friday, Saturday (closed Wednesday, Sunday)

Open access

Specialises in business, employment and law with over 35,000 items in stock.

Imperial War Museum

Department of Printed Books, Lambeth Road,
London SE1 6HZ
☏ 01–735 8922

Open 10.00 am to 5.00 pm Monday to Friday

Access open for reference purposes but at least 24 hours' notice must be given for intended visits.

A large collection of material on 20th-century life with detailed coverage of the two world wars and other conflicts. Books; pamphlets and periodicals including many produced for short periods in unlikely wartime settings; technical drawings and maps; biographies including privately printed memoirs; foreign language material. Also holds research material in the Departments of Art; Documents; Exhibits and Firearms; Film;

Sound & Records, and Photographs (see also **Photo Libraries**).

Italian Institute

39 Belgrave Square, London SW1X 8NX
☏ 01–235 1461

Open 9.30 am to 5.00 pm

Open access for reference

A collection of over 20,000 volumes relating to all aspects of Italian culture. Texts are mostly in Italian, with some in English.

Library of the Religious Society of Friends

Friend's House, Euston Road, London NW1 2BJ
☏ 01–387 3601

Open 10.00 am to 5.00 pm Tuesday to Friday (closed last full week November and week preceding Spring Bank Holiday)

Access open for reference purposes to members of the Society of Friends and to *bona fide* researchers on introduction or letter of recommendation

Quaker history, thought and activities from the 17th century onwards. Supporting collections on peace, anti-slavery and other subjects in which Quakers have maintained longstanding interest. Also archives and manuscripts relating to the Society of Friends.

Liverpool City Libraries

William Brown Street, Liverpool LE3 8EW
☏ 051–207 2147

Open 9.00 am to 9.00 pm Monday to Friday; 9.00 am to 5.00 pm Saturday

Access to all the libraries open to the public

Arts and Recreations Library (ext. 33) 50,000 volumes covering all subjects in arts and recreation.

Commercial and Social Sciences Library (ext. 29) Business and trade directories plus all UK statutes and law reports. Serves as a depository library for UNO and EEC reports.

General, Religion and Philosophy Library and Hornby Library (ext. 31) Contains stock of 68,000 volumes, 24,000 maps plus book plates, prints and autographed letters. *Special collections* Walter Crane and Edward Lear illustrations.

International Library (ext. 20) Open shelf and reserve stocks on language, literature, geography and history. Special interest is the collection on British history with much on politicians and statesmen. 20,000 copies of British, American and European plays plus language tapes in twenty languages.

Music Library (ext. 49) Extensive stock relating to all aspects of music. Includes 128,000 volumes and music scores, 18,500 records and over 3000 cassettes. *Special collections* Carl Rosa Opera Company Collection and Earl of Sefton's early printed piano music.

Record Office and Local History Department (ext. 34) Printed and audiovisual material relating to Liverpool, Merseyside, Lancashire and Cheshire together with archive material mainly on Liverpool. Some restrictions on access, e.g. 30-year rule applies to archives.

Science and Technology Library (ext. 7) Extensive stock dealing with all aspects of science and technology including British and European standards and patents.

London Borough of Camden Information and Reference Services

Swiss Cottage Library, 88 Avenue Road, London NW3 3HA
☏ 01–586 5989

Open 9.30 am to 8.00 pm Monday, Thursday; 9.30 am to 6.00 pm Tuesday; 9.30 to 5.00 pm Friday, Saturday (closed Wednesday)

Open access

Over 60,000 volumes and 600 periodical titles.

London College of Printing

Library, Elephant and Castle, London SE1 6SB
☏ 01–735 8484

Open 9.00 am to 7.00 pm Monday to Thursday; 9.00 am to 5.45 pm Fridays (term time); 9.00 am to 4.30 pm (vacations)

Access Open to members of the public on payment of an annual subscription fee of £10.00

Books, periodicals, slides, videos and computer software on all aspects of the art of the book: printing, management, film/photograph, graphic arts. *Special collections* Private press books and the history and development of printing and books. The London College of Printing is a constituent college of the London Institute.

London Library

14 St James's Square, London SW1Y 4LG
☏ 01-930 7705/6

Open 9.30 am to 5.30 pm Monday to Saturday (Thursday till 7.30 pm) **Closed** Sundays

Annual Membership Fee £75

With over a million books and 6700 members, the London Library 'is the most distinguished private library in the world; probably the largest, certainly the best loved'. Wholly independent of public funding, there are no restrictions on membership. Anybody can apply, pay the subscription and take up to ten books home immediately; fifteen if the member lives more than twenty miles from St James's Square. Particularly strong in European languages, but stock excludes specialist collections on science and technology, medicine and law.
The London Library Trust was founded in 1952 with the object of making the resources of the library accessible to scholars and students who cannot afford the full annual membership fee; making grants for original research work at the Library; purchasing works of scholarship for the Library which it might not otherwise acquire. Last year's grants totalled almost £5000.

Medical Library

Marylebone Library, Marylebone Road,
London NW1 5PS
☏ 01–798 1039

Open 9.30 am to 7.00 pm Monday to Friday; 9.30 am to 5.00 pm Saturday

Open access for reference

Books, pamphlets and periodicals covering all aspects of medicine and the health services.

Ministry of Agriculture, Fisheries and Food

Main Library, 3 Whitehall Place,
London SW1A 2HH
☏ 01–270 8419/8420/8421 Fax 01–270 8125

Open 9.30 am to 5.00 pm Monday to Friday

Access for reference purposes to all researchers

Large stock of volumes on temperate agriculture, horticulture and fisheries. *Special collections* Agriculture and poultry genetics.

National Library of Scotland

George IV Bridge, Edinburgh EH1 1EW
☏ 031–226 4531

Open 9.30 am to 8.30 pm Monday to Friday; 9.30 am to 1.00 pm Saturday. **Closed** Map Room at 5.00 pm Monday to Friday; library on public holidays

Access to reading rooms and Map rooms for research not easily done elsewhere, via ticket

Collection of over 4 million volumes. The library receives all British and Irish publications. Large stock of newspapers and periodicals. Many *special collections* including early Scottish books, theology, polar studies, baking, phrenology and liturgies. Also large collections of maps, music and manuscripts including personal archives of notable Scottish persons.

National Library of Wales

Aberystwyth, Dyfed SY23 3BU
☏ 0970 623816

Open 9.30 am to 6.00 pm Monday to Friday; 9.30 am to 5.00 pm Saturday and general holidays

Access to reading room and Map room by reader's ticket available on application

Collection of over 3 million books including large collections of periodicals, maps and manuscripts. Particular emphasis on humanities in foreign material, and on Wales and other Celtic areas in all collections.

National Sound Archive

See **British Library National Sound Archive**

Northern Listening Service

See **British Library National Sound Archive**

New Zealand High Commission Library

80 Haymarket, London SW1Y 4TO
☏ 01–930 8422 Fax 01–839 4580

Books, periodicals, official publications covering New Zealand, South Pacific, Antarctica. Works by New Zealand authors.

Office of Population Censuses & Surveys

St Catherine's House, 10 Kingsway,
London WC2B 6JP
☏ 01–242 0262

Open 8.30 am to 4.30 pm Monday to Friday

Open access for reference purposes

Population censuses and vital statistics reports from most countries. Law and administration of birth, marriage and death registration, demography, epidemiology, psychology, survey methodology.

The Polish Library

238–246 King Street, London W6 0RF
☎ 01–741 0474

Open 10.00 am to 8.00 pm Monday, Wednesday; 10.00 am to 5.00 pm Tuesday, Friday; 10.00 am to 1.00 pm Thursday, Saturday

Access Open for reference and loans to all scholars and those interested in Polish affairs

Books, pamphlets, periodicals, maps, music, photographs on all aspects of Polish culture. *Special collections* Emigré publications; Joseph Conrad and related works; Polish underground publications.

Press Association

85 Fleet Street, London EC4P 4BE
☎ 01–353 7440

Open 9.00 am to 5.00 pm

The national news agency offers public access to millions of b&w and colour photographs, and newscuttings. *Pictures* Personal callers welcome, or phone ext. 3201. *Cuttings* Contact News Features department, ext. 3147, or the Librarian on ext. 3160. Set scale of charges.

Poetry Library

South Bank Centre, Royal Festival Hall (Level 5, Red Side), London SE1 8XX
☎ 01–921 0664/0940/0943

Open 11.00 am to 8.00 pm daily

Access Membership free and open to all on production of proof of identity and permanent address. Members may borrow up to four books for up to four weeks at a time

A collection of 45,000 titles of modern poetry since 1912, representing all English-speaking countries and including translations into English by contemporary poets. Two copies of each title are kept, one for loan and one for reference. A wide range of poetry magazines and periodicals from all over the world are kept. Also cassettes, records and videos for consultation.
An information service compiles lists of poetry magazines, competitions, publishers, bookshops, groups and workshops, which are available from the Library on receipt of a large s.a.e. It has noticeboards for lost quotations through which it tries to trace the author, and fragments of poetry sent in by the public.

Public Record Office

Ruskin Avenue, Kew, Richmond, Surrey TW9 4DU
☎ 01–876 3444

Open 9.30 am to 5.00 pm Monday to Friday

Access for reference purposes by reader's ticket, available free of charge on production of identity and proof of address

Also at Chancery Lane, London WC2A 1LR
☎ 01–405 0741

Over 84 miles of shelving house the national repository of records of central Government in the UK and law courts of England and Wales, which extend in time from the 11th–20th century; medieval records; the records of the State Paper Office from early 16th–late 18th century; the records of the Privy Council Office and the Lord Chamberlain's and Lord Steward's Departments are held at Chancery Lane.
Modern Government department records, together with those of the Copyright Office are held at Kew. These date mostly from the late 18th century. Under the Public Records Act records are normally only open to inspection when they are 30 years old.

Royal Geographical Society

1 Kensington Gore, London SW7 2AR
☎ 01–589 4566

Open 10.00 am to 5.00 pm Monday to Friday (Map Room closed 1.00 pm to 2.00 pm)

Access Library and Reading Rooms solely for use of Fellows and Members, except by special arrangement. Map Room open to public.

Books and periodicals on geography, topography, cartography, voyages and travels. Map Room houses map sheets, atlases and expedition reports, plus photographs on travel and exploration.

Royal Society

Library, 6 Carlton House Terrace, London SW1Y 5AG
☎ 01–839 5561 Telex 917876

Open 10.00 am to 5.00 pm Monday to Friday

Access Private library, open for research purposes to *bona fide* researchers on application to the Librarian

Science, history of science, scientists' biographies. Recent science policy reports and publications of international scientific unions, and national academies from all over the world.

Royal Society of Medicine

Library, 1 Wimpole Street, London W1M 8AE
☎ 01–408 2119 Fax 01–408 0062

Open 9.30 am to 9.00 pm Monday to Friday; 10.00 am to 5.00 pm Saturday

Access for reference purposes only, on introduction by Fellow of the Society; also temporary membership may be granted.

Books, periodicals on general medicine, biochemistry, biomedical science. Some historical material.

Science Fiction Foundation Research Library

Polytechnic of East London, Longbridge Road, Dagenham, Essex RM8 2AS
☎ 01–590 7722 ext. 2177

Open 9.30 am to 3.30 pm Monday, Tuesday and Thursday during term times; open on an irregular basis during vacations

Access open for research purposes to *bona fide* researchers, but telephone first

The largest collection outside the USA of science fiction and related material – including autobiographies and critical works. *Special collection* Runs of 'pulp' magazines dating back to the 1920s.

Science Museum Library

South Kensington, London SW7 5NH
☎ 01–938 8234 Fax 01–938 8118

Open 10.00 am to 5.30 pm Monday to Saturday

Open access for reference purposes

National reference library of pure and applied science, with a large collection of source material on the history of science and technology.

Sheffield City Libraries

Central Library, Surrey Street, Sheffield S1 1XZ
☎ 0742 734711
Archives 0742 734756

Open 9.30 am to 9.00 pm Monday to Friday; 9.00 am to 4.30 pm Saturday

Open access to the public, but prior arrangement should be made for consulting archive material

Stocks the Fairbank collection of maps, draft plans and surveying books, together with manuscript collections and parochial records relating to the area.

Arts and Social Sciences Reference Library
☎ 0742 734747–9

Open 9.30 am to 9.00 pm Monday to Friday; 9.00 am to 4.00 pm Saturday

Open access to all for reference purposes

A comprehensive collection of books, periodicals and newspapers covering all aspects of arts and the humanities (excluding music).

Audio Visual and Music Library
☎ 0742 734733

Open 9.30 am to 8.00 pm Monday, Wednesday, Friday; 9.30 am to 5.30 pm Tuesday and Thursday; 9.30 am to 4.30 pm Saturday

Open access for reference purposes, loans with tickets

An extensive range of books, records, scores etc. related to music. Also a video cassette loan service.

Business Library
☎ 0742 734736–8

Open 9.30 am to 5.30 pm Monday to Friday; 9.00 am to 4.30 pm Saturday

Open access for reference purposes

A large stock of business and trade directories, plus overseas telephone directories and reference works with business emphasis.

Local Studies Library
☎ 0742 734753

Open 9.30 am to 5.30 pm Monday to Friday; 9.00 am to 4.30 pm Saturday

Open access for reference use (advance notice advisable)

Extensive material covering all aspects of Sheffield and its population, including maps and taped oral histories.

Science and Technology Reference Library
☎ 0742 734753

Open 9.30 am to 5.30 pm Monday to Friday; 9.00 am to 4.00 pm Saturday

Open access for reference

Extensive coverage of science and technology as well as commerce and commercial law. British patents and British and European standards with emphasis on metals. (Sheffield also houses the *World Metal Index*.)

Sheffield Information Service
☎ 0742 734760/734761

Open 9.30 am to 5.30 pm Monday to Friday; 9.00 am to 4.30 pm Saturday

Full local information service covering all aspects of the Sheffield community.

Spanish Institute Library

102 Eaton Square, London SW1W 9AN
☎ 01–235 1484/5

Open 10.00 am to 6.00 pm Monday to Friday

Access non-members may use the library for reference purposes.

Spanish literature, history, art, philosophy. Books, slides, tapes, records and films.

Trades Union Congress

Library, Congress House, Great Russell Street, London WC1B 3LS
☎ 01–636 4030 ext. 220/221/222
Fax 01–636 0632

Open 10.00 am to 5.00 pm Monday to Friday

Access open to researchers by appointment only

Industrial relations, wages and conditions of employment, trade unions, economics, industrial health, international trade union activities, other areas covered by TUC policy. Also a small collection of photographs.

United Nations London Information Centre

20 Buckingham Gate, London SW1E 6LB
☎ 01–630 1981 Telex 23737

Open 10.00 am to 1.00 pm and 2.00 pm to 5.00 pm Monday, Wednesday and Thursday

Open access for reference

A full stock of official publications and documentation from the United Nations.

The Weiner Library

4 Devonshire Street, London W1N 2BH
☎ 01–636 7247/8

Open 10.00 am to 5.30 pm Monday to Friday

Access through letter of introduction. Readers needing to use the Library for any length of time should become member.

Private library – one of the leading research centres on European history since the First World War, with special reference to the era of totalitarianism and to Jewish affairs. FOUNDED by Dr Weiner in Amsterdam in 1933, it holds much material that is not available elsewhere. Books, periodicals, press archives, documents, pamphlets, leaflets and brochures. Much of the material can be consulted on microfilm.

Westminister History and Archives Department

Victoria Library, 160 Buckingham Palace Road, London SW1W 9UD
☎ 01–798 2180

Open 9.30 am to 7.00 pm Monday to Friday; 9.30 am to 1.00 pm and 2.00 pm to 5.00 pm Saturday

Open access for reference books

Comprehensive coverage of the history of Westminster and selective coverage of general London history. 18,000 books, together with a large stock of prints, photographs, and theatre programmes.

Filling the Space Between the Words

A Guide to Picture Libraries

by Brian Shuel

So you want to use a Picture Library? But you have heard all these stories about how they rip you off, charge you to go through the door, *look* at their pictures, *use* them, *keep* them for more time than it takes even a half-way competent publisher to produce your material ... and if you have the misfortune to *lose* the things, well, you might as well sell the family silver, the car, the house ...

We're not so bad really. We're just trying to make a living, same as you, and it's an expensive business. Pictures are little different from any other commodity – the price you pay for them is based on what it costs to produce them. If they are in some way special – by a famous photographer, for example, or unique images of an historic event – then you can reasonably expect to pay more for them. So, assuming you have now reassessed your views, you will want to know how to approach a picture library.

The British Association of Picture Libraries and Agencies (BAPLA) has just over 200 members – a door to something like 200 million images: photographs, mostly, but some libraries deal in prints, engravings, labels, posters, and much more.

There are, roughly speaking, four types of library within BAPLA. Two of these could be described as 'General', though they are quite different from one another; one deals only in colour transparencies: the work of numerous photographers (on a 50–50 basis), with up-to-date material on every subject under the sun; the other in black and white, produced mostly by news agencies and magazines during the last hundred years. These libraries supply illustrations for today's steady flow of historical books, articles and TV documentaries. **The Hulton Picture Company**, for example, which started as the archive of *Picture Post*, has since added many collections and has recently acquired the much coveted Keystone Collection. With around 25 million images, they are by far the biggest member of BAPLA. Half a dozen members specialise in 'hot news' pictures for today's newspapers and magazines.

The other two groups are 'The Specialists'. Many libraries deal in a single subject, handling the work of a great number of photographers. One such category is 'Natural History' which has as many as 22 member libraries. Other specialist libraries cover entertainment, gardening, landscapes, science, sport and travel.

Finally, there are the 'One-man Bands', which constitute a large group, maybe 50 libraries in all. They tend to be specialist, too, for no individual can produce enough pictures of enough subjects to justify calling himself a 'general' library. Also, he is probably especially interested in, or even seriously obsessed by, his chosen subject. Thus, as an enthusiast and authority on his subject he often has much more to offer than mere pictures. BAPLA has specialist authorities on a diverse range of subjects: cricket, steam locomotives, food, mountaineering, snooker, children, inland waterways, jazz, opera, ballet, golf, traditional customs, anthropology, ancient civilizations, gardening, Iceland, wine ...

The fact is that between all of us we are practically bound to have whatever you need. Moreover, unless you are a professional, or an exceptionally good amateur photographer, the quality will be far better than you can muster by other means, short of commissioning original pictures, which is probably the best plan if you can afford it. Which brings us back to the money. You may think that picture libraries are extortionate but they are still cheaper than any other professional method of illustrating books. This is how they work.

All BAPLA members operate in more or less the same way, so, having first consulted the BAPLA Directory (price £6), you ring up the appropriate libraries and explain what you are looking for. You need to be very specific about what you want because already money is about to change hands. Service fees are charged by most libraries, not all, and some charge only for requested pictures which are not used. Ask before you order. Service fees cover the cost of research, postage and packing and will be anywhere from £10–25 – not much for one library, but they do add up if you 'trawl' for pictures among several. And it would be so easy to ring up 20 libraries when you are looking for just one picture – without the fee, all that time and effort would be for nothing.

Reproduction fees are the basis of our business. They are unlikely to vary much between members, but they do vary a lot according to use. A quarter page b&w picture for a low print-run, UK only book could attract around £50; for a wraparound colour cover, with world rights, this would be around £500. Again, ask first – we have nothing to hide.

In addition, there are two other types of fee, but you will not have to pay these if you behave yourselves!

Every delivery note gives a 'Return By' date. That is the date upon which your *free* loan of the pictures expires. It is up to you to schedule the loan well, make sure that you get on with the work and keep the library informed of progress. If holding fees come into effect, they are to compensate for the time that the pictures are out of circulation and no longer, therefore, potential income earners. One well-known author called for pictures from several libraries a couple of years ago but before they arrived he went off for a holiday in Ireland. While he was there he fell in love, and stayed for a year. When he eventually came home he found a pile of packages, dozens of increasingly irate letters, and bills for holding fees totalling £22,000. Fortunately his previous book had been a great success and he could afford it. Beware.

Finally there are loss fees which apply if you *lose* the pictures. You may not think so, but this is quite easy to do. So look after any pictures that you get from a library. They are valuable property and if you lose them it is likely to cost you at least £400 a picture – much more if they are irreplaceable or exceptionally expensive to re-shoot. A photographer in America was recently awarded $35,000 for the loss of his unique picture of Salvador Dali with two nude models. The fee is calculated not only on its presumed intrinsic value but also on the loss of its potential earnings to the owner.

So there you are. Picture Libraries, certainly members of BAPLA, can provide you with first-class, comparatively cheap images, and they are run by well informed, charming and enthusiastic professionals – just waiting to hear from you.

Picture Libraries

AA Photo Library

Fanum House, Basingstoke,
Hampshire RG21 2EA
☎ 0256 491588 Telex 858538

Colour coverage of landscape, towns, villages, places of interest and lesser known areas of Britain, commissioned by the Automobile Association's Publication Division.

Ace Photo Agency

22 Maddox Street, Mayfair, London W1R 9PG
☎ 01–629 0303
Telex 915342 COTMEX G Fax 01–495 6100

Colour files include lifestyles, business, industry, sports, celebrities, glamour, skies and sunsets, still life, special effects, arts, natural history and much more. Visitors are welcome, and a 60pp catalogue is available. Commissions undertaken.

Action Plus

54–8 Tanner Street, London SE1 3LL
☎ 01–403 1558
Telex 8951182 GECOMS C Fax 01–403 1526

Colour and b&w coverage of over 100 international sports and leisure activities. Visitors welcome. Commissions undertaken.

Adams Picture Library

156 New Cavendish Street, London W1M 7JF
☎ 01–636 1468 Fax 01–436 7131

Represent the work of over 300 photographers. Subjects include families, people at work and play, glamour, humour, natural history, microbiology, landscapes, seascapes, clouds, buildings, monuments, London, British Isles (in depth), aerial views, art, music, vehicles, special effects. Brochure Available.

Adlib Foto Agency

33 Albury Avenue, Isleworth,
Middlesex TW7 5HY
☎ 01–847 3777
Telex 924150 ADLIB G Fax 01–568 2402

Specialist collections include cars, children, girls, landscapes, nature, rock bands, the ocean and travel.

Adlib Sports Scene

33 Albury Avenue, Isleworth,
Middlesex TW7 5HY
☎ 01–847 3777
Telex 924150 ADLIB G Fax 01–568 2402

Specialises in sports photography, covering cricket, football, golf, motor racing, snooker, tennis and many others. Provides promotional material for the sponsors of sporting events, and also can provide book packages for publishers. Also see **Football International.**

Malcolm Aird Associates

18 Upper Park Road, London NW3 2UP
☎ 0787 210111

Rural and urban Britain, landscapes, people at work, industry, modern transport and commercial aircraft.

Alba Pictures

The Sutors, 28 Broadstone Park, Inverness,
Highland IV2 3LA
☎ 0463 233717

Scottish landscapes, mountaineering in Britain and around the world, world travel, general landscape shots, volcanoes, glaciers, aerial shots, and miscellaneous abstract shots.

All-Action Picture Library

32 Great Sutton Street, London EC1V 0DX
☎ 01–608 2988/9

Sport, royalty, pop and celebrities. Worldwide

coverage of all aspects of football including recent World Cup tournaments. Library list available. Commissions undertaken.

Allsport (UK) Ltd

Allsport House, 3 Greenlea Park, Prince George's Road, London SW19 2JD
☏ 01–685 1010
Telex 8955022 ASPORT G Fax 01–648 5240

A large specialist sports library, covering 130 different sports and top sports personalities. Represented in 27 countries worldwide.

A.M. Photo Agency

40 Croft Close, Rowton, Chester CH3 7QQ
☏ 0244 332060

Colour coverage of UK, especially NW England and N Wales. Sport, leisure, natural history, transport.

Ancient Art and Architecture Collection

6 Kenton Road, Harrow-on-the-Hill, Middlesex HA1 2BL
☏ 01–422 1214 Telex 268048

Colour and b&w coverage of civilisations of the world: arts, cities, architecture, landscapes and peoples both past and present. Country by Country catalogues available.

Heather Angel/Biofotos

Highways, 6 Vicarage Hill, Farnham, Surrey GU9 8HJ
☏ 0252 716700
Fax 0252 727464 FAO Heather Angel

Worldwide natural history, wildlife and landscapes. Tropical rain forest flora and fauna, and all types of plants and animals taken in natural habitats from Africa, Asia (notably China), Australasia, South America and USA. Catalogue available. Commissions undertaken.

Animal Photography

4 Marylebone Mews, New Cavendish Street, London W1M 7LF
☏ 01–935 0503

Colour and b&w coverage of horses, dogs, cats, the Galapagos Islands, East Africa, and zoos. Commissions undertaken.

Aquila Photographics

PO Box 1, Haydon House, Alcester Road, Studley, Warwickshire B80 7AN
☏ 052785 2357

Colour and b&w coverage of all natural history, specialising in birds. British and European wildlife, also North America, Africa and Australia.

Arcaid

6 Latchmere Road, Kingston-upon-Thames, Surrey KT2 5TW
☏ 01–546 4352 Fax 01–541 5230

Historic and contemporary architecture and interior design by leading architectural photographers. Covers international and British subjects, single images or series with background information. Visitors welcome by appointment. Commissions undertaken.

Ardea London Ltd

35 Brodrick Road, London SW17 7DX
☏ 01–672 2067/8787
Telex 896691 TLX1RG prefix Ardeaphotos

Colour and b&w coverage of natural history: creatures in wild habitat, domestic animals, deserts, rain forests, Antarctic, Aborigines, farming, conservation.

Art Directors Photo Library

Image House, 86 Haverstock Hill, London NW3 2BD
☏ 01–485 9325/267 6930 Fax 01–485 7776

Work from international photographers includes computer graphics, Hi-Tech, industry, business, space, personalities, life styles, travel, skies, still life, entertainment, fashion, cars (vintage and modern), and coverage of USA, Europe, Asia, Africa and the Tropics. Catalogue available.

Aspect Picture Library Ltd

40 Rostrevor Road, London SW6 5AD
☏ 01–736 1998/731 7362
Telex 934999 TXLINK G quote MBX 219994671

Colour and b&w worldwide coverage of countries, events, industry, travel. Large files on art, paintings, space, China, Middle East.

Associated Sports Photography
21–3 Green Walk, Leicester LE3 6SE
☎ 0533 320310 Fax 0533 311123

Colour and b&w coverage of all sports, including major international events and personalities.

Aviation Photographic International
15 Downs Vine Road, Swindon, Wilts SN3 1NS
☎ 0793 47179

Coverage of all aspects of aviation, both civil and military. Also ships and vehicles. Commissions undertaken for photography and research.

Aviemore Photographic
Main Road, Aviemore, Highland PH22 1RH
☎ 0479 810371

Colour and b&w coverage of Scotland. Sports, tourism, landscapes.

Clive Barda
50 Agate Road, London W6 0AH
☎ 01–741 0805/6
Telex 291829 BARDA Fax 01–563 0538

Colour and b&w pictures of all aspects of classical music and opera. Also interiors of opera houses and concert halls.

Barnaby's Picture Library
19 Rathbone Street, London W1P 1AF
☎ 01–636 6128 Fax 01–637 4317

Colour and b&w coverage of a wide range of subjects: nature, transport, industry, historical, including collection on Hitler. Commissions undertaken.

BBC Hulton Picture Library
See **Hulton Picture Company**

Beken of Cowes Ltd
16 Birmingham Road, Cowes
Isle of Wight PO31 7BH
☎ 0983 297311 Fax 0983 291059

Maritime subjects from 1888 to the present day. Commissions undertaken.

Ivan J. Belcher Colour Picture Library
34 Berry Croft, Abingdon, Oxfordshire OX14 1JL
☎ 0235 21524

Colour pictures of locations all over Britain.

Anthony Blake
54 Hill Rise, Richmond, Surrey TW10 6UB
☎ 01–940 7583 Fax 01–948 1224

Colour coverage of all aspects of food and wine: cooking, restaurants, farming, vineyards, fishing. Catalogue available. Commissions undertaken.

John Blake Picture Library
26 Malvern Drive, Thornbury, Bristol,
Avon BS12 2HY
☎ 0454 418321/413240

Colour and b&w coverage of topography of Britain, Europe and USA. Also horse trials and mountaineering. Commissions undertaken.

BMV Picturebank
79 Farringdon Road, London EC1M 3JY
☎ 01–405 5021 Fax 01–831 2982

Specialists in world travel, covering most popular resorts. Also general file. Commissions undertaken.

Janet and Colin Bord
Melysfan, Llangwm, Corwen, Clwyd LL21 0RD
☎ 049082 472

Colour and b&w coverage of prehistoric sites, churches, countryside and folklore of Britain and Ireland; also collections of Welsh life and landscapes, and worldwide supernatural phenomena.

Michael Boys Syndication
Red House, Newbourn, Woodbridge,
Suffolk IP12 4PX
☎ 0473 36333

Colour collections on interiors, gardens, lighting, cookery, travel.

Bridgeman Art Library
19 Chepstow Road, London W2 5BP
☎ 01–727 4065/229 7420
Telex 265208 ARTPIX Fax 01–792 8509

Colour coverage of paintings and works of art from antiquity to the present day, also furniture, glass, ceramics, silver and needlework. Catalogue available. Commissions undertaken.

Britain on View Photographic Library
Thames Tower, Black's Road, London W6 9EL
☎ 01–846 9000
Telex 21231 Fax 01–563 0302

Colour and b&w coverage of Great Britain: countryside, coast, towns, villages, historic buildings and landmarks. Also specialised file on London.

British Film Institute
Stills, Posters and Designs Collection,
21 Stephen Street, London W1P 1PL
☎ 01–255 1444
Telex 27624 Fax 01–436 7950

The history of world cinematography from *c.*1895 to the present day, with emphasis on British cinema and television. Callers by appointment. Catalogue available.

Bubbles Photolibrary
23A Benwell Road, London N7 7BL
☎ 01–609 4547

Babies, children, pregnancy and women's health. Commissions undertaken.

Business Magazine Picture Library
234 King's Road, London SW3 5UA
☎ 01–351 7351
Telex 914549 ITNMAG G Fax 01–351 2794

Portraits of international business personalities and company profiles, filed by issue.

Camera Press
Russell Court, Coram Street,
London WC1H 0NB
☎ 01–837 4488
Telex 21654 Fax 01–278 5126

Colour and b&w coverage of British royalty, events and personalities throughout the world. Also features on photo journalism and educational subjects.

Camerapix Picture Library
8 Ruston Mews, London W11 1RB
☎ 01–221 0249/0077

Colour coverage of assignments and expeditions in Africa, Asia and the Middle East. Indigenous cultures, industry, landscapes, political leaders, African wildlife. Also an outstanding Islamic portfolio. Material not available in London may be accessed from the Nairobi collection.

The Casement Collection
2 Frobisher Crescent, Stanwell, Staines,
Middlesex TW19 7DX
☎ 0784 254918

Colour and b&w travel library, particularly strong on North America and the Gulf. Not just beaches and palm trees. Based on Jack Casement's collection, with additions by other photographers.

J Allan Cash Ltd
74 South Ealing Road, London W5 4QB
☎ 01–840 4141

Colour and b&w coverage of travel, natural history, people, space, sport, animals. New material regularly contributed by 250 plus photographers.

Celtic Picture Agency
4 Rhodfa Gwilym, St Asaph, Clwyd LL17 0UU
☎ 074574 395

Environment, conservation, tourism, scenery, farming, historic sites. Commissions undertaken.

Central Press Photos Ltd
See the **Hulton Picture Company**

Cephas Picture Library
20 Trafalgar Drive, Walton on Thames,
Surrey KT12 1NZ
☎ 0932 241903 Fax 0932 68481

A general picture library with coverage of countries and people round the world. Also a comprehensive collection on vineyards and winemaking in Europe and Britain. Commissions undertaken.

Christian Aid Photo Library
PO Box 100, London SE1 7RT
☎ 01–620 4444 Fax 01–620 0719

Pictures from Africa, Asia and Latin America, relating to small-scale community based programmes. Mostly development themes: agriculture, health, education, urban and rural life.

The Cinema Museum (incorporating the Ronald Grant Archive)
The Old Fire Station, 46 Renfrew Road,
London SE11 4NA
☏ 01–820 9991

Colour and b&w coverage (including stills) of the motion picture industry throughout its history. Also small collections on theatre, variety, television and popular music.

John Cleare/Mountain Camera
Hill Cottage, Fonthill Gifford, Salisbury,
Wiltshire SP3 6QW
☏ 0747 89320 Fax 0722 332335

Colour and b&w coverage of mountains and wilderness, expeditions, landscapes from all continents, geographical features and cities.

Stephanie Colasanti
38 Hillside Court, 409 Finchley Road,
London NW3 6HQ
☏ 01–435 3695

Colour coverage of Europe, Africa, Asia, Caribbean, South America. People, animals, towns, agriculture, landscapes, carnivals, markets, archaeology, religion and ancient civilisations. Travel assignments undertaken.

Bruce Coleman Ltd
17 Windsor Street, Uxbridge,
Middlesex UB8 1AB
☏ 0895 57094
Telex 932439 Fax 0895 72357

Colour coverage of natural history, ecology, archaeology, anthropology, horticulture, agriculture, science, and social documentary. Incorporates World Wildlife Fund International Colour Library.

Colorsport
44 St Peter's Street, London N1 8JT
☏ 01–359 2714
Telex 24224 ref 970 Fax 01–226 4328

Colour and b&w coverage of sport, sports personalities, football from 1881, cricket from 1920s. Can be selected in library or sent.

Colour Library International
See **The Photo Source**

Compix
Commonwealth Institute, Kensington High
Street, London W8 6NQ
☏ 01–603 4535 ext. 237 Telex 8955822

Colour coverage of the lives and people of the Commonwealth. Information leaflet available.

Conway Picture Library
24 Bride Lane, Fleet Street, London EC4Y 8DR
☏ 01–353 9665/6 Telex 8814206 Popper G

Magazine photo collections from women's journals 1940s–1960s. Colour and b&w coverage of personalities, fashion, features. Also has a transport section, including naval shipping from 19th century.

Countryside Commission
Visual Resources Service, John Dower House,
Crescent Place, Cheltenham,
Gloucestershire GL50 3RA
☏ 0242 521381 ext. 280

Landscapes of England and Wales, National Parks, countryside recreation and rural occupations.

James Davis Travel Photography
30 Hengistbury Road, New Milton,
Hampshire BH25 7LU
☏ 0425 610328

Travel collection. People, places, emotive scenes and tourism. Commissions undertaken.

Peter Dazeley Photography
The Studios, 5 Heathmans Road, Parsons Green,
London SW6 4TJ
☏ 01–736 3171 Fax 01–736 3356

Colour and b&w coverage of golf: players, courses and tournaments over the last two decades.

Design Council Picture Library
28 Haymarket, London SW1Y 4SU
☏ 01–839 8000
Telex 8812963 Fax 01–925 2130

Colour and b&w coverage of all aspects of design. *Special collections*: Britain Can Make It

(1946); Enterprise Scotland (1947); Festival of Britain (1951). Callers welcome by appointment.

Douglas Dickins Photo Library

2 Wessex Gardens, Golders Green,
London NW11 9RT
☎ 01–455 6221

Colour and b&w coverage of educational work in India and Asia as a whole; historic sites in Britain and scenery, people, religions, customs, archaeology worldwide.

CM Dixon

The Orchard, Marley Lane, Kingston, Canterbury,
Kent CT4 6HJ
☎ 0227 830075

Colour coverage of ancient civilisations, archaeology and art. Also ethnology, mythology, world religion, museum objects, geography, geology, meteorology, landscapes, people and places from many countries including most of Europe, USSR, Ethiopia, Iceland, Morocco, Sri Lanka, Tunisia, Turkey.

Dominic Photography

9A Netherton Grove, London SW10 9TQ
☎ 01–352 6118

Colour and b&w coverage of the entertainment world from 1957 onwards: dance, opera, theatre, ballet, films and television.

Patrick Eagar Photography

5 Ennerdale Road, Kew Gardens,
Surrey TW9 3PG
☎ 01–940 9269 Fax 01–332 1229

Colour and b&w coverage of cricket from 1965. Test matches, overseas tours and all aspects of the sport. Also a wine collection, mostly in colour, of vineyards, grapes, cellars and winemakers of France, other European countries, Australia and New Zealand.

English Heritage Historic Buildings and Monuments Commission for England

Fortress House, 23 Savile Row,
London W1X 2HE
☎ 01–734 6010 Fax 01–434 1799

Coverage of all English Heritage properties: castles, abbeys, mills, Roman ruins, standing stones, churches, gardens, paintings. Also English Civil War and Tournament re-enactments. Contemporary and archive photographs.

Robert Estall Photographs

Falcon House, 12–14 Swan Street, Boxford,
Colchester, Essex CO6 5NZ
☎ 0787 210111

Colour coverage of many subjects, including standing stones, megalithic sites, cheese-making, domestic and farm animals, sites involving haunting and legends, African tribal portraits and adornments.

Greg Evans Photo Library

91 Charlotte Street, London W1P 1LB
☎ 01–636 8238/9 Fax 01–436 2318

Colour coverage of a wide range of subjects, including travel, winter skiing, UK scenery, families, industry, abstracts, natural history. Visitors welcome. Commissions undertaken.

Mary Evans Picture Library

1 Tranquil Vale, Blackheath, London SE3 0BU
☎ 01–318 0034 Fax 01–852 7211

A general historical collection up to 1939 – prints and ephemera and some photographs. Social conditions, technology, the paranormal. *Special collections*: Sigmund Freud Photographs; Society for Psychical Research; London University Harry Price Collection; The Fawcett Library (women's rights).

Eyeline Photos

259 London Road, Cheltenham Gl52 7YG
☎ 0242 513567
Telex 43432 DSA Eyeline Fax 0242 573498

Colour and b&w coverage of sport, with emphasis on sailing and powerboating. Also various watersports, equestrian events and pigeon racing. Commissions undertaken.

Falklands Pictorial

Vision House, 16 Broadfield Road, Heeley,
Sheffield S8 0XJ
☎ 0742 589299

Colour and b&w photographs showing all aspects of Falklands life from 1880 to the present day.

Farmers Publishing Group Picture Library
Carew House, Wallington, Surrey SM6 0DX
☎ 01–661 4738
Telex 892084 BISPRS G Fax 01–647 4892

Large agricultural collection. B&W coverage of all aspects of farming and country life. Colour brochure available.

Feature-Pix Colour Library
21 Great Chapel Street, London W1V 3AQ
☎ 01–437 2121 Fax 01–439 1307

Colour collection aimed at the travel and holiday market. Popular resort areas updated regularly. Commissions undertaken.

Financial Times Picture Collection
Number One, Southwark Bridge,
London SE1 9HL
☎ 01–873 3484 Fax 01–407 5700/01–873 3076

Industry, banking, agriculture, personalities – statesmen, politicians and financial figures around the world.

Football International
33 Albury Avenue, Isleworth,
Middlesex TW7 5HY
☎ 01–847 3777
Telex 924150 ADLIB G Fax 01–568 2402

Every aspect of football, including World Cups and international championships. Archive material dating back to 1930.

Werner Forman Archive Ltd
36 Camden Square, London NW1 9XA
☎ 01–267 1034
Telex 295931 UNICOM G Fax 01–267 6026

Colour and b&w coverage of ancient civilisations, the Near and Far East and primitive societies around the world. Vikings, Ancient Mexico, North American Indians, Ancient Japan, Assyria, Egypt and China. A number of rare collections. Subject lists available.

Fotoflite
Chart Road Industrial Estate, Godinton Road,
Ashford, Kent TN23 1ES
☎ 0233 37529 Fax 0233 45618

Aerial photography of 14,000 ships of all types, naval and private. Constantly updated.

Fox Photos Ltd
See the **Hulton Picture Company**

The John R Freeman Reference Library
Harleyson House, 74 Newman Street,
London W1
☎ 01–636 4537

Coverage of fine arts, etc.

Leslie Garland
69 Fern Avenue, Jesmond, Newcastle upon Tyne
NE2 2QU
☎ 091 281 3442

Colour and b&w coverage of construction, travel and leisure. Bridges, building, civil engineering, council estates, flood mitigation schemes, micro-tunnelling, sea defence works, backpacking, climbing, countryside, landscapes. Shot in Europe, Northern England, Scotland and the Far East.

GeoScience Features
6 Orchard Drive, Wye, near Ashford,
Kent TN25 5AU
☎ 0233 812707

Colour and b&w coverage of earth sciences and natural history. Geography, geology, ecology, plants, weather, wildlife, Iceland, earthquakes, tidal waves and volcanos. Commissions undertaken.

Fay Godwin's Photo Files
36 Camden Square, London NW1 9XA
☎ 01–267 1034 Fax 01–267 6026

Colour and b&w specialist collections: Iceland, West Indies, Yorkshire factories and mills, North Sea oil, Scotch whisky distilleries, British and American writers, landscapes, animals, children, social services.

Martin and Dorothy Grace
40 Clipstone Avenue, Mapperley,
Nottingham NG3 5JZ
☎ 0602 208248

Colour coverage of Britain's natural history. Specialising in trees, shrubs and wild flowers.

Also birds and butterflies, habitats, landscapes, ecology. Subject lists are available.

Greater London Photograph Library

Greater London Record Office & History Library, 40 Northampton Road, London EC1R 0HB
☏ 01–633 6759

A large collection of photographs of London, mostly topographical and architectural. Subjects include education, local authority housing, transport, the Thames, parks, churches, hospitals, war damage, pubs, theatres and cinemas. Also major redevelopments: The South Bank, The City, Covent Garden and Docklands.

Sally and Richard Greenhill

357A Liverpool Road, London N1 1NL
☏ 01–607 8549

Colour and b&w photographs of a social documentary nature. Child development, pregnancy, urban scenes. Also Modern China, Hong Kong, USA, longhouse life in Sarawak, Indian maharajas and other material from around the world.

Greenpeace Communications Ltd

124 Cannon Workshops, West India Dock, London E14 9SA
☏ 01–515 0275 Fax 01–538 1177

Colour and b&w coverage of environmental issues and Greenpeace campaigns and direct actions. Whales, seals, dolphins, pollution, acid rain, Antarctica, kangaroos, Sellafield, the South Pacific, and much more.

Susan Griggs Agency Ltd

17 Victoria Grove, London W8 5RW
☏ 01–584 6738
Telex 265871 ref WQQ122 Fax 01–584 1732

Colour coverage of peoples and scenes worldwide, also subjects including animals, children, gardens, interiors, nudes, transport. Visitors welcome by appointment. Subject lists available. Commissions undertaken.

V K Guy Ltd

Silver Birches, Troutbeck, Windermere, Cumbria LA23 1PN
☏ 05394 33519 Fax 05394 32971

British landscapes and architectural heritage. Colour brochure available.

Sonia Halliday Photographs

22 Bates Lane, Weston Turville, Bucks HP22 5SL
☏ 029 661 2266

Stained glass; Biblical subjects in all media; Middle Eastern archaeology, architecture, ethnology, industry; Turkish illuminated manuscripts; mosaics; murals; tapestries; cave paintings; African bushmen; mythology; landscapes and cloudscapes from around the world.

Tom Hanley

61 Stephendale Road, Fulham, London SW6 2LT
☏ 01–731 3225

Colour and b&w coverage of London, England, Europe, Canada, India, the Philipines, Brazil, China, Japan, Korea, Taiwan, the Seychelles, Cayman Islands, USA. Also pop artists of the 60s, Atlantic sailing by Blyth & Ridgeway, First World War trenches, removal of London Bridge to America, and much more.

Robert Harding Picture Library

17A Newman Street, London W1P 3HD
☏ 01–637 8969

Colour coverage of a wide range of subjects including children, beauty, art, architecture, cities, computer graphics, women, fashion, landscapes, space, sport, technology, transport, travel. Specialist collections include: Tutankhamun, The Chinese Exhibition, Alistair Cowin's Beauty Bank, The Victor Kennett Collection, The Equinox Picture Library and The Financial Times colour material.

Harpur Garden Library

44 Roxwell Road, Chelmsford, Essex CM1 2NB
☏ 0245 257527

Colour coverage of gardens in Britain and USA, and unusual plants.

Michael Holland

119 Queen's Road, Loughton, Essex IG10 1RR
☏ 01–508 4358 Fax 01–508 3359

Colour coverage of art history, from pre-history to the 19th century. Architecture, objects, coins, ceramics, tapestries, glass, ivories, jewellery, miniatures, early scientific instruments, early toys, and much more.

Holt Studios

The Courtyard, 24 High Street, Hungerford, Berkshire RG17 0NF
☏ 0488 83523 Fax 0488 83511

World agriculture and horticulture both from a pictorial and a technical point of view. Commissions undertaken worldwide.

Hulton Picture Company

Unique House, 21–31 Woodfield Road, London W9 2BA
☏ 01–266 2662/2660 Fax 01–266 2414

With more than 20 million photographs, engravings and maps, the Hulton Picture Company provides a complete visual history of 20th-century Britain. Based on the Picture Post Collection, it was owned by the BBC since 1958 but has recently been sold to Brian Deutsch. The Keystone Collection, comprising the Fox, Central and Three Lions Agencies, is now also under the Hulton Picture Company's umbrella. Open 9.00 am – 6.00 pm Monday to Friday.

The Robert Hunt Library

1st Floor, 58 Charlotte Road, London EC2A 3QT
☏ 01–739 3536 Fax 01–729 4072

Colour and b&w coverage of warfare, arts, film stars, animals, sport, crime, disasters and royalty (British, European, Middle Eastern, Asian and tribal). Callers welcome. Subject list available.

The Hutchison Library

118B Holland Park Avenue, London W11 4UA
☏ 01–229 2743

Colour and b&w worldwide coverage of agriculture, architecture, industry, landscape, war, disasters, transport. Collections include: Disappearing World (ethnic minorities); Puttkamer (Amazon Indians); Long Search (world religions); Felix Greene (China, North Vietnam, Tibet); Tribal Eye; Shogun Experience; Spirit of Asia; New Pacific and also collections on pregnancy, birth and human relations.

The Illustrated London News Picture Library

20 Upper Ground, London SE1 9FP
☏ 01–928 6969 Telex 8955803 SCLDNG

Engravings, photographs and illustrations from 1842 to the present day, taken from magazines published by Illustrated Newspapers: *Illustrated London News; Graphic; Sphere; Tatler; Sketch; Illustrated Sporting and Dramatic News; Illustrated War News 1914–18; Bystander,* and *Britannia & Eve.* Social history, London, Industrial Revolution, wars, travel.

The Image Bank

3rd Floor, 7 Langley Street, London WC2 4AY
☏ 01–240 9621/6 Fax 01–831 1489

Colour photographs from 300 top world photographers on all subjects. 31 offices world wide from which material not available in London can be called up. Commissions undertaken. Brochure available.

Images Colour Library

Kingswood House, 180 Hunslet Road, Leeds LS10 1AF
☏ 0532 433389 Fax 0532 425605
9 Rosemount Road, London NW3 6NG
☏ Tel 01–435 8175

Editorial and advertising photography. Special collections include agriculture, archaeology and the occult. Catalogue available. Visitors welcome.

Impact Photos

26–7 Great Sutton Street, London EC1V 0DX
☏ 01–251 5191 Fax 01–608 0114

Colour coverage of travel subjects. Agriculture, landscapes, personalities, current affairs, industry, horticulture. Commissions undertaken. Subject list available.

Imperial War Museum Department of Photographs

Lambeth Road, London SE1
☏ 01–735 8922 Fax 01–582 5374

A national archive of photographs of war in this century. Mostly the two World Wars but also other conflicts involving Britain and the Commonwealth. Mostly b&w. Callers welcome 10.00 am – 5.00 pm.

Innes Photographic Library
11–13 The Square, Hessle, North Humberside HU13 0AF
☎ 0482 649271 Fax 0482 647189

In depth coverage of Humberside, and the Yorkshire and Lincolnshire Wolds. Special collections include the construction of the Humber Bridge and b&w coverage of the Hull fishing fleet. Commissions undertaken. Visitors welcome.

International Centre for Conservation Education Photo Library
Greenfield House, Guiting Power, Cheltenham, Gloucestershire GL54 5TZ
☎ 045 15 549 Fax 045 15705

Colour and b&w coverage of conservation, environmental issues, scenery and wildlife in Britain, Africa, South East Asia, and the Middle East. Income from the library supports the Centre's work in conservation education in developing countries.

International Photobank
33 Barrs Avenue, New Milton, Hampshire BH25 5HL
☎ 0425 620359 Fax 0425 638151

Colour and b&w coverage of travel subjects: places, people, folklore, events.

IPA Picture Library
Crown House, Crown Lane, East Burnham, near Slough, Buckinghamshire SL2 3SG
☎ 02814 5177 Telex 847031 ARABIA G

Colour and b&w coverage of the Islamic world. Events, development, lifestyles, people, heritage, nature.

JAS Photographic Ltd
92–4 Church Road, Mitcham, Surrey CR4 3TD
☎ 01–685 9393 Fax 01–685 9479

Colour and b&w aerial photographs of most parts of UK. Some very detailed urban work. Also architectural photography. Commissions undertaken.

Camilla Jessel Photo Library
Riverside House, Riverside, Twickenham, Middlesex TW1 3DJ
☎ 01–892 1470 Fax 01–744 1217

Colour and b&w coverage of babies and children. Childbirth, newborns, children in hospital, race relations, socially disadvantaged children (UK, Africa, USA), Royal Ballet School, Royal Ballet on stage, child and adult musicians.

The Kennel Club Library
1–4 Clarges Street, London W1Y 8AB
☎ 01–493 6651 ext. 207

Dogs and the dog world. Mostly b&w with some material dating back to 1870.

The Keystone Collection
See the **Hulton Picture Company**

The Kobal Collection
28-32 Shelton Street, London WC2H 9HP
☎ 01–240 9565 Fax 01–836 3381

Colour and b&w coverage of Hollywood films: portraits, stills, publicity shots, posters, ephemera. Callers welcome by appointment.

Landscape Only
c/o Parr Joyce Partnership, 60 Poland Street, London W1V 3DF
☎ 01–427 2655/734 7344

Colour and b&w coverage of landscape and related subjects.

Frank Lane Picture Agency Ltd
Pages Green House, Wetheringsett, Stowmarket, Suffolk IP14 5QA
☎ 0728 860789 Fax 0728 860222

Colour and b&w coverage of natural history and weather. Represents Silvestris Fotoservice from Germany.

Andre Laubier Picture Library
4 St James Park, Bath, Avon BA1 2SS
☎ 0225 20688

Photographs, maps, stereographs, posters and greeting cards from 1935 to the present day. Travel, natural history, architecture, art, industry, religion, transport, sport, customs, crafts, abstracts, special effects. Visitors by appointment only.

Linz Images Ltd

No 1 Upstairs, West Centre, St Helier, Jersey, Channel Islands
☎ 0534 76412

Colour coverage of the Channel Islands. Also California, Hawaii, Morocco, Canaries, St Lucia, Gambia, Kenya, Australia and New Zealand. Commissions undertaken.

London Features International Ltd

Unit 3, London Close, Boscobel Street, London NW8 8PS
☎ 01–723 4204 Telex 25884 LONPIX G

Colour and b&w coverage of international showbusiness, pop, royalty, sport, politics, personalities.

Magnum Photos Ltd

Moreland Building, 2nd Floor, 23–5 Old Street, London EC1V 9HL
☎ 01–490 1771 Fax 01–608 0020

Founded in 1947 by Cartier Bresson. Coverage of world events from the Second World War to the present day. Also a large collection of personalities.

The Martin Library

45 Stainforth Road, Newbury Park, Ilford, Essex IG2 7EL
☎ 01–590 4144

Wildlife photography by Frank Martin.

S & O Mathews Photography

Stitches Farm House, Eridge, East Sussex TN3 9JB
☎ 089 285 2848 Fax 0892 665 024

British landscape, life, people, natural history.

Lee Miller Archives

Burgh Hill House, Chiddingly, near Lewes, East Sussex BN8 6JF
☎ 0825 872 691

The work of Lee Miller (1907–1977). Surrealist and contemporary art, poets and writers, fashion, London during the Blitz, Middle East, Egypt, Balkans in the 1930s, war in Europe, liberation of Dachau.

Monitor Syndication

17 Old Street, London EC1V 9HL
☎ 01–253 7071
Telex 24718 Fax 01–251 4405

Colour and b&w coverage of leading international personalities. Syndication to international, national and local media.

David Muscroft Photography and Picture Library

Vision House, 16 Broomfield Road, Heeley, Sheffield S8 0XJ
☎ 0742 589299 Fax 0742 550113

Colour and b&w coverage of snooker. All aspects of the game from the 19th century onwards. Also other sporting subjects and general file.

NAAS Ltd (News Afro Asian Service)

49 Goodge Street, London W1P 1FB
☎ 01–580 7448 Fax 01–631 1265

Colour and b&w coverage of Asia, Middle East and Northern Africa. All aspects of life in these areas. Commissions undertaken.

National History Photographic Agency (NHPA)

See **NHPA**

National Magazines Picture Library

72 Broadwick Street, London W1V 2BP
☎ 01–439 7144 Telex 263879 NATMAG G

Syndication of photographs commissioned for National Magazines' publications. Includes cookery section from *Good Housekeeping*, and fashion and beauty from *Harpers & Queen* and *Company*. Also interior and antiques. Visitors by appointment only.

National Medical Slide Bank

Holly House, 220 New London Road, Chelmsford, Essex CM2 9BJ
☎ 0245 283351 Telex 94012063 GMAL G

Colour coverage of clinical and general medicine and pathology, drawn from the collections of hospitals and medical schools.

The National Trust Photo Library

36 Queen Anne's Gate, London SW1H 9AS
☎ 01–222 9251 Fax 01–222 5097

Colour and b&w coverage of National Trust properties. Buildings, nature reserves, paintings, furniture, coastlines.

Natural Science Photos

33 Woodland Drive, Watford, Hertfordshire WD1 3BY
☎ 0923 245265 (24 hours)

Colour coverage of natural science subjects worldwide. Also botany, horticulture, freshwater angling and ethnic. Commissions undertaken.

Network Photographers

3–4 Kirby Street, London EC1N 8TS
☎ 01–831 3633 Fax 01–831 4468

Colour and b&w coverage of the UK, including industry, agriculture, arts, politics, news, sport and leisure, science. Foreign material also available. Commissions undertaken. List available.

NHPA (Natural History Photographic Agency)

Little Tye, 57 High Street, Ardingly, Sussex RH17 6TB
☎ 0444 892514
Telex 878110 BEEBEE G Fax 0444 892168

Colour and b&w coverage of natural history. Specialist files include Bushman culture; high speed subjects (birds, bats, frogs, insects – also splashes and explosions).

The Northern Picture Library

Unit 2, Bentinck Industrial Estate, Ellesmere Street, Chester Road, Manchester M15 4LN
☎ 061–834 1255 Fax 061–832 6270

Colour coverage of landscapes and topography of Britain and the world. Also trees, animals, industry, farming, sport, flowers. Commissions undertaken.

Observer Colour Library

PO Box 33, Edenbridge, Kent TN8 5PB
☎ 034 286313 Telex 95351 TOPHAM G

Half a million pictures from the *Observer* magazine.

Only Horses Picture Library

27 Greenway Gardens, Greenford, Middlesex UB6 9AF
☎ 01–578 9047

Colour and b&w coverage of all aspects of the horse. Foaling, retirement, racing, show jumping, eventing, veterinary, polo, breeds, personalities.

George Outram Picture Library

195 Albion Street, Glasgow G1 1QP
☎ 041–552 6255 Telex 779818

Mostly b&w photographs from *c.*1900 from the *Glasgow Herald* and *Evening Times*. Current affairs, Scotland, Glasgow, Clydesdale shipbuilding and engineering, personalities, World Wars I and II, sport.

Oxford Scientific Films Stills

Long Hanborough, Oxford OX7 2LD
☎ 0993 881881
Telex 83147 VIA OR OSF Fax 0993 882808

Natural history subjects photographed by Oxford Scientific Films. Animals, plants, histology, embryology, conservation, industry, high speed and time lapse. Commissions undertaken. Visitors by appointment.

Hugh Palmer

Knapp House, Shenington, near Banbury, Oxon OX15 6NE
☎ 0295 87433

Extensive coverage of gardens from Britain and Europe, also stately homes, conservatories and garden buildings.

Panos Pictures

8 Alfred Place, London WC1E 7EB
☎ 01–631 1590 Fax 01–436 8293

Colour and b&w coverage of Third World, with emphasis on environment and development. A leaflet is available. All profits from this library go to the Panos Institute to further its work in international sustainable development.

Parr Joyce Partnership

60 Poland Street, London W1V 3DF
☎ 01–734 7344

Still life, nudes, water sports, fairgrounds, food, people from Britain and Europe.

David Paterson Library

88 Cavendish Road, London SW12 0DF
☎ 01–673 2414

Travel, landscapes, nature, mountains from the UK, Europe, North Africa, the Himalayas, Japan and Scotland.

Penrose Pictures

Burgh Hill House, Chiddingly, near Lewes, East Sussex BN8 6JF
☎ 0825 872691/0825 872733

Colour and b&w coverage of farming, rural life, forestry, flora and fauna, ethnic subjects, landscapes from Britain, Turkey, Afghanistan, Iran, India, Australia, New Zealand, Peru, Colombia, Ecuador, Central America, USA, Canada.

The Photo Co-op

61 Webbs Road, London SW11 6RX
☎ 01–228 8949 Fax 01–675 3506

Colour and b&w coverage of contemporary social issues including babies and children, disablement, education, the elderly, environment, family, health, housing, homelessness, trade unions, race, women's issues, youth. Open 10.00 am – 6.00 pm. List available.

Photo Flora

46 Jacoby Place, Priory Road, Edgbaston, Birmingham B5 7UN
☎ 021–471 3300

Colour coverage of British and European wild plants. Most British species, rare and common; habitat pictures; also coverage of North India, Nepal, Egypt, Turkey and the Mediterranean.

Photo Library International

PO Box 75, Leeds LS7 3NZ
☎ 0532 623005
Telex 55293 Chacom G/PLI Fax 0532 625366

Colour coverage includes Yorkshire views, aspects of industry.

Photo Resources

The Orchard, Marley Lane, Kingston, Canterbury, Kent CT4 6JH
☎ 0227 830075

Colour and b&w coverage of archaeology, art, ancient art, ethnology, mythology, world religion, museum objects.

The Photo Source

Unit C1, Enterprise Business Estate, 2 Millharbour, Mastmaker Road, London E14 9TE
☎ 01–987 1212
Telex 888258 Fax 01–538 3309

Colour coverage of travel, glamour, people, animals, industry. Colour catalogue available. Incorporates Colour Library International.

Photofile International

17 Victoria Grove, London W8 5RW
☎ 01–584 6738 Telex 8956130

People, families, travel, sport, industrial, landscapes. Colour catalogue available.

The Photographers' Library

81A Endell Street, London WC2H 9AJ
☎ 01–836 5591/240 5554 Fax 01–379 4650

Covers principal European, North American, African and Far Eastern centres. Industry, transport, sport, families, landscapes, skyscapes and seascapes. Brochure available.

Photos Horticultural

169 Valley Road, Ipswich, Suffolk IP1 4PJ
☎ 0473 257329 Fax 0473 233974

Colour and b&w coverage of all aspects of gardening in Britain and abroad. Commissions undertaken.

PictureBank Photo Library Ltd

Parman House, 30–36 Fife Road, Kingston upon Thames, London KT1 1EU
☎ 01–547 2344
Telex 928017 Fax 01–547 2241

Colour coverage of girls, models, children, families, hotels, London, Europe, travel, technology, animals, sport, paintings. Commissions undertaken. Visitors welcome.

Pictures Colour Library

Suite B3, 16–16A Baldwins Gardens,
London EC1N 7RJ
☏ 01–831 2120 Fax 01–831 1336

Landscapes, travel, people, children, food, interiors, architecture, industry, glamour and still life. Visitors welcome.

Pitkin Pictorials Ltd

North Way, Andover, Hants SP10 5BE
☏ 0264 334303
Telex 47214 Fax 0264 334110

Colour and b&w coverage of architecture: cathedrals, churches and stately homes.

Planet Earth Pictures/Seaphot

4 Harcourt Street, London W1H 1DS
☏ 01–262 4427/8
Telex 28221 REDFOT G Fax 01–706 4042

Marine and natural history photographs. All aspects of the sea, including underwater. Wildlife and landscapes around the world, and sports. Commissions undertaken, especially underwater.

Axel Poignant Archive

115 Bedford Mansions, Bedford Avenue,
London WC1B 3AG
☏ 01–636 2555

Anthropological and ethnographic subjects, especially Australia and the South Pacific. Also Scandinavia (early history and mythology), Sicily and England.

Popperfoto

Paul Popper Ltd, 24 Bride Lane, Fleet Street,
London EC4Y 8DR
☏ 01–353 9665/6 Telex 8814206 Popper G

Includes early colour from 1940s, and b&w from 1870 to the present day. Subjects include Scott's 1910–1912 Antarctic expedition, wars, royalty, sport, politics, transport, crime, topography, history, and social conditions worldwide.

Fiona Pragoff

9 Lancashire Court, New Bond Street,
London W1Y 9AD
☏ 01–629 5075

Children, ranging from babies to teenagers, both on location and in the studio.

Premaphotos Wildlife

2 Willoughby Close, Kings Coughton, Alcester,
Warwickshire B49 5QJ
☏ 0789 762938

Natural history worldwide. Subjects include flowering and non-flowering plants, fungi, slime moulds, fruits and seeds, galls, leaf mines, seashore life, amphibians, insects, spiders, habitats, scenery and also cultivated cactuses. Commissions undertaken. Visitors welcome.

Press Association

See **Library Services**

Press-tige Pictures

3 Newmarket Road, Cringleford,
Norwich NR4 6UE
☏ 0603 54345

Colour and b&w photographs of natural history subjects, also geography, tourism and agriculture around the world. Some highspeed and scientific. Commissions undertaken.

Professional Sport

8 Apollo Studios, Charlton Kings Mews,
London NW5 2SA
☏ 01–482 2311 Fax 01–482 2441

Colour and b&w coverage of tennis, golf, soccer, athletics, boxing, winter sports and many minor sports.

QA Photos Library

8 Stade Street, Hythe, Kent CT21 6BD
☏ 0303 68233

The Channel tunnel – construction shots and related aspects since 1986.

Quadrant Picture Library

Quadrant House, The Quadrant, Sutton,
Surrey SM2 5AS
☏ 01–661 3427/8
Telex 892084 BISPRS G(EST) Fax 01–661 8933

Colour and b&w coverage of transport and motor sport from early 1900s to the present day. Also motoring artwork from the '20s and '30s.

Redferns

7 Bramley Road, London W10 6SZ
☎ 01–792 9914 Fax 01–792 0921

Colour and b&w coverage of pop, jazz, easy listening, heavy metal, country and folk music. Includes over 2500 artists and an early American jazz collection. List available.

Reflex Picture Agency Ltd

83 Clerkenwell Road, London EC1R 5BX
☎ 01–405 8545

Colour and b&w coverage of events worldwide. People and places, politics, inner cities, industry, unemployment, strikes, demonstrations. Photographers based in Iran and South Africa. Commissions undertaken. Lists available. Visitors welcome by appointment.

Relay Photos Ltd

2 Queensborough Mews, London W2 3SG
☎ 01–402 2178 Fax 01–706 4564

Colour and b&w coverage of pop personalities in the last 20 years. Constantly updated.

Remote Source

13 Chapter Street, London SW1P 4NY
☎ 01–630 7102 Telex 266774 EXPIOR G

Expedition photographs from remote, unusual and adventurous destinations. Commissions undertaken.

Repfoto London

74 Creffield Road, London W3 9PS
☎ 01–992 2936 Fax 01–992 9641

A specialist service for the rock music industry. Incorporates the Rock Library: colour and b&w photographs from the last 15 years.

Retna Pictures Ltd

1 Fitzroy Mews, off Cleveland Street,
London W1P 5DQ
☎ 01–388 3444 Fax 01–388 7151

Colour and b&w coverage of rock and pop performers, actors, actresses, entertainers and celebrities.

Retrographic Archive Collection

164 Kensington Park Road, London W11 2ER
☎ 01–727 9378/9426

Original graphics from the past: packaging, typography, fashion, advertising, magazine and label art from 1860–1960. Food, alcohol, chocolate, shipping labels, pharmaceutics, USA printers' sample books for tiles, wallpaper and textiles, Middle Eastern and Third World products, performing arts, circus, classical music, optical toys. Visitors welcome by appointment.

Reuter and UPI

c/o Popperfoto, 24 Bride Lane, Fleet Street,
London EC4Y 8DR
☎ 01–353 9665/6
Telex 8814206 Popper G Fax 01–936 2153

Daily news coverage worldwide. The UPI collection covers 1920s to the present day.

Rex Features Ltd

18 Vine Hill, London EC1R 5DX
☎ 01–278 7294/8
Telex 25491 Fax 01–837 4812

Established in the 1950s. Colour and b&w coverage of news, politics, personalities, show business, glamour, humour, art, medicine, science, landscapes, celebrities, royalties.

Ann Ronan Picture Library

Wheel Cottage, Bishops Hull, Taunton,
Somerset TA1 5EP
☎ 0823 252737 Fax 0823 336785

History of science and technology in the form of 150,000 illustrations from printed sources AD 1500–1920. Personalities, scientific experiments, manufacturing, mining, agriculture, transport, child labour, cookery, communications, medicine.

RoSPA (The Royal Society for the Prevention of Accidents)

Cannon House, The Priory, Queensway,
Birmingham B4 6BS
☎ 021–200 2461 Telex 336546

Colour and b&w coverage of all aspects of safety: road, occupational, home, water, education, police and fire service.

Science Photo Library

112 Westbourne Grove, London W2 5RU
☎ 01–727 4712/229 9847

Colour and b&w coverage of all aspects of science, technology and medicine. Subjects include laboratories, industry, hospitals, astronomy, biology, botany, chemistry, computers, earth sciences, genetics, landscapes, physics, satellite imagery, space, zoology.

Sealand Aerial Photography

Goodwood Airfield, Chichester,
West Sussex PO18 0PH
☎ 0243 781025

Colour coverage of subjects throughout the UK. Operations carried out throughout the year.

Sefton Photo Library

30–30A Mason Street, Manchester M4 5EY
☎ 061–834 9423/832 7670

Colour and b&w coverage of general subjects: sport, farming, animals, sunsets, historic transport, personalities. Also, many industrial subjects, and aspects of the North of England and Wales. Collection, too, of Victorian and Edwardian scenes. Commissions undertaken.

Phil Shelton Golf Picture Library

3 Grimsdyke Crescent, Arkley, Barnet,
Hertfordshire EN5 4AH
☎ 01–440 1986 Fax 01–440 9348

Colour and b&w coverage of golf, including major championships, tournaments and the Ryder Cup.

Brian and Sal Shuel

13 Woodberry Crescent, London N10 1PJ
☎ 01–883 2531 Fax 01–883 9215

A personal collection (colour and b&w) of British customs, bridges, and London. Also b&w 'fun' photos from the last 25 years. Visitors welcome by appointment.

Skyscan Balloon Photography

Stanway Grounds Farm, Stanway, Cheltenham,
Gloucestershire GL54 5DR
☎ 0242 69357 (24 hours) Fax 0242 69671

Colour and b&w aerial views taken from a tethered balloon. Industrial, cities, countryside, coasts, stately homes, heritage sites. Commissions undertaken.

South American Pictures

48 Station Road, Woodbridge, Suffolk IP12 4AT
☎ 03943 3963/3279

Colour and b&w images of South America and Mexico, including archaelogy and the Amazon. Frequently updated. There is an archival section, with pictures and documents from most countries.

Space Frontiers Ltd

The Telegraph Colour Library, Unit C1,
Enterprise Business Estate, Mastmaker Road, 2
Millharbour, London E14 9TE
☎ 01–987 0121
Telex 888258 Fax 01–538 3309

US manned and unmanned space programmes, orbital views of Earth's surface and weather, spacecraft, constellations, comets, nebulae, planets, men and machines in free space and on the Moon.

Spectrum Colour Library

146 Oxford Street, London W1N 9DL
☎ 01–637 1587/2108 Fax 01–637 3681

A large collection including travel, sport, people, pets, scenery, industry, British and European cities. Visitors welcome.

Split Second

1A Doughty Street, Gray's Inn Road,
London WC1N 2PH
☎ 01–831 4316 Fax 01–831 4322

Sports and live action.

Frank Spooner Pictures

Suite 820/1 Africa House, Kingsway,
London WC2B 6AY
☎ 01–405 9943
Telex 262501 Fax 01–831 2483

Handles UK distribution of Gamma Presse Images of Paris. Subjects include war, fashion, politics, travel, adventure, sport, personalities, films, animals. Branches in New York and Paris.

Sporting Pictures (UK) Ltd

7A Lamb's Conduit Passage, London WC1R 4RG
☎ 01–405 4500/1844
Telex 27924 Fax 01–831 7991

Colour and b&w coverage of professional, amateur and leisure sports, including coverage of major names and events of the last 15 years. Visitors welcome. Commissions undertaken.

Steam Locomotives of the World

The Square, Newton Harcourt,
Leicestershire LE8 0FQ
☏ 0537592068/0625615491

Colour coverage of the last steam locomotives in the world taken on expeditions over the last 15 years. Dramatic locations and situations.

Stockphotos

3rd Floor, 7 Langley Street, London WC2N 4AY
☏ 01–240 7361

British landscapes and general UK material, also USA.

Tony Stone Worldwide

28 Finchley Road, London NW8 6ES
☏ 01–586 7671/586 3222 Fax 01–722 9305

Colour coverage of subjects of international interest including travel, wildlife, industry, sports, people, historic transport. Catalogue available.

Jessica Strang

86 Cambridge Gardens, London W10 6HS
☏ 01–969 7292 Telex 268312 WESCOM G

Current architecture and design; vanishing architecture of London, and specialist and idiosyncratic collections. Also sculpture, architecture, markets, local colour of Bali, Malaysia, Singapore, Burma, Australia, America, Sicily, Corsica, Spain, Holland and France.

Survival Anglia Photo Library

Brook House, 113 Park Lane, London W1Y 4DX
☏ 01–321 0101 Fax 01–493 2598

Colour and b&w coverage of all aspects of natural history. Catalogue available.

Swift Picture Library

Claremont, Redwood Close, Ringwood,
Hants BH24 1PR
☏ 0425 478333 Fax 0425 471525

Colour coverage of scenery and natural history. Britain, West Greenland, parts of Africa and Europe. Commissions undertaken. Visitors welcome.

Syndication International

4–12 Dorrington Street, London EC1N 7TB
☏ 01–404 0004
Telex 267503 SYNINT Fax 01–430 2437

Photographs, text and cartoons from the Mirror Group newspapers and IPC magazines. Colour and b&w photographs on a variety of subjects.

Telefocus

Floor A3, British Telecom Centre, 81 Newgate Street, London EC1A 7AJ
☏ 01–356 6591/2/3
Telex 8811510 Fax 01–356 6591/6630

Coverage of telecommunications, optical fibres, research labs, satellites, rural locations, telephone cable laying, staff at work. Also an historical collection including Alexander Graham Bell, early cable ships and early telephone exchanges.

The Telegraph Colour Library

Unit C1, Enterprise Business Estate, Mastmaker Road, 2 Millharbour, London E14 9TE
☏ 01–987 1212
Telex 888258 Fax 01–538 3309

Colour coverage of a wide range of subjects, including photographs commissioned by the *Sunday Telegraph* magazine. Good travel and space collections. Catalogue available.

Three Lions

See the **Hulton Picture Company**

Patrick Thurston Colour Library

10 Willis Road, Cambridge CB1 2AQ
☏ 0223 352547 Fax 0223 66274

Colour coverage of Britain: scenery, people, museums, churches, coastline. Also Amsterdam, Bangkok, Edinburgh, London, Rome, Venice, Elba, Finland, Iceland. Commissions undertaken.

Topham Picture Library

PO Box 33, Edenbridge, Kent TN8 5PB
☏ 034 286 313
Telex 95351 TOPHAM G Fax 034 286 244

Colour and b&w coverage of news, personalities, war, royalty, topography, natural history.

Also *The Observer* colour library and *Private Eye* cartoons.

Trades Union Congress

See under **Library Services**

Tessa Traeger

7 Rossetti Studios, 72 Flood Street,
London SW3 5TF
☎ 01-352 3641

Food, gardens, travel, artists. Visitors welcome.

Tropic Photographic Library

156 Meols Parade, Meols, Wirral,
Merseyside LA7 6AN
☎ 051-632 1698

Colour and b&w coverage of the developing world, with extensive files on all areas and much material from sensitive and remote locations. Commissions undertaken.

United Press International (UPI 1932–1970)

PO Box 33, Edenbridge, Kent TN8 5PB
☎ 034 286 313
Telex 95351 TOPHAM G Fax 034 286 244

An international news file commencing 1932.

Universal Pictorial Press & Agency Ltd

30–34 New Bridge Street, London EC4V 6BN
☎ 01-248 6730
Telex G 8952718 UNIPIX Fax 01-489 8932

Colour and b&w coverage of news, royalty, politics, sport, arts, and many other subjects. Commissions undertaken for press and public relations.

USSR Photo Library

Conifers House, Cheapside Lane, Denham,
Uxbridge UB9 5AE
☎ 0895 834814

Images of the Soviet Union: cities, museums, cathedrals, resorts, traditional costumes and dances, craftsmen at work.

The Victoria and Albert Museum Picture Library

The Victoria and Albert Museum, South
Kensington, London SW7 2RL
☎ 01-838 8354 Telex 268831 VICART G

Colour and b&w coverage of decorative and applied arts, including ceramics, ivories, furniture, costumes, textiles, stage, musical instruments, toys, and Indian, Far Eastern and Islamic objects.

Viewfinder Colour Photo Library

The Production House, 147A St Michael's Hill,
Cotham, Bristol BS2 8DB
☎ 0272 731729/237268

Colour coverage of industry, agriculture, people, travel. Detailed coverage of South West England, Wales and the Channel Islands. Stock list available.

The Vintage Magazine Company Ltd

7–8 Greenland Place, London NW1 0AP
☎ 01-482 5083 Fax 01-482 4429

A large collection of movie stills, and photographs covering music, glamour, social history, theatre posters, ephemera, postcards.

Visionbank Library Ltd (incorporating England Scene)

Riverside, Studio B5, Metropolitan Wharf,
Wapping Wall, London E1 9SS
☎ 01-702 0023 Fax 01-480 7336

Extensive worldwide coverage of many subjects. Large collection of England.

Visnews Still Service

Cumberland Avenue, Park Royal,
London NW10 7EH
☎ 01-453 4233/4227
Telex 22678 VIS LDN G Fax 01-695 0620

Colour coverage of international political leaders, personalities and locations. Stills service available from Visnews' international coverage, BBC news, clients' own video, or Aston caption generator.

VS Photo Library

See **Ace Photo Agency**

John Walmsley Picture Library
27 Wyeths Road, Epsom, Surrey KT17 4EB
☎ 0372 743374

Education: schools, colleges, universities, in-service training, skill centres, at home. Commissions undertaken. Subject list available.

Waterways Picture Library
39 Manor Court Road, Hanwell, London W7 3EJ
☎ 01–840 1659

Colour and b&w coverage of rivers, canals, bridges, locks, aqueducts, tunnels, holidays, canal art, fishing, wildlife, town and country. Commissions undertaken.

West Air Photography
40 Alexandra Parade,
Weston super Mare BS23 1QZ
☎ 0934 621333 Fax 0934 635421

Colour and b&w aerial coverage of locations all over England and South Wales. Commissions undertaken.

Eric Whitehead Picture Library and Agency
PO Box 33, Kendal, Cumbria LA9 4SU
☎ 0539 33166

Snooker, indoor bowling, mountaineering, landscapes, heritage, major events in the North of England. Commissions undertaken.

Elizabeth Whiting and Associates
21 Albert Street, London NW1 7LU
☎ 01–388 2828 Fax 01–387 1615

Interior decoration and home interest – many different types of home represented.

Janine Wiedel
6 Stirling Road, London SW9 9EE
☎ 01–737 0007

Social documentary over the last 20 years. Education, industry, women's issues, childbirth, ethnic groups (Eskimos, Gypsies, Asian and black communities in UK), Arctic, Iceland, Galapagos Islands, Iran, Europe, USA. Commissions undertaken. Leaflets available. Visitors welcome by appointment.

Andy Williams Photo Library
3 Levylsdene, Merrow, Guildford,
Surrey GU1 2RS
☎ 0483 572778

Colour coverage of British Isles and Continent. London, castles, historic houses, gardens, cottages, golf, waterfalls, windmills, lighthouses. Commissions undertaken. Visitors welcome.

David Williams Picture Library
50 Burlington Avenue, Glasgow G12 0LH
☎ 041–339 7823

Colour coverage of Scotland and Iceland. Landscapes, historical sites, geology and geomorphology.

S&I Williams Power Pix International Picture Library
Castle Lodge, Wenvoe, Cardiff CF5 6AD
☎ 0222 595163
Telex 995411 Fax 0222 593905

Colour coverage of a wide range of subjects including abstracts, agriculture, aviation, glamour, landscapes, natural history, people, sport, sub-acqua, yachting, America, Australia, Canada, Europe, India, Japan and Great Britain. Commissions undertaken. Catalogue available.

Vaughan Williams Memorial Library
English Folk Song and Dance Society, Cecil Sharp House, 2 Regent's Park Road,
London NW1 7AY
☎ 01–485 2206

Colour and b&w coverage of traditional/folk music, dance and customs worldwide, focussing on Britain and other English-speaking nations. Photographs date from the late 19th century to the present day. (Also see **Library Services**).

Roger Wood Library
45 Victoria Road, Deal, Kent CT14 7AY
☎ 0304 372786
Telex 477719 a/b/MARFIL attn Roger Wood
Fax 0304 365766 (attn Wood)

Colour and b&w coverage of the Middle East, especially antiquities and tourism. Egypt, North Africa, Iran, some Gulf States, Greece, Turkey, Ethiopia, Pakistan, Bangladesh.

Woodmansterne Publications Ltd

Watford Business Park, Watford WD1 8RD
☎ 0923 228236/245788 Fax 0923 245788

Colour coverage of Britain, Europe and the Holy Land. Architecture, cathedrals, interiors, painting, sculpture, natural history, butterflies, volcanoes, transport, space exploration, opera and ballet, sunsets, state occasions.

Michael Woodward Licensing

Parlington Hall, Parlington, Aberford, West Yorkshire LS25 3EG
☎ 0532 813913
Telex 55293 Fax 0532 813911

Represent over 100 illustrators, artists and photographers, with extensive files on most subjects.

The Woolverton Colour Library

Hatters End, Lawton Cross, Kingsland, Leominster, Herefordshire HR6 9AU
☎ 05447 584

Colour coverage of UK, France, Germany, Austria, Switzerland, Belgium, Sicily, Yugoslavia and Greece. Alpine and British wild flowers. Visitors welcome.

World Press Network

112 Westbourne Park Road, London W2 5PL
☎ 01–221 5587 Fax 01–229 6720

Colour and b&w coverage of beauty, fashion, relationships, food, home and family, news, sport, business, Australia (politics, celebrities). Offices in Australia and New York.

World Wildlife Fund International Library

See **Bruce Coleman Ltd**

George Wright

Mountover Farm, Rampisham, Dorchester, Dorset DT2 0PL
☎ 093583 333

Colour coverage of English gardens, landscapes and countryside; people and events; British and European regional cooking. Also some coverage of Middle East, India, Nepal and USA.

York Archaeological Trust for Excavation and Research Ltd

1 Pavement, York YO1 2NA
☎ 0904 643211

Colour and b&w coverage of the antiquities, archaeology and architecture of the City of York and the surrounding area.

Proofreading

The ultimate responsibility for checking proofs rests with the author.

Make an absolute minimum of alterations, as distinct from correcting misprints. Making alterations at proof stage is wasteful in time and effort, and is very expensive. An author is liable to be charged for all corrections in excess of the allowance agreed in his contract. (Remember this allowance is a proportion of the typesetting cost and not a proportion of the length of the book.) Alterations may cause delay and can result in new errors being introduced. They can also have knock-on effects throughout the book on cross-references and an index.

The author normally receives page proofs – that is, the type matter will have already been divided into numbered pages. The proofs will not reflect the quality of the finished book, especially if, as is often the case, they take the form of photocopies.

It is a great help in working out the cost of the corrections if you mark the proofs with red ink for printer's errors (that is, any deviation from the typescript as it was sent to him); and blue or black ink for your alterations or additions.

The following paragraph shows the commonest correction marks and how they can be employed. Where more than one correction is required on the same line, marginal marks can be divided between left and right margin space logically and as appropriate. All corrections (margin marks) should be followed by a diagonal line (/) to indicate that the correction is finished.

INTRODUCtiON

Straddling the top of Europe, the Nordic races have been for
much of their history culurally sheltered on the south and west
by the sea and on the esat by the forest and swamps which
separated Finland from the inhabited areas of Russia
Naturally, they tended to look inwards and, irrespective of
political differences to develop a common set of values Down
the centuries, the achievements of one country - from the
Icelandic sagas to the sWedish invention of teh ball-bearing -
were adopted by the others as part of the Nordic creative genius.
So, today, a Swede will take pride in a Finns design, a Norwegian
looks to Swedish technology to multiply wealth from North Sea
oil and a Dane acknowledges the mid night sun as part of his
heritage, even though geographically he is ill suited ever to it.

Text Marks	Function	Margin Marks
	Delete character(s), word(s) or line	
	Insert character(s), word(s)	

Mark in text	Instruction	Mark in margin
⋏	Insert space	#⋏/
⋏	Insert comma	,⋏/
⋏	Insert full stop	⊙⋏/
⋏	Insert colon	⊙⋏/
⋏	Insert semicolon	;⋏/
⋏	Insert apostrophe, quotation marks	’⋏/‘⋏/’⋏
mid night	Close up space	⁀‿/
N/aturally	Delete character(s), punctuation, words, etc. and close up	∂/
text (dotted underline)	Retain character(s), word(s), punctuation, which have been marked for deletion	(stet)/
INTRODucTION	Change lower case (lc) character(s) to upper case (caps)	(caps) or ≡/
E/Urope	Change to lower case, not caps	(l.c.)
FOUNDED	Set in small caps	(s.c.) or =/
(Russia)	Wrong face/typesize	(w.f.)
sagas	Set in italics	(itals) or ⎯/
INTRODUCTION	Set in bold	(bold) or ~/
text	Set in bold italics	(bold itals) or ~/
(text)	Set in roman, not itals	(roms) or ⊥/
	Run on text (no new line or para.)	(R/o)
∽	Transpose characters or words	(trs) or ∽/
3 2 4 1 (over words numbering them in new order)	Transpose words (when above method not easy to use)	1 2 3 4 (listing new order required)
[text	Take over to next line	(t/o)/
text]	Take back to previous line (commonly used to correct widows)	(t/b)/

text text	Take over to start new para.	N.P. /
or more commonly in front of text		
text	Indent	/
text	Cancel indent	/
text	Correct horizontal alignment	═/
text	Correct vertical alignment	‖/

Tax and the Writer

'No man in this country is under the smallest obligation, moral or other, to arrange his affairs as to enable the Inland Revenue to put the largest possible shovel in his stores.

The Inland Revenue is not slow, and quite rightly, to take every advantage which is open to it ... for the purpose of depleting the taxpayer's pockets. And the taxpayer is, in like manner, entitled to be astute to prevent as far as he honestly can the depletion of his means by the Inland Revenue.'

LORD CLYDE
Ayrshire Pullman v. Inland Revenue Commissioners, 1929.

Value Added Tax

Value Added Tax (VAT) is a tax currently levied at 15% on:

(a) the total value of taxable goods and services supplied to consumers,
(b) the importation of goods into the UK,
(c) certain services from abroad if a taxable person receives them in the UK for the purpose of their business.

Who is Taxable?

A writer resident in the UK whose turnover from writing and any other business, craft or art on a self-employed basis is greater than £23,600 annually, or exceeds £8000 in one quarter before deducting agent's commission, must register with HM Customs & Excise as a taxable person. Penalties will be claimed in the case of late registration. A writer whose turnover is below these limits is exempt from the requirement to register for VAT, but may apply for voluntary registration, and this will be allowed at the discretion of HM Customs & Excise.

A taxable person collects VAT on outputs (turnover) and deducts VAT paid on inputs (taxable expenses) and where VAT collected exceeds VAT paid, must remit the difference to HM Customs & Excise. In the event that input exceeds output, the difference will be repaid by HM Customs & Excise.

Outputs (Turnover)

A writer's outputs are taxable services supplied to publishers, broadcasting organisations, theatre managements, film companies, educational institutions, etc. A taxable writer must invoice, i.e. collect from, all the persons (either individuals or organisations) in the UK for whom supplies have been made, for fees, royalties or other considerations plus VAT. An unregistered writer cannot and must not invoice for VAT. A taxable writer is not obliged to collect VAT on royalties or other fees paid by publishers or others overseas for supplies. In practice agents usually collect VAT for the registered author.

Taxable at the standard rate	*Taxable at the zero rate*	*Exempt*
Rent of certain commercial premises	Books	Rent of non-commercial premises
	Periodicals	
Advertisements in newspapers, magazines, journals and periodicals	Lighting	Rates
	Heating	Postage
Agent's commission (unless it relates to monies from overseas, when it is zero-rated)	Coach, rail, and air travel	Services supplied by unregistered persons
		Subscriptions to the **Society of Authors, PEN, NUJ,** etc.
Accountant's fees		Wages and salaries
Solicitor's fees re business matters		Insurance
		Taxicab fares
Agency services (typing, copying, etc.)		
Stationery and typewriters		
Artists' materials		
Photographic equipment		
Tape recorders and tapes		
Hotel accommodation		
Motor-car expenses		*Outside the Scope of VAT*
Telephone		P.L.R. (Public Lending Rights)
		Profit Shares
Theatres and concerts		Dividend income

NB This list is not exhaustive

Remit to Customs

The taxable writer adds up the VAT which has been paid on taxable inputs, deducts it from the VAT received and remits the balance to Customs. Business with HM Customs is conducted through the local VAT Offices of HM Customs which are listed in local telephone directories, except for tax returns which are sent direct to the Customs and Excise VAT Central Unit, Alexander House, 21 Victoria Avenue, Southend-on-Sea, Essex SS99 1AA.

Accounting

A taxable writer is obliged to account to HM Customs & Excise at quarterly intervals. Accounts must be completed and sent to VAT Central Unit within 28 days of the accounting date. It should be noted that only invoices are necessary to complete a VAT return, not receipts.

Since the 1st October 1987, it has been possible to account for the VAT liability under the Cash Accounting Scheme (Note 731), whereby the author accounts for the output tax when the invoice is paid or royalties, etc. are received. The same applies to the input tax, but as most purchases are probably on a 'cash basis', this will not make a considerable difference to the author's input tax. This scheme is only applicable to those with a taxable turnover of less than £250,000 and, therefore, is available to the majority of authors. The advantage of this scheme is that the author does not have to account for VAT before receiving payment, thereby relieving the author of a cash flow problem. To join or transfer to this scheme, application must be made to the VAT office to which the author is assigned.

Registration

A writer will be given a VAT Registration Number which must be quoted on all VAT correspondence. It is the responsibility of those registered to inform those to whom they make supplies of their Registration Number. A writer who would not normally be required to register as taxable may, on receipt of a single large payment, for example in respect of film rights or a paperback edition, find that the quarterly or annual turnover has risen above the limits and is liable to register. If the local VAT Office is satisfied that the turnover will not exceed £23,600 in the next 12 months, they may not insist on registration.

Voluntary Registration

A writer whose turnover is below the limits may apply to register. If the writer is paying a relatively large amount of VAT on taxable inputs – agent's commissions, accountant's fees, equipment, materials, or agency services, etc. – it may make a significant improvement in the net income to be able to offset the VAT on these inputs. An author who pays relatively little VAT may find it easier, and no more expensive, to remain unregistered.

Fees and Royalties

A taxable writer must notify those to whom he makes supplies of the Tax Registration Number at the first opportunity. One method of accounting for and paying VAT on fees and royalties is the use of multiple stationery for 'self-billing', one copy of the royalty statement being used by the author as the VAT invoice. A second method is for the recipient of taxable outputs to pay fees, including authors' royalties, without VAT. The taxable author then renders a tax invoice for the VAT element and a second payment, of the VAT element, will be made. This scheme is cumbersome but will involve only taxable authors. Fees and royalties from abroad will count as payments for exported services and will accordingly be zero-rated.

Agents and Accountants

A writer is responsible to HM Customs for making VAT returns and payments. Neither an agent nor an accountant nor a solicitor can take this over, although they can be helpful in preparing and keeping VAT returns and accounts. Their professional fees or commission will, except in rare cases where the adviser or agent is himself unregistered, be taxable at the standard rate and will represent some of a writer's taxable inputs. An agent's commission in respect of zero-rated fees and royalties received from abroad is not liable for VAT.

Income Tax – Schedule D

An unregistered writer can claim some of the VAT paid on taxable inputs as a business expense allowable against income tax. However, certain taxable inputs fall into categories which cannot be claimed under the income tax regulations. A taxable writer, who has already offset VAT on inputs, cannot charge it as a business expense for the purposes of income tax.

Certain Services From Abroad

A taxable author who resides in the United Kingdom and who receives certain services from abroad must account for VAT on those services at the appropriate tax rate on the sum paid for them. Examples of the type of services concerned include: services of lawyers, accountants, consultants, provisions of information and copyright permissions.

Income Tax

What is a professional writer for tax purposes?

Writers are professionals while they are writing regularly with the intention of making a profit; or while they are gathering material, researching or otherwise preparing a publication.

A professional freelance writer is taxed under Case II of Schedule D of the *Income and Corporation Taxes Act 1970*. The taxable income is the amount received, either directly or by an agent, on his behalf, less expenses wholly and exclusively laid out for the purposes of the profession. If expenses exceed income, the loss can either be carried forward and set against future income from writing or set against other income which is subject to tax in the same year. If tax has been paid on that other income, a repayment can be obtained, or the sum can be offset against other tax liabilities. Special loss relief can apply in the opening year of the profession. Losses made in the first four years can be set against income of up to five earlier years.

Where a writer receives very occasional payments for isolated articles, it may not be possible to establish that these are profits arising from carrying on a continuing profession. In such circumstances these 'isolated transactions' may be assessed under Case VI of Schedule D of the *Income and Corporation Taxes Act 1970*. Again, expenses may be deducted in arriving at the taxable income, but, if expenses exceed income, the loss can only be set against the profits from future isolated transactions, or other income assessable under Case VI.

Expenses

A writer can normally claim the following expenses:

(a) Secretarial, typing, proofreading, research. Where payments for these are made to the author's wife or husband, they should be recorded and entered in the author's tax return, or (in the case of a married woman her husband's tax return) as earned income which is subject to the usual personal allowances.

(b) Telephone, telegrams, postage, stationery, printing, maintenance and insurance or equipment, dictation tapes, batteries, office requisites used for the profession.

(c) Periodicals, books (including presentation copies and reference books) and other publications necessary for the profession, but amounts received from the sale of books should be deducted.

(d) Hotels, fares, car running expenses (including repairs, petrol, oil, garaging, parking, cleaning, insurance, licence, road fund tax, depreciation), hire of cars or taxis in connection with:
   (i) business discussions with agents, publishers, co-authors, collaborators, researchers, illustrators, etc.
   (ii) travel at home and abroad to collect background material.

(e) Publishing and advertising expenses, including costs of proof corrections, indexing, photographs, etc.

(f) Subscriptions to societies and associations, press cutting agencies, libraries, etc. incurred wholly for the purpose of the profession.

(g) Premiums to pension schemes such as the *Society of Authors Retirement Benefits Scheme*. For contributors born in 1954 and later, the maximum premium is now $17\frac{1}{2}$% of net earned income. Higher limits apply for those born before 1954.

(h) Rent, general rates, and water rates, etc., the proportion being determined by the ratio which the number of rooms are used exclusively for the profession bears to the total number of rooms in the residence. But see note on *Capital Gains Tax* below.

(i) Lighting, heating and cleaning. A carefully estimated figure of the business use of these costs can be claimed as a proportion of the total.

(j) Accountancy charges and legal charges incurred wholly in the course of the profession including cost of defending libel actions, damages in so far as they are not covered by insurance and libel insurance premiums. However, where in a libel case, damages are awarded to punish the author for having acted maliciously the action becomes quasi-criminal and costs and damages may not be allowed.

(k) TV and video rental (which may be apportioned for private use), and cinema or theatre tickets, if wholly for the purpose of the profession, e.g. playwriting.

(l) Capital allowances for equipment, e.g. car, TV, radio, hi-fi sets, tape and video recorders, dictaphones, typewriters, desks, bookshelves, filing cabinets, photographic equipment. Allowances vary in the Finance Acts depending upon political and economic views prevailing. At present they are set at 25%. On motor cars the allowance is 25% in the first year and 25% of the reduced balance in each successive year limited to £2000 each year. The total allowances in the case of all assets must not exceed the difference between cost and eventual sale price. Allowances will be reduced to exclude personal (non-professional) use where necessary.

(m) Lease rent. The cost of lease rent of equipment is allowable; also of cars, subject to restrictions for private use and for expensive cars.

NB It is always advisable to keep detailed records. Diary entries of appointments, notes of fares and receipted bills are much more convincing to the Inland Revenue than round figure estimates.

(n) Gifts to charitable bodies are allowed, subject to certain conditions, provided they are reasonable in amount and for a cause connected with the donor's professional activities. Tax relief is also available for three years (minimum) covenants to charities.

Capital Gains Tax

The exemption from Capital Gains Tax which applies to an individual's main residence does not apply to any part of that residence which is used exclusively for business purposes. The effect of this is that the appropriate proportion of any increase in value of the residence since 31st March 1982 can be taxed, when the residence is sold, at the maximum rate of 40% (at present).

Writers who own their houses should bear this in mind before claiming expenses for the use of a room for writing purposes. Arguments in favour of making such claims are that they afford some relief now, while Capital Gains Tax in its present form may not stay for ever. Also, where a new house is bought in place of an old one, the gain made on the sale of the first study may be set off against the cost of the study in the new house, thus postponing the tax payment until the final sale. For this relief to apply, each house must have a study, and the author must continue his profession throughout. On death there is an exemption of the total Capital Gains of the estate.

NB Writers can claim that their use is non-exclusive and restrict their claim to the cost of extra lighting, heating and cleaning so that no Capital Gains Tax liability arises.

Can a writer average-out his income over a number of years for tax purposes?

Under Section 389 of the *Income and Corporation Taxes Act 1970*, a writer may in certain circumstances spread over two or three fiscal years lump sum payments, whenever received, and royalties received during two years from the date of first publication or performance of work. Points to note are:

(a) The relief can only be claimed if the writer has been engaged in preparing and collecting material and writing the work for more than twelve months.

(b) If the period of preparing and writing the work exceeds twelve months but does not exceed twenty-four months, one-half of the advances and/or royalties will be regarded as income from the year preceding that of receipt. If the period of preparing and writing exceeds twenty-four months, one-third of the amount received would be regarded as income from each of the two years preceding that of receipt.

(c) For a writer on a very large income, who otherwise fulfils the conditions required, a claim under these sections could result in a tax saving. If his income is not large he should consider the implication, in the various fiscal years concerned, of possible loss of benefit from personal and other allowances and changes in the standard rate of income tax.

It is also possible to average out income within the terms of publishers' contracts, but professional advice should be taken before signature. Where a husband and wife collaborate as writers, advice should be taken as to whether a formal partnership agreement should be made or whether the publishing agreement should be in joint names.

Is a lump sum paid for an outright sale of the copyright or part of the copyright exempt from tax?

No. All the money received from the marketing of literary work, by whatever means, is taxable. Some writers, in spite of clear judicial decisions to the contrary, still seem to think that an outright sale of, for instance, the film rights in a book, is not subject to tax.

Is there any relief where old copyrights are sold?

Section 390 of the *Income and Corporation Taxes Act 1970* gives relief 'where not less than ten years after the first publication of the work the author of a literary, dramatic, musical or artistic work assigns the copyright therein wholly or partially, or grants any interest in the copyright by licence, and:

(a) the consideration for the assignment or grant consists wholly or partially of a lump sum payment, the whole amount of which would, but for this section, be included in computing the amount of his/her profits or gains for a single year of assessment, and
(b) the copyright or interest is not assigned or granted for a period of less than two years.'

In such cases, the amount received may be spread forward in equal yearly instalments for a maximum of six years, or, where the copyright or interest is assigned or granted for a period of less than six years, for the number of whole years in that period. A 'lump sum payment' is defined to include a non-returnable advance on account of royalties.

It should be noted that a claim may not be made under this section in respect of a payment if a prior claim has been made under Section 389 of the *Income and Corporation Taxes Act 1970* (see section on spreading lump sum payments over two or three years) or vice versa.

Are royalties payable on publication of a book abroad subject to both foreign tax as well as UK tax?

Where there is a Double Taxation Agreement between the country concerned and the UK, then on the completion of certain formalities no tax is deductible at source by the foreign payer, but such income is taxable in the UK in the ordinary way. When there is no Double Taxation agreement, credit will be given against UK tax for overseas tax paid. A complete list of countries with which the UK has conventions for the avoidance of double taxation may be obtained from the Inspector of Foreign Dividends, Lynwood Road, Thames Ditton, Surrey KT7 0DP or the local tax office.

Residence Abroad

Writers residing abroad will, of course, be subject to the tax laws ruling in their country of residence, and as a general rule royalty income paid from the United Kingdom can be exempted from deduction of UK tax at source, providing the author is carrying on his profession abroad. A writer who is intending to go and live abroad should make early application for future royalties to be paid without deduction of tax to HM Inspector of Taxes, Claims Branch, Magdalen House, Stanley Precinct, Bootle, Merseyside L69 9BB. In certain circumstances writers resident in the Irish Republic are exempt from Irish Income Tax on their authorship earnings.

Are grants or prizes taxable?

The law is uncertain. Some Arts Council grants are now deemed to be taxable, whereas most prizes and awards are not, though it depends on the conditions in each case. When submitting a statement of income and expenses, such items should be excluded, but reference made to them in a covering letter to the Inspector of Taxes.

What if I disagree with a tax assessment?

Income tax law requires the Inspector of Taxes to make an assessment each year calculating the amount of income tax payable on the 'profits' of the profession. Even though accounts may have already been submitted the assessment can quite possibly be estimated and overstated.

The taxpayer has the right of appeal within 30 days of receipt of the assessment and can request that the tax payable should be reduced to the correct liability which he must estimate as accurately as possible. However, if he underestimates the amount, interest can become payable on the amount by which he underpays when the correct liability is known.

What is the item 'Class 4 N.I.C.' which appears on my tax assessment?

All taxpayers who are self-employed pay an additional national insurance contribution if their earned income exceeds a figure which is varied each year. This contribution is described as Class 4 and is calculated in the tax assessment. It is additional to the self-employed Class 2 (stamp) contribution but confers no additional benefits and is a form of levy. It applies to men aged under 65 and women under 60. Tax relief is given on half the Class 4 contributions.

Anyone wondering how best to order his affairs for tax purposes, should consult an accountant with specialised knowledge in this field. Experience shows that a good accountant is well worth his fee which, incidentally, so far as it relates to matters other than personal tax work, is an allowable expense.

The information contained in this section is adapted from **The Society of Authors** *Quick Guides to Taxation* (Nos. 4 and 7) with the kind help of A.P. Kernon, FCA.

Companies Index

The following codes have been used to classify the index entries

A Publishers (UK)
B Poetry Presses
C Poetry Magazines
D Poetry - Specialist and other organisations
E Packagers
F Agents (UK)
G Newspapers (national)
H Newspapers (regional)
I Magazines
J Television
K Radio
L Film, TV and video producers
M Theatre producers
N Publishers (US)
O Agents (US)
P US Press and Journals
Q Professional Associations
R Regional Arts Associations
S Busaries/fellowships
T Prizes
U Libraries
V Picture libraries

Subject Index

Children's: Publishers (UK) *(cont)*

Children's: Packagers

Children's: Agents (UK)

Children's: Magazines

Children's: Film, TV and video producers

Children's: Theatre producers

Children's: Publishers (US)

Children's: Agents (US)

Drama: Publishers (UK) *(cont)*

Education: Publishers (UK) *(cont)*

Education: Packagers

Education: Magazines

Education: Film, TV and video producers

Education: Publishers (US)

Education: Agents (US)

Education: Professional Associations

Education: Regional Arts Associations

Education: Prizes

Education: Picture libraries

Electronics: Publishers (UK)

Electronics: Magazines

Encyclopedias: Publishers (UK)

Encyclopedias: Packagers

Encyclopedias: Publishers (US)

Fiction: Agents (US) *(cont)*

History: Publishers (UK) *(cont)*

History: Packagers

History: Agents (UK)

History: Magazines

History: Publishers (US)

History: Agents (US)

History: Prizes

History: Libraries

History: Picture libraries

Home Economics: Publishers (UK)

Home Economics: Magazines

Home Interests: Magazines

Leisure and Hobbies: Magazines *(cont)*

Poetry: Publishers (UK) *(cont)*

Poetry: Poetry Presses

Poetry: Poetry magazines

Poetry: Poetry magazines (*cont*)

Poetry: Poetry - other organisations

Poetry: Poetry - specialist organisations

Poetry: Packagers

Poetry: Magazines

Poetry: Publishers (US)

Poetry: Agents (US)

Poetry: Professional Associations

Poetry: Regional Arts Associations

Science: Publishers (UK) (*cont*)

Television: Agents (UK) *(cont)*

Television: Magazines

Television: Film, TV and video producers

Television: Film, TV and video producers *(cont)*

Video: Film, TV and video producers *(cont)*